TIDE TABLES 2014

Aberdeen, 30
Belfast, 58
Brest, 88
Brest – Tidal coefficients 2014, 96
Bristol (Avonmouth), 52
Calais, 74
Cherbourg, 80
Cobh, 54
Cuxhaven, 66
Dieppe, 76
Dover, 14
Dublin, 56
Dunkerque,72
Esbjerg, 62
Galway, 60
Gibraltar, 94
Greenock, 42
Helgoland, 64
Holyhead, 46
Immingham, 24
Le Havre, 78
Leith, 28
Lerwick, 34
Lisbon, 92
Liverpool (Gladstone Dock), 44
London Bridge, 18
Lowestoft, 22
Milford Haven, 48
Oban, 40
Plymouth, 2
Poole Harbour, 6
Portland, 4
Portsmouth, 10
Pointe de Grave, 90
R Tyne (N Shields), 26
Sheerness, 16
Shoreham, 12
St Helier, 84
St Malo, 86
Southampton, 8
Stornoway, 38
St Peter Port, 82
Swansea, 50
Ullapool, 36
Vlissingen (Flushing), 70
Walton-on-the-Naze, 20
Wick, 32
Wilhelmshaven, 68

Summer time figures are enclosed within a shaded box. See title to each table for necessary adjustments.

○ Full Moon
● New Moon
☾/☽ Half moon – first or last quarter

PLYMOUTH (DEVONPORT)
LAT 50°22′N
LONG 4°11′W

TIMES AND HEIGHTS OF HIGH AND LOW WATER (Heights in Metres)

TIME ZONE UT
For Summer Time (area enclosed in shaded box) add 1 hour

2014

JANUARY

Date	Day	Time	m	Time	m	Time	m	Time	m	Moon
1	W	0513	5.6	1135	0.8	1741	5.5	2358	0.8	●
2	TH	0604	5.8	1227	0.6	1833	5.6			
3	F	0048	0.6	0654	5.9	1316	0.5	1923	5.6	
4	SA	0135	0.6	0742	5.9	1402	0.5	2011	5.5	
5	SU	0220	0.7	0830	5.8	1447	0.6	2057	5.4	
6	M	0303	0.9	0915	5.6	1530	0.9	2142	5.2	
7	TU	0346	1.2	1001	5.3	1614	1.2	2227	4.9	
8	W	0430	1.5	1048	5.0	1700	1.6	2319	4.7	☽
9	TH	0521	1.9	1145	4.7	1755	1.9			
10	F	0023	4.5	0623	2.1	1255	4.5	1903	2.1	
11	SA	0134	4.5	0744	2.2	1405	4.5	2023	2.1	
12	SU	0239	4.6	0903	2.0	1507	4.6	2130	1.9	
13	M	0335	4.8	1002	1.8	1600	4.8	2222	1.6	
14	TU	0423	5.0	1050	1.5	1646	4.9	2307	1.4	
15	W	0505	5.2	1132	1.3	1727	5.1	2346	1.3	
16	TH	0543	5.3	1210	1.2	1805	5.1			○
17	F	0022	1.2	0619	5.4	1244	1.1	1841	5.2	
18	SA	0054	1.2	0655	5.4	1314	1.2	1917	5.2	
19	SU	0122	1.2	0730	5.3	1342	1.2	1951	5.1	
20	M	0149	1.3	0802	5.3	1409	1.3	2022	5.0	
21	TU	0217	1.4	0832	5.2	1436	1.4	2051	4.9	
22	W	0246	1.5	0904	5.0	1507	1.5	2123	4.8	
23	TH	0321	1.6	0941	4.9	1546	1.7	2205	4.7	
24	F	0406	1.8	1029	4.7	1636	1.9	2301	4.6	☾
25	SA	0507	2.0	1132	4.6	1748	2.0			
26	SU	0013	4.5	0635	2.1	1249	4.5	1923	2.0	
27	M	0136	4.6	0807	1.9	1413	4.7	2045	1.8	
28	TU	0255	4.9	0922	1.6	1530	4.9	2154	1.4	
29	W	0401	5.2	1027	1.1	1633	5.2	2254	1.0	
30	TH	0458	5.5	1124	0.7	1729	5.4	2347	0.6	●
31		0550	5.8	1215	0.4					

FEBRUARY

Date	Day	Time	m	Time	m	Time	m	Time	m	Moon
1	SA	0036	0.4	0640	5.9	1303	0.2	1909	5.6	
2	SU	0122	0.3	0728	5.9	1348	0.2	1955	5.6	
3	M	0205	0.3	0812	5.8	1429	0.3	2036	5.5	
4	TU	0244	0.6	0854	5.6	1508	0.6	2114	5.3	
5	W	0322	0.9	0932	5.3	1545	1.0	2148	5.0	
6	TH	0359	1.3	1007	5.0	1623	1.5	2222	4.7	☽
7	F	0441	1.7	1045	4.6	1708	1.9	2307	4.5	
8	SA	0533	2.1	1147	4.3	1806	2.2			
9	SU	0032	4.3	0643	2.3	1326	4.2	1922	2.3	
10	M	0203	4.3	0820	2.3	1439	4.3	2056	2.2	
11	TU	0307	4.6	0939	2.0	1536	4.5	2159	1.8	
12	W	0358	4.8	1030	1.6	1624	4.8	2246	1.5	
13	TH	0442	5.1	1112	1.3	1706	5.0	2326	1.2	
14	F	0522	5.2	1150	1.1	1745	5.1			○
15	SA	0002	1.1	0600	5.3	1224	1.0	1822	5.2	
16	SU	0034	1.0	0637	5.4	1254	1.0	1858	5.2	
17	M	0104	1.0	0712	5.4	1322	1.0	1931	5.2	
18	TU	0131	1.0	0744	5.3	1349	1.0	2001	5.1	
19	W	0158	1.1	0813	5.2	1416	1.1	2029	5.0	
20	TH	0227	1.2	0843	5.1	1446	1.2	2058	4.9	
21	F	0300	1.3	0918	4.9	1522	1.4	2136	4.8	
22	SA	0341	1.6	1003	4.7	1607	1.7	2229	4.6	☾
23	SU	0437	1.8	1105	4.5	1712	2.0	2341	4.5	
24	M	0600	2.0	1224	4.4	1850	2.1			
25	TU	0109	4.5	0744	1.9	1357	4.5	2026	1.8	
26	W	0236	4.8	0908	1.6	1517	4.8	2141	1.4	
27	TH	0345	5.1	1014	1.1	1621	5.1	2241	0.9	
28	F	0442	5.5	1109	0.6	1715	5.4	2333	0.5	

MARCH

Date	Day	Time	m	Time	m	Time	m	Time	m	Moon
1	SA	0534	5.7	1159	0.3	1804	5.6			●
2	SU	0020	0.3	0622	5.8	1245	0.1	1849	5.7	
3	M	0104	0.2	0707	5.9	1327	0.1	1931	5.6	
4	TU	0144	0.2	0749	5.8	1406	0.3	2009	5.5	
5	W	0221	0.4	0827	5.5	1441	0.6	2040	5.3	
6	TH	0255	0.8	0858	5.2	1515	1.0	2107	5.1	
7	F	0329	1.2	0926	4.9	1549	1.5	2135	4.8	
8	SA	0406	1.6	0957	4.6	1628	1.9	2213	4.5	☽
9	SU	0454	2.1	1044	4.2	1722	2.2	2311	4.3	
10	M	0559	2.3	1222	4.0	1833	2.4			
11	TU	0113	4.2	0720	2.3	1406	4.1	1959	2.3	
12	W	0233	4.4	0901	2.1	1507	4.4	2123	2.0	
13	TH	0328	4.7	0958	1.7	1556	4.7	2215	1.6	
14	F	0414	4.9	1041	1.4	1639	4.9	2256	1.3	
15	SA	0455	5.1	1119	1.1	1719	5.1	2333	1.1	
16	SU	0535	5.3	1154	0.9	1757	5.2			○
17	M	0007	0.9	0613	5.3	1227	0.8	1834	5.2	
18	TU	0040	0.8	0649	5.3	1258	0.8	1908	5.3	
19	W	0111	0.8	0722	5.3	1328	0.8	1939	5.2	
20	TH	0141	0.9	0754	5.3	1358	0.9	2008	5.2	
21	F	0212	1.0	0826	5.1	1429	1.1	2040	5.1	
22	SA	0246	1.1	0903	5.0	1506	1.3	2119	4.9	
23	SU	0328	1.4	0950	4.7	1552	1.6	2211	4.7	
24	M	0424	1.7	1051	4.5	1656	1.9	2321	4.5	☾
25	TU	0546	1.9	1211	4.4	1831	2.1			
26	W	0052	4.5	0729	1.9	1347	4.5	2011	1.8	
27	TH	0220	4.8	0853	1.5	1505	4.8	2125	1.4	
28	F	0328	5.1	0957	1.0	1605	5.1	2223	0.9	
29	SA	0424	5.4	1050	0.6	1656	5.4	2313	0.6	
30	SU	0514	5.6	1138	0.3	1742	5.5	2359	0.3	●
31		0600	5.7	1222	0.2					

APRIL

Date	Day	Time	m	Time	m	Time	m	Time	m	Moon
1	TU	0041	0.2	0643	5.7	1303	0.2	1904	5.6	
2	W	0120	0.3	0723	5.6	1340	0.4	1938	5.5	
3	TH	0156	0.5	0757	5.4	1414	0.7	2006	5.3	
4	F	0229	0.8	0826	5.1	1446	1.1	2032	5.1	
5	SA	0302	1.2	0853	4.8	1518	1.5	2101	4.9	
6	SU	0337	1.6	0926	4.6	1555	1.9	2139	4.6	
7	M	0421	2.0	1011	4.3	1645	2.2	2230	4.4	☽
8	TU	0522	2.2	1119	4.1	1752	2.4	2346	4.2	
9	W	0635	2.3	1318	4.1	1907	2.3			
10	TH	0143	4.3	0752	2.1	1428	4.3	2022	2.1	
11	F	0248	4.6	0903	1.8	1520	4.6	2125	1.7	
12	SA	0337	4.8	0955	1.5	1605	4.8	2214	1.4	
13	SU	0422	5.0	1038	1.2	1647	5.0	2256	1.1	
14	M	0504	5.2	1118	1.0	1728	5.2	2336	0.9	
15	TU	0545	5.3	1156	0.8	1806	5.3			○
16	W	0013	0.8	0623	5.3	1233	0.8	1842	5.3	
17	TH	0050	0.7	0701	5.3	1308	0.8	1917	5.4	
18	F	0125	0.7	0737	5.3	1343	0.9	1951	5.3	
19	SA	0201	0.8	0814	5.2	1419	1.0	2028	5.2	
20	SU	0240	1.0	0856	5.0	1459	1.3	2111	5.1	
21	M	0325	1.3	0944	4.8	1548	1.6	2202	4.9	
22	TU	0423	1.6	1045	4.6	1653	1.8	2310	4.7	☾
23	W	0539	1.8	1205	4.4	1818	2.0			
24	TH	0037	4.6	0710	1.7	1332	4.5	1949	1.8	
25	F	0200	4.8	0830	1.4	1443	4.8	2101	1.4	
26	SA	0306	5.0	0933	1.1	1541	5.0	2159	1.1	
27	SU	0401	5.3	1026	0.8	1631	5.3	2249	0.8	
28	M	0451	5.4	1114	0.6	1717	5.4	2335	0.6	
29	TU	0536	5.5	1157	0.5	1759	5.5			●
30	W	0017	0.5	0618	5.5	1238	0.5	1836	5.5	

MAY

Date	Day	Time	m	Time	m	Time	m	Time	m	Moon
1	TH	0057	0.6	0656	5.4	1315	0.7	1908	5.4	
2	F	0132	0.7	0729	5.2	1349	0.9	1937	5.3	
3	SA	0205	1.0	0759	5.0	1420	1.2	2005	5.2	
4	SU	0237	1.3	0830	4.8	1452	1.5	2037	5.0	
5	M	0311	1.6	0905	4.6	1526	1.8	2115	4.8	
6	TU	0351	1.9	0948	4.4	1610	2.1	2201	4.5	
7	W	0444	2.1	1045	4.2	1710	2.3	2300	4.4	☽
8	TH	0550	2.2	1204	4.2	1820	2.3			
9	F	0020	4.3	0658	2.1	1330	4.3	1928	2.1	
10	SA	0148	4.5	0803	1.9	1432	4.5	2031	1.9	
11	SU	0250	4.7	0901	1.6	1523	4.8	2127	1.6	
12	M	0342	4.9	0953	1.3	1610	5.0	2217	1.3	
13	TU	0429	5.1	1041	1.1	1654	5.2	2303	1.0	
14	W	0514	5.2	1126	0.9	1736	5.3	2347	0.8	○
15	TH	0558	5.3	1209	0.8	1818	5.4			
16	F	0030	0.7	0640	5.3	1251	0.7	1858	5.5	
17	SA	0113	0.7	0723	5.3	1332	0.8	1939	5.5	
18	SU	0155	0.7	0807	5.3	1415	0.9	2021	5.4	
19	M	0239	0.9	0853	5.1	1459	1.1	2107	5.3	
20	TU	0327	1.1	0943	4.9	1549	1.4	2159	5.1	
21	W	0422	1.3	1042	4.7	1648	1.6	2301	4.9	☾
22	TH	0528	1.5	1153	4.6	1758	1.8			
23	F	0017	4.8	0643	1.6	1308	4.6	1917	1.8	
24	SA	0133	4.8	0758	1.5	1414	4.7	2030	1.6	
25	SU	0238	4.9	0903	1.3	1512	4.9	2131	1.3	
26	M	0335	5.0	0959	1.1	1604	5.1	2224	1.1	
27	TU	0426	5.1	1048	0.9	1650	5.2	2311	0.9	
28	W	0512	5.2	1133	0.8	1732	5.3	2355	0.8	●
29	TH	0554	5.2	1214	0.8	1810	5.4			
30	F	0034	0.8	0632	5.2	1252	0.9	1843	5.3	
31	SA	0111	0.9	0706	5.1	1326	1.1			

JUNE

Date	Day	Time	m	Time	m	Time	m	Time	m	Moon
1	SU	0145	1.1	0739	5.0	1358	1.2	1946	5.2	
2	M	0217	1.3	0813	4.9	1429	1.4	2020	5.1	
3	TU	0248	1.5	0849	4.7	1500	1.7	2056	4.9	
4	W	0322	1.7	0929	4.6	1536	1.9	2137	4.7	
5	TH	0402	1.9	1015	4.4	1622	2.1	2224	4.6	☽
6	F	0457	2.0	1111	4.3	1725	2.2	2322	4.5	
7	SA	0604	2.0	1218	4.3	1835	2.1			
8	SU	0030	4.5	0710	1.9	1329	4.5	1941	2.0	
9	M	0146	4.6	0813	1.7	1433	4.7	2043	1.7	
10	TU	0253	4.8	0912	1.5	1528	4.9	2140	1.4	
11	W	0351	5.0	1007	1.2	1619	5.1	2234	1.1	
12	TH	0444	5.1	1059	1.0	1708	5.3	2325	0.9	
13	F	0534	5.3	1149	0.8	1755	5.5			○
14	SA	0015	0.7	0623	5.4	1238	0.7	1842	5.6	
15	SU	0103	0.6	0712	5.4	1324	0.7	1928	5.6	
16	M	0150	0.6	0800	5.4	1411	0.7	2015	5.6	
17	TU	0237	0.6	0849	5.3	1457	0.9	2103	5.5	
18	W	0324	0.8	0938	5.1	1544	1.1	2152	5.3	
19	TH	0413	1.1	1031	4.9	1634	1.4	2246	5.0	☾
20	F	0506	1.3	1129	4.8	1731	1.6	2350	4.8	
21	SA	0608	1.6	1235	4.6	1838	1.8			
22	SU	0100	4.7	0718	1.7	1341	4.6	1952	1.8	
23	M	0207	4.7	0829	1.6	1441	4.7	2101	1.7	
24	TU	0307	4.7	0931	1.5	1536	4.9	2200	1.5	
25	W	0401	4.9	1024	1.3	1625	5.0	2250	1.3	
26	TH	0449	5.0	1111	1.2	1708	5.2	2335	1.1	
27	F	0532	5.0	1154	1.1	1747	5.3			●
28	SA	0016	1.0	0610	5.1	1233	1.1	1822	5.3	
29	SU	0053	1.0	0647	5.1	1307	1.1	1856	5.3	
30	M	0127	1.1	0722	5.0	1338	1.2	1930	5.2	

SUNRISE AND SUNSET TIMES

PLYMOUTH
At 50°22′N 4°11′W

		Sunrise	Sunset
UT			
Jan	01	0817	1623
	15	0811	1641
Feb	01	0752	1709
	15	0729	1733
Mar	01	0700	1759
	15	0630	1822
BST			
Apr	01	0653	1949
	15	0623	2012
May	01	0552	2037
	15	0529	2058
Jun	01	0511	2119
	15	0505	2130
Jul	01	0510	2131
	15	0523	2122
Aug	01	0545	2100
	15	0606	2035
Sep	01	0632	2001
	15	0653	1930
Oct	01	0717	1854
	15	0740	1824
UT			
Nov	01	0708	1652
	15	0731	1631
Dec	01	0755	1616
	15	0811	1613

PLYMOUTH (DEVONPORT)
LAT 50°22′N
LONG 4°11′W

TIMES AND HEIGHTS OF HIGH AND LOW WATER (Heights in Metres)

TIME ZONE UT
For Summer Time (area enclosed in shaded box) add 1 hour

2014

JULY

Date	Time	m	Date	Time	m
1 TU	0157 0757 1407 2004	1.2 5.0 1.3 5.2	16 W	0226 0837 1445 2051	0.4 5.4 0.6 5.6
2 W	0225 0832 1435 2038	1.3 4.8 1.5 5.0	17 TH	0310 0922 1528 2136	0.6 5.3 0.8 5.4
3 TH	0253 0907 1504 2113	1.5 4.7 1.6 4.9	18 F	0353 1008 1611 2222	0.9 5.1 1.2 5.1
4 F	0324 0945 1538 2151	1.6 4.6 1.8 4.8	19 SA ☾	0438 1057 1659 2314	1.2 4.8 1.5 4.8
5 SA ☽	0403 1028 1624 2238	1.8 4.5 2.0 4.6	20 SU	0529 1155 1756	1.6 4.6 1.8
6 SU	0457 1122 1730 2337	1.9 4.4 2.1 4.5	21 M	0022 0631 1304 1908	4.5 1.9 4.5 2.0
7 M	0612 1227 1851	2.0 4.5 2.0	22 TU	0136 0749 1411 2030	4.4 2.0 4.5 2.0
8 TU	0047 0728 1340 2004	4.5 1.9 4.6 1.8	23 W	0242 0904 1511 2138	4.5 1.8 4.7 1.8
9 W	0206 0837 1449 2110	4.6 1.6 4.8 1.5	24 TH	0339 1003 1602 2232	4.6 1.6 4.9 1.5
10 TH	0318 0940 1550 2211	4.8 1.4 5.1 1.2	25 F	0428 1052 1646 2317	4.8 1.4 5.1 1.3
11 F	0420 1038 1645 2308	5.1 1.1 5.4 0.9	26 SA ●	0511 1135 1726 2358	4.9 1.2 5.2 1.1
12 SA ○	0515 1133 1737	5.3 0.8 5.6	27 SU	0550 1213 1803	5.0 1.1 5.3
13 SU	0001 0608 1226 1827	0.6 5.4 0.6 5.7	28 M	0035 0627 1248 1838	1.0 5.1 1.1 5.3
14 M	0052 0659 1315 1916	0.4 5.5 0.5 5.8	29 TU	0107 0703 1318 1913	1.0 5.1 1.1 5.3
15 TU	0140 0749 1401 2004	0.3 5.5 0.5 5.8	30 W	0135 0738 1344 1946	1.1 5.1 1.2 5.2
			31 TH	0200 0811 1410 2018	1.2 5.0 1.3 5.1

AUGUST

Date	Time	m	Date	Time	m
1 F	0225 0843 1436 2048	1.3 4.9 1.4 5.0	16 SA	0327 0937 1544 2150	0.8 5.2 1.1 5.1
2 SA	0252 0914 1506 2121	1.4 4.8 1.6 4.9	17 SU ☾	0406 1015 1626 2229	1.3 4.9 1.5 4.7
3 SU	0326 0951 1545 2203	1.6 4.6 1.7 4.7	18 M	0451 1101 1716 2325	1.7 4.6 2.0 4.4
4 M ☽	0409 1039 1637 2258	1.8 4.5 2.0 4.6	19 TU	0547 1218 1823	2.1 4.4 2.2
5 TU	0512 1143 1758	2.0 4.5 2.1	20 W	0103 0701 1341 1956	4.2 2.3 4.4 2.2
6 W	0009 0644 1300 1932	4.5 2.0 4.5 2.0	21 TH	0219 0836 1446 2118	4.3 2.1 4.5 2.0
7 TH	0133 0809 1419 2048	4.5 1.8 4.8 1.7	22 F	0318 0942 1539 2212	4.5 1.8 4.8 1.6
8 F	0256 0921 1528 2154	4.8 1.5 5.1 1.2	23 SA	0407 1031 1624 2256	4.7 1.5 5.0 1.3
9 SA	0402 1023 1627 2254	5.0 1.1 5.4 0.8	24 SU	0449 1112 1703 2335	4.9 1.2 5.2 1.1
10 SU ○	0500 1120 1720 2348	5.3 0.7 5.6 0.5	25 M ●	0527 1150 1741	5.1 1.1 5.3
11 M	0553 1211 1811	5.5 0.5 5.8	26 TU	0010 0604 1223 1817	1.0 5.2 1.0 5.4
12 TU	0037 0643 1300 1900	0.2 5.6 0.3 5.9	27 W	0041 0640 1253 1852	1.0 5.2 1.0 5.4
13 W	0124 0731 1344 1947	0.1 5.6 0.3 5.9	28 TH	0108 0715 1319 1925	1.0 5.2 1.1 5.3
14 TH	0208 0316 1426 2031	0.2 5.6 0.4 5.7	29 F	0134 0747 1345 1956	1.1 5.1 1.2 5.2
15 F	0248 0858 1505 2111	0.5 5.4 0.7 5.4	30 SA	0159 0817 1411 2024	1.2 5.0 1.3 5.1
			31 SU	0226 0846 1441 2056	1.3 4.9 1.4 5.0

SEPTEMBER

Date	Time	m	Date	Time	m
1 M	0258 0920 1517 2136	1.5 4.8 1.6 4.3	16 TU ☾	0414 1005 1641 2225	1.9 4.6 2.1 4.3
2 TU ☽	0338 1008 1606 2232	1.7 4.6 1.9 4.6	17 W	0506 1101 1744	2.3 4.4 2.4
3 W	0435 1112 1721 2344	2.0 4.5 2.1 4.4	18 TH	0007 0617 1302 1908	4.1 2.5 4.3 2.4
4 TH	0609 1231 1909	2.2 4.5 2.1	19 F	0151 0752 1416 2047	4.2 2.4 4.5 2.1
5 F	0113 0750 1359 2032	4.5 2.0 4.7 1.7	20 SA	0252 0911 1511 2143	4.4 2.0 4.7 1.8
6 SA	0242 0907 1512 2140	4.7 1.6 5.1 1.2	21 SU	0340 1001 1556 2226	4.7 1.7 5.0 1.4
7 SU	0350 1009 1611 2239	5.1 1.1 5.4 0.8	22 M	0422 1042 1637 2304	5.0 1.4 5.2 1.2
8 M	0445 1104 1703 2330	5.4 0.7 5.7 0.4	23 TU	0501 1119 1715 2338	5.2 1.2 5.4 1.0
9 TU ○	0535 1154 1753	5.6 0.4 5.9	24 W ●	0538 1153 1753	5.3 1.0 5.4
10 W	0018 0623 1240 1840	0.2 5.7 0.2 5.9	25 TH	0010 0615 1224 1828	1.0 5.3 1.0 5.4
11 TH	0103 0708 1323 1924	0.1 5.7 0.2 5.9	26 F	0040 0650 1254 1902	1.0 5.3 1.0 5.4
12 F	0144 0750 1402 2005	0.3 5.6 0.4 5.7	27 SA	0108 0722 1322 1934	1.0 5.3 1.1 5.3
13 SA	0222 0827 1439 2042	0.5 5.5 0.7 5.4	28 SU	0136 0752 1351 2004	1.1 5.2 1.2 5.2
14 SU	0258 0900 1516 2113	0.9 5.2 1.2 5.0	29 M	0205 0823 1423 2038	1.2 5.1 1.3 5.0
15 M	0334 0930 1554 2144	1.4 4.9 1.6 4.7	30 TU	0238 0859 1500 2121	1.5 5.0 1.6 4.8

OCTOBER

Date	Time	m	Date	Time	m
1 W ☽	0320 0948 1550 2216	1.7 4.8 1.9 4.6	16 TH	0430 1018 1707 2255	2.3 4.5 2.4 4.2
2 TH	0417 1051 1705 2328	2.0 4.6 2.1 4.4	17 F	0536 1134 1820	2.5 4.3 2.5
3 F	0548 1211 1851	2.2 4.6 2.1	18 SA	0104 0654 1331 1945	4.2 2.5 4.4 2.3
4 SA	0101 0734 1342 2017	4.5 2.1 4.8 1.7	19 SU	0214 0816 1433 2055	4.4 2.3 4.7 2.0
5 SU	0230 0851 1455 2124	4.8 1.6 5.1 1.3	20 M	0305 0916 1521 2143	4.7 1.9 4.9 1.6
6 M	0334 0952 1554 2220	5.1 1.2 5.5 0.8	21 TU	0349 1001 1605 2223	5.0 1.6 5.1 1.4
7 TU	0427 1045 1645 2310	5.4 0.8 5.7 0.5	22 W	0430 1042 1646 2301	5.2 1.3 5.3 1.2
8 W ○	0515 1133 1733 2356	5.6 0.5 5.8 0.3	23 TH ●	0510 1119 1725 2337	5.3 1.1 5.4 1.0
9 TH	0600 1217 1818	5.7 0.4 5.9	24 F	0548 1155 1804	5.4 1.0 5.4
10 F	0038 0642 1259 1900	0.3 5.8 0.4 5.8	25 SA	0011 0624 1230 1840	1.0 5.4 1.0 5.4
11 SA	0119 0721 1338 1938	0.5 5.7 0.6 5.6	26 SU	0045 0659 1303 1915	1.0 5.4 1.0 5.4
12 SU	0156 0755 1414 2012	0.7 5.5 0.9 5.3	27 M	0118 0733 1337 1950	1.1 5.4 1.1 5.3
13 M	0230 0825 1449 2041	1.1 5.3 1.3 5.0	28 TU	0152 0808 1414 2028	1.2 5.3 1.3 5.1
14 TU	0304 0853 1525 2111	1.5 5.0 1.7 4.7	29 W	0229 0848 1455 2113	1.4 5.2 1.5 4.9
15 W ☾	0341 0929 1609 2152	1.9 4.8 2.1 4.4	30 TH	0313 0937 1547 2208	1.7 5.0 1.8 4.7
			31 F ☽	0412 1038 1659 2318	2.0 4.8 2.0 4.6

NOVEMBER

Date	Time	m	Date	Time	m
1 SA	0534 1154 1831	2.2 4.7 2.0	16 SU	0601 1205 1842	2.5 4.5 2.4
2 SU	0047 0711 1321 1954	4.6 2.1 4.9 1.8	17 M	0110 0712 1333 1949	4.4 2.4 4.6 2.2
3 M	0210 0828 1433 2101	4.8 1.7 5.1 1.4	18 TU	0217 0817 1435 2048	4.6 2.1 4.8 1.9
4 TU	0313 0930 1532 2157	5.1 1.3 5.4 1.0	19 W	0309 0913 1526 2138	4.8 1.8 5.0 1.6
5 W	0406 1022 1624 2247	5.4 1.0 5.6 0.8	20 TH	0355 1001 1613 2223	5.1 1.5 5.2 1.3
6 TH ○	0453 1110 1711 2332	5.6 0.7 5.7 0.6	21 F	0439 1045 1657 2305	5.3 1.3 5.3 1.2
7 F	0537 1155 1756	5.7 0.6 5.7	22 SA ●	0520 1128 1739 2346	5.4 1.1 5.4 1.0
8 SA	0015 0617 1237 1837	0.6 5.7 0.7 5.6	23 SU	0600 1209 1820	5.5 1.0 5.4
9 SU	0055 0655 1315 1914	0.7 5.6 0.8 5.4	24 M	0026 0639 1250 1900	1.0 5.6 1.0 5.4
10 M	0131 0728 1351 1946	0.9 5.5 1.0 5.2	25 TU	0106 0719 1330 1941	1.0 5.6 1.0 5.4
11 TU	0205 0757 1426 2016	1.2 5.3 1.3 5.0	26 W	0146 0759 1412 2024	1.1 5.5 1.1 5.2
12 W	0238 0828 1501 2049	1.6 5.1 1.7 4.8	27 TH	0228 0843 1457 2110	1.3 5.4 1.3 5.1
13 TH	0313 0905 1540 2130	1.9 4.9 2.0 4.6	28 F	0314 0932 1548 2203	1.5 5.2 1.5 4.9
14 F ☾	0354 0950 1629 2223	2.2 4.7 2.3 4.4	29 SA ☽	0409 1028 1649 2307	1.8 5.0 1.7 4.7
15 SA	0451 1047 1732 2336	2.4 4.5 2.4 4.3	30 SU	0516 1136 1803	2.0 4.9 1.9

DECEMBER

Date	Time	m	Date	Time	m
1 M	0023 0637 1253 1922	4.7 2.0 4.9 1.8	16 TU	0609 1212 1848	2.4 4.5 2.2
2 TU	0139 0757 1405 2032	4.8 1.9 5.0 1.6	17 W	0106 0720 1328 1953	4.5 2.3 4.6 2.1
3 W	0245 0903 1507 2132	5.0 1.6 5.1 1.3	18 TH	0216 0824 1437 2053	4.6 2.0 4.7 1.8
4 TH	0341 1000 1602 2224	5.2 1.3 5.3 1.1	19 F	0314 0922 1536 2147	4.9 1.7 4.9 1.5
5 F	0430 1050 1651 2311	5.4 1.1 5.4 1.0	20 SA	0406 1015 1628 2238	5.1 1.4 5.1 1.3
6 SA ○	0515 1135 1736 2354	5.5 1.0 5.4 0.9	21 SU	0453 1105 1716 2326	5.3 1.2 5.3 1.1
7 SU	0556 1218 1817	5.6 0.9 5.4	22 M ●	0538 1153 1803	5.5 0.9 5.4
8 M	0034 0633 1257 1854	1.0 5.6 1.0 5.3	23 TU	0013 0623 1240 1848	0.9 5.6 0.8 5.5
9 TU	0111 0707 1333 1927	1.1 5.5 1.1 5.2	24 W	0058 0708 1325 1934	0.8 5.7 0.7 5.5
10 W	0145 0738 1407 1959	1.3 5.4 1.3 5.1	25 TH	0143 0753 1410 2019	0.9 5.7 0.8 5.4
11 TH	0217 0811 1439 2033	1.5 5.3 1.5 4.9	26 F	0227 0838 1455 2106	1.0 5.6 0.9 5.3
12 F	0248 0847 1512 2111	1.7 5.1 1.8 4.7	27 SA	0312 0925 1542 2154	1.1 5.5 1.1 5.1
13 SA	0321 0926 1549 2155	1.9 4.9 2.0 4.6	28 SU ☽	0359 1015 1632 2248	1.4 5.2 1.4 4.9
14 SU ☾	0401 1012 1636 2247	2.2 4.7 2.2 4.4	29 M	0452 1113 1729 2351	1.7 5.0 1.7 4.7
15 M	0457 1106 1738 2351	2.3 4.6 2.3 4.4	30 TU	0556 1221 1839	1.9 4.8 1.9
			31 W	0103 0715 1334 1957	4.7 2.0 4.7 1.9

PORTLAND
LAT 50°34′N
LONG 2°26′W

TIMES AND HEIGHTS OF HIGH AND LOW WATER (Heights in Metres)

TIME ZONE UT
For Summer Time (area enclosed in shaded box) add 1 hour

Double low waters occur at Portland. The predictions are for the first low water. The second low water occus from 3 to 4 hours later and, at springs, may be lower that the first

2014

JANUARY

Date	Day	Time	m	Time	m	Time	m	Time	m
1	W ●	0616	2.2	1116	0.3	1844	2.1	2336	0.2
2	TH	0708	2.3	1206	0.2	1936	2.1		
3	F	0025	0.1	0756	2.4	1254	0.1	2024	2.2
4	SA	0112	0.1	0842	2.4	1341	0.1	2108	2.1
5	SU	0157	0.2	0925	2.3	1427	0.2	2150	2.0
6	M	0240	0.3	1006	2.1	1513	0.3	2230	1.9
7	TU	0324	0.4	1046	1.9	1601	0.4	2311	1.7
8	W ☽	0411	0.6	1128	1.7	1652	0.5	2356	1.6
9	TH	0506	0.7	1215	1.6	1751	0.6		
10	F	0053	1.5	0613	0.8	1319	1.5	1857	0.7
11	SA	0213	1.5	0735	0.8	1444	1.4	2007	0.7
12	SU	0328	1.5	0852	0.8	1555	1.5	2107	0.6
13	M	0426	1.7	0946	0.7	1652	1.6	2156	0.5
14	TU	0513	1.8	1030	0.6	1741	1.6	2241	0.4
15	W	0557	1.9	1112	0.4	1825	1.7	2324	0.4
16	TH ○	0636	2.0	1153	0.3	1905	1.8		
17	F	0005	0.3	0713	2.0	1232	0.3	1941	1.8
18	SA	0044	0.2	0749	2.0	1308	0.2	2015	1.8
19	SU	0118	0.2	0822	2.0	1338	0.2	2047	1.8
20	M	0146	0.3	0853	1.9	1402	0.3	2116	1.7
21	TU	0211	0.3	0920	1.8	1426	0.3	2141	1.6
22	W	0236	0.3	0946	1.7	1454	0.3	2208	1.5
23	TH	0306	0.4	1017	1.6	1530	0.4	2244	1.5
24	F ☾	0346	0.5	1058	1.5	1620	0.5	2337	1.4
25	SA	0447	0.6	1157	1.4	1735	0.6		
26	SU	0053	1.4	0618	0.7	1320	1.4	1906	0.6
27	M	0231	1.5	0755	0.6	1501	1.5	2029	0.5
28	TU	0356	1.7	0913	0.5	1627	1.6	2138	0.4
29	W	0504	1.9	1015	0.4	1736	1.8	2236	0.2
30	TH ●	0603	2.1	1108	0.2	1835	2.0	2327	0.1
31	F	0657	2.3	1157	0.1	1926	2.1		

FEBRUARY

Date	Day	Time	m	Time	m	Time	m	Time	m
1	SA	0014	0.0	0745	2.4	1244	0.0	2012	2.2
2	SU	0059	0.0	0829	2.4	1328	-0.1	2053	2.2
3	M	0142	0.0	0910	2.3	1410	0.0	2131	2.1
4	TU	0221	0.1	0947	2.2	1450	0.1	2205	1.9
5	W	0300	0.2	1020	1.9	1530	0.3	2236	1.7
6	TH ☽	0339	0.4	1052	1.7	1610	0.4	2308	1.6
7	F	0421	0.6	1127	1.5	1657	0.6	2349	1.4
8	SA	0519	0.7	1214	1.3	1800	0.7		
9	SU	0047	1.4	0643	0.8	1326	1.2	1920	0.7
10	M	0220	1.4	0822	0.8	1519	1.3	2035	0.7
11	TU	0349	1.5	0926	0.7	1628	1.4	2132	0.6
12	W	0446	1.6	1010	0.5	1720	1.5	2219	0.4
13	TH	0533	1.8	1051	0.4	1805	1.7	2302	0.3
14	F ○	0616	1.9	1131	0.3	1847	1.8	2343	0.2
15	SA	0657	2.0	1209	0.2	1926	1.9		
16	SU	0022	0.1	0735	2.1	1245	0.1	2001	1.9
17	M	0057	0.1	0810	2.0	1316	0.1	2033	1.9
18	TU	0128	0.1	0841	2.0	1343	0.1	2101	1.8
19	W	0155	0.1	0908	1.9	1409	0.2	2124	1.7
20	TH	0221	0.2	0934	1.7	1437	0.2	2148	1.6
21	F	0249	0.3	1002	1.6	1508	0.3	2220	1.5
22	SA ☾	0324	0.4	1039	1.5	1550	0.4	2304	1.5
23	SU	0417	0.5	1132	1.4	1656	0.5		
24	M	0011	1.4	0547	0.6	1251	1.3	1841	0.6
25	TU	0149	1.4	0740	0.6	1438	1.4	2017	0.6
26	W	0331	1.6	0905	0.5	1614	1.6	2128	0.4
27	TH	0447	1.8	1006	0.3	1724	1.8	2225	0.2
28	F	0548	2.1	1057	0.1	1821	2.0	2314	0.1

MARCH

Date	Day	Time	m	Time	m	Time	m	Time	m
1	SA ●	0641	2.3	1143	0.0	1910	2.2	2359	0.0
2	SU	0728	2.4	1227	-0.1	1954	2.2		
3	M	0042	-0.1	0811	2.4	1309	-0.2	2033	2.2
4	TU	0122	-0.1	0849	2.3	1348	-0.1	2108	2.1
5	W	0200	0.0	0923	2.1	1425	0.0	2138	2.0
6	TH	0235	0.1	0953	1.9	1459	0.2	2203	1.8
7	F	0309	0.3	1019	1.7	1532	0.4	2229	1.6
8	SA ☽	0344	0.5	1050	1.4	1604	0.6	2303	1.4
9	SU	0427	0.7	1132	1.3	1650	0.7	2352	1.3
10	M	0553	0.8	1236	1.2	1829	0.8		
11	TU	0137	1.3	0744	0.8	1427	1.2	1959	0.7
12	W	0251	1.4	0858	0.6	1601	1.3	2102	0.6
13	TH	0408	1.5	0943	0.5	1653	1.5	2151	0.5
14	F	0501	1.7	1023	0.3	1739	1.7	2235	0.3
15	SA	0549	1.9	1102	0.2	1822	1.8	2316	0.2
16	SU ○	0632	2.0	1140	0.1	1902	1.9	2355	0.1
17	M	0713	2.1	1216	0.0	1939	2.0		
18	TU	0030	0.0	0750	2.1	1249	0.0	2013	2.0
19	W	0103	0.0	0823	2.0	1320	0.0	2042	1.9
20	TH	0134	0.1	0852	1.9	1350	0.1	2107	1.9
21	F	0204	0.1	0919	1.8	1421	0.2	2132	1.7
22	SA	0236	0.2	0949	1.7	1454	0.3	2204	1.6
23	SU	0314	0.3	1028	1.5	1536	0.4	2247	1.5
24	M ☾	0408	0.5	1122	1.4	1643	0.6	2352	1.5
25	TU	0540	0.6	1240	1.4	1828	0.7		
26	W	0127	1.5	0729	0.6	1429	1.4	2003	0.6
27	TH	0310	1.6	0851	0.5	1600	1.6	2113	0.5
28	F	0426	1.8	0950	0.3	1706	1.8	2208	0.3
29	SA	0527	2.0	1039	0.1	1800	2.0	2255	0.1
30	SU ●	0620	2.2	1124	0.0	1848	2.2	2340	0.0
31	M	0707	2.3	1206	-0.1	1931	2.2		

APRIL

Date	Day	Time	m	Time	m	Time	m	Time	m
1	TU	0021	0.0	0748	2.3	1247	-0.1	2009	2.2
2	W	0101	0.0	0826	2.2	1324	-0.1	2042	2.1
3	TH	0137	0.0	0858	2.1	1359	0.1	2110	2.0
4	F	0212	0.1	0926	1.8	1431	0.2	2133	1.8
5	SA	0244	0.3	0951	1.6	1459	0.4	2156	1.6
6	SU	0315	0.5	1020	1.4	1522	0.6	2225	1.5
7	M ☽	0349	0.6	1100	1.3	1552	0.7	2307	1.4
8	TU	0453	0.7	1201	1.2	1712	0.8		
9	W	0015	1.3	0654	0.7	1333	1.2	1915	0.8
10	TH	0146	1.4	0814	0.6	1515	1.3	2026	0.7
11	F	0314	1.5	0906	0.5	1615	1.5	2118	0.5
12	SA	0419	1.6	0948	0.4	1704	1.7	2202	0.4
13	SU	0512	1.8	1028	0.2	1749	1.8	2244	0.3
14	M	0600	1.9	1106	0.1	1832	2.0	2323	0.2
15	TU ○	0645	2.0	1143	0.1	1912	2.1		
16	W	0000	0.1	0726	2.1	1220	0.0	1949	2.1
17	TH	0037	0.1	0803	2.1	1256	0.1	2022	2.1
18	F	0113	0.1	0836	2.0	1332	0.1	2052	2.0
19	SA	0150	0.1	0908	1.9	1409	0.2	2122	1.9
20	SU	0228	0.2	0942	1.7	1448	0.3	2157	1.8
21	M	0313	0.3	1025	1.6	1537	0.5	2243	1.6
22	TU ☾	0413	0.5	1122	1.5	1645	0.6	2346	1.6
23	W	0535	0.6	1241	1.4	1814	0.7		
24	TH	0115	1.5	0709	0.6	1417	1.5	1941	0.7
25	F	0247	1.6	0827	0.4	1536	1.7	2050	0.5
26	SA	0400	1.8	0926	0.3	1639	1.8	2146	0.4
27	SU	0501	1.9	1015	0.2	1734	2.0	2234	0.3
28	M	0554	2.1	1100	0.1	1822	2.1	2318	0.2
29	TU ●	0642	2.1	1143	0.0	1905	2.2	2359	0.1
30	W	0726	2.2	1223	0.0	1944	2.2		

MAY

Date	Day	Time	m	Time	m	Time	m	Time	m
1	TH	0039	0.1	0803	2.1	1301	0.1	2017	2.1
2	F	0117	0.1	0835	2.0	1336	0.2	2044	2.0
3	SA	0152	0.2	0902	1.8	1408	0.3	2106	1.8
4	SU	0225	0.3	0928	1.6	1436	0.4	2130	1.7
5	M	0255	0.4	0958	1.5	1459	0.6	2158	1.6
6	TU	0325	0.5	1036	1.3	1526	0.7	2232	1.5
7	W ☽	0407	0.6	1130	1.2	1618	0.8	2326	1.4
8	TH	0531	0.7	1246	1.2	1808	0.8		
9	F	0048	1.4	0712	0.6	1413	1.3	1938	0.7
10	SA	0216	1.4	0816	0.5	1525	1.5	2037	0.6
11	SU	0330	1.6	0904	0.4	1621	1.7	2125	0.5
12	M	0431	1.7	0947	0.3	1711	1.8	2208	0.4
13	TU	0525	1.8	1028	0.2	1759	2.0	2250	0.3
14	W ○	0615	2.0	1110	0.1	1843	2.1	2331	0.2
15	TH	0701	2.0	1152	0.1	1926	2.1		
16	F	0013	0.1	0744	2.1	1235	0.1	2005	2.1
17	SA	0056	0.1	0824	2.0	1317	0.2	2042	2.1
18	SU	0139	0.2	0903	2.0	1401	0.2	2120	2.0
19	M	0224	0.2	0944	1.9	1447	0.3	2200	1.9
20	TU	0314	0.3	1030	1.7	1538	0.5	2247	1.8
21	W ☾	0411	0.4	1125	1.6	1639	0.6	2346	1.7
22	TH	0519	0.5	1234	1.6	1751	0.7		
23	F	0100	1.6	0637	0.5	1352	1.6	1909	0.7
24	SA	0218	1.6	0753	0.5	1505	1.7	2021	0.6
25	SU	0329	1.7	0856	0.4	1609	1.8	2120	0.5
26	M	0432	1.8	0949	0.3	1705	1.9	2211	0.4
27	TU	0528	1.9	1036	0.3	1755	2.0	2256	0.4
28	W ●	0618	1.9	1119	0.2	1840	2.1	2339	0.3
29	TH	0703	2.0	1200	0.2	1920	2.1		
30	F	0020	0.3	0742	1.9	1240	0.2	1953	2.1
31	SA	0059	0.2	0816	1.9	1317	0.3	2021	2.0

JUNE

Date	Day	Time	m	Time	m	Time	m	Time	m
1	SU	0136	0.3	0844	1.8	1352	0.3	2047	1.9
2	M	0210	0.3	0911	1.7	1422	0.4	2114	1.8
3	TU	0240	0.4	0942	1.6	1446	0.5	2142	1.7
4	W	0305	0.5	1017	1.4	1511	0.6	2212	1.5
5	TH ☽	0336	0.5	1059	1.4	1549	0.7	2250	1.4
6	F	0423	0.6	1158	1.3	1650	0.7	2349	1.4
7	SA	0533	0.6	1312	1.3	1817	0.7		
8	SU	0112	1.4	0655	0.6	1430	1.4	1937	0.7
9	M	0236	1.5	0805	0.5	1536	1.6	2039	0.6
10	TU	0348	1.6	0901	0.4	1634	1.8	2131	0.5
11	W	0450	1.7	0953	0.3	1727	1.9	2220	0.4
12	TH	0547	1.9	1043	0.2	1818	2.1	2309	0.3
13	F ○	0640	2.0	1132	0.2	1906	2.2	2356	0.2
14	SA	0730	2.1	1220	0.1	1952	2.2		
15	SU	0043	0.1	0817	2.1	1307	0.1	2036	2.2
16	M	0131	0.1	0901	2.1	1354	0.2	2119	2.2
17	TU	0218	0.1	0945	2.0	1441	0.3	2202	2.1
18	W	0307	0.2	1029	1.9	1529	0.4	2247	1.9
19	TH ☾	0359	0.3	1117	1.8	1622	0.5	2337	1.8
20	F	0456	0.4	1212	1.7	1721	0.6		
21	SA	0034	1.7	0600	0.5	1317	1.6	1829	0.7
22	SU	0143	1.6	0712	0.5	1429	1.6	1944	0.7
23	M	0255	1.6	0822	0.5	1537	1.7	2053	0.7
24	TU	0403	1.6	0922	0.5	1637	1.8	2150	0.6
25	W	0503	1.7	1013	0.4	1729	1.9	2237	0.5
26	TH	0556	1.8	1058	0.4	1816	1.9	2320	0.4
27	F ●	0643	1.8	1140	0.3	1858	2.0		
28	SA	0001	0.3	0723	1.8	1220	0.3	1933	2.0
29	SU	0042	0.3	0758	1.8	1259	0.3	2004	2.0
30	M	0120	0.3	0828	1.8	1336	0.3	2033	1.9

SUNRISE AND SUNSET TIMES
PORTLAND
AT 50°34′N 2°26′ W

UT		Sunrise	Sunset
Jan	01	0811	1616
	15	0805	1634
Feb	01	0745	1702
	15	0721	1727
Mar	01	0654	1751
	15	0623	1815
BST			
Apr	01	0646	1942
	15	0616	2005
May	01	0544	2030
	15	0522	2051
Jun	01	0503	2113
	15	0457	2124
Jul	01	0502	2125
	15	0515	2116
Aug	01	0537	2054
	15	0558	2029
Sep	01	0624	1954
	15	0645	1923
Oct	01	0710	1848
	15	0732	1818
UT			
Nov	01	0701	1645
	15	0725	1624
Dec	01	0749	1608
	15	0804	1605

PANTAENIUS
Yacht Insurance

JULY

Date	Day	Time	m	Time	m	Time	m	Time	m
1	TU	0154	0.3	0857	1.7	1408	0.3	2102	1.8
2	W	0223	0.3	0927	1.7	1433	0.4	2130	1.7
3	TH	0245	0.4	0957	1.6	1455	0.5	2157	1.6
4	F	0310	0.4	1029	1.5	1524	0.5	2227	1.5
5	SA ☽	0345	0.4	1109	1.4	1606	0.6	2307	1.4
6	SU	0435	0.5	1205	1.4	1709	0.7		
7	M	0006	1.4	0544	0.5	1324	1.4	1830	0.7
8	TU	0129	1.4	0705	0.5	1447	1.5	1951	0.6
9	W	0301	1.5	0822	0.5	1558	1.7	2101	0.5
10	TH	0418	1.6	0927	0.4	1700	1.9	2200	0.4
11	F	0524	1.8	1025	0.3	1757	2.0	2254	0.3
12	SA O	0623	1.9	1118	0.2	1851	2.2	2345	0.2
13	SU	0718	2.1	1208	0.1	1941	2.3		
14	M	0033	0.1	0807	2.2	1257	0.1	2027	2.4
15	TU	0121	0.0	0853	2.2	1343	0.1	2111	2.3
16	W	0207	0.0	0935	2.1	1427	0.1	2153	2.2
17	TH	0253	0.1	1015	2.0	1512	0.2	2233	2.0
18	F	0339	0.2	1056	1.8	1558	0.4	2315	1.8
19	SA ☾	0428	0.4	1140	1.7	1648	0.5		
20	SU	0000	1.6	0523	0.5	1234	1.6	1748	0.7
21	M	0058	1.5	0628	0.6	1345	1.5	1904	0.8
22	TU	0217	1.4	0747	0.7	1505	1.5	2029	0.8
23	W	0337	1.4	0859	0.6	1612	1.6	2133	0.7
24	TH	0441	1.5	0952	0.6	1706	1.7	2219	0.6
25	F	0534	1.6	1036	0.5	1754	1.8	2300	0.5
26	SA ●	0621	1.7	1117	0.4	1836	1.9	2341	0.4
27	SU	0703	1.8	1158	0.3	1914	2.0		
28	M	0020	0.3	0738	1.9	1238	0.2	1946	2.0
29	TU	0059	0.2	0810	1.9	1315	0.2	2018	2.0
30	W	0133	0.2	0840	1.8	1348	0.2	2047	1.9
31	TH	0201	0.2	0909	1.8	1413	0.3	2116	1.8

AUGUST

Date	Day	Time	m	Time	m	Time	m	Time	m
1	F	0223	0.3	0935	1.7	1435	0.3	2141	1.7
2	SA	0246	0.3	1000	1.6	1459	0.4	2206	1.6
3	SU	0315	0.4	1031	1.5	1532	0.5	2238	1.5
4	M ☽	0354	0.4	1114	1.4	1622	0.6	2326	1.4
5	TU	0455	0.5	1218	1.4	1741	0.7		
6	W	0036	1.4	0623	0.6	1352	1.4	1918	0.7
7	TH	0218	1.4	0757	0.6	1526	1.6	2043	0.6
8	F	0354	1.6	0913	0.5	1638	1.8	2148	0.4
9	SA	0507	1.8	1014	0.3	1740	2.0	2243	0.3
10	SU O	0609	2.0	1106	0.2	1835	2.2	2333	0.1
11	M	0703	2.1	1155	0.0	1926	2.4		
12	TU	0021	0.0	0751	2.2	1242	0.0	2012	2.5
13	W	0107	-0.1	0835	2.3	1326	0.0	2054	2.4
14	TH	0150	-0.1	0915	2.2	1408	0.0	2133	2.3
15	F	0232	0.0	0952	2.1	1449	0.2	2210	2.1
16	SA	0314	0.2	1028	1.9	1530	0.3	2246	1.8
17	SU ☾	0356	0.4	1103	1.7	1615	0.5	2322	1.6
18	M	0443	0.6	1144	1.5	1710	0.7		
19	TU	0008	1.4	0543	0.7	1244	1.4	1826	0.8
20	W	0126	1.3	0706	0.8	1429	1.4	2009	0.8
21	TH	0316	1.3	0833	0.7	1548	1.5	2116	0.7
22	F	0422	1.4	0927	0.6	1642	1.7	2158	0.6
23	SA	0512	1.6	1010	0.5	1727	1.8	2236	0.5
24	SU	0556	1.7	1051	0.4	1809	1.9	2315	0.3
25	M ●	0637	1.8	1131	0.3	1848	2.0	2354	0.2
26	TU	0713	1.9	1211	0.2	1923	2.1		
27	W	0031	0.2	0747	2.0	1249	0.1	1956	2.1
28	TH	0106	0.1	0818	1.9	1321	0.2	2028	2.0
29	F	0134	0.2	0846	1.9	1348	0.2	2056	1.9
30	SA	0158	0.2	0911	1.8	1412	0.3	2120	1.8
31	SU	0222	0.3	0934	1.7	1436	0.4	2145	1.7

SEPTEMBER

Date	Day	Time	m	Time	m	Time	m	Time	m
1	M	0248	0.4	1002	1.6	1505	0.4	2217	1.5
2	TU ☽	0322	0.5	1041	1.5	1549	0.6	2301	1.4
3	W	0416	0.6	1139	1.4	1712	0.7		
4	TH	0010	1.4	0557	0.7	1310	1.4	1904	0.7
5	F	0155	1.4	0745	0.7	1459	1.6	2034	0.6
6	SA	0341	1.6	0903	0.5	1618	1.8	2137	0.4
7	SU	0453	1.8	1001	0.4	1721	2.1	2229	0.2
8	M	0552	2.0	1051	0.2	1815	2.3	2317	0.1
9	TU O	0644	2.2	1138	0.1	1905	2.4		
10	W	0002	0.0	0730	2.3	1222	0.0	1950	2.5
11	TH	0046	-0.1	0812	2.3	1305	0.0	2031	2.4
12	F	0128	0.0	0850	2.3	1345	0.0	2109	2.3
13	SA	0207	0.1	0924	2.1	1423	0.2	2143	2.0
14	SU	0244	0.2	0955	1.9	1501	0.4	2213	1.8
15	M	0321	0.4	1023	1.7	1542	0.6	2243	1.5
16	TU ☾	0359	0.6	1055	1.5	1632	0.7	2322	1.3
17	W	0451	0.8	1142	1.4	1751	0.9		
18	TH	0026	1.2	0618	0.9	1259	1.4	1937	0.8
19	F	0258	1.3	0753	0.9	1512	1.5	2048	0.7
20	SA	0401	1.4	0855	0.7	1607	1.6	2127	0.6
21	SU	0445	1.6	0939	0.6	1652	1.8	2205	0.5
22	M	0525	1.7	1021	0.4	1733	1.9	2243	0.3
23	TU	0604	1.9	1101	0.3	1814	2.0	2322	0.2
24	W ●	0642	2.0	1141	0.2	1853	2.1	2358	0.2
25	TH	0718	2.1	1217	0.2	1930	2.1		
26	F	0032	0.1	0751	2.1	1251	0.2	2003	2.1
27	SA	0103	0.2	0821	2.0	1320	0.2	2033	2.0
28	SU	0131	0.2	0847	1.9	1348	0.3	2100	1.9
29	M	0158	0.3	0911	1.8	1416	0.4	2127	1.7
30	TU	0227	0.4	0940	1.7	1449	0.5	2201	1.6

OCTOBER

Date	Day	Time	m	Time	m	Time	m	Time	m
1	W ☽	0301	0.5	1018	1.6	1537	0.6	2248	1.5
2	TH	0355	0.7	1116	1.5	1706	0.7		
3	F	0000	1.4	0545	0.8	1244	1.5	1855	0.7
4	SA	0150	1.4	0732	0.8	1437	1.6	2019	0.6
5	SU	0329	1.6	0847	0.6	1556	1.8	2119	0.4
6	M	0435	1.8	0943	0.4	1657	2.1	2210	0.2
7	TU	0530	2.1	1032	0.3	1751	2.2	2256	0.1
8	W O	0619	2.2	1117	0.2	1840	2.4	2340	0.0
9	TH	0705	2.3	1200	0.1	1925	2.4		
10	F	0022	0.0	0745	2.3	1242	0.1	2006	2.3
11	SA	0102	0.0	0822	2.3	1321	0.2	2043	2.2
12	SU	0139	0.2	0854	2.1	1358	0.3	2114	2.0
13	M	0214	0.3	0920	2.0	1435	0.4	2141	1.7
14	TU	0246	0.5	0943	1.8	1512	0.6	2208	1.5
15	W ☾	0315	0.7	1011	1.6	1557	0.7	2245	1.3
16	TH	0347	0.8	1051	1.5	1710	0.8	2342	1.2
17	F	0512	1.0	1154	1.4	1845	0.9		
18	SA	0133	1.2	0701	1.0	1328	1.4	1959	0.8
19	SU	0323	1.4	0814	0.8	1506	1.5	2048	0.6
20	M	0407	1.6	0905	0.7	1603	1.7	2129	0.5
21	TU	0447	1.8	0948	0.5	1651	1.8	2208	0.4
22	W	0527	1.9	1029	0.4	1736	2.0	2245	0.3
23	TH ●	0607	2.1	1107	0.3	1820	2.1	2322	0.2
24	F	0647	2.1	1144	0.3	1901	2.1	2357	0.2
25	SA	0724	2.2	1219	0.2	1939	2.1		
26	SU	0031	0.2	0757	2.1	1253	0.3	2012	2.0
27	M	0106	0.3	0827	2.1	1328	0.3	2043	1.9
28	TU	0140	0.3	0855	2.0	1404	0.4	2115	1.8
29	W	0216	0.5	0928	1.9	1445	0.5	2154	1.7
30	TH	0257	0.6	1008	1.7	1541	0.6	2244	1.6
31	F ☽	0358	0.7	1105	1.6	1703	0.7	2357	1.5

NOVEMBER

Date	Day	Time	m	Time	m	Time	m	Time	m
1	SA	0532	0.8	1228	1.6	1835	0.7		
2	SU	0138	1.5	0707	0.8	1411	1.7	1953	0.6
3	M	0307	1.7	0823	0.7	1528	1.8	2054	0.5
4	TU	0410	1.9	0921	0.6	1630	2.0	2145	0.3
5	W	0504	2.1	1010	0.4	1725	2.1	2232	0.2
6	TH O	0553	2.2	1056	0.3	1815	2.2	2315	0.2
7	F	0638	2.3	1139	0.3	1901	2.2	2357	0.2
8	SA	0720	2.3	1220	0.2	1942	2.2		
9	SU	0036	0.2	0756	2.3	1259	0.3	2018	2.1
10	M	0114	0.3	0826	2.1	1337	0.3	2048	1.9
11	TU	0148	0.4	0850	2.0	1413	0.4	2114	1.7
12	W	0219	0.5	0913	1.8	1449	0.6	2141	1.6
13	TH	0245	0.7	0940	1.7	1525	0.7	2216	1.4
14	F ☾	0308	0.8	1013	1.6	1612	0.8	2305	1.3
15	SA	0348	0.9	1102	1.5	1740	0.8		
16	SU	0018	1.3	0547	1.0	1220	1.4	1900	0.8
17	M	0153	1.3	0723	0.9	1349	1.5	1959	0.7
18	TU	0309	1.5	0824	0.8	1506	1.6	2046	0.5
19	W	0402	1.7	0911	0.6	1607	1.7	2127	0.4
20	TH	0449	1.9	0953	0.5	1659	1.9	2206	0.3
21	F	0534	2.0	1033	0.4	1748	2.0	2246	0.3
22	SA ●	0617	2.1	1112	0.3	1835	2.0	2326	0.2
23	SU	0659	2.2	1151	0.3	1918	2.1		
24	M	0007	0.2	0738	2.2	1232	0.3	1957	2.0
25	TU	0048	0.3	0814	2.2	1314	0.3	2035	2.0
26	W	0130	0.3	0850	2.1	1357	0.4	2113	1.9
27	TH	0213	0.4	0927	2.0	1445	0.4	2155	1.8
28	F	0300	0.5	1010	1.9	1540	0.5	2245	1.7
29	SA ☽	0357	0.7	1104	1.8	1647	0.6	2348	1.6
30	SU	0508	0.8	1213	1.7	1803	0.6		

DECEMBER

Date	Day	Time	m	Time	m	Time	m	Time	m
1	M	0109	1.6	0630	0.8	1338	1.7	1917	0.6
2	TU	0231	1.7	0748	0.8	1456	1.7	2022	0.5
3	W	0339	1.8	0854	0.7	1601	1.8	2118	0.4
4	TH	0437	1.9	0948	0.6	1659	1.9	2207	0.4
5	F	0528	2.1	1036	0.5	1751	2.0	2253	0.3
6	SA O	0614	2.1	1120	0.4	1839	2.0	2335	0.3
7	SU	0656	2.2	1201	0.4	1922	2.0		
8	M	0015	0.3	0733	2.2	1241	0.3	1958	2.0
9	TU	0054	0.3	0804	2.1	1320	0.3	2029	1.9
10	W	0130	0.4	0830	2.0	1356	0.4	2055	1.7
11	TH	0202	0.5	0856	1.9	1430	0.5	2123	1.6
12	F	0229	0.6	0924	1.8	1458	0.5	2156	1.5
13	SA	0250	0.7	0953	1.7	1524	0.6	2234	1.4
14	SU ☾	0320	0.7	1028	1.5	1602	0.7	2326	1.3
15	M	0409	0.8	1121	1.5	1709	0.7		
16	TU	0038	1.3	0536	0.9	1239	1.4	1837	0.7
17	W	0200	1.4	0718	0.8	1406	1.5	1945	0.6
18	TH	0312	1.6	0823	0.7	1522	1.6	2039	0.5
19	F	0410	1.7	0914	0.6	1624	1.7	2129	0.4
20	SA	0502	1.9	1001	0.5	1720	1.8	2216	0.3
21	SU	0552	2.1	1046	0.4	1813	1.9	2304	0.2
22	M ●	0639	2.2	1132	0.3	1902	2.0	2351	0.2
23	TU	0725	2.2	1218	0.2	1949	2.1		
24	W	0037	0.2	0808	2.3	1305	0.2	2032	2.1
25	TH	0123	0.2	0850	2.2	1351	0.2	2114	2.0
26	F	0208	0.3	0931	2.1	1438	0.3	2155	1.9
27	SA	0254	0.4	1013	2.0	1529	0.3	2239	1.8
28	SU ☽	0344	0.5	1059	1.9	1624	0.4	2329	1.7
29	M	0440	0.6	1152	1.7	1726	0.5		
30	TU	0029	1.6	0547	0.7	1258	1.6	1834	0.6
31	W	0144	1.6	0704	0.8	1416	1.6	1945	0.6

POOLE HARBOUR

LAT 50°42′N
LONG 1°59′W

TIMES AND HEIGHTS OF HIGH AND LOW WATER (Heights in Metres)

TIME ZONE UT
For Summer Time (area enclosed in shaded box) add 1 hour

Sea level is above mean tide level from 2·0 hours after LW to 2·0 hours before the next LW and HW will occur between 5·0 hours after LW and 3·0 hours before the next LW

2014

JANUARY

Day		Time	m	Time	m	Time	m	Time	m
1	W ●	0329	0.5	0848	2.3	1556	0.3	2119	2.2
2	TH	0419	0.4	0934	2.4	1644	0.2	2204	2.3
3	F	0506	0.4	1018	2.5	1730	0.2	2247	2.3
4	SA	0554	0.5	1100	2.4	1816	0.2	2330	2.2
5	SU	0642	0.6	1141	2.3	1903	0.4		
6	M	0433	2.1	0732	0.7	1217	2.2	1953	0.5
7	TU	0518	2.1	0824	0.9	1247	2.0	2046	0.7
8	W ☽	0604	2.1	0923	1.0	1825	1.8	2147	0.9
9	TH	0654	2.0	1030	1.1	1922	1.8	2257	1.1
10	F	0750	2.0	1138	1.2	2030	1.8		
11	SA	0004	1.1	0856	2.0	1241	1.1	2143	1.8
12	SU	0105	1.1	1003	1.9	1339	1.0	2248	1.8
13	M	0200	1.0	1104	1.9	1429	0.9	2343	1.9
14	TU	0248	1.0	0621	1.9	1515	0.8	1900	1.8
15	W	0333	0.9	0717	2.0	1557	0.7	2042	1.9
16	TH O	0413	0.8	0823	2.1	1634	0.6	2114	2.0
17	F	0449	0.8	0918	2.1	1707	0.6	2157	2.0
18	SA	0521	0.8	1003	2.1	1737	0.6	2238	2.0
19	SU	0553	0.8	1043	2.1	1808	0.6	2319	1.9
20	M	0626	0.8	1109	2.0	1842	0.6		
21	TU	0405	1.9	0702	0.8	1021	1.9	1920	0.7
22	W	0447	2.0	0742	0.9	1039	1.9	2002	0.7
23	TH	0531	1.9	0827	0.9	1117	1.8	2050	0.8
24	F ☾	0619	1.9	0921	1.0	1207	1.8	2149	1.0
25	SA	0708	1.9	1027	1.1	1935	1.7	2300	1.0
26	SU	0802	1.8	1140	1.0	2034	1.7		
27	M	0011	1.0	0623	1.8	1250	0.9	1852	1.7
28	TU	0119	0.9	0704	1.9	1354	0.7	1938	1.9
29	W	0220	0.7	0751	2.1	1451	0.5	2025	2.0
30	TH ●	0315	0.5	0838	2.3	1542	0.3	2108	2.2
31	F	0405	0.4	0922	2.4	1629	0.1	2150	2.3

FEBRUARY

Day		Time	m	Time	m	Time	m	Time	m
1	SA	0451	0.3	1004	2.5	1713	0.0	2230	2.3
2	SU	0537	0.3	1044	2.5	1757	0.1	2309	2.3
3	M	0621	0.4	1121	2.4	1841	0.2	2346	2.1
4	TU	0706	0.5	1156	2.2	1926	0.5		
5	W	0452	2.0	0753	0.7	1220	2.0	2013	0.7
6	TH ☽	0534	2.0	0844	0.9	1755	1.8	2106	1.0
7	F	0619	1.9	0944	1.1	1847	1.8	2213	1.2
8	SA	0710	1.9	1101	1.2	1954	1.8	2335	1.3
9	SU	0816	1.8	1215	1.2	2112	1.8		
10	M	0045	1.2	0931	1.8	1317	1.1	2220	1.8
11	TU	0142	1.1	1037	1.8	1409	0.9	2318	1.8
12	W	0231	1.0	1134	1.8	1455	0.8	2035	1.7
13	TH	0315	0.9	0653	1.9	1536	0.7		
14	F O	0354	0.8	0803	2.0	1613	0.6	2052	2.0
15	SA	0428	0.7	0900	2.1	1645	0.5	2133	2.1
16	SU	0459	0.7	0944	2.2	1715	0.5	2213	2.1
17	M	0530	0.6	1023	2.2	1746	0.5	2250	2.1
18	TU	0602	0.6	1058	2.1	1818	0.5	2326	2.0
19	W	0636	0.6	1126	2.0	1853	0.6		
20	TH	0422	1.9	0713	0.7	1018	1.9	1932	0.7
21	F	0505	1.9	0754	0.8	1054	1.9	2016	0.8
22	SA ☾	0550	1.9	0843	0.9	1814	1.8	2110	1.0
23	SU	0637	1.8	0947	1.0	1904	1.8	2224	1.1
24	M	0725	1.8	1109	1.0	1957	1.7	2349	1.1
25	TU	0610	1.8	1230	0.9	1853	1.7		
26	W	0105	1.0	0652	1.9	1338	0.7	1931	1.9
27	TH	0208	0.8	0738	2.0	1435	0.5	2013	2.0
28	F	0301	0.6	0824	2.2	1525	0.2	2053	2.2

MARCH

Day		Time	m	Time	m	Time	m	Time	m
1	SA ●	0349	0.4	0905	2.4	1611	0.1	2131	2.3
2	SU	0433	0.3	0945	2.5	1653	0.0	2209	2.3
3	M	0516	0.2	1023	2.5	1736	0.1	2245	2.3
4	TU	0558	0.3	1059	2.3	1817	0.3	2319	2.2
5	W	0640	0.5	1133	2.2	1859	0.5	2348	2.0
6	TH	0723	0.7	1159	1.9	1942	0.8		
7	F	0503	1.9	0803	0.9	1725	1.8	2028	1.0
8	SA ☽	0542	1.9	0857	1.0	1810	1.8	2122	1.2
9	SU	0621	1.8	1034	1.2	1910	1.8	2258	1.4
10	M	0633	1.7	1141	1.2	2039	1.8		
11	TU	0021	1.3	0900	1.7	1249	1.1	2149	1.8
12	W	0119	1.2	1010	1.7	1342	1.0	2247	1.8
13	TH	0207	1.1	1107	1.7	1428	0.9	2339	1.9
14	F	0249	1.0	0637	1.8	1508	0.7	1950	1.8
15	SA	0327	0.8	0745	1.9	1544	0.6	2026	2.0
16	SU O	0401	0.7	0838	2.1	1617	0.5	2106	2.1
17	M	0433	0.6	0921	2.2	1649	0.5	2145	2.2
18	TU	0505	0.5	1001	2.2	1721	0.4	2223	2.2
19	W	0539	0.5	1039	2.2	1755	0.5	2259	2.1
20	TH	0613	0.5	1115	2.1	1830	0.6	2335	2.0
21	F	0649	0.6	1151	1.9	1908	0.7	2219	1.9
22	SA	0730	0.7	1704	1.9	1952	0.9	2300	1.8
23	SU	0818	0.8	1750	1.9	2046	1.0		
24	M ☾	0609	1.8	0920	1.0	1841	1.9	2205	1.2
25	TU	0655	1.7	1051	1.0	1933	1.8	2338	1.1
26	W	0550	1.8	1213	0.9	2025	1.8		
27	TH	0052	1.0	0634	1.9	1319	0.7	1918	1.9
28	F	0151	0.8	0720	2.0	1415	0.5	1955	2.0
29	SA	0243	0.6	0804	2.1	1504	0.3	2033	2.2
30	SU ●	0330	0.4	0845	2.3	1549	0.2	2109	2.3
31	M	0413	0.3	0923	2.4	1632	0.2	2143	2.3

APRIL

Day		Time	m	Time	m	Time	m	Time	m
1	TU	0454	0.3	1000	2.4	1713	0.3	2217	2.3
2	W	0535	0.3	1036	2.3	1753	0.4	2249	2.2
3	TH	0616	0.5	1110	2.1	1834	0.7	2318	2.0
4	F	0656	0.6	1142	1.9	1915	0.9	2251	1.9
5	SA	0737	0.8	1656	1.9	1958	1.1		
6	SU	0504	1.8	0821	1.0	1733	1.9	2045	1.3
7	M ☽	0530	1.8	0910	1.1	1807	1.9	2144	1.4
8	TU	0557	1.7	1015	1.2	1839	1.8	2342	1.4
9	W	0633	1.6	1206	1.2	2109	1.8		
10	TH	0045	1.3	0933	1.6	1304	1.1	2209	1.8
11	F	0134	1.2	1031	1.7	1351	1.0	2300	1.9
12	SA	0216	1.0	0636	1.7	1431	0.8	1922	1.9
13	SU	0253	0.9	0726	1.9	1508	0.7	1958	2.0
14	M	0329	0.7	0815	2.0	1544	0.6	2037	2.2
15	TU O	0404	0.6	0858	2.1	1620	0.5	2117	2.2
16	W	0440	0.5	0940	2.2	1656	0.5	2156	2.3
17	TH	0516	0.4	1020	2.2	1733	0.5	2236	2.2
18	F	0553	0.5	1101	2.1	1812	0.6	2315	2.1
19	SA	0632	0.5	1143	2.0	1853	0.8	2356	2.0
20	SU	0716	0.7	1648	2.0	1941	0.9		
21	M	0042	1.9	0807	0.8	1735	2.0	2042	1.1
22	TU ☾	0138	1.8	0914	0.9	1828	2.0	2205	1.2
23	W	0239	1.8	1036	0.9	1925	1.9	2324	1.1
24	TH	0522	1.8	1150	0.9	2027	1.9		
25	F	0030	1.0	0612	1.8	1254	0.8	1858	1.9
26	SA	0128	0.9	0659	1.9	1349	0.6	1934	2.0
27	SU	0220	0.7	0744	2.0	1439	0.5	2011	2.1
28	M	0307	0.5	0824	2.1	1526	0.4	2044	2.2
29	TU ●	0351	0.4	0901	2.2	1609	0.4	2116	2.3
30	W	0433	0.4	0937	2.2	1651	0.5	2147	2.3

MAY

Day		Time	m	Time	m	Time	m	Time	m
1	TH	0514	0.4	1012	2.2	1732	0.6	2220	2.2
2	F	0554	0.5	1048	2.1	1812	0.8	2251	2.1
3	SA	0633	0.7	1126	1.9	1852	1.0	2229	1.9
4	SU	0711	0.8	1629	1.9	1933	1.1	2244	1.8
5	M	0751	0.9	1702	1.9	2017	1.3	2318	1.8
6	TU	0836	1.0	1738	1.9	2107	1.3		
7	W ☽	0541	1.7	0927	1.1	1822	1.9	2205	1.4
8	TH	0631	1.7	1027	1.2	1922	1.9	2318	1.4
9	F	0744	1.6	1138	1.2	2059	1.9		
10	SA	0034	1.3	0934	1.6	1248	1.1	2205	1.9
11	SU	0125	1.1	0627	1.7	1340	0.9	1857	1.9
12	M	0209	0.9	0707	1.8	1426	0.8	1929	2.0
13	TU	0252	0.8	0752	2.0	1509	0.7	2008	2.2
14	W O	0334	0.6	0837	2.1	1552	0.6	2051	2.3
15	TH	0415	0.5	0921	2.2	1634	0.5	2135	2.3
16	F	0456	0.4	1005	2.2	1715	0.6	2218	2.3
17	SA	0538	0.4	1049	2.2	1759	0.7	2302	2.3
18	SU	0621	0.5	1134	2.1	1846	0.8	2346	2.2
19	M	0709	0.6	1638	2.0	1939	0.9		
20	TU	0032	2.1	0803	0.7	1727	2.1	2041	1.1
21	W ☾	0119	1.9	0906	0.8	1820	2.1	2151	1.1
22	TH	0208	1.8	1015	0.9	1915	2.1	2259	1.1
23	F	0258	1.8	1123	0.9	2014	2.0		
24	SA	0003	1.0	0552	1.8	1225	0.8	2119	2.0
25	SU	0101	0.9	0642	1.8	1322	0.8	1916	2.0
26	M	0155	0.8	0726	1.9	1415	0.7	1951	2.0
27	TU	0244	0.7	0807	2.0	1503	0.7	2023	2.1
28	W ●	0331	0.6	0843	2.1	1549	0.7	2050	2.2
29	TH	0414	0.6	0916	2.1	1632	0.7	2117	2.2
30	F	0455	0.6	0950	2.1	1713	0.8	2152	2.2
31	SA	0534	0.6	1027	2.1	1753	0.9	2229	2.1

JUNE

Day		Time	m	Time	m	Time	m	Time	m
1	SU	0612	0.7	1108	2.0	1831	1.0	2301	2.0
2	M	0648	0.8	1605	1.9	1908	1.1	2228	1.9
3	TU	0724	0.9	1637	2.0	1949	1.2	2257	1.8
4	W	0806	0.9	1716	2.0	2034	1.2	2335	1.8
5	TH ☽	0852	1.0	1802	2.0	2125	1.3		
6	F	0620	1.7	0946	1.1	1854	2.0	2222	1.3
7	SA	0720	1.7	1044	1.1	1953	1.9	2324	1.2
8	SU	0828	1.7	1147	1.1	2100	1.9		
9	M	0026	1.1	0939	1.7	1248	1.0	2206	1.9
10	TU	0124	1.0	0509	1.8	1345	0.9	1905	2.0
11	W	0216	0.8	0733	1.9	1438	0.8	1945	2.1
12	TH	0305	0.6	0822	2.0	1526	0.6	2034	2.3
13	F O	0353	0.5	0908	2.2	1614	0.6	2121	2.4
14	SA	0438	0.4	0955	2.3	1700	0.6	2208	2.4
15	SU	0524	0.3	1039	2.3	1747	0.6	2252	2.4
16	M	0610	0.4	1123	2.2	1836	0.7	2336	2.3
17	TU	0659	0.5	1208	2.1	1928	0.8		
18	W	0018	2.2	0751	0.6	1716	2.1	2025	0.9
19	TH ☾	0059	2.1	0847	0.7	1805	2.1	2126	1.0
20	F	0137	1.9	0948	0.8	1856	2.1	2230	1.1
21	SA	0720	1.8	1053	0.9	1952	2.1	2334	1.1
22	SU	0822	1.8	1157	1.0	2051	2.1		
23	M	0034	1.0	0932	1.8	1257	1.0	2156	2.0
24	TU	0131	0.9	1042	1.8	1353	1.0	2300	2.0
25	W	0224	0.8	1143	1.9	1444	0.9	2010	2.0
26	TH	0312	0.7	0834	1.9	1532	0.9	2025	2.1
27	F ●	0357	0.7	0901	2.0	1616	0.9	2042	2.2
28	SA	0439	0.6	0929	2.0	1657	0.9	2125	2.2
29	SU	0517	0.6	1006	2.1	1735	0.9	2209	2.2
30	M	0552	0.7	1046	2.0	1809	1.0	2250	2.1

SUNRISE AND SUNSET TIMES

POOLE

At 50°42′N 1°59′ W

		Sunrise	Sunset
UT			
Jan	01	0810	1614
	15	0803	1632
Feb	01	0744	1700
	15	0720	1725
Mar	01	0652	1749
	15	0622	1813
BST			
Apr	01	0644	1941
	15	0614	2003
May	01	0542	2029
	15	0519	2050
Jun	01	0500	2112
	15	0455	2122
Jul	01	0459	2124
	15	0512	2115
Aug	01	0535	2053
	15	0556	2028
Sep	01	0622	1953
	15	0643	1922
Oct	01	0708	1846
	15	0731	1816
UT			
Nov	01	0659	1643
	15	0723	1621
Dec	01	0748	1606
	15	0803	1603

JULY

Date	Day	Time	m	Time	m	Time	m	Time	m
1	TU	0624	0.7	1129	2.0	1843	1.0	2315	2.0
2	W	0658	0.8	1613	2.0	1919	1.0	2241	1.9
3	TH	0736	0.8	1653	2.0	2001	1.1	2308	1.8
4	F	0819	0.9	1737	2.0	2048	1.1	2343	1.8
5	SA ☽	0908	1.0	1826	2.0	2142	1.2		
6	SU	0650	1.8	1005	1.0	1919	2.0	2242	1.2
7	M	0750	1.8	1106	1.1	2018	1.9	2344	1.1
8	TU	0855	1.8	1210	1.0	2121	1.9		
9	W	0047	1.0	1002	1.8	1312	1.0	1849	2.0
10	TH	0147	0.8	0720	1.9	1411	0.8	1933	2.1
11	F	0242	0.6	0811	2.0	1506	0.7	2023	2.3
12	SA	0334	0.4	0858	2.2	1557	0.6	○ 2111	2.4
13	SU	0422	0.3	0944	2.3	1646	0.5	2157	2.5
14	M	0509	0.2	1027	2.4	1733	0.5	2240	2.5
15	TU	0555	0.2	1109	2.3	1821	0.5	2322	2.5
16	W	0642	0.3	1150	2.3	1909	0.7		
17	TH	0001	2.3	0730	0.5	1656	2.1	2001	0.8
18	F	0038	2.1	0821	0.7	1742	2.1	2056	1.0
19	SA	0106	1.9	0918	0.9	1830	2.1	☾ 2159	1.1
20	SU	0656	1.9	1022	1.0	1923	2.1	2305	1.1
21	M	0758	1.9	1130	1.1	2022	2.0		
22	TU	0010	1.1	0908	1.9	1235	1.2	2126	2.0
23	W	0110	1.0	1017	1.9	1335	1.1	2231	2.0
24	TH	0206	0.9	1120	1.9	1428	1.1	2002	1.9
25	F	0255	0.8	1214	1.9	1516	1.0	1855	2.0
26	SA	0340	0.7	1301	1.9	1600	0.9	● 2003	2.1
27	SU	0421	0.6	0906	2.0	1639	0.9	2101	2.2
28	M	0457	0.6	0942	2.1	1714	0.9	2148	2.2
29	TU	0530	0.6	1021	2.1	1745	0.9	2229	2.2
30	W	0559	0.7	1101	2.1	1816	0.9	2306	2.1
31	TH	0630	0.7	1139	2.0	1849	0.9	2242	2.0

AUGUST

Date	Day	Time	m	Time	m	Time	m	Time	m
1	F	0705	0.7	1627	2.0	1928	0.9	2239	1.9
2	SA	0745	0.8	1710	2.0	2011	1.0	2304	1.9
3	SU	0830	0.9	1756	2.0	2102	1.1		
4	M	0620	1.8	0924	1.0	1846	2.0	☽ 2202	1.1
5	TU	0714	1.8	1029	1.1	1939	1.9	2310	1.1
6	W	0815	1.8	1138	1.1	2036	1.9		
7	TH	0018	1.0	0922	1.8	1246	1.0	1837	2.0
8	F	0124	0.9	0713	1.9	1352	0.9	1923	2.1
9	SA	0224	0.6	0801	2.0	1450	0.7	2012	2.3
10	SU	0318	0.4	0847	2.2	1542	0.6	○ 2058	2.5
11	M	0406	0.2	0930	2.3	1630	0.4	2142	2.6
12	TU	0452	0.1	1011	2.4	1715	0.4	2224	2.6
13	W	0536	0.1	1051	2.4	1800	0.4	2304	2.6
14	TH	0620	0.2	1129	2.3	1845	0.5	2342	2.4
15	F	0705	0.4	1205	2.2	1932	0.7		
16	SA	0016	2.2	0753	0.7	1714	2.1	2024	0.9
17	SU	0039	1.9	0845	0.9	1800	2.1	☾ 2124	1.1
18	M	0627	1.9	0949	1.2	1850	2.0	2236	1.2
19	TU	0730	1.9	1105	1.3	1950	2.0	2347	1.2
20	W	0844	1.9	1217	1.3	2101	1.9		
21	TH	0050	1.1	0954	1.9	1318	1.2	2208	1.9
22	F	0146	1.0	1055	2.0	1410	1.1	2309	1.9
23	SA	0235	0.9	1149	2.0	1457	1.0	1834	2.0
24	SU	0319	0.7	1236	2.0	1539	0.9	1936	2.1
25	M	0359	0.6	0834	2.0	1617	0.8	● 2036	2.2
26	TU	0433	0.6	0914	2.1	1649	0.8	2124	2.3
27	W	0504	0.6	0954	2.2	1718	0.8	2206	2.3
28	TH	0533	0.6	1032	2.2	1748	0.8	2243	2.2
29	F	0603	0.6	1108	2.1	1820	0.8	2314	2.1
30	SA	0636	0.7	1600	2.0	1855	0.8	2210	2.0
31	SU	0712	0.8	1642	2.0	1935	0.9	2232	1.9

SEPTEMBER

Date	Day	Time	m	Time	m	Time	m	Time	m
1	M	0754	0.9	1726	2.0	2021	1.0		
2	TU	0550	1.9	0844	1.0	1813	1.9	☽ 2122	1.1
3	W	0640	1.9	0952	1.2	1901	1.9	2240	1.1
4	TH	0736	1.8	1114	1.2	1748	1.9	2358	1.0
5	F	0838	1.8	1231	1.1	1823	2.0		
6	SA	0107	0.9	0705	1.9	1338	1.0	1909	2.1
7	SU	0207	0.6	0748	2.1	1434	0.7	1957	2.3
8	M	0259	0.4	0831	2.2	1524	0.5	2042	2.5
9	TU	0346	0.2	0911	2.4	1610	0.4	○ 2123	2.6
10	W	0431	0.1	0950	2.5	1654	0.3	2204	2.6
11	TH	0514	0.1	1028	2.5	1737	0.4	2243	2.6
12	F	0556	0.3	1104	2.4	1820	0.5	2320	2.4
13	SA	0639	0.5	1138	2.2	1904	0.7	2355	2.1
14	SU	0724	0.8	1645	2.0	1952	0.9		
15	M	0508	1.9	0814	1.0	1727	2.0	2048	1.1
16	TU	0556	1.9	0914	1.3	1813	2.0	☾ 2201	1.2
17	W	0658	1.9	1039	1.4	1914	1.9	2320	1.2
18	TH	0819	1.9	1155	1.4	2037	1.9		
19	F	0025	1.2	0928	2.0	1255	1.3	2146	1.9
20	SA	0120	1.0	1027	2.0	1346	1.2	2244	1.9
21	SU	0208	0.9	1119	2.0	1432	1.1	1825	1.9
22	M	0251	0.8	1206	2.0	1512	0.9	1919	2.0
23	TU	0330	0.7	0800	2.1	1548	0.8	2013	2.2
24	W	0404	0.6	0843	2.2	1620	0.7	● 2059	2.3
25	TH	0434	0.6	0924	2.3	1650	0.7	2141	2.3
26	F	0505	0.6	1002	2.3	1721	0.7	2220	2.3
27	SA	0537	0.6	1039	2.2	1754	0.7	2256	2.2
28	SU	0610	0.7	1112	2.1	1828	0.7	2331	2.0
29	M	0646	0.8	1142	2.0	1907	0.8		
30	TU	0440	2.0	0727	0.9	1659	2.0	1952	0.9

OCTOBER

Date	Day	Time	m	Time	m	Time	m	Time	m
1	W	0525	2.0	0816	1.1	1744	1.9	☽ 2049	1.1
2	TH	0614	1.9	0925	1.2	1829	1.9	2217	1.1
3	F	0707	1.9	1101	1.3	1730	1.9	2341	1.0
4	SA	0807	1.9	1219	1.2	1807	2.0		
5	SU	0049	0.8	0651	2.0	1322	1.0	1853	2.1
6	M	0146	0.6	0730	2.1	1415	0.7	1938	2.2
7	TU	0237	0.4	0811	2.2	1504	0.5	2022	2.4
8	W	0324	0.3	0849	2.4	1549	0.4	○ 2103	2.5
9	TH	0408	0.2	0926	2.4	1632	0.4	2142	2.5
10	F	0450	0.3	1003	2.5	1714	0.4	2221	2.5
11	SA	0532	0.4	1037	2.4	1756	0.5	2258	2.3
12	SU	0615	0.6	1109	2.2	1838	0.7	2334	2.1
13	M	0658	0.9	1131	2.0	1923	0.9		
14	TU	0443	2.0	0745	1.1	1654	1.9	2012	1.1
15	W	0527	2.0	0838	1.3	1730	1.9	☾ 2111	1.2
16	TH	0618	2.0	0956	1.5	1729	1.8	2240	1.3
17	F	0740	1.9	1123	1.4	1757	1.8	2351	1.2
18	SA	0852	2.0	1225	1.4	2115	1.8		
19	SU	0047	1.1	0952	2.0	1316	1.3	2213	1.8
20	M	0135	1.0	1043	2.0	1400	1.1	1832	1.8
21	TU	0217	0.9	1129	2.0	1439	1.0	1907	2.0
22	W	0254	0.8	0734	2.1	1515	0.8	1952	2.1
23	TH	0329	0.7	0812	2.2	1549	0.7	● 2036	2.2
24	F	0404	0.6	0853	2.3	1623	0.6	2117	2.3
25	SA	0438	0.6	0933	2.3	1657	0.6	2158	2.3
26	SU	0514	0.6	1011	2.3	1733	0.6	2239	2.2
27	M	0550	0.7	1050	2.2	1810	0.7	2321	2.1
28	TU	0629	0.8	1130	2.1	1850	0.7		
29	W	0423	2.0	0713	1.0	1215	2.0	1937	0.9
30	TH	0509	2.0	0805	1.1	1312	1.9	2036	1.0
31	F	0600	2.0	0919	1.3	1811	1.9	☽ 2200	1.0

NOVEMBER

Date	Day	Time	m	Time	m	Time	m	Time	m
1	SA	0654	2.0	1048	1.3	1704	1.9	2320	1.0
2	SU	0756	2.0	1200	1.1	1748	1.9		
3	M	0025	0.8	0634	2.0	1300	1.0	1835	2.0
4	TU	0121	0.7	0711	2.1	1353	0.8	1920	2.1
5	W	0213	0.5	0750	2.2	1442	0.6	2003	2.2
6	TH	0300	0.5	0828	2.3	1527	0.5	○ 2043	2.3
7	F	0346	0.4	0903	2.4	1611	0.4	2121	2.4
8	SA	0429	0.5	0937	2.4	1653	0.4	2159	2.3
9	SU	0511	0.6	1010	2.3	1734	0.5	2236	2.2
10	M	0554	0.8	1042	2.2	1816	0.7	2315	2.1
11	TU	0636	1.0	1108	2.1	1857	0.8		
12	W	0420	2.0	0719	1.1	1041	1.9	1940	1.0
13	TH	0458	2.0	0805	1.3	1107	1.8	2025	1.1
14	F	0532	2.0	0854	1.4	1717	1.8	☾ 2116	1.2
15	SA	0558	2.0	0957	1.5	1753	1.8	2222	1.2
16	SU	0630	1.9	1134	1.4	1833	1.7	2353	1.2
17	M	0857	1.9	1233	1.3	2124	1.7		
18	TU	0047	1.1	0956	1.9	1318	1.2	2221	1.8
19	W	0131	1.0	1046	1.9	1358	1.0	1856	1.8
20	TH	0212	0.9	0714	2.0	1437	0.9	1933	2.0
21	F	0253	0.8	0744	2.1	1516	0.7	2015	2.1
22	SA	0334	0.7	0822	2.2	1557	0.6	● 2058	2.2
23	SU	0414	0.6	0907	2.3	1636	0.5	2142	2.2
24	M	0454	0.6	0952	2.3	1716	0.5	2227	2.2
25	TU	0536	0.7	1037	2.3	1758	0.5	2312	2.1
26	W	0619	0.8	1122	2.2	1842	0.6		
27	TH	0414	2.0	0707	0.9	1208	2.1	1930	0.7
28	F	0500	2.1	0802	1.0	1257	2.0	2028	0.8
29	SA	0550	2.1	0909	1.2	1349	1.9	☽ 2138	0.9
30	SU	0643	2.1	1024	1.2	1443	1.8	2251	0.9

DECEMBER

Date	Day	Time	m	Time	m	Time	m	Time	m
1	M	0740	2.0	1133	1.1	1732	1.8	2357	0.9
2	TU	0843	2.0	1235	1.0	1820	1.9		
3	W	0056	0.8	0656	2.0	1330	0.9	1906	2.0
4	TH	0150	0.7	0734	2.1	1421	0.7	1948	2.0
5	F	0239	0.7	0811	2.1	1508	0.6	2028	2.1
6	SA	0327	0.6	0844	2.2	1553	0.5	○ 2104	2.1
7	SU	0411	0.6	0914	2.3	1636	0.5	2139	2.2
8	M	0454	0.7	0944	2.3	1717	0.5	2215	2.1
9	TU	0536	0.8	1018	2.2	1757	0.6	2254	2.0
10	W	0616	0.9	1053	2.1	1835	0.7		
11	TH	0358	1.9	0654	1.0	1027	2.0	1911	0.8
12	F	0430	2.0	0733	1.1	1044	1.9	1950	0.9
13	SA	0501	2.0	0814	1.2	1118	1.8	2032	1.0
14	SU	0538	2.0	0901	1.3	1751	1.8	☾ 2122	1.1
15	M	0622	2.0	0956	1.3	1843	1.7	2221	1.1
16	TU	0715	1.9	1059	1.3	1947	1.7	2325	1.1
17	W	0825	1.9	1206	1.2	2111	1.7		
18	TH	0029	1.1	0945	1.9	1307	1.1	2222	1.8
19	F	0127	1.0	0657	1.9	1359	0.9	1918	1.8
20	SA	0218	0.8	0723	2.0	1448	0.7	2000	2.0
21	SU	0307	0.7	0805	2.2	1534	0.5	2046	2.1
22	M	0354	0.6	0855	2.3	1619	0.4	● 2132	2.2
23	TU	0438	0.6	0944	2.4	1702	0.3	2217	2.2
24	W	0524	0.6	1029	2.4	1747	0.3	2301	2.2
25	TH	0610	0.6	1113	2.3	1832	0.4	2346	2.1
26	F	0657	0.7	1157	2.3	1920	0.5		
27	SA	0449	2.0	0749	0.8	1239	2.1	2012	0.6
28	SU	0536	2.1	0846	1.0	1321	2.0	☽ 2111	0.8
29	M	0625	2.1	0952	1.1	1404	1.8	2219	0.9
30	TU	0717	2.0	1102	1.1	1940	1.8	2328	0.9
31	W	0815	2.0	1208	1.0	2049	1.8		

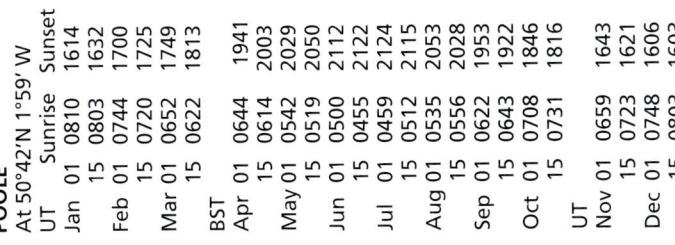

SOUTHAMPTON
LAT 50°54'N
LONG 1°24'W

TIMES AND HEIGHTS OF HIGH AND LOW WATER (Heights in Metres)

TIME ZONE UT
For Summer Time (area enclosed in shaded box) add 1 hour

HIGH WATERS – IMPORTANT NOTE. DOUBLE HIGH WATERS OCCUR AT SOUTHAMPTON. THE PREDICTIONS ARE FOR THE FIRST HIGH WATER

2014

JANUARY

Date	Day	Time	m	Time	m	Time	m	Time	m
1	W ●	0348	0.8	1025	4.8	1614	0.5	2250	4.8
2	TH	0437	0.6	1108	4.9	1702	0.3	2336	4.8
3	F	0524	0.5	1154	4.9	1748	0.2		
4	SA	0022	4.8	0611	0.5	1240	4.8	1834	0.3
5	SU	0111	4.7	0656	0.6	1329	4.7	1919	0.5
6	M	0204	4.6	0743	0.8	1422	4.5	2006	0.8
7	TU	0310	4.5	0831	1.1	1526	4.3	2056	1.1
8	W ☽	0531	4.4	0926	1.4	1648	4.1	2154	1.5
9	TH	0549	4.2	1030	1.7	1748	3.9	2300	1.7
10	F	0624	4.1	1141	1.8	1846	3.8		
11	SA	0011	1.9	0719	4.0	1251	1.8	1956	3.8
12	SU	0116	1.8	0825	4.0	1351	1.6	2239	4.0
13	M	0213	1.7	1045	4.1	1442	1.4	2328	4.1
14	TU	0302	1.5	1000	4.2	1528	1.2	2213	4.2
15	W	0349	1.3	1035	4.3	1612	1.0	2317	4.3
16	TH O	0431	1.1	1112	4.4	1652	0.9	2349	4.4
17	F	0510	1.1	1148	4.4	1730	0.9		
18	SA	0021	4.4	0545	1.1	1219	4.4	1801	0.9
19	SU	0046	4.4	0612	1.1	1247	4.4	1825	1.0
20	M	0109	4.4	0638	1.1	1316	4.4	1851	1.0
21	TU	0138	4.4	0709	1.1	1350	4.4	1925	1.0
22	W	0216	4.4	0746	1.1	1432	4.3	2005	1.1
23	TH	0300	4.3	0830	1.2	1519	4.2	2052	1.3
24	F ☾	0351	4.2	0922	1.5	1614	4.0	2148	1.5
25	SA	0448	4.1	1028	1.7	1718	3.9	2301	1.7
26	SU	0559	4.0	1148	1.8	2002	3.9		
27	M	0026	1.8	0817	4.1	1310	1.6	2053	4.1
28	TU	0145	1.5	0856	4.3	1419	1.2	2127	4.3
29	W	0247	1.2	0932	4.5	1515	0.8	2159	4.5
30	TH ●	0339	0.8	1012	4.7	1604	0.4	2239	4.7
31	F	0426	0.5	1053	4.8	1650	0.2	2321	4.8

FEBRUARY

Date	Day	Time	m	Time	m	Time	m	Time	m
1	SA	0511	0.3	1137	4.9	1734	0.0		
2	SU	0005	4.8	0555	0.2	1221	4.8	1817	0.1
3	M	0051	4.7	0638	0.3	1308	4.7	1859	0.3
4	TU	0140	4.6	0720	0.5	1357	4.5	1941	0.6
5	W	0238	4.4	0803	0.9	1456	4.3	2025	1.0
6	TH ☽	0455	4.3	0851	1.2	1642	4.1	2117	1.4
7	F	0505	4.1	0947	1.6	1720	3.9	2218	1.8
8	SA	0543	3.9	1056	1.9	1811	3.7	2334	2.0
9	SU	0635	3.8	1218	2.0	1913	3.6		
10	M	0052	2.0	0737	3.7	1327	1.8	2157	3.8
11	TU	0154	1.9	1012	3.9	1421	1.6	2255	4.0
12	W	0244	1.6	0935	4.0	1508	1.3	2334	4.1
13	TH	0329	1.3	1009	4.2	1550	1.0	2243	4.2
14	F O	0410	1.1	1047	4.3	1629	0.8	2315	4.4
15	SA	0448	0.9	1123	4.4	1706	0.7	2349	4.4
16	SU	0521	0.9	1155	4.4	1737	0.7		
17	M	0016	4.4	0549	0.9	1222	4.4	1804	0.8
18	TU	0041	4.4	0615	0.8	1251	4.5	1830	0.7
19	W	0111	4.5	0646	0.8	1326	4.5	1902	0.7
20	TH	0148	4.5	0722	0.8	1406	4.5	1940	0.8
21	F	0231	4.4	0803	0.9	1452	4.3	2024	1.0
22	SA ☾	0320	4.3	0851	1.2	1546	4.1	2115	1.4
23	SU	0418	4.1	0950	1.6	1651	3.9	2224	1.8
24	M	0533	3.9	1118	1.8	1940	3.8		
25	TU	0010	1.9	0757	4.0	1302	1.6	2036	4.0
26	W	0143	1.6	0843	4.2	1412	1.2	2118	4.3
27	TH	0239	1.2	0919	4.4	1503	0.8	2149	4.5
28	F	0327	0.8	0957	4.6	1549	0.4	2225	4.7

MARCH

Date	Day	Time	m	Time	m	Time	m	Time	m
1	SA ●	0412	0.4	1037	4.7	1633	0.1	2304	4.7
2	SU	0454	0.2	1119	4.8	1715	0.0	2347	4.7
3	M	0536	0.1	1202	4.7	1756	0.0		
4	TU	0030	4.7	0617	0.2	1246	4.6	1836	0.2
5	W	0115	4.5	0656	0.4	1333	4.4	1916	0.6
6	TH	0205	4.4	0736	0.8	1428	4.3	1957	1.0
7	F	0418	4.3	0818	1.1	1625	4.1	2042	1.4
8	SA ☽	0430	4.0	0907	1.5	1654	3.9	2139	1.8
9	SU	0507	3.8	101[illegible]	1.9	1739	3.7	2254	2.1
10	M	0557	3.6	1134	2.0	1835	3.6		
11	TU	0021	2.1	0656	3.6	1254	1.9	1947	3.6
12	W	0129	2.0	0832	3.6	1352	1.7	2216	3.9
13	TH	0220	1.7	0900	3.8	1440	1.4	2300	4.1
14	F	0303	1.4	0941	4.1	1522	1.1	2209	4.2
15	SA	0343	1.1	1019	4.3	1601	0.8	2243	4.4
16	SU O	0419	0.9	1055	4.4	1637	0.7	2317	4.4
17	M	0452	0.8	1127	4.4	1709	0.6	2346	4.5
18	TU	0522	0.7	1156	4.5	1738	0.6		
19	W	0014	4.5	0552	0.6	1227	4.6	1808	0.6
20	TH	0046	4.6	0625	0.6	1303	4.6	1842	0.6
21	F	0124	4.6	0701	0.6	1345	4.5	1920	0.7
22	SA	0207	4.5	0742	0.8	1432	4.4	2003	1.0
23	SU	0257	4.3	0828	1.1	1528	4.1	2054	1.4
24	M ☾	0358	4.0	0928	1.5	1642	3.9	2207	1.8
25	TU	0525	3.8	1105	1.7	1917	3.9		
26	W	0010	1.9	0732	3.9	1250	1.6	2017	4.1
27	TH	0130	1.6	0824	4.1	1354	1.2	2103	4.3
28	F	0222	1.2	0902	4.3	1443	0.8	2134	4.5
29	SA	0308	0.8	0939	4.5	1528	0.5	2208	4.6
30	SU ●	0352	0.5	1019	4.6	1612	0.2	2246	4.7
31	M	0433	0.2	1100	4.6	1653	0.1	2327	4.7

APRIL

Date	Day	Time	m	Time	m	Time	m	Time	m
1	TU	0514	0.2	1142	4.6	1733	0.2		
2	W	0008	4.6	0554	0.3	1225	4.5	1813	0.4
3	TH	0049	4.5	0633	0.5	1310	4.4	1852	0.7
4	F	0133	4.3	0711	0.8	1404	4.2	1930	1.0
5	SA	0223	4.2	0748	1.1	1604	4.2	2011	1.4
6	SU	0348	4.0	0832	1.4	1628	4.0	2102	1.8
7	M ☽	0428	3.8	0929	1.8	1707	3.8	2211	2.1
8	TU	0519	3.6	1043	2.0	1758	3.7	2334	2.2
9	W	0617	3.5	1203	2.0	1859	3.7		
10	TH	0051	2.1	0721	3.6	1310	1.8	2132	3.8
11	F	0146	1.8	0822	3.8	1402	1.6	2058	4.0
12	SA	0230	1.5	0910	4.0	1446	1.2	2135	4.2
13	SU	0309	1.2	0950	4.2	1525	1.0	2211	4.4
14	M	0345	0.9	1026	4.4	1602	0.8	2245	4.5
15	TU O	0420	0.7	1058	4.5	1638	0.6	2316	4.6
16	W	0454	0.6	1130	4.5	1712	0.6	2347	4.6
17	TH	0529	0.5	1205	4.6	1747	0.6		
18	F	0023	4.7	0606	0.5	1245	4.6	1824	0.6
19	SA	0104	4.6	0645	0.6	1329	4.6	1905	0.8
20	SU	0150	4.5	0728	0.8	1419	4.4	1951	1.1
21	M	0243	4.3	0817	1.1	1522	4.2	2047	1.5
22	TU ☾	0350	4.1	0922	1.4	1801	4.1	2208	1.8
23	W	0516	3.9	1052	1.6	1858	4.1	2343	1.8
24	TH	0703	3.9	1217	1.5	1957	4.2		
25	F	0059	1.5	0801	4.1	1323	1.3	2045	4.3
26	SA	0155	1.3	0842	4.2	1416	1.0	2117	4.5
27	SU	0243	0.9	0921	4.3	1503	0.7	2151	4.5
28	M	0328	0.6	1002	4.4	1547	0.5	2229	4.6
29	TU ●	0411	0.5	1043	4.4	1629	0.5	2308	4.5
30	W	0452	0.4	1127	4.4	1711	0.5	2348	4.5

MAY

Date	Day	Time	m	Time	m	Time	m	Time	m
1	TH	0532	0.5	1211	4.4	1751	0.7		
2	F	0027	4.4	0612	0.6	1258	4.3	1830	0.9
3	SA	0106	4.3	0649	0.9	1515	4.3	1909	1.2
4	SU	0149	4.2	0724	1.1	1543	4.2	1946	1.4
5	M	0237	4.0	0802	1.4	1605	4.1	2029	1.7
6	TU	0335	3.9	0849	1.6	1636	4.0	2125	2.0
7	W ☽	0437	3.7	0952	1.8	1723	3.9	2231	2.1
8	TH	0538	3.6	1059	1.9	1820	3.8	2339	2.1
9	F	0642	3.6	1205	1.9	1921	3.9		
10	SA	0044	1.9	0746	3.7	1306	1.7	2018	4.0
11	SU	0139	1.7	0839	3.9	1358	1.4	2102	4.2
12	M	0224	1.3	0921	4.1	1444	1.2	2140	4.4
13	TU	0306	1.0	0957	4.3	1526	0.9	2214	4.5
14	W O	0347	0.7	1031	4.5	1607	0.7	2247	4.6
15	TH	0428	0.5	1107	4.6	1648	0.6	2324	4.7
16	F	0509	0.4	1146	4.7	1730	0.6		
17	SA	0004	4.7	0551	0.4	1230	4.7	1812	0.6
18	SU	0048	4.7	0634	0.5	1317	4.6	1858	0.8
19	M	0137	4.6	0721	0.7	1411	4.5	1947	1.0
20	TU	0232	4.4	0813	1.0	1515	4.3	2045	1.3
21	W ☾	0337	4.2	0915	1.2	1751	4.3	2154	1.5
22	TH	0453	4.0	1026	1.4	1841	4.2	2307	1.6
23	F	0623	4.0	1138	1.5	1934	4.3		
24	SA	0018	1.6	0733	4.0	1245	1.4	2022	4.3
25	SU	0122	1.4	0821	4.1	1344	1.2	2057	4.4
26	M	0215	1.2	0904	4.2	1435	1.1	2132	4.4
27	TU	0303	0.9	0948	4.2	1522	0.9	2212	4.4
28	W ●	0348	0.8	1033	4.3	1607	0.8	2252	4.4
29	TH	0431	0.7	1122	4.3	1650	0.8	2332	4.4
30	F	0513	0.7	1351	4.4	1733	0.9		
31	SA	0010	4.3	0554	0.8	1416	4.4	1813	1.0

JUNE

Date	Day	Time	m	Time	m	Time	m	Time	m
1	SU	0047	4.3	0631	0.9	1449	4.3	1850	1.2
2	M	0125	4.2	0705	1.1	1523	4.3	1924	1.4
3	TU	0204	4.1	0737	1.3	1550	4.2	1958	1.6
4	W	0247	4.0	0814	1.4	1547	4.1	2040	1.7
5	TH ☽	0335	3.9	0901	1.6	1637	4.0	2134	1.9
6	F	0431	3.7	1001	1.8	1738	3.9	2236	1.9
7	SA	0550	3.7	1105	1.8	1842	3.9	2339	1.9
8	SU	0712	3.7	1207	1.7	1942	4.0		
9	M	0039	1.7	0812	3.9	1307	1.6	2032	4.2
10	TU	0137	1.4	0857	4.1	1403	1.3	2111	4.3
11	W	0230	1.1	0932	4.3	1454	1.1	2146	4.5
12	TH	0320	0.8	1008	4.5	1543	0.8	2224	4.6
13	F O	0407	0.6	1047	4.6	1630	0.6	2304	4.7
14	SA	0453	0.4	1130	4.7	1717	0.6	2348	4.8
15	SU	0539	0.3	1216	4.7	1803	0.6		
16	M	0034	4.7	0626	0.4	1304	4.7	1850	0.7
17	TU	0123	4.6	0713	0.5	1357	4.6	1939	0.8
18	W	0216	4.5	0802	0.7	1458	4.5	2031	1.1
19	TH ☾	0317	4.3	0857	1.0	1739	4.5	2129	1.3
20	F	0428	4.1	0956	1.3	1819	4.3	2232	1.5
21	SA	0548	4.0	1101	1.4	1857	4.3	2340	1.6
22	SU	0656	4.0	1208	1.5	1942	4.2		
23	M	0047	1.6	0758	4.0	1312	1.5	2030	4.2
24	TU	0147	1.4	0853	4.0	1409	1.4	2114	4.2
25	W	0240	1.2	0942	4.1	1501	1.3	2156	4.3
26	TH	0328	1.0	1029	4.2	1548	1.1	2237	4.3
27	F ●	0413	0.9	1117	4.2	1634	1.0	2315	4.3
28	SA	0456	0.8	1215	4.3	1716	1.0	2353	4.3
29	SU	0537	0.8	1336	4.3	1756	1.1		
30	M	0028	4.3	0615	0.9	1419	4.3	1832	1.2

SUNRISE AND SUNSET TIMES

SOUTHAMPTON
At 50°54'N 1°24'W

		Sunrise	Sunset
UT			
Jan	01	0808	1610
	15	0802	1629
Feb	01	0742	1657
	15	0718	1722
Mar	01	0650	1747
	15	0619	1810
BST			
Apr	01	0641	1938
	15	0611	2001
May	01	0539	2027
	15	0516	2049
Jun	01	0457	2110
	15	0451	2121
Jul	01	0456	2123
	15	0509	2113
Aug	01	0532	2051
	15	0553	2026
Sep	01	0619	1951
	15	0641	1920
Oct	01	0706	1843
	15	0729	1813
UT			
Nov	01	0658	1640
	15	0722	1618
Dec	01	0746	1603
	15	0802	1600

JULY

		Time	m
1	TU	0102 0646 1339 1901	4.2 1.1 4.3 1.3
2	W	0135 0712 1406 1928	4.2 1.2 4.3 1.4
3	TH	0209 0742 1440 2003	4.1 1.2 4.2 1.4
4	F	0249 0821 1521 2048	4.1 1.3 4.2 1.5
5	SA ☽	0335 0910 1609 2143	4.0 1.5 4.1 1.7
6	SU	0427 1009 1703 2247	3.9 1.6 4.0 1.8
7	M	0528 1117 1813 2354	3.8 1.7 4.0 1.7
8	TU	0756 1224 2009	3.8 1.7 4.1
9	W	0059 0848 1329 2051	1.5 4.0 1.5 4.3
10	TH	0202 0922 1430 2127	1.3 4.2 1.2 4.5
11	F	0300 0954 1525 2206	0.9 4.4 0.9 4.6
12	SA O	0352 1033 1616 2248	0.6 4.6 0.7 4.8
13	SU	0441 1116 1704 2332	0.3 4.8 0.5 4.8
14	M	0528 1200 1751	0.2 4.8 0.4
15	TU	0017 0613 1247 1836	4.8 0.2 4.8 0.4
16	W	0104 0658 1338 1922	4.7 0.3 4.7 0.6
17	TH	0155 0744 1434 2009	4.6 0.5 4.5 0.8
18	F	0252 0832 1717 2101	4.4 0.8 4.5 1.1
19	SA ☾	0404 0926 1745 2159	4.2 1.2 4.4 1.4
20	SU	0525 1027 1805 2305	4.0 1.5 4.2 1.7
21	M	0622 1134 1853	3.9 1.7 4.1
22	TU	0015 0728 1243 1954	1.7 3.8 1.8 4.0
23	W	0122 1008 1347 2055	1.7 3.9 1.7 4.0
24	TH	0220 1112 1442 2139	1.5 4.1 1.5 4.1
25	F	0309 1200 1530 2216	1.2 4.2 1.3 4.2
26	SA ●	0355 1058 1616 2253	1.0 4.2 1.1 4.3
27	SU	0437 1132 1658 2331	0.9 4.3 1.0 4.3
28	M	0517 1208 1736	0.8 4.4 1.0
29	TU	0005 0554 1239 1810	4.3 0.9 4.4 1.1
30	W	0037 0624 1304 1835	4.3 1.0 4.4 1.2
31	TH	0105 0645 1330 1859	4.3 1.0 4.4 1.2

AUGUST

		Time	m
1	F	0137 0712 1402 1931	4.3 1.1 4.4 1.2
2	SA	0214 0748 1441 2012	4.3 1.1 4.3 1.3
3	SU	0258 0831 1528 2100	4.2 1.2 4.2 1.4
4	M ☽	0350 0923 1621 2200	4.1 1.5 4.1 1.6
5	TU	0447 1030 1723 2314	3.9 1.7 4.0 1.8
6	W	0558 1150 1954	3.8 1.8 4.0
7	TH	0032 0836 1307 2041	1.7 4.0 1.7 4.2
8	F	0146 0920 1417 2114	1.4 4.2 1.4 4.4
9	SA	0248 0946 1514 2151	1.0 4.5 1.0 4.6
10	SU O	0340 1020 1604 2232	0.6 4.7 0.7 4.8
11	M	0428 1100 1650 2314	0.3 4.8 0.4 4.9
12	TU	0512 1143 1735 2358	0.1 4.9 0.3 4.9
13	W	0556 1228 1818	0.1 4.8 0.3
14	TH	0044 0639 1316 1900	4.8 0.2 4.7 0.5
15	F	0132 0721 1409 1945	4.6 0.5 4.6 0.7
16	SA	0227 0806 1648 2032	4.4 0.8 4.5 1.1
17	SU ☾	0456 0856 1703 2126	4.2 1.3 4.3 1.5
18	M	0504 0955 1727 2231	4.0 1.6 4.1 1.8
19	TU	0552 1104 1814 2346	3.8 1.9 3.9 1.9
20	W	0651 1218 1912	3.7 2.0 3.8
21	TH	0057 0945 1325 2200	1.9 3.8 1.9 3.9
22	F	0157 1046 1421 2258	1.7 4.0 1.7 4.0
23	SA	0247 1133 1510 2152	1.4 4.2 1.4 4.2
24	SU	0332 1037 1553 2228	1.1 4.3 1.2 4.3
25	M ●	0413 1101 1634 2305	0.9 4.4 1.0 4.4
26	TU	0452 1135 1711 2340	0.8 4.4 1.0 4.4
27	W	0528 1207 1742	0.8 4.5 1.0
28	TH	0010 0556 1232 1807	4.4 0.9 4.5 1.0
29	F	0037 0618 1258 1831	4.4 0.9 4.5 1.0
30	SA	0108 0645 1330 1903	4.5 0.9 4.5 1.0
31	SU	0145 0720 1409 1942	4.4 1.0 4.5 1.1

SEPTEMBER

		Time	m
1	M	0229 0801 1455 2026	4.4 1.1 4.4 1.3
2	TU ☽	0319 0849 1549 2121	4.2 1.4 4.2 1.6
3	W	0419 0952 1654 2241	4.0 1.8 4.0 1.9
4	TH	0536 1127 1933	3.8 2.0 4.0
5	F	0018 0817 1301 2026	1.8 4.0 1.8 4.2
6	SA	0138 0906 1409 2101	1.5 4.3 1.5 4.4
7	SU	0236 0935 1501 2135	1.0 4.5 1.0 4.6
8	M	0325 1005 1548 2214	0.6 4.7 0.6 4.8
9	TU O	0410 1042 1633 2255	0.3 4.9 0.4 4.9
10	W	0453 1124 1715 2338	0.1 4.9 0.2 4.9
11	TH	0535 1207 1756	0.1 4.8 0.3
12	F	0022 0616 1252 1837	4.8 0.3 4.7 0.5
13	SA	0108 0657 1341 1919	4.6 0.6 4.6 0.8
14	SU	0201 0740 1614 2003	4.4 0.9 4.5 1.1
15	M	0423 0826 1625 2053	4.2 1.4 4.2 1.5
16	TU ☾	0440 0923 1653 2158	4.0 1.8 4.0 1.9
17	W	0521 1035 1738 2315	3.9 2.1 3.8 2.0
18	TH	0613 1151 1833	3.7 2.2 3.7
19	F	0026 0910 1258 1936	2.0 3.8 2.1 3.7
20	SA	0127 1011 1355 2230	1.8 4.0 1.8 4.0
21	SU	0218 1056 1443 2124	1.5 4.2 1.5 4.1
22	M	0303 1129 1526 2201	1.2 4.3 1.2 4.3
23	TU	0344 1029 1605 2238	1.0 4.4 1.0 4.4
24	W ●	0422 1103 1640 2313	0.9 4.5 0.9 4.5
25	TH	0457 1135 1711 2343	0.8 4.6 0.9 4.5
26	F	0525 1202 1738	0.9 4.6 0.9
27	SA	0011 0552 1229 1806	4.6 0.9 4.6 0.9
28	SU	0043 0622 1303 1840	4.6 0.9 4.6 0.9
29	M	0122 0657 1343 1918	4.6 1.0 4.6 1.0
30	TU	0206 0738 1430 2002	4.5 1.2 4.4 1.3

OCTOBER

		Time	m
1	W ☽	0257 0825 1526 2055	4.3 1.5 4.2 1.6
2	TH	0401 0929 1638 2222	4.0 1.9 4.0 1.9
3	F	0654 1122 1910	4.0 2.1 4.0
4	SA	0010 0756 1252 2007	1.8 4.1 1.8 4.2
5	SU	0122 0849 1352 2044	1.5 4.4 1.5 4.4
6	M	0216 0921 1442 2117	1.1 4.6 1.1 4.6
7	TU	0303 0948 1527 2155	0.7 4.8 0.7 4.7
8	W O	0348 1024 1611 2235	0.5 4.9 0.4 4.8
9	TH	0430 1104 1652 2318	0.3 4.9 0.3 4.8
10	F	0512 1145 1733	0.3 4.8 0.4
11	SA	0001 0553 1228 1814	4.7 0.5 4.7 0.6
12	SU	0046 0633 1313 1854	4.6 0.7 4.5 0.9
13	M	0137 0715 1407 1935	4.4 1.1 4.4 1.2
14	TU	0356 0759 1549 2022	4.3 1.5 4.2 1.6
15	W ☾	0415 0852 1617 2121	4.1 1.9 4.0 1.9
16	TH	0451 1002 1703 2236	4.0 2.1 3.8 2.1
17	F	0537 1118 1755 2348	3.8 2.2 3.7 2.1
18	SA	0634 1225 1855	3.8 2.2 3.7
19	SU	0050 0742 1323 1957	2.0 3.9 2.0 3.8
20	M	0143 1014 1411 2051	1.7 4.2 1.7 4.1
21	TU	0229 0922 1453 2132	1.5 4.3 1.4 4.3
22	W	0310 0957 1531 2211	1.2 4.5 1.2 4.4
23	TH ●	0348 1032 1606 2245	1.0 4.6 1.0 4.5
24	F	0422 1104 1639 2316	0.9 4.6 0.9 4.6
25	SA	0455 1134 1711 2348	0.9 4.7 0.8 4.7
26	SU	0527 1206 1745	0.8 4.7 0.8
27	M	0023 0603 1242 1822	4.7 0.9 4.7 0.8
28	TU	0104 0641 1324 1902	4.7 1.0 4.6 1.0
29	W	0150 0724 1413 1948	4.5 1.2 4.5 1.2
30	TH	0245 0814 1511 2043	4.4 1.5 4.2 1.6
31	F ☽	0354 0923 1627 2211	4.2 1.9 4.0 1.8

NOVEMBER

		Time	m
1	SA	0634 1105 1845 2344	4.2 2.0 4.0 1.8
2	SU	0733 1226 1943	4.3 1.8 4.1
3	M	0053 0828 1326 2024	1.5 4.4 1.5 4.3
4	TU	0149 0904 1417 2059	1.3 4.6 1.2 4.5
5	W	0238 0931 1504 2139	1.0 4.7 0.9 4.6
6	TH O	0323 1007 1548 2220	0.7 4.8 0.6 4.6
7	F	0407 1045 1631 2302	0.6 4.8 0.5 4.6
8	SA	0449 1126 1712 2346	0.6 4.7 0.6 4.6
9	SU	0531 1207 1754	0.7 4.6 0.7
10	M	0031 0613 1249 1833	4.5 0.9 4.5 0.9
11	TU	0122 0653 1333 1912	4.4 1.2 4.4 1.2
12	W	0334 0735 1424 1954	4.4 1.5 4.2 1.5
13	TH	0355 0820 1526 2041	4.2 1.8 4.0 1.8
14	F ☾	0419 0916 1623 2143	4.1 2.1 3.9 2.0
15	SA	0503 1024 1718 2253	4.0 2.2 3.8 2.1
16	SU	0555 1135 1818 2359	3.9 2.2 3.7 2.1
17	M	0654 1238 1920	3.9 2.1 3.8
18	TU	0057 0755 1328 2019	1.9 4.1 1.9 4.0
19	W	0146 0846 1412 2106	1.7 4.3 1.6 4.2
20	TH	0229 0927 1452 2146	1.4 4.4 1.3 4.4
21	F	0310 1004 1531 2220	1.2 4.6 1.0 4.5
22	SA ●	0350 1036 1610 2253	1.0 4.7 0.8 4.6
23	SU	0429 1109 1650 2328	0.9 4.7 0.7 4.7
24	M	0508 1146 1729	0.8 4.8 0.6
25	TU	0007 0549 1227 1810	4.7 0.8 4.8 0.7
26	W	0051 0632 1311 1854	4.7 0.9 4.7 0.8
27	TH	0140 0718 1400 1942	4.6 1.1 4.5 1.1
28	F	0235 0810 1458 2037	4.5 1.4 4.3 1.3
29	SA ☽	0342 0914 1608 2148	4.3 1.7 4.2 1.6
30	SU	0615 1031 1817 2307	4.3 1.8 4.1 1.6

DECEMBER

		Time	m
1	M	0706 1149 1910	4.3 1.7 4.1
2	TU	0018 0758 1255 2000	1.6 4.4 1.6 4.2
3	W	0119 0839 1351 2043	1.4 4.5 1.3 4.3
4	TH	0212 0914 1441 2126	1.2 4.5 1.1 4.4
5	F	0300 0952 1527 2211	1.1 4.6 0.9 4.4
6	SA O	0347 1032 1612 2256	0.9 4.6 0.7 4.5
7	SU	0431 1113 1654 2344	0.9 4.6 0.7 4.5
8	M	0514 1153 1736	0.9 4.5 0.8
9	TU	0210 0556 1231 1817	4.5 1.0 4.5 0.9
10	W	0239 0636 1309 1854	4.5 1.2 4.4 1.1
11	TH	0313 0713 1350 1928	4.4 1.4 4.3 1.3
12	F	0239 0747 1434 2002	4.3 1.6 4.1 1.5
13	SA	0330 0825 1523 2044	4.2 1.8 4.0 1.7
14	SU ☾	0422 0913 1622 2139	4.1 2.0 3.8 1.9
15	M	0517 1015 1736 2245	4.0 2.1 3.8 2.0
16	TU	0617 1121 1847 2351	4.0 2.1 3.7 2.0
17	W	0719 1224 1953	4.0 2.0 3.9
18	TH	0051 0817 1321 2048	1.9 4.1 1.7 4.0
19	F	0146 0903 1413 2129	1.6 4.3 1.4 4.2
20	SA	0236 0940 1501 2201	1.3 4.5 1.1 4.4
21	SU	0323 1014 1548 2235	1.1 4.6 0.8 4.6
22	M ●	0409 1050 1633 2312	0.9 4.8 0.6 4.7
23	TU	0454 1129 1718 2354	0.7 4.8 0.5 4.8
24	W	0539 1212 1802	0.7 4.9 0.4
25	TH	0038 0624 1257 1847	4.8 0.7 4.8 0.5
26	F	0127 0710 1346 1933	4.7 0.8 4.7 0.7
27	SA	0219 0759 1440 2023	4.6 1.0 4.5 1.0
28	SU ☽	0321 0853 1544 2121	4.4 1.3 4.3 1.3
29	M	0553 0956 1705 2228	4.4 1.5 4.1 1.5
30	TU	0632 1109 1828 2341	4.3 1.7 4.0 1.6
31	W	0715 1224 1929	4.3 1.7 4.0

PORTSMOUTH
LAT 50°48′N
LONG 1°07′W

TIMES AND HEIGHTS OF HIGH AND LOW WATER (Heights in Metres)

TIME ZONE UT
For Summer Time (area enclosed in shaded box) add 1 hour

2014

JANUARY

Day	Time	m	Day	Time	m
1 W ●	0352 1047 1620 2317	0.9 4.9 0.6 4.8	16 TH O	0438 1131 1658	1.2 4.5 1.0
2 TH	0442 1132 1707	0.7 5.0 0.4	17 F	0000 0515 1209 1732	4.5 1.1 4.5 0.9
3 F	0005 0529 1219 1753	4.9 0.6 5.0 0.4	18 SA	0038 0548 1243 1804	4.5 1.1 4.5 0.9
4 SA	0056 0616 1307 1839	4.9 0.6 4.9 0.4	19 SU	0111 0617 1313 1833	4.5 1.1 4.5 1.0
5 SU	0152 0702 1359 1925	4.9 0.7 4.8 0.6	20 M	0141 0647 1343 1902	4.5 1.1 4.4 1.0
6 M	0255 0751 1458 2014	4.8 0.9 4.6 0.9	21 TU	0212 0718 1416 1935	4.5 1.1 4.4 1.0
7 TU	0353 0843 1559 2108	4.7 1.2 4.4 1.2	22 W	0247 0754 1455 2013	4.4 1.2 4.3 1.1
8 W ☽	0443 0945 1656 2213	4.5 1.5 4.2 1.5	23 TH	0330 0837 1542 2058	4.3 1.3 4.1 1.3
9 TH	0534 1055 1755 2323	4.3 1.7 4.0 1.7	24 F ☾	0421 0929 1641 2154	4.2 1.5 4.0 1.5
10 F	0631 1204 1858	4.2 1.8 3.9	25 SA	0522 1035 1752 2308	4.1 1.7 3.9 1.7
11 SA	0029 0732 1307 2004	1.8 4.1 1.7 3.9	26 SU	0633 1202 1911	4.0 1.7 3.9
12 SU	0129 0833 1404 2108	1.8 4.1 1.6 4.0	27 M	0040 0747 1323 2027	1.7 4.1 1.5 4.1
13 M	0224 0926 1454 2200	1.7 4.2 1.4 4.2	28 TU	0151 0852 1425 2127	1.5 4.4 1.2 4.4
14 TU	0313 1010 1539 2242	1.5 4.3 1.2 4.3	29 W	0250 0945 1519 2218	1.2 4.6 0.8 4.6
15 W	0358 1051 1620 2322	1.3 4.4 1.1 4.4	30 TH ●	0342 1032 1608 2305	0.9 4.8 0.5 4.8
			31 F	0431 1117 1655 2352	0.6 4.9 0.3 4.9

FEBRUARY

Day	Time	m	Day	Time	m
1 SA	0517 1203 1739	0.5 4.9 0.2	16 SU	0012 0524 1220 1740	4.5 0.9 4.5 0.8
2 SU	0039 0601 1249 1822	4.9 0.4 4.9 0.3	17 M	0044 0555 1251 1811	4.5 0.9 4.5 0.8
3 M	0131 0644 1339 1905	4.9 0.5 4.8 0.4	18 TU	0114 0624 1320 1840	4.5 0.9 4.5 0.8
4 TU	0228 0728 1433 1949	4.8 0.7 4.6 0.7	19 W	0144 0655 1351 1911	4.5 0.9 4.5 0.8
5 W	0321 0814 1529 2035	4.7 1.0 4.4 1.1	20 TH	0216 0729 1427 1947	4.5 0.9 4.4 0.9
6 TH ☽	0407 0904 1623 2129	4.5 1.3 4.2 1.4	21 F	0255 0809 1512 2030	4.4 1.0 4.2 1.1
7 F	0453 1009 1719 2242	4.2 1.6 4.0 1.8	22 SA ☾	0344 0857 1610 2122	4.2 1.3 4.1 1.4
8 SA	0548 1127 1823 2357	4.0 1.8 3.8 1.9	23 SU	0448 0959 1726 2232	4.0 1.5 3.9 1.7
9 SU	0655 1237 1935	3.8 1.9 3.7	24 M	0606 1133 1854	3.9 1.7 3.9
10 M	0105 0803 1341 2043	1.9 3.8 1.7 3.8	25 TU	0028 0729 1312 2014	1.8 4.0 1.5 4.1
11 TU	0206 0902 1434 2138	1.8 4.0 1.5 4.0	26 W	0144 0837 1414 2114	1.5 4.2 1.2 4.3
12 W	0256 0949 1518 2221	1.6 4.1 1.3 4.2	27 TH	0241 0929 1506 2203	1.2 4.5 0.8 4.6
13 TH	0339 1031 1558 2259	1.4 4.3 1.1 4.4	28 F	0331 1016 1553 2248	0.8 4.7 0.5 4.8
14 F O	0417 1109 1635 2337	1.2 4.4 0.9 4.5			
15 SA	0453 1146 1709	1.0 4.5 0.8			

MARCH

Day	Time	m	Day	Time	m
1 SA ●	0416 1100 1638 2333	0.6 4.8 0.3 4.9	16 SU O	0424 1121 1640 2342	1.0 4.4 0.8 4.5
2 SU	0500 1144 1721	0.4 4.9 0.2	17 M	0457 1154 1714	0.8 4.5 0.7
3 M	0018 0542 1230 1802	4.9 0.3 4.8 0.3	18 TU	0014 0529 1225 1746	4.6 0.7 4.5 0.7
4 TU	0105 0623 1317 1843	4.9 0.4 4.8 0.4	19 W	0045 0601 1256 1817	4.6 0.7 4.6 0.7
5 W	0154 0704 1407 1923	4.8 0.6 4.6 0.7	20 TH	0116 0633 1329 1850	4.6 0.7 4.6 0.7
6 TH	0240 0744 1457 2003	4.6 0.9 4.5 1.1	21 F	0150 0709 1408 1927	4.5 0.7 4.5 0.9
7 F	0323 0826 1547 2048	4.4 1.2 4.2 1.4	22 SA	0230 0749 1456 2011	4.4 0.9 4.3 1.1
8 SA ☽	0406 0916 1639 2149	4.2 1.6 4.0 1.8	23 SU	0321 0837 1558 2103	4.3 1.2 4.1 1.4
9 SU	0457 1040 1743 2323	3.9 1.8 3.7 2.0	24 M ☾	0428 0938 1715 2219	4.0 1.5 4.0 1.7
10 M	0610 1202 1902	3.6 1.9 3.6	25 TU	0549 1127 1842	3.9 1.7 3.9
11 TU	0033 0729 1309 2013	2.0 3.6 1.9 3.7	26 W	0024 0712 1258 1958	1.8 4.0 1.5 4.1
12 W	0141 0834 1405 2111	1.9 3.8 1.7 4.0	27 TH	0133 0818 1357 2057	1.5 4.2 1.2 4.4
13 TH	0232 0924 1449 2154	1.7 4.0 1.4 4.2	28 F	0226 0910 1448 2145	1.2 4.4 0.9 4.6
14 F	0312 1006 1528 2233	1.4 4.2 1.1 4.4	29 SA	0313 0956 1534 2229	0.9 4.6 0.6 4.8
15 SA	0349 1045 1605 2309	1.2 4.4 0.9 4.5	30 SU ●	0357 1040 1617 2312	0.6 4.7 0.4 4.8
			31 M	0440 1124 1700 2355	0.4 4.8 0.4 4.8

APRIL

Day	Time	m	Day	Time	m
1 TU	0521 1209 1740	0.4 4.7 0.4	16 W	0502 1158 1720	0.7 4.6 0.7
2 W	0038 0601 1255 1819	4.8 0.5 4.7 0.6	17 TH	0015 0537 1234 1756	4.7 0.6 4.6 0.7
3 TH	0121 0639 1343 1857	4.7 0.7 4.6 0.8	18 F	0051 0614 1313 1833	4.7 0.6 4.6 0.7
4 F	0202 0717 1429 1935	4.6 0.9 4.5 1.1	19 SA	0130 0653 1357 1914	4.6 0.7 4.6 0.9
5 SA	0243 0754 1515 2016	4.4 1.2 4.3 1.4	20 SU	0215 0736 1451 2000	4.5 0.9 4.4 1.1
6 SU	0324 0836 1600 2105	4.1 1.5 4.1 1.8	21 M	0311 0827 1557 2058	4.3 1.1 4.3 1.4
7 M ☽	0409 0933 1655 2236	3.9 1.8 3.8 2.0	22 TU ☾	0418 0932 1710 2223	4.1 1.4 4.1 1.7
8 TU	0508 1115 1815 2357	3.6 2.0 3.7 2.1	23 W	0534 1114 1826	4.0 1.6 4.1
9 W	0645 1225 1935	3.5 1.9 3.7	24 TH	0001 0650 1232 1937	1.7 4.0 1.4 4.3
10 TH	0102 0759 1322 2035	2.0 3.7 1.8 3.9	25 F	0108 0755 1332 2036	1.5 4.2 1.2 4.4
11 F	0154 0853 1409 2122	1.8 3.9 1.5 4.2	26 SA	0202 0849 1423 2124	1.2 4.3 1.0 4.6
12 SA	0236 0937 1450 2201	1.5 4.1 1.3 4.3	27 SU	0250 0935 1510 2207	1.0 4.5 0.8 4.7
13 SU	0314 1016 1529 2237	1.2 4.3 1.0 4.5	28 M	0335 1020 1554 2249	0.8 4.6 0.7 4.7
14 M	0350 1051 1607 2310	1.0 4.4 0.9 4.6	29 TU ●	0418 1105 1637 2331	0.6 4.6 0.7 4.7
15 TU O	0426 1124 1644 2342	0.8 4.5 0.7 4.6	30 W	0459 1151 1718	0.6 4.6 0.7

MAY

Day	Time	m	Day	Time	m
1 TH	0013 0539 1237 1757	4.7 0.7 4.6 0.8	16 F	0517 1214 1738	0.6 4.7 0.7
2 F	0054 0617 1323 1835	4.6 0.8 4.6 1.0	17 SA	0030 0558 1300 1820	4.8 0.5 4.7 0.7
3 SA	0134 0654 1407 1913	4.5 1.0 4.5 1.2	18 SU	0115 0642 1350 1905	4.7 0.6 4.7 0.9
4 SU	0213 0729 1449 1951	4.4 1.2 4.3 1.5	19 M	0204 0728 1450 1955	4.6 0.8 4.6 1.1
5 M	0252 0808 1530 2033	4.2 1.4 4.2 1.7	20 TU	0302 0821 1555 2054	4.4 1.0 4.5 1.3
6 TU	0334 0854 1615 2130	4.0 1.6 4.0 1.9	21 W ☾	0408 0926 1659 2209	4.3 1.3 4.4 1.5
7 W ☽	0424 0959 1711 2256	3.8 1.8 3.9 2.0	22 TH	0516 1045 1804 2327	4.1 1.4 4.3 1.6
8 TH	0528 1126 1832	3.6 1.9 3.8	23 F	0624 1158 1909	4.1 1.4 4.3
9 F	0006 0705 1229 1948	2.0 3.6 1.8 3.9	24 SA	0034 0727 1300 2008	1.5 4.1 1.3 4.4
10 SA	0103 0813 1321 2041	1.8 3.8 1.6 4.1	25 SU	0133 0824 1355 2100	1.3 4.2 1.2 4.5
11 SU	0150 0901 1408 2123	1.6 4.0 1.4 4.3	26 M	0224 0915 1444 2145	1.2 4.3 1.1 4.6
12 M	0233 0942 1451 2200	1.3 4.2 1.2 4.5	27 TU	0312 1003 1531 2228	1.0 4.4 1.0 4.6
13 TU	0314 1018 1533 2235	1.1 4.4 1.0 4.6	28 W ●	0356 1050 1615 2310	0.9 4.5 1.0 4.6
14 W O	0355 1055 1615 2312	0.8 4.5 0.8 4.7	29 TH	0439 1136 1658 2352	0.8 4.5 1.0 4.6
15 TH	0436 1133 1656 2350	0.7 4.7 0.7 4.8	30 F	0521 1222 1739	0.8 4.5 1.0
			31 SA	0032 0559 1306 1817	4.5 0.9 4.5 1.1

JUNE

Day	Time	m	Day	Time	m
1 SU	0112 0635 1348 1853	4.5 1.0 4.5 1.3	16 M	0101 0632 1342 1856	4.8 0.5 4.8 0.7
2 M	0149 0709 1427 1928	4.4 1.2 4.4 1.4	17 TU	0152 0719 1442 1946	4.7 0.6 4.8 0.9
3 TU	0225 0743 1504 2005	4.3 1.3 4.3 1.6	18 W	0250 0810 1544 2040	4.6 0.8 4.7 1.1
4 W	0305 0822 1543 2048	4.1 1.5 4.2 1.7	19 TH ☾	0352 0907 1641 2143	4.4 1.1 4.6 1.3
5 TH ☽	0350 0910 1628 2141	4.0 1.6 4.1 1.8	20 F	0454 1014 1737 2252	4.3 1.3 4.5 1.5
6 F	0442 1008 1721 2246	3.8 1.8 4.0 1.9	21 SA	0556 1123 1836 2359	4.2 1.4 4.4 1.5
7 SA	0542 1119 1823 2357	3.8 1.8 4.0 1.9	22 SU	0658 1227 1936	4.1 1.5 4.3
8 SU	0654 1226 1932	3.8 1.7 4.1	23 M	0102 0759 1326 2032	1.5 4.1 1.5 4.3
9 M	0057 0805 1323 2032	1.7 3.9 1.5 4.2	24 TU	0159 0858 1421 2123	1.4 4.2 1.4 4.4
10 TU	0150 0859 1413 2119	1.4 4.1 1.3 4.4	25 W	0250 0951 1511 2209	1.2 4.3 1.3 4.4
11 W	0240 0945 1502 2203	1.2 4.4 1.1 4.6	26 TH	0338 1039 1557 2252	1.1 4.3 1.2 4.5
12 TH	0327 1029 1550 2247	0.9 4.5 0.9 4.7	27 F ●	0422 1123 1641 2333	1.0 4.4 1.1 4.5
13 F O	0414 1114 1636 2330	0.7 4.7 0.8 4.8	28 SA	0504 1205 1723	0.9 4.5 1.1
14 SA	0500 1200 1723	0.5 4.8 0.7	29 SU	0013 0542 1247 1800	4.5 0.9 4.5 1.1
15 SU	0014 0545 1248 1809	4.8 0.5 4.8 0.7	30 M	0052 0617 1326 1834	4.4 1.0 4.5 1.2

SUNRISE AND SUNSET TIMES

PORTSMOUTH
At 50°48′N 1°07′ W

UT		Sunrise	Sunset
Jan	01	0807	1610
	15	0800	1628
Feb	01	0740	1656
	15	0717	1721
Mar	01	0649	1746
	15	0618	1809
BST			
Apr	01	0640	1937
	15	0610	2000
May	01	0538	2026
	15	0515	2047
Jun	01	0457	2109
	15	0451	2120
Jul	01	0455	2121
	15	0508	2112
Aug	01	0531	2050
	15	0552	2025
Sep	01	0618	1950
	15	0640	1918
Oct	01	0705	1842
	15	0628	1812
UT			
Nov	01	0656	1639
	15	0720	1618
Dec	01	0745	1602
	15	0800	1559

PORTSMOUTH
LAT 50°48′N
LONG 1°07′W

TIMES AND HEIGHTS OF HIGH AND LOW WATER (Heights in Metres)

TIME ZONE UT
For Summer Time (area enclosed in shaded box) add 1 hour

2014

JULY

Date	Day	Time	m
1	TU	0128 0649 1403 1905	4.4 1.1 4.5 1.3
2	W	0201 0719 1436 1937	4.3 1.2 4.4 1.4
3	TH	0236 0752 1511 2013	4.2 1.3 4.3 1.5
4	F	0316 0832 1552 2057	4.1 1.4 4.2 1.6
5	SA ☽	0403 0918 1640 2150	4.0 1.5 4.2 1.7
6	SU	0457 1016 1734 2254	3.9 1.6 4.1 1.7
7	M	0600 1126 1836	3.9 1.7 4.1
8	TU	0006 0710 1239 1943	1.7 3.9 1.6 4.2
9	W	0113 0821 1342 2047	1.5 4.1 1.5 4.3
10	TH	0212 0921 1438 2140	1.3 4.3 1.2 4.5
11	F	0306 1012 1531 2227	1.0 4.5 1.0 4.7
12	SA ○	0358 1059 1622 2312	0.7 4.7 0.8 4.8
13	SU	0446 1146 1710 2358	0.5 4.8 0.6 4.9
14	M	0533 1234 1756	0.4 4.9 0.5
15	TU	0044 0618 1327 1842	4.9 0.3 4.9 0.6
16	W	0135 0704 1425 1929	4.8 0.4 4.9 0.7
17	TH	0231 0751 1526 2019	4.7 0.7 4.8 0.9
18	F	0331 0843 1618 2114	4.5 1.0 4.7 1.2
19	SA ☾	0430 0942 1708 2218	4.4 1.3 4.5 1.5
20	SU	0528 1050 1803 2326	4.2 1.5 4.3 1.6
21	M	0629 1157 1903	4.0 1.7 4.1
22	TU	0032 0735 1301 2005	1.7 3.9 1.7 4.1
23	W	0135 0843 1400 2103	1.6 4.0 1.7 4.2
24	TH	0231 0942 1454 2151	1.5 4.1 1.5 4.3
25	F	0320 1025 1541 2233	1.3 4.3 1.4 4.4
26	SA ●	0404 1105 1624 2313	1.1 4.4 1.2 4.4
27	SU	0445 1144 1704 2353	1.0 4.5 1.1 4.5
28	M	0522 1223 1740	0.9 4.5 1.1
29	TU	0030 0555 1301 1812	4.5 0.9 4.5 1.1
30	W	0105 0625 1335 1840	4.4 1.0 4.5 1.1
31	TH	0135 0653 1405 1909	4.4 1.0 4.5 1.2

AUGUST

Date	Day	Time	m
1	F	0206 0723 1438 1942	4.3 1.1 4.4 1.2
2	SA	0242 0758 1516 2020	4.3 1.2 4.4 1.3
3	SU	0325 0839 1601 2108	4.2 1.3 4.2 1.5
4	M ☽	0418 0930 1654 2207	4.0 1.5 4.1 1.6
5	TU	0521 1036 1758 2323	3.9 1.7 4.0 1.7
6	W	0636 1204 1912	3.9 1.8 4.1
7	TH	0046 0758 1322 2025	1.6 4.0 1.6 4.3
8	F	0155 0906 1424 2122	1.3 4.3 1.3 4.5
9	SA	0252 0957 1519 2210	1.0 4.6 1.0 4.7
10	SU ○	0344 1043 1608 2255	0.7 4.8 0.7 4.9
11	M	0432 1129 1655 2339	0.4 4.9 0.5 4.9
12	TU	0517 1215 1740	0.3 5.0 0.4
13	W	0025 0601 1305 1824	4.9 0.3 5.0 0.5
14	TH	0113 0644 1359 1908	4.9 0.4 4.9 0.6
15	F	0206 0728 1458 1954	4.7 0.6 4.8 0.9
16	SA	0305 0815 1548 2044	4.6 1.0 4.6 1.2
17	SU ☾	0402 0909 1635 2144	4.4 1.3 4.4 1.5
18	M	0458 1018 1727 2256	4.1 1.7 4.2 1.7
19	TU	0600 1131 1830	3.9 1.9 4.0
20	W	0006 0710 1238 1938	1.8 3.8 2.0 3.9
21	TH	0111 0824 1341 2041	1.8 3.9 1.9 4.0
22	F	0209 0930 1435 2131	1.6 4.1 1.7 4.2
23	SA	0258 1007 1521 2212	1.4 4.3 1.4 4.3
24	SU	0341 1043 1602 2252	1.2 4.4 1.2 4.4
25	M ●	0420 1120 1640 2330	1.0 4.5 1.1 4.5
26	TU	0456 1157 1714	0.9 4.6 1.0
27	W	0006 0528 1232 1745	4.5 0.9 4.6 1.0
28	TH	0039 0558 1304 1813	4.5 0.9 4.6 1.0
29	F	0108 0627 1333 1842	4.5 1.0 4.5 1.0
30	SA	0136 0655 1403 1913	4.5 1.0 4.5 1.1
31	SU	0209 0728 1438 1949	4.4 1.1 4.4 1.1

SEPTEMBER

Date	Day	Time	m
1	M	0250 0807 1522 2033	4.3 1.2 4.3 1.3
2	TU ☽	0343 0855 1619 2130	4.1 1.5 4.1 1.6
3	W	0452 0959 1728 2249	4.0 1.8 4.0 1.8
4	TH	0615 1147 1851	3.9 1.9 4.0
5	F	0035 0744 1314 2009	1.7 4.0 1.7 4.2
6	SA	0144 0850 1414 2105	1.4 4.3 1.4 4.5
7	SU	0239 0940 1505 2152	1.0 4.6 1.0 4.7
8	M	0328 1025 1552 2236	0.7 4.9 0.7 4.9
9	TU ○	0414 1109 1637 2319	0.4 5.0 0.5 5.0
10	W	0458 1153 1720	0.3 5.0 0.4
11	TH	0004 0540 1239 1802	5.0 0.3 5.0 0.5
12	F	0050 0622 1328 1844	4.9 0.5 4.9 0.6
13	SA	0140 0703 1419 1927	4.8 0.7 4.8 0.9
14	SU	0235 0746 1509 2011	4.6 1.1 4.6 1.2
15	M	0331 0834 1555 2105	4.4 1.5 4.3 1.6
16	TU ☾	0426 0942 1646 2224	4.1 1.8 4.1 1.9
17	W	0526 1104 1750 2337	3.9 2.0 3.8 2.0
18	TH	0639 1212 1906	3.8 2.1 3.7
19	F	0042 0756 1315 2014	1.9 3.8 2.0 3.9
20	SA	0140 0905 1410 2107	1.8 4.1 1.8 4.1
21	SU	0229 0943 1455 2149	1.5 4.3 1.5 4.3
22	M	0311 1018 1534 2228	1.3 4.5 1.3 4.4
23	TU	0349 1053 1610 2305	1.1 4.6 1.1 4.5
24	W ●	0425 1128 1644 2340	1.0 4.7 1.0 4.6
25	TH	0458 1201 1716	0.9 4.7 1.0
26	F	0011 0530 1232 1746	4.6 0.9 4.7 0.9
27	SA	0040 0600 1301 1816	4.6 0.9 4.6 0.9
28	SU	0110 0631 1331 1848	4.6 1.0 4.6 1.0
29	M	0144 0705 1406 1925	4.5 1.1 4.5 1.1
30	TU	0226 0744 1452 2009	4.4 1.2 4.4 1.3

OCTOBER

Date	Day	Time	m
1	W ☽	0322 0833 1553 2105	4.2 1.5 4.2 1.6
2	TH	0437 0939 1709 2231	4.1 1.9 4.0 1.8
3	F	0603 1151 1834	4.0 2.0 4.0
4	SA	0025 0727 1303 1948	1.7 4.1 1.7 4.2
5	SU	0127 0831 1358 2044	1.4 4.4 1.4 4.5
6	M	0220 0921 1447 2131	1.1 4.7 1.1 4.7
7	TU	0307 1004 1532 2215	0.8 4.9 0.8 4.9
8	W ○	0352 1047 1616 2258	0.6 5.0 0.6 4.9
9	TH	0435 1130 1659 2343	0.5 5.0 0.5 4.9
10	F	0517 1213 1740	0.5 5.0 0.6
11	SA	0028 0558 1258 1820	4.9 0.6 4.9 0.7
12	SU	0116 0638 1342 1901	4.8 0.9 4.7 1.0
13	M	0207 0719 1427 1942	4.6 1.2 4.6 1.3
14	TU	0259 0803 1513 2027	4.4 1.5 4.3 1.6
15	W ☾	0350 0859 1602 2136	4.2 1.9 4.1 1.9
16	TH	0446 1031 1700 2302	4.0 2.1 3.8 2.0
17	F	0557 1141 1822	3.8 2.2 3.7
18	SA	0006 0714 1242 1937	2.0 3.9 2.1 3.8
19	SU	0103 0821 1336 2036	1.9 4.0 1.9 4.0
20	M	0152 0909 1420 2122	1.7 4.3 1.7 4.2
21	TU	0234 0948 1459 2202	1.5 4.5 1.4 4.4
22	W	0313 1024 1535 2238	1.2 4.6 1.2 4.5
23	TH ●	0350 1058 1611 2312	1.1 4.7 1.0 4.6
24	F	0427 1130 1646 2343	1.0 4.7 0.9 4.7
25	SA	0502 1200 1720	0.9 4.8 0.9
26	SU	0015 0536 1233 1754	4.7 0.9 4.8 0.8
27	M	0050 0611 1307 1830	4.7 1.0 4.7 0.9
28	TU	0129 0649 1347 1910	4.7 1.1 4.6 1.0
29	W	0216 0732 1436 1956	4.5 1.3 4.4 1.3
30	TH	0317 0823 1540 2053	4.4 1.6 4.2 1.5
31	F ☽	0432 0933 1655 2222	4.2 1.9 4.1 1.7

NOVEMBER

Date	Day	Time	m
1	SA	0548 1131 1813	4.2 1.9 4.1
2	SU	0001 0703 1240 1923	1.7 4.3 1.7 4.2
3	M	0103 0807 1335 2021	1.5 4.5 1.4 4.4
4	TU	0155 0859 1424 2109	1.2 4.7 1.2 4.6
5	W	0243 0943 1510 2155	1.0 4.8 0.9 4.7
6	TH ○	0329 1025 1554 2240	0.8 4.9 0.8 4.8
7	F	0413 1107 1637 2325	0.7 4.9 0.7 4.8
8	SA	0455 1150 1719	0.8 4.9 0.7
9	SU	0011 0537 1233 1759	4.8 0.9 4.8 0.8
10	M	0058 0617 1315 1839	4.7 1.0 4.7 1.0
11	TU	0146 0657 1357 1917	4.6 1.3 4.5 1.2
12	W	0232 0737 1439 1957	4.5 1.5 4.3 1.5
13	TH	0318 0822 1523 2043	4.3 1.8 4.1 1.8
14	F ☾	0405 0924 1613 2156	4.1 2.1 3.9 2.0
15	SA	0501 1055 1715 2318	4.0 2.2 3.8 2.0
16	SU	0614 1200 1844	3.9 2.1 3.7
17	M	0017 0730 1254 1954	2.0 4.0 2.0 3.9
18	TU	0108 0827 1339 2048	1.8 4.2 1.8 4.1
19	W	0153 0913 1420 2132	1.6 4.4 1.5 4.3
20	TH	0235 0951 1459 2210	1.4 4.5 1.3 4.4
21	F	0316 1025 1539 2244	1.2 4.7 1.1 4.6
22	SA ●	0356 1059 1618 2318	1.0 4.7 0.9 4.7
23	SU	0436 1134 1658 2355	0.9 4.8 0.8 4.8
24	M	0516 1210 1738	0.9 4.8 0.7
25	TU	0035 0556 1250 1818	4.8 0.9 4.8 0.8
26	W	0120 0639 1334 1902	4.8 1.0 4.7 0.9
27	TH	0211 0725 1426 1949	4.7 1.2 4.6 1.1
28	F	0314 0817 1529 2046	4.5 1.4 4.4 1.3
29	SA ☽	0422 0924 1639 2200	4.4 1.6 4.2 1.5
30	SU	0528 1053 1748 2326	4.4 1.7 4.2 1.6

DECEMBER

Date	Day	Time	m
1	M	0634 1208 1854	4.4 1.7 4.2
2	TU	0032 0737 1308 1954	1.5 4.5 1.5 4.3
3	W	0129 0833 1400 2049	1.4 4.6 1.3 4.4
4	TH	0220 0922 1448 2139	1.2 4.7 1.1 4.5
5	F	0307 1006 1534 2227	1.1 4.7 1.0 4.6
6	SA ○	0353 1049 1619 2314	1.0 4.8 0.9 4.6
7	SU	0437 1131 1702 2359	1.0 4.7 0.8 4.7
8	M	0520 1213 1743	1.0 4.7 0.9
9	TU	0044 0600 1254 1821	4.6 1.1 4.6 1.0
10	W	0128 0639 1334 1857	4.6 1.3 4.5 1.1
11	TH	0209 0715 1412 1932	4.5 1.4 4.4 1.3
12	F	0249 0751 1450 2008	4.4 1.6 4.2 1.5
13	SA	0327 0830 1532 2050	4.3 1.8 4.1 1.7
14	SU ☾	0410 0919 1621 2144	4.1 2.0 3.9 1.9
15	M	0501 1026 1719 2258	4.0 2.1 3.8 2.0
16	TU	0601 1147 1833	4.0 2.1 3.8
17	W	0011 0717 1248 1958	1.9 4.0 1.9 3.9
18	TH	0107 0825 1338 2056	1.8 4.2 1.7 4.1
19	F	0157 0913 1424 2140	1.6 4.4 1.4 4.3
20	SA	0244 0953 1510 2220	1.3 4.5 1.1 4.5
21	SU	0330 1033 1555 2259	1.1 4.7 0.9 4.7
22	M ●	0416 1113 1640 2340	0.9 4.8 0.7 4.8
23	TU	0501 1153 1724	0.8 4.9 0.6
24	W	0023 0545 1236 1808	4.8 0.7 4.9 0.5
25	TH	0110 0629 1322 1853	4.8 0.8 4.8 0.6
26	F	0203 0716 1414 1939	4.8 0.9 4.7 0.8
27	SA	0303 0806 1513 2031	4.7 1.1 4.5 1.0
28	SU ☽	0405 0903 1618 2132	4.6 1.3 4.4 1.3
29	M	0504 1014 1722 2247	4.5 1.5 4.2 1.5
30	TU	0603 1131 1825 2359	4.4 1.6 4.1 1.6
31	W	0705 1238 1929	4.3 1.6 4.1

SHOREHAM
LAT 50°50'N
LONG 0°15'W

TIMES AND HEIGHTS OF HIGH AND LOW WATER (Heights in Metres)

TIME ZONE UT
For Summer Time (area enclosed in shaded box) add 1 hour

2014

JANUARY

Date	Day	Time	m
1	W ●	0431 1040 1658 2311	0.8 6.5 0.5 6.5
2	TH	0521 1129 1748	0.6 6.6 0.4
3	F	0001 0610 1219 1836	6.6 0.5 6.7 0.3
4	SA	0051 0659 1308 1925	6.7 0.5 6.6 0.3
5	SU	0140 0748 1357 2015	6.6 0.6 6.4 0.5
6	M	0227 0838 1445 2104	6.5 0.8 6.2 0.7
7	TU	0315 0930 1535 2155	6.2 1.0 5.8 1.0
8	W ☽	0405 1025 1628 2251	5.9 1.3 5.5 1.4
9	TH	0459 1128 1728 2357	5.5 1.6 5.1 1.7
10	F	0602 1240 1840	5.2 1.8 4.9
11	SA	0109 0716 1347 2001	1.8 5.1 1.7 5.0
12	SU	0214 0829 1446 2105	1.8 5.2 1.6 5.2
13	M	0309 0925 1536 2156	1.6 5.5 1.4 5.5
14	TU	0357 1011 1620 2238	1.4 5.7 1.1 5.7
15	W	0438 1050 1659 2315	1.2 5.8 1.0 5.9
16	TH O	0515 1124 1735 2348	1.1 5.9 0.9 6.0
17	F	0550 1154 1810	1.0 6.0 0.9
18	SA	0018 0624 1223 1844	6.0 1.0 6.0 0.9
19	SU	0046 0657 1251 1916	6.0 1.0 5.9 0.9
20	M	0112 0728 1321 1946	6.0 1.1 5.9 1.0
21	TU	0141 0758 1353 2014	5.9 1.2 5.8 1.1
22	W	0215 0830 1430 2048	5.8 1.3 5.7 1.2
23	TH	0254 0911 1513 2132	5.7 1.4 5.5 1.4
24	F ☾	0341 1003 1605 2228	5.5 1.6 5.2 1.7
25	SA	0441 1111 1716 2344	5.2 1.8 5.0 1.8
26	SU	0605 1235 1854	5.1 1.7 5.0
27	M	0112 0732 1354 2010	1.7 5.3 1.5 5.3
28	TU	0227 0839 1500 2113	1.5 5.7 1.1 5.8
29	W	0327 0937 1555 2209	1.1 6.1 0.7 6.2
30	TH ●	0420 1030 1646 2302	0.7 6.4 0.4 6.5
31	F	0509 1121 1734 2351	0.5 6.6 0.2 6.7

FEBRUARY

Date	Day	Time	m
1	SA	0557 1209 1822	0.3 6.7 0.2
2	SU	0039 0643 1257 1908	6.8 0.3 6.7 0.2
3	M	0124 0730 1342 1953	6.8 0.4 6.6 0.3
4	TU	0207 0815 1424 2037	6.6 0.5 6.3 0.6
5	W	0248 0858 1507 2120	6.3 0.8 6.0 0.9
6	TH ☽	0330 0943 1552 2206	5.9 1.2 5.5 1.3
7	F	0417 1034 1645 2300	5.5 1.6 5.1 1.7
8	SA	0513 1143 1749	5.0 1.9 4.8
9	SU	0023 0621 1315 1910	2.0 4.8 2.0 4.7
10	M	0147 0750 1421 2041	2.0 4.8 1.8 4.9
11	TU	0248 0903 1514 2136	1.8 5.1 1.5 5.3
12	W	0337 0952 1559 2218	1.5 5.4 1.2 5.6
13	TH	0418 1030 1638 2254	1.3 5.7 1.0 5.8
14	F O	0455 1103 1713 2326	1.1 5.9 0.9 6.0
15	SA	0529 1133 1748 2355	0.9 6.0 0.8 6.0
16	SU	0603 1200 1822	0.9 6.0 0.8
17	M	0021 0635 1230 1853	6.1 0.9 6.1 0.8
18	TU	0048 0705 1300 1921	6.1 0.9 6.1 0.8
19	W	0118 0732 1332 1948	6.1 0.9 6.0 0.9
20	TH	0151 0804 1407 2022	6.0 1.0 5.9 1.0
21	F	0228 0843 1447 2105	5.9 1.1 5.7 1.2
22	SA ☾	0312 0932 1537 2159	5.6 1.4 5.4 1.5
23	SU	0408 1037 1643 2314	5.3 1.6 5.0 1.8
24	M	0528 1204 1827	5.0 1.8 4.9
25	TU	0050 0711 1335 1955	1.8 5.1 1.6 5.2
26	W	0213 0826 1446 2102	1.5 5.5 1.2 5.7
27	TH	0315 0927 1542 2159	1.1 5.9 0.7 6.1
28	F	0407 1020 1631 2250	0.7 6.3 0.4 6.5

MARCH

Date	Day	Time	m
1	SA ●	0454 1109 1718 2337	0.4 6.6 0.2 6.7
2	SU	0540 1156 1803	0.2 6.7 0.1
3	M	0021 0624 1240 1846	6.8 0.2 6.7 0.2
4	TU	0103 0707 1322 1928	6.7 0.3 6.6 0.3
5	W	0142 0748 1401 2007	6.6 0.5 6.3 0.5
6	TH	0219 0826 1438 2045	6.3 0.7 6.0 0.9
7	F	0256 0904 1519 2125	5.9 1.1 5.6 1.3
8	SA ☽	0337 0947 1607 2212	5.4 1.5 5.1 1.7
9	SU	0430 1042 1709 2317	4.9 1.9 4.7 2.1
10	M	0537 1210 1821	4.6 2.1 4.6
11	TU	0111 0654 1350 1959	2.2 4.5 2.0 4.7
12	W	0221 0829 1446 2106	2.0 4.8 1.7 5.1
13	TH	0311 0923 1531 2149	1.6 5.2 1.4 5.5
14	F	0352 1002 1610 2224	1.3 5.5 1.1 5.8
15	SA	0428 1034 1646 2255	1.1 5.8 0.9 5.9
16	SU O	0503 1104 1721 2324	0.9 5.9 0.8 6.1
17	M	0537 1135 1755 2353	0.8 6.1 0.7 6.1
18	TU	0610 1206 1828	0.7 6.1 0.7
19	W	0023 0640 1239 1856	6.2 0.7 6.2 0.7
20	TH	0055 0711 1312 1927	6.2 0.7 6.2 0.7
21	F	0130 0745 1349 2004	6.2 0.8 6.1 0.9
22	SA	0208 0826 1431 2049	6.0 0.9 5.8 1.1
23	SU	0252 0915 1521 2145	5.7 1.2 5.5 1.5
24	M ☾	0349 1020 1630 2301	5.3 1.5 5.1 1.7
25	TU	0511 1147 1812	5.0 1.7 5.0
26	W	0037 0654 1319 1940	1.8 5.0 1.5 5.2
27	TH	0158 0812 1429 2049	1.4 5.4 1.1 5.7
28	F	0259 0913 1524 2144	1.0 5.8 0.7 6.1
29	SA	0349 1005 1612 2232	0.6 6.2 0.4 6.5
30	SU ●	0435 1053 1657 2317	0.4 6.4 0.3 6.6
31	M	0520 1138 1740 2359	0.3 6.6 0.2 6.7

APRIL

Date	Day	Time	m
1	TU	0602 1220 1822	0.3 6.6 0.3
2	W	0039 0642 1300 1901	6.6 0.4 6.4 0.4
3	TH	0116 0721 1337 1939	6.4 0.5 6.2 0.7
4	F	0150 0757 1412 2015	6.1 0.8 6.0 0.9
5	SA	0224 0833 1450 2053	5.8 1.1 5.6 1.3
6	SU	0301 0913 1535 2138	5.4 1.4 5.2 1.7
7	M ☽	0349 1003 1633 2236	5.0 1.8 4.8 2.0
8	TU	0457 1109 1740 2355	4.6 2.0 4.6 2.2
9	W	0609 1250 1852	4.5 2.1 4.7
10	TH	0139 0722 1406 2007	2.1 4.6 1.8 5.0
11	F	0235 0829 1455 2101	1.7 5.0 1.5 5.3
12	SA	0318 0916 1535 2140	1.4 5.3 1.2 5.7
13	SU	0356 0954 1613 2215	1.1 5.7 1.0 5.9
14	M	0432 1030 1649 2250	0.9 5.9 0.8 6.1
15	TU O	0507 1106 1725 2324	0.8 6.1 0.7 6.2
16	W	0543 1143 1800 2359	0.7 6.2 0.7 6.3
17	TH	0617 1219 1835	0.6 6.3 0.7
18	F	0035 0653 1257 1912	6.3 0.6 6.2 0.7
19	SA	0113 0733 1337 1954	6.2 0.6 6.1 0.8
20	SU	0155 0817 1423 2043	6.0 0.8 5.9 1.1
21	M	0243 0910 1517 2141	5.7 1.1 5.6 1.3
22	TU ☾	0342 1014 1628 2255	5.4 1.3 5.3 1.6
23	W	0503 1135 1757	5.1 1.5 5.2
24	TH	0021 0635 1259 1920	1.6 5.1 1.4 5.3
25	F	0137 0752 1407 2027	1.4 5.3 1.1 5.7
26	SA	0237 0853 1501 2122	1.0 5.7 0.8 6.0
27	SU	0328 0946 1550 2210	0.7 6.0 0.6 6.3
28	M	0414 1033 1635 2254	0.5 6.2 0.5 6.4
29	TU ●	0458 1117 1718 2336	0.5 6.3 0.5 6.4
30	W	0540 1159 1759	0.5 6.3 0.5

MAY

Date	Day	Time	m
1	TH	0015 0619 1238 1837	6.4 0.5 6.3 0.7
2	F	0051 0657 1314 1914	6.2 0.6 6.1 0.8
3	SA	0124 0732 1349 1949	6.0 0.8 5.9 1.0
4	SU	0157 0808 1425 2027	5.7 1.0 5.7 1.3
5	M	0231 0847 1506 2111	5.4 1.3 5.4 1.6
6	TU	0314 0933 1557 2203	5.1 1.6 5.1 1.9
7	W ☽	0414 1030 1659 2306	4.8 1.8 4.8 2.0
8	TH	0525 1138 1804	4.6 2.0 4.8
9	F	0021 0631 1255 1907	2.0 4.7 1.9 5.0
10	SA	0137 0733 1402 2004	1.8 4.9 1.7 5.2
11	SU	0232 0826 1451 2052	1.5 5.2 1.4 5.6
12	M	0316 0913 1534 2136	1.2 5.5 1.2 5.8
13	TU	0356 0957 1615 2217	1.0 5.8 1.0 6.1
14	W O	0436 1039 1655 2257	0.8 6.0 0.8 6.2
15	TH	0515 1121 1735 2337	0.6 6.2 0.7 6.3
16	F	0557 1203 1817	0.5 6.3 0.6
17	SA	0019 0639 1246 1901	6.4 0.5 6.3 0.6
18	SU	0102 0724 1332 1948	6.3 0.5 6.2 0.7
19	M	0148 0813 1421 2039	6.1 0.7 6.1 0.9
20	TU	0239 0907 1517 2137	5.9 0.9 5.8 1.1
21	W ☾	0339 1008 1621 2245	5.6 1.1 5.6 1.3
22	TH	0450 1119 1734 2359	5.3 1.3 5.4 1.4
23	F	0609 1232 1851	5.2 1.3 5.5
24	SA	0110 0724 1339 1958	1.3 5.3 1.2 5.6
25	SU	0211 0828 1436 2056	1.1 5.5 1.1 5.8
26	M	0304 0923 1527 2146	0.9 5.7 0.9 6.0
27	TU	0352 1012 1613 2232	0.8 5.9 0.8 6.1
28	W ●	0437 1058 1657 2314	0.7 6.0 0.8 6.2
29	TH	0519 1139 1738 2353	0.7 6.1 0.8 6.1
30	F	0559 1218 1817	0.7 6.1 0.9
31	SA	0029 0636 1254 1853	6.0 0.8 6.0 0.9

JUNE

Date	Day	Time	m
1	SU	0102 0712 1329 1928	5.9 0.9 5.9 1.1
2	M	0134 0747 1402 2005	5.7 1.0 5.7 1.2
3	TU	0206 0825 1437 2045	5.5 1.2 5.5 1.4
4	W	0242 0906 1517 2131	5.3 1.4 5.3 1.6
5	TH ☽	0326 0953 1606 2224	5.0 1.6 5.1 1.8
6	F	0424 1049 1709 2325	4.8 1.8 5.0 1.9
7	SA	0538 1152 1815	4.8 1.8 5.0
8	SU	0030 0644 1258 1915	1.8 4.9 1.8 5.2
9	M	0134 0743 1400 2010	1.6 5.1 1.6 5.4
10	TU	0231 0836 1454 2101	1.4 5.4 1.3 5.7
11	W	0320 0926 1543 2148	1.1 5.7 1.1 6.0
12	TH	0407 1014 1629 2234	0.8 6.0 0.9 6.2
13	F O	0453 1102 1715 2320	0.6 6.2 0.7 6.4
14	SA	0539 1150 1803	0.5 6.4 0.6
15	SU	0007 0626 1239 1850	6.4 0.4 6.4 0.6
16	M	0055 0715 1327 1940	6.4 0.4 6.4 0.6
17	TU	0144 0806 1417 2031	6.3 0.5 6.3 0.7
18	W	0235 0858 1510 2126	6.1 0.7 6.1 0.9
19	TH ☾	0330 0954 1605 2226	5.8 0.9 5.9 1.1
20	F	0429 1056 1705 2332	5.6 1.1 5.7 1.3
21	SA	0535 1202 1812	5.3 1.3 5.5
22	SU	0040 0648 1309 1923	1.4 5.2 1.4 5.4
23	M	0144 0800 1411 2028	1.4 5.2 1.4 5.5
24	TU	0241 0901 1505 2124	1.2 5.4 1.3 5.7
25	W	0333 0954 1554 2212	1.1 5.6 1.1 5.8
26	TH	0419 1040 1639 2256	1.0 5.8 1.0 5.9
27	F ●	0501 1122 1720 2334	0.9 5.9 1.0 5.9
28	SA	0541 1200 1758	0.9 6.0 1.0
29	SU	0009 0617 1236 1834	5.9 0.9 6.0 1.0
30	M	0042 0652 1308 1908	5.9 0.9 5.9 1.0

SUNRISE AND SUNSET TIMES

SHOREHAM
At 50°50'N 0°15'W

		Sunrise	Sunset
UT			
Jan	01	0803	1606
	15	0757	1624
Feb	01	0737	1653
	15	0713	1718
Mar	01	0645	1742
	15	0615	1806
BST			
Apr	01	0637	1934
	15	0607	1957
May	01	0535	2022
	15	0512	2044
Jun	01	0453	2105
	15	0447	2116
Jul	01	0452	2118
	15	0505	2108
Aug	01	0527	2046
	15	0548	2021
Sep	01	0615	1946
	15	0636	1915
Oct	01	0701	1839
	15	0724	1809
UT			
Nov	01	0653	1636
	15	0717	1614
Dec	01	0741	1558
	15	0757	1555

SHOREHAM
LAT 50°50′N
LONG 0°15′W

TIMES AND HEIGHTS OF HIGH AND LOW WATER (Heights in Metres)

TIME ZONE UT
For Summer Time (area enclosed in shaded box) add 1 hour

2014

JULY

Date	Day	Time	m	Time	m	Time	m	Time	m
1	TU	0111	5.8	0727	1.0	1338	5.8	1944	1.1
2	W	0141	5.6	0802	1.1	1406	5.7	2020	1.2
3	TH	0212	5.5	0837	1.2	1438	5.6	2057	1.4
4	F	0248	5.4	0914	1.4	1516	5.4	2139	1.6
5	SA	0331	5.2	0958	1.6	1603	5.2	☽ 2231	1.7
6	SU	0425	5.0	1053	1.7	1704	5.1	2334	1.8
7	M	0540	4.9	1201	1.8	1823	5.1		
8	TU	0043	1.7	0700	5.0	1314	1.7	1932	5.3
9	W	0151	1.5	0805	5.3	1420	1.5	2032	5.6
10	TH	0252	1.2	0902	5.7	1518	1.2	2126	6.0
11	F	0345	0.9	0956	6.0	1610	0.9	2217	6.2
12	SA	0435	0.6	1048	6.3	1700	0.6	O 2307	6.4
13	SU	0524	0.4	1139	6.5	1749	0.5	2357	6.5
14	M	0613	0.3	1229	6.6	1838	0.4		
15	TU	0046	6.6	0702	0.3	1318	6.6	1927	0.4
16	W	0135	6.5	0752	0.3	1406	6.6	2017	0.5
17	TH	0224	6.3	0841	0.5	1453	6.4	2107	0.7
18	F	0312	6.0	0932	0.7	1541	6.1	2200	1.0
19	SA	0403	5.7	1026	1.1	1633	5.7	☾ 2259	1.3
20	SU	0500	5.3	1127	1.4	1731	5.4		
21	M	0006	1.6	0606	5.0	1238	1.7	1840	5.2
22	TU	0117	1.6	0728	5.0	1347	1.7	1959	5.1
23	W	0220	1.6	0842	5.1	1446	1.6	2105	5.3
24	TH	0315	1.4	0938	5.4	1537	1.4	2156	5.6
25	F	0401	1.2	1024	5.7	1622	1.2	2239	5.7
26	SA	0443	1.0	1105	5.9	1702	1.1	● 2317	5.9
27	SU	0521	0.9	1141	6.0	1739	1.0	2350	5.9
28	M	0557	0.9	1214	6.0	1813	1.0		
29	TU	0019	5.9	0631	0.9	1244	6.0	1847	1.0
30	W	0047	5.9	0704	0.9	1309	6.0	1920	1.0
31	TH	0114	5.8	0736	1.0	1335	5.9	1952	1.1

AUGUST

Date	Day	Time	m	Time	m	Time	m	Time	m
1	F	0143	5.8	0806	1.1	1405	5.8	2022	1.2
2	SA	0216	5.6	0836	1.2	1440	5.7	2057	1.4
3	SU	0255	5.5	0914	1.4	1522	5.5	2142	1.5
4	M	0343	5.2	1005	1.6	1615	5.3	☽ 2242	1.7
5	TU	0445	5.0	1112	1.8	1728	5.1	2359	1.8
6	W	0619	4.9	1237	1.8	1901	5.2		
7	TH	0121	1.6	0741	5.2	1357	1.6	2011	5.5
8	F	0232	1.3	0846	5.6	1502	1.2	2110	5.9
9	SA	0330	0.9	0943	6.0	1556	0.9	2204	6.3
10	SU	0421	0.6	1036	6.4	1645	0.6	O 2255	6.5
11	M	0509	0.3	1126	6.6	1734	0.4	2345	6.7
12	TU	0557	0.2	1215	6.8	1821	0.3		
13	W	0033	6.7	0644	0.2	1302	6.8	1908	0.3
14	TH	0120	6.6	0731	0.3	1347	6.7	1955	0.4
15	F	0205	6.4	0817	0.5	1430	6.5	2041	0.7
16	SA	0249	6.1	0903	0.8	1513	6.1	2127	1.0
17	SU	0335	5.7	0950	1.2	1600	5.7	☾ 2218	1.4
18	M	0426	5.3	1044	1.6	1653	5.3	2323	1.8
19	TU	0528	4.9	1200	1.9	1758	4.9		
20	W	0048	1.9	0648	4.8	1323	2.0	1925	4.8
21	TH	0159	1.8	0821	4.9	1427	1.8	2045	5.1
22	F	0255	1.6	0920	5.3	1518	1.6	2138	5.4
23	SA	0341	1.3	1005	5.6	1602	1.3	2219	5.7
24	SU	0421	1.1	1043	5.9	1640	1.1	2255	5.9
25	M	0458	0.9	1117	6.0	1715	1.0	● 2326	6.0
26	TU	0532	0.9	1148	6.1	1749	0.9	2353	6.0
27	W	0606	0.8	1214	6.1	1823	0.9		
28	TH	0019	6.0	0639	0.9	1239	6.1	1854	0.9
29	F	0047	6.0	0709	0.9	1306	6.1	1923	1.0
30	SA	0117	6.0	0735	1.0	1336	6.0	1951	1.1
31	SU	0149	5.9	0804	1.1	1410	5.9	2025	1.2

SEPTEMBER

Date	Day	Time	m	Time	m	Time	m	Time	m
1	M	0227	5.7	0844	1.3	1451	5.6	2110	1.4
2	TU	0312	5.4	0935	1.6	1541	5.3	☽ 2208	1.7
3	W	0412	5.1	1042	1.9	1652	5.0	2327	1.9
4	TH	0551	4.9	1213	1.9	1838	5.0		
5	F	0059	1.7	0724	5.1	1341	1.7	1955	5.4
6	SA	0217	1.4	0833	5.6	1448	1.3	2058	5.9
7	SU	0315	0.9	0930	6.1	1541	0.8	2152	6.3
8	M	0405	0.5	1022	6.5	1629	0.5	2242	6.6
9	TU	0451	0.3	1110	6.8	1715	0.3	O 2329	6.7
10	W	0537	0.2	1156	6.9	1801	0.3		
11	TH	0015	6.8	0622	0.2	1241	6.9	1845	0.3
12	F	0100	6.7	0706	0.3	1323	6.7	1929	0.5
13	SA	0142	6.5	0748	0.6	1403	6.4	2011	0.7
14	SU	0222	6.2	0830	0.9	1443	6.1	2052	1.1
15	M	0305	5.7	0912	1.3	1526	5.6	2137	1.5
16	TU	0354	5.3	1001	1.7	1617	5.1	☾ 2231	1.9
17	W	0453	4.9	1106	2.1	1721	4.8		
18	TH	0002	2.2	0604	4.7	1252	2.2	1838	4.7
19	F	0131	2.1	0747	4.8	1402	2.0	2017	4.9
20	SA	0229	1.8	0852	5.2	1454	1.7	2112	5.3
21	SU	0315	1.5	0937	5.6	1536	1.4	2152	5.6
22	M	0355	1.2	1013	5.9	1614	1.1	2226	5.9
23	TU	0430	1.0	1045	6.1	1648	1.0	2255	6.0
24	W	0505	0.9	1114	6.1	1722	0.9	● 2323	6.1
25	TH	0539	0.9	1140	6.2	1756	0.9	2352	6.1
26	F	0612	0.9	1208	6.2	1828	0.9		
27	SA	0022	6.2	0641	0.9	1239	6.2	1856	0.9
28	SU	0054	6.1	0709	1.0	1311	6.1	1927	1.0
29	M	0128	6.0	0742	1.1	1346	6.0	2004	1.1
30	TU	0206	5.9	0824	1.3	1428	5.7	2050	1.4

OCTOBER

Date	Day	Time	m	Time	m	Time	m	Time	m
1	W	0252	5.5	0917	1.6	1519	5.4	☽ 2149	1.7
2	TH	0355	5.2	1026	1.9	1633	5.0	2308	1.9
3	F	0535	5.0	1158	1.9	1821	5.0		
4	SA	0042	1.8	0707	5.2	1325	1.7	1940	5.4
5	SU	0159	1.4	0817	5.7	1431	1.2	2043	5.8
6	M	0257	1.0	0914	6.1	1523	0.8	2136	6.2
7	TU	0346	0.6	1004	6.5	1610	0.5	2225	6.5
8	W	0431	0.4	1050	6.7	1654	0.4	O 2311	6.7
9	TH	0515	0.3	1134	6.8	1738	0.3	2355	6.7
10	F	0559	0.4	1216	6.8	1821	0.4		
11	SA	0037	6.6	0640	0.5	1257	6.6	1902	0.6
12	SU	0118	6.4	0721	0.7	1335	6.3	1942	0.8
13	M	0156	6.1	0800	1.0	1412	6.0	2021	1.1
14	TU	0236	5.8	0840	1.4	1452	5.6	2102	1.5
15	W	0322	5.4	0925	1.8	1541	5.1	☾ 2151	1.9
16	TH	0419	5.0	1022	2.1	1644	4.8	2256	2.2
17	F	0525	4.8	1144	2.3	1754	4.6		
18	SA	0041	2.2	0639	4.8	1324	2.2	1913	4.8
19	SU	0152	2.0	0803	5.1	1420	1.8	2028	5.1
20	M	0242	1.7	0854	5.5	1504	1.5	2111	5.5
21	TU	0323	1.4	0932	5.8	1543	1.2	2145	5.8
22	W	0400	1.2	1004	6.0	1618	1.0	2218	6.0
23	TH	0435	1.0	1036	6.2	1653	0.9	● 2251	6.1
24	F	0510	0.9	1108	6.2	1728	0.9	2325	6.2
25	SA	0544	0.9	1141	6.3	1801	0.8	2359	6.3
26	SU	0616	0.9	1215	6.3	1835	0.8		
27	M	0034	6.3	0650	1.0	1251	6.2	1910	0.9
28	TU	0112	6.2	0729	1.1	1330	6.1	1951	1.0
29	W	0154	6.0	0814	1.2	1414	5.8	2040	1.3
30	TH	0244	5.7	0908	1.5	1509	5.5	2139	1.5
31	F	0348	5.4	1017	1.7	1622	5.2	☽ 2254	1.7

NOVEMBER

Date	Day	Time	m	Time	m	Time	m	Time	m
1	SA	0517	5.2	1141	1.8	1759	5.1		
2	SU	0020	1.7	0644	5.4	1302	1.6	1918	5.4
3	M	0135	1.4	0755	5.7	1407	1.3	2023	5.7
4	TU	0234	1.1	0852	6.1	1501	0.9	2117	6.1
5	W	0324	0.8	0942	6.4	1549	0.7	2206	6.4
6	TH	0410	0.6	1028	6.6	1634	0.5	O 2252	6.5
7	F	0454	0.6	1111	6.6	1717	0.5	2335	6.5
8	SA	0537	0.6	1153	6.6	1800	0.6		
9	SU	0017	6.5	0618	0.7	1232	6.4	1839	0.7
10	M	0056	6.3	0657	0.9	1309	6.2	1918	0.9
11	TU	0133	6.1	0734	1.1	1344	5.9	1955	1.1
12	W	0211	5.9	0813	1.4	1422	5.6	2034	1.4
13	TH	0253	5.5	0856	1.7	1506	5.2	2119	1.7
14	F	0343	5.2	0947	1.9	1603	4.9	☾ 2214	2.0
15	SA	0443	5.0	1048	2.2	1709	4.7	2320	2.1
16	SU	0548	4.9	1203	2.2	1815	4.7		
17	M	0040	2.1	0651	5.0	1326	2.0	1918	4.9
18	TU	0151	1.9	0751	5.3	1421	1.7	2014	5.2
19	W	0241	1.6	0840	5.6	1505	1.4	2100	5.6
20	TH	0324	1.4	0922	5.9	1545	1.2	2142	5.9
21	F	0403	1.2	1001	6.1	1623	1.0	2222	6.1
22	SA	0440	1.0	1039	6.3	1700	0.9	● 2301	6.2
23	SU	0518	0.9	1117	6.4	1739	0.8	2341	6.3
24	M	0556	0.9	1156	6.4	1818	0.7		
25	TU	0021	6.4	0636	0.9	1237	6.3	1859	0.8
26	W	0103	6.3	0720	0.9	1320	6.2	1945	0.9
27	TH	0149	6.2	0808	1.1	1408	6.0	2034	1.0
28	F	0240	5.9	0902	1.3	1502	5.7	2132	1.3
29	SA	0340	5.7	1006	1.5	1608	5.4	☽ 2239	1.4
30	SU	0453	5.5	1119	1.6	1728	5.3	2353	1.5

DECEMBER

Date	Day	Time	m	Time	m	Time	m	Time	m
1	M	0612	5.5	1233	1.5	1848	5.3		
2	TU	0105	1.5	0724	5.6	1340	1.4	1956	5.5
3	W	0208	1.3	0826	5.9	1438	1.1	2055	5.8
4	TH	0302	1.1	0920	6.1	1529	0.9	2147	6.0
5	F	0351	0.9	1008	6.3	1615	0.8	2234	6.2
6	SA	0436	0.8	1052	6.3	1700	0.7	O 2318	6.3
7	SU	0519	0.8	1133	6.3	1742	0.7	2359	6.3
8	M	0600	0.9	1212	6.3	1821	0.8		
9	TU	0038	6.2	0637	1.0	1248	6.1	1858	0.9
10	W	0114	6.1	0713	1.1	1322	5.9	1934	1.0
11	TH	0149	5.9	0750	1.3	1355	5.7	2011	1.2
12	F	0224	5.7	0829	1.5	1431	5.4	2051	1.4
13	SA	0302	5.5	0913	1.7	1512	5.2	2137	1.7
14	SU	0348	5.2	1004	1.9	1606	4.9	☾ 2229	1.9
15	M	0449	5.0	1103	2.0	1718	4.8	2331	2.0
16	TU	0556	5.0	1209	2.1	1826	4.8		
17	W	0038	2.0	0658	5.1	1317	1.9	1926	5.0
18	TH	0145	1.9	0754	5.4	1418	1.6	2021	5.3
19	F	0242	1.6	0845	5.7	1508	1.3	2110	5.7
20	SA	0330	1.3	0931	6.0	1554	1.1	2156	6.0
21	SU	0413	1.1	1015	6.2	1637	0.8	2241	6.2
22	M	0456	0.9	1059	6.4	1720	0.7	● 2326	6.4
23	TU	0540	0.8	1142	6.5	1804	0.6		
24	W	0011	6.5	0624	0.7	1227	6.5	1849	0.5
25	TH	0057	6.5	0711	0.7	1313	6.4	1937	0.6
26	F	0143	6.4	0759	0.8	1401	6.3	2026	0.7
27	SA	0233	6.2	0851	0.9	1452	6.0	2119	0.9
28	SU	0326	6.0	0948	1.1	1549	5.7	☽ 2217	1.1
29	M	0425	5.8	1052	1.4	1654	5.4	2322	1.4
30	TU	0532	5.5	1201	1.5	1807	5.3		
31	W	0033	1.5	0646	5.4	1311	1.5	1925	5.2

DOVER

LAT 51°07′N
LONG 1°19′E

TIMES AND HEIGHTS OF HIGH AND LOW WATER (Heights in Metres)

TIME ZONE UT
For Summer Time (area enclosed in shaded box) add 1 hour

2014

JANUARY

Date	Day	Time	m
1	W	0534 1026 1804 ● 2252	1.0 6.8 0.8 6.9
2	TH	0631 1114 1859 2340	0.8 6.9 0.7 7.0
3	F	0724 1202 1950	0.6 7.0 0.7
4	SA	0027 0814 1251 2036	7.1 0.5 6.9 0.7
5	SU	0114 0901 1339 2118	7.1 0.6 6.7 0.8
6	M	0203 0945 1430 2200	6.9 0.7 6.5 1.0
7	TU	0253 1029 1523 2243	6.7 1.0 6.2 1.3
8	W	0346 1116 1620 ☽ 2333	6.4 1.3 5.9 1.7
9	TH	0444 1209 1725	6.0 1.7 5.6
10	F	0032 0550 1311 1839	2.0 5.7 1.9 5.4
11	SA	0139 0706 1417 1954	2.1 5.6 2.0 5.5
12	SU	0248 0820 1525 2056	2.0 5.6 1.9 5.7
13	M	0355 0919 1627 2145	1.8 5.8 1.7 6.0
14	TU	0451 1006 1715 2226	1.6 6.0 1.5 6.2
15	W	0535 1044 1754 2302	1.4 6.2 1.4 6.4
16	TH	0612 1117 1827 O 2335	1.2 6.3 1.3 6.5
17	F	0645 1149 1858	1.2 6.3 1.2
18	SA	0007 0716 1219 1929	6.5 1.1 6.3 1.2
19	SU	0035 0749 1246 2002	6.5 1.1 6.3 1.2
20	M	0101 0823 1310 2034	6.5 1.2 6.3 1.3
21	TU	0127 0856 1339 2107	6.4 1.2 6.2 1.3
22	W	0159 0930 1414 2142	6.4 1.3 6.2 1.5
23	TH	0239 1007 1458 2222	6.3 1.5 6.0 1.7
24	F	0327 1052 1552 ☾ 2313	6.1 1.7 5.7 1.9
25	SA	0428 1153 1706	5.8 1.9 5.5
26	SU	0026 0556 1317 1853	2.1 5.6 1.9 5.5
27	M	0156 0725 1437 2006	2.0 5.8 1.7 5.8
28	TU	0310 0832 1546 2105	1.7 6.1 1.4 6.1
29	W	0418 0930 1653 2158	1.3 6.4 1.1 6.5
30	TH	0524 1022 1757 ● 2246	0.9 6.7 0.8 6.8
31	F	0625 1110 1853 2332	0.6 6.9 0.6 7.1

FEBRUARY

Date	Day	Time	m
1	SA	0719 1155 1942	0.4 7.0 0.5
2	SU	0016 0807 1239 2024	7.2 0.3 7.0 0.5
3	M	0100 0849 1322 2102	7.2 0.3 6.8 0.6
4	TU	0143 0927 1407 2138	7.1 0.5 6.6 0.8
5	W	0228 1004 1453 2214	6.8 0.8 6.3 1.1
6	TH	0314 1042 1543 ☽ 2254	6.4 1.2 6.0 1.6
7	F	0406 1128 1640 2345	6.0 1.7 5.6 2.0
8	SA	0506 1226 1748	5.6 2.1 5.3
9	SU	0054 0619 1335 1908	2.2 5.3 2.2 5.2
10	M	0209 0746 1446 2027	2.2 5.3 2.1 5.4
11	TU	0320 0901 1552 2125	2.0 5.5 1.9 5.7
12	W	0421 0950 1648 2207	1.7 5.8 1.6 6.1
13	TH	0510 1026 1731 2241	1.4 6.1 1.4 6.3
14	F	0549 1056 1807 O 2312	1.2 6.2 1.2 6.4
15	SA	0624 1125 1839 2341	1.1 6.3 1.1 6.5
16	SU	0657 1153 1911	1.0 6.4 1.1
17	M	0009 0730 1221 1943	6.5 1.0 6.4 1.0
18	TU	0035 0804 1246 2015	6.6 1.0 6.4 1.0
19	W	0102 0836 1314 2047	6.6 1.0 6.5 1.1
20	TH	0134 0907 1349 2119	6.6 1.1 6.5 1.2
21	F	0212 0941 1431 2157	6.5 1.3 6.3 1.5
22	SA	0257 1023 1522 ☾ 2245	6.3 1.6 5.9 1.8
23	SU	0355 1119 1631 2353	5.9 1.8 5.5 2.0
24	M	0524 1241 1831	5.5 2.0 5.4
25	TU	0126 0714 1413 1952	2.0 5.6 1.9 5.6
26	W	0249 0826 1529 2055	1.7 5.9 1.5 6.1
27	TH	0404 0925 1642 2149	1.3 6.3 1.1 6.5
28	F	0515 1017 1747 2236	0.9 6.6 0.8 6.8

MARCH

Date	Day	Time	m
1	SA	0615 1102 1840 ● 2320	0.5 6.8 0.5 7.1
2	SU	0706 1144 1926	0.3 7.0 0.4
3	M	0001 0750 1223 2005	7.2 0.2 7.0 0.4
4	TU	0042 0828 1302 2040	7.2 0.3 6.9 0.5
5	W	0122 0903 1342 2112	7.0 0.5 6.7 0.7
6	TH	0202 0935 1424 2144	6.8 0.8 6.4 1.1
7	F	0244 1007 1510 2216	6.4 1.3 6.1 1.5
8	SA	0331 1043 1603 ☽ 2258	6.0 1.7 5.7 1.9
9	SU	0429 1135 1707	5.5 2.2 5.3
10	M	0006 0538 1253 1821	2.3 5.2 2.4 5.1
11	TU	0130 0701 1409 1945	2.4 5.1 2.3 5.3
12	W	0243 0820 1516 2053	2.1 5.3 2.0 5.6
13	TH	0346 0923 1614 2137	1.8 5.7 1.7 5.9
14	F	0437 0957 1700 2211	1.5 6.0 1.4 6.2
15	SA	0519 1026 1739 2241	1.2 6.2 1.2 6.4
16	SU	0557 1055 1814 O 2311	1.1 6.3 1.1 6.5
17	M	0633 1125 1848 2340	0.9 6.4 1.0 6.6
18	TU	0708 1153 1922	0.9 6.5 0.9
19	W	0008 0742 1222 1955	6.7 0.8 6.6 0.9
20	TH	0039 0815 1253 2027	6.7 0.9 6.7 1.0
21	F	0113 0847 1330 2101	6.7 1.0 6.6 1.1
22	SA	0152 0922 1413 2141	6.6 1.2 6.4 1.3
23	SU	0238 1005 1506 2230	6.3 1.5 6.0 1.6
24	M	0338 1100 1620 ☾ 2337	5.8 1.8 5.6 1.9
25	TU	0517 1222 1814	5.5 2.0 5.4
26	W	0109 0702 1355 1935	2.0 5.5 1.9 5.7
27	TH	0232 0815 1513 2040	1.7 5.9 1.6 6.1
28	F	0350 0914 1626 2133	1.3 6.2 1.2 6.5
29	SA	0501 1004 1729 2220	0.9 6.6 0.8 6.8
30	SU	0558 1048 1819 ● 2303	0.6 6.8 0.6 7.0
31	M	0646 1127 1903 2343	0.4 6.9 0.5 7.1

APRIL

Date	Day	Time	m
1	TU	0728 1204 1941	0.3 6.9 0.5
2	W	0022 0804 1241 2014	7.0 0.4 6.8 0.6
3	TH	0101 0836 1320 2046	6.9 0.7 6.7 0.8
4	F	0139 0906 1359 2114	6.7 1.0 6.5 1.1
5	SA	0218 0932 1442 2142	6.3 1.3 6.2 1.5
6	SU	0302 1000 1531 2217	5.9 1.7 5.8 1.9
7	M	0356 1040 1631 ☽ 2313	5.5 2.1 5.4 2.2
8	TU	0502 1157 1739	5.2 2.4 5.2
9	W	0044 0616 1327 1852	2.4 5.1 2.4 5.2
10	TH	0201 0733 1435 2002	2.2 5.2 2.1 5.5
11	F	0302 0833 1532 2052	1.9 5.5 1.8 5.8
12	SA	0354 0914 1620 2130	1.5 5.9 1.5 6.1
13	SU	0440 0948 1703 2203	1.3 6.1 1.3 6.3
14	M	0523 1021 1743 2236	1.1 6.3 1.1 6.5
15	TU	0604 1054 1822 O 2309	0.9 6.5 1.0 6.6
16	W	0643 1126 1859 2343	0.8 6.6 0.9 6.7
17	TH	0721 1200 1936	0.8 6.7 0.9
18	F	0018 0756 1237 2012	6.8 0.8 6.7 0.9
19	SA	0056 0831 1318 2050	6.7 0.9 6.7 1.0
20	SU	0140 0910 1406 2132	6.6 1.1 6.4 1.2
21	M	0231 0955 1504 2224	6.2 1.4 6.1 1.5
22	TU	0338 1053 1619 ☾ 2333	5.9 1.7 5.8 1.8
23	W	0511 1213 1750	5.6 1.9 5.6
24	TH	0056 0644 1337 1911	1.8 5.6 1.8 5.8
25	F	0214 0757 1451 2017	1.6 5.9 1.6 6.1
26	SA	0329 0856 1601 2112	1.3 6.1 1.2 6.4
27	SU	0438 0945 1702 2200	1.0 6.4 1.0 6.6
28	M	0535 1028 1753 2243	0.7 6.6 0.8 6.8
29	TU	0623 1106 1837 ● 2324	0.6 6.7 0.7 6.8
30	W	0703 1143 1915	0.6 6.7 0.7

MAY

Date	Day	Time	m
1	TH	0002 0738 1221 1949	6.8 0.7 6.7 0.8
2	F	0041 0810 1259 2020	6.7 0.9 6.6 1.0
3	SA	0118 0837 1338 2048	6.5 1.1 6.5 1.2
4	SU	0155 0901 1418 2116	6.2 1.4 6.2 1.4
5	M	0236 0929 1502 2150	5.9 1.7 5.9 1.7
6	TU	0325 1007 1554 2237	5.6 2.0 5.6 2.0
7	W	0425 1100 1655 ☽ 2347	5.3 2.2 5.4 2.2
8	TH	0532 1225 1801	5.2 2.3 5.3
9	F	0108 0639 1343 1904	2.1 5.2 2.2 5.5
10	SA	0213 0739 1444 1959	1.9 5.5 1.9 5.7
11	SU	0309 0827 1536 2043	1.6 5.8 1.7 6.0
12	M	0359 0908 1625 2123	1.4 6.0 1.4 6.3
13	TU	0448 0946 1711 2202	1.1 6.3 1.2 6.5
14	W	0535 1024 1755 O 2241	1.0 6.5 1.0 6.6
15	TH	0619 1102 1838 2321	0.9 6.7 0.9 6.8
16	F	0702 1142 1920	0.8 6.8 0.8
17	SA	0002 0742 1225 2002	6.8 0.8 6.8 0.8
18	SU	0046 0823 1312 2045	6.7 0.9 6.7 0.9
19	M	0135 0906 1403 2132	6.6 1.0 6.6 1.0
20	TU	0231 0955 1502 2226	6.3 1.2 6.3 1.3
21	W	0336 1052 1608 ☾ 2329	6.0 1.5 6.1 1.5
22	TH	0453 1201 1720	5.8 1.7 5.9
23	F	0040 0616 1312 1837	1.5 5.7 1.7 5.9
24	SA	0149 0729 1420 1948	1.5 5.8 1.6 6.0
25	SU	0259 0830 1527 2047	1.3 6.0 1.4 6.2
26	M	0408 0922 1631 2138	1.2 6.2 1.2 6.4
27	TU	0508 1006 1725 2223	1.0 6.3 1.1 6.5
28	W	0557 1046 1810 ● 2305	1.0 6.5 1.0 6.6
29	TH	0638 1124 1850 2344	1.0 6.5 1.0 6.5
30	F	0714 1202 1926	1.0 6.6 1.0
31	SA	0022 0745 1241 1957	6.5 1.1 6.6 1.1

JUNE

Date	Day	Time	m
1	SU	0059 0812 1318 2026	6.4 1.3 6.5 1.2
2	M	0135 0837 1355 2055	6.2 1.4 6.3 1.4
3	TU	0211 0906 1431 2129	6.0 1.5 6.1 1.5
4	W	0249 0943 1510 2210	5.8 1.7 5.9 1.7
5	TH	0336 1027 1600 ☽ 2301	5.5 1.9 5.6 1.9
6	F	0437 1123 1701	5.4 2.1 5.5
7	SA	0008 0544 1238 1806	2.0 5.3 2.2 5.5
8	SU	0120 0647 1351 1906	1.9 5.4 2.0 5.6
9	M	0223 0742 1452 1959	1.7 5.6 1.8 5.9
10	TU	0320 0830 1548 2047	1.5 5.9 1.5 6.2
11	W	0414 0915 1640 2133	1.3 6.2 1.3 6.4
12	TH	0507 0959 1731 2219	1.1 6.5 1.0 6.6
13	F	0557 1044 1820 O 2304	0.9 6.7 0.9 6.8
14	SA	0647 1130 1909 2351	0.8 6.8 0.7 6.8
15	SU	0735 1216 1958	0.8 6.9 0.7
16	M	0039 0822 1305 2046	6.8 0.8 6.9 0.7
17	TU	0130 0908 1356 2134	6.7 0.8 6.8 0.8
18	W	0224 0954 1450 2223	6.5 1.0 6.6 0.9
19	TH	0322 1044 1547 ☾ 2317	6.3 1.2 6.4 1.2
20	F	0425 1139 1648	6.0 1.4 6.1
21	SA	0015 0535 1241 1756	1.4 5.8 1.6 5.9
22	SU	0118 0651 1345 1911	1.5 5.7 1.7 5.9
23	M	0223 0759 1452 2020	1.6 5.7 1.7 5.9
24	TU	0333 0857 1558 2118	1.5 5.9 1.5 6.1
25	W	0438 0946 1657 2207	1.4 6.1 1.3 6.2
26	TH	0531 1028 1746 2250	1.3 6.3 1.2 6.3
27	F	0614 1107 1828 ● 2328	1.2 6.4 1.1 6.4
28	SA	0650 1145 1904	1.2 6.5 1.1
29	SU	0004 0721 1222 1935	6.3 1.2 6.5 1.1
30	M	0040 0749 1257 2005	6.3 1.3 6.5 1.2

SUNRISE AND SUNSET TIMES

DOVER
At 51°07′N 1°19′E

		Sunrise	Sunset
UT			
Jan	01	0759	1558
	15	0752	1617
Feb	01	0732	1646
	15	0708	1711
Mar	01	0639	1736
	15	0609	1800
BST			
Apr	01	0630	1928
	15	0600	1951
May	01	0528	2017
	15	0504	2039
Jun	01	0445	2101
	15	0439	2112
Jul	01	0444	2113
	15	0457	2104
Aug	01	0520	2041
	15	0541	2016
Sep	01	0608	1940
	15	0630	1909
Oct	01	0655	1832
	15	0718	1802
UT			
Nov	01	0647	1629
	15	0711	1607
Dec	01	0736	1551
	15	0752	1548

DOVER
LAT 51°07′N
LONG 1°19′E

TIMES AND HEIGHTS OF HIGH AND LOW WATER (Heights in Metres)

TIME ZONE UT
For Summer Time (area enclosed in shaded box) add 1 hour

2014

JULY

Date	Day	Time	m	Time	m	Time	m	Time	m
1	TU	0112	6.2	0816	1.3	1329	6.4	2035	1.2
2	W	0141	6.1	0846	1.4	1357	6.2	2109	1.3
3	TH	0208	5.9	0920	1.5	1427	6.1	2145	1.5
4	F	0240	5.8	0958	1.7	1504	6.0	2226	1.6
5	SA	0323	5.7	1041	1.9	1553	5.8	☽ 2314	1.8
6	SU	0421	5.5	1135	2.0	1657	5.6		
7	M	0019	1.9	0543	5.4	1251	2.1	1813	5.6
8	TU	0136	1.9	0659	5.5	1408	2.0	1921	5.8
9	W	0243	1.7	0759	5.8	1514	1.7	2020	6.0
10	TH	0344	1.4	0853	6.1	1613	1.4	2114	6.3
11	F	0443	1.2	0943	6.4	1710	1.1	2205	6.6
12	SA	0540	0.9	1032	6.7	1806	0.8	○ 2254	6.8
13	SU	0636	0.8	1120	6.9	1902	0.6	2342	6.9
14	M	0730	0.7	1207	7.0	1954	0.5		
15	TU	0030	6.9	0818	0.6	1254	7.1	2042	0.4
16	W	0119	6.8	0902	0.6	1342	7.0	2126	0.5
17	TH	0208	6.7	0943	0.8	1431	6.9	2209	0.7
18	F	0300	6.4	1024	1.0	1522	6.6	2254	1.0
19	SA	0354	6.1	1111	1.3	1617	6.3	☾ 2344	1.4
20	SU	0455	5.8	1205	1.7	1718	5.9		
21	M	0043	1.7	0604	5.6	1309	1.9	1830	5.7
22	TU	0148	1.9	0722	5.5	1418	1.9	1951	5.6
23	W	0258	1.8	0833	5.6	1528	1.8	2101	5.8
24	TH	0409	1.7	0928	5.9	1633	1.6	2154	6.0
25	F	0506	1.5	1013	6.2	1725	1.4	2236	6.2
26	SA	0551	1.4	1051	6.4	1807	1.2	● 2312	6.3
27	SU	0628	1.3	1126	6.5	1842	1.2	2344	6.3
28	M	0658	1.3	1200	6.5	1913	1.1		
29	TU	0015	6.3	0725	1.3	1232	6.5	1942	1.1
30	W	0045	6.3	0753	1.2	1300	6.5	2013	1.1
31	TH	0109	6.2	0824	1.3	1324	6.4	2045	1.2

AUGUST

Date	Day	Time	m	Time	m	Time	m	Time	m
1	F	0132	6.2	0856	1.3	1350	6.3	2118	1.3
2	SA	0202	6.1	0930	1.5	1424	6.3	2153	1.5
3	SU	0240	6.0	1007	1.7	1507	6.1	2233	1.7
4	M	0329	5.8	1051	1.9	1602	5.8	☽ 2325	1.9
5	TU	0434	5.5	1153	2.1	1721	5.6		
6	W	0043	2.0	0621	5.4	1325	2.1	1855	5.6
7	TH	0210	1.9	0739	5.7	1445	1.8	2005	5.9
8	F	0320	1.6	0839	6.0	1551	1.5	2104	6.3
9	SA	0424	1.3	0932	6.4	1654	1.1	2157	6.6
10	SU	0526	1.0	1022	6.8	1755	0.8	○ 2246	6.8
11	M	0625	0.7	1108	7.0	1852	0.5	2332	7.0
12	TU	0718	0.6	1153	7.2	1943	0.4		
13	W	0016	7.0	0804	0.5	1238	7.2	2028	0.3
14	TH	0101	6.9	0844	0.5	1323	7.2	2108	0.4
15	F	0146	6.8	0921	0.7	1408	7.0	2146	0.7
16	SA	0233	6.5	0958	1.0	1455	6.7	2225	1.1
17	SU	0323	6.2	1039	1.4	1546	6.3	☾ 2309	1.5
18	M	0419	5.8	1128	1.8	1643	5.8		
19	TU	0005	1.9	0523	5.5	1233	2.1	1752	5.5
20	W	0114	2.2	0641	5.3	1347	2.2	1919	5.4
21	TH	0228	2.2	0805	5.5	1502	2.0	2046	5.6
22	F	0340	1.9	0908	5.8	1609	1.7	2140	5.9
23	SA	0440	1.7	0953	6.1	1702	1.5	2219	6.1
24	SU	0526	1.4	1030	6.4	1743	1.3	2250	6.3
25	M	0602	1.3	1102	6.5	1816	1.2	● 2318	6.4
26	TU	0632	1.3	1133	6.6	1847	1.1	2347	6.4
27	W	0659	1.2	1202	6.6	1917	1.1		
28	TH	0013	6.4	0729	1.2	1228	6.6	1948	1.1
29	F	0037	6.4	0800	1.2	1252	6.5	2020	1.1
30	SA	0101	6.4	0832	1.2	1319	6.5	2051	1.2
31	SU	0131	6.4	0903	1.4	1353	6.5	2123	1.4

SEPTEMBER

Date	Day	Time	m	Time	m	Time	m	Time	m
1	M	0209	6.3	0938	1.6	1434	6.3	2201	1.6
2	TU	0256	6.0	1021	1.8	1527	5.9	☽ 2250	1.9
3	W	0358	5.6	1119	2.1	1645	5.6		
4	TH	0001	2.1	0556	5.4	1249	2.2	1841	5.6
5	F	0143	2.1	0723	5.6	1421	1.9	1955	5.9
6	SA	0301	1.7	0826	6.1	1533	1.5	2055	6.3
7	SU	0409	1.3	0920	6.5	1640	1.1	2147	6.6
8	M	0512	1.0	1008	6.9	1742	0.7	2234	6.9
9	TU	0609	0.7	1053	7.1	1837	0.5	○ 2318	7.0
10	W	0659	0.6	1136	7.3	1925	0.3	2359	7.1
11	TH	0742	0.5	1218	7.3	2007	0.4		
12	F	0039	7.0	0820	0.6	1301	7.2	2044	0.5
13	SA	0121	6.9	0855	0.8	1343	7.0	2119	0.8
14	SU	0205	6.6	0929	1.1	1427	6.6	2153	1.2
15	M	0253	6.3	1006	1.5	1516	6.2	2232	1.7
16	TU	0346	5.9	1049	1.9	1612	5.7	☾ 2323	2.2
17	W	0448	5.5	1152	2.3	1719	5.4		
18	TH	0037	2.5	0600	5.3	1314	2.4	1839	5.2
19	F	0156	2.4	0725	5.4	1431	2.2	2018	5.4
20	SA	0308	2.2	0838	5.7	1537	1.9	2114	5.8
21	SU	0407	1.8	0924	6.1	1629	1.5	2151	6.1
22	M	0453	1.5	1000	6.3	1710	1.3	2219	6.3
23	TU	0530	1.4	1031	6.5	1744	1.2	2246	6.4
24	W	0601	1.2	1100	6.6	1816	1.1	● 2314	6.5
25	TH	0631	1.2	1128	6.6	1849	1.1	2341	6.5
26	F	0703	1.1	1155	6.7	1923	1.0		
27	SA	0007	6.6	0736	1.1	1223	6.7	1955	1.1
28	SU	0035	6.6	0808	1.2	1253	6.7	2027	1.2
29	M	0108	6.6	0841	1.3	1328	6.6	2100	1.4
30	TU	0147	6.4	0917	1.5	1411	6.3	2138	1.6

OCTOBER

Date	Day	Time	m	Time	m	Time	m	Time	m
1	W	0235	6.1	1001	1.8	1505	5.9	☽ 2228	1.9
2	TH	0340	5.7	1100	2.1	1631	5.6	2337	2.2
3	F	0538	5.5	1227	2.2	1829	5.6		
4	SA	0120	2.2	0703	5.7	1401	1.9	1941	5.9
5	SU	0242	1.8	0808	6.1	1515	1.5	2042	6.3
6	M	0351	1.4	0902	6.5	1623	1.1	2133	6.6
7	TU	0453	1.0	0950	6.9	1724	0.8	2218	6.9
8	W	0548	0.8	1035	7.1	1816	0.6	○ 2259	7.0
9	TH	0635	0.7	1116	7.2	1902	0.5	2338	7.1
10	F	0717	0.6	1157	7.2	1942	0.5		
11	SA	0017	7.0	0754	0.7	1238	7.1	2017	0.7
12	SU	0058	6.9	0828	0.9	1319	6.9	2050	1.0
13	M	0140	6.7	0901	1.2	1401	6.5	2121	1.4
14	TU	0225	6.3	0934	1.6	1448	6.1	2152	1.8
15	W	0316	6.0	1010	1.9	1543	5.7	☾ 2231	2.2
16	TH	0414	5.6	1103	2.3	1646	5.4	2342	2.6
17	F	0520	5.4	1229	2.5	1758	5.2		
18	SA	0112	2.6	0634	5.4	1349	2.3	1920	5.3
19	SU	0225	2.4	0748	5.6	1453	2.0	2026	5.7
20	M	0324	2.0	0841	5.9	1544	1.7	2107	6.0
21	TU	0411	1.7	0919	6.2	1628	1.4	2139	6.2
22	W	0451	1.5	0952	6.4	1707	1.2	2209	6.4
23	TH	0527	1.3	1023	6.6	1745	1.1	● 2240	6.6
24	F	0603	1.2	1054	6.7	1822	1.0	2310	6.7
25	SA	0639	1.1	1125	6.7	1858	1.0	2341	6.7
26	SU	0714	1.1	1158	6.8	1933	1.1		
27	M	0014	6.8	0749	1.1	1233	6.7	2007	1.1
28	TU	0052	6.7	0825	1.2	1313	6.6	2043	1.3
29	W	0135	6.5	0905	1.4	1359	6.3	2125	1.6
30	TH	0227	6.2	0952	1.6	1458	6.0	2215	1.8
31	F	0337	5.9	1051	1.9	1627	5.7	☽ 2324	2.1

NOVEMBER

Date	Day	Time	m	Time	m	Time	m	Time	m
1	SA	0512	5.7	1214	2.0	1808	5.7		
2	SU	0057	2.1	0636	5.8	1339	1.8	1921	5.9
3	M	0216	1.8	0743	6.1	1452	1.5	2022	6.2
4	TU	0325	1.5	0840	6.5	1600	1.2	2114	6.5
5	W	0428	1.2	0929	6.7	1701	0.9	2159	6.7
6	TH	0523	1.0	1015	6.9	1753	0.8	○ 2240	6.8
7	F	0610	0.8	1057	7.0	1838	0.7	2319	6.9
8	SA	0652	0.8	1138	7.0	1917	0.8	2358	6.9
9	SU	0730	0.9	1217	6.9	1952	1.0		
10	M	0037	6.8	0805	1.0	1257	6.7	2023	1.2
11	TU	0118	6.7	0837	1.3	1338	6.4	2051	1.5
12	W	0200	6.4	0907	1.5	1421	6.1	2118	1.8
13	TH	0246	6.1	0939	1.8	1511	5.8	2151	2.1
14	F	0338	5.8	1022	2.1	1609	5.5	☾ 2239	2.4
15	SA	0437	5.5	1125	2.3	1715	5.3	2357	2.6
16	SU	0543	5.4	1248	2.3	1823	5.3		
17	M	0124	2.5	0649	5.5	1357	2.1	1926	5.5
18	TU	0229	2.2	0746	5.7	1454	1.9	2016	5.8
19	W	0323	1.9	0831	6.0	1544	1.6	2056	6.1
20	TH	0411	1.6	0910	6.3	1630	1.3	2133	6.3
21	F	0454	1.4	0947	6.5	1714	1.2	2208	6.5
22	SA	0536	1.2	1023	6.6	1756	1.0	● 2244	6.7
23	SU	0617	1.1	1101	6.8	1837	1.0	2321	6.8
24	M	0657	1.0	1139	6.8	1916	1.0		
25	TU	0000	6.9	0736	1.0	1220	6.8	1955	1.1
26	W	0043	6.8	0817	1.1	1305	6.7	2035	1.2
27	TH	0130	6.7	0901	1.2	1355	6.4	2120	1.4
28	F	0224	6.5	0950	1.4	1454	6.2	2211	1.6
29	SA	0327	6.2	1048	1.6	1608	5.9	☽ 2314	1.8
30	SU	0440	6.0	1157	1.7	1734	5.8		

DECEMBER

Date	Day	Time	m	Time	m	Time	m	Time	m
1	M	0029	1.9	0559	5.9	1310	1.7	1851	5.8
2	TU	0142	1.8	0712	6.0	1420	1.6	1956	6.0
3	W	0251	1.7	0814	6.2	1531	1.4	2052	6.2
4	TH	0359	1.4	0909	6.4	1637	1.2	2141	6.4
5	F	0458	1.2	0957	6.6	1731	1.0	2223	6.6
6	SA	0547	1.1	1041	6.7	1816	1.0	○ 2303	6.7
7	SU	0631	1.0	1122	6.7	1855	1.0	2342	6.7
8	M	0710	1.0	1201	6.7	1929	1.1		
9	TU	0020	6.7	0745	1.1	1240	6.5	2000	1.3
10	W	0059	6.6	0816	1.2	1317	6.4	2027	1.4
11	TH	0137	6.5	0845	1.4	1355	6.1	2053	1.6
12	F	0215	6.3	0916	1.6	1435	5.9	2125	1.8
13	SA	0255	6.0	0952	1.8	1520	5.6	2205	2.0
14	SU	0341	5.8	1038	2.0	1618	5.4	☾ 2255	2.2
15	M	0440	5.5	1137	2.1	1725	5.3		
16	TU	0003	2.4	0547	5.4	1252	2.2	1830	5.3
17	W	0124	2.3	0650	5.5	1401	2.0	1928	5.5
18	TH	0232	2.1	0745	5.8	1500	1.7	2017	5.8
19	F	0330	1.8	0832	6.0	1555	1.5	2101	6.1
20	SA	0422	1.5	0917	6.3	1646	1.2	2143	6.4
21	SU	0511	1.2	1000	6.6	1734	1.1	2224	6.6
22	M	0557	1.0	1043	6.7	1820	0.9	● 2307	6.8
23	TU	0644	0.9	1126	6.8	1906	0.9	2350	6.9
24	W	0730	0.8	1211	6.8	1951	0.9		
25	TH	0036	7.0	0815	0.8	1258	6.8	2034	0.9
26	F	0124	6.9	0902	0.9	1348	6.6	2119	1.0
27	SA	0214	6.8	0949	1.0	1442	6.4	2205	1.2
28	SU	0309	6.5	1039	1.2	1542	6.1	☽ 2257	1.5
29	M	0410	6.3	1135	1.4	1651	5.9	2358	1.7
30	TU	0518	6.0	1238	1.6	1809	5.7		
31	W	0104	1.9	0634	5.9	1345	1.7	1924	5.7

SHEERNESS

LAT 51°27'N
LONG 0°45'E

TIMES AND HEIGHTS OF HIGH AND LOW WATER (Heights in Metres)

TIME ZONE UT
For Summer Time (area enclosed in shaded box) add 1 hour

2014

JANUARY

Date	Day	Time	m
1	W ●	0603 1208 1827	0.7 5.9 0.7
2	TH	0032 0700 1259 1918	5.9 0.5 6.1 0.6
3	F	0119 0752 1348 2005	6.0 0.4 6.2 0.6
4	SA	0205 0842 1436 2050	6.0 0.3 6.2 0.6
5	SU	0251 0928 1524 2132	6.0 0.3 6.1 0.7
6	M	0337 1012 1612 2213	5.9 0.4 5.9 0.9
7	TU	0424 1054 1702 2255	5.7 0.6 5.6 1.1
8	W ☽	0515 1139 1756 2344	5.5 0.8 5.4 1.2
9	TH	0612 1232 1856	5.3 1.1 5.1
10	F	0045 0717 1338 2002	1.4 5.1 1.3 5.0
11	SA	0159 0828 1447 2111	1.5 4.9 1.3 5.0
12	SU	0312 0940 1552 2215	1.4 5.0 1.3 5.1
13	M	0420 1042 1648 2308	1.3 5.1 1.3 5.3
14	TU	0518 1132 1733 2352	1.1 5.3 1.2 5.4
15	W	0604 1215 1811	0.9 5.4 1.1
16	TH O	0030 0643 1252 1844	5.5 0.8 5.5 1.0
17	F	0105 0718 1325 1916	5.6 0.8 5.6 0.9
18	SA	0136 0751 1357 1949	5.6 0.7 5.6 0.9
19	SU	0207 0824 1429 2022	5.6 0.7 5.6 0.9
20	M	0238 0857 1502 2056	5.6 0.7 5.6 0.9
21	TU	0310 0929 1536 2127	5.5 0.8 5.5 1.0
22	W	0344 0959 1612 2157	5.4 0.9 5.4 1.1
23	TH	0420 1029 1653 2232	5.3 1.0 5.2 1.2
24	F ☾	0504 1106 1743 2321	5.2 1.1 5.1 1.3
25	SA	0600 1201 1846	5.1 1.2 5.0
26	SU	0028 0713 1324 2002	1.4 5.0 1.3 5.0
27	M	0205 0836 1500 2118	1.4 5.0 1.2 5.1
28	TU	0333 0952 1612 2226	1.2 5.3 1.0 5.4
29	W	0446 1059 1716 2326	0.9 5.6 0.8 5.6
30	TH ●	0553 1156 1814	0.7 5.9 0.7
31	F	0018 0652 1248 1905	5.8 0.4 6.1 0.6

FEBRUARY

Date	Day	Time	m
1	SA	0105 0743 1335 1952	6.0 0.2 6.2 0.5
2	SU	0150 0829 1421 2035	6.1 0.1 6.2 0.5
3	M	0234 0912 1505 2114	6.1 0.1 6.1 0.6
4	TU	0317 0950 1548 2151	6.0 0.3 5.9 0.7
5	W	0359 1025 1632 2226	5.9 0.5 5.7 0.9
6	TH ☽	0444 1059 1718 2305	5.6 0.8 5.3 1.1
7	F	0533 1138 1810 2355	5.3 1.1 5.0 1.4
8	SA	0632 1235 1913	5.0 1.4 4.8
9	SU	0107 0746 1355 2027	1.5 4.7 1.6 4.7
10	M	0236 0908 1513 2143	1.5 4.7 1.6 4.8
11	TU	0354 1019 1619 2243	1.4 4.9 1.4 5.1
12	W	0457 1112 1711 2330	1.1 5.2 1.2 5.3
13	TH	0545 1155 1752	0.9 5.4 1.1
14	F O	0009 0624 1231 1826	5.4 0.8 5.5 1.0
15	SA	0044 0658 1304 1858	5.6 0.7 5.6 0.9
16	SU	0115 0731 1335 1931	5.6 0.6 5.7 0.8
17	M	0146 0804 1406 2005	5.7 0.6 5.7 0.8
18	TU	0217 0838 1438 2039	5.7 0.6 5.7 0.8
19	W	0248 0911 1511 2109	5.7 0.6 5.6 0.9
20	TH	0321 0938 1546 2135	5.6 0.8 5.5 1.0
21	F	0357 1003 1625 2206	5.5 0.9 5.4 1.1
22	SA ☾	0439 1036 1711 2251	5.4 1.0 5.2 1.2
23	SU	0532 1129 1811 2356	5.2 1.2 5.0 1.3
24	M	0644 1250 1929	5.0 1.4 4.9
25	TU	0135 0811 1436 2053	1.4 5.0 1.3 5.0
26	W	0315 0936 1553 2208	1.2 5.2 1.1 5.3
27	TH	0434 1046 1701 2309	0.9 5.6 0.9 5.6
28	F	0544 1143 1800	0.6 5.9 0.7

MARCH

Date	Day	Time	m
1	SA ●	0001 0639 1233 1849	5.8 0.3 6.1 0.6
2	SU	0048 0726 1318 1934	6.0 0.2 6.2 0.5
3	M	0131 0809 1401 2015	6.1 0.1 6.2 0.4
4	TU	0212 0848 1442 2053	6.2 0.2 6.1 0.5
5	W	0253 0923 1521 2127	6.1 0.3 5.9 0.6
6	TH	0333 0953 1600 2158	5.9 0.6 5.6 0.8
7	F	0413 1021 1639 2231	5.6 0.9 5.3 1.0
8	SA ☽	0457 1054 1723 2312	5.3 1.2 5.0 1.3
9	SU	0550 1141 1820	4.9 1.5 4.7
10	M	0013 0700 1257 1936	1.5 4.6 1.7 4.5
11	TU	0154 0827 1433 2100	1.6 4.6 1.7 4.6
12	W	0320 0945 1545 2209	1.4 4.8 1.5 4.9
13	TH	0425 1042 1641 2259	1.2 5.1 1.3 5.2
14	F	0515 1126 1726 2340	1.0 5.3 1.1 5.4
15	SA	0556 1203 1802	0.8 5.5 1.0
16	SU O	0016 0631 1236 1836	5.5 0.7 5.6 0.9
17	M	0049 0705 1308 1910	5.6 0.6 5.7 0.8
18	TU	0121 0740 1340 1946	5.7 0.5 5.8 0.7
19	W	0153 0816 1413 2021	5.8 0.5 5.8 0.7
20	TH	0226 0849 1447 2053	5.8 0.6 5.8 0.8
21	F	0301 0919 1523 2121	5.7 0.7 5.7 0.9
22	SA	0339 0946 1602 2154	5.6 0.9 5.5 0.9
23	SU	0423 1022 1649 2240	5.5 1.0 5.3 1.1
24	M ☾	0518 1117 1748 2347	5.2 1.2 5.0 1.2
25	TU	0630 1239 1906	5.0 1.4 4.9
26	W	0127 0757 1417 2032	1.3 5.0 1.4 4.9
27	TH	0303 0922 1534 2149	1.1 5.3 1.2 5.2
28	F	0422 1030 1642 2250	0.8 5.6 0.9 5.5
29	SA	0528 1126 1741 2341	0.5 5.8 0.8 5.8
30	SU ●	0620 1214 1829	0.4 6.0 0.6
31	M	0027 0704 1257 1912	5.9 0.3 6.1 0.5

APRIL

Date	Day	Time	m
1	TU	0109 0744 1337 1952	6.1 0.3 6.1 0.4
2	W	0150 0820 1416 2029	6.1 0.3 6.0 0.5
3	TH	0229 0853 1453 2104	6.0 0.5 5.8 0.6
4	F	0308 0922 1529 2134	5.8 0.7 5.6 0.8
5	SA	0346 0948 1604 2203	5.6 1.0 5.3 1.0
6	SU	0427 1019 1643 2239	5.3 1.2 5.0 1.2
7	M ☽	0514 1101 1732 2331	4.9 1.5 4.7 1.4
8	TU	0616 1203 1841	4.6 1.7 4.5
9	W	0053 0734 1338 2005	1.6 4.5 1.8 4.5
10	TH	0235 0855 1501 2120	1.5 4.7 1.7 4.7
11	F	0342 0958 1601 2217	1.2 5.0 1.4 5.0
12	SA	0434 1046 1649 2302	1.0 5.3 1.2 5.3
13	SU	0518 1126 1730 2341	0.8 5.5 1.0 5.5
14	M	0558 1203 1808	0.7 5.6 0.9
15	TU O	0018 0635 1239 1846	5.6 0.7 5.8 0.8
16	W	0054 0713 1314 1925	5.7 0.6 5.8 0.7
17	TH	0129 0752 1350 2004	5.8 0.6 5.9 0.6
18	F	0206 0829 1426 2042	5.9 0.6 5.8 0.7
19	SA	0245 0904 1505 2117	5.8 0.7 5.7 0.7
20	SU	0327 0939 1547 2156	5.7 0.9 5.6 0.8
21	M	0415 1020 1636 2245	5.6 1.0 5.3 0.9
22	TU ☾	0513 1116 1736 2353	5.3 1.2 5.1 1.1
23	W	0624 1232 1852	5.2 1.4 5.0
24	TH	0124 0745 1358 2013	1.1 5.2 1.3 5.0
25	F	0249 0903 1511 2126	0.9 5.3 1.2 5.3
26	SA	0402 1010 1618 2228	0.7 5.6 1.0 5.5
27	SU	0505 1105 1716 2319	0.6 5.8 0.8 5.7
28	M	0556 1152 1805	0.5 5.9 0.7
29	TU ●	0005 0638 1235 1848	5.8 0.5 5.9 0.6
30	W	0048 0715 1314 1929	5.9 0.5 5.9 0.5

MAY

Date	Day	Time	m
1	TH	0128 0751 1352 2007	5.9 0.6 5.9 0.5
2	F	0208 0823 1427 2043	5.9 0.7 5.7 0.6
3	SA	0246 0853 1502 2114	5.7 0.9 5.6 0.8
4	SU	0324 0920 1535 2142	5.5 1.1 5.4 1.0
5	M	0402 0950 1612 2215	5.3 1.2 5.1 1.1
6	TU	0445 1029 1655 2259	5.0 1.4 4.9 1.3
7	W ☽	0537 1121 1752	4.8 1.6 4.7
8	TH	0000 0640 1231 1905	1.4 4.6 1.8 4.6
9	F	0128 0752 1358 2020	1.4 4.7 1.7 4.7
10	SA	0246 0900 1508 2124	1.3 4.9 1.5 4.9
11	SU	0344 0957 1603 2217	1.1 5.2 1.3 5.2
12	M	0434 1045 1651 2304	0.9 5.4 1.1 5.4
13	TU	0520 1129 1737 2346	0.8 5.6 0.9 5.6
14	W O	0604 1210 1822	0.7 5.8 0.8
15	TH	0027 0647 1250 1906	5.7 0.6 5.9 0.7
16	F	0109 0730 1330 1951	5.9 0.6 5.9 0.6
17	SA	0151 0812 1410 2035	5.9 0.6 5.9 0.5
18	SU	0234 0853 1452 2119	5.9 0.7 5.8 0.6
19	M	0321 0935 1538 2204	5.9 0.8 5.6 0.6
20	TU	0412 1020 1629 2255	5.7 1.0 5.5 0.7
21	W ☾	0509 1113 1728 2358	5.5 1.1 5.3 0.8
22	TH	0616 1219 1837	5.4 1.3 5.2
23	F	0112 0727 1332 1950	0.9 5.3 1.3 5.2
24	SA	0225 0839 1442 2100	0.9 5.4 1.2 5.3
25	SU	0334 0944 1548 2203	0.8 5.5 1.1 5.4
26	M	0436 1041 1649 2257	0.8 5.6 1.0 5.5
27	TU	0528 1130 1741 2346	0.8 5.7 0.8 5.6
28	W ●	0610 1213 1827	0.8 5.7 0.7
29	TH	0030 0648 1254 1909	5.7 0.8 5.7 0.6
30	F	0111 0723 1331 1948	5.7 0.8 5.7 0.6
31	SA	0151 0756 1406 2024	5.7 0.8 5.6 0.7

JUNE

Date	Day	Time	m
1	SU	0228 0828 1440 2056	5.6 0.9 5.5 0.8
2	M	0304 0857 1513 2126	5.5 1.1 5.4 0.9
3	TU	0340 0928 1548 2158	5.4 1.2 5.3 1.0
4	W	0419 1004 1627 2236	5.2 1.3 5.1 1.1
5	TH ☽	0502 1048 1712 2323	5.0 1.5 4.9 1.2
6	F	0553 1140 1809	4.9 1.6 4.8
7	SA	0022 0653 1246 1917	1.3 4.8 1.7 4.7
8	SU	0136 0800 1403 2027	1.3 4.9 1.6 4.9
9	M	0249 0905 1513 2130	1.2 5.1 1.4 5.1
10	TU	0350 1003 1612 2226	1.0 5.3 1.2 5.3
11	W	0444 1055 1707 2317	0.9 5.6 1.0 5.6
12	TH	0535 1144 1759	0.8 5.7 0.8
13	F O	0006 0624 1230 1851	5.7 0.7 5.9 0.7
14	SA	0053 0712 1314 1941	5.9 0.6 5.9 0.5
15	SU	0139 0759 1358 2030	6.0 0.6 5.9 0.4
16	M	0226 0844 1443 2119	6.1 0.6 5.9 0.4
17	TU	0315 0929 1530 2206	6.0 0.7 5.8 0.4
18	W	0405 1014 1619 2254	5.9 0.8 5.7 0.5
19	TH ☾	0459 1102 1713 2346	5.7 1.0 5.5 0.6
20	F	0558 1156 1814	5.5 1.1 5.4
21	SA	0046 0701 1300 1921	0.8 5.4 1.2 5.3
22	SU	0152 0808 1408 2030	0.9 5.3 1.3 5.2
23	M	0259 0914 1517 2137	1.0 5.3 1.2 5.3
24	TU	0402 1015 1622 2238	1.0 5.4 1.1 5.4
25	W	0459 1109 1721 2330	1.0 5.5 1.0 5.5
26	TH	0545 1156 1810	1.0 5.6 0.9
27	F ●	0016 0624 1237 1853	5.5 1.0 5.6 0.8
28	SA	0058 0659 1314 1931	5.6 1.0 5.6 0.7
29	SU	0136 0733 1349 2007	5.6 1.0 5.6 0.7
30	M	0211 0805 1421 2040	5.6 1.0 5.6 0.7

SUNRISE AND SUNSET TIMES

SHEERNESS
At 51°27'N 0°45'E

		Sunrise	Sunset
UT			
Jan	01	0802	1559
	15	0756	1618
Feb	01	0735	1647
	15	0711	1712
Mar	01	0642	1738
	15	0611	1802
BST			
Apr	01	0632	1930
	15	0601	1954
May	01	0529	2020
	15	0505	2042
Jun	01	0446	2105
	15	0440	2116
Jul	01	0445	2117
	15	0458	2107
Aug	01	0521	2045
	15	0543	2019
Sep	01	0610	1943
	15	0632	1911
Oct	01	0658	1835
	15	0721	1804
UT			
Nov	01	0651	1630
	15	0715	1608
Dec	01	0740	1552
	15	0756	1548

SHEERNESS
LAT 51°27′N
LONG 0°45′E

TIMES AND HEIGHTS OF HIGH AND LOW WATER (Heights in Metres)

TIME ZONE UT
For Summer Time (area enclosed in shaded box) add 1 hour

2014

JULY

Date	Day	Time	m
1	TU	0245 0837 1453 2111	5.6 1.0 5.5 0.8
2	W	0318 0909 1526 2142	5.5 1.1 5.4 0.9
3	TH	0353 0942 1600 2215	5.4 1.2 5.3 1.0
4	F	0431 1018 1639 2253	5.2 1.3 5.2 1.1
5	SA ☽	0513 1100 1724 2337	5.1 1.4 5.0 1.2
6	SU	0603 1151 1820	5.0 1.5 4.9
7	M	0033 0705 1258 1930	1.3 4.9 1.6 4.9
8	TU	0150 0815 1422 2044	1.3 5.0 1.5 5.0
9	W	0308 0924 1536 2152	1.2 5.2 1.3 5.3
10	TH	0412 1026 1640 2253	1.0 5.5 1.0 5.5
11	F	0511 1121 1741 2348	0.9 5.7 0.8 5.8
12	SA ○	0606 1212 1839	0.7 5.9 0.6
13	SU	0039 0657 1300 1933	6.0 0.7 6.0 0.4
14	M	0128 0747 1346 2023	6.1 0.6 6.1 0.2
15	TU	0216 0833 1431 2110	6.2 0.6 6.1 0.2
16	W	0303 0917 1516 2155	6.2 0.6 6.0 0.2
17	TH	0350 0959 1603 2238	6.0 0.7 5.9 0.4
18	F	0439 1041 1651 2322	5.8 0.9 5.7 0.6
19	SA ☾	0531 1127 1745	5.6 1.1 5.5
20	SU	0010 0628 1222 1847	0.9 5.4 1.3 5.3
21	M	0110 0732 1331 1957	1.1 5.2 1.4 5.1
22	TU	0219 0841 1446 2111	1.3 5.1 1.4 5.1
23	W	0328 0949 1600 2219	1.3 5.2 1.3 5.2
24	TH	0431 1049 1705 2316	1.3 5.3 1.1 5.4
25	F	0523 1138 1756	1.2 5.5 0.9
26	SA ●	0002 0604 1220 1837	5.5 1.1 5.6 0.8
27	SU	0043 0639 1257 1913	5.6 1.1 5.6 0.8
28	M	0118 0712 1330 1947	5.6 1.0 5.7 0.7
29	TU	0150 0744 1401 2019	5.6 1.0 5.7 0.7
30	W	0222 0817 1431 2051	5.6 0.9 5.7 0.7
31	TH	0253 0849 1502 2123	5.6 1.0 5.6 0.8

AUGUST

Date	Day	Time	m
1	F	0326 0921 1534 2153	5.5 1.1 5.5 0.9
2	SA	0400 0952 1609 2223	5.4 1.2 5.4 1.0
3	SU	0438 1024 1648 2257	5.3 1.3 5.2 1.2
4	M ☽	0523 1106 1738 2344	5.2 1.4 5.1 1.3
5	TU	0619 1205 1844	5.0 1.5 5.0
6	W	0055 0730 1333 2005	1.4 5.0 1.5 5.0
7	TH	0231 0848 1507 2124	1.3 5.1 1.3 5.2
8	F	0346 1000 1620 2233	1.1 5.4 1.1 5.5
9	SA	0450 1102 1727 2333	0.9 5.6 0.8 5.8
10	SU ○	0549 1155 1828	0.8 5.9 0.5
11	M	0025 0643 1244 1921	6.1 0.7 6.1 0.3
12	TU	0114 0732 1329 2009	6.2 0.6 6.2 0.2
13	W	0200 0817 1413 2053	6.3 0.5 6.2 0.1
14	TH	0244 0859 1456 2135	6.2 0.6 6.2 0.2
15	F	0328 0939 1540 2213	6.1 0.7 6.1 0.4
16	SA	0413 1016 1625 2249	5.9 0.9 5.8 0.7
17	SU ☾	0459 1055 1714 2328	5.6 1.1 5.5 1.0
18	M	0550 1142 1811	5.3 1.3 5.2
19	TU	0019 0651 1248 1922	1.3 5.0 1.5 4.9
20	W	0133 0803 1415 2043	1.6 4.9 1.5 4.9
21	TH	0253 0919 1536 2158	1.6 5.0 1.4 5.1
22	F	0403 1025 1645 2256	1.5 5.2 1.2 5.3
23	SA	0459 1116 1735 2342	1.3 5.4 1.0 5.5
24	SU	0542 1157 1815	1.2 5.6 0.9
25	M ●	0021 0617 1234 1849	5.6 1.1 5.7 0.8
26	TU	0055 0650 1306 1921	5.7 1.0 5.7 0.7
27	W	0125 0721 1336 1953	5.7 0.9 5.8 0.7
28	TH	0155 0754 1406 2026	5.8 0.9 5.8 0.7
29	F	0226 0828 1437 2059	5.8 0.9 5.7 0.7
30	SA	0258 0859 1508 2129	5.7 1.0 5.7 0.9
31	SU	0331 0927 1542 2155	5.6 1.1 5.5 1.0

SEPTEMBER

Date	Day	Time	m
1	M	0407 0955 1621 2224	5.5 1.2 5.4 1.2
2	TU ☽	0450 1033 1709 2308	5.3 1.3 5.2 1.3
3	W	0543 1131 1813	5.1 1.5 5.0
4	TH	0019 0654 1259 1936	1.5 5.0 1.5 5.0
5	F	0202 0818 1445 2102	1.5 5.0 1.4 5.2
6	SA	0323 0936 1603 2216	1.3 5.3 1.0 5.6
7	SU	0430 1041 1713 2316	1.0 5.6 0.7 5.9
8	M	0532 1136 1813	0.8 5.9 0.5
9	TU ○	0008 0625 1224 1903	6.1 0.7 6.1 0.3
10	W	0055 0712 1308 1948	6.3 0.6 6.2 0.2
11	TH	0139 0756 1351 2030	6.3 0.5 6.3 0.2
12	F	0221 0837 1433 2108	6.2 0.6 6.2 0.4
13	SA	0302 0914 1515 2142	6.1 0.7 6.1 0.6
14	SU	0343 0949 1557 2213	5.8 0.9 5.8 0.9
15	M	0425 1024 1642 2246	5.5 1.1 5.5 1.2
16	TU ☾	0510 1104 1735 2330	5.2 1.3 5.1 1.5
17	W	0606 1202 1844	4.9 1.6 4.8
18	TH	0039 0718 1338 2006	1.8 4.7 1.7 4.7
19	F	0213 0840 1505 2126	1.8 4.7 1.5 4.9
20	SA	0328 0951 1612 2227	1.6 5.0 1.2 5.2
21	SU	0427 1045 1703 2313	1.4 5.3 1.0 5.5
22	M	0513 1127 1744 2351	1.2 5.5 0.9 5.6
23	TU	0550 1203 1819	1.1 5.7 0.8
24	W ●	0024 0623 1236 1851	5.7 1.0 5.7 0.7
25	TH	0055 0656 1307 1924	5.8 0.9 5.8 0.7
26	F	0126 0730 1339 1958	5.8 0.9 5.8 0.7
27	SA	0158 0805 1411 2032	5.9 0.9 5.8 0.7
28	SU	0231 0838 1445 2103	5.8 0.9 5.8 0.9
29	M	0305 0908 1521 2131	5.7 1.1 5.7 1.0
30	TU	0342 0937 1602 2202	5.6 1.2 5.5 1.2

OCTOBER

Date	Day	Time	m
1	W ☽	0425 1017 1651 2249	5.4 1.3 5.3 1.4
2	TH	0518 1116 1755	5.1 1.4 5.1
3	F	0001 0628 1245 1917	1.6 5.0 1.5 5.0
4	SA	0139 0753 1427 2044	1.6 5.0 1.3 5.2
5	SU	0301 0913 1546 2157	1.3 5.3 1.0 5.6
6	M	0408 1019 1655 2257	1.1 5.6 0.7 5.9
7	TU	0509 1113 1752 2347	0.9 5.9 0.5 6.1
8	W ○	0603 1201 1840	0.8 6.0 0.4
9	TH	0032 0649 1245 1922	6.2 0.6 6.2 0.4
10	F	0115 0732 1328 2002	6.2 0.6 6.2 0.4
11	SA	0156 0812 1409 2037	6.1 0.6 6.2 0.6
12	SU	0235 0850 1451 2110	6.0 0.7 6.0 0.8
13	M	0314 0924 1532 2139	5.8 0.9 5.7 1.1
14	TU	0352 0956 1614 2208	5.5 1.1 5.4 1.3
15	W ☾	0432 1031 1703 2248	5.2 1.3 5.1 1.6
16	TH	0521 1120 1803 2345	4.9 1.5 4.8 1.8
17	F	0627 1239 1918	4.7 1.7 4.7
18	SA	0115 0747 1421 2037	2.0 4.6 1.6 4.8
19	SU	0243 0903 1528 2143	1.8 4.8 1.4 5.0
20	M	0345 1002 1620 2233	1.6 5.1 1.1 5.3
21	TU	0434 1048 1704 2314	1.3 5.4 1.0 5.5
22	W	0515 1128 1742 2349	1.1 5.6 0.9 5.7
23	TH ●	0552 1203 1818	1.0 5.7 0.8
24	F	0023 0628 1238 1853	5.8 0.9 5.8 0.7
25	SA	0058 0705 1313 1930	5.9 0.9 5.8 0.7
26	SU	0132 0743 1348 2007	5.9 0.8 5.9 0.8
27	M	0207 0821 1425 2042	5.9 0.8 5.8 0.9
28	TU	0244 0856 1505 2115	5.8 0.9 5.8 1.0
29	W	0323 0932 1550 2153	5.6 1.0 5.6 1.2
30	TH	0408 1015 1642 2242	5.4 1.1 5.4 1.3
31	F ☽	0502 1115 1746 2350	5.2 1.2 5.2 1.5

NOVEMBER

Date	Day	Time	m
1	SA	0611 1238 1904	5.0 1.3 5.2
2	SU	0115 0731 1409 2024	1.5 5.1 1.2 5.3
3	M	0234 0848 1524 2134	1.4 5.3 0.9 5.5
4	TU	0341 0954 1631 2234	1.2 5.5 0.8 5.8
5	W	0443 1050 1727 2325	1.0 5.7 0.6 5.9
6	TH ○	0537 1139 1814	0.8 5.9 0.6
7	F	0010 0625 1224 1855	6.0 0.7 6.0 0.6
8	SA	0053 0708 1307 1932	6.0 0.6 6.0 0.6
9	SU	0132 0750 1349 2007	6.0 0.6 6.0 0.7
10	M	0211 0828 1430 2039	5.9 0.7 5.9 0.9
11	TU	0248 0903 1510 2108	5.7 0.9 5.7 1.1
12	W	0324 0933 1550 2137	5.5 1.0 5.4 1.3
13	TH	0401 1004 1633 2213	5.2 1.2 5.1 1.5
14	F ☾	0443 1044 1723 2300	5.0 1.4 4.9 1.7
15	SA	0536 1140 1823	4.8 1.5 4.7
16	SU	0004 0645 1304 1932	1.9 4.6 1.6 4.7
17	M	0132 0759 1429 2041	1.9 4.7 1.5 4.8
18	TU	0249 0905 1529 2139	1.7 4.9 1.3 5.1
19	W	0346 1000 1618 2229	1.5 5.1 1.1 5.4
20	TH	0434 1048 1703 2312	1.2 5.4 0.9 5.6
21	F	0518 1130 1744 2352	1.1 5.6 0.9 5.7
22	SA ●	0601 1210 1825	0.9 5.7 0.8
23	SU	0031 0643 1251 1905	5.8 0.8 5.8 0.7
24	M	0110 0726 1331 1946	5.9 0.7 5.9 0.7
25	TU	0149 0809 1412 2026	5.9 0.7 5.9 0.8
26	W	0229 0852 1456 2106	5.8 0.7 5.9 0.9
27	TH	0311 0935 1543 2149	5.7 0.8 5.7 1.0
28	F	0358 1022 1636 2237	5.5 0.9 5.6 1.2
29	SA ☽	0451 1117 1736 2336	5.4 1.0 5.4 1.3
30	SU	0554 1226 1845	5.2 1.0 5.3

DECEMBER

Date	Day	Time	m
1	M	0047 0706 1342 1958	1.4 5.2 1.0 5.3
2	TU	0201 0819 1454 2107	1.4 5.2 1.0 5.4
3	W	0310 0927 1601 2209	1.3 5.4 0.9 5.5
4	TH	0415 1027 1659 2303	1.1 5.5 0.9 5.7
5	F	0514 1120 1748 2350	1.0 5.6 0.8 5.7
6	SA ○	0605 1207 1829	0.8 5.7 0.8
7	SU	0033 0650 1252 1906	5.8 0.7 5.8 0.8
8	M	0114 0731 1334 1941	5.8 0.7 5.8 0.9
9	TU	0152 0810 1413 2013	5.7 0.7 5.7 1.0
10	W	0227 0844 1451 2043	5.6 0.8 5.6 1.1
11	TH	0301 0914 1528 2112	5.5 0.9 5.4 1.2
12	F	0335 0943 1605 2145	5.3 1.0 5.3 1.3
13	SA	0412 1017 1646 2224	5.2 1.1 5.1 1.5
14	SU ☾	0454 1100 1733 2313	5.0 1.3 4.9 1.6
15	M	0546 1153 1829	4.8 1.4 4.8
16	TU	0013 0649 1303 1934	1.8 4.7 1.5 4.7
17	W	0129 0801 1424 2040	1.8 4.7 1.4 4.9
18	TH	0248 0907 1528 2141	1.6 4.9 1.2 5.2
19	F	0350 1006 1623 2235	1.4 5.2 1.1 5.4
20	SA	0445 1058 1713 2324	1.1 5.4 0.9 5.6
21	SU	0535 1146 1800	1.0 5.6 0.8
22	M ●	0009 0624 1232 1845	5.8 0.8 5.8 0.7
23	TU	0053 0714 1317 1931	5.9 0.6 5.9 0.7
24	W	0135 0802 1402 2016	5.9 0.5 6.0 0.7
25	TH	0218 0850 1447 2059	5.9 0.5 6.0 0.7
26	F	0302 0936 1535 2143	5.9 0.5 5.9 0.8
27	SA	0348 1021 1625 2227	5.8 0.6 5.8 1.0
28	SU ☽	0438 1109 1720 2316	5.6 0.7 5.5 1.1
29	M	0534 1202 1821	5.4 0.9 5.3
30	TU	0014 0638 1307 1927	1.3 5.3 1.0 5.2
31	W	0124 0749 1418 2036	1.3 5.2 1.1 5.2

LONDON BRIDGE
LAT 51°30'N
LONG 0°05'W

TIMES AND HEIGHTS OF HIGH AND LOW WATER

TIME ZONE UT
For Summer Time (area enclosed in shaded box) add 1 hour

2014

JANUARY

Date	Day	Time	m	Time	m	Time	m	Time	m
1	W ●	0104	6.9	0755	0.6	1329	7.3	2014	0.7
2	TH	0157	7.1	0854	0.4	1420	7.4	2109	0.7
3	F	0247	7.2	0946	0.2	1510	7.5	2158	0.6
4	SA	0334	7.2	1033	0.1	1559	7.5	2242	0.6
5	SU	0420	7.2	1115	0.1	1646	7.4	2321	0.7
6	M	0505	7.1	1153	0.2	1734	7.2		
7	TU	0000	0.8	0550	6.9	1230	0.4	1823	6.9
8	W ☽	0040	1.0	0640	6.7	1310	0.6	1916	6.6
9	TH	0125	1.2	0735	6.4	1357	0.9	2013	6.3
10	F	0221	1.4	0837	6.2	1454	1.2	2114	6.1
11	SA	0327	1.5	0943	6.1	1557	1.3	2222	6.0
12	SU	0438	1.5	1052	6.1	1704	1.3	2333	6.1
13	M	0550	1.2	1157	6.3	1811	1.3		
14	TU	0029	6.4	0651	1.0	1249	6.5	1907	1.1
15	W	0115	6.5	0740	0.8	1333	6.7	1952	1.1
16	TH O	0154	6.7	0823	0.7	1411	6.8	2032	1.1
17	F	0229	6.7	0901	0.7	1445	6.8	2106	1.1
18	SA	0300	6.8	0936	0.6	1516	6.9	2137	1.0
19	SU	0330	6.8	1008	0.6	1546	6.9	2208	1.0
20	M	0400	6.8	1038	0.6	1618	6.9	2239	1.0
21	TU	0431	6.8	1106	0.6	1651	6.8	2309	1.1
22	W	0505	6.6	1131	0.7	1727	6.6	2338	1.2
23	TH	0541	6.5	1158	0.8	1807	6.4		
24	F ☾	0011	1.2	0623	6.4	1234	0.9	1853	6.2
25	SA	0055	1.3	0714	6.2	1321	1.0	1952	6.0
26	SU	0154	1.5	0823	6.1	1430	1.3	2116	6.0
27	M	0321	1.5	0955	6.2	1616	1.3	2235	6.2
28	TU	0504	1.3	1110	6.5	1736	1.0	2346	6.5
29	W	0627	0.9	1216	6.9	1854	0.9		
30	TH ●	0048	6.8	0743	0.6	1315	7.2	2003	0.7
31	F	0144	7.1	0844	0.2	1408	7.4	2059	0.6

FEBRUARY

Date	Day	Time	m	Time	m	Time	m	Time	m
1	SA	0233	7.3	0935	0.0	1457	7.5	2147	0.5
2	SU	0319	7.4	1020	-0.1	1543	7.6	2230	0.5
3	M	0402	7.4	1100	-0.1	1628	7.5	2308	0.5
4	TU	0444	7.4	1134	0.1	1711	7.2	2341	0.7
5	W	0525	7.1	1203	0.4	1753	6.9		
6	TH ☽	0013	0.9	0607	6.8	1231	0.7	1836	6.5
7	F	0047	1.1	0653	6.5	1304	1.0	1924	6.2
8	SA	0128	1.4	0749	6.2	1353	1.3	2021	5.9
9	SU	0229	1.6	0856	5.9	1506	1.6	2130	5.7
10	M	0350	1.6	1011	5.8	1622	1.6	2253	5.8
11	TU	0506	1.4	1127	6.1	1736	1.4		
12	W	0000	6.1	0616	1.1	1226	6.4	1839	1.2
13	TH	0050	6.5	0712	0.8	1311	6.6	1929	1.1
14	F O	0132	6.7	0758	0.7	1350	6.7	2012	1.0
15	SA	0208	6.8	0838	0.6	1424	6.8	2050	1.0
16	SU	0240	6.9	0915	0.6	1454	6.9	2125	0.9
17	M	0310	6.9	0949	0.5	1523	7.0	2157	0.9
18	TU	0339	7.0	1021	0.4	1555	7.0	2229	0.8
19	W	0410	7.0	1049	0.5	1628	6.9	2257	0.9
20	TH	0444	6.9	1112	0.6	1703	6.7	2323	1.0
21	F	0520	6.7	1136	0.7	1741	6.5	2353	1.1
22	SA ☾	0600	6.6	1209	0.8	1825	6.3		
23	SU	0032	1.1	0650	6.4	1253	1.0	1921	6.1
24	M	0126	1.3	0755	6.2	1358	1.3	2040	5.9
25	TU	0249	1.5	0928	6.2	1553	1.4	2209	6.1
26	W	0441	1.3	1050	6.4	1718	1.1	2328	6.4
27	TH	0613	0.9	1202	6.8	1842	0.9		
28	F	0034	6.8	0731	0.4	1303	7.2	1949	0.6

MARCH

Shaded on the page (Summer Time): 30–31 March.

Date	Day	Time	m	Time	m	Time	m	Time	m
1	SA ●	0128	7.1	0828	0.1	1354	7.4	2043	0.5
2	SU	0215	7.3	0917	0.0	1440	7.5	2130	0.4
3	M	0258	7.5	1000	-0.1	1523	7.5	2211	0.4
4	TU	0339	7.5	1037	0.0	1603	7.4	2248	0.4
5	W	0418	7.5	1107	0.3	1642	7.2	2318	0.6
6	TH	0457	7.3	1128	0.5	1720	6.8	2343	0.8
7	F	0536	6.9	1149	0.8	1757	6.4		
8	SA ☽	0010	1.0	0616	6.5	1218	1.0	1837	6.1
9	SU	0044	1.2	0704	6.1	1259	1.4	1927	5.8
10	M	0134	1.5	0808	5.8	1404	1.7	2037	5.6
11	TU	0258	1.7	0928	5.7	1541	1.8	2204	5.6
12	W	0425	1.5	1048	5.9	1700	1.6	2322	6.0
13	TH	0535	1.2	1152	6.2	1806	1.3		
14	F	0017	6.4	0635	0.9	1242	6.5	1859	1.1
15	SA	0102	6.6	0725	0.7	1322	6.7	1945	1.0
16	SU O	0140	6.8	0808	0.6	1356	6.8	2027	0.9
17	M	0213	6.9	0848	0.5	1427	6.9	2105	0.9
18	TU	0244	7.0	0924	0.5	1458	7.0	2141	0.8
19	W	0315	7.1	0958	0.4	1531	7.0	2215	0.7
20	TH	0349	7.1	1027	0.5	1606	6.9	2244	0.8
21	F	0424	7.1	1052	0.6	1642	6.8	2310	0.8
22	SA	0502	6.9	1118	0.7	1720	6.5	2340	0.9
23	SU	0544	6.7	1152	0.9	1805	6.3		
24	M ☾	0018	1.0	0635	6.5	1238	1.1	1902	6.1
25	TU	0112	1.2	0743	6.2	1347	1.4	2021	5.9
26	W	0239	1.4	0913	6.2	1539	1.4	2151	6.1
27	TH	0425	1.1	1035	6.5	1702	1.1	2311	6.4
28	F	0600	0.8	1147	6.8	1825	0.8		
29	SA	0017	6.8	0712	0.4	1247	7.1	1929	0.6
30	SU ●	0109	7.1	0806	0.1	1336	7.2	2021	0.5
31	M	0154	7.2	0852	0.1	1419	7.3	2107	0.4

APRIL

Shaded on the page (Summer Time): all of April.

Date	Day	Time	m	Time	m	Time	m	Time	m
1	TU	0235	7.4	0933	0.2	1459	7.3	2148	0.4
2	W	0313	7.5	1007	0.3	1537	7.2	2223	0.4
3	TH	0352	7.5	1033	0.5	1613	7.1	2252	0.5
4	F	0430	7.2	1051	0.7	1648	6.8	2314	0.7
5	SA	0507	6.9	1114	0.8	1723	6.4	2340	0.9
6	SU	0546	6.5	1144	1.1	1800	6.1		
7	M ☽	0012	1.1	0628	6.1	1221	1.4	1844	5.8
8	TU	0056	1.4	0723	5.8	1314	1.7	1946	5.6
9	W	0203	1.6	0841	5.6	1442	1.9	2114	5.5
10	TH	0339	1.5	1000	5.7	1616	1.7	2233	5.8
11	F	0451	1.2	1107	6.1	1724	1.4	2335	6.2
12	SA	0550	0.9	1201	6.4	1821	1.1		
13	SU	0023	6.5	0644	0.7	1245	6.6	1911	1.0
14	M	0105	6.8	0732	0.6	1322	6.8	1957	0.9
15	TU O	0141	6.9	0816	0.6	1358	6.9	2040	0.8
16	W	0216	7.1	0856	0.5	1434	7.0	2121	0.7
17	TH	0252	7.2	0934	0.5	1511	7.0	2159	0.6
18	F	0330	7.2	1007	0.5	1548	6.9	2233	0.6
19	SA	0408	7.2	1037	0.6	1626	6.8	2303	0.7
20	SU	0449	7.0	1108	0.7	1708	6.5	2334	0.7
21	M	0535	6.8	1146	0.9	1755	6.3		
22	TU ☾	0014	0.8	0629	6.6	1237	1.2	1854	6.1
23	W	0111	1.0	0740	6.4	1353	1.4	2012	6.1
24	TH	0241	1.1	0902	6.4	1523	1.3	2135	6.2
25	F	0408	0.9	1017	6.6	1641	1.1	2250	6.5
26	SA	0534	0.7	1127	6.8	1759	0.9	2354	6.8
27	SU	0645	0.4	1226	7.0	1903	0.7		
28	M	0047	7.0	0738	0.3	1315	7.0	1955	0.5
29	TU ●	0131	7.1	0823	0.4	1357	7.1	2041	0.5
30	W	0211	7.2	0902	0.5	1436	7.1	2122	0.4

MAY

Shaded on the page (Summer Time): all of May.

Date	Day	Time	m	Time	m	Time	m	Time	m
1	TH	0250	7.3	0935	0.6	1512	7.1	2158	0.4
2	F	0328	7.3	0959	0.7	1547	6.9	2227	0.5
3	SA	0405	7.2	1019	0.8	1621	6.7	2250	0.7
4	SU	0443	6.9	1046	0.9	1655	6.4	2316	0.8
5	M	0520	6.5	1118	1.1	1730	6.2	2348	1.0
6	TU	0559	6.2	1153	1.3	1810	6.0		
7	W ☽	0026	1.2	0645	5.9	1238	1.6	1900	5.7
8	TH	0119	1.4	0747	5.7	1340	1.8	2014	5.6
9	F	0237	1.4	0906	5.7	1506	1.8	2140	5.7
10	SA	0358	1.3	1013	6.0	1628	1.6	2245	6.0
11	SU	0501	1.0	1111	6.3	1733	1.3	2339	6.4
12	M	0557	0.8	1201	6.6	1830	1.1		
13	TU	0025	6.7	0650	0.7	1247	6.8	1924	0.9
14	W O	0108	6.9	0741	0.6	1330	6.9	2014	0.8
15	TH	0150	7.1	0828	0.6	1412	7.0	2101	0.6
16	F	0232	7.3	0912	0.6	1454	7.0	2145	0.5
17	SA	0314	7.3	0953	0.6	1536	7.0	2225	0.4
18	SU	0358	7.3	1030	0.6	1619	6.8	2303	0.4
19	M	0443	7.1	1108	0.7	1703	6.7	2339	0.5
20	TU	0532	7.0	1151	0.9	1753	6.5		
21	W ☾	0022	0.6	0628	6.7	1244	1.1	1851	6.4
22	TH	0120	0.7	0735	6.6	1350	1.2	2002	6.3
23	F	0232	0.8	0845	6.6	1502	1.2	2114	6.4
24	SA	0343	0.8	0953	6.6	1613	1.1	2223	6.5
25	SU	0455	0.7	1101	6.7	1726	0.9	2327	6.7
26	M	0609	0.7	1202	6.7	1833	0.8		
27	TU	0023	6.8	0705	0.7	1254	6.8	1928	0.6
28	W ●	0110	6.9	0752	0.7	1337	6.8	2015	0.5
29	TH	0152	7.0	0831	0.8	1416	6.9	2057	0.5
30	F	0230	7.1	0905	0.8	1452	6.9	2135	0.5
31	SA	0308	7.1	0933	0.9	1526	6.8	2206	0.6

JUNE

Shaded on the page (Summer Time): all of June.

Date	Day	Time	m	Time	m	Time	m	Time	m
1	SU	0345	7.0	0957	0.9	1600	6.7	2232	0.7
2	M	0421	6.8	1026	1.0	1633	6.5	2300	0.7
3	TU	0457	6.6	1059	1.1	1707	6.4	2331	0.8
4	W	0533	6.4	1134	1.2	1744	6.2		
5	TH ☽	0005	1.0	0613	6.2	1212	1.4	1826	6.0
6	F	0045	1.1	0700	6.0	1257	1.5	1918	5.8
7	SA	0136	1.2	0802	5.8	1356	1.7	2031	5.7
8	SU	0244	1.3	0917	5.9	1511	1.6	2150	5.9
9	M	0403	1.1	1022	6.1	1636	1.4	2252	6.3
10	TU	0508	0.9	1120	6.4	1746	1.1	2347	6.6
11	W	0608	0.8	1214	6.7	1850	0.9		
12	TH	0038	6.9	0706	0.7	1305	6.9	1949	0.7
13	F O	0128	7.1	0804	0.7	1354	7.0	2043	0.5
14	SA	0215	7.3	0857	0.6	1441	7.1	2134	0.3
15	SU	0303	7.4	0945	0.6	1527	7.1	2221	0.2
16	M	0350	7.4	1029	0.6	1613	7.0	2304	0.1
17	TU	0438	7.3	1111	0.6	1659	6.9	2345	0.2
18	W	0527	7.2	1153	0.7	1747	6.8		
19	TH ☾	0027	0.3	0620	7.0	1240	0.8	1841	6.7
20	F	0115	0.5	0719	6.8	1333	1.0	1942	6.6
21	SA	0210	0.6	0821	6.6	1434	1.1	2046	6.5
22	SU	0309	0.8	0924	6.5	1539	1.1	2151	6.5
23	M	0412	0.9	1030	6.4	1648	1.1	2257	6.5
24	TU	0521	1.0	1136	6.5	1800	1.0	2358	6.6
25	W	0629	1.0	1232	6.6	1901	0.8		
26	TH	0050	6.7	0721	0.9	1319	6.7	1951	0.6
27	F ●	0136	6.9	0804	0.9	1400	6.7	2035	0.5
28	SA	0216	6.9	0842	0.9	1437	6.8	2114	0.5
29	SU	0254	7.0	0916	1.0	1511	6.8	2148	0.6
30	M	0329	6.9	0945	1.0	1543	6.7	2218	0.6

SUNRISE AND SUNSET TIMES

LONDON BRIDGE
At 51°30'N 0°05'W

		Sunrise	Sunset
UT			
Jan	01	0806	1602
	15	0759	1621
Feb	01	0738	1650
	15	0714	1716
Mar	01	0645	1741
	15	0614	1805
BST			
Apr	01	0636	1934
	15	0605	1957
May	01	0532	2024
	15	0508	2046
Jun	01	0449	2108
	15	0443	2119
Jul	01	0448	2121
	15	0501	2111
Aug	01	0524	2048
	15	0546	2023
Sep	01	0613	1947
	15	0635	1915
Oct	01	0701	1838
	15	0724	1807
UT			
Nov	01	0654	1633
	15	0718	1611
Dec	01	0744	1555
	15	0800	1551

LONDON BRIDGE
LAT 51°30'N
LONG 0°05'W

TIMES AND HEIGHTS OF HIGH AND LOW WATER

TIME ZONE UT
For Summer Time (area enclosed in shaded box) add 1 hour

2014

JULY

Date	Day	Time	m	Time	m	Time	m	Time	m
1	TU	0402	6.8	1014	1.0	1614	6.7	2247	0.6
2	W	0435	6.7	1046	1.0	1646	6.6	2317	0.7
3	TH	0508	6.6	1119	1.1	1720	6.4	2346	0.8
4	F	0544	6.4	1151	1.2	1757	6.3		
5	SA ☽	0016	0.9	0623	6.2	1226	1.3	1839	6.1
6	SU	0052	1.0	0711	6.0	1311	1.4	1931	5.9
7	M	0141	1.1	0814	5.9	1410	1.5	2045	5.9
8	TU	0250	1.2	0934	6.0	1533	1.5	2207	6.1
9	W	0421	1.1	1042	6.3	1705	1.2	2313	6.5
10	TH	0532	0.9	1145	6.6	1818	0.9		
11	F	0013	6.9	0638	0.8	1244	6.8	1927	0.6
12	SA O	0108	7.2	0746	0.7	1337	7.0	2030	0.4
13	SU	0201	7.4	0846	0.6	1427	7.2	2125	0.2
14	M	0250	7.5	0938	0.5	1515	7.3	2214	0.0
15	TU	0339	7.6	1024	0.5	1601	7.3	2258	-0.1
16	W	0426	7.5	1106	0.4	1645	7.3	2338	-0.1
17	TH	0513	7.3	1146	0.5	1731	7.1		
18	F	0015	0.1	0601	7.1	1226	0.7	1818	6.9
19	SA ☾	0054	0.4	0653	6.8	1309	0.9	1912	6.7
20	SU	0137	0.7	0748	6.5	1359	1.1	2011	6.5
21	M	0229	0.9	0848	6.3	1500	1.3	2115	6.3
22	TU	0330	1.1	0953	6.1	1608	1.3	2223	6.3
23	W	0436	1.2	1106	6.2	1722	1.1	2333	6.4
24	TH	0549	1.2	1209	6.4	1833	0.9		
25	F	0031	6.6	0652	1.1	1300	6.6	1927	0.7
26	SA ●	0119	6.8	0740	1.0	1343	6.7	2012	0.6
27	SU	0201	6.9	0822	1.0	1420	6.8	2052	0.5
28	M	0238	6.9	0900	1.0	1454	6.8	2128	0.5
29	TU	0311	6.9	0932	1.0	1524	6.9	2200	0.5
30	W	0340	6.9	1003	0.9	1553	6.9	2230	0.5
31	TH	0410	6.9	1033	0.9	1623	6.8	2259	0.5

AUGUST

Date	Day	Time	m	Time	m	Time	m	Time	m
1	F	0441	6.8	1103	1.0	1655	6.7	2325	0.7
2	SA	0515	6.6	1131	1.1	1729	6.5	2349	0.8
3	SU	0551	6.4	1159	1.2	1807	6.3		
4	M ☽	0018	0.9	0632	6.2	1236	1.3	1853	6.2
5	TU	0059	1.0	0725	6.0	1327	1.4	1954	6.0
6	W	0157	1.2	0843	5.9	1441	1.5	2124	6.1
7	TH	0337	1.3	1007	6.1	1631	1.3	2243	6.4
8	F	0504	1.1	1119	6.4	1751	0.9	2350	6.8
9	SA	0617	0.9	1223	6.8	1911	0.6		
10	SU O	0051	7.2	0733	0.7	1320	7.1	2017	0.3
11	M	0145	7.4	0834	0.6	1410	7.3	2112	0.0
12	TU	0235	7.6	0926	0.4	1457	7.4	2200	-0.2
13	W	0322	7.6	1012	0.4	1541	7.5	2242	-0.2
14	TH	0407	7.6	1052	0.4	1624	7.5	2320	-0.1
15	F	0451	7.4	1129	0.5	1706	7.3	2352	0.2
16	SA	0535	7.0	1203	0.7	1750	7.1		
17	SU ☾	0022	0.5	0619	6.7	1239	0.9	1836	6.7
18	M	0055	0.9	0708	6.3	1319	1.2	1930	6.4
19	TU	0140	1.2	0804	6.0	1415	1.4	2034	6.1
20	W	0245	1.5	0910	5.8	1528	1.5	2147	6.0
21	TH	0359	1.5	1030	5.9	1644	1.3	2304	6.2
22	F	0515	1.4	1141	6.2	1759	1.0		
23	SA	0008	6.5	0622	1.1	1235	6.5	1858	0.7
24	SU	0057	6.8	0715	1.0	1319	6.7	1945	0.6
25	M ●	0139	6.9	0759	0.9	1357	6.9	2025	0.5
26	TU	0215	6.9	0838	0.9	1430	6.9	2102	0.5
27	W	0246	6.9	0914	0.9	1500	7.0	2136	0.5
28	TH	0314	7.0	0946	0.9	1528	7.0	2207	0.5
29	F	0343	7.0	1017	0.9	1557	7.0	2236	0.5
30	SA	0414	6.9	1047	0.9	1629	6.9	2300	0.7
31	SU	0447	6.7	1112	1.0	1703	6.7	2322	0.8

SEPTEMBER

Date	Day	Time	m	Time	m	Time	m	Time	m
1	M	0522	6.5	1137	1.1	1741	6.6	2349	0.9
2	TU ☽	0602	6.3	1210	1.2	1826	6.4		
3	W	0027	1.1	0652	6.0	1257	1.3	1924	6.2
4	TH	0122	1.3	0802	5.9	1406	1.5	2050	6.1
5	F	0306	1.5	0936	6.0	1605	1.3	2218	6.4
6	SA	0443	1.2	1055	6.3	1731	0.9	2331	6.8
7	SU	0601	0.9	1204	6.8	1857	0.5		
8	M	0034	7.2	0718	0.7	1301	7.1	2001	0.2
9	TU O	0128	7.4	0817	0.5	1350	7.3	2053	0.0
10	W	0215	7.6	0907	0.4	1435	7.5	2139	-0.1
11	TH	0300	7.6	0952	0.3	1517	7.6	2219	0.0
12	F	0343	7.5	1032	0.4	1558	7.6	2254	0.2
13	SA	0424	7.3	1107	0.5	1638	7.4	2322	0.5
14	SU	0503	7.0	1137	0.7	1719	7.1	2344	0.8
15	M	0542	6.6	1205	0.9	1802	6.7		
16	TU ☾	0010	1.1	0623	6.2	1239	1.2	1849	6.3
17	W	0048	1.4	0713	5.9	1326	1.4	1951	5.9
18	TH	0150	1.7	0821	5.6	1444	1.6	2108	5.8
19	F	0321	1.8	0945	5.6	1606	1.4	2226	6.0
20	SA	0441	1.6	1103	6.0	1717	1.1	2335	6.3
21	SU	0548	1.3	1201	6.4	1819	0.8		
22	M	0027	6.7	0643	1.0	1248	6.7	1909	0.6
23	TU	0109	6.8	0730	0.9	1327	6.8	1952	0.6
24	W ●	0145	6.9	0811	0.9	1401	6.9	2031	0.6
25	TH	0216	7.0	0849	0.9	1431	7.0	2107	0.5
26	F	0245	7.0	0925	0.8	1500	7.1	2140	0.5
27	SA	0315	7.0	0959	0.8	1532	7.1	2210	0.6
28	SU	0348	7.0	1029	0.8	1606	7.1	2235	0.7
29	M	0422	6.8	1055	0.9	1642	6.9	2259	0.9
30	TU	0458	6.6	1120	1.0	1721	6.7	2329	1.0

OCTOBER

Date	Day	Time	m	Time	m	Time	m	Time	m
1	W ☽	0538	6.3	1153	1.1	1808	6.5		
2	TH	0008	1.2	0629	6.1	1240	1.2	1906	6.3
3	F	0104	1.5	0737	5.9	1347	1.4	2031	6.2
4	SA	0252	1.6	0911	6.0	1547	1.3	2157	6.4
5	SU	0424	1.3	1033	6.3	1712	0.9	2311	6.8
6	M	0543	1.0	1142	6.7	1836	0.5		
7	TU	0014	7.1	0656	0.7	1239	7.1	1937	0.2
8	W O	0108	7.3	0754	0.5	1327	7.3	2028	0.1
9	TH	0154	7.4	0844	0.4	1411	7.4	2112	0.2
10	F	0236	7.4	0929	0.4	1452	7.6	2151	0.3
11	SA	0317	7.4	1009	0.4	1532	7.6	2224	0.5
12	SU	0355	7.2	1043	0.5	1612	7.4	2247	0.7
13	M	0433	6.9	1110	0.7	1651	7.1	2306	1.0
14	TU	0509	6.5	1134	0.9	1731	6.7	2333	1.2
15	W ☾	0546	6.2	1204	1.2	1815	6.3		
16	TH	0008	1.5	0628	5.9	1245	1.4	1908	5.9
17	F	0059	1.8	0727	5.6	1349	1.6	2022	5.7
18	SA	0221	2.0	0854	5.5	1522	1.6	2139	5.8
19	SU	0357	1.9	1014	5.7	1634	1.3	2248	6.1
20	M	0507	1.5	1118	6.1	1733	1.0	2345	6.4
21	TU	0604	1.2	1208	6.5	1826	0.8		
22	W	0030	6.7	0654	1.0	1251	6.7	1913	0.7
23	TH ●	0109	6.8	0739	1.0	1327	6.9	1956	0.7
24	F	0143	6.9	0821	0.9	1400	7.0	2035	0.7
25	SA	0216	7.0	0901	0.8	1434	7.1	2112	0.7
26	SU	0251	7.0	0939	0.8	1509	7.2	2144	0.7
27	M	0327	7.0	1013	0.7	1546	7.2	2214	0.8
28	TU	0403	6.8	1043	0.8	1625	7.1	2243	0.9
29	W	0441	6.6	1111	0.9	1708	6.9	2318	1.0
30	TH	0524	6.4	1146	0.9	1757	6.6		
31	F ☽	0002	1.2	0616	6.2	1234	1.1	1858	6.4

NOVEMBER

Date	Day	Time	m	Time	m	Time	m	Time	m
1	SA	0102	1.5	0723	6.0	1347	1.2	2018	6.3
2	SU	0239	1.6	0851	6.1	1529	1.1	2137	6.5
3	M	0402	1.4	1009	6.3	1648	0.8	2248	6.7
4	TU	0518	1.1	1118	6.7	1807	0.6	2352	7.0
5	W	0630	0.8	1216	6.9	1909	0.4		
6	TH O	0046	7.1	0729	0.6	1305	7.1	1959	0.4
7	F	0133	7.2	0819	0.5	1348	7.3	2043	0.5
8	SA	0214	7.2	0904	0.5	1429	7.4	2121	0.6
9	SU	0253	7.2	0944	0.5	1509	7.4	2153	0.8
10	M	0331	7.0	1019	0.6	1548	7.3	2214	0.9
11	TU	0407	6.8	1045	0.7	1627	7.0	2235	1.1
12	W	0441	6.5	1108	0.9	1705	6.6	2305	1.3
13	TH	0516	6.3	1137	1.1	1745	6.3	2340	1.5
14	F ☾	0553	6.0	1214	1.2	1829	6.0		
15	SA	0021	1.7	0638	5.8	1302	1.4	1925	5.8
16	SU	0118	1.9	0743	5.5	1414	1.6	2043	5.7
17	M	0239	2.0	0917	5.6	1540	1.5	2152	5.9
18	TU	0410	1.8	1025	5.9	1644	1.2	2252	6.2
19	W	0516	1.5	1122	6.2	1739	1.0	2345	6.5
20	TH	0612	1.2	1209	6.6	1831	0.8		
21	F	0030	6.7	0703	1.0	1252	6.8	1919	0.8
22	SA ●	0112	6.9	0752	0.9	1331	7.0	2004	0.8
23	SU	0152	7.0	0838	0.8	1411	7.1	2047	0.8
24	M	0232	7.0	0922	0.7	1452	7.2	2127	0.8
25	TU	0313	7.0	1003	0.6	1533	7.3	2204	0.8
26	W	0353	6.9	1040	0.6	1616	7.2	2240	0.8
27	TH	0434	6.7	1115	0.6	1701	7.0	2320	1.0
28	F	0519	6.6	1152	0.7	1752	6.8		
29	SA ☽	0007	1.2	0610	6.4	1241	0.9	1852	6.6
30	SU	0107	1.4	0713	6.3	1349	1.0	2003	6.5

DECEMBER

Date	Day	Time	m	Time	m	Time	m	Time	m
1	M	0220	1.4	0830	6.2	1505	1.0	2114	6.5
2	TU	0335	1.4	0943	6.4	1615	0.9	2222	6.6
3	W	0448	1.2	1051	6.5	1730	0.8	2328	6.7
4	TH	0601	1.0	1152	6.7	1837	0.7		
5	F	0026	6.8	0702	0.8	1245	6.9	1930	0.7
6	SA O	0114	6.9	0754	0.6	1330	7.0	2015	0.8
7	SU	0157	6.9	0841	0.5	1412	7.1	2054	0.9
8	M	0236	6.9	0922	0.5	1452	7.2	2127	1.0
9	TU	0312	6.9	0958	0.6	1530	7.1	2151	1.1
10	W	0346	6.8	1027	0.7	1607	6.9	2215	1.1
11	TH	0420	6.6	1050	0.8	1643	6.7	2246	1.2
12	F	0452	6.4	1119	0.9	1718	6.5	2319	1.3
13	SA	0526	6.2	1151	1.0	1755	6.3	2355	1.5
14	SU ☾	0604	6.1	1227	1.2	1838	6.0		
15	M	0036	1.6	0649	5.8	1311	1.3	1930	5.9
16	TU	0126	1.8	0748	5.7	1409	1.5	2044	5.8
17	W	0232	1.9	0921	5.7	1533	1.4	2155	5.9
18	TH	0406	1.8	1029	6.0	1647	1.2	2256	6.2
19	F	0524	1.5	1126	6.3	1746	1.0	2352	6.5
20	SA	0625	1.1	1218	6.7	1842	0.9		
21	SU	0043	6.8	0723	0.9	1306	7.0	1937	0.8
22	M ●	0131	6.9	0817	0.7	1353	7.2	2029	0.8
23	TU	0218	7.0	0909	0.6	1438	7.3	2118	0.8
24	W	0302	7.1	0956	0.4	1524	7.4	2204	0.7
25	TH	0346	7.1	1041	0.3	1610	7.4	2246	0.7
26	F	0430	7.0	1121	0.3	1656	7.2	2327	0.8
27	SA	0514	6.9	1200	0.4	1745	7.0		
28	SU ☽	0010	0.9	0601	6.7	1243	0.5	1839	6.8
29	M	0058	1.1	0657	6.6	1333	0.7	1941	6.6
30	TU	0155	1.3	0803	6.4	1432	0.9	2046	6.4
31	W	0301	1.4	0912	6.4	1537	1.0	2152	6.4

WALTON-ON-THE-NAZE
LAT 51°51'N
LONG 1°17'E

TIMES AND HEIGHTS OF HIGH AND LOW WATER (Heights in Metres)

TIME ZONE UT
For Summer Time (area enclosed in shaded box) add 1 hour

2014

JANUARY

Date	Day		Time	m	Time	m	Time	m	Time	m
1	W	●	0505	0.5	1110	4.4	1719	0.5	2340	4.3
2	TH		0558	0.3	1200	4.5	1809	0.5		
3	F		0029	4.4	0649	0.2	1250	4.6	1856	0.5
4	SA		0117	4.5	0738	0.1	1339	4.6	1943	0.6
5	SU		0204	4.5	0826	0.1	1428	4.5	2029	0.7
6	M		0251	4.4	0913	0.2	1518	4.3	2116	0.8
7	TU		0338	4.2	1001	0.3	1610	4.1	2206	0.9
8	W	☽	0429	4.1	1052	0.5	1706	3.9	2302	1.0
9	TH		0525	3.9	1148	0.7	1807	3.7		
10	F		0006	1.1	0631	3.7	1251	0.8	1914	3.6
11	SA		0119	1.1	0743	3.6	1400	1.0	2025	3.6
12	SU		0235	1.1	0850	3.7	1510	1.0	2126	3.7
13	M		0344	0.9	0946	3.8	1605	1.0	2216	3.9
14	TU		0435	0.7	1033	3.9	1647	0.9	2259	4.0
15	W		0516	0.6	1113	4.0	1723	0.8	2336	4.0
16	TH	○	0552	0.5	1149	4.0	1756	0.8		
17	F		0011	4.1	0624	0.4	1225	4.1	1826	0.8
18	SA		0044	4.2	0655	0.4	1259	4.1	1855	0.8
19	SU		0117	4.2	0726	0.4	1333	4.1	1924	0.7
20	M		0149	4.1	0757	0.4	1406	4.0	1955	0.8
21	TU		0222	4.1	0828	0.4	1439	4.0	2029	0.8
22	W		0255	4.0	0900	0.5	1516	3.9	2106	0.9
23	TH		0332	3.9	0937	0.6	1557	3.8	2149	1.0
24	F	☾	0415	3.8	1023	0.7	1647	3.7	2245	1.1
25	SA		0510	3.7	1127	0.8	1751	3.6		
26	SU		0004	1.1	0620	3.7	1253	0.9	1906	3.6
27	M		0137	1.0	0742	3.7	1410	0.8	2025	3.7
28	TU		0251	0.8	0859	3.8	1515	0.7	2137	3.9
29	W		0355	0.6	1003	4.1	1614	0.6	2236	4.1
30	TH	●	0454	0.4	1058	4.3	1708	0.6	2327	4.3
31	F		0548	0.2	1149	4.5	1758	0.5		

FEBRUARY

Date	Day		Time	m	Time	m	Time	m	Time	m
1	SA		0015	4.4	0638	0.1	1237	4.6	1844	0.5
2	SU		0101	4.6	0725	0.0	1324	4.6	1929	0.5
3	M		0146	4.6	0809	0.0	1410	4.5	2012	0.6
4	TU		0229	4.5	0850	0.1	1455	4.3	2053	0.7
5	W		0312	4.3	0929	0.3	1541	4.1	2135	0.8
6	TH	☽	0356	4.1	1009	0.5	1629	3.8	2222	0.9
7	F		0444	3.9	1056	0.8	1722	3.6	2318	1.0
8	SA		0543	3.6	1156	1.0	1825	3.4		
9	SU		0029	1.1	0658	3.4	1308	1.1	1942	3.4
10	M		0156	1.1	0818	3.5	1434	1.2	2057	3.5
11	TU		0323	1.0	0923	3.6	1542	1.1	2153	3.7
12	W		0417	0.8	1013	3.7	1627	1.0	2237	3.9
13	TH		0457	0.6	1054	3.9	1704	0.9	2315	4.0
14	F	○	0530	0.5	1131	4.0	1736	0.8	2349	4.1
15	SA		0601	0.4	1205	4.0	1806	0.7		
16	SU		0022	4.2	0630	0.4	1238	4.1	1834	0.7
17	M		0056	4.2	0700	0.3	1311	4.1	1904	0.6
18	TU		0128	4.2	0731	0.3	1343	4.1	1935	0.6
19	W		0200	4.2	0801	0.4	1416	4.0	2008	0.7
20	TH		0232	4.1	0831	0.4	1451	4.0	2044	0.7
21	F		0307	4.1	0906	0.5	1531	3.9	2124	0.8
22	SA	☾	0349	4.0	0949	0.7	1618	3.8	2216	0.9
23	SU		0441	3.8	1053	0.8	1718	3.6	2332	1.0
24	M		0550	3.7	1223	1.0	1834	3.5		
25	TU		0110	1.0	0717	3.6	1348	0.9	2004	3.5
26	W		0232	0.8	0845	3.8	1458	0.8	2123	3.8
27	TH		0341	0.5	0952	4.0	1559	0.7	2223	4.0
28	F		0441	0.3	1047	4.3	1653	0.6	2313	4.3

MARCH

Date	Day		Time	m	Time	m	Time	m	Time	m
1	SA	●	0533	0.1	1135	4.4	1741	0.5	2358	4.4
2	SU		0620	0.0	1220	4.5	1827	0.5		
3	M		0041	4.6	0703	0.0	1304	4.5	1909	0.4
4	TU		0123	4.6	0743	0.1	1347	4.4	1951	0.5
5	W		0203	4.5	0820	0.2	1428	4.3	2029	0.5
6	TH		0243	4.4	0853	0.4	1509	4.0	2106	0.6
7	F		0322	4.1	0927	0.6	1551	3.8	2146	0.8
8	SA	☽	0406	3.9	1008	0.8	1638	3.6	2235	0.9
9	SU		0500	3.6	1104	1.1	1736	3.4	2340	1.1
10	M		0612	3.3	1220	1.3	1849	3.3		
11	TU		0107	1.1	0736	3.3	1349	1.3	2013	3.3
12	W		0240	1.0	0851	3.5	1507	1.2	2118	3.5
13	TH		0344	0.8	0945	3.7	1558	1.0	2207	3.7
14	F		0426	0.6	1028	3.8	1637	0.9	2246	3.9
15	SA		0500	0.5	1104	3.9	1710	0.8	2321	4.0
16	SU	○	0531	0.4	1138	4.0	1740	0.7	2355	4.1
17	M		0601	0.4	1212	4.1	1810	0.6		
18	TU		0028	4.2	0631	0.3	1246	4.2	1842	0.6
19	W		0103	4.3	0702	0.3	1320	4.2	1915	0.5
20	TH		0136	4.3	0733	0.3	1355	4.1	1950	0.5
21	F		0211	4.2	0805	0.4	1431	4.0	2026	0.6
22	SA		0248	4.1	0842	0.5	1511	3.9	2108	0.7
23	SU		0331	4.0	0929	0.7	1558	3.8	2202	0.8
24	M	☾	0425	3.9	1036	0.9	1657	3.6	2318	0.9
25	TU		0534	3.7	1206	1.0	1815	3.5		
26	W		0054	0.8	0705	3.6	1330	1.0	1948	3.5
27	TH		0216	0.7	0833	3.8	1440	0.9	2106	3.8
28	F		0326	0.5	0939	4.0	1541	0.7	2205	4.0
29	SA		0424	0.3	1031	4.2	1634	0.6	2253	4.2
30	SU	●	0513	0.2	1117	4.3	1721	0.5	2337	4.4
31	M		0557	0.1	1200	4.4	1806	0.4		

APRIL

Date	Day		Time	m	Time	m	Time	m	Time	m
1	TU		0017	4.5	0637	0.1	1241	4.4	1848	0.4
2	W		0058	4.5	0714	0.2	1322	4.3	1929	0.4
3	TH		0136	4.4	0748	0.4	1401	4.2	2006	0.5
4	F		0214	4.3	0819	0.5	1439	4.0	2041	0.6
5	SA		0253	4.1	0850	0.7	1517	3.8	2117	0.7
6	SU		0334	3.8	0927	0.9	1559	3.6	2159	0.8
7	M	☽	0424	3.6	1017	1.1	1652	3.4	2257	1.0
8	TU		0530	3.4	1129	1.3	1800	3.3		
9	W		0017	1.1	0648	3.3	1301	1.4	1915	3.3
10	TH		0144	1.0	0802	3.4	1420	1.2	2026	3.4
11	F		0252	0.8	0903	3.6	1518	1.1	2122	3.6
12	SA		0342	0.7	0951	3.7	1602	0.9	2207	3.8
13	SU		0422	0.5	1030	3.9	1638	0.8	2246	4.0
14	M		0456	0.5	1107	4.0	1712	0.7	2323	4.1
15	TU	○	0529	0.4	1143	4.1	1746	0.6	2359	4.2
16	W		0602	0.3	1219	4.2	1821	0.5		
17	TH		0037	4.3	0635	0.3	1258	4.2	1857	0.5
18	F		0115	4.3	0709	0.4	1336	4.2	1935	0.5
19	SA		0154	4.3	0746	0.4	1416	4.1	2016	0.5
20	SU		0235	4.2	0829	0.6	1459	3.9	2102	0.5
21	M		0322	4.1	0922	0.8	1548	3.8	2200	0.6
22	TU	☾	0418	3.9	1031	0.9	1649	3.6	2316	0.7
23	W		0529	3.7	1152	1.0	1806	3.6		
24	TH		0042	0.7	0655	3.7	1309	1.0	1930	3.6
25	F		0158	0.5	0814	3.8	1418	0.9	2043	3.8
26	SA		0306	0.4	0919	4.0	1519	0.8	2142	4.0
27	SU		0403	0.4	1012	4.1	1613	0.7	2231	4.2
28	M		0450	0.3	1057	4.2	1700	0.6	2314	4.3
29	TU	●	0532	0.3	1138	4.3	1745	0.5	2354	4.4
30	W		0610	0.3	1218	4.3	1828	0.4		

MAY

Date	Day		Time	m	Time	m	Time	m	Time	m
1	TH		0033	4.4	0646	0.4	1258	4.2	1908	0.4
2	F		0112	4.3	0720	0.5	1336	4.1	1946	0.4
3	SA		0149	4.2	0751	0.7	1412	4.0	2021	0.5
4	SU		0228	4.1	0821	0.8	1448	3.9	2054	0.6
5	M		0308	3.9	0855	0.9	1527	3.7	2132	0.7
6	TU		0353	3.6	0938	1.1	1615	3.5	2221	0.8
7	W	☽	0450	3.5	1036	1.2	1716	3.4	2327	0.9
8	TH		0559	3.4	1158	1.4	1824	3.4		
9	F		0049	1.0	0707	3.4	1327	1.3	1929	3.4
10	SA		0159	0.9	0809	3.5	1431	1.1	2029	3.6
11	SU		0253	0.7	0903	3.7	1520	1.0	2122	3.8
12	M		0339	0.6	0950	3.9	1603	0.8	2208	4.0
13	TU		0420	0.5	1032	4.0	1642	0.7	2250	4.1
14	W	○	0458	0.5	1114	4.1	1722	0.6	2332	4.3
15	TH		0536	0.4	1156	4.2	1803	0.5		
16	F		0014	4.4	0613	0.4	1239	4.3	1844	0.4
17	SA		0058	4.4	0653	0.4	1323	4.2	1927	0.4
18	SU		0142	4.4	0736	0.5	1407	4.2	2013	0.4
19	M		0228	4.3	0824	0.6	1454	4.1	2104	0.4
20	TU		0318	4.2	0919	0.8	1545	3.9	2203	0.5
21	W	☾	0415	4.0	1022	0.9	1645	3.8	2312	0.5
22	TH		0523	3.9	1132	1.0	1753	3.8		
23	F		0025	0.5	0636	3.8	1244	1.0	1905	3.8
24	SA		0134	0.5	0748	3.9	1352	0.9	2015	3.9
25	SU		0240	0.5	0854	3.9	1455	0.8	2116	4.0
26	M		0338	0.5	0949	4.0	1552	0.7	2207	4.1
27	TU		0427	0.5	1036	4.1	1642	0.6	2252	4.2
28	W	●	0508	0.5	1119	4.1	1727	0.5	2333	4.2
29	TH		0546	0.6	1159	4.2	1810	0.4		
30	F		0012	4.3	0622	0.6	1238	4.2	1851	0.4
31	SA		0051	4.2	0657	0.7	1315	4.1	1928	0.4

JUNE

Date	Day		Time	m	Time	m	Time	m	Time	m
1	SU		0129	4.2	0730	0.7	1350	4.1	2003	0.5
2	M		0207	4.0	0800	0.8	1426	4.0	2035	0.5
3	TU		0245	3.9	0831	0.9	1503	3.9	2110	0.6
4	W		0326	3.8	0910	1.0	1544	3.7	2151	0.7
5	TH	☽	0412	3.6	0956	1.1	1634	3.6	2242	0.8
6	F		0506	3.5	1053	1.2	1732	3.5	2347	0.9
7	SA		0609	3.5	1210	1.3	1835	3.5		
8	SU		0101	0.9	0712	3.5	1334	1.2	1937	3.6
9	M		0204	0.8	0812	3.6	1435	1.0	2036	3.7
10	TU		0257	0.7	0908	3.8	1527	0.9	2131	3.9
11	W		0345	0.6	1000	4.0	1615	0.7	2221	4.1
12	TH		0431	0.6	1049	4.1	1702	0.6	2309	4.3
13	F	○	0515	0.5	1137	4.2	1749	0.4	2356	4.4
14	SA		0600	0.5	1224	4.3	1836	0.3		
15	SU		0043	4.5	0644	0.5	1312	4.4	1924	0.3
16	M		0131	4.5	0731	0.5	1359	4.3	2013	0.2
17	TU		0220	4.5	0820	0.6	1447	4.3	2104	0.2
18	W		0311	4.3	0911	0.7	1537	4.2	2158	0.3
19	TH	☾	0406	4.2	1006	0.8	1631	4.1	2257	0.4
20	F		0506	4.0	1107	0.9	1730	4.0	2359	0.5
21	SA		0611	3.9	1213	1.0	1836	3.9		
22	SU		0103	0.6	0718	3.8	1322	1.0	1944	3.9
23	M		0208	0.7	0825	3.8	1429	0.9	2049	3.9
24	TU		0312	0.7	0926	3.9	1534	0.8	2145	4.0
25	W		0406	0.8	1017	4.0	1629	0.7	2233	4.0
26	TH		0450	0.8	1102	4.1	1716	0.6	2316	4.1
27	F	●	0529	0.7	1143	4.1	1757	0.5	2355	4.1
28	SA		0604	0.7	1220	4.1	1835	0.4		
29	SU		0033	4.2	0639	0.7	1257	4.2	1910	0.4
30	M		0111	4.1	0711	0.8	1331	4.1	1943	0.5

SUNRISE AND SUNSET TIMES

WALTON-ON-THE-NAZE
At 51°51'N 1°17'E

		Sunrise	Sunset
UT			
Jan	01	0802	1555
	15	0755	1614
Feb	01	0734	1643
	15	0709	1709
Mar	01	0640	1735
	15	0609	1800
BST			
Apr	01	0630	1929
	15	0558	1952
May	01	0526	2019
	15	0502	2042
Jun	01	0442	2104
	15	0435	2116
Jul	01	0440	2117
	15	0454	2107
Aug	01	0517	2044
	15	0539	2018
Sep	01	0607	1942
	15	0630	1909
Oct	01	0656	1832
	15	0719	1801
UT			
Nov	01	0649	1627
	15	0714	1604
Dec	01	0740	1548
	15	0756	1544

WALTON-ON-THE-NAZE
LAT 51°51'N
LONG 1°17'E

TIMES AND HEIGHTS OF HIGH AND LOW WATER (Heights in Metres)

TIME ZONE UT
For Summer Time (area enclosed in shaded box) add 1 hour

2014

JULY

Date	Time	m
1 TU	0147 0741 1405 2015	4.1 0.8 4.1 0.5
2 W	0223 0811 1440 2047	4.0 0.8 4.0 0.5
3 TH	0259 0845 1516 2122	3.9 0.9 3.9 0.6
4 F	0336 0924 1555 2201	3.8 1.0 3.8 0.7
5 SA ☽	0419 1010 1641 2249	3.7 1.1 3.7 0.8
6 SU	0510 1107 1737 2354	3.6 1.2 3.6 0.9
7 M	0614 1225 1844	3.6 1.2 3.6
8 TU	0112 0722 1350 1953	0.9 3.6 1.1 3.7
9 W	0218 0830 1454 2058	0.8 3.7 0.9 3.9
10 TH	0316 0933 1551 2157	0.7 3.9 0.7 4.1
11 F	0409 1029 1645 2250	0.6 4.1 0.5 4.3
12 SA O	0500 1121 1737 2341	0.6 4.2 0.4 4.5
13 SU	0549 1210 1828	0.6 4.4 0.2
14 M	0030 0636 1258 1917	4.6 0.5 4.5 0.2
15 TU	0119 0723 1345 2006	4.6 0.5 4.5 0.1
16 W	0207 0809 1431 2053	4.6 0.6 4.5 0.2
17 TH	0256 0856 1518 2140	4.4 0.7 4.4 0.2
18 F	0346 0944 1607 2229	4.2 0.8 4.3 0.4
19 SA ☾	0440 1037 1700 2323	4.0 0.9 4.1 0.6
20 SU	0539 1138 1802	3.9 1.0 3.9
21 M	0024 0643 1246 1911	0.8 3.7 1.0 3.8
22 TU	0131 0754 1401 2022	0.9 3.7 1.0 3.8
23 W	0245 0902 1519 2124	1.0 3.8 0.9 3.8
24 TH	0348 0958 1619 2216	1.0 3.9 0.8 3.9
25 F	0436 1045 1705 2301	0.9 4.0 0.6 4.0
26 SA ●	0514 1126 1743 2339	0.9 4.1 0.5 4.1
27 SU	0547 1202 1817	0.8 4.1 0.5
28 M	0016 0619 1237 1849	4.1 0.8 4.2 0.4
29 TU	0051 0650 1310 1920	4.2 0.8 4.2 0.4
30 W	0126 0720 1343 1950	4.1 0.8 4.2 0.5
31 TH	0159 0749 1415 2020	4.1 0.8 4.1 0.5

AUGUST

Date	Time	m
1 F	0231 0821 1447 2050	4.0 0.8 4.1 0.6
2 SA	0304 0856 1521 2123	3.9 0.9 4.0 0.7
3 SU	0342 0935 1601 2203	3.8 1.0 3.9 0.8
4 M ☽	0427 1024 1650 2259	3.7 1.1 3.8 0.9
5 TU	0525 1133 1754	3.6 1.2 3.7
6 W	0021 0637 1308 1912	1.0 3.6 1.1 3.7
7 TH	0146 0756 1426 2031	1.0 3.7 1.0 3.8
8 F	0252 0910 1530 2138	0.8 3.8 0.7 4.1
9 SA	0351 1012 1630 2235	0.7 4.1 0.5 4.3
10 SU O	0445 1105 1724 2326	0.7 4.3 0.3 4.5
11 M	0535 1153 1815	0.6 4.4 0.2
12 TU	0014 0622 1240 1902	4.6 0.5 4.6 0.1
13 W	0102 0708 1325 1948	4.7 0.5 4.7 0.1
14 TH	0148 0752 1409 2031	4.6 0.6 4.6 0.2
15 F	0234 0835 1453 2112	4.5 0.6 4.5 0.3
16 SA	0320 0919 1537 2154	4.3 0.7 4.3 0.5
17 SU ☾	0409 1006 1626 2241	4.0 0.8 4.1 0.8
18 M	0502 1100 1723 2337	3.8 1.0 3.9 1.0
19 TU	0604 1207 1835	3.6 1.1 3.7
20 W	0047 0718 1328 1953	1.2 3.5 1.1 3.6
21 TH	0213 0835 1459 2103	1.2 3.6 1.0 3.7
22 F	0327 0936 1602 2157	1.1 3.8 0.8 3.9
23 SA	0416 1024 1646 2241	1.0 3.9 0.7 4.0
24 SU	0454 1104 1721 2319	0.9 4.1 0.6 4.1
25 M ●	0526 1139 1752 2353	0.9 4.2 0.5 4.1
26 TU	0557 1211 1822	0.8 4.2 0.5
27 W	0027 0627 1244 1851	4.2 0.8 4.3 0.4
28 TH	0100 0656 1316 1920	4.2 0.7 4.3 0.5
29 F	0131 0726 1347 1949	4.2 0.7 4.2 0.5
30 SA	0203 0758 1418 2017	4.1 0.8 4.2 0.6
31 SU	0235 0831 1452 2048	4.0 0.8 4.1 0.7

SEPTEMBER

Date	Time	m
1 M	0312 0907 1530 2126	3.9 0.9 4.0 0.8
2 TU ☽	0354 0953 1618 2220	3.8 1.0 3.9 1.0
3 W	0449 1059 1720 2344	3.7 1.1 3.7 1.1
4 TH	0601 1236 1841	3.6 1.1 3.7
5 F	0119 0727 1402 2011	1.1 3.6 0.9 3.8
6 SA	0231 0851 1511 2123	1.0 3.8 0.7 4.1
7 SU	0333 0955 1612 2220	0.8 4.0 0.4 4.3
8 M	0427 1047 1706 2309	0.7 4.3 0.3 4.5
9 TU O	0517 1133 1755 2355	0.6 4.5 0.2 4.6
10 W	0603 1217 1840	0.5 4.6 0.1
11 TH	0040 0648 1301 1923	4.6 0.5 4.7 0.2
12 F	0125 0731 1343 2002	4.6 0.5 4.7 0.3
13 SA	0208 0813 1424 2039	4.4 0.6 4.5 0.5
14 SU	0251 0854 1506 2116	4.2 0.7 4.3 0.7
15 M	0334 0936 1551 2157	4.0 0.8 4.1 0.9
16 TU ☾	0422 1024 1644 2250	3.7 0.9 3.8 1.2
17 W	0520 1126 1755	3.5 1.1 3.6
18 TH	0001 0633 1247 1917	1.4 3.4 1.1 3.5
19 F	0130 0755 1419 2033	1.4 3.5 1.1 3.6
20 SA	0252 0903 1529 2130	1.3 3.6 0.9 3.8
21 SU	0346 0953 1614 2214	1.1 3.8 0.7 4.0
22 M	0425 1033 1649 2252	1.0 4.0 0.6 4.1
23 TU	0500 1108 1720 2325	0.9 4.1 0.5 4.1
24 W ●	0531 1141 1750 2358	0.8 4.2 0.5 4.2
25 TH	0601 1213 1819	0.7 4.3 0.5
26 F	0030 0631 1247 1848	4.2 0.7 4.3 0.5
27 SA	0103 0703 1319 1917	4.2 0.7 4.3 0.5
28 SU	0136 0736 1353 1947	4.2 0.7 4.3 0.6
29 M	0210 0810 1428 2020	4.1 0.7 4.2 0.7
30 TU	0247 0848 1508 2101	4.0 0.8 4.1 0.9

OCTOBER

Date	Time	m
1 W ☽	0330 0935 1557 2158	3.9 0.9 4.0 1.0
2 TH	0424 1042 1659 2324	3.7 1.0 3.8 1.2
3 F	0535 1216 1821	3.6 1.0 3.7
4 SA	0056 0705 1341 1953	1.2 3.6 0.8 3.8
5 SU	0209 0829 1450 2105	1.0 3.8 0.6 4.1
6 M	0311 0933 1551 2202	0.9 4.0 0.4 4.3
7 TU	0406 1025 1644 2250	0.7 4.3 0.3 4.5
8 W O	0455 1111 1731 2334	0.6 4.5 0.2 4.5
9 TH	0542 1153 1814	0.5 4.6 0.2
10 F	0017 0626 1235 1854	4.6 0.5 4.6 0.3
11 SA	0100 0710 1316 1932	4.5 0.5 4.6 0.5
12 SU	0141 0752 1356 2007	4.4 0.5 4.5 0.6
13 M	0221 0831 1437 2040	4.2 0.6 4.2 0.8
14 TU	0301 0909 1519 2117	4.0 0.7 4.0 1.0
15 W ☾	0343 0952 1608 2204	3.7 0.8 3.7 1.2
16 TH	0435 1046 1713 2310	3.5 1.0 3.5 1.4
17 F	0543 1159 1831	3.4 1.1 3.4
18 SA	0039 0659 1324 1946	1.5 3.4 1.1 3.5
19 SU	0202 0812 1435 2049	1.4 3.5 1.0 3.7
20 M	0304 0909 1528 2137	1.2 3.7 0.8 3.9
21 TU	0350 0954 1609 2217	1.0 3.9 0.7 4.0
22 W	0428 1031 1644 2252	0.9 4.0 0.6 4.1
23 TH ●	0502 1107 1716 2326	0.8 4.2 0.6 4.2
24 F	0534 1142 1747	0.7 4.3 0.5
25 SA	0001 0607 1218 1818	4.3 0.6 4.3 0.5
26 SU	0037 0642 1255 1850	4.3 0.6 4.4 0.6
27 M	0114 0718 1332 1924	4.3 0.6 4.3 0.6
28 TU	0152 0755 1411 2002	4.2 0.6 4.3 0.7
29 W	0231 0838 1455 2049	4.1 0.6 4.2 0.9
30 TH	0316 0929 1545 2150	3.9 0.7 4.0 1.1
31 F ☽	0410 1038 1648 2309	3.7 0.8 3.8 1.2

NOVEMBER

Date	Time	m
1 SA	0520 1202 1809	3.6 0.8 3.8
2 SU	0031 0644 1319 1933	1.2 3.6 0.7 3.9
3 M	0144 0804 1427 2043	1.1 3.8 0.5 4.1
4 TU	0247 0909 1528 2141	0.9 4.0 0.4 4.2
5 W	0343 1002 1620 2230	0.8 4.2 0.4 4.3
6 TH O	0434 1048 1706 2314	0.7 4.4 0.4 4.4
7 F	0522 1131 1749 2356	0.5 4.5 0.4 4.4
8 SA	0607 1211 1828	0.5 4.5 0.5
9 SU	0036 0651 1252 1905	4.4 0.4 4.5 0.6
10 M	0117 0732 1332 1940	4.3 0.5 4.3 0.8
11 TU	0155 0810 1412 2012	4.2 0.5 4.2 0.9
12 W	0232 0846 1452 2044	4.0 0.6 4.0 1.0
13 TH	0310 0924 1537 2123	3.8 0.7 3.8 1.2
14 F ☾	0355 1009 1631 2216	3.6 0.9 3.6 1.4
15 SA	0454 1109 1739 2330	3.5 1.0 3.4 1.5
16 SU	0602 1226 1848	3.4 1.0 3.4
17 M	0104 0709 1338 1951	1.5 3.4 1.0 3.5
18 TU	0214 0812 1436 2047	1.3 3.6 0.9 3.7
19 W	0307 0905 1524 2134	1.1 3.7 0.8 3.9
20 TH	0351 0951 1605 2216	1.0 3.9 0.7 4.0
21 F	0430 1033 1643 2256	0.8 4.1 0.6 4.2
22 SA ●	0508 1113 1718 2335	0.7 4.2 0.6 4.3
23 SU	0546 1153 1754	0.6 4.3 0.6
24 M	0016 0625 1235 1830	4.3 0.5 4.4 0.6
25 TU	0058 0706 1317 1910	4.3 0.4 4.4 0.6
26 W	0140 0749 1401 1954	4.3 0.4 4.4 0.7
27 TH	0224 0835 1448 2045	4.2 0.5 4.3 0.8
28 F	0310 0929 1539 2143	4.0 0.5 4.1 1.0
29 SA ☽	0404 1032 1640 2251	3.9 0.6 3.9 1.1
30 SU	0507 1144 1752	3.8 0.6 3.9

DECEMBER

Date	Time	m
1 M	0003 0621 1254 1907	1.1 3.8 0.6 3.9
2 TU	0115 0736 1400 2017	1.1 3.8 0.6 3.9
3 W	0220 0843 1502 2118	1.0 3.9 0.6 4.1
4 TH	0321 0939 1557 2211	0.8 4.1 0.6 4.2
5 F	0416 1028 1645 2256	0.7 4.2 0.6 4.2
6 SA O	0506 1112 1728 2338	0.6 4.3 0.6 4.3
7 SU	0552 1153 1807	0.5 4.3 0.6
8 M	0019 0635 1234 1844	4.3 0.4 4.3 0.7
9 TU	0057 0715 1312 1918	4.2 0.4 4.2 0.8
10 W	0134 0752 1351 1950	4.2 0.5 4.1 0.9
11 TH	0209 0825 1429 2019	4.1 0.5 4.0 1.0
12 F	0245 0859 1509 2053	3.9 0.6 3.8 1.1
13 SA	0323 0936 1552 2135	3.8 0.7 3.7 1.2
14 SU ☾	0408 1021 1643 2226	3.6 0.8 3.5 1.3
15 M	0504 1119 1744 2333	3.5 0.9 3.5 1.4
16 TU	0608 1233 1848	3.4 1.0 3.5
17 W	0107 0713 1342 1949	1.4 3.5 0.9 3.6
18 TH	0217 0815 1438 2047	1.2 3.6 0.9 3.7
19 F	0311 0911 1528 2140	1.0 3.8 0.8 3.9
20 SA	0359 1001 1613 2228	0.8 4.0 0.7 4.1
21 SU	0444 1048 1655 2315	0.7 4.1 0.6 4.2
22 M ●	0529 1134 1737	0.5 4.3 0.6
23 TU	0000 0613 1220 1819	4.3 0.4 4.4 0.6
24 W	0046 0658 1306 1903	4.4 0.3 4.5 0.6
25 TH	0131 0744 1352 1949	4.4 0.2 4.5 0.6
26 F	0217 0832 1440 2038	4.3 0.2 4.4 0.7
27 SA	0303 0923 1531 2130	4.2 0.3 4.2 0.8
28 SU ☽	0353 1018 1626 2228	4.1 0.4 4.0 0.9
29 M	0448 1118 1729 2332	4.0 0.5 3.9 1.0
30 TU	0553 1223 1837	3.9 0.6 3.8
31 W	0041 0704 1329 1948	1.0 3.8 0.7 3.8

LOWESTOFT
LAT 52°28′N
LONG 1°45′E

TIMES AND HEIGHTS OF HIGH AND LOW WATER (Heights in Metres)

TIME ZONE UT
For Summer Time (area enclosed in shaded box) add 1 hour

2014

JANUARY

Date	Day	Time	m
1	W ●	0248 0854 1507 2113	0.7 2.5 0.7 2.6
2	TH	0342 0946 1557 2158	0.5 2.6 0.6 2.7
3	F	0434 1037 1644 2245	0.4 2.6 0.7 2.7
4	SA	0523 1126 1730 2331	0.3 2.6 0.7 2.8
5	SU	0611 1215 1814	0.3 2.5 0.8
6	M	0017 0658 1306 1857	2.7 0.4 2.4 0.9
7	TU	0105 0747 1403 1943	2.7 0.5 2.3 1.0
8	W ☽	0156 0841 1519 2036	2.6 0.6 2.2 1.1
9	TH	0257 0945 1630 2148	2.4 0.8 2.2 1.2
10	F	0416 1054 1731 2314	2.3 0.9 2.2 1.2
11	SA	0530 1157 1829	2.3 1.0 2.2
12	SU	0025 0640 1255 1923	1.1 2.2 1.0 2.3
13	M	0127 0747 1347 2007	1.0 2.3 1.0 2.4
14	TU	0218 0837 1430 2044	0.9 2.3 1.0 2.4
15	W	0300 0917 1507 2117	0.8 2.3 1.0 2.5
16	TH O	0339 0953 1539 2148	0.7 2.3 0.9 2.5
17	F	0414 1025 1607 2220	0.7 2.3 0.9 2.6
18	SA	0447 1055 1636 2253	0.6 2.3 0.9 2.6
19	SU	0520 1126 1708 2328	0.6 2.3 0.9 2.6
20	M	0553 1158 1742	0.6 2.3 0.9
21	TU	0004 0626 1234 1819	2.5 0.7 2.3 0.9
22	W	0042 0702 1312 1859	2.5 0.7 2.2 1.0
23	TH	0122 0742 1355 1945	2.4 0.8 2.2 1.1
24	F ☾	0207 0830 1449 2039	2.4 0.9 2.2 1.1
25	SA	0303 0932 1608 2151	2.3 0.9 2.1 1.2
26	SU	0422 1055 1727 2326	2.3 1.0 2.2 1.1
27	M	0544 1205 1825	2.3 0.9 2.3
28	TU	0035 0649 1304 1916	0.9 2.3 0.9 2.4
29	W	0137 0750 1359 2006	0.8 2.4 0.8 2.5
30	TH ●	0236 0846 1453 2055	0.6 2.5 0.7 2.6
31	F	0331 0937 1544 2141	0.4 2.6 0.7 2.7

FEBRUARY

Date	Day	Time	m
1	SA	0422 1023 1630 2227	0.2 2.6 0.6 2.8
2	SU	0508 1108 1713 2312	0.2 2.6 0.6 2.8
3	M	0552 1153 1754 2357	0.2 2.5 0.7 2.8
4	TU	0635 1238 1834	0.3 2.4 0.8
5	W	0042 0718 1326 1916	2.7 0.5 2.3 0.9
6	TH ☽	0131 0803 1421 2003	2.5 0.7 2.2 1.0
7	F	0228 0857 1535 2103	2.4 0.9 2.1 1.1
8	SA	0349 1013 1645 2239	2.2 1.1 2.1 1.2
9	SU	0510 1130 1748	2.2 1.1 2.1
10	M	0000 0629 1235 1851	1.1 2.2 1.2 2.2
11	TU	0105 0739 1330 1943	1.0 2.2 1.1 2.3
12	W	0157 0826 1414 2022	0.9 2.2 1.1 2.3
13	TH	0240 0903 1450 2054	0.8 2.3 1.0 2.4
14	F O	0316 0933 1519 2124	0.7 2.3 0.9 2.5
15	SA	0350 1001 1548 2156	0.6 2.3 0.8 2.5
16	SU	0423 1029 1618 2230	0.6 2.3 0.8 2.6
17	M	0455 1059 1650 2305	0.5 2.4 0.8 2.6
18	TU	0528 1131 1724 2340	0.6 2.3 0.8 2.5
19	W	0600 1205 1759	0.6 2.3 0.8
20	TH	0016 0634 1242 1836	2.5 0.7 2.3 0.9
21	F	0055 0711 1323 1919	2.4 0.7 2.2 0.9
22	SA ☾	0140 0755 1413 2012	2.4 0.8 2.2 1.0
23	SU	0236 0852 1516 2120	2.3 1.0 2.1 1.0
24	M	0357 1018 1643 2303	2.2 1.0 2.2 1.0
25	TU	0531 1144 1753	2.2 1.0 2.2
26	W	0018 0642 1248 1851	0.8 2.3 1.0 2.3
27	TH	0122 0744 1346 1945	0.7 2.4 0.9 2.4
28	F	0223 0837 1440 2035	0.5 2.5 0.8 2.6

MARCH

Date	Day	Time	m
1	SA ●	0316 0922 1529 2122	0.3 2.5 0.6 2.7
2	SU	0404 1005 1613 2208	0.2 2.5 0.5 2.8
3	M	0447 1047 1654 2252	0.2 2.5 0.5 2.8
4	TU	0528 1128 1733 2337	0.2 2.5 0.6 2.7
5	W	0608 1209 1812	0.4 2.4 0.6
6	TH	0021 0646 1251 1851	2.6 0.6 2.3 0.7
7	F	0108 0725 1335 1935	2.4 0.8 2.2 0.9
8	SA ☽	0203 0809 1427 2029	2.3 1.0 2.1 1.0
9	SU	0322 0908 1540 2158	2.2 1.2 2.1 1.1
10	M	0447 1058 1654 2331	2.1 1.3 2.1 1.0
11	TU	0606 1209 1800	2.1 1.3 2.1
12	W	0033 0717 1306 1901	0.9 2.2 1.2 2.2
13	TH	0126 0803 1350 1947	0.9 2.2 1.1 2.3
14	F	0209 0838 1424 2022	0.8 2.3 1.0 2.3
15	SA	0245 0906 1453 2055	0.7 2.3 0.9 2.4
16	SU O	0319 0932 1523 2129	0.6 2.3 0.8 2.5
17	M	0352 1000 1556 2204	0.5 2.4 0.7 2.5
18	TU	0426 1030 1630 2240	0.5 2.4 0.7 2.5
19	W	0500 1104 1706 2316	0.5 2.4 0.7 2.5
20	TH	0535 1139 1742 2354	0.5 2.4 0.7 2.5
21	F	0609 1216 1820	0.6 2.3 0.7
22	SA	0035 0647 1259 1903	2.4 0.7 2.3 0.8
23	SU	0123 0731 1347 1956	2.4 0.9 2.2 0.8
24	M ☾	0223 0827 1447 2108	2.3 1.0 2.2 0.9
25	TU	0352 0950 1605 2250	2.2 1.1 2.2 0.8
26	W	0526 1125 1723	2.2 1.1 2.2
27	TH	0002 0635 1231 1825	0.7 2.3 1.0 2.3
28	F	0106 0734 1330 1922	0.6 2.4 0.9 2.4
29	SA	0204 0822 1423 2013	0.4 2.4 0.8 2.5
30	SU ●	0256 0903 1510 2101	0.3 2.5 0.7 2.6
31	M	0341 0943 1553 2147	0.3 2.5 0.6 2.7

APRIL

Date	Day	Time	m
1	TU	0423 1023 1634 2233	0.3 2.5 0.5 2.7
2	W	0502 1103 1713 2318	0.4 2.5 0.5 2.6
3	TH	0539 1142 1751	0.5 2.4 0.6
4	F	0002 0614 1221 1830	2.5 0.7 2.3 0.7
5	SA	0049 0649 1300 1911	2.3 0.9 2.3 0.8
6	SU	0141 0727 1343 2000	2.2 1.1 2.2 0.9
7	M ☽	0254 0811 1437 2110	2.1 1.2 2.1 1.0
8	TU	0417 0921 1549 2252	2.1 1.4 2.1 1.0
9	W	0528 1132 1703 2354	2.1 1.3 2.1 0.9
10	TH	0636 1228 1804	2.1 1.3 2.1
11	F	0044 0727 1312 1857	0.8 2.2 1.2 2.2
12	SA	0128 0803 1347 1941	0.8 2.2 1.0 2.3
13	SU	0206 0832 1420 2020	0.7 2.3 0.9 2.4
14	M	0242 0859 1454 2058	0.6 2.3 0.8 2.4
15	TU O	0319 0930 1531 2137	0.5 2.4 0.7 2.5
16	W	0356 1003 1610 2216	0.5 2.4 0.6 2.5
17	TH	0434 1039 1650 2255	0.5 2.5 0.6 2.5
18	F	0511 1116 1729 2337	0.5 2.5 0.6 2.5
19	SA	0550 1156 1811	0.6 2.4 0.6
20	SU	0023 0630 1240 1858	2.4 0.8 2.4 0.7
21	M	0115 0716 1330 1954	2.3 0.9 2.3 0.7
22	TU ☾	0220 0812 1428 2108	2.2 1.1 2.3 0.7
23	W	0354 0930 1537 2235	2.2 1.2 2.2 0.7
24	TH	0517 1101 1654 2343	2.2 1.2 2.2 0.6
25	F	0622 1208 1800	2.3 1.1 2.3
26	SA	0044 0717 1308 1858	0.5 2.4 1.0 2.4
27	SU	0141 0803 1402 1951	0.5 2.4 0.8 2.5
28	M	0232 0843 1450 2042	0.4 2.4 0.7 2.5
29	TU ●	0317 0922 1534 2130	0.4 2.5 0.6 2.6
30	W	0358 1001 1615 2216	0.5 2.5 0.5 2.5

MAY

Date	Day	Time	m
1	TH	0436 1039 1655 2302	0.5 2.5 0.5 2.5
2	F	0512 1117 1733 2346	0.7 2.4 0.6 2.4
3	SA	0545 1153 1811	0.8 2.4 0.6
4	SU	0031 0617 1231 1851	2.3 0.9 2.4 0.7
5	M	0119 0651 1311 1935	2.2 1.1 2.3 0.8
6	TU	0217 0731 1358 2029	2.1 1.2 2.2 0.9
7	W ☽	0335 0819 1453 2150	2.1 1.3 2.2 0.9
8	TH	0444 0927 1603 2305	2.1 1.4 2.1 0.9
9	F	0543 1129 1713 2357	2.1 1.3 2.1 0.9
10	SA	0635 1219 1810	2.2 1.2 2.2
11	SU	0042 0717 1302 1859	0.8 2.2 1.1 2.2
12	M	0123 0752 1342 1945	0.7 2.3 1.0 2.3
13	TU	0204 0826 1424 2028	0.6 2.4 0.8 2.4
14	W O	0246 0901 1507 2111	0.6 2.4 0.7 2.4
15	TH	0328 0938 1551 2154	0.5 2.5 0.6 2.5
16	F	0410 1016 1636 2239	0.5 2.5 0.5 2.5
17	SA	0452 1057 1721 2326	0.6 2.5 0.5 2.5
18	SU	0535 1140 1808	0.7 2.5 0.5
19	M	0016 0619 1226 1857	2.4 0.8 2.5 0.5
20	TU	0111 0706 1316 1954	2.4 0.9 2.4 0.5
21	W ☾	0215 0800 1411 2101	2.3 1.0 2.4 0.6
22	TH	0344 0907 1514 2214	2.2 1.1 2.3 0.6
23	F	0459 1029 1628 2319	2.3 1.2 2.3 0.6
24	SA	0601 1140 1737	2.3 1.1 2.3
25	SU	0019 0655 1243 1837	0.6 2.3 1.0 2.3
26	M	0116 0742 1341 1934	0.6 2.4 0.9 2.4
27	TU	0208 0823 1431 2028	0.6 2.4 0.8 2.4
28	W ●	0253 0903 1517 2118	0.6 2.5 0.6 2.4
29	TH	0334 0941 1559 2205	0.7 2.5 0.6 2.4
30	F	0412 1019 1639 2249	0.7 2.5 0.6 2.4
31	SA	0447 1055 1717 2332	0.8 2.5 0.6 2.3

JUNE

Date	Day	Time	m
1	SU	0519 1130 1754	0.9 2.5 0.6
2	M	0012 0548 1206 1831	2.2 1.0 2.4 0.7
3	TU	0053 0621 1244 1910	2.2 1.0 2.4 0.7
4	W	0136 0658 1327 1953	2.1 1.1 2.3 0.8
5	TH ☽	0228 0742 1414 2045	2.1 1.2 2.3 0.9
6	F	0343 0834 1508 2151	2.1 1.3 2.2 0.9
7	SA	0449 0940 1616 2300	2.1 1.3 2.2 0.9
8	SU	0542 1110 1725 2355	2.1 1.3 2.2 0.8
9	M	0630 1215 1821	2.2 1.2 2.2
10	TU	0043 0713 1307 1912	0.8 2.3 1.0 2.3
11	W	0130 0754 1356 2001	0.7 2.4 0.9 2.3
12	TH	0217 0834 1445 2050	0.6 2.4 0.7 2.4
13	F O	0304 0915 1535 2139	0.6 2.5 0.6 2.5
14	SA	0351 0957 1624 2228	0.6 2.6 0.5 2.5
15	SU	0437 1041 1713 2317	0.6 2.6 0.4 2.5
16	M	0523 1126 1802	0.7 2.6 0.3
17	TU	0007 0608 1213 1851	2.5 0.8 2.6 0.4
18	W	0100 0654 1301 1944	2.4 0.9 2.6 0.4
19	TH ☾	0159 0743 1353 2041	2.3 1.0 2.5 0.5
20	F	0317 0840 1451 2146	2.3 1.1 2.4 0.6
21	SA	0432 0951 1603 2252	2.2 1.1 2.4 0.7
22	SU	0533 1109 1717 2354	2.3 1.1 2.3 0.7
23	M	0629 1218 1822	2.3 1.1 2.3
24	TU	0052 0721 1321 1925	0.8 2.3 1.0 2.3
25	W	0146 0806 1416 2023	0.8 2.4 0.8 2.3
26	TH	0234 0846 1503 2112	0.8 2.4 0.7 2.3
27	F ●	0315 0924 1545 2156	0.8 2.5 0.6 2.3
28	SA	0352 1000 1625 2236	0.9 2.5 0.6 2.3
29	SU	0425 1035 1701 2314	0.9 2.5 0.6 2.3
30	M	0455 1108 1736 2348	0.9 2.5 0.6 2.3

SUNRISE AND SUNSET TIMES

LOWESTOFT
At 52°28′N 1°45′E

		Sunrise	Sunset
UT			
Jan	01	0804	1550
	15	0756	1609
Feb	01	0734	1640
	15	0709	1706
Mar	01	0639	1732
	15	0607	1758
BST			
Apr	01	0627	1927
	15	0555	1952
May	01	0522	2020
	15	0457	2043
Jun	01	0436	2106
	15	0430	2117
Jul	01	0435	2119
	15	0449	2109
Aug	01	0513	2045
	15	0536	2018
Sep	01	0604	1941
	15	0627	1908
Oct	01	0654	1830
	15	0718	1758
UT			
Nov	01	0649	1623
	15	0715	1600
Dec	01	0741	1543
	15	0757	1539

LOWESTOFT
LAT 52°28′N
LONG 1°45′E

TIMES AND HEIGHTS OF HIGH AND LOW WATER (Heights in Metres)

TIME ZONE UT
For Summer Time (area enclosed in shaded box) add 1 hour

2014

JULY

Day	Time	m	Day	Time	m
1 TU	0524 1142 1810	0.9 2.5 0.6	16 W	0554 1155 1837	0.7 2.8 0.3
2 W	0022 0555 1219 1843	2.2 1.0 2.5 0.7	17 TH	0040 0637 1242 1923	2.5 0.8 2.7 0.4
3 TH	0058 0631 1258 1920	2.2 1.0 2.4 0.8	18 F	0133 0722 1331 2013	2.4 0.9 2.6 0.5
4 F	0137 0712 1340 2001	2.2 1.1 2.4 0.8	19 SA	0235 0811 1427 ☾ 2111	2.3 1.0 2.5 0.7
5 SA	0223 0758 1426 ☽ 2051	2.1 1.2 2.3 0.9	20 SU	0355 0913 1540 2220	2.2 1.1 2.4 0.8
6 SU	0325 0853 1521 2154	2.1 1.2 2.3 0.9	21 M	0459 1038 1700 2328	2.2 1.2 2.3 0.9
7 M	0448 1005 1636 2307	2.1 1.3 2.2 0.9	22 TU	0559 1156 1812	2.3 1.1 2.3
8 TU	0546 1132 1747	2.2 1.2 2.2	23 W	0030 0657 1304 1924	1.0 2.3 1.0 2.3
9 W	0008 0636 1236 1845	0.9 2.3 1.0 2.3	24 TH	0129 0748 1402 2021	1.0 2.4 0.9 2.3
10 TH	0102 0724 1332 1941	0.8 2.4 0.9 2.4	25 F	0218 0829 1449 2105	1.0 2.4 0.8 2.3
11 F	0153 0809 1427 2035	0.8 2.5 0.7 2.4	26 SA	0259 0906 1529 ● 2143	1.0 2.5 0.7 2.3
12 SA	0244 0854 1521 ○ 2127	0.7 2.6 0.5 2.5	27 SU	0334 0939 1606 2218	0.9 2.5 0.6 2.4
13 SU	0335 0939 1613 2217	0.7 2.6 0.4 2.6	28 M	0404 1012 1640 2249	0.9 2.6 0.6 2.3
14 M	0423 1025 1702 2305	0.6 2.7 0.3 2.6	29 TU	0433 1044 1713 2319	0.9 2.6 0.6 2.3
15 TU	0510 1110 1750 2352	0.7 2.8 0.2 2.5	30 W	0501 1118 1744 2350	0.9 2.6 0.6 2.3
			31 TH	0533 1153 1816	0.9 2.6 0.7

AUGUST

Day	Time	m	Day	Time	m
1 F	0023 0607 1230 1848	2.3 1.0 2.5 0.7	16 SA	0102 0658 1309 1941	2.4 0.8 2.7 0.6
2 SA	0059 0645 1308 1925	2.3 1.0 2.5 0.8	17 SU	0154 0745 1404 ☾ 2032	2.3 0.9 2.5 0.8
3 SU	0140 0728 1351 2008	2.2 1.1 2.4 0.9	18 M	0301 0841 1519 2139	2.3 1.1 2.4 1.0
4 M	0229 0818 1442 ☽ 2102	2.2 1.2 2.3 1.0	19 TU	0416 1006 1644 2300	2.2 1.1 2.3 1.1
5 TU	0334 0922 1551 2217	2.2 1.2 2.3 1.0	20 W	0521 1134 1801	2.3 1.1 2.2
6 W	0459 1054 1718 2337	2.2 1.2 2.3 1.0	21 TH	0010 0624 1243 1916	1.2 2.3 1.0 2.3
7 TH	0601 1211 1826	2.3 1.0 2.3	22 F	0111 0722 1341 2009	1.2 2.4 0.9 2.3
8 F	0038 0654 1312 1927	0.9 2.4 0.9 2.4	23 SA	0200 0806 1427 2049	1.1 2.4 0.8 2.3
9 SA	0133 0744 1410 2024	0.9 2.5 0.7 2.5	24 SU	0239 0842 1505 2123	1.1 2.5 0.7 2.4
10 SU	0227 0833 1506 ○ 2115	0.8 2.6 0.5 2.6	25 M	0312 0913 1540 ● 2153	1.0 2.6 0.7 2.4
11 M	0319 0919 1558 2201	0.7 2.7 0.3 2.6	26 TU	0340 0944 1612 2220	0.9 2.6 0.6 2.4
12 TU	0408 1005 1646 2246	0.7 2.8 0.2 2.6	27 W	0408 1017 1643 2248	0.9 2.6 0.6 2.4
13 W	0452 1050 1731 2330	0.6 2.9 0.2 2.6	28 TH	0438 1051 1714 2319	0.8 2.6 0.6 2.4
14 TH	0535 1135 1814	0.7 2.9 0.3	29 F	0511 1126 1746 2352	0.9 2.6 0.7 2.4
15 F	0015 0616 1221 1857	2.5 0.7 2.8 0.4	30 SA	0545 1202 1818	0.9 2.6 0.7
			31 SU	0027 0621 1240 1853	2.4 0.9 2.5 0.8

SEPTEMBER

Day	Time	m	Day	Time	m
1 M	0107 0702 1322 1934	2.3 1.0 2.4 0.9	16 TU	0210 0814 1458 ☾ 2047	2.3 1.0 2.3 1.2
2 TU	0153 0751 1413 ☽ 2025	2.3 1.1 2.4 1.0	17 W	0319 0933 1625 2224	2.3 1.1 2.2 1.3
3 W	0250 0853 1522 2134	2.3 1.1 2.3 1.1	18 TH	0432 1107 1741 2344	2.3 1.1 2.2 1.3
4 TH	0407 1027 1700 2309	2.3 1.1 2.3 1.1	19 F	0537 1213 1854	2.3 1.0 2.3
5 F	0525 1150 1814	2.3 1.0 2.4	20 SA	0044 0639 1308 1946	1.3 2.3 0.9 2.3
6 SA	0017 0624 1253 1917	1.1 2.4 0.8 2.4	21 SU	0133 0729 1354 2025	1.2 2.4 0.8 2.4
7 SU	0115 0718 1352 2011	1.0 2.5 0.6 2.5	22 M	0211 0807 1432 2056	1.1 2.5 0.8 2.4
8 M	0210 0808 1448 2058	0.9 2.7 0.4 2.6	23 TU	0242 0840 1506 2122	1.0 2.5 0.7 2.4
9 TU	0302 0856 1538 ○ 2141	0.8 2.8 0.3 2.6	24 W	0311 0913 1538 ● 2148	0.9 2.6 0.6 2.5
10 W	0349 0943 1624 2224	0.7 2.9 0.2 2.6	25 TH	0341 0948 1610 2217	0.9 2.6 0.6 2.5
11 TH	0432 1029 1707 2306	0.6 2.9 0.3 2.6	26 F	0414 1024 1643 2249	0.8 2.6 0.6 2.5
12 F	0514 1114 1748 2348	0.6 2.9 0.4 2.5	27 SA	0449 1100 1716 2323	0.8 2.6 0.7 2.5
13 SA	0555 1200 1828	0.7 2.8 0.5	28 SU	0525 1137 1750 2359	0.8 2.6 0.7 2.5
14 SU	0031 0636 1248 1908	2.5 0.8 2.6 0.8	29 M	0602 1216 1826	0.9 2.5 0.8
15 M	0117 0721 1343 1952	2.4 0.9 2.5 1.0	30 TU	0039 0643 1301 1907	2.4 0.9 2.4 0.9

OCTOBER

Day	Time	m	Day	Time	m
1 W	0126 0733 1355 ☽ 1958	2.4 1.0 2.4 1.1	16 TH	0224 0856 1557 2101	2.3 1.1 2.2 1.4
2 TH	0221 0836 1507 2104	2.3 1.0 2.3 1.2	17 F	0331 1030 1708 2304	2.3 1.1 2.2 1.5
3 F	0329 1010 1651 2242	2.3 1.0 2.3 1.2	18 SA	0443 1135 1816	2.3 1.0 2.3
4 SA	0448 1130 1803 2355	2.4 0.9 2.4 1.2	19 SU	0006 0544 1228 1911	1.4 2.3 0.9 2.3
5 SU	0555 1233 1903	2.4 0.7 2.5	20 M	0055 0637 1313 1951	1.3 2.3 0.9 2.4
6 M	0054 0651 1331 1953	1.1 2.5 0.6 2.5	21 TU	0133 0722 1352 2021	1.2 2.4 0.8 2.4
7 TU	0150 0743 1426 2037	0.9 2.7 0.5 2.6	22 W	0206 0802 1427 2047	1.1 2.5 0.7 2.5
8 W	0241 0832 1515 ○ 2119	0.8 2.8 0.4 2.6	23 TH	0238 0840 1501 ● 2115	1.0 2.5 0.7 2.5
9 TH	0328 0921 1600 2200	0.7 2.8 0.3 2.7	24 F	0313 0918 1537 2147	0.9 2.6 0.6 2.6
10 F	0411 1008 1641 2241	0.6 2.8 0.4 2.6	25 SA	0351 0957 1613 2221	0.8 2.6 0.6 2.6
11 SA	0453 1055 1720 2322	0.6 2.8 0.5 2.6	26 SU	0430 1036 1650 2257	0.8 2.6 0.7 2.6
12 SU	0535 1141 1758	0.7 2.7 0.7	27 M	0509 1116 1727 2336	0.8 2.6 0.8 2.6
13 M	0003 0615 1230 1835	2.5 0.7 2.5 0.9	28 TU	0550 1159 1806	0.8 2.5 0.9
14 TU	0045 0659 1324 1914	2.5 0.8 2.4 1.1	29 W	0018 0634 1248 1849	2.5 0.8 2.4 1.0
15 W	0130 0749 1433 ☾ 1959	2.4 1.0 2.3 1.3	30 TH	0105 0726 1345 1940	2.5 0.9 2.4 1.1
			31 F	0159 0830 1459 ☽ 2044	2.4 0.9 2.3 1.2

NOVEMBER

Day	Time	m	Day	Time	m
1 SA	0301 0954 1639 2212	2.4 0.9 2.3 1.3	16 SU	0340 1047 1725 2306	2.3 1.0 2.2 1.5
2 SU	0415 1109 1747 2329	2.4 0.8 2.4 1.2	17 M	0451 1142 1819	2.3 1.0 2.2
3 M	0526 1210 1844	2.5 0.7 2.5	18 TU	0003 0549 1228 1903	1.4 2.3 0.9 2.3
4 TU	0030 0625 1308 1933	1.1 2.5 0.6 2.5	19 W	0047 0640 1309 1939	1.3 2.3 0.9 2.4
5 W	0127 0719 1402 2016	1.0 2.6 0.5 2.6	20 TH	0126 0726 1347 2011	1.1 2.4 0.8 2.4
6 TH	0220 0811 1451 ○ 2057	0.9 2.7 0.5 2.6	21 F	0206 0809 1426 2044	1.0 2.5 0.7 2.5
7 F	0308 0902 1535 2137	0.7 2.7 0.5 2.6	22 SA	0247 0852 1506 ● 2119	0.9 2.5 0.7 2.6
8 SA	0353 0951 1616 2218	0.6 2.7 0.6 2.6	23 SU	0330 0934 1547 2157	0.8 2.5 0.7 2.6
9 SU	0436 1039 1654 2258	0.6 2.6 0.7 2.6	24 M	0413 1017 1628 2236	0.7 2.6 0.7 2.6
10 M	0517 1126 1731 2338	0.6 2.5 0.8 2.6	25 TU	0458 1102 1710 2317	0.7 2.6 0.7 2.6
11 TU	0558 1213 1805	0.7 2.4 1.0	26 W	0543 1149 1753	0.6 2.5 0.8
12 W	0017 0639 1303 1840	2.5 0.8 2.3 1.1	27 TH	0001 0631 1240 1837	2.6 0.7 2.4 1.0
13 TH	0058 0724 1359 1918	2.5 0.9 2.2 1.3	28 F	0049 0723 1336 1927	2.6 0.7 2.4 1.1
14 F	0143 0817 1513 ☾ 2003	2.4 1.0 2.2 1.4	29 SA	0140 0823 1445 ☽ 2024	2.5 0.7 2.3 1.2
15 SA	0236 0930 1624 2102	2.3 1.0 2.2 1.5	30 SU	0237 0933 1618 2137	2.5 0.7 2.3 1.2

DECEMBER

Day	Time	m	Day	Time	m
1 M	0345 1044 1725 2257	2.4 0.7 2.3 1.2	16 TU	0349 1040 1723 2236	2.3 1.0 2.2 1.4
2 TU	0500 1146 1821	2.4 0.7 2.4	17 W	0502 1138 1812 2355	2.2 1.0 2.2 1.3
3 W	0004 0603 1244 1911	1.1 2.5 0.7 2.4	18 TH	0602 1226 1856	2.3 0.9 2.3
4 TH	0105 0701 1339 1956	1.0 2.5 0.7 2.5	19 F	0047 0653 1312 1937	1.1 2.3 0.8 2.4
5 F	0202 0757 1429 2038	0.9 2.5 0.7 2.5	20 SA	0136 0742 1356 2016	1.0 2.4 0.8 2.5
6 SA	0252 0851 1513 ○ 2119	0.8 2.5 0.7 2.6	21 SU	0223 0830 1441 2056	0.9 2.4 0.7 2.5
7 SU	0338 0941 1554 2159	0.7 2.5 0.8 2.6	22 M	0311 0917 1526 ● 2136	0.7 2.5 0.7 2.6
8 M	0421 1028 1632 2238	0.6 2.5 0.8 2.6	23 TU	0400 1004 1612 2218	0.6 2.5 0.7 2.7
9 TU	0502 1113 1706 2315	0.6 2.4 0.9 2.6	24 W	0448 1051 1657 2302	0.5 2.6 0.7 2.7
10 W	0541 1155 1738 2352	0.7 2.4 1.0 2.5	25 TH	0536 1139 1742 2346	0.5 2.5 0.8 2.7
11 TH	0620 1236 1809	0.7 2.3 1.1	26 F	0624 1228 1826	0.5 2.5 0.9
12 F	0029 0658 1319 1843	2.5 0.8 2.2 1.2	27 SA	0033 0713 1320 1912	2.7 0.5 2.4 1.0
13 SA	0110 0739 1406 1923	2.4 0.9 2.2 1.2	28 SU	0122 0806 1420 ☽ 2002	2.6 0.6 2.3 1.1
14 SU	0155 0826 1510 ☾ 2011	2.4 1.0 2.1 1.3	29 M	0215 0906 1544 2103	2.5 0.7 2.2 1.2
15 M	0246 0927 1626 2109	2.3 1.0 2.1 1.4	30 TU	0318 1014 1656 2222	2.5 0.7 2.3 1.2
			31 W	0438 1121 1755 2340	2.4 0.8 2.3 1.1

IMMINGHAM
LAT 53°38′N
LONG 0°11′W

TIMES AND HEIGHTS OF HIGH AND LOW WATER (Heights in Metres)

TIME ZONE UT
For Summer Time (area enclosed in shaded box) add 1 hour

2014

JANUARY

Day	Time	m	Day	Time	m
1 W ●	0521	7.2	16 TH O	0005	1.4
	1141	1.1		0602	6.6
	1741	7.4		1212	1.6
				1811	7.0
2 TH	0012	0.9	17 F	0044	1.3
	0613	7.4		0636	6.7
	1232	1.0		1248	1.6
	1827	7.6		1845	7.0
3 F	0104	0.6	18 SA	0120	1.3
	0703	7.5		0709	6.7
	1320	0.9		1320	1.6
	1912	7.7		1917	7.0
4 SA	0153	0.5	19 SU	0152	1.3
	0751	7.4		0741	6.7
	1405	0.9		1349	1.6
	1956	7.7		1948	7.0
5 SU	0240	0.5	20 M	0222	1.4
	0838	7.3		0814	6.7
	1449	1.1		1417	1.6
	2041	7.6		2018	6.9
6 M	0325	0.8	21 TU	0249	1.5
	0925	7.0		0845	6.6
	1533	1.4		1447	1.7
	2128	7.3		2047	6.8
7 TU	0411	1.1	22 W	0319	1.6
	1016	6.7		0919	6.4
	1618	1.8		1521	1.9
	2220	6.9		2122	6.6
8 W ☽	0500	1.6	23 TH	0355	1.8
	1113	6.3		0959	6.2
	1708	2.2		1602	2.1
	2321	6.5		2206	6.4
9 TH	0554	2.0	24 F ☾	0442	2.0
	1215	6.0		1048	6.0
	1808	2.5		1657	2.3
				2302	6.2
10 F	0029	6.2	25 SA	0546	2.2
	0658	2.3		1154	5.9
	1319	5.9		1809	2.5
	1925	2.6			
11 SA	0141	6.0	26 SU	0015	6.0
	0809	2.4		0701	2.3
	1423	5.9		1321	5.9
	2044	2.5		1931	2.5
12 SU	0249	6.0	27 M	0150	6.0
	0912	2.3		0819	2.2
	1522	6.1		1439	6.1
	2147	2.2		2051	2.2
13 M	0350	6.2	28 TU	0313	6.3
	1005	2.1		0929	1.9
	1613	6.4		1543	6.5
	2238	1.9		2203	1.7
14 TU	0441	6.4	29 W	0419	6.7
	1051	1.9		1031	1.5
	1657	6.7		1638	7.0
	2323	1.6		2306	1.2
15 W	0524	6.5	30 TH ●	0516	7.1
	1133	1.8		1127	1.2
	1736	6.9		1728	7.4
			31 F	0002	0.8
				0607	7.3
				1219	0.9
				1814	7.7

FEBRUARY

Day	Time	m	Day	Time	m
1 SA	0053	0.4	16 SU	0100	1.2
	0654	7.5		0646	6.8
	1306	0.7		1302	1.4
	1859	7.8		1855	7.1
2 SU	0140	0.3	17 M	0133	1.2
	0738	7.5		0718	6.9
	1350	0.7		1331	1.4
	1942	7.9		1927	7.1
3 M	0223	0.4	18 TU	0202	1.2
	0820	7.4		0749	6.9
	1432	0.8		1359	1.4
	2024	7.7		1956	7.1
4 TU	0304	0.6	19 W	0228	1.3
	0900	7.1		0819	6.8
	1510	1.1		1428	1.4
	2107	7.4		2026	7.0
5 W	0343	1.0	20 TH	0255	1.4
	0942	6.8		0850	6.7
	1548	1.5		1459	1.6
	2151	7.0		2059	6.8
6 TH ☽	0420	1.6	21 F	0326	1.6
	1027	6.3		0927	6.5
	1628	2.0		1537	1.8
	2242	6.5		2141	6.6
7 F	0502	2.1	22 SA ☾	0407	1.9
	1121	5.9		1013	6.2
	1716	2.4		1626	2.1
	2347	6.0		2235	6.2
8 SA	0556	2.5	23 SU	0508	2.2
	1229	5.7		1114	5.9
	1821	2.7		1738	2.3
				2347	5.9
9 SU	0105	5.7	24 M	0630	2.4
	0711	2.8		1239	5.8
	1341	5.6		1906	2.4
	2004	2.8			
10 M	0222	5.7	25 TU	0135	5.9
	0839	2.7		0756	2.4
	1449	5.8		1414	6.0
	2124	2.5		2034	2.1
11 TU	0330	5.9	26 W	0307	6.2
	0941	2.4		0913	2.0
	1547	6.1		1524	6.4
	2217	2.1		2151	1.6
12 W	0424	6.1	27 TH	0413	6.6
	1030	2.1		1017	1.6
	1634	6.5		1621	6.9
	2302	1.7		2253	1.1
13 TH	0506	6.4	28 F	0507	7.0
	1113	1.8		1112	1.2
	1714	6.7		1711	7.3
	2344	1.4		2347	0.6
14 F O	0542	6.6			
	1152	1.6			
	1749	6.9			
15 SA	0023	1.3			
	0614	6.7			
	1229	1.5			
	1822	7.0			

MARCH

Day	Time	m	Day	Time	m
1 SA ●	0555	7.3	16 SU O	0547	6.7
	1202	0.8		1204	1.4
	1758	7.6		1755	7.0
2 SU	0035	0.4	17 M	0032	1.1
	0638	7.5		0619	6.9
	1249	0.7		1239	1.3
	1841	7.8		1829	7.1
3 M	0120	0.3	18 TU	0107	1.1
	0718	7.5		0651	7.0
	1331	0.6		1310	1.2
	1924	7.8		1903	7.1
4 TU	0201	0.4	19 W	0137	1.1
	0756	7.4		0723	7.0
	1411	0.7		1341	1.2
	2004	7.7		1935	7.2
5 W	0238	0.7	20 TH	0206	1.1
	0831	7.2		0754	7.0
	1447	1.0		1412	1.2
	2044	7.4		2008	7.1
6 TH	0311	1.1	21 F	0235	1.3
	0906	6.8		0827	6.9
	1520	1.4		1445	1.3
	2123	6.9		2044	6.9
7 F	0342	1.6	22 SA	0308	1.5
	0942	6.4		0904	6.7
	1554	1.8		1524	1.5
	2207	6.4		2127	6.6
8 SA ☽	0418	2.1	23 SU	0349	1.8
	1025	6.0		0951	6.4
	1637	2.2		1614	1.9
	2304	5.9		2222	6.2
9 SU	0505	2.6	24 M ☾	0448	2.2
	1130	5.6		1051	6.0
	1735	2.6		1726	2.2
				2339	5.8
10 M	0027	5.5	25 TU	0611	2.5
	0611	2.9		1216	5.9
	1258	5.5		1853	2.2
	1856	2.8			
11 TU	0152	5.4	26 W	0134	5.8
	0747	3.0		0739	2.4
	1413	5.6		1352	6.0
	2052	2.6		2021	2.0
12 W	0302	5.7	27 TH	0258	6.2
	0912	2.6		0856	2.1
	1515	5.9		1504	6.4
	2149	2.2		2136	1.5
13 TH	0358	6.0	28 F	0400	6.6
	1004	2.2		0959	1.6
	1605	6.3		1601	6.9
	2234	1.8		2235	1.0
14 F	0441	6.3	29 SA	0452	7.0
	1047	1.9		1053	1.2
	1645	6.6		1651	7.3
	2315	1.4		2326	0.7
15 SA	0516	6.6	30 SU ●	0536	7.2
	1127	1.6		1142	0.9
	1721	6.8		1737	7.5
	2355	1.2			
			31 M	0013	0.5
				0616	7.4
				1228	0.7
				1821	7.6

APRIL

Day	Time	m	Day	Time	m
1 TU	0056	0.5	16 W	0036	1.0
	0654	7.4		0624	7.1
	1310	0.7		1247	1.1
	1903	7.6		1839	7.2
2 W	0135	0.6	17 TH	0112	1.0
	0729	7.3		0659	7.1
	1349	0.8		1323	1.1
	1943	7.5		1916	7.2
3 TH	0210	0.9	18 F	0146	1.0
	0803	7.1		0734	7.1
	1423	1.0		1359	1.0
	2021	7.2		1954	7.1
4 F	0241	1.2	19 SA	0220	1.2
	0834	6.9		0810	7.1
	1455	1.3		1438	1.1
	2059	6.8		2036	7.0
5 SA	0310	1.7	20 SU	0258	1.4
	0906	6.5		0850	6.9
	1528	1.7		1521	1.4
	2138	6.3		2123	6.6
6 SU	0343	2.1	21 M	0343	1.8
	0943	6.1		0939	6.5
	1609	2.1		1615	1.6
	2226	5.8		2222	6.2
7 M ☽	0426	2.5	22 TU ☾	0442	2.1
	1035	5.8		1040	6.2
	1702	2.4		1725	1.9
	2341	5.4		2344	5.9
8 TU	0527	2.9	23 W	0559	2.4
	1201	5.5		1202	6.1
	1813	2.7		1845	1.9
9 W	0112	5.4	24 TH	0124	6.0
	0646	3.0		0720	2.4
	1329	5.5		1329	6.2
	1943	2.6		2004	1.7
10 TH	0224	5.6	25 F	0239	6.2
	0820	2.8		0834	2.1
	1435	5.8		1439	6.5
	2103	2.2		2112	1.4
11 F	0321	5.9	26 SA	0339	6.6
	0925	2.4		0936	1.7
	1526	6.1		1537	6.8
	2154	1.9		2210	1.1
12 SA	0405	6.2	27 SU	0430	6.9
	1012	2.0		1030	1.3
	1608	6.4		1629	7.1
	2238	1.5		2300	0.9
13 SU	0441	6.5	28 M	0513	7.1
	1054	1.7		1119	1.1
	1646	6.7		1716	7.2
	2320	1.3		2347	0.8
14 M	0515	6.7	29 TU ●	0552	7.2
	1133	1.5		1205	0.9
	1724	6.9		1801	7.3
	2359	1.1			
15 TU O	0550	6.9	30 W	0029	0.8
	1210	1.3		0628	7.2
	1802	7.0		1249	0.9
				1843	7.3

MAY

Day	Time	m	Day	Time	m
1 TH	0108	0.9	16 F	0048	1.0
	0704	7.2		0638	7.2
	1328	0.9		1308	0.9
	1924	7.2		1902	7.2
2 F	0143	1.1	17 SA	0129	1.0
	0737	7.0		0718	7.3
	1403	1.1		1351	0.9
	2002	6.9		1946	7.2
3 SA	0214	1.4	18 SU	0210	1.1
	0808	6.9		0758	7.2
	1436	1.3		1436	0.9
	2038	6.6		2032	7.0
4 SU	0244	1.7	19 M	0252	1.3
	0839	6.6		0842	7.1
	1509	1.6		1523	1.1
	2115	6.3		2123	6.7
5 M	0317	2.0	20 TU	0340	1.6
	0914	6.3		0932	6.8
	1548	1.9		1618	1.3
	2157	5.9		2223	6.4
6 TU	0356	2.4	21 W ☾	0436	1.9
	0959	6.0		1032	6.5
	1636	2.2		1721	1.5
	2255	5.6		2340	6.2
7 W ☽	0448	2.7	22 TH	0543	2.2
	1104	5.7		1146	6.3
	1737	2.4		1829	1.6
8 TH	0013	5.5	23 F	0059	6.1
	0555	2.9		0655	2.2
	1228	5.6		1303	6.3
	1846	2.4		1939	1.6
9 F	0128	5.5	24 SA	0209	6.2
	0711	2.8		0806	2.1
	1339	5.7		1411	6.4
	1957	2.3		2044	1.5
10 SA	0229	5.8	25 SU	0310	6.4
	0823	2.6		0910	1.8
	1437	6.0		1512	6.6
	2101	2.0		2142	1.4
11 SU	0319	6.1	26 M	0402	6.6
	0923	2.2		1006	1.6
	1525	6.3		1607	6.8
	2153	1.7		2234	1.3
12 M	0402	6.4	27 TU	0447	6.8
	1012	1.9		1057	1.3
	1610	6.5		1657	6.9
	2240	1.4		2321	1.2
13 TU	0442	6.7	28 W ●	0527	6.9
	1058	1.6		1145	1.2
	1653	6.8		1743	6.9
	2324	1.2			
14 W O	0521	6.9	29 TH	0004	1.2
	1142	1.3		0605	7.0
	1736	7.0		1229	1.1
				1826	6.9
15 TH	0007	1.1	30 F	0044	1.3
	0600	7.1		0641	7.0
	1225	1.1		1310	1.1
	1818	7.1		1907	6.9
			31 SA	0120	1.4
				0716	7.0
				1347	1.2
				1944	6.7

JUNE

Day	Time	m	Day	Time	m
1 SU	0153	1.5	16 M	0200	1.0
	0748	6.9		0749	7.5
	1421	1.3		1432	0.6
	2019	6.6		2029	7.2
2 M	0224	1.7	17 TU	0245	1.1
	0820	6.7		0835	7.4
	1454	1.5		1521	0.7
	2054	6.4		2120	7.0
3 TU	0255	1.9	18 W	0332	1.3
	0854	6.5		0924	7.1
	1530	1.8		1611	1.0
	2132	6.1		2216	6.7
4 W	0331	2.2	19 TH ☾	0423	1.6
	0933	6.2		1020	6.9
	1612	2.0		1706	1.2
	2218	5.9		2319	6.4
5 TH ☽	0414	2.4	20 F	0520	1.9
	1022	6.0		1124	6.6
	1702	2.1		1806	1.5
	2315	5.7			
6 F	0509	2.6	21 SA	0026	6.2
	1125	5.8		0624	2.2
	1800	2.2		1233	6.4
				1909	1.7
7 SA	0022	5.7	22 SU	0132	6.1
	0613	2.7		0735	2.2
	1236	5.8		1342	6.3
	1901	2.2		2014	1.8
8 SU	0129	5.8	23 M	0234	6.2
	0721	2.6		0843	2.1
	1342	5.9		1447	6.3
	2005	2.1		2115	1.8
9 M	0229	6.0	24 TU	0332	6.3
	0827	2.4		0944	1.9
	1441	6.1		1547	6.4
	2105	1.8		2209	1.7
10 TU	0322	6.3	25 W	0421	6.5
	0928	2.0		1038	1.6
	1535	6.4		1641	6.5
	2200	1.6		2257	1.6
11 W	0410	6.6	26 TH	0504	6.7
	1024	1.7		1127	1.4
	1626	6.7		1729	6.6
	2252	1.4		2342	1.6
12 TH	0455	6.9	27 F ●	0544	6.8
	1116	1.4		1212	1.3
	1715	6.9		1812	6.7
	2341	1.2			
13 F O	0539	7.1	28 SA	0023	1.5
	1207	1.0		0621	6.9
	1804	7.1		1254	1.2
				1850	6.7
14 SA	0029	1.0	29 SU	0101	1.5
	0622	7.3		0656	7.0
	1256	0.8		1332	1.2
	1852	7.3		1926	6.7
15 SU	0115	0.9	30 M	0135	1.6
	0705	7.4		0730	6.9
	1345	0.7		1407	1.3
	1941	7.3		1959	6.6

SUNRISE AND SUNSET TIMES

IMMINGHAM
At 53°38′N 0°11′W

		Sunrise	Sunset
UT			
Jan	01	0818	1551
	15	0809	1612
Feb	01	0746	1643
	15	0719	1711
Mar	01	0649	1738
	15	0615	1805
BST			
Apr	01	0634	1936
	15	0601	2002
May	01	0526	2031
	15	0500	2056
Jun	01	0438	2120
	15	0430	2132
Jul	01	0435	2133
	15	0450	2122
Aug	01	0516	2057
	15	0540	2029
Sep	01	0610	1951
	15	0634	1916
Oct	01	0703	1837
	15	0728	1804
UT			
Nov	01	0700	1628
	15	0727	1603
Dec	01	0754	1545
	15	0811	1540

IMMINGHAM
LAT 53°38'N
LONG 0°11'W

TIMES AND HEIGHTS OF HIGH AND LOW WATER (Heights in Metres)

TIME ZONE UT
For Summer Time (area enclosed in shaded box) add 1 hour

2014

JULY

Date	Day	Time	m
1	TU	0206 0802 1439 2032	1.7 6.8 1.4 6.5
2	W	0236 0834 1511 2106	1.8 6.7 1.6 6.4
3	TH	0307 0909 1545 2144	1.9 6.5 1.8 6.2
4	F	0343 0947 1625 2228	2.1 6.3 1.9 6.0
5	SA ☽	0427 1033 1713 2322	2.3 6.1 2.1 5.9
6	SU	0522 1132 1811	2.5 5.9 2.2
7	M	0029 0628 1244 1916	5.8 2.6 5.9 2.2
8	TU	0141 0739 1359 2023	5.9 2.5 6.0 2.0
9	W	0245 0850 1506 2127	6.1 2.2 6.3 1.8
10	TH	0342 0956 1606 2226	6.5 1.8 6.6 1.5
11	F	0433 1056 1702 2321	6.8 1.4 6.9 1.3
12	SA O	0522 1153 1755	7.2 1.0 7.2
13	SU	0013 0608 1246 1845	1.0 7.4 0.6 7.3
14	M	0102 0653 1336 1934	0.9 7.6 0.4 7.4
15	TU	0149 0738 1423 2020	0.8 7.7 0.4 7.4
16	W	0233 0823 1509 2107	0.9 7.7 0.5 7.2
17	TH	0318 0910 1555 2155	1.1 7.5 0.8 6.9
18	F	0403 1000 1642 2248	1.4 7.1 1.2 6.6
19	SA ☾	0451 1057 1734 2347	1.8 6.7 1.6 6.2
20	SU	0548 1201 1833	2.2 6.3 2.0
21	M	0050 0657 1312 1941	6.0 2.4 6.1 2.3
22	TU	0156 0817 1423 2049	5.9 2.4 6.0 2.3
23	W	0259 0925 1531 2147	6.1 2.2 6.1 2.2
24	TH	0355 1021 1628 2237	6.3 1.9 6.3 2.0
25	F	0442 1110 1715 2322	6.6 1.6 6.5 1.8
26	SA ●	0523 1154 1756	6.8 1.4 6.6
27	SU	0003 0600 1236 1831	1.6 6.9 1.2 6.7
28	M	0042 0635 1313 1904	1.6 7.0 1.2 6.7
29	TU	0117 0709 1348 1936	1.5 7.0 1.2 6.7
30	W	0147 0741 1420 2007	1.6 7.0 1.3 6.7
31	TH	0215 0813 1449 2039	1.6 6.9 1.4 6.6

AUGUST

Date	Day	Time	m
1	F	0243 0843 1516 2112	1.7 6.8 1.6 6.5
2	SA	0314 0915 1547 2148	1.9 6.6 1.8 6.3
3	SU	0351 0954 1628 2232	2.1 6.4 2.0 6.1
4	M ☽	0440 1044 1723 2331	2.3 6.1 2.2 5.9
5	TU	0545 1152 1834	2.5 5.9 2.3
6	W	0052 0702 1324 1949	5.8 2.5 5.9 2.3
7	TH	0213 0821 1449 2102	6.0 2.3 6.2 2.0
8	F	0319 0937 1556 2207	6.4 1.9 6.5 1.7
9	SA	0415 1042 1654 2305	6.8 1.4 6.9 1.3
10	SU O	0505 1140 1746 2358	7.3 0.9 7.2 1.0
11	M	0553 1232 1835	7.6 0.5 7.5
12	TU	0046 0638 1321 1920	0.8 7.8 0.3 7.6
13	W	0133 0722 1406 2003	0.7 7.9 0.2 7.5
14	TH	0216 0806 1449 2044	0.7 7.9 0.4 7.3
15	F	0257 0850 1529 2126	0.9 7.6 0.8 7.0
16	SA	0337 0935 1610 2211	1.3 7.2 1.3 6.6
17	SU ☾	0419 1027 1653 2303	1.8 6.7 1.8 6.2
18	M	0506 1128 1745	2.2 6.2 2.4
19	TU	0007 0610 1243 1857	5.9 2.6 5.8 2.7
20	W	0118 0748 1400 2022	5.8 2.7 5.7 2.7
21	TH	0227 0906 1511 2126	5.9 2.4 5.9 2.5
22	F	0328 1002 1610 2216	6.2 2.0 6.2 2.2
23	SA	0418 1049 1656 2301	6.5 1.7 6.4 1.9
24	SU	0459 1131 1734 2341	6.8 1.4 6.6 1.7
25	M ●	0536 1211 1807	7.0 1.2 6.8
26	TU	0019 0610 1249 1838	1.5 7.1 1.1 6.9
27	W	0055 0643 1324 1909	1.5 7.1 1.2 6.9
28	TH	0125 0716 1355 1940	1.5 7.1 1.2 6.9
29	F	0153 0748 1422 2010	1.5 7.1 1.3 6.8
30	SA	0219 0817 1447 2040	1.6 6.9 1.5 6.7
31	SU	0248 0848 1514 2113	1.7 6.8 1.7 6.5

SEPTEMBER

Date	Day	Time	m
1	M	0323 0925 1551 2154	1.9 6.6 1.9 6.3
2	TU ☽	0408 1013 1643 2249	2.2 6.2 2.3 6.0
3	W	0512 1121 1759	2.4 5.9 2.5
4	TH	0008 0635 1304 1924	5.8 2.5 5.8 2.5
5	F	0145 0802 1439 2044	6.0 2.3 6.1 2.2
6	SA	0258 0922 1546 2151	6.4 1.8 6.6 1.8
7	SU	0356 1028 1642 2248	6.9 1.3 7.0 1.4
8	M	0446 1123 1732 2339	7.3 0.8 7.3 1.0
9	TU O	0533 1213 1817	7.7 0.4 7.5
10	W	0027 0618 1300 1859	0.8 7.9 0.3 7.6
11	TH	0112 0702 1343 1938	0.7 8.0 0.3 7.6
12	F	0154 0744 1422 2016	0.7 7.9 0.6 7.4
13	SA	0233 0827 1459 2053	0.9 7.6 1.0 7.1
14	SU	0310 0909 1534 2132	1.3 7.2 1.5 6.7
15	M	0346 0956 1609 2218	1.7 6.6 2.0 6.2
16	TU ☾	0428 1054 1653 2320	2.2 6.1 2.6 5.9
17	W	0525 1211 1758	2.6 5.7 3.0
18	TH	0039 0656 1332 1940	5.7 2.8 5.6 3.0
19	F	0153 0839 1444 2059	5.8 2.6 5.8 2.8
20	SA	0257 0935 1542 2151	6.1 2.2 6.1 2.3
21	SU	0349 1020 1628 2234	6.4 1.8 6.4 2.0
22	M	0431 1102 1705 2314	6.7 1.5 6.7 1.7
23	TU	0507 1141 1737 2352	6.9 1.3 6.9 1.5
24	W ●	0541 1218 1808	7.1 1.2 7.0
25	TH	0027 0615 1254 1839	1.4 7.2 1.1 7.0
26	F	0059 0649 1326 1911	1.4 7.2 1.2 7.1
27	SA	0128 0722 1354 1942	1.4 7.2 1.3 7.0
28	SU	0157 0754 1420 2012	1.5 7.1 1.4 6.9
29	M	0228 0827 1450 2046	1.6 6.9 1.6 6.7
30	TU	0304 0906 1527 2127	1.7 6.6 1.9 6.5

OCTOBER

Date	Day	Time	m
1	W ☽	0349 0956 1618 2222	2.0 6.3 2.3 6.2
2	TH	0454 1107 1734 2340	2.3 5.9 2.6 5.9
3	F	0619 1257 1903	2.4 5.8 2.6
4	SA	0119 0746 1425 2024	6.1 2.2 6.1 2.3
5	SU	0234 0905 1530 2131	6.5 1.7 6.6 1.9
6	M	0333 1007 1624 2227	6.9 1.2 7.0 1.4
7	TU	0424 1100 1711 2317	7.3 0.8 7.3 1.1
8	W O	0511 1148 1754	7.6 0.6 7.5
9	TH	0005 0556 1234 1833	0.8 7.8 0.5 7.6
10	F	0049 0640 1316 1911	0.7 7.8 0.6 7.5
11	SA	0131 0723 1354 1947	0.8 7.7 0.8 7.4
12	SU	0209 0804 1428 2022	1.0 7.4 1.2 7.1
13	M	0244 0845 1459 2057	1.3 7.0 1.7 6.8
14	TU	0318 0928 1532 2135	1.7 6.6 2.1 6.4
15	W ☾	0357 1020 1612 2227	2.1 6.0 2.6 6.0
16	TH	0449 1133 1709 2349	2.5 5.7 3.0 5.7
17	F	0600 1254 1829	2.8 5.5 3.2
18	SA	0111 0743 1405 2010	5.7 2.7 5.7 3.0
19	SU	0218 0854 1504 2114	5.9 2.3 6.0 2.6
20	M	0312 0942 1552 2200	6.3 2.0 6.3 2.2
21	TU	0355 1024 1630 2241	6.6 1.6 6.6 1.9
22	W	0433 1105 1704 2320	6.8 1.4 6.9 1.6
23	TH ●	0509 1143 1737 2356	7.0 1.3 7.0 1.5
24	F	0546 1220 1811	7.1 1.2 7.1
25	SA	0031 0622 1255 1844	1.4 7.2 1.2 7.2
26	SU	0105 0659 1327 1917	1.3 7.2 1.3 7.2
27	M	0139 0735 1359 1951	1.3 7.1 1.4 7.1
28	TU	0215 0814 1434 2028	1.4 7.0 1.6 6.9
29	W	0255 0857 1514 2111	1.6 6.7 1.9 6.7
30	TH	0343 0950 1606 2206	1.8 6.4 2.2 6.4
31	F ☽	0447 1103 1717 2320	2.1 6.0 2.5 6.2

NOVEMBER

Date	Day	Time	m
1	SA	0605 1242 1840	2.2 6.0 2.6
2	SU	0050 0726 1402 1958	6.2 2.0 6.2 2.4
3	M	0206 0840 1506 2106	6.5 1.7 6.6 2.0
4	TU	0307 0941 1600 2203	6.9 1.3 6.9 1.6
5	W	0400 1034 1647 2254	7.2 1.0 7.2 1.2
6	TH O	0449 1122 1729 2342	7.4 0.9 7.3 1.0
7	F	0536 1207 1808	7.5 0.9 7.4
8	SA	0027 0620 1249 1845	0.9 7.5 1.0 7.4
9	SU	0110 0703 1326 1922	1.0 7.4 1.1 7.3
10	M	0148 0745 1400 1956	1.1 7.2 1.4 7.1
11	TU	0223 0824 1431 2029	1.4 6.9 1.7 6.9
12	W	0256 0903 1502 2103	1.7 6.5 2.1 6.6
13	TH	0333 0947 1539 2146	2.0 6.1 2.4 6.2
14	F ☾	0418 1043 1627 2246	2.3 5.8 2.8 5.9
15	SA	0518 1158 1731	2.5 5.6 3.0
16	SU	0009 0627 1311 1848	5.7 2.6 5.6 3.0
17	M	0123 0742 1413 2006	5.8 2.5 5.9 2.8
18	TU	0222 0847 1505 2109	6.0 2.2 6.2 2.5
19	W	0312 0938 1548 2159	6.3 1.9 6.5 2.1
20	TH	0355 1024 1628 2242	6.6 1.6 6.7 1.8
21	F	0437 1106 1706 2324	6.8 1.4 7.0 1.6
22	SA ●	0518 1147 1743	7.0 1.3 7.1
23	SU	0005 0559 1227 1821	1.4 7.1 1.2 7.3
24	M	0046 0641 1305 1858	1.2 7.2 1.2 7.3
25	TU	0126 0723 1344 1936	1.1 7.2 1.3 7.3
26	W	0208 0806 1424 2016	1.2 7.1 1.4 7.2
27	TH	0252 0853 1507 2101	1.3 6.9 1.7 7.0
28	F	0342 0946 1558 2155	1.5 6.6 2.0 6.7
29	SA ☽	0440 1054 1700 2301	1.7 6.3 2.3 6.5
30	SU	0548 1215 1812	1.8 6.2 2.4

DECEMBER

Date	Day	Time	m
1	M	0020 0700 1329 1927	6.4 1.9 6.2 2.4
2	TU	0134 0810 1434 2037	6.5 1.8 6.4 2.1
3	W	0240 0912 1532 2138	6.6 1.6 6.6 1.8
4	TH	0338 1007 1621 2232	6.8 1.4 6.9 1.5
5	F	0430 1057 1705 2322	7.0 1.3 7.1 1.3
6	SA O	0519 1142 1745	7.1 1.3 7.2
7	SU	0008 0605 1225 1824	1.2 7.1 1.3 7.2
8	M	0052 0648 1303 1901	1.1 7.1 1.4 7.2
9	TU	0131 0728 1337 1936	1.2 7.0 1.5 7.1
10	W	0206 0805 1409 2008	1.3 6.8 1.7 7.0
11	TH	0239 0840 1439 2040	1.5 6.6 1.9 6.8
12	F	0313 0916 1513 2116	1.8 6.3 2.2 6.5
13	SA	0351 0958 1552 2200	2.0 6.0 2.4 6.2
14	SU ☾	0437 1051 1641 2257	2.3 5.8 2.7 5.9
15	M	0534 1157 1743	2.4 5.7 2.9
16	TU	0010 0637 1307 1853	5.8 2.5 5.7 2.9
17	W	0121 0742 1409 2003	5.8 2.4 5.9 2.7
18	TH	0223 0844 1504 2107	6.0 2.1 6.2 2.4
19	F	0318 0940 1552 2203	6.3 1.9 6.5 2.0
20	SA	0408 1030 1637 2254	6.6 1.6 6.8 1.7
21	SU	0455 1118 1720 2342	6.9 1.4 7.1 1.3
22	M ●	0542 1203 1802	7.1 1.2 7.3
23	TU	0030 0628 1249 1843	1.1 7.2 1.1 7.4
24	W	0117 0713 1332 1924	0.9 7.3 1.1 7.5
25	TH	0203 0759 1416 2007	0.8 7.2 1.2 7.5
26	F	0248 0846 1500 2052	0.9 7.1 1.3 7.3
27	SA	0336 0936 1546 2142	1.0 6.8 1.6 7.1
28	SU ☽	0427 1033 1639 2240	1.3 6.5 1.9 6.8
29	M	0524 1140 1740 2348	1.6 6.3 2.2 6.5
30	TU	0628 1249 1851	1.9 6.1 2.4
31	W	0101 0737 1357 2006	6.3 2.0 6.1 2.3

RIVER TYNE (NORTH SHIELDS)
LAT 55°01'N
LONG 1°26'W

TIMES AND HEIGHTS OF HIGH AND LOW WATER (Heights in Metres)

TIME ZONE UT
For Summer Time (area enclosed in shaded box) add 1 hour

2014

JANUARY

Day	Time	m	Day	Time	m
1 W ●	0245 0908 1503 2136	5.1 0.9 5.3 0.6	16 TH O	0333 0940 1544 2207	4.7 1.3 4.9 1.0
2 TH	0335 0956 1548 2226	5.3 0.8 5.4 0.4	17 F	0406 1012 1615 2240	4.8 1.2 5.0 0.9
3 F	0424 1043 1633 2314	5.4 0.7 5.5 0.3	18 SA	0438 1042 1645 2312	4.8 1.2 5.0 0.9
4 SA	0513 1128 1720	5.3 0.8 5.5	19 SU	0511 1113 1717 2344	4.8 1.2 5.0 1.0
5 SU	0002 0602 1214 1808	0.4 5.2 1.0 5.4	20 M	0544 1144 1750	4.7 1.3 4.9
6 M	0050 0654 1300 1900	0.6 5.0 1.2 5.2	21 TU	0018 0618 1217 1824	1.0 4.6 1.4 4.8
7 TU	0140 0748 1350 1956	0.8 4.7 1.4 4.9	22 W	0054 0656 1253 1903	1.2 4.5 1.5 4.7
8 W ☽	0234 0846 1448 2057	1.2 4.5 1.7 4.6	23 TH	0133 0739 1335 1950	1.3 4.4 1.7 4.5
9 TH	0335 0948 1557 2205	1.5 4.3 1.9 4.4	24 F ☾	0221 0831 1430 2048	1.5 4.3 1.8 4.4
10 F	0443 1056 1714 2319	1.7 4.2 1.9 4.3	25 SA	0322 0935 1544 2200	1.7 4.2 1.9 4.2
11 SA	0554 1205 1828	1.8 4.2 1.9	26 SU	0439 1048 1712 2321	1.7 4.2 1.9 4.3
12 SU	0031 0658 1305 1929	4.3 1.8 4.4 1.7	27 M	0556 1202 1830	1.6 4.3 1.6
13 M	0130 0749 1354 2017	4.4 1.7 4.5 1.5	28 TU	0038 0704 1307 1937	4.5 1.4 4.6 1.2
14 TU	0218 0831 1435 2058	4.5 1.5 4.7 1.3	29 W	0142 0804 1401 2035	4.8 1.2 4.9 0.8
15 W	0257 0907 1511 2134	4.6 1.4 4.8 1.1	30 TH ●	0235 0856 1449 2126	5.1 0.9 5.2 0.5
			31 F	0324 0944 1534 2214	5.3 0.7 5.4 0.3

FEBRUARY

Day	Time	m	Day	Time	m
1 SA	0411 1029 1618 2300	5.4 0.6 5.6 0.2	16 SU	0415 1023 1623 2249	4.8 1.0 5.0 0.8
2 SU	0456 1112 1703 2345	5.3 0.6 5.6 0.2	17 M	0446 1052 1653 2320	4.8 1.0 5.0 0.8
3 M	0542 1153 1749	5.2 0.7 5.4	18 TU	0517 1123 1725 2352	4.8 1.0 5.0 0.8
4 TU	0027 0627 1235 1835	0.4 5.0 0.9 5.2	19 W	0549 1154 1758	4.8 1.1 4.9
5 W	0110 0714 1318 1925	0.8 4.7 1.2 4.9	20 TH	0026 0624 1229 1836	1.0 4.7 1.2 4.8
6 TH ☽	0155 0805 1407 2021	1.2 4.5 1.5 4.6	21 F	0102 0705 1308 1921	1.2 4.5 1.4 4.6
7 F	0246 0902 1508 2125	1.6 4.2 1.8 4.2	22 SA ☾	0146 0754 1400 2019	1.4 4.4 1.6 4.4
8 SA	0351 1009 1628 2241	1.9 4.0 2.0 4.0	23 SU	0245 0857 1512 2134	1.6 4.2 1.8 4.2
9 SU	0510 1125 1757	2.0 4.0 2.0	24 M	0406 1015 1646 2302	1.8 4.1 1.8 4.2
10 M	0003 0630 1237 1908	4.0 2.0 4.1 1.8	25 TU	0534 1137 1814	1.7 4.2 1.5
11 TU	0111 0729 1333 1959	4.1 1.8 4.3 1.5	26 W	0026 0649 1249 1925	4.4 1.5 4.5 1.1
12 W	0200 0813 1416 2039	4.3 1.6 4.6 1.3	27 TH	0131 0750 1345 2022	4.7 1.2 4.9 0.7
13 TH	0240 0849 1452 2114	4.5 1.4 4.7 1.1	28 F	0223 0842 1433 2112	5.0 0.9 5.2 0.4
14 F O	0314 0922 1524 2147	4.6 1.3 4.9 0.9			
15 SA	0345 0953 1554 2218	4.8 1.1 5.0 0.8			

MARCH

Day	Time	m	Day	Time	m
1 SA ●	0310 0927 1517 2158	5.2 0.7 5.4 0.2	16 SU O	0318 0929 1528 2151	4.7 1.1 4.9 0.7
2 SU	0353 1010 1600 2241	5.3 0.5 5.5 0.1	17 M	0348 0959 1558 2222	4.8 0.9 5.0 0.7
3 M	0435 1051 1643 2322	5.3 0.5 5.5 0.2	18 TU	0418 1030 1628 2254	4.9 0.9 5.0 0.6
4 TU	0516 1131 1726	5.2 0.6 5.4	19 W	0450 1102 1701 2327	4.9 0.8 5.0 0.7
5 W	0000 0557 1210 1810	0.5 5.0 0.8 5.1	20 TH	0523 1135 1737	4.9 0.9 5.0
6 TH	0038 0640 1249 1856	0.8 4.7 1.1 4.8	21 F	0001 0559 1211 1817	0.9 4.8 1.0 4.8
7 F	0117 0725 1332 1947	1.2 4.5 1.4 4.5	22 SA	0039 0640 1253 1906	1.1 4.6 1.2 4.6
8 SA ☽	0200 0816 1426 2048	1.6 4.2 1.7 4.1	23 SU	0125 0730 1347 2006	1.3 4.4 1.4 4.4
9 SU	0256 0919 1540 220[illegible]	2.0 4.0 1.9 3.9	24 M ☾	0225 0834 1459 2124	1.6 4.2 1.6 4.2
10 M	0419 1036 1713 2325	2.2 3.9 2.0 3.8	25 TU	0348 0953 1632 2252	1.8 4.1 1.6 4.2
11 TU	0552 1157 1835	2.2 3.9 1.8	26 W	0518 1116 1759	1.8 4.2 1.4
12 W	0040 07[illegible]0 13[illegible]1 1929	4.0 2.0 4.2 1.6	27 TH	0013 0633 1230 1909	4.4 1.5 4.5 1.0
13 TH	0133 0747 1348 2011	4.2 1.7 4.4 1.3	28 F	0116 0733 1327 2005	4.7 1.2 4.8 0.7
14 F	0213 0324 1425 2046	4.4 1.5 4.6 1.1	29 SA	0207 0823 1415 2053	4.9 0.9 5.1 0.4
15 SA	0247 0858 1458 2119	4.6 1.2 4.8 0.9	30 SU ●	0251 0908 1458 2136	5.1 0.7 5.3 0.3
			31 M	0332 0950 1541	5.2 0.5 5.4

APRIL

Day	Time	m	Day	Time	m
1 TU	0411 1030 1622 2255	5.2 0.5 5.4 0.4	16 W	0350 1007 1604 2229	5.0 0.8 5.0 0.6
2 W	0450 1108 1704 2332	5.1 0.6 5.2 0.6	17 TH	0424 1043 1641 2305	5.0 0.7 5.0 0.7
3 TH	0529 1146 1747	5.0 0.7 5.0	18 F	0500 1120 1722 2343	5.0 0.7 5.0 0.8
4 F	0006 0607 1224 1831	1.0 4.8 1.0 4.7	19 SA	0540 1201 1807	4.9 0.8 4.8
5 SA	0042 0649 1305 1919	1.3 4.5 1.3 4.4	20 SU	0025 0624 1248 1859	1.1 4.8 1.0 4.6
6 SU	0121 0735 1353 2014	1.6 4.3 1.6 4.1	21 M	0114 0716 1345 2003	1.3 4.6 1.2 4.4
7 M ☽	0210 0833 1455 2120	2.0 4.0 1.8 3.9	22 TU ☾	0215 0820 1456 2119	1.6 4.4 1.3 4.3
8 TU	0322 0943 1618 2236	2.2 3.9 1.9 3.8	23 W	0334 0936 1621 2239	1.8 4.3 1.3 4.2
9 W	0456 1102 1741 2353	2.2 3.9 1.8 3.9	24 TH	0459 1055 1740 2354	1.7 4.3 1.2 4.4
10 TH	0614 1214 1844	2.1 4.0 1.6	25 F	0611 1206 1847	1.5 4.5 1.0
11 F	0052 0708 1307 1931	4.1 1.8 4.2 1.4	26 SA	0055 0711 1306 1942	4.6 1.3 4.7 0.8
12 SA	0136 0750 1348 2010	4.3 1.5 4.5 1.1	27 SU	0146 0802 1355 2030	4.8 1.0 4.9 0.6
13 SU	0213 0826 1424 2045	4.5 1.3 4.7 0.9	28 M	0230 0847 1440 2113	5.0 0.8 5.1 0.6
14 M	0246 0859 1457 2119	4.7 1.1 4.8 0.8	29 TU ●	0309 0929 1522 2152	5.0 0.7 5.1 0.6
15 TU O	0318 0933 1530 2154	4.9 0.9 5.0 0.6	30 W	0348 1009 1604 2229	5.1 0.6 5.1 0.7

MAY

Day	Time	m	Day	Time	m
1 TH	0425 1048 1645 2304	5.0 0.7 5.0 0.9	16 F	0402 1027 1626 2247	5.1 0.6 5.1 0.7
2 F	0503 1125 1727 2338	4.9 0.8 4.8 1.1	17 SA	0442 1110 1712 2330	5.1 0.6 5.0 0.8
3 SA	0540 1203 1809	4.8 1.0 4.6	18 SU	0525 1156 1801	5.0 0.6 4.9
4 SU	0013 0619 1242 1853	1.3 4.6 1.2 4.4	19 M	0016 0612 1247 1856	1.0 4.9 0.8 4.7
5 M	0050 0702 1325 1943	1.6 4.4 1.4 4.2	20 TU	0107 0706 1343 1958	1.2 4.8 0.9 4.6
6 TU	0134 0753 1418 2040	1.9 4.2 1.6 4.0	21 W ☾	0206 0808 1449 2107	1.5 4.6 1.1 4.4
7 W ☽	0232 0853 1524 2144	2.1 4.0 1.7 3.9	22 TH	0317 0918 1602 2218	1.6 4.5 1.1 4.3
8 TH	0350 1001 1638 2252	2.2 3.9 1.8 3.9	23 F	0432 1031 1715 2328	1.7 4.5 1.1 4.4
9 F	0510 1111 1745 2356	2.1 4.0 1.6 4.0	24 SA	0543 1141 1821	1.6 4.5 1.1
10 SA	0615 1213 1840	1.9 4.1 1.4	25 SU	0030 0645 1243 1918	4.5 1.4 4.6 1.0
11 SU	0049 0705 1303 1926	4.2 1.7 4.3 1.2	26 M	0123 0740 1336 2007	4.7 1.2 4.7 0.9
12 M	0132 0748 1345 2007	4.5 1.4 4.5 1.0	27 TU	0209 0828 1423 2050	4.8 1.0 4.8 0.9
13 TU	0210 0827 1425 2047	4.7 1.2 4.7 0.8	28 W ●	0250 0911 1507 2130	4.9 0.9 4.9 0.9
14 W O	0247 0906 1503 2126	4.9 0.9 4.9 0.7	29 TH	0328 0952 1549 2206	4.9 0.8 4.9 1.0
15 TH	0324 0946 1543 2206	5.0 0.8 5.0 0.7	30 F	0405 1031 1629 2241	4.9 0.8 4.8 1.1
			31 SA	0441 1107 1708	4.9 0.8 4.7

JUNE

Day	Time	m	Day	Time	m
1 SU	0518 1143 1748 2348	4.8 0.9 4.6 1.3	16 M	0513 1150 1753	5.2 0.4 5.1
2 M	0555 1220 1829	4.7 1.1 4.4	17 TU	0007 0601 1241 1847	0.9 5.2 0.5 4.9
3 TU	0024 0634 1300 1912	1.5 4.6 1.2 4.3	18 W	0056 0653 1334 1944	1.1 5.0 0.7 4.7
4 W	0104 0718 1345 2000	1.7 4.4 1.4 4.1	19 TH ☾	0150 0751 1432 2045	1.3 4.9 0.9 4.5
5 TH ☽	0150 0809 1437 2054	1.9 4.2 1.6 4.0	20 F	0251 0855 1536 2150	1.5 4.7 1.1 4.4
6 F	0248 0906 1538 2153	2.0 4.1 1.6 4.0	21 SA	0400 1003 1644 2256	1.6 4.5 1.2 4.3
7 SA	0359 1008 1643 2255	2.1 4.1 1.6 4.0	22 SU	0511 1113 1751	1.6 4.4 1.3
8 SU	0511 1112 1745 2355	2.0 4.1 1.5 4.2	23 M	0002 0619 1221 1853	4.4 1.5 4.5 1.3
9 M	0613 1212 1840	1.8 4.3 1.4	24 TU	0100 0720 1320 1946	4.5 1.4 4.5 1.3
10 TU	0048 0706 1307 1930	4.4 1.5 4.5 1.2	25 W	0150 0812 1411 2031	4.6 1.2 4.6 1.2
11 W	0136 0755 1355 2017	4.6 1.3 4.7 1.0	26 TH	0233 0857 1455 2111	4.7 1.1 4.7 1.2
12 TH	0219 0842 1441 2103	4.8 1.0 4.9 0.8	27 F ●	0312 0937 1535 2147	4.8 0.9 4.7 1.2
13 F O	0301 0928 1527 2148	5.0 0.7 5.1 0.7	28 SA	0348 1015 1613 2221	4.9 0.9 4.7 1.2
14 SA	0343 1015 1614 2234	5.2 0.5 5.2 0.7	29 SU	0423 1050 1650 2254	4.9 0.9 4.7 1.2
15 SU	0427 1102 1702 2320	5.2 0.4 5.2 0.8	30 M	0457 1124 1725 2326	4.9 0.9 4.7 1.3

SUNRISE AND SUNSET TIMES

RIVER TYNE
At 55°01'N 1°26'W

UT		Sunrise	Sunset
Jan	01	0831	1548
	15	0821	1609
Feb	01	0756	1643
	15	0728	1712
Mar	01	0656	1742
	15	0621	1810
BST			
Apr	01	0637	1943
	15	0602	2010
May	01	0526	2041
	15	0458	2107
Jun	01	0434	2134
	15	0426	2147
Jul	01	0431	2148
	15	0447	2136
Aug	01	0515	2108
	15	0540	2039
Sep	01	0612	1958
	15	0638	1922
Oct	01	0708	1841
	15	0735	1807
UT			
Nov	01	0710	1628
	15	0738	1602
Dec	01	0807	1542
	15	0825	1537

RIVER TYNE (NORTH SHIELDS)
LAT 55°01'N
LONG 1°26'W

TIMES AND HEIGHTS OF HIGH AND LOW WATER (Heights in Metres)

TIME ZONE UT
For Summer Time (area enclosed in shaded box) add 1 hour

2014

JULY

Day	Time	m	Day	Time	m
1 TU	0531 1158 1802 2359	4.8 1.0 4.6 1.3	16 W	0545 1226 1829	5.4 0.3 5.1
2 W	0607 1233 1840	4.7 1.1 4.5	17 TH	0038 0635 1315 1921	0.9 5.3 0.5 4.8
3 TH	0034 0645 1313 1921	1.5 4.6 1.2 4.3	18 F	0127 0729 1406 2017	1.1 5.0 0.8 4.6
4 F	0114 0728 1355 2007	1.6 4.5 1.4 4.2	19 SA	0221 0828 1503 ☾ 2116	1.4 4.8 1.2 4.4
5 SA	0200 0816 1446 ☽ 2059	1.8 4.3 1.5 4.1	20 SU	0324 0933 1608 2222	1.6 4.5 1.4 4.3
6 SU	0257 0912 1545 2159	1.9 4.2 1.6 4.1	21 M	0438 1045 1719 2331	1.7 4.3 1.6 4.2
7 M	0408 1016 1652 2303	2.0 4.1 1.6 4.1	22 TU	0555 1200 1829	1.7 4.3 1.7
8 TU	0522 1125 1758	1.9 4.2 1.5	23 W	0037 0704 1306 1928	4.3 1.6 4.3 1.6
9 W	0007 0629 1233 1858	4.3 1.6 4.4 1.3	24 TH	0132 0759 1359 2015	4.5 1.4 4.4 1.5
10 TH	0105 0728 1332 1954	4.5 1.3 4.6 1.1	25 F	0217 0843 1443 2054	4.7 1.2 4.6 1.4
11 F	0156 0823 1425 2045	4.8 1.0 4.9 0.9	26 SA	0256 0921 1520 ● 2129	4.8 1.0 4.7 1.3
12 SA	0242 0914 1514 O 2134	5.1 0.7 5.1 0.7	27 SU	0331 0956 1555 2202	4.9 0.9 4.7 1.2
13 SU	0327 1003 1602 2221	5.3 0.4 5.3 0.6	28 M	0403 1029 1628 2233	5.0 0.8 4.8 1.1
14 M	0412 1051 1650 2307	5.4 0.2 5.3 0.6	29 TU	0435 1101 1700 2303	5.0 0.8 4.8 1.1
15 TU	0458 1139 1739 2352	5.5 0.2 5.2 0.7	30 W	0506 1133 1733 2334	5.0 0.9 4.7 1.2
			31 TH	0539 1206 1807	4.9 0.9 4.6

AUGUST

Day	Time	m	Day	Time	m
1 F	0007 0613 1241 1843	1.3 4.8 1.1 4.5	16 SA	0100 0703 1335 1943	1.0 5.1 0.9 4.6
2 SA	0042 0651 1318 1923	1.4 4.7 1.2 4.4	17 SU	0149 0759 1426 ☾ 2039	1.3 4.7 1.3 4.4
3 SU	0122 0734 1402 2011	1.6 4.5 1.4 4.3	18 M	0248 0903 1528 2144	1.6 4.4 1.7 4.2
4 M	0211 0827 1456 ☽ 2109	1.8 4.3 1.6 4.2	19 TU	0404 1016 1644 2257	1.8 4.2 1.9 4.1
5 TU	0317 0933 1607 2218	1.9 4.2 1.7 4.2	20 W	0530 1137 1805	1.9 4.1 2.0
6 W	0440 1050 1724 2331	1.9 4.2 1.7 4.3	21 TH	0011 0646 1249 1909	4.2 1.7 4.2 1.8
7 TH	0600 1209 1835	1.7 4.4 1.5	22 F	0111 0741 1343 1956	4.4 1.5 4.4 1.7
8 F	0039 0708 1316 1936	4.5 1.3 4.6 1.2	23 SA	0158 0824 1424 2035	4.6 1.3 4.5 1.5
9 SA	0136 0807 1411 2030	4.8 0.9 4.9 1.0	24 SU	0236 0900 1500 2108	4.8 1.1 4.7 1.3
10 SU	0225 0900 1500 O 2118	5.1 0.6 5.2 0.7	25 M	0309 0933 1532 ● 2139	4.9 0.9 4.8 1.2
11 M	0310 0949 1546 2205	5.4 0.3 5.4 0.6	26 TU	0340 1004 1602 2209	5.0 0.8 4.9 1.1
12 TU	0354 1036 1632 2249	5.6 0.1 5.4 0.5	27 W	0410 1035 1632 2239	5.1 0.8 4.9 1.0
13 W	0439 1121 1718 2332	5.6 0.1 5.3 0.6	28 TH	0440 1105 1703 2309	5.1 0.8 4.9 1.1
14 TH	0525 1205 1804	5.6 0.3 5.2	29 F	0511 1137 1735 2340	5.0 0.9 4.8 1.1
15 F	0015 0612 1250 1852	0.8 5.4 0.5 4.9	30 SA	0544 1209 1809	4.9 1.0 4.7
			31 SU	0014 0620 1245 1847	1.3 4.8 1.2 4.6

SEPTEMBER

Day	Time	m	Day	Time	m
1 M	0052 0702 1326 1933	1.4 4.6 1.4 4.4	16 TU	0213 0832 1442 ☾ 2103	1.6 4.3 1.9 4.2
2 TU	0140 0756 1419 ☽ 2031	1.6 4.4 1.6 4.3	17 W	0326 0944 1601 2216	1.9 4.0 2.2 4.1
3 W	0245 0905 1532 2143	1.8 4.2 1.8 4.2	18 TH	0456 1106 1731 2336	1.9 4.0 2.2 4.1
4 TH	0412 1029 1659 2304	1.8 4.2 1.8 4.3	19 F	0617 1221 1842	1.8 4.1 2.0
5 F	0540 1153 1817	1.6 4.4 1.6	20 SA	0041 0713 1317 1930	4.3 1.6 4.3 1.8
6 SA	0017 0653 1302 1920	4.5 1.3 4.7 1.3	21 SU	0130 0755 1358 2009	4.5 1.3 4.5 1.6
7 SU	0117 0752 1356 2013	4.9 0.8 5.0 1.0	22 M	0209 0831 1433 2042	4.7 1.1 4.7 1.4
8 M	0206 0844 1443 2101	5.2 0.5 5.3 0.7	23 TU	0242 0904 1504 2114	4.9 1.0 4.8 1.2
9 TU	0251 0931 1527 O 2145	5.5 0.2 5.4 0.6	24 W	0313 0935 1534 ● 2144	5.0 0.8 4.9 1.1
10 W	0335 1015 1610 2228	5.6 0.1 5.5 0.5	25 TH	0342 1006 1603 2214	5.1 0.8 5.0 1.0
11 TH	0418 1058 1653 2310	5.7 0.2 5.4 0.6	26 F	0413 1037 1634 2245	5.1 0.8 5.0 1.0
12 F	0502 1139 1736 2351	5.6 0.4 5.2 0.7	27 SA	0445 1109 1706 2318	5.1 0.8 5.0 1.0
13 SA	0548 1220 1820	5.3 0.7 5.0	28 SU	0519 1142 1740 2353	5.0 1.0 4.9 1.2
14 SU	0033 0636 1301 1907	1.0 5.0 1.1 4.7	29 M	0557 1217 1819	4.9 1.2 4.8
15 M	0119 0730 1346 2000	1.3 4.7 1.5 4.4	30 TU	0032 0642 1300 1906	1.3 4.7 1.4 4.6

OCTOBER

Day	Time	m	Day	Time	m
1 W	0122 0738 1354 ☽ 2004	1.5 4.5 1.7 4.4	16 TH	0245 0906 1507 2128	1.9 4.0 2.3 4.1
2 TH	0229 0850 1510 2118	1.7 4.3 1.9 4.3	17 F	0406 1020 1639 2245	2.0 3.9 2.3 4.1
3 F	0355 1016 1640 2240	1.7 4.2 1.9 4.3	18 SA	0528 1137 1758 2357	1.9 4.0 2.2 4.2
4 SA	0523 1138 1759 2355	1.5 4.4 1.7 4.6	19 SU	0630 1237 1853	1.7 4.2 2.0
5 SU	0636 1245 1902	1.2 4.7 1.4	20 M	0051 0717 1323 1935	4.4 1.5 4.5 1.7
6 M	0056 0734 1339 1954	4.9 0.8 5.0 1.1	21 TU	0134 0755 1400 2011	4.6 1.3 4.7 1.5
7 TU	0147 0824 1424 2041	5.2 0.5 5.2 0.8	22 W	0210 0830 1432 2045	4.8 1.1 4.8 1.3
8 W	0232 0909 1506 O 2125	5.4 0.4 5.4 0.6	23 TH	0243 0903 1504 ● 2117	5.0 0.9 5.0 1.1
9 TH	0315 0952 1547 2207	5.6 0.3 5.4 0.6	24 F	0315 0936 1535 2150	5.1 0.8 5.1 1.0
10 F	0358 1033 1627 2248	5.6 0.4 5.4 0.6	25 SA	0348 1010 1607 2224	5.1 0.8 5.1 0.9
11 SA	0441 1112 1708 2328	5.5 0.6 5.2 0.8	26 SU	0423 1044 1641 2300	5.1 0.9 5.1 1.0
12 SU	0526 1150 1749	5.2 0.9 5.0	27 M	0501 1120 1718 2339	5.1 1.0 5.0 1.0
13 M	0009 0612 1228 1832	1.0 4.9 1.3 4.8	28 TU	0543 1159 1759	4.9 1.2 4.9
14 TU	0052 0703 1308 1921	1.3 4.6 1.7 4.5	29 W	0023 0631 1245 1847	1.2 4.8 1.4 4.7
15 W	0142 0800 1357 ☾ 2019	1.6 4.3 2.0 4.2	30 TH	0115 0729 1340 1946	1.3 4.5 1.7 4.6
			31 F	0220 0841 1453 ☽ 2058	1.5 4.4 1.9 4.4

NOVEMBER

Day	Time	m	Day	Time	m
1 SA	0341 1001 1619 2217	1.5 4.3 1.9 4.5	16 SU	0422 1036 1652 2254	1.9 4.0 2.3 4.1
2 SU	0503 1118 1735 2331	1.4 4.5 1.8 4.6	17 M	0530 1142 1759 2358	1.8 4.1 2.1 4.3
3 M	0613 1224 1839	1.2 4.7 1.5	18 TU	0627 1236 1852	1.7 4.3 1.9
4 TU	0034 0712 1318 1933	4.9 0.9 4.9 1.2	19 W	0050 0713 1321 1935	4.4 1.4 4.5 1.6
5 W	0127 0802 1404 2021	5.1 0.8 5.1 1.0	20 TH	0134 0754 1359 2014	4.6 1.3 4.8 1.4
6 TH	0214 0848 1446 O 2105	5.3 0.6 5.2 0.8	21 F	0212 0832 1434 2051	4.8 1.1 4.9 1.2
7 F	0258 0930 1526 2148	5.4 0.6 5.3 0.7	22 SA	0249 0909 1509 ● 2128	5.0 1.0 5.1 1.0
8 SA	0341 1009 1605 2229	5.4 0.7 5.3 0.7	23 SU	0327 0946 1544 2207	5.1 0.9 5.2 0.9
9 SU	0424 1047 1644 2309	5.2 0.9 5.2 0.8	24 M	0406 1025 1621 2248	5.1 0.9 5.2 0.8
10 M	0507 1123 1723 2349	5.1 1.2 5.0 1.0	25 TU	0448 1106 1701 2331	5.1 1.0 5.2 0.9
11 TU	0551 1158 1803	4.8 1.4 4.8	26 W	0534 1148 1746	5.0 1.1 5.1
12 W	0029 0637 1236 1846	1.3 4.6 1.7 4.6	27 TH	0018 0624 1236 1834	0.9 4.9 1.4 5.0
13 TH	0113 0727 1319 1937	1.5 4.3 2.0 4.4	28 F	0111 0721 1329 1931	1.1 4.7 1.6 4.8
14 F	0204 0824 1413 ☾ 2036	1.7 4.1 2.2 4.2	29 SA	0211 0827 1434 ☽ 2037	1.2 4.5 1.8 4.7
15 SA	0308 0927 1528 2144	1.9 4.0 2.3 4.1	30 SU	0322 0939 1550 2150	1.3 4.4 1.9 4.6

DECEMBER

Day	Time	m	Day	Time	m
1 M	0436 1051 1705 2303	1.3 4.5 1.8 4.6	16 TU	0422 1036 1649 2253	1.9 4.0 2.2 4.1
2 TU	0546 1158 1813	1.3 4.6 1.6	17 W	0527 1139 1757 2358	1.8 4.2 2.1 4.2
3 W	0010 0648 1256 1912	4.7 1.2 4.7 1.4	18 TH	0626 1235 1854	1.6 4.4 1.8
4 TH	0109 0742 1345 2004	4.9 1.1 4.9 1.2	19 F	0054 0716 1324 1942	4.4 1.5 4.6 1.6
5 F	0200 0829 1429 2051	5.0 1.0 5.0 1.0	20 SA	0143 0802 1406 2027	4.6 1.3 4.8 1.3
6 SA	0246 0911 1509 O 2134	5.1 1.0 5.1 0.9	21 SU	0227 0846 1446 2110	4.9 1.1 5.0 1.0
7 SU	0329 0950 1548 2215	5.1 1.0 5.2 0.9	22 M	0310 0928 1525 ● 2154	5.0 0.9 5.2 0.8
8 M	0411 1026 1625 2253	5.0 1.1 5.1 0.9	23 TU	0353 1011 1606 2239	5.2 0.9 5.3 0.6
9 TU	0451 1101 1702 2330	4.9 1.3 5.0 1.0	24 W	0438 1055 1648 2324	5.2 0.9 5.3 0.6
10 W	0531 1135 1739	4.8 1.4 4.9	25 TH	0525 1139 1733	5.2 1.0 5.3
11 TH	0007 0611 1209 1817	1.2 4.6 1.6 4.8	26 F	0011 0614 1225 1821	0.6 5.1 1.1 5.2
12 F	0046 0654 1246 1900	1.3 4.5 1.8 4.6	27 SA	0101 0707 1315 1914	0.8 4.9 1.3 5.0
13 SA	0128 0741 1329 1948	1.5 4.3 2.0 4.4	28 SU	0155 0806 1410 ☽ 2014	1.0 4.7 1.5 4.8
14 SU	0217 0834 1423 ☾ 2045	1.7 4.1 2.1 4.2	29 M	0256 0910 1516 2122	1.2 4.5 1.7 4.7
15 M	0316 0932 1532 2147	1.8 4.0 2.3 4.1	30 TU	0404 1018 1631 2234	1.4 4.4 1.8 4.5
			31 W	0515 1128 1745 2347	1.5 4.4 1.7 4.5

LEITH
LAT 55°59′N
LONG 3°11′W

TIMES AND HEIGHTS OF HIGH AND LOW WATER (Heights in Metres)

TIME ZONE UT
For Summer Time (area enclosed in shaded box) add 1 hour

2014

JANUARY

Date	Day	Time	m	Time	m	Time	m	Time	m
1	W ●	0156	5.7	0759	0.9	1413	5.8	2030	0.7
2	TH	0244	5.9	0851	0.8	1459	5.9	2123	0.4
3	F	0331	6.0	0940	0.7	1545	6.0	2213	0.3
4	SA	0419	5.9	1027	0.7	1632	6.0	2301	0.4
5	SU	0508	5.8	1112	0.9	1722	5.8	2347	0.6
6	M	0559	5.5	1155	1.2	1814	5.6		
7	TU	0032	0.9	0654	5.2	1238	1.5	1912	5.3
8	W ☽	0119	1.3	0753	5.0	1327	1.8	2016	5.0
9	TH	0215	1.7	0855	4.8	1435	2.0	2121	4.8
10	F	0330	1.9	0958	4.7	1555	2.1	2227	4.7
11	SA	0447	2.0	1104	4.7	1710	2.0	2335	4.7
12	SU	0552	2.0	1209	4.8	1814	1.8		
13	M	0037	4.8	0638	1.8	1304	5.0	1904	1.6
14	TU	0128	4.9	0713	1.7	1349	5.1	1944	1.4
15	W	0210	5.1	0744	1.5	1427	5.3	2018	1.2
16	TH O	0245	5.2	0816	1.4	1501	5.3	2050	1.1
17	F	0317	5.2	0848	1.3	1532	5.4	2121	1.0
18	SA	0349	5.3	0921	1.2	1604	5.4	2153	1.0
19	SU	0422	5.2	0953	1.2	1636	5.3	2225	1.0
20	M	0456	5.2	1022	1.3	1709	5.3	2256	1.1
21	TU	0532	5.1	1046	1.5	1743	5.1	2323	1.3
22	W	0611	5.0	1111	1.6	1821	5.0	2353	1.4
23	TH	0654	4.9	1146	1.8	1905	4.9		
24	F ☾	0034	1.6	0743	4.7	1240	2.0	1959	4.7
25	SA	0137	1.8	0843	4.6	1403	2.1	2111	4.6
26	SU	0311	2.0	0955	4.6	1559	2.1	2232	4.7
27	M	0448	1.8	1108	4.8	1722	1.8	2346	4.9
28	TU	0557	1.6	1213	5.1	1829	1.4		
29	W	0049	5.3	0654	1.3	1309	5.4	1928	0.9
30	TH ●	0143	5.6	0748	1.0	1358	5.7	2023	0.5
31	F	0230	5.8	0838	0.7	1444	6.0	2114	0.2

FEBRUARY

Date	Day	Time	m	Time	m	Time	m	Time	m
1	SA	0316	6.0	0926	0.5	1529	6.1	2200	0.1
2	SU	0402	6.0	1010	0.5	1615	6.1	2244	0.2
3	M	0448	5.8	1052	0.7	1702	5.9	2325	0.4
4	TU	0535	5.6	1129	0.9	1751	5.7		
5	W	0002	0.8	0624	5.3	1202	1.3	1843	5.3
6	TH ☽	0032	1.3	0717	4.9	1237	1.6	1940	5.0
7	F	0106	1.7	0814	4.7	1333	2.0	2042	4.7
8	SA	0208	2.1	0915	4.5	1505	2.2	2148	4.4
9	SU	0355	2.3	1022	4.4	1644	2.2	2301	4.4
10	M	0519	2.2	1137	4.5	1759	1.9		
11	TU	0016	4.5	0615	2.0	1243	4.7	1851	1.7
12	W	0112	4.7	0654	1.8	1330	5.0	1930	1.4
13	TH	0153	4.9	0727	1.6	1408	5.2	2002	1.2
14	F O	0226	5.1	0759	1.3	1441	5.3	2032	1.0
15	SA	0256	5.2	0832	1.2	1512	5.4	2104	0.9
16	SU	0326	5.3	0906	1.0	1542	5.4	2136	0.8
17	M	0358	5.3	0938	1.0	1613	5.4	2208	0.8
18	TU	0430	5.3	1006	1.1	1645	5.4	2236	0.9
19	W	0505	5.3	1024	1.2	1718	5.3	2256	1.1
20	TH	0542	5.1	1044	1.3	1756	5.2	2317	1.3
21	F	0622	5.0	1117	1.5	1839	5.0	2354	1.5
22	SA ☾	0709	4.8	1205	1.7	1932	4.8		
23	SU	0053	1.8	0805	4.6	1320	2.0	2040	4.6
24	M	0237	2.0	0920	4.5	1532	2.0	2208	4.6
25	TU	0430	2.0	1042	4.6	1711	1.7	2328	4.8
26	W	0543	1.7	1154	4.9	1821	1.3		
27	TH	0034	5.2	0641	1.3	1252	5.3	1920	0.8
28	F	0127	5.5	0733	0.9	1341	5.7	2011	0.4

MARCH

Date	Day	Time	m	Time	m	Time	m	Time	m
1	SA ●	0213	5.8	0821	0.6	1426	5.9	2057	0.2
2	SU	0257	5.9	0906	0.4	1511	6.1	2141	0.1
3	M	0341	5.9	0949	0.4	1556	6.1	2222	0.2
4	TU	0425	5.8	1029	0.5	1641	5.9	2259	0.5
5	W	0509	5.5	1104	0.8	1727	5.6	2329	0.9
6	TH	0554	5.2	1130	1.1	1815	5.3	2347	1.3
7	F	0641	4.9	1157	1.5	1906	4.9		
8	SA ☽	0016	1.8	0733	4.6	1245	1.9	2003	4.6
9	SU	0109	2.2	0832	4.4	1403	2.2	2106	4.3
10	M	0244	2.4	0937	4.3	1612	2.2	2216	4.2
11	TU	0440	2.4	1052	4.3	1731	2.0	2340	4.3
12	W	0543	2.2	1208	4.5	1824	1.7		
13	TH	0043	4.6	0627	1.9	1301	4.8	1903	1.5
14	F	0125	4.8	0703	1.6	1340	5.0	1936	1.2
15	SA	0158	5.0	0737	1.3	1414	5.2	2007	1.0
16	SU O	0229	5.2	0811	1.1	1446	5.4	2039	0.8
17	M	0259	5.3	0845	0.9	1517	5.4	2113	0.7
18	TU	0331	5.4	0919	0.9	1548	5.5	2145	0.7
19	W	0404	5.4	0948	0.9	1621	5.5	2215	0.8
20	TH	0439	5.4	1009	1.0	1657	5.4	2236	1.0
21	F	0516	5.3	1028	1.1	1736	5.3	2256	1.2
22	SA	0558	5.1	1102	1.3	1822	5.1	2334	1.5
23	SU	0644	4.9	1153	1.5	1916	4.9		
24	M ☾	0040	1.8	0741	4.7	1317	1.8	2026	4.6
25	TU	0234	2.0	0857	4.5	1527	1.8	2152	4.6
26	W	0415	2.0	1022	4.6	1700	1.5	2312	4.8
27	TH	0525	1.7	1134	4.9	1808	1.2		
28	F	0017	5.1	0621	1.3	1233	5.3	1903	0.8
29	SA	0109	5.4	0711	1.0	1322	5.6	1952	0.5
30	SU ●	0154	5.6	0759	0.7	1407	5.8	2036	0.3
31	M	0236	5.8	0844	0.5	1451	5.9	[illegible]	[illegible]

APRIL

Date	Day	Time	m	Time	m	Time	m	Time	m
1	TU	0318	5.8	0927	0.4	1535	5.9	2156	0.4
2	W	0401	5.6	1006	0.5	1620	5.7	2230	0.7
3	TH	0443	5.5	1040	0.8	1704	5.5	2255	1.0
4	F	0525	5.2	1105	1.1	1749	5.2	2309	1.4
5	SA	0609	4.9	1129	1.4	1836	4.9	2339	1.8
6	SU	0656	4.7	1211	1.7	1927	4.5		
7	M ☽	0028	2.1	0750	4.4	1314	2.0	2024	4.3
8	TU	0143	2.4	0852	4.3	1510	2.2	2126	4.2
9	W	0346	2.4	0959	4.2	1645	2.0	2237	4.2
10	TH	0459	2.2	1113	4.4	1740	1.8	2350	4.4
11	F	0549	1.9	1215	4.6	1823	1.5		
12	SA	0041	4.7	0629	1.6	1301	4.9	1859	1.3
13	SU	0120	5.0	0706	1.4	1339	5.1	1934	1.0
14	M	0155	5.2	0743	1.1	1414	5.3	2009	0.8
15	TU O	0229	5.3	0819	0.9	1449	5.4	2044	0.7
16	W	0304	5.5	0856	0.8	1523	5.5	2121	0.7
17	TH	0339	5.5	0932	0.8	1600	5.5	2156	0.8
18	F	0416	5.5	1005	0.8	1639	5.5	2231	0.9
19	SA	0455	5.4	1037	0.9	1722	5.4	2305	1.2
20	SU	0539	5.2	1116	1.1	1811	5.2	2351	1.5
21	M	0628	5.0	1217	1.4	1908	4.9		
22	TU ☾	0101	1.8	0726	4.8	1341	1.6	2017	4.8
23	W	0228	1.9	0842	4.7	1519	1.6	2137	4.7
24	TH	0352	1.9	1003	4.7	1640	1.4	2251	4.9
25	F	0459	1.6	1112	5.0	1745	1.1	2355	5.1
26	SA	0555	1.3	1211	5.2	1841	0.9		
27	SU	0047	5.3	0646	1.1	1302	5.4	1928	0.7
28	M	0133	5.5	0735	0.8	1348	5.6	2011	0.6
29	TU ●	0216	5.6	0821	0.6	1433	5.6	2052	0.6
30	W	0257	5.6	0905	0.6	1517	5.6	2129	0.7

MAY

Date	Day	Time	m	Time	m	Time	m	Time	m
1	TH	0339	5.5	0944	0.6	1600	5.5	2200	0.9
2	F	0420	5.4	1018	0.8	1643	5.3	2223	1.2
3	SA	0500	5.2	1044	1.1	1725	5.1	2242	1.4
4	SU	0540	5.0	1110	1.3	1808	4.9	2313	1.7
5	M	0623	4.8	1147	1.5	1853	4.6	2357	2.0
6	TU	0712	4.6	1239	1.8	1944	4.4		
7	W ☽	0058	2.2	0807	4.4	1348	2.0	2039	4.3
8	TH	0225	2.4	0908	4.3	1531	2.0	2139	4.3
9	F	0401	2.3	1012	4.4	1643	1.8	2243	4.4
10	SA	0501	2.0	1116	4.5	1732	1.6	2343	4.6
11	SU	0548	1.8	1211	4.7	1815	1.4		
12	M	0034	4.9	0630	1.5	1259	5.0	1854	1.1
13	TU	0119	5.1	0710	1.2	1341	5.2	1934	0.9
14	W O	0159	5.3	0751	1.0	1421	5.4	2015	0.8
15	TH	0237	5.5	0834	0.8	1501	5.5	2058	0.7
16	F	0316	5.6	0918	0.7	1541	5.6	2142	0.7
17	SA	0356	5.6	1004	0.6	1625	5.6	2227	0.9
18	SU	0439	5.5	1051	0.7	1711	5.5	2314	1.1
19	M	0525	5.4	1141	0.9	1802	5.3		
20	TU	0003	1.4	0616	5.2	1236	1.1	1859	5.1
21	W ☾	0101	1.6	0716	5.0	1341	1.3	2006	4.9
22	TH	0209	1.8	0828	4.9	1457	1.3	2118	4.8
23	F	0322	1.8	0941	4.9	1612	1.3	2226	4.9
24	SA	0428	1.7	1048	5.0	1717	1.2	2329	5.0
25	SU	0527	1.5	1149	5.1	1814	1.1		
26	M	0025	5.1	0621	1.3	1243	5.2	1903	1.0
27	TU	0114	5.3	0713	1.0	1332	5.3	1946	1.0
28	W ●	0158	5.4	0800	0.9	1418	5.4	2025	1.0
29	TH	0240	5.4	0844	0.8	1501	5.4	2100	1.0
30	F	0320	5.4	0923	0.8	1543	5.3	2130	1.1
31	SA	0400	5.3	0956	0.9	1623	5.2		

JUNE

Date	Day	Time	m	Time	m	Time	m	Time	m
1	SU	0437	5.2	1024	1.0	1701	5.1	2221	1.4
2	M	0515	5.1	1053	1.2	1740	4.9	2253	1.6
3	TU	0554	4.9	1127	1.4	1821	4.8	2332	1.8
4	W	0637	4.7	1210	1.5	1906	4.6		
5	TH ☽	0020	2.0	0724	4.6	1303	1.7	1955	4.5
6	F	0124	2.2	0818	4.5	1407	1.9	2051	4.4
7	SA	0243	2.2	0918	4.4	1524	1.9	2150	4.5
8	SU	0401	2.1	1021	4.5	1634	1.7	2251	4.6
9	M	0501	1.9	1122	4.7	1729	1.5	2350	4.8
10	TU	0552	1.6	1219	4.9	1817	1.3		
11	W	0043	5.1	0639	1.3	1310	5.1	1903	1.1
12	TH	0130	5.3	0727	1.0	1357	5.4	1951	0.9
13	F O	0214	5.5	0817	0.8	1441	5.6	2041	0.8
14	SA	0256	5.7	0908	0.6	1526	5.7	2130	0.7
15	SU	0340	5.7	0959	0.4	1612	5.8	2219	0.8
16	M	0425	5.7	1049	0.4	1700	5.7	2307	0.9
17	TU	0513	5.6	1139	0.5	1751	5.5	2355	1.1
18	W	0605	5.5	1229	0.8	1846	5.3		
19	TH ☾	0045	1.3	0702	5.3	1324	1.0	1948	5.1
20	F	0141	1.6	0808	5.1	1426	1.3	2053	4.9
21	SA	0247	1.7	0917	5.0	1536	1.4	2158	4.8
22	SU	0356	1.7	1023	4.9	1645	1.5	2301	4.9
23	M	0501	1.7	1126	4.9	1747	1.5		
24	TU	0002	5.0	0601	1.5	1227	5.0	1838	1.4
25	W	0056	5.1	0656	1.3	1320	5.1	1921	1.4
26	TH	0143	5.2	0744	1.1	1406	5.1	1958	1.3
27	F ●	0226	5.3	0826	1.0	1448	5.2	2032	1.2
28	SA	0305	5.3	0903	0.9	1526	5.2	2102	1.2
29	SU	0341	5.3	0935	0.9	1602	5.2	2132	1.2
30	M	0416	5.3	1005	1.0	1637	5.1	2203	1.3

SUNRISE AND SUNSET TIMES
Leith
At 55°59′N 3°11′W

UT		Sunrise	Sunset
Jan	01	0844	1549
	15	0834	1611
Feb	01	0807	1646
	15	0738	1717
Mar	01	0704	1747
	15	0628	1816
BST			
Apr	01	0643	1951
	15	0607	2020
May	01	0529	2052
	15	0500	2119
Jun	01	0435	2147
	15	0426	2201
Jul	01	0431	2201
	15	0448	2149
Aug	01	0517	2120
	15	0544	2049
Sep	01	0617	2007
	15	0644	1930
Oct	01	0716	1848
	15	0744	1812
UT			
Nov	01	0720	1632
	15	0749	1605
Dec	01	0820	1544
	15	0838	1538

LEITH
LAT 55°59′N
LONG 3°11′W

TIMES AND HEIGHTS OF HIGH AND LOW WATER (Heights in Metres)

TIME ZONE UT
For Summer Time (area enclosed in shaded box) add 1 hour

2014

JULY

Date	Day	Time	m	Time	m	Time	m	Time	m
1	TU	0451	5.2	1035	1.0	1713	5.1	2234	1.4
2	W	0527	5.1	1108	1.2	1751	5.0	2307	1.5
3	TH	0604	5.0	1143	1.3	1831	4.8	2343	1.7
4	F	0645	4.8	1224	1.5	1916	4.7		
5	SA ☽	0028	1.9	0731	4.7	1314	1.7	2005	4.6
6	SU	0131	2.1	0825	4.6	1416	1.8	2103	4.6
7	M	0251	2.1	0930	4.5	1532	1.8	2207	4.6
8	TU	0412	2.0	1039	4.6	1647	1.7	2311	4.8
9	W	0519	1.8	1144	4.8	1748	1.5		
10	TH	0011	5.0	0615	1.4	1244	5.1	1842	1.2
11	F	0106	5.3	0710	1.1	1337	5.4	1934	1.0
12	SA ○	0154	5.5	0805	0.7	1424	5.7	2027	0.8
13	SU	0239	5.8	0859	0.4	1510	5.9	2117	0.6
14	M	0324	5.9	0950	0.2	1557	5.9	2206	0.6
15	TU	0410	6.0	1039	0.2	1644	5.9	2252	0.7
16	W	0458	5.9	1125	0.3	1734	5.7	2337	0.9
17	TH	0548	5.7	1211	0.6	1826	5.4		
18	F	0021	1.1	0642	5.5	1257	0.9	1922	5.2
19	SA ☾	0108	1.5	0743	5.2	1347	1.3	2024	4.9
20	SU	0206	1.7	0849	4.9	1452	1.7	2127	4.8
21	M	0322	1.9	0955	4.8	1610	1.9	2231	4.7
22	TU	0439	1.9	1103	4.7	1721	1.9	2338	4.8
23	W	0549	1.7	1210	4.8	1818	1.8		
24	TH	0039	4.9	0647	1.5	1308	4.9	1900	1.6
25	F	0130	5.1	0733	1.3	1354	5.0	1934	1.5
26	SA ●	0211	5.2	0810	1.1	1433	5.1	2006	1.3
27	SU	0248	5.3	0843	1.0	1507	5.2	2039	1.2
28	M	0322	5.4	0914	0.9	1539	5.2	2111	1.1
29	TU	0354	5.4	0944	0.9	1611	5.2	2144	1.1
30	W	0426	5.3	1015	0.9	1645	5.2	2214	1.2
31	TH	0459	5.3	1046	1.0	1720	5.1	2242	1.3

AUGUST

Date	Day	Time	m	Time	m	Time	m	Time	m
1	F	0534	5.2	1115	1.2	1758	5.0	2306	1.5
2	SA	0611	5.0	1144	1.3	1839	4.9	2336	1.7
3	SU	0652	4.9	1221	1.6	1925	4.8		
4	M ☽	0022	1.9	0741	4.7	1316	1.8	2019	4.6
5	TU	0139	2.1	0845	4.6	1438	1.9	2125	4.6
6	W	0326	2.1	1002	4.6	1615	1.9	2237	4.7
7	TH	0455	1.8	1117	4.8	1728	1.7	2345	5.0
8	F	0601	1.5	1223	5.1	1827	1.4		
9	SA	0044	5.3	0700	1.0	1319	5.4	1920	1.0
10	SU ○	0135	5.6	0755	0.6	1407	5.8	2011	0.7
11	M	0221	5.9	0847	0.3	1453	6.0	2101	0.5
12	TU	0305	6.1	0936	0.0	1538	6.0	2148	0.4
13	W	0351	6.1	1021	0.0	1624	6.0	2232	0.5
14	TH	0438	6.1	1105	0.2	1711	5.8	2314	0.7
15	F	0527	5.9	1146	0.6	1800	5.5	2353	1.0
16	SA	0618	5.5	1223	1.0	1853	5.2		
17	SU ☾	0032	1.4	0715	5.2	1301	1.5	1951	4.9
18	M	0123	1.8	0819	4.8	1355	1.9	2053	4.7
19	TU	0245	2.0	0925	4.6	1530	2.2	2158	4.6
20	W	0422	2.0	1036	4.5	1657	2.2	2310	4.6
21	TH	0540	1.9	1151	4.6	1758	2.0		
22	F	0018	4.8	0637	1.6	1252	4.8	1840	1.8
23	SA	0110	5.0	0717	1.4	1337	5.0	1912	1.6
24	SU	0151	5.2	0750	1.2	1413	5.1	1944	1.4
25	M ●	0226	5.3	0819	1.0	1444	5.2	2016	1.2
26	TU	0258	5.4	0849	0.9	1513	5.3	2050	1.1
27	W	0329	5.5	0920	0.8	1544	5.4	2123	1.0
28	TH	0400	5.4	0951	0.8	1617	5.3	2153	1.1
29	F	0432	5.4	1021	0.9	1651	5.3	2215	1.2
30	SA	0505	5.3	1045	1.1	1727	5.2	2234	1.3
31	SU	0541	5.2	1104	1.3	1806	5.1	2301	1.5

SEPTEMBER

Date	Day	Time	m	Time	m	Time	m	Time	m
1	M	0623	5.0	1134	1.5	1850	4.9	2343	1.7
2	TU ☽	0712	4.8	1226	1.8	1943	4.7		
3	W	0051	2.0	0814	4.7	1402	2.1	2050	4.6
4	TH	0256	2.1	0934	4.6	1556	2.0	2209	4.7
5	F	0441	1.8	1056	4.8	1713	1.8	2322	4.9
6	SA	0551	1.4	1205	5.1	1812	1.4		
7	SU	0024	5.3	0649	1.0	1301	5.5	1903	1.1
8	M	0115	5.7	0741	0.5	1348	5.8	1952	0.7
9	TU ○	0200	6.0	0830	0.2	1432	6.0	2040	0.5
10	W	0245	6.2	0916	0.0	1516	6.0	2126	0.4
11	TH	0330	6.2	0959	0.1	1600	6.0	2209	0.4
12	F	0416	6.1	1040	0.3	1646	5.8	2250	0.7
13	SA	0504	5.8	1117	0.7	1733	5.5	2326	1.0
14	SU	0554	5.5	1146	1.2	1822	5.2	2357	1.4
15	M	0648	5.1	1210	1.7	1917	4.9		
16	TU ☾	0040	1.8	0747	4.7	1257	2.1	2017	4.6
17	W	0158	2.1	0851	4.5	1429	2.4	2122	4.5
18	TH	0359	2.2	1000	4.4	1623	2.4	2233	4.5
19	F	0518	2.0	1119	4.5	1727	2.2	2346	4.7
20	SA	0611	1.7	1225	4.7	1811	2.0		
21	SU	0041	4.9	0649	1.5	1310	4.9	1846	1.7
22	M	0123	5.1	0721	1.2	1345	5.1	1919	1.4
23	TU	0158	5.3	0750	1.0	1415	5.3	1952	1.2
24	W ●	0230	5.4	0821	0.9	1444	5.4	2026	1.0
25	TH	0301	5.5	0852	0.8	1516	5.5	2100	1.0
26	F	0332	5.5	0924	0.8	1548	5.5	2130	1.0
27	SA	0405	5.5	0954	0.9	1622	5.4	2154	1.1
28	SU	0440	5.4	1017	1.0	1659	5.3	2212	1.2
29	M	0518	5.3	1036	1.3	1738	5.2	2241	1.4
30	TU	0601	5.1	1108	1.5	1823	5.0	2326	1.6

OCTOBER

Date	Day	Time	m	Time	m	Time	m	Time	m
1	W ☽	0652	4.9	1202	1.9	1916	4.8		
2	TH	0041	1.9	0755	4.7	1353	2.1	2023	4.7
3	F	0247	2.0	0916	4.7	1539	2.1	2146	4.7
4	SA	0427	1.7	1037	4.9	1654	1.8	2301	5.0
5	SU	0536	1.3	1145	5.2	1752	1.5		
6	M	0002	5.3	0632	0.9	1241	5.5	1842	1.1
7	TU	0054	5.7	0722	0.6	1328	5.8	1930	0.8
8	W ○	0139	5.9	0808	0.4	1411	5.9	2018	0.6
9	TH	0224	6.1	0852	0.3	1453	6.0	2103	0.5
10	F	0309	6.1	0934	0.3	1537	5.9	2147	0.5
11	SA	0355	5.9	1013	0.6	1621	5.7	2226	0.8
12	SU	0442	5.7	1045	1.0	1706	5.4	2300	1.1
13	M	0530	5.4	1105	1.4	1752	5.2	2326	1.4
14	TU	0620	5.0	1126	1.8	1842	4.9		
15	W ☾	0003	1.8	0714	4.7	1211	2.2	1938	4.6
16	TH	0104	2.1	0812	4.5	1322	2.5	2041	4.5
17	F	0308	2.2	0915	4.3	1528	2.6	2146	4.4
18	SA	0434	2.1	1025	4.4	1643	2.4	2256	4.6
19	SU	0528	1.9	1136	4.6	1733	2.1	2358	4.8
20	M	0609	1.6	1228	4.8	1813	1.8		
21	TU	0045	5.0	0643	1.4	1307	5.1	1849	1.5
22	W	0123	5.2	0716	1.2	1341	5.3	1925	1.3
23	TH ●	0158	5.4	0749	1.0	1414	5.4	2000	1.1
24	F	0232	5.5	0822	0.9	1447	5.5	2035	1.0
25	SA	0307	5.5	0856	0.8	1522	5.6	2110	1.0
26	SU	0342	5.6	0930	0.9	1557	5.6	2142	1.0
27	M	0419	5.5	1001	1.1	1635	5.5	2211	1.1
28	TU	0500	5.4	1030	1.3	1716	5.4	2246	1.3
29	W	0546	5.3	1108	1.6	1802	5.2	2339	1.5
30	TH	0639	5.1	1217	1.9	1856	5.0		
31	F ☽	0101	1.7	0742	4.9	1346	2.1	2004	4.8

NOVEMBER

Date	Day	Time	m	Time	m	Time	m	Time	m
1	SA	0236	1.7	0900	4.8	1515	2.1	2125	4.9
2	SU	0405	1.6	1016	4.9	1628	1.9	2238	5.0
3	M	0513	1.3	1123	5.2	1727	1.6	2340	5.3
4	TU	0610	1.0	1218	5.4	1819	1.3		
5	W	0033	5.6	0659	0.8	1307	5.6	1908	1.0
6	TH ○	0121	5.7	0745	0.7	1351	5.8	1956	0.8
7	F	0207	5.8	0828	0.6	1433	5.8	2043	0.7
8	SA	0252	5.8	0909	0.7	1516	5.8	2126	0.7
9	SU	0338	5.7	0945	0.9	1559	5.6	2205	0.9
10	M	0423	5.5	1013	1.2	1642	5.4	2237	1.1
11	TU	0507	5.3	1030	1.5	1725	5.2	2301	1.4
12	W	0553	5.0	1056	1.8	1810	5.0	2333	1.6
13	TH	0640	4.8	1136	2.1	1859	4.7		
14	F ☾	0021	1.9	0731	4.6	1233	2.3	1954	4.6
15	SA	0128	2.1	0826	4.4	1354	2.5	2055	4.5
16	SU	0316	2.2	0926	4.4	1540	2.5	2157	4.5
17	M	0430	2.0	1028	4.5	1645	2.3	2300	4.6
18	TU	0520	1.8	1128	4.7	1734	2.0	2356	4.8
19	W	0602	1.6	1220	4.9	1816	1.7		
20	TH	0043	5.0	0639	1.4	1304	5.2	1855	1.5
21	F	0126	5.2	0716	1.2	1343	5.4	1934	1.2
22	SA ●	0205	5.4	0754	1.0	1421	5.5	2013	1.0
23	SU	0244	5.5	0833	0.9	1458	5.6	2054	0.9
24	M	0322	5.6	0914	0.9	1536	5.7	2137	0.9
25	TU	0403	5.6	0956	1.0	1616	5.6	2222	0.9
26	W	0447	5.6	1041	1.2	1700	5.5	2310	1.0
27	TH	0535	5.4	1129	1.4	1747	5.4		
28	F	0002	1.2	0627	5.2	1224	1.7	1841	5.2
29	SA ☽	0102	1.4	0728	5.0	1329	1.9	1945	5.0
30	SU	0214	1.5	0839	4.9	1443	2.0	2101	5.0

DECEMBER

Date	Day	Time	m	Time	m	Time	m	Time	m
1	M	0333	1.5	0951	4.9	1555	1.9	2213	5.0
2	TU	0443	1.4	1057	5.1	1659	1.7	2317	5.2
3	W	0544	1.3	1156	5.2	1756	1.5		
4	TH	0014	5.3	0637	1.2	1248	5.4	1849	1.2
5	F	0106	5.4	0724	1.1	1335	5.5	1940	1.0
6	SA ○	0154	5.5	0806	1.0	1418	5.6	2026	0.9
7	SU	0240	5.6	0844	1.0	1501	5.6	2109	0.9
8	M	0323	5.5	0918	1.1	1542	5.5	2146	0.9
9	TU	0405	5.4	0945	1.3	1622	5.4	2217	1.1
10	W	0445	5.3	1007	1.4	1700	5.3	2241	1.2
11	TH	0525	5.1	1035	1.6	1739	5.1	2311	1.4
12	F	0606	4.9	1110	1.8	1821	4.9	2349	1.6
13	SA	0650	4.7	1153	2.1	1908	4.7		
14	SU ☾	0038	1.8	0738	4.6	1250	2.3	2000	4.6
15	M	0139	2.0	0832	4.5	1407	2.4	2059	4.5
16	TU	0256	2.1	0930	4.5	1537	2.4	2201	4.5
17	W	0416	2.0	1031	4.6	1646	2.2	2303	4.6
18	TH	0515	1.8	1131	4.8	1739	1.9		
19	F	0002	4.8	0603	1.6	1227	5.0	1826	1.6
20	SA	0055	5.1	0647	1.4	1315	5.3	1910	1.3
21	SU	0141	5.3	0731	1.2	1358	5.5	1956	1.1
22	M ●	0224	5.5	0816	1.0	1439	5.7	2043	0.8
23	TU	0306	5.7	0903	0.9	1519	5.8	2132	0.7
24	W	0349	5.8	0950	0.9	1601	5.8	2221	0.6
25	TH	0434	5.8	1037	1.0	1646	5.8	2309	0.7
26	F	0521	5.6	1124	1.1	1734	5.7	2357	0.8
27	SA	0612	5.4	1211	1.4	1826	5.5		
28	SU ☽	0047	1.1	0709	5.2	1303	1.6	1925	5.2
29	M	0144	1.3	0813	5.0	1405	1.8	2035	5.1
30	TU	0253	1.6	0922	4.9	1518	1.9	2147	5.0
31	W	0409	1.7	1029	4.9	1630	1.9	2254	4.9

ABERDEEN
LAT 57°09'N
LONG 2°05'W

TIMES AND HEIGHTS OF HIGH AND LOW WATER (Heights in Metres)

TIME ZONE UT
For Summer Time (area enclosed in shaded box) add 1 hour

2014

JANUARY

Date	Day	Time	m	Date	Day	Time	m
1	W ●	0040 0643 1256 1910	4.4 0.9 4.5 0.6	16	TH O	0127 0717 1337 1943	4.0 1.2 4.2 1.0
2	TH	0129 0730 1341 1959	4.5 0.8 4.6 0.4	17	F	0200 0748 1408 2015	4.0 1.2 4.2 0.9
3	F	0218 0816 1427 2047	4.6 0.7 4.7 0.4	18	SA	0232 0819 1439 2047	4.0 1.1 4.2 0.9
4	SA	0307 0902 1514 2136	4.5 0.8 4.7 0.4	19	SU	0305 0850 1510 2119	4.0 1.1 4.2 0.9
5	SU	0357 0948 1602 2225	4.4 0.9 4.6 0.6	20	M	0338 0921 1543 2153	4.0 1.2 4.2 1.0
6	M	0449 1036 1655 2316	4.2 1.1 4.4 0.8	21	TU	0413 0954 1618 2228	3.9 1.3 4.1 1.1
7	TU	0543 1129 1751	4.0 1.3 4.2	22	W	0451 1031 1658 2308	3.8 1.4 3.9 1.2
8	W ☽	0011 0640 1228 1852	1.1 3.8 1.5 3.9	23	TH	0536 1114 1746 2357	3.7 1.5 3.8 1.4
9	TH	0111 0743 1334 2000	1.3 3.6 1.7 3.7	24	F ☾	0630 1211 1847	3.6 1.7 3.7
10	F	0218 0852 1452 2115	1.6 3.6 1.8 3.6	25	SA	0100 0734 1326 1958	1.5 3.5 1.7 3.6
11	SA	0336 1002 1611 2227	1.6 3.6 1.7 3.6	26	SU	0214 0843 1449 2115	1.6 3.6 1.7 3.6
12	SU	0440 1100 1709 2325	1.6 3.7 1.5 3.7	27	M	0331 0955 1609 2231	1.5 3.7 1.5 3.8
13	M	0528 1147 1755	1.5 3.9 1.3	28	TU	0443 1100 1716 2335	1.3 3.9 1.2 4.1
14	TU	0011 0608 1228 1833	3.8 1.4 4.0 1.2	29	W	0541 1154 1810	1.1 4.2 0.8
15	W	0051 0643 1304 1909	3.9 1.3 4.1 1.1	30	TH ●	0029 0631 1242 1900	4.3 0.9 4.4 0.5
				31	F	0118 0717 1328	4.5 0.7 4.6

FEBRUARY

Date	Day	Time	m	Date	Day	Time	m
1	SA	0205 0802 1412 2033	4.5 0.6 4.7 0.2	16	SU	0209 0758 1417 2024	4.1 1.0 4.3 0.7
2	SU	0250 0845 1457 2117	4.5 0.6 4.7 0.3	17	M	0239 0828 1447 2055	4.1 0.9 4.3 0.7
3	M	0336 0927 1542 2202	4.4 0.7 4.6 0.5	18	TU	0310 0858 1519 2126	4.1 1.0 4.2 0.8
4	TU	0422 1010 1630 2246	4.2 0.9 4.4 0.7	19	W	0343 0930 1553 2159	4.0 1.0 4.1 0.9
5	W	0510 1056 1721 2333	4.0 1.1 4.1 1.1	20	TH	0419 1004 1632 2236	3.9 1.1 4.0 1.1
6	TH ☽	0601 1147 1818	3.8 1.4 3.8	21	F	0500 1045 1718 2322	3.8 1.3 3.9 1.2
7	F	0025 0658 1249 1921	1.4 3.6 1.6 3.6	22	SA ☾	0551 1138 1817	3.7 1.4 3.7
8	SA	0128 0805 1406 2037	1.7 3.4 1.8 3.4	23	SU	0023 0655 1253 1933	1.5 3.5 1.6 3.6
9	SU	0250 0921 1543 2200	1.8 3.4 1.8 3.4	24	M	0143 0811 1423 2055	1.6 3.5 1.6 3.6
10	M	0415 1032 1649 2306	1.8 3.5 1.6 3.5	25	TU	0311 0929 1554 2218	1.6 3.6 1.4 3.7
11	TU	0509 1126 1737 2355	1.7 3.7 1.4 3.7	26	W	0429 1041 1703 2324	1.4 3.8 1.0 4.0
12	W	0550 1208 1815	1.5 3.9 1.2	27	TH	0528 1138 1758	1.1 4.1 0.7
13	TH	0034 0625 1245 1850	3.8 1.3 4.0 1.0	28	F	0017 0617 1227 1845	4.2 0.9 4.4 0.4
14	F O	0108 0658 1317 1922	3.9 1.2 4.1 0.9				
15	SA	0139 0728 1347 1953	4.0 1.1 4.2 0.8				

MARCH

Date	Day	Time	m	Date	Day	Time	m
1	SA ●	0103 0701 1311 1930	4.4 0.6 4.6 0.2	16	SU O	0112 0704 1322 1925	4.0 1.0 4.1 0.7
2	SU	0147 0744 1354 2013	4.5 0.5 4.7 0.2	17	M	0142 0734 1352 1956	4.1 0.9 4.2 0.6
3	M	0228 0824 1437 2054	4.5 0.5 4.7 0.3	18	TU	0212 0805 1423 2028	4.1 0.8 4.3 0.6
4	TU	0310 0904 1520 2134	4.4 0.6 4.6 0.5	19	W	0243 0836 1456 2100	4.1 0.8 4.2 0.7
5	W	0351 0944 1605 2213	4.2 0.7 4.3 0.8	20	TH	0317 0909 1532 2134	4.1 0.8 4.2 0.8
6	TH	0435 1026 1652 2254	4.0 1.0 4.1 1.1	21	F	0353 0945 1613 2212	4.0 0.9 4.0 1.0
7	F	0521 1112 1745 2340	3.8 1.2 3.7 1.5	22	SA	0435 1028 1702 2300	3.9 1.1 3.9 1.2
8	SA ☽	0614 1208 1846	3.5 1.5 3.5	23	SU	0525 1123 1804	3.7 1.2 3.7
9	SU	0038 0716 1321 1957	1.8 3.4 1.7 3.3	24	M ☾	0003 0630 1240 1921	1.5 3.6 1.4 3.5
10	M	0157 0831 1459 2122	1.9 3.3 1.8 3.2	25	TU	0126 0747 1410 2044	1.6 3.5 1.4 3.5
11	TU	0340 0952 1620 2237	1.9 3.4 1.6 3.4	26	W	0256 0907 1540 2207	1.6 3.6 1.2 3.7
12	W	0443 1054 1710 2328	1.7 3.5 1.4 3.5	27	TH	0414 1022 1648 2310	1.4 3.8 0.9 3.9
13	TH	0526 1140 1749	1.5 3.7 1.2	28	F	0512 1120 1741	1.1 4.0 0.6
14	F	0007 0601 1218 1823	3.7 1.3 3.9 1.0	29	SA	0001 0559 1209 1827	4.1 0.9 4.3 0.4
15	SA	0041 0633 1251 1854	3.9 1.1 4.0 0.8	30	SU ●	0045 0643 1252 1910	4.3 0.7 4.5 0.3
				31	M	0125 0724 1334	4.4 0.5 4.5

APRIL

Date	Day	Time	m	Date	Day	Time	m
1	TU	0204 0803 1416 2028	4.4 0.5 4.5 0.4	16	W	0144 0742 1400 2002	4.2 0.7 4.2 0.6
2	W	0243 0842 1458 2105	4.3 0.5 4.4 0.6	17	TH	0218 0817 1437 2038	4.2 0.7 4.2 0.7
3	TH	0322 0921 1541 2142	4.2 0.7 4.2 0.9	18	F	0254 0854 1517 2116	4.2 0.7 4.2 0.8
4	F	0402 1001 1627 2219	4.0 0.9 3.9 1.2	19	SA	0333 0935 1602 2159	4.1 0.8 4.1 1.0
5	SA	0444 1043 1716 2301	3.8 1.1 3.7 1.5	20	SU	0417 1023 1655 2250	4.0 0.9 3.9 1.2
6	SU	0532 1134 1813 2353	3.6 1.4 3.4 1.7	21	M	0510 1122 1800 2355	3.8 1.0 3.7 1.4
7	M ☽	0631 1239 1917	3.4 1.6 3.2	22	TU ☾	0616 1235 1914	3.7 1.2 3.6
8	TU	0105 0738 1400 2031	1.9 3.3 1.7 3.2	23	W	0114 0730 1359 2031	1.6 3.6 1.2 3.6
9	W	0237 0855 1530 2150	2.0 3.3 1.6 3.3	24	TH	0237 0846 1520 2149	1.5 3.6 1.1 3.7
10	TH	0401 1008 1630 2248	1.8 3.4 1.4 3.4	25	F	0352 0959 1627 2251	1.4 3.8 0.9 3.9
11	F	0451 1101 1712 2331	1.6 3.6 1.2 3.6	26	SA	0450 1059 1720 2340	1.2 4.0 0.7 4.0
12	SA	0529 1142 1748	1.4 3.7 1.0	27	SU	0539 1149 1806	0.9 4.1 0.6
13	SU	0007 0602 1218 1821	3.8 1.2 3.9 0.8	28	M	0023 0623 1234 1848	4.1 0.7 4.3 0.5
14	M	0040 0635 1252 1854	3.9 1.0 4.0 0.7	29	TU ●	0103 0704 1316 1926	4.2 0.6 4.3 0.6
15	TU O	0112 0708 1325 1928	4.1 0.8 4.2 0.6	30	W	0141 0744 1358 2004	4.2 0.6 4.3 0.7

MAY

Date	Day	Time	m	Date	Day	Time	m
1	TH	0219 0823 1439 2039	4.2 0.6 4.2 0.8	16	F	0156 0801 1422 2021	4.3 0.6 4.3 0.7
2	F	0256 0901 1521 2114	4.1 0.7 4.0 1.0	17	SA	0236 0844 1507 2104	4.3 0.6 4.2 0.8
3	SA	0334 0939 1604 2150	4.0 0.9 3.8 1.2	18	SU	0318 0930 1556 2151	4.2 0.6 4.1 0.9
4	SU	0413 1020 1650 2229	3.8 1.0 3.6 1.4	19	M	0405 1022 1652 2244	4.1 0.7 4.0 1.1
5	M	0457 1105 1741 2316	3.7 1.2 3.5 1.6	20	TU	0500 1121 1755 2346	4.0 0.8 3.8 1.3
6	TU	0549 1200 1838	3.5 1.4 3.3	21	W ☾	0603 1228 1901	3.8 0.9 3.7
7	W ☽	0016 0649 1306 1939	1.8 3.4 1.5 3.2	22	TH	0057 0711 1340 2011	1.5 3.7 1.0 3.6
8	TH	0133 0755 1419 2047	1.9 3.3 1.5 3.3	23	F	0210 0822 1453 2123	1.5 3.7 1.0 3.7
9	F	0252 0904 1528 2153	1.9 3.3 1.4 3.4	24	SA	0323 0934 1601 2226	1.4 3.8 1.0 3.8
10	SA	0358 1009 1623 2245	1.7 3.4 1.3 3.5	25	SU	0426 1037 1657 2318	1.2 3.9 0.9 3.9
11	SU	0447 1059 1706 2328	1.5 3.6 1.1 3.7	26	M	0519 1131 1745	1.1 4.0 0.9
12	M	0527 1141 1745	1.3 3.8 0.9	27	TU	0002 0605 1218 1827	4.0 0.9 4.0 0.8
13	TU	0005 0604 1221 1822	3.9 1.0 4.0 0.8	28	W ●	0043 0648 1302 1905	4.1 0.8 4.1 0.8
14	W O	0042 0642 1259 1901	4.1 0.8 4.1 0.7	29	TH	0122 0728 1343 1942	4.1 0.7 4.1 0.9
15	TH	0118 0721 1339 1940	4.2 0.7 4.2 0.6	30	F	0159 0806 1424 2017	4.1 0.7 4.0 1.0
				31	SA	0235 0843 1504	4.1 0.8 3.9

JUNE

Date	Day	Time	m	Date	Day	Time	m
1	SU	0311 0920 1543 2127	4.0 0.8 3.8 1.2	16	M	0306 0925 1548 2142	4.4 0.4 4.3 0.8
2	M	0348 0958 1625 2203	3.9 1.0 3.7 1.4	17	TU	0355 1016 1642 2233	4.3 0.5 4.1 1.0
3	TU	0428 1038 1709 2244	3.8 1.1 3.6 1.5	18	W	0448 1111 1740 2329	4.2 0.6 4.0 1.2
4	W	0513 1124 1758 2332	3.7 1.2 3.5 1.6	19	TH ☾	0546 1210 1840	4.1 0.8 3.8
5	TH ☽	0605 1217 1851	3.5 1.4 3.4	20	F	0031 0649 1314 1943	1.3 3.9 1.0 3.7
6	F	0032 0702 1318 1948	1.8 3.4 1.4 3.3	21	SA	0138 0756 1421 2051	1.4 3.8 1.1 3.6
7	SA	0142 0802 1422 2050	1.8 3.4 1.4 3.4	22	SU	0250 0907 1531 2158	1.5 3.7 1.2 3.7
8	SU	0251 0906 1523 2151	1.7 3.4 1.4 3.5	23	M	0401 1016 1634 2255	1.4 3.7 1.2 3.8
9	M	0353 1009 1619 2244	1.6 3.5 1.2 3.7	24	TU	0501 1115 1726 2344	1.2 3.8 1.2 3.9
10	TU	0447 1103 1708 2331	1.4 3.7 1.1 3.9	25	W	0550 1206 1809	1.1 3.9 1.1
11	W	0534 1151 1754	1.1 3.9 0.9	26	TH	0027 0634 1250 1848	4.0 1.0 3.9 1.1
12	TH	0014 0619 1237 1839	4.1 0.9 4.1 0.8	27	F ●	0106 0713 1331 1924	4.1 0.9 3.9 1.1
13	F O	0056 0704 1323 1923	4.2 0.7 4.2 0.7	28	SA	0142 0750 1409 1958	4.1 0.8 4.0 1.1
14	SA	0138 0749 1409 2008	4.3 0.5 4.3 0.7	29	SU	0217 0826 1445 2031	4.1 0.8 3.9 1.1
15	SU	0221 0836 1457 2055	4.4 0.4 4.3 0.7	30	M	0251 0900 1521 2104	4.1 0.8 3.9 1.1

SUNRISE AND SUNSET TIMES

ABERDEEN
At 57°09'N 2°05'W

UT		Sunrise	Sunset
Jan	01	0847	1537
	15	0836	1600
Feb	01	0808	1637
	15	0737	1709
Mar	01	0701	1741
	15	0624	1812
BST			
Apr	01	0637	1948
	15	0600	2018
May	01	0520	2053
	15	0449	2122
Jun	01	0422	2151
	15	0412	2206
Jul	01	0418	2206
	15	0435	2152
Aug	01	0506	2121
	15	0535	2049
Sep	01	0610	2005
	15	0639	1927
Oct	01	0712	1843
	15	0742	1805
UT			
Nov	01	0719	1623
	15	0751	1555
Dec	01	0822	1532
	15	0842	1525

ABERDEEN
LAT 57°09'N
LONG 2°05'W

TIMES AND HEIGHTS OF HIGH AND LOW WATER (Heights in Metres)

TIME ZONE UT
For Summer Time (area enclosed in shaded box) add 1 hour

2014

JULY

Date	Day	Time	m	Time	m	Time	m	Time	m
1	TU	0325	4.0	0935	0.9	1557	3.8	2138	1.2
2	W	0401	4.0	1011	1.0	1636	3.7	2214	1.3
3	TH	0439	3.8	1049	1.1	1718	3.6	2253	1.5
4	F	0523	3.7	1133	1.2	1805	3.5	2341	1.6
5	SA ☽	0613	3.6	1224	1.3	1858	3.5		
6	SU	0040	1.7	0711	3.5	1324	1.4	1956	3.4
7	M	0150	1.7	0814	3.5	1429	1.4	2058	3.5
8	TU	0301	1.6	0921	3.5	1535	1.4	2202	3.6
9	W	0409	1.5	1029	3.7	1637	1.2	2259	3.8
10	TH	0509	1.2	1127	3.9	1732	1.0	2350	4.0
11	F	0601	0.9	1220	4.1	1822	0.9		
12	SA O	0036	4.3	0649	0.6	1309	4.3	1909	0.7
13	SU	0121	4.4	0737	0.4	1357	4.4	1955	0.6
14	M	0206	4.6	0825	0.2	1445	4.5	2041	0.6
15	TU	0252	4.6	0913	0.2	1534	4.4	2127	0.7
16	W	0339	4.5	1002	0.3	1624	4.3	2215	0.8
17	TH	0430	4.4	1052	0.5	1717	4.1	2305	1.0
18	F	0524	4.2	1144	0.8	1812	3.9		
19	SA ☾	0001	1.2	0623	4.0	1241	1.0	1911	3.7
20	SU	0104	1.4	0728	3.8	1344	1.3	2017	3.6
21	M	0216	1.5	0840	3.6	1458	1.5	2127	3.6
22	TU	0338	1.5	0956	3.6	1612	1.5	2233	3.7
23	W	0445	1.4	1102	3.6	1708	1.4	2326	3.8
24	TH	0537	1.2	1154	3.7	1753	1.3		
25	F	0011	3.9	0619	1.1	1238	3.8	1831	1.2
26	SA ●	0050	4.0	0657	0.9	1316	3.9	1905	1.2
27	SU	0125	4.1	0732	0.8	1350	4.0	1938	1.1
28	M	0157	4.2	0805	0.8	1423	4.0	2010	1.0
29	TU	0229	4.2	0837	0.8	1455	4.0	2041	1.0
30	W	0300	4.2	0909	0.8	1528	3.9	2112	1.1
31	TH	0333	4.1	0942	0.9	1602	3.9	2144	1.2

AUGUST

Date	Day	Time	m	Time	m	Time	m	Time	m
1	F	0408	4.0	1016	1.0	1639	3.8	2219	1.3
2	SA	0446	3.9	1054	1.1	1721	3.7	2300	1.4
3	SU	0531	3.8	1138	1.3	1811	3.6	2351	1.6
4	M ☽	0627	3.6	1235	1.4	1910	3.5		
5	TU	0100	1.7	0733	3.5	1345	1.5	2016	3.5
6	W	0220	1.7	0847	3.5	1500	1.5	2126	3.6
7	TH	0340	1.5	1003	3.7	1614	1.4	2233	3.8
8	F	0450	1.2	1110	3.9	1715	1.1	2329	4.1
9	SA	0546	0.9	1205	4.1	1807	0.9		
10	SU O	0018	4.3	0635	0.5	1255	4.4	1854	0.7
11	M	0104	4.5	0723	0.3	1342	4.5	1939	0.6
12	TU	0149	4.7	0809	0.1	1427	4.6	2023	0.5
13	W	0234	4.8	0855	0.1	1513	4.5	2107	0.6
14	TH	0319	4.7	0940	0.3	1559	4.3	2151	0.7
15	F	0407	4.5	1025	0.5	1647	4.1	2237	0.9
16	SA	0459	4.3	1112	0.9	1739	3.9	2329	1.2
17	SU ☾	0556	4.0	1204	1.2	1836	3.7		
18	M	0029	1.5	0659	3.7	1306	1.5	1940	3.5
19	TU	0142	1.6	0812	3.5	1421	1.7	2053	3.5
20	W	0314	1.7	0934	3.4	1550	1.8	2207	3.6
21	TH	0429	1.5	1045	3.5	1650	1.6	2305	3.7
22	F	0520	1.3	1138	3.7	1734	1.5	2351	3.9
23	SA	0601	1.1	1219	3.8	1811	1.3		
24	SU	0029	4.0	0636	1.0	1255	3.9	1844	1.2
25	M ●	0103	4.1	0709	0.8	1327	4.0	1916	1.1
26	TU	0134	4.2	0740	0.8	1357	4.1	1946	1.0
27	W	0204	4.3	0810	0.7	1427	4.1	2015	1.0
28	TH	0234	4.3	0841	0.7	1458	4.1	2046	1.0
29	F	0306	4.2	0912	0.8	1530	4.0	2117	1.1
30	SA	0339	4.1	0944	0.9	1604	4.0	2150	1.2
31	SU	0416	4.0	1019	1.1	1644	3.9	2229	1.3

SEPTEMBER

Date	Day	Time	m	Time	m	Time	m	Time	m
1	M	0500	3.9	1101	1.3	1731	3.7	2318	1.5
2	TU ☽	0555	3.7	1157	1.5	1831	3.6		
3	W	0026	1.6	0706	3.6	1311	1.6	1942	3.6
4	TH	0152	1.6	0825	3.6	1437	1.6	2057	3.6
5	F	0321	1.5	0946	3.7	1557	1.5	2210	3.8
6	SA	0434	1.2	1056	3.9	1700	1.2	2310	4.1
7	SU	0531	0.8	1151	4.2	1751	1.0		
8	M	0000	4.4	0619	0.5	1238	4.4	1836	0.7
9	TU O	0046	4.6	0705	0.3	1322	4.6	1920	0.6
10	W	0129	4.8	0749	0.2	1405	4.6	2002	0.5
11	TH	0213	4.8	0831	0.2	1447	4.5	2044	0.6
12	F	0257	4.7	0913	0.4	1530	4.4	2126	0.7
13	SA	0343	4.5	0955	0.7	1615	4.2	2210	0.9
14	SU	0433	4.2	1038	1.0	1704	3.9	2258	1.2
15	M	0528	3.9	1125	1.4	1758	3.7	2356	1.5
16	TU ☾	0631	3.6	1223	1.7	1901	3.5		
17	W	0106	1.7	0741	3.4	1338	1.9	2012	3.5
18	TH	0239	1.7	0903	3.4	1516	2.0	2131	3.5
19	F	0403	1.6	1019	3.5	1624	1.8	2235	3.7
20	SA	0454	1.4	1113	3.6	1709	1.6	2323	3.8
21	SU	0534	1.2	1153	3.8	1746	1.4		
22	M	0001	4.0	0608	1.0	1227	3.9	1819	1.3
23	TU	0035	4.1	0640	0.9	1258	4.1	1850	1.1
24	W ●	0107	4.2	0711	0.8	1328	4.2	1920	1.0
25	TH	0137	4.3	0741	0.7	1358	4.2	1950	0.9
26	F	0208	4.3	0812	0.7	1428	4.2	2021	0.9
27	SA	0240	4.3	0843	0.8	1500	4.2	2053	1.0
28	SU	0315	4.2	0916	0.9	1535	4.1	2128	1.1
29	M	0354	4.1	0952	1.1	1615	4.0	2208	1.2
30	TU	0439	3.9	1035	1.3	1701	3.9	2259	1.4

OCTOBER

Date	Day	Time	m	Time	m	Time	m	Time	m
1	W ☽	0537	3.8	1132	1.5	1802	3.7		
2	TH	0008	1.5	0650	3.6	1250	1.7	1916	3.6
3	F	0135	1.5	0810	3.6	1418	1.7	2033	3.7
4	SA	0303	1.4	0931	3.7	1539	1.6	2147	3.9
5	SU	0416	1.1	1040	4.0	1642	1.3	2249	4.1
6	M	0512	0.8	1133	4.2	1732	1.0	2340	4.4
7	TU	0601	0.5	1218	4.4	1818	0.8		
8	W O	0025	4.6	0644	0.4	1301	4.5	1900	0.6
9	TH	0109	4.7	0726	0.3	1341	4.6	1941	0.6
10	F	0152	4.7	0807	0.4	1421	4.5	2022	0.6
11	SA	0236	4.6	0846	0.6	1502	4.4	2103	0.7
12	SU	0321	4.4	0925	0.9	1544	4.2	2145	0.9
13	M	0409	4.1	1004	1.2	1629	4.0	2231	1.2
14	TU	0501	3.9	1048	1.5	1719	3.8	2323	1.4
15	W ☾	0600	3.6	1140	1.8	1819	3.6		
16	TH	0027	1.7	0704	3.4	1250	2.0	1925	3.5
17	F	0146	1.8	0817	3.4	1417	2.1	2039	3.5
18	SA	0315	1.7	0934	3.4	1543	2.0	2151	3.6
19	SU	0416	1.5	1034	3.6	1635	1.8	2245	3.7
20	M	0459	1.3	1117	3.8	1715	1.6	2327	3.9
21	TU	0535	1.2	1154	3.9	1750	1.4		
22	W	0003	4.1	0608	1.0	1227	4.1	1821	1.2
23	TH ●	0037	4.2	0639	0.9	1258	4.2	1853	1.0
24	F	0110	4.3	0711	0.8	1329	4.3	1926	0.9
25	SA	0143	4.3	0744	0.8	1401	4.3	1959	0.9
26	SU	0219	4.3	0818	0.8	1435	4.3	2035	0.9
27	M	0257	4.3	0854	1.0	1512	4.3	2113	1.0
28	TU	0339	4.2	0934	1.1	1553	4.2	2157	1.1
29	W	0427	4.0	1020	1.3	1642	4.0	2251	1.2
30	TH	0527	3.9	1119	1.6	1742	3.9	2359	1.4
31	F ☽	0639	3.7	1234	1.7	1855	3.8		

NOVEMBER

Date	Day	Time	m	Time	m	Time	m	Time	m
1	SA	0120	1.4	0754	3.7	1357	1.7	2009	3.8
2	SU	0242	1.3	0911	3.8	1515	1.6	2122	3.9
3	M	0353	1.1	1019	4.0	1619	1.4	2227	4.1
4	TU	0451	0.9	1112	4.2	1712	1.2	2320	4.3
5	W	0540	0.7	1158	4.3	1759	0.9		
6	TH O	0007	4.5	0624	0.6	1240	4.4	1842	0.8
7	F	0052	4.5	0705	0.6	1320	4.5	1923	0.7
8	SA	0135	4.5	0744	0.7	1359	4.5	2004	0.7
9	SU	0219	4.4	0822	0.9	1438	4.4	2044	0.8
10	M	0302	4.3	0859	1.1	1517	4.3	2125	1.0
11	TU	0347	4.1	0936	1.3	1558	4.1	2206	1.2
12	W	0435	3.9	1015	1.6	1643	3.9	2252	1.4
13	TH	0526	3.7	1100	1.8	1735	3.7	2346	1.6
14	F ☾	0623	3.5	1157	2.0	1834	3.6		
15	SA	0050	1.7	0723	3.4	1311	2.1	1938	3.5
16	SU	0202	1.7	0831	3.4	1430	2.1	2047	3.5
17	M	0313	1.7	0938	3.5	1542	1.9	2153	3.6
18	TU	0411	1.5	1032	3.7	1634	1.7	2245	3.8
19	W	0454	1.3	1115	3.9	1715	1.5	2328	3.9
20	TH	0532	1.2	1152	4.0	1751	1.3		
21	F	0006	4.1	0608	1.0	1228	4.2	1827	1.1
22	SA ●	0044	4.2	0644	0.9	1303	4.3	1904	1.0
23	SU	0122	4.3	0721	0.9	1338	4.4	1942	0.9
24	M	0201	4.4	0800	0.9	1415	4.4	2023	0.8
25	TU	0243	4.3	0840	1.0	1455	4.4	2106	0.8
26	W	0329	4.3	0923	1.1	1539	4.3	2153	0.9
27	TH	0420	4.1	1011	1.3	1628	4.2	2246	1.0
28	F	0518	4.0	1108	1.5	1726	4.1	2349	1.1
29	SA ☽	0624	3.9	1215	1.6	1833	4.0		
30	SU	0100	1.2	0732	3.8	1329	1.7	1943	3.9

DECEMBER

Date	Day	Time	m	Time	m	Time	m	Time	m
1	M	0213	1.2	0844	3.8	1443	1.6	2055	3.9
2	TU	0325	1.2	0953	3.9	1553	1.5	2204	4.0
3	W	0428	1.1	1050	4.0	1652	1.3	2303	4.1
4	TH	0520	1.0	1139	4.2	1742	1.1	2353	4.2
5	F	0606	1.0	1222	4.3	1828	1.0		
6	SA O	0039	4.3	0647	1.0	1303	4.4	1910	0.9
7	SU	0123	4.3	0725	1.0	1341	4.4	1950	0.8
8	M	0205	4.3	0802	1.1	1419	4.4	2029	0.9
9	TU	0246	4.2	0837	1.2	1456	4.3	2106	1.0
10	W	0327	4.1	0912	1.3	1533	4.2	2144	1.1
11	TH	0408	3.9	0948	1.5	1612	4.0	2223	1.2
12	F	0452	3.8	1026	1.6	1655	3.9	2306	1.4
13	SA	0539	3.6	1110	1.8	1745	3.7	2357	1.5
14	SU ☾	0631	3.5	1205	1.9	1841	3.6		
15	M	0056	1.6	0728	3.4	1315	2.0	1941	3.5
16	TU	0201	1.7	0830	3.5	1428	2.0	2047	3.5
17	W	0306	1.6	0934	3.6	1537	1.9	2152	3.6
18	TH	0405	1.5	1030	3.7	1633	1.7	2249	3.8
19	F	0455	1.4	1117	3.9	1720	1.4	2337	3.9
20	SA	0539	1.2	1159	4.1	1803	1.2		
21	SU	0021	4.1	0621	1.0	1239	4.3	1845	1.0
22	M ●	0104	4.3	0703	0.9	1319	4.4	1928	0.8
23	TU	0148	4.4	0746	0.9	1359	4.5	2013	0.6
24	W	0232	4.4	0829	0.9	1442	4.5	2058	0.6
25	TH	0319	4.4	0914	0.9	1526	4.5	2146	0.6
26	F	0409	4.3	1001	1.1	1615	4.4	2237	0.7
27	SA	0503	4.1	1052	1.2	1709	4.3	2332	0.9
28	SU ☽	0602	4.0	1150	1.4	1810	4.1		
29	M	0034	1.1	0704	3.8	1256	1.6	1915	4.0
30	TU	0141	1.3	0811	3.7	1408	1.6	2027	3.9
31	W	0253	1.4	0923	3.8	1525	1.6	2142	3.8

WICK

LAT 58°26′N
LONG 3°05′W

TIMES AND HEIGHTS OF HIGH AND LOW WATER (Heights in Metres)

TIME ZONE UT
For Summer Time (area enclosed in shaded box) add 1 hour

2014

JANUARY

Date	Day	Time	m	Time	m	Time	m	Time	m
1	W ●	0428	0.8	1050	3.7	1657	0.6	2324	3.7
2	TH	0514	0.7	1138	3.8	1745	0.5		
3	F	0014	3.7	0559	0.7	1225	3.9	1832	0.4
4	SA	0103	3.7	0645	0.8	1312	3.9	1921	0.4
5	SU	0151	3.6	0730	0.9	1359	3.8	2011	0.6
6	M	0240	3.4	0816	1.0	1448	3.6	2103	0.8
7	TU	0332	3.2	0907	1.2	1540	3.4	2159	1.0
8	W ☽	0427	3.1	1006	1.4	1639	3.2	2302	1.2
9	TH	0527	2.9	1119	1.5	1743	3.1		
10	F	0015	1.3	0632	2.9	1245	1.5	1853	3.0
11	SA	0131	1.4	0742	2.9	1403	1.4	2008	3.0
12	SU	0230	1.4	0845	3.1	1459	1.3	2110	3.0
13	M	0315	1.3	0935	3.2	1543	1.2	2159	3.1
14	TU	0353	1.3	1017	3.3	1621	1.1	2240	3.2
15	W	0427	1.2	1055	3.4	1656	0.9	2317	3.2
16	TH O	0459	1.1	1129	3.5	1730	0.9	2351	3.3
17	F	0531	1.1	1202	3.5	1802	0.8		
18	SA	0024	3.3	0601	1.0	1235	3.5	1834	0.8
19	SU	0057	3.3	0632	1.0	1306	3.5	1906	0.8
20	M	0130	3.2	0703	1.1	1339	3.4	1939	0.9
21	TU	0204	3.1	0736	1.1	1413	3.3	2013	1.0
22	W	0241	3.1	0811	1.2	1450	3.2	2052	1.1
23	TH	0323	3.0	0852	1.3	1535	3.1	2140	1.2
24	F ☾	0413	2.9	0945	1.4	1630	3.0	2249	1.3
25	SA	0516	2.9	1110	1.5	1741	2.9		
26	SU	0009	1.3	0627	2.9	1242	1.5	1900	3.0
27	M	0125	1.3	0738	3.0	1403	1.3	2016	3.1
28	TU	0233	1.1	0845	3.2	1507	1.0	2125	3.3
29	W	0329	1.0	0944	3.4	1559	0.7	2222	3.5
30	TH ●	0417	0.8	1036	3.7	1647	0.5	2313	3.6
31	F	0502	0.7	1124	3.8	1733	0.3		

FEBRUARY

Date	Day	Time	m	Time	m	Time	m	Time	m
1	SA	0000	3.7	0545	0.6	1211	3.9	1818	0.2
2	SU	0047	3.7	0627	0.6	1256	3.9	1902	0.3
3	M	0131	3.6	0709	0.7	1340	3.8	1945	0.5
4	TU	0215	3.4	0750	0.8	1425	3.7	2029	0.7
5	W	0259	3.2	0833	1.0	1511	3.4	2114	1.0
6	TH ☽	0347	3.0	0922	1.2	1603	3.2	2208	1.2
7	F	0442	2.9	1029	1.4	1705	2.9	2316	1.5
8	SA	0546	2.8	1159	1.5	1818	2.8		
9	SU	0046	1.6	0659	2.8	1338	1.5	1940	2.7
10	M	0206	1.5	0814	2.9	1441	1.3	2051	2.8
11	TU	0257	1.4	0912	3.0	1527	1.2	2141	2.9
12	W	0336	1.3	0956	3.2	1604	1.0	2222	3.1
13	TH	0410	1.2	1034	3.3	1637	0.9	2257	3.2
14	F O	0441	1.0	1109	3.4	1709	0.8	2330	3.2
15	SA	0511	0.9	1141	3.5	1740	0.7		
16	SU	0002	3.3	0541	0.9	1213	3.5	1810	0.7
17	M	0033	3.3	0611	0.8	1244	3.5	1840	0.7
18	TU	0105	3.3	0641	0.8	1316	3.4	1911	0.7
19	W	0137	3.2	0713	0.9	1349	3.4	1944	0.8
20	TH	0212	3.2	0747	1.0	1425	3.3	2020	0.9
21	F	0251	3.1	0826	1.1	1509	3.1	2103	1.1
22	SA ☾	0338	3.0	0914	1.2	1603	3.0	2204	1.3
23	SU	0438	2.9	1031	1.4	1714	2.9	2336	1.4
24	M	0553	2.8	1218	1.3	1841	2.8		
25	TU	0105	1.3	0712	2.9	1350	1.2	2004	3.0
26	W	0220	1.2	0825	3.1	1456	0.9	2115	3.2
27	TH	0316	1.0	0927	3.3	1547	0.6	2210	3.4
28	F	0403	0.8	1020	3.6	1633	0.4	2258	3.5

MARCH

Date	Day	Time	m	Time	m	Time	m	Time	m
1	SA ●	0445	0.6	1107	3.8	1716	0.2	2343	3.6
2	SU	0526	0.5	1152	3.9	1757	0.2		
3	M	0025	3.6	0606	0.5	1236	3.9	1837	0.3
4	TU	0106	3.5	0646	0.5	1318	3.7	1916	0.5
5	W	0146	3.4	0725	0.7	1400	3.5	1954	0.7
6	TH	0225	3.2	0804	0.9	1443	3.3	2032	1.0
7	F	0307	3.0	0848	1.1	1530	3.0	2115	1.3
8	SA ☽	0356	2.9	0946	1.3	1628	2.8	2215	1.5
9	SU	0458	2.7	1112	1.4	1740	2.6	2344	1.6
10	M	06[illegible]2	2.7	1258	1.4	1904	2.6		
11	TU	0129	1.6	0731	2.7	1411	1.3	2022	2.7
12	W	0231	1.5	0838	2.8	1459	1.1	2115	2.8
13	TH	0312	1.3	0927	3.0	1537	1.0	2155	3.0
14	F	0346	1.1	1006	3.1	1610	0.8	2231	3.1
15	SA	0417	1.0	1041	3.3	1641	0.7	2303	3.2
16	SU O	0447	0.9	1115	3.4	1712	0.6	2335	3.3
17	M	0517	0.8	1147	3.4	1742	0.6		
18	TU	0006	3.3	0547	0.7	1220	3.5	1813	0.5
19	W	0039	3.3	0619	0.7	1254	3.4	1845	0.6
20	TH	0112	3.3	0653	0.7	1329	3.4	1919	0.7
21	F	0148	3.2	0729	0.8	1408	3.3	1957	0.8
22	SA	0228	3.1	0810	0.9	1453	3.1	2041	1.0
23	SU	0315	3.0	0901	1.1	1549	2.9	2143	1.2
24	M ☾	0413	2.9	1023	1.2	1704	2.8	2318	1.4
25	TU	0529	2.8	1208	1.2	1831	2.8		
26	W	0050	1.3	0650	2.9	1336	1.0	1953	2.9
27	TH	0205	1.2	0805	3.0	1440	0.8	2101	3.1
28	F	0259	1.0	0908	3.3	1530	0.5	2153	3.3
29	SA	0345	0.8	1001	3.5	1613	0.4	2239	3.4
30	SU ●	0426	0.6	1048	3.6	1654	0.3	2321	3.5
31	M	0506	0.5	1132	3.7	1733	0.3		

APRIL

Date	Day	Time	m	Time	m	Time	m	Time	m
1	TU	0001	3.5	0545	0.4	1215	3.7	1810	0.4
2	W	0040	3.5	0624	0.5	1256	3.6	1847	0.6
3	TH	0117	3.4	0702	0.6	1336	3.4	1922	0.8
4	F	0154	3.2	0741	0.8	1417	3.2	1957	1.0
5	SA	0233	3.1	0822	1.0	1501	2.9	2034	1.2
6	SU	0316	2.9	0914	1.2	1553	2.7	2124	1.5
7	M ☽	0411	2.7	1029	1.3	1701	2.6	2246	1.6
8	TU	0522	2.6	1157	1.3	1817	2.5		
9	W	0023	1.6	0637	2.6	1323	1.3	1934	2.6
10	TH	0147	1.5	0748	2.7	1419	1.1	2035	2.7
11	F	0236	1.3	0844	2.8	1500	1.0	2119	2.9
12	SA	0314	1.2	0928	3.0	1536	0.8	2156	3.0
13	SU	0347	1.0	1007	3.1	1608	0.7	2231	3.1
14	M	0419	0.8	1043	3.3	1640	0.6	2305	3.3
15	TU O	0451	0.7	1119	3.4	1713	0.5	2339	3.3
16	W	0525	0.6	1156	3.4	1747	0.5		
17	TH	0014	3.4	0600	0.6	1234	3.4	1822	0.6
18	F	0050	3.4	0638	0.6	1314	3.3	1900	0.7
19	SA	0129	3.3	0718	0.6	1357	3.2	1942	0.8
20	SU	0211	3.2	0805	0.8	1446	3.1	2031	1.0
21	M	0300	3.1	0903	0.9	1545	2.9	2136	1.2
22	TU ☾	0400	3.0	1027	1.0	1659	2.8	2305	1.3
23	W	0513	2.9	1156	1.0	1819	2.8		
24	TH	0029	1.3	0630	2.9	1316	0.9	1935	2.9
25	F	0142	1.2	0742	3.0	1419	0.7	2040	3.0
26	SA	0238	1.0	0846	3.2	1509	0.6	2132	3.2
27	SU	0324	0.8	0941	3.3	1552	0.5	2217	3.3
28	M	0406	0.7	1028	3.4	1631	0.5	2259	3.4
29	TU ●	0447	0.6	1113	3.5	1708	0.5	2338	3.4
30	W	0526	0.5	1155	3.4	1745	0.6		

MAY

Date	Day	Time	m	Time	m	Time	m	Time	m
1	TH	0015	3.4	0605	0.5	1235	3.4	1820	0.7
2	F	0052	3.3	0644	0.6	1314	3.2	1855	0.9
3	SA	0127	3.2	0722	0.7	1354	3.1	1929	1.0
4	SU	0204	3.1	0802	0.9	1435	2.9	2005	1.2
5	M	0245	3.0	0849	1.0	1522	2.7	2049	1.4
6	TU	0332	2.8	0949	1.2	1619	2.6	2152	1.5
7	W ☽	0431	2.7	1101	1.2	1726	2.5	2316	1.6
8	TH	0540	2.6	1214	1.2	1834	2.5		
9	F	0036	1.5	0647	2.7	1321	1.1	1936	2.6
10	SA	0143	1.4	0748	2.7	1413	1.0	2029	2.8
11	SU	0232	1.2	0841	2.9	1455	0.9	2114	2.9
12	M	0312	1.1	0927	3.0	1533	0.8	2154	3.1
13	TU	0349	0.9	1010	3.2	1609	0.7	2233	3.3
14	W O	0426	0.7	1052	3.3	1646	0.6	2312	3.4
15	TH	0504	0.6	1134	3.4	1724	0.5	2351	3.5
16	F	0545	0.5	1217	3.4	1805	0.6		
17	SA	0032	3.5	0627	0.5	1303	3.4	1847	0.7
18	SU	0115	3.4	0714	0.5	1350	3.3	1933	0.8
19	M	0201	3.3	0805	0.6	1442	3.1	2025	1.0
20	TU	0251	3.2	0907	0.7	1541	3.0	2129	1.1
21	W ☾	0349	3.1	1020	0.8	1649	2.9	2244	1.2
22	TH	0457	3.0	1135	0.8	1759	2.8		
23	F	0000	1.3	0607	3.0	1249	0.8	1907	2.9
24	SA	0113	1.2	0716	3.0	1354	0.8	2012	3.0
25	SU	0214	1.1	0822	3.1	1446	0.7	2108	3.1
26	M	0305	0.9	0920	3.2	1530	0.7	2155	3.2
27	TU	0350	0.8	1011	3.2	1610	0.7	2237	3.3
28	W ●	0431	0.7	1056	3.3	1647	0.7	2317	3.3
29	TH	0511	0.6	1137	3.3	1723	0.8	2354	3.4
30	F	0550	0.6	1217	3.2	1759	0.8		
31	SA	0030	3.3	0628	0.7	1255	3.1		

JUNE

Date	Day	Time	m	Time	m	Time	m	Time	m
1	SU	0105	3.3	0705	0.7	1333	3.0	1906	1.0
2	M	0141	3.2	0743	0.8	1411	2.9	1941	1.1
3	TU	0218	3.1	0824	0.9	1453	2.8	2020	1.3
4	W	0300	2.9	0911	1.0	1539	2.7	2107	1.4
5	TH ☽	0347	2.8	1009	1.1	1633	2.6	2212	1.5
6	F	0443	2.7	1113	1.2	1734	2.6	2328	1.5
7	SA	0547	2.7	1216	1.2	1835	2.7		
8	SU	0038	1.4	0649	2.7	1317	1.1	1933	2.8
9	M	0141	1.3	0749	2.8	1410	1.0	2027	2.9
10	TU	0234	1.1	0846	3.0	1457	0.9	2117	3.1
11	W	0320	1.0	0939	3.1	1540	0.8	2203	3.3
12	TH	0404	0.8	1028	3.3	1623	0.7	2248	3.4
13	F O	0448	0.6	1117	3.4	1707	0.6	2333	3.5
14	SA	0534	0.4	1205	3.5	1752	0.6		
15	SU	0018	3.6	0620	0.4	1253	3.5	1837	0.6
16	M	0104	3.6	0709	0.4	1342	3.4	1924	0.7
17	TU	0151	3.5	0801	0.4	1434	3.3	2015	0.9
18	W	0241	3.4	0858	0.5	1528	3.1	2110	1.0
19	TH ☾	0335	3.3	1001	0.7	1628	3.0	2215	1.2
20	F	0436	3.2	1107	0.8	1730	2.9	2325	1.2
21	SA	0541	3.0	1216	0.9	1835	2.9		
22	SU	0040	1.2	0649	3.0	1326	1.0	1941	2.9
23	M	0152	1.2	0759	3.0	1424	1.0	2042	3.0
24	TU	0250	1.1	0903	3.0	1512	1.0	2134	3.1
25	W	0338	0.9	0956	3.1	1553	1.0	2218	3.2
26	TH	0420	0.8	1041	3.1	1630	0.9	2259	3.3
27	F ●	0459	0.7	1122	3.1	1705	0.9	2336	3.3
28	SA	0536	0.7	1200	3.1	1740	0.9		
29	SU	0011	3.3	0611	0.7	1237	3.1	1813	0.9
30	M	0046	3.3	0646	0.7	1312	3.1	1845	1.0

SUNRISE AND SUNSET TIMES

WICK
At 58°26′N 3°05′W

		Sunrise	Sunset
UT			
Jan	01	0901	1531
	15	0848	1556
Feb	01	0818	1635
	15	0745	1709
Mar	01	0708	1743
	15	0628	1815
BST			
Apr	01	0640	1954
	15	0600	2026
May	01	0518	2103
	15	0445	2134
Jun	01	0416	2206
	15	0405	2221
Jul	01	0411	2221
	15	0430	2206
Aug	01	0503	2133
	15	0534	2058
Sep	01	0611	2012
	15	0642	1932
Oct	01	0717	1846
	15	0748	1807
UT			
Nov	01	0728	1623
	15	0801	1552
Dec	01	0835	1527
	15	0856	1519

WICK
LAT 58°26′N
LONG 3°05′W

TIMES AND HEIGHTS OF HIGH AND LOW WATER (Heights in Metres)

TIME ZONE UT
For Summer Time (area enclosed in shaded box) add 1 hour

2014

JULY

Date	Day	Time	m
1	TU	0120 0721 1347 1918	3.3 0.7 3.0 1.0
2	W	0154 0757 1423 1953	3.2 0.8 2.9 1.1
3	TH	0230 0835 1502 2031	3.1 0.9 2.9 1.2
4	F	0310 0919 1546 2116	3.0 1.0 2.8 1.3
5	SA	0356 1013 1638 ☽ 2219	2.9 1.1 2.7 1.4
6	SU	0451 1118 1738 2338	2.8 1.2 2.7 1.4
7	M	0556 1223 1842	2.8 1.2 2.8
8	TU	0051 0704 1327 1944	1.4 2.8 1.1 2.9
9	W	0159 0811 1427 2043	1.2 2.9 1.0 3.1
10	TH	0258 0914 1519 2138	1.0 3.1 0.9 3.3
11	F	0348 1010 1607 2228	0.8 3.3 0.8 3.4
12	SA	0436 1103 1653 ○ 2316	0.6 3.4 0.7 3.6
13	SU	0524 1152 1739	0.4 3.5 0.6
14	M	0003 0610 1241 1824	3.7 0.2 3.6 0.6
15	TU	0050 0658 1329 1909	3.8 0.2 3.5 0.6
16	W	0137 0747 1417 1956	3.7 0.3 3.4 0.8
17	TH	0225 0837 1506 2044	3.6 0.5 3.2 0.9
18	F	0315 0931 1559 2141	3.4 0.7 3.1 1.1
19	SA	0411 1031 1657 ☾ 2248	3.2 0.9 2.9 1.2
20	SU	0513 1138 1759	3.0 1.1 2.8
21	M	0008 0621 1255 1907	1.3 2.9 1.2 2.8
22	TU	0133 0737 1404 2016	1.3 2.8 1.2 2.9
23	W	0238 0847 1456 2114	1.2 2.9 1.2 3.1
24	TH	0327 0942 1538 2200	1.0 3.0 1.2 3.2
25	F	0408 1027 1614 2241	0.9 3.0 1.1 3.3
26	SA	0444 1106 1648 ● 2317	0.8 3.1 1.0 3.4
27	SU	0518 1141 1720 2351	0.7 3.2 1.0 3.4
28	M	0551 1215 1752	0.7 3.2 0.9
29	TU	0024 0623 1248 1823	3.4 0.7 3.2 0.9
30	W	0057 0655 1320 1854	3.4 0.7 3.1 0.9
31	TH	0129 0727 1353 1926	3.3 0.7 3.1 1.0

AUGUST

Date	Day	Time	m
1	F	0202 0800 1428 2000	3.2 0.8 3.0 1.1
2	SA	0238 0837 1507 2038	3.1 0.9 2.9 1.2
3	SU	0319 0920 1553 2126	3.0 1.1 2.9 1.3
4	M	0409 1019 1649 ☽ 2240	2.9 1.2 2.8 1.4
5	TU	0513 1137 1757	2.8 1.3 2.8
6	W	0012 0630 1254 1908	1.4 2.8 1.2 2.9
7	TH	0134 0746 1405 2015	1.3 2.9 1.1 3.1
8	F	0242 0857 1504 2116	1.0 3.1 1.0 3.3
9	SA	0336 0957 1553 2210	0.7 3.3 0.8 3.5
10	SU	0424 1049 1639 ○ 2259	0.5 3.5 0.7 3.7
11	M	0510 1137 1723 2347	0.3 3.6 0.6 3.8
12	TU	0555 1223 1806	0.2 3.7 0.5
13	W	0033 0639 1309 1849	3.9 0.2 3.6 0.5
14	TH	0118 0723 1354 1932	3.8 0.3 3.5 0.7
15	F	0204 0808 1438 2016	3.7 0.5 3.3 0.8
16	SA	0251 0855 1526 2106	3.5 0.8 3.1 1.1
17	SU	0342 0948 1619 ☾ 2211	3.2 1.1 3.0 1.3
18	M	0443 1053 1721 2335	3.0 1.3 2.8 1.4
19	TU	0554 1216 1832	2.8 1.5 2.8
20	W	0112 0714 1342 1947	1.4 2.7 1.5 2.9
21	TH	0222 0830 1439 2050	1.2 2.8 1.4 3.0
22	F	0311 0925 1521 2138	1.1 2.9 1.3 3.1
23	SA	0349 1007 1555 2218	1.0 3.0 1.2 3.3
24	SU	0423 1044 1627 2254	0.8 3.1 1.0 3.4
25	M	0455 1118 1658 ● 2328	0.7 3.2 1.0 3.4
26	TU	0526 1150 1728 2359	0.7 3.3 0.9 3.5
27	W	0556 1221 1758	0.6 3.3 0.8
28	TH	0031 0626 1252 1828	3.5 0.6 3.3 0.9
29	F	0102 0657 1323 1900	3.4 0.7 3.2 0.9
30	SA	0135 0729 1357 1933	3.3 0.8 3.2 1.0
31	SU	0210 0803 1434 2010	3.2 0.9 3.1 1.1

SEPTEMBER

Date	Day	Time	m
1	M	0251 0842 1518 2055	3.1 1.1 3.0 1.2
2	TU	0340 0935 1613 ☽ 2201	3.0 1.3 2.9 1.4
3	W	0445 1101 1722 2347	2.9 1.4 2.9 1.4
4	TH	0608 1231 1840	2.8 1.4 2.9
5	F	0118 0730 1349 1952	1.2 2.9 1.3 3.1
6	SA	0228 0844 1449 2056	1.0 3.1 1.1 3.3
7	SU	0321 0942 1537 2151	0.7 3.3 0.9 3.6
8	M	0408 1032 1621 2241	0.4 3.5 0.7 3.8
9	TU	0451 1118 1703 ○ 2327	0.3 3.7 0.5 3.9
10	W	0534 1202 1745	0.2 3.7 0.5
11	TH	0012 0615 1245 1826	3.9 0.2 3.7 0.5
12	F	0057 0656 1326 1907	3.9 0.4 3.5 0.6
13	SA	0140 0736 1408 1949	3.7 0.6 3.4 0.8
14	SU	0225 0817 1451 2035	3.4 0.9 3.2 1.1
15	M	0314 0901 1540 2135	3.2 1.2 3.0 1.3
16	TU	0412 1001 1641 ☾ 2259	2.9 1.5 2.9 1.4
17	W	0523 1126 1752	2.7 1.6 2.8
18	TH	0040 0643 1309 1909	1.4 2.7 1.6 2.8
19	F	0155 0803 1414 2018	1.3 2.8 1.5 3.0
20	SA	0244 0859 1456 2109	1.2 2.9 1.4 3.1
21	SU	0322 0941 1531 2150	1.0 3.0 1.2 3.2
22	M	0355 1017 1602 2226	0.9 3.2 1.1 3.4
23	TU	0426 1049 1633 2259	0.8 3.3 1.0 3.4
24	W	0457 1121 1703 ● 2332	0.7 3.3 0.9 3.5
25	TH	0527 1152 1733	0.7 3.4 0.8
26	F	0004 0557 1223 1804	3.5 0.7 3.4 0.8
27	SA	0037 0628 1256 1837	3.5 0.7 3.4 0.9
28	SU	0111 0701 1330 1911	3.4 0.8 3.3 0.9
29	M	0149 0736 1408 1950	3.3 1.0 3.3 1.0
30	TU	0231 0817 1452 2038	3.2 1.1 3.1 1.2

OCTOBER

Date	Day	Time	m
1	W	0323 0910 1547 ☽ 2147	3.0 1.3 3.0 1.3
2	TH	0431 1039 1656 2334	2.9 1.5 3.0 1.3
3	F	0555 1213 1816	2.9 1.5 3.0
4	SA	0102 0717 1331 1930	1.2 3.0 1.3 3.1
5	SU	0211 0828 1431 2035	0.9 3.2 1.1 3.4
6	M	0303 0924 1519 2131	0.7 3.4 0.9 3.6
7	TU	0348 1013 1602 2221	0.5 3.6 0.8 3.8
8	W	0430 1057 1643 ○ 2307	0.4 3.7 0.6 3.9
9	TH	0510 1139 1724 2351	0.4 3.7 0.6 3.9
10	F	0550 1219 1805	0.4 3.7 0.6
11	SA	0034 0628 1259 1845	3.8 0.6 3.6 0.7
12	SU	0117 0705 1338 1926	3.6 0.8 3.4 0.9
13	M	0200 0743 1419 2010	3.4 1.1 3.3 1.1
14	TU	0247 0822 1503 2103	3.1 1.3 3.1 1.3
15	W	0340 0911 1558 ☾ 2218	2.9 1.6 2.9 1.4
16	TH	0447 1028 1707 2345	2.7 1.7 2.8 1.5
17	F	0601 1204 1821	2.7 1.8 2.8
18	SA	0109 0717 1331 1930	1.4 2.7 1.7 2.9
19	SU	0205 0819 1422 2028	1.3 2.9 1.5 3.0
20	M	0247 0905 1500 2113	1.1 3.0 1.3 3.2
21	TU	0322 0943 1533 2152	1.0 3.2 1.2 3.3
22	W	0355 1017 1605 2228	0.9 3.3 1.1 3.4
23	TH	0426 1050 1637 ● 2303	0.8 3.4 0.9 3.5
24	F	0457 1123 1709 2338	0.7 3.5 0.9 3.5
25	SA	0529 1156 1743	0.7 3.5 0.8
26	SU	0014 0603 1231 1818	3.5 0.8 3.5 0.8
27	M	0053 0639 1308 1857	3.5 0.9 3.5 0.9
28	TU	0134 0718 1349 1940	3.4 1.0 3.4 1.0
29	W	0220 0802 1435 2032	3.3 1.2 3.3 1.1
30	TH	0315 0858 1529 2146	3.1 1.4 3.2 1.2
31	F	0422 1022 1637 ☽ 2318	3.0 1.5 3.1 1.2

NOVEMBER

Date	Day	Time	m
1	SA	0542 1149 1754	3.0 1.5 3.1
2	SU	0040 0657 1307 1906	1.1 3.0 1.4 3.2
3	M	0148 0806 1408 2012	0.9 3.2 1.2 3.4
4	TU	0242 0903 1458 2110	0.8 3.4 1.0 3.5
5	W	0327 0951 1543 2201	0.7 3.5 0.9 3.6
6	TH	0408 1035 1625 ○ 2248	0.6 3.6 0.8 3.7
7	F	0448 1116 1706 2333	0.6 3.7 0.7 3.7
8	SA	0526 1156 1747	0.7 3.7 0.7
9	SU	0015 0603 1235 1827	3.6 0.8 3.6 0.8
10	M	0057 0639 1312 1907	3.5 1.0 3.5 0.9
11	TU	0138 0715 1351 1949	3.3 1.2 3.4 1.0
12	W	0221 0751 1432 2035	3.1 1.4 3.2 1.2
13	TH	0308 0833 1519 2134	3.0 1.5 3.1 1.3
14	F	0404 0930 1617 ☾ 2244	2.8 1.7 2.9 1.4
15	SA	0510 1052 1725 2358	2.7 1.8 2.9 1.4
16	SU	0618 1215 1832	2.7 1.8 2.9
17	M	0107 0721 1329 1933	1.4 2.8 1.6 3.0
18	TU	0201 0816 1420 2027	1.2 3.0 1.5 3.1
19	W	0243 0901 1501 2113	1.1 3.1 1.3 3.2
20	TH	0320 0941 1537 2155	1.0 3.3 1.2 3.3
21	F	0355 1018 1612 2235	0.9 3.4 1.0 3.4
22	SA	0430 1055 1648 ● 2315	0.9 3.5 0.9 3.5
23	SU	0506 1133 1726 2356	0.8 3.6 0.8 3.6
24	M	0543 1211 1806	0.8 3.7 0.8
25	TU	0039 0623 1253 1849	3.5 0.9 3.6 0.8
26	W	0125 0707 1336 1937	3.5 1.0 3.6 0.8
27	TH	0213 0754 1423 2031	3.4 1.1 3.5 0.9
28	F	0307 0849 1516 2139	3.2 1.3 3.4 1.0
29	SA	0410 0959 1619 ☽ 2255	3.1 1.4 3.3 1.1
30	SU	0520 1118 1730	3.0 1.5 3.2

DECEMBER

Date	Day	Time	m
1	M	0010 0630 1234 1839	1.1 3.1 1.4 3.2
2	TU	0121 0738 1343 1947	1.0 3.1 1.3 3.3
3	W	0220 0839 1440 2050	1.0 3.3 1.2 3.4
4	TH	0308 0930 1528 2145	0.9 3.4 1.0 3.5
5	F	0350 1016 1612 2234	0.9 3.5 0.9 3.5
6	SA	0429 1058 1653 ○ 2318	0.9 3.6 0.8 3.5
7	SU	0507 1137 1734	0.9 3.6 0.8
8	M	0000 0543 1215 1813	3.5 1.0 3.6 0.8
9	TU	0040 0618 1252 1851	3.4 1.1 3.5 0.9
10	W	0118 0653 1328 1929	3.3 1.2 3.5 1.0
11	TH	0157 0727 1405 2009	3.2 1.3 3.3 1.1
12	F	0237 0803 1445 2053	3.0 1.4 3.2 1.2
13	SA	0322 0845 1531 2146	2.9 1.5 3.1 1.3
14	SU	0414 0941 1624 ☾ 2250	2.8 1.7 3.0 1.4
15	M	0514 1058 1727 2356	2.8 1.7 2.9 1.4
16	TU	0617 1215 1832	2.8 1.7 2.9
17	W	0101 0717 1326 1933	1.4 2.9 1.6 3.0
18	TH	0158 0813 1423 2030	1.3 3.0 1.5 3.1
19	F	0245 0902 1509 2123	1.2 3.2 1.3 3.2
20	SA	0327 0947 1550 2211	1.1 3.4 1.1 3.4
21	SU	0407 1030 1631 2257	0.9 3.5 0.9 3.5
22	M	0447 1113 1714 ● 2342	0.9 3.7 0.7 3.6
23	TU	0529 1156 1757	0.8 3.7 0.6
24	W	0028 0612 1240 1843	3.6 0.8 3.8 0.6
25	TH	0115 0657 1325 1931	3.6 0.9 3.8 0.6
26	F	0203 0743 1412 2022	3.5 1.0 3.7 0.7
27	SA	0255 0833 1502 2120	3.3 1.1 3.5 0.8
28	SU	0350 0931 1559 ☽ 2225	3.2 1.3 3.4 1.0
29	M	0452 1041 1703 2336	3.1 1.4 3.3 1.1
30	TU	0558 1157 1812	3.0 1.4 3.2
31	W	0050 0705 1317 1923	1.2 3.0 1.4 3.1

LERWICK
LAT 60°09'N
LONG 1°08'W

TIMES AND HEIGHTS OF HIGH AND LOW WATER (Heights in Metres)

TIME ZONE UT
For Summer Time (area enclosed in shaded box) add 1 hour

2014

JANUARY

Date	Day	Time	m	Time	m	Time	m	Time	m
1	W ●	0412	0.6	1025	2.3	1641	0.4	2302	2.3
2	TH	0459	0.6	1113	2.4	1729	0.3	2355	2.3
3	F	0545	0.6	1202	2.5	1816	0.3		
4	SA	0045	2.3	0630	0.6	1251	2.5	1903	0.3
5	SU	0135	2.2	0716	0.6	1340	2.4	1951	0.4
6	M	0223	2.1	0803	0.7	1429	2.3	2042	0.5
7	TU	0312	2.0	0853	0.8	1520	2.1	2138	0.7
8	W ☽	0404	1.9	0952	0.9	1615	2.0	2245	0.8
9	TH	0503	1.8	1109	1.0	1722	1.9		
10	F	0004	0.9	0613	1.8	1238	1.0	1839	1.8
11	SA	0116	1.0	0721	1.8	1349	1.0	1950	1.8
12	SU	0213	1.0	0820	1.9	1445	0.9	2049	1.9
13	M	0301	0.9	0910	2.0	1530	0.8	2138	1.9
14	TU	0341	0.9	0952	2.1	1609	0.7	2219	2.0
15	W	0416	0.9	1030	2.2	1644	0.7	2256	2.0
16	TH O	0449	0.8	1106	2.2	1716	0.6	2331	2.0
17	F	0521	0.8	1140	2.2	1748	0.6		
18	SA	0004	2.0	0551	0.8	1212	2.2	1820	0.6
19	SU	0037	2.0	0621	0.8	1242	2.2	1852	0.6
20	M	0108	2.0	0653	0.8	1314	2.1	1926	0.6
21	TU	0141	2.0	0727	0.8	1348	2.1	2003	0.7
22	W	0218	1.9	0805	0.9	1427	2.0	2045	0.8
23	TH	0302	1.9	0850	0.9	1515	1.9	2133	0.8
24	F ☾	0354	1.8	0945	1.0	1613	1.9	2233	0.9
25	SA	0455	1.8	1100	1.0	1722	1.8	2353	0.9
26	SU	0606	1.8	1236	1.0	1844	1.8		
27	M	0110	0.9	0721	1.9	1350	0.9	2000	1.9
28	TU	0215	0.8	0825	2.0	1450	0.7	2103	2.0
29	W	0310	0.7	0920	2.2	1542	0.5	2159	2.2
30	TH ●	0359	0.6	1012	2.3	1630	0.3	2252	2.3
31	F	0445	0.5	1101	2.4	1716	0.2	2342	2.3

FEBRUARY

Date	Day	Time	m	Time	m	Time	m	Time	m
1	SA	0529	0.5	1149	2.5	1800	0.2		
2	SU	0028	2.3	0612	0.4	1235	2.5	1844	0.2
3	M	0113	2.2	0655	0.5	1320	2.4	1927	0.3
4	TU	0156	2.1	0738	0.6	1405	2.3	2012	0.5
5	W	0239	2.0	0824	0.7	1451	2.1	2059	0.7
6	TH ☽	0324	1.9	0915	0.8	1540	1.9	2153	0.9
7	F	0415	1.8	1023	1.0	1639	1.8	2308	1.0
8	SA	0521	1.7	1201	1.0	1800	1.7		
9	SU	0039	1.1	0643	1.7	1325	1.0	1925	1.7
10	M	0150	1.0	0753	1.8	1427	0.9	2030	1.7
11	TU	0243	1.0	0847	1.9	1513	0.8	2118	1.8
12	W	0324	0.9	0931	2.0	1551	0.7	2159	1.9
13	TH	0359	0.8	1010	2.1	1623	0.6	2235	2.0
14	F O	0430	0.7	1045	2.1	1654	0.5	2308	2.0
15	SA	0500	0.7	1118	2.2	1724	0.5	2340	2.0
16	SU	0529	0.6	1149	2.2	1755	0.5		
17	M	0011	2.0	0559	0.6	1220	2.2	1826	0.5
18	TU	0041	2.0	0630	0.6	1250	2.1	1859	0.5
19	W	0112	2.0	0704	0.6	1323	2.1	1934	0.6
20	TH	0147	2.0	0742	0.7	1401	2.0	2014	0.6
21	F	0227	1.9	0825	0.8	1446	1.9	2059	0.8
22	SA ☾	0316	1.8	0918	0.9	1544	1.8	2156	0.9
23	SU	0416	1.8	1028	0.9	1656	1.7	2315	0.9
24	M	0530	1.7	1210	0.9	1824	1.7		
25	TU	0050	0.9	0655	1.8	1334	0.8	1949	1.8
26	W	0201	0.8	0808	1.9	1437	0.6	2053	1.9
27	TH	0257	0.7	0906	2.1	1529	0.4	2148	2.1
28	F	0345	0.6	0957	2.2	1615	0.2	2237	2.2

MARCH

Date	Day	Time	m	Time	m	Time	m	Time	m
1	SA ●	0429	0.4	1046	2.3	1658	0.1	2323	2.2
2	SU	0511	0.3	1131	2.4	1739	0.1		
3	M	0006	2.2	0551	0.3	1215	2.4	1820	0.2
4	TU	0047	2.2	0632	0.4	1258	2.3	1900	0.3
5	W	0126	2.1	0714	0.5	1339	2.2	1941	0.5
6	TH	0204	2.0	0757	0.6	1422	2.0	2023	0.7
7	F	0245	1.9	0844	0.7	1508	1.8	2108	0.9
8	SA ☽	0330	1.8	0944	0.9	1600	1.7	2210	1.0
9	SU	0425	1.7	1114	0.9	1713	1.5	2349	1.1
10	M	0551	1.6	1247	0.9	1853	1.5		
11	TU	0116	1.1	0718	1.6	1356	0.9	2001	1.6
12	W	0216	1.0	0816	1.7	1444	0.8	2050	1.7
13	TH	0259	0.9	0902	1.8	1522	0.7	2130	1.8
14	F	0333	0.8	0941	1.9	1554	0.6	2205	1.9
15	SA	0404	0.7	1017	2.0	1624	0.5	2239	1.9
16	SU O	0433	0.6	1051	2.1	1655	0.4	2311	2.0
17	M	0504	0.5	1123	2.1	1726	0.4	2341	2.0
18	TU	0536	0.5	1154	2.1	1758	0.4		
19	W	0012	2.0	0609	0.5	1227	2.1	1832	0.4
20	TH	0045	2.0	0644	0.5	1302	2.1	1909	0.5
21	F	0120	2.0	0724	0.5	1342	2.0	1949	0.6
22	SA	0200	1.9	0809	0.6	1430	1.9	2036	0.7
23	SU	0248	1.8	0903	0.7	1530	1.8	2134	0.8
24	M ☾	0349	1.7	1013	0.8	1645	1.7	2254	0.9
25	TU	0504	1.7	1155	0.7	1814	1.6		
26	W	0034	0.9	0634	1.7	1319	0.6	1937	1.7
27	TH	0145	0.8	0750	1.8	1420	0.5	2039	1.9
28	F	0240	0.6	0848	2.0	1511	0.3	2130	2.0
29	SA	0327	0.5	0939	2.1	1555	0.2	2217	2.1
30	SU ●	0409	0.4	1027	2.2	1636	0.2	2300	2.1
31	M	0450	0.3	1111	2.3	1716	0.2	2340	2.1

APRIL

Date	Day	Time	m	Time	m	Time	m	Time	m
1	TU	0531	0.3	1153	2.2	1755	0.2		
2	W	0018	2.1	0611	0.3	1235	2.2	1833	0.4
3	TH	0054	2.1	0651	0.4	1315	2.0	1911	0.5
4	F	0131	2.0	0733	0.5	1356	1.9	1949	0.7
5	SA	0209	1.9	0818	0.6	1439	1.7	2030	0.9
6	SU	0251	1.8	0911	0.8	1528	1.6	2122	1.0
7	M ☽	0340	1.6	1025	0.8	1628	1.5	2248	1.0
8	TU	0442	1.6	1149	0.8	1801	1.5		
9	W	0021	1.0	0624	1.5	1303	0.8	1920	1.5
10	TH	0132	1.0	0735	1.6	1358	0.7	2012	1.6
11	F	0221	0.9	0824	1.7	1440	0.6	2053	1.7
12	SA	0258	0.7	0905	1.8	1515	0.5	2129	1.8
13	SU	0331	0.6	0943	1.9	1549	0.4	2204	1.9
14	M	0404	0.5	1018	2.0	1622	0.4	2238	2.0
15	TU O	0437	0.5	1054	2.0	1657	0.3	2311	2.0
16	W	0512	0.4	1130	2.1	1732	0.3	2346	2.1
17	TH	0549	0.4	1207	2.1	1809	0.4		
18	F	0021	2.1	0628	0.4	1248	2.0	1848	0.4
19	SA	0100	2.0	0711	0.4	1333	1.9	1932	0.6
20	SU	0142	1.9	0800	0.5	1426	1.8	2022	0.7
21	M	0232	1.9	0856	0.5	1528	1.7	2121	0.8
22	TU ☾	0335	1.8	1007	0.6	1639	1.6	2240	0.9
23	W	0448	1.7	1139	0.6	1802	1.6		
24	TH	0013	0.8	0612	1.7	1257	0.5	1917	1.7
25	F	0123	0.7	0727	1.8	1358	0.4	2017	1.8
26	SA	0219	0.6	0827	1.9	1449	0.4	2107	1.9
27	SU	0306	0.5	0919	2.0	1533	0.3	2153	2.0
28	M	0350	0.4	1007	2.1	1614	0.3	2235	2.0
29	TU ●	0431	0.3	1051	2.1	1653	0.3	2314	2.1
30	W	0512	0.3	1133	2.1	1731	0.4	2351	2.1

MAY

Date	Day	Time	m	Time	m	Time	m	Time	m
1	TH	0552	0.3	1213	2.0	1808	0.5		
2	F	0026	2.0	0631	0.4	1253	1.9	1845	0.6
3	SA	0103	2.0	0712	0.5	1333	1.8	1921	0.7
4	SU	0140	1.9	0755	0.6	1415	1.7	2000	0.8
5	M	0220	1.8	0842	0.7	1500	1.6	2045	0.9
6	TU	0305	1.7	0940	0.7	1550	1.5	2149	1.0
7	W ☽	0357	1.6	1050	0.8	1651	1.5	2316	1.0
8	TH	0501	1.5	1157	0.8	1816	1.5		
9	F	0028	1.0	0631	1.5	1257	0.7	1921	1.6
10	SA	0127	0.9	0735	1.6	1348	0.6	2008	1.6
11	SU	0214	0.8	0822	1.7	1431	0.6	2048	1.8
12	M	0254	0.7	0904	1.8	1511	0.5	2127	1.9
13	TU	0333	0.6	0945	1.9	1550	0.4	2205	2.0
14	W O	0412	0.4	1026	2.0	1629	0.4	2243	2.1
15	TH	0451	0.4	1108	2.0	1709	0.4	2323	2.1
16	F	0532	0.3	1152	2.1	1751	0.4		
17	SA	0003	2.1	0615	0.3	1239	2.0	1834	0.4
18	SU	0047	2.1	0702	0.3	1330	2.0	1920	0.5
19	M	0134	2.0	0753	0.3	1425	1.9	2012	0.6
20	TU	0227	1.9	0849	0.4	1524	1.8	2110	0.7
21	W ☾	0327	1.8	0956	0.5	1627	1.7	2219	0.8
22	TH	0433	1.8	1115	0.5	1738	1.7	2342	0.8
23	F	0548	1.7	1230	0.5	1849	1.7		
24	SA	0055	0.7	0701	1.8	1333	0.5	1949	1.8
25	SU	0156	0.7	0803	1.8	1426	0.5	2041	1.8
26	M	0247	0.6	0858	1.9	1512	0.5	2128	1.9
27	TU	0333	0.5	0948	1.9	1553	0.5	2211	2.0
28	W ●	0416	0.4	1034	1.9	1632	0.5	2251	2.0
29	TH	0456	0.4	1116	1.9	1710	0.5	2328	2.0
30	F	0536	0.4	1156	1.9	1747	0.6		
31	SA	0005	2.0	0614	0.4	1235	1.9		

JUNE

Date	Day	Time	m	Time	m	Time	m	Time	m
1	SU	0041	2.0	0653	0.5	1313	1.8	1858	0.7
2	M	0117	1.9	0732	0.5	1351	1.7	1934	0.8
3	TU	0154	1.8	0814	0.6	1432	1.7	2014	0.8
4	W	0235	1.8	0859	0.7	1515	1.6	2101	0.9
5	TH ☽	0321	1.7	0953	0.7	1604	1.6	2202	0.9
6	F	0413	1.6	1056	0.7	1700	1.5	2322	0.9
7	SA	0514	1.6	1200	0.7	1807	1.6		
8	SU	0031	0.9	0626	1.6	1257	0.7	1913	1.6
9	M	0128	0.8	0733	1.7	1349	0.6	2005	1.7
10	TU	0218	0.7	0826	1.8	1436	0.6	2051	1.9
11	W	0304	0.6	0915	1.9	1522	0.5	2135	2.0
12	TH	0349	0.5	1003	2.0	1606	0.5	2220	2.1
13	F O	0433	0.4	1051	2.1	1651	0.4	2304	2.2
14	SA	0519	0.3	1141	2.1	1736	0.4	2350	2.2
15	SU	0605	0.2	1232	2.1	1822	0.4		
16	M	0037	2.2	0653	0.2	1324	2.0	1909	0.5
17	TU	0128	2.1	0743	0.2	1417	1.9	1959	0.6
18	W	0220	2.1	0836	0.3	1510	1.9	2052	0.7
19	TH ☾	0315	2.0	0935	0.4	1605	1.8	2152	0.7
20	F	0413	1.9	1043	0.5	1707	1.7	2306	0.8
21	SA	0520	1.8	1158	0.6	1814	1.7		
22	SU	0026	0.8	0632	1.8	1307	0.7	1918	1.7
23	M	0134	0.7	0740	1.8	1404	0.7	2015	1.8
24	TU	0231	0.7	0840	1.8	1454	0.7	2106	1.9
25	W	0320	0.6	0934	1.8	1537	0.7	2152	2.0
26	TH	0404	0.5	1020	1.9	1617	0.6	2233	2.0
27	F ●	0444	0.5	1101	1.9	1654	0.6	2311	2.0
28	SA	0521	0.5	1140	1.9	1729	0.6	2347	2.0
29	SU	0557	0.4	1216	1.9	1803	0.7		
30	M	0022	2.0	0632	0.5	1251	1.9	1836	0.7

SUNRISE AND SUNSET TIMES

LERWICK
At 60°09'N 1°08'W

		Sunrise	Sunset
UT			
Jan	01	0908	1509
	15	0853	1535
Feb	01	0819	1618
	15	0743	1655
Mar	01	0703	1732
	15	0621	1807
BST			
Apr	01	0629	1949
	15	0547	2023
May	01	0502	2103
	15	0426	2138
Jun	01	0352	2214
	15	0339	2231
Jul	01	0345	2231
	15	0407	2213
Aug	01	0444	2136
	15	0518	2058
Sep	01	0559	2008
	15	0632	1926
Oct	01	0710	1837
	15	0744	1755
UT			
Nov	01	0728	1608
	15	0804	1534
Dec	01	0841	1506
	15	0903	1456

LERWICK

LAT 60°09'N
LONG 1°08'W

TIMES AND HEIGHTS OF HIGH AND LOW WATER (Heights in Metres)

TIME ZONE UT
For Summer Time (area enclosed in shaded box) add 1 hour

2014

JULY

Date	Day	Time	m
1	TU	0056 0707 1326 1909	2.0 0.5 1.8 0.7
2	W	0130 0743 1401 1944	1.9 0.5 1.8 0.8
3	TH	0206 0822 1440 2023	1.9 0.6 1.7 0.8
4	F	0247 0905 1523 2110	1.8 0.7 1.7 0.9
5	SA ☽	0334 0956 1613 2208	1.7 0.7 1.6 0.9
6	SU	0428 1059 1710 2327	1.7 0.8 1.6 0.9
7	M	0531 1208 1815	1.7 0.8 1.7
8	TU	0044 0644 1311 1922	0.9 1.7 0.7 1.7
9	W	0146 0753 1407 2020	0.8 1.8 0.7 1.9
10	TH	0240 0851 1459 2111	0.7 1.9 0.6 2.0
11	F	0330 0945 1549 2200	0.5 2.0 0.5 2.1
12	SA ○	0419 1038 1636 2249	0.3 2.1 0.5 2.2
13	SU	0506 1130 1723 2338	0.2 2.2 0.4 2.3
14	M	0553 1221 1808	0.1 2.2 0.4
15	TU	0026 0639 1310 1853	2.3 0.1 2.1 0.4
16	W	0116 0726 1359 1940	2.3 0.2 2.0 0.5
17	TH	0205 0815 1447 2028	2.2 0.3 1.9 0.6
18	F	0255 0907 1537 2122	2.1 0.5 1.8 0.7
19	SA ☾	0348 1007 1632 2230	1.9 0.6 1.8 0.8
20	SU	0450 1121 1736 2357	1.8 0.8 1.7 0.8
21	M	0603 1239 1847	1.7 0.8 1.7
22	TU	0115 0719 1345 1951	0.8 1.7 0.9 1.8
23	W	0219 0825 1438 2047	0.8 1.7 0.8 1.9
24	TH	0309 0920 1523 2134	0.7 1.8 0.8 2.0
25	F	0352 1004 1602 2215	0.6 1.8 0.7 2.0
26	SA ●	0429 1044 1637 2253	0.5 1.9 0.7 2.1
27	SU	0503 1120 1710 2328	0.5 1.9 0.7 2.1
28	M	0536 1154 1741	0.5 1.9 0.6
29	TU	0001 0608 1226 1811	2.1 0.5 1.9 0.6
30	W	0033 0640 1258 1843	2.1 0.5 1.9 0.7
31	TH	0104 0713 1329 1915	2.0 0.5 1.9 0.7

AUGUST

Date	Day	Time	m
1	F	0136 0748 1404 1952	2.0 0.6 1.8 0.8
2	SA	0213 0827 1444 2033	1.9 0.7 1.8 0.8
3	SU	0257 0911 1531 2124	1.8 0.7 1.7 0.9
4	M ☽	0350 1005 1627 2231	1.8 0.8 1.7 0.9
5	TU	0453 1118 1731	1.7 0.9 1.7
6	W	0003 0608 1239 1845	0.9 1.7 0.9 1.8
7	TH	0121 0729 1345 1954	0.8 1.8 0.8 1.9
8	F	0222 0835 1443 2052	0.7 1.9 0.7 2.0
9	SA	0316 0932 1534 2144	0.5 2.0 0.6 2.2
10	SU ○	0405 1024 1621 2234	0.3 2.1 0.5 2.3
11	M	0451 1115 1706 2322	0.2 2.2 0.4 2.4
12	TU	0536 1203 1750	0.1 2.2 0.4
13	W	0010 0620 1249 1833	2.4 0.1 2.2 0.4
14	TH	0057 0704 1334 1917	2.4 0.2 2.1 0.5
15	F	0143 0749 1418 2003	2.3 0.4 2.0 0.6
16	SA	0230 0836 1504 2054	2.1 0.6 1.9 0.7
17	SU ☾	0321 0929 1554 2157	2.0 0.8 1.8 0.8
18	M	0418 1038 1654 2330	1.8 0.9 1.7 0.9
19	TU	0532 1209 1812	1.7 1.0 1.7
20	W	0057 0659 1324 1926	0.9 1.6 1.0 1.8
21	TH	0203 0809 1421 2025	0.8 1.7 1.0 1.9
22	F	0253 0901 1506 2112	0.7 1.8 0.9 1.9
23	SA	0333 0943 1543 2153	0.7 1.9 0.8 2.0
24	SU	0408 1020 1616 2230	0.6 1.9 0.7 2.1
25	M ●	0439 1054 1646 2304	0.5 2.0 0.7 2.1
26	TU	0510 1126 1716 2336	0.5 2.0 0.6 2.2
27	W	0540 1157 1746	0.5 2.0 0.6
28	TH	0006 0610 1227 1816	2.1 0.5 2.0 0.6
29	F	0036 0642 1257 1849	2.1 0.5 2.0 0.7
30	SA	0108 0716 1330 1925	2.1 0.6 2.0 0.7
31	SU	0144 0754 1408 2006	2.0 0.7 1.9 0.8

SEPTEMBER

Date	Day	Time	m
1	M	0227 0837 1454 2056	1.9 0.8 1.9 0.9
2	TU ☽	0320 0929 1550 2200	1.8 0.9 1.8 0.9
3	W	0427 1040 1657 2334	1.7 0.9 1.8 0.9
4	TH	0547 1215 1817	1.7 1.0 1.8
5	F	0103 0714 1330 1934	0.8 1.8 0.9 1.9
6	SA	0207 0822 1428 2035	0.7 1.9 0.8 2.1
7	SU	0301 0918 1518 2128	0.5 2.1 0.6 2.2
8	M	0348 1008 1603 2217	0.3 2.2 0.5 2.3
9	TU ○	0432 1055 1647 2304	0.2 2.3 0.4 2.4
10	W	0515 1140 1729 2349	0.1 2.3 0.4 2.5
11	TH	0557 1223 1811	0.2 2.3 0.4
12	F	0034 0639 1305 1854	2.4 0.3 2.2 0.4
13	SA	0119 0721 1346 1938	2.3 0.5 2.1 0.6
14	SU	0204 0804 1429 2027	2.1 0.7 2.0 0.7
15	M	0253 0852 1516 2127	1.9 0.9 1.9 0.9
16	TU ☾	0347 0954 1611 2256	1.8 1.0 1.8 1.0
17	W	0457 1129 1729	1.7 1.1 1.7
18	TH	0028 0630 1255 1855	0.9 1.6 1.1 1.8
19	F	0136 0743 1356 1956	0.9 1.7 1.0 1.8
20	SA	0227 0833 1441 2044	0.8 1.8 0.9 1.9
21	SU	0306 0914 1518 2125	0.7 1.9 0.9 2.0
22	M	0339 0950 1549 2201	0.6 2.0 0.8 2.1
23	TU	0409 1024 1619 2235	0.6 2.0 0.7 2.1
24	W ●	0439 1055 1649 2307	0.5 2.1 0.6 2.2
25	TH	0510 1126 1720 2338	0.5 2.1 0.6 2.2
26	F	0541 1156 1752	0.5 2.1 0.6
27	SA	0010 0614 1227 1826	2.2 0.5 2.1 0.6
28	SU	0044 0649 1301 1904	2.1 0.6 2.1 0.7
29	M	0122 0727 1339 1947	2.1 0.7 2.0 0.7
30	TU	0206 0811 1424 2038	2.0 0.8 2.0 0.8

OCTOBER

Date	Day	Time	m
1	W ☽	0303 0905 1522 2143	1.9 0.9 1.9 0.9
2	TH	0413 1017 1632 2316	1.8 1.0 1.8 0.9
3	F	0535 1157 1755	1.7 1.0 1.8
4	SA	0046 0702 1313 1915	0.8 1.8 0.9 1.9
5	SU	0150 0807 1411 2017	0.6 2.0 0.8 2.1
6	M	0243 0900 1500 2109	0.5 2.1 0.7 2.2
7	TU	0329 0948 1544 2157	0.4 2.2 0.5 2.3
8	W ○	0412 1033 1626 2244	0.3 2.3 0.4 2.4
9	TH	0453 1115 1708 2329	0.3 2.3 0.4 2.4
10	F	0534 1156 1750	0.3 2.3 0.4
11	SA	0012 0613 1236 1832	2.4 0.5 2.2 0.5
12	SU	0056 0654 1315 1916	2.2 0.6 2.2 0.6
13	M	0140 0735 1356 2003	2.1 0.8 2.1 0.7
14	TU	0227 0818 1440 2059	1.9 1.0 1.9 0.9
15	W ☾	0317 0912 1531 2213	1.8 1.1 1.8 1.0
16	TH	0417 1034 1635 2338	1.7 1.2 1.8 1.0
17	F	0543 1206 1807	1.6 1.2 1.7
18	SA	0051 0702 1317 1918	0.9 1.7 1.1 1.8
19	SU	0147 0756 1407 2009	0.9 1.8 1.0 1.9
20	M	0228 0838 1445 2051	0.8 1.9 0.9 2.0
21	TU	0303 0915 1518 2128	0.7 2.0 0.8 2.1
22	W	0335 0950 1550 2204	0.6 2.1 0.7 2.1
23	TH ●	0407 1023 1622 2238	0.6 2.1 0.7 2.2
24	F	0440 1055 1656 2312	0.5 2.2 0.6 2.2
25	SA	0514 1128 1731 2348	0.5 2.2 0.6 2.2
26	SU	0550 1202 1809	0.6 2.2 0.6
27	M	0026 0627 1239 1849	2.2 0.6 2.2 0.6
28	TU	0108 0708 1319 1935	2.1 0.7 2.1 0.7
29	W	0157 0755 1406 2028	2.0 0.8 2.1 0.7
30	TH	0257 0850 1505 2132	1.9 1.0 2.0 0.8
31	F ☽	0405 0959 1615 2258	1.8 1.0 1.9 0.8

NOVEMBER

Date	Day	Time	m
1	SA	0521 1132 1734	1.8 1.0 1.9
2	SU	0024 0642 1250 1852	0.8 1.9 1.0 2.0
3	M	0128 0746 1350 1956	0.7 2.0 0.9 2.1
4	TU	0222 0839 1440 2050	0.6 2.1 0.7 2.2
5	W	0308 0926 1526 2139	0.5 2.2 0.6 2.3
6	TH ○	0351 1010 1609 2226	0.5 2.3 0.5 2.3
7	F	0432 1052 1651 2311	0.5 2.3 0.5 2.3
8	SA	0512 1132 1733 2354	0.5 2.3 0.5 2.3
9	SU	0551 1210 1815	0.6 2.3 0.5
10	M	0036 0630 1249 1857	2.2 0.7 2.2 0.6
11	TU	0119 0709 1328 1941	2.1 0.9 2.1 0.7
12	W	0202 0749 1410 2030	1.9 1.0 2.0 0.8
13	TH	0248 0834 1455 2127	1.8 1.1 1.9 0.9
14	F ☾	0338 0934 1547 2235	1.7 1.2 1.8 1.0
15	SA	0438 1057 1651 2345	1.7 1.2 1.8 1.0
16	SU	0600 1214 1819	1.7 1.2 1.8
17	M	0047 0708 1316 1923	0.9 1.7 1.1 1.8
18	TU	0138 0756 1403 2011	0.9 1.8 1.0 1.9
19	W	0220 0837 1443 2052	0.8 1.9 0.9 2.0
20	TH	0259 0914 1520 2132	0.7 2.1 0.8 2.1
21	F	0336 0951 1557 2210	0.7 2.2 0.7 2.2
22	SA ●	0413 1027 1635 2250	0.6 2.2 0.6 2.2
23	SU	0451 1105 1714 2331	0.6 2.3 0.6 2.2
24	M	0530 1143 1755	0.6 2.3 0.5
25	TU	0015 0611 1224 1839	2.2 0.7 2.3 0.5
26	W	0103 0655 1308 1927	2.2 0.7 2.2 0.6
27	TH	0155 0743 1357 2019	2.1 0.8 2.2 0.6
28	F	0251 0837 1454 2119	2.0 0.9 2.1 0.7
29	SA ☽	0353 0939 1558 2232	1.9 1.0 2.0 0.7
30	SU	0500 1057 1709 2354	1.9 1.0 2.0 0.8

DECEMBER

Date	Day	Time	m
1	M	0613 1220 1825	1.9 1.0 2.0
2	TU	0103 0719 1326 1932	0.7 1.9 0.9 2.0
3	W	0200 0815 1422 2031	0.7 2.0 0.8 2.1
4	TH	0250 0905 1511 2124	0.7 2.1 0.7 2.2
5	F	0334 0951 1556 2213	0.7 2.2 0.6 2.2
6	SA ○	0415 1034 1638 2258	0.7 2.3 0.6 2.2
7	SU	0454 1113 1720 2341	0.7 2.3 0.6 2.2
8	M	0533 1151 1800	0.7 2.3 0.6
9	TU	0020 0610 1229 1840	2.1 0.8 2.2 0.6
10	W	0100 0646 1306 1920	2.1 0.9 2.2 0.7
11	TH	0138 0723 1343 2000	2.0 0.9 2.1 0.8
12	F	0218 0800 1423 2044	1.9 1.0 2.0 0.9
13	SA	0300 0843 1507 2135	1.8 1.1 1.9 0.9
14	SU ☾	0347 0938 1556 2237	1.8 1.2 1.8 1.0
15	M	0441 1057 1655 2343	1.7 1.2 1.8 1.0
16	TU	0549 1214 1808	1.7 1.2 1.8
17	W	0043 0700 1315 1920	1.0 1.8 1.1 1.8
18	TH	0136 0754 1406 2014	0.9 1.9 1.0 1.9
19	F	0223 0839 1452 2101	0.8 2.0 0.9 2.0
20	SA	0307 0921 1534 2147	0.8 2.1 0.8 2.1
21	SU	0350 1003 1617 2232	0.7 2.2 0.6 2.2
22	M ●	0433 1046 1700 2319	0.6 2.3 0.5 2.3
23	TU	0515 1129 1744	0.6 2.4 0.4
24	W	0007 0559 1214 1829	2.3 0.6 2.4 0.4
25	TH	0056 0644 1301 1916	2.2 0.7 2.4 0.4
26	F	0147 0730 1350 2006	2.2 0.7 2.3 0.5
27	SA	0238 0820 1442 2100	2.1 0.8 2.2 0.6
28	SU ☽	0332 0915 1539 2202	2.0 0.9 2.1 0.7
29	M	0431 1020 1642 2317	1.9 1.0 2.0 0.8
30	TU	0538 1145 1755	1.9 1.0 1.9
31	W	0035 0648 1304 1909	0.8 1.9 1.0 1.9

ULLAPOOL
LAT 57°54′N
LONG 5°10′W

TIMES AND HEIGHTS OF HIGH AND LOW WATER (Heights in Metres)

TIME ZONE UT
For Summer Time (area enclosed in shaded box) add 1 hour

2014

JANUARY

Day	Time	m	Day	Time	m
1 W ●	0030 0627 1254 1854	1.0 5.5 0.8 5.4	16 TH O	0107 0705 1337 1925	1.4 5.0 1.3 4.9
2 TH	0117 0712 1342 1941	0.8 5.7 0.6 5.4	17 F	0140 0733 1409 1955	1.3 5.1 1.2 4.9
3 F	0202 0757 1429 2028	0.7 5.8 0.5 5.4	18 SA	0212 0801 1440 2025	1.2 5.1 1.1 4.9
4 SA	0247 0844 1515 2117	0.7 5.7 0.6 5.2	19 SU	0243 0829 1512 2056	1.2 5.1 1.2 4.8
5 SU	0333 0933 1602 2208	0.9 5.5 0.7 5.0	20 M	0314 0900 1543 2130	1.3 5.0 1.3 4.7
6 M	0420 1025 1650 2303	1.1 5.2 1.1 4.7	21 TU	0347 0934 1617 2208	1.4 4.8 1.4 4.5
7 TU	0509 1125 1741	1.5 4.9 1.4	22 W	0423 1013 1655 2255	1.6 4.7 1.6 4.4
8 W ☽	0007 0605 1232 1838	4.4 1.8 4.6 1.8	23 TH	0505 1100 1740 2356	1.8 4.5 1.8 4.2
9 TH	0121 0711 1345 1945	4.2 2.1 4.3 2.0	24 F ☾	0556 1205 1838	2.0 4.3 2.0
10 F	0240 0830 1501 2104	4.1 2.2 4.2 2.1	25 SA	0112 0702 1330 1953	4.1 2.2 4.2 2.1
11 SA	0350 0950 1607 2215	4.2 2.2 4.3 2.1	26 SU	0227 0826 1452 2118	4.2 2.2 4.2 2.0
12 SU	0445 1054 1700 2310	4.4 2.0 4.4 1.9	27 M	0336 0949 1606 2230	4.4 2.0 4.4 1.7
13 M	0528 1143 1743 2354	4.6 1.8 4.5 1.7	28 TU	0437 1057 1707 2328	4.7 1.6 4.7 1.4
14 TU	0604 1225 1820	4.8 1.6 4.7	29 W	0529 1153 1758	5.1 1.2 5.0
15 W	0032 0636 1302 1853	1.5 4.9 1.4 4.8	30 TH ●	0018 0615 1244 1844	1.0 5.5 0.7 5.3
			31 F	0105 0659 1330 1928	0.7 5.7 0.4 5.5

FEBRUARY

Day	Time	m	Day	Time	m
1 SA	0149 0742 1415 2010	0.5 5.9 0.3 5.5	16 SU	0151 0738 1417 1959	1.1 5.1 0.9 5.0
2 SU	0232 0825 1458 2053	0.5 5.8 0.3 5.3	17 M	0221 0805 1446 2029	1.0 5.1 0.9 5.0
3 M	0314 0909 1540 2137	0.6 5.6 0.5 5.1	18 TU	0251 0835 1516 2100	1.0 5.1 1.0 4.9
4 TU	0357 0955 1622 2223	0.9 5.3 0.9 4.8	19 W	0323 0907 1549 2136	1.1 5.0 1.1 4.7
5 W	0441 1047 1706 2318	1.2 4.9 1.3 4.4	20 TH	0358 0945 1625 2219	1.2 4.8 1.3 4.5
6 TH ☽	0529 1149 1754	1.6 4.5 1.7	21 F	0437 1030 1707 2314	1.5 4.5 1.6 4.3
7 F	0028 0626 1303 1852	4.1 2.0 4.1 2.1	22 SA ☾	0525 1131 1759	1.7 4.3 1.9
8 SA	0152 0743 1425 2013	4.0 2.3 4.0 2.3	23 SU	0031 0627 1302 1914	4.1 2.0 4.1 2.1
9 SU	0317 0919 1543 2145	4.0 2.3 4.0 2.3	24 M	0156 0755 1434 2053	4.1 2.1 4.1 2.1
10 M	0421 1035 1641 2250	4.1 2.1 4.1 2.1	25 TU	0314 0932 1555 2215	4.3 1.9 4.3 1.8
11 TU	0509 1126 1726 2336	4.3 1.9 4.3 1.8	26 W	0421 1045 1658 2315	4.6 1.5 4.6 1.4
12 W	0546 1207 1803	4.6 1.6 4.5	27 TH	0514 1141 1747	5.0 1.1 5.0
13 TH	0014 0617 1243 1834	1.6 4.8 1.4 4.7	28 F	0004 0559 1230 1829	1.0 5.4 0.6 5.3
14 F O	0049 0646 1316 1904	1.4 4.9 1.2 4.9			
15 SA	0120 0712 1347 1932	1.2 5.1 1.0 5.0			

MARCH

Day	Time	m	Day	Time	m
1 SA ●	0050 0641 1314 1909	0.6 5.7 0.3 5.4	16 SU O	0055 0645 1319 1905	1.1 5.0 0.9 5.0
2 SU	0132 0722 1355 1948	0.4 5.8 0.2 5.5	17 M	0126 0712 1349 1932	0.9 5.1 0.8 5.1
3 M	0212 0803 1435 2026	0.4 5.7 0.2 5.3	18 TU	0156 0740 1419 2002	0.8 5.1 0.7 5.1
4 TU	0252 0844 1514 2105	0.5 5.5 0.5 5.1	19 W	0227 0811 1450 2035	0.8 5.1 0.8 5.0
5 W	0332 0926 1552 2146	0.7 5.2 0.8 4.8	20 TH	0301 0846 1523 2111	0.9 5.0 0.9 4.9
6 TH	0413 1012 1632 2231	1.1 4.8 1.2 4.4	21 F	0337 0926 1600 2155	1.0 4.8 1.1 4.6
7 F	0457 1108 1714 2331	1.5 4.3 1.7 4.1	22 SA	0418 1015 1643 2251	1.2 4.5 1.4 4.4
8 SA ☽	0548 1220 1805	1.9 4.0 2.1	23 SU	0506 1122 1736	1.5 4.2 1.8
9 SU	0056 0656 1344 1917	3.9 2.2 3.8 2.4	24 M ☾	0009 0610 1255 1852	4.2 1.8 4.0 2.0
10 M	0229 0837 1507 2103	3.8 2.3 3.8 2.4	25 TU	0135 0739 1424 2035	4.1 1.9 4.0 2.1
11 TU	0346 1005 1613 2220	3.9 2.2 3.9 2.2	26 W	0254 0918 1544 2159	4.2 1.8 4.2 1.8
12 W	0439 1059 1700 2309	4.1 1.9 4.2 1.9	27 TH	0402 1029 1644 2258	4.5 1.4 4.5 1.4
13 TH	0519 1140 1737 2348	4.4 1.6 4.4 1.6	28 F	0456 1124 1731 2346	4.9 1.0 4.8 1.0
14 F	0551 1216 1809	4.6 1.3 4.6	29 SA	0541 1210 1811	5.2 0.6 5.1
15 SA	0022 0619 1248 1837	1.3 4.8 1.1 4.8	30 SU ●	0030 0622 1253 1848	0.7 5.4 0.4 5.3
			31 M	0112 0701 1333 1925	0.5 5.5 0.3 5.3

APRIL

Day	Time	m	Day	Time	m
1 TU	0152 0740 1410 2001	0.4 5.5 0.4 5.2	16 W	0131 0716 1352 1938	0.7 5.1 0.6 5.1
2 W	0231 0820 1447 2037	0.5 5.3 0.6 5.0	17 TH	0205 0751 1426 2014	0.7 5.1 0.7 5.1
3 TH	0309 0901 1524 2114	0.7 5.0 0.9 4.8	18 F	0242 0831 1503 2055	0.7 4.9 0.8 5.0
4 F	0349 0945 1601 2154	1.0 4.6 1.2 4.5	19 SA	0322 0917 1543 2143	0.8 4.7 1.0 4.7
5 SA	0430 1036 1641 2243	1.4 4.2 1.6 4.1	20 SU	0406 1014 1629 2243	1.1 4.5 1.3 4.5
6 SU	0517 1141 1727 2356	1.8 3.9 2.0 3.9	21 M	0458 1127 1726 2358	1.3 4.2 1.7 4.3
7 M ☽	0616 1257 1828	2.1 3.7 2.3	22 TU ☾	0604 1250 1842	1.6 4.0 1.9
8 TU	0126 0742 1418 2003	3.7 2.2 3.7 2.4	23 W	0117 0729 1410 2015	4.2 1.7 4.0 1.9
9 W	0251 0916 1529 2134	3.8 2.1 3.8 2.3	24 TH	0232 0857 1525 2134	4.3 1.6 4.2 1.7
10 TH	0354 1018 1623 2231	3.9 1.9 4.0 2.0	25 F	0339 1006 1625 2235	4.5 1.3 4.4 1.4
11 F	0440 1103 1703 2313	4.2 1.6 4.3 1.7	26 SA	0435 1101 1712 2325	4.7 1.0 4.7 1.1
12 SA	0516 1140 1737 2350	4.4 1.3 4.5 1.4	27 SU	0521 1148 1752	5.0 0.8 4.9
13 SU	0546 1214 1807	4.6 1.1 4.7	28 M	0010 0603 1230 1828	0.8 5.1 0.6 5.1
14 M	0024 0614 1247 1835	1.1 4.8 0.9 4.9	29 TU ●	0053 0643 1310 1904	0.7 5.2 0.6 5.1
15 TU O	0057 0644 1319 1905	0.9 5.0 0.7 5.1	30 W	0133 0722 1347 1939	0.6 5.1 0.6 5.1

MAY

Day	Time	m	Day	Time	m
1 TH	0211 0801 1423 2014	0.7 5.0 0.8 4.9	16 F	0147 0738 1408 1959	0.6 5.0 0.7 5.2
2 F	0249 0841 1459 2050	0.8 4.7 1.0 4.7	17 SA	0229 0824 1449 2045	0.6 4.9 0.8 5.1
3 SA	0328 0923 1536 2128	1.1 4.5 1.3 4.5	18 SU	0313 0916 1533 2136	0.7 4.8 1.0 4.9
4 SU	0408 1010 1615 2211	1.3 4.2 1.6 4.2	19 M	0401 1016 1622 2237	0.9 4.5 1.2 4.7
5 M	0451 1105 1657 2306	1.6 4.0 1.9 4.0	20 TU	0455 1124 1719 2345	1.1 4.3 1.5 4.5
6 TU	0542 1210 1749	1.9 3.8 2.1	21 W ☾	0558 1235 1829	1.3 4.2 1.7
7 W ☽	0021 0646 1320 1859	3.8 2.0 3.7 2.3	22 TH	0056 0710 1348 1948	4.4 1.5 4.1 1.8
8 TH	0140 0808 1430 2026	3.8 2.1 3.7 2.3	23 F	0207 0826 1500 2103	4.4 1.5 4.2 1.7
9 F	0251 0920 1532 2137	3.8 1.9 3.9 2.1	24 SA	0315 0936 1602 2208	4.4 1.4 4.3 1.5
10 SA	0347 1014 1619 2228	4.0 1.7 4.1 1.8	25 SU	0414 1035 1652 2303	4.5 1.2 4.5 1.3
11 SU	0431 1058 1658 2311	4.2 1.5 4.4 1.5	26 M	0504 1125 1735 2352	4.7 1.1 4.7 1.1
12 M	0508 1136 1733 2350	4.4 1.2 4.6 1.2	27 TU	0548 1209 1813	4.8 1.0 4.9
13 TU	0543 1213 1807	4.7 1.0 4.9	28 W ●	0036 0629 1250 1848	1.0 4.8 0.9 4.9
14 W O	0028 0618 1251 1841	1.0 4.9 0.8 5.1	29 TH	0117 0708 1327 1923	0.9 4.8 0.9 4.9
15 TH	0107 0656 1329 1919	0.8 5.0 0.7 5.2	30 F	0156 0746 1404 1957	0.9 4.8 1.0 4.9
			31 SA	0233 0824 1439	1.0 4.6 1.1

JUNE

Day	Time	m	Day	Time	m
1 SU	0310 0903 1515 2106	1.1 4.5 1.3 4.6	16 M	0305 0910 1525 2127	0.5 4.9 0.8 5.2
2 M	0348 0944 1552 2144	1.2 4.3 1.5 4.4	17 TU	0354 1006 1614 2223	0.6 4.7 1.0 5.0
3 TU	0427 1029 1631 2228	1.4 4.1 1.7 4.2	18 W	0445 1106 1707 2325	0.9 4.5 1.3 4.7
4 W	0510 1122 1715 2322	1.6 4.0 1.9 4.0	19 TH ☾	0541 1211 1807	1.1 4.3 1.5
5 TH ☽	0559 1223 1808	1.8 3.8 2.1	20 F	0031 0642 1320 1915	4.5 1.4 4.2 1.7
6 F	0031 0659 1329 1914	3.9 1.9 3.8 2.2	21 SA	0140 0750 1431 2029	4.4 1.5 4.1 1.8
7 SA	0142 0808 1432 2029	3.9 1.9 3.9 2.1	22 SU	0250 0902 1538 2141	4.3 1.6 4.2 1.7
8 SU	0246 0914 1529 2134	3.9 1.8 4.1 2.0	23 M	0355 1008 1634 2244	4.3 1.6 4.4 1.6
9 M	0341 1010 1617 2229	4.1 1.6 4.3 1.7	24 TU	0450 1104 1720 2336	4.4 1.5 4.5 1.4
10 TU	0430 1058 1700 2317	4.3 1.4 4.6 1.4	25 W	0537 1151 1800	4.5 1.4 4.7
11 W	0515 1143 1741	4.5 1.1 4.8	26 TH	0022 0618 1233 1836	1.2 4.6 1.3 4.8
12 TH	0002 0558 1227 1821	1.1 4.8 0.9 5.1	27 F ●	0104 0656 1311 1909	1.1 4.7 1.2 4.8
13 F O	0048 0643 1310 1903	0.8 4.9 0.7 5.2	28 SA	0142 0732 1347 1941	1.0 4.7 1.2 4.9
14 SA	0133 0729 1354 1948	0.6 5.0 0.7 5.3	29 SU	0217 0806 1421 2012	1.0 4.6 1.2 4.8
15 SU	0218 0818 1439 2036	0.5 5.0 0.7 5.3	30 M	0252 0840 1455 2043	1.1 4.6 1.2 4.7

SUNRISE AND SUNSET TIMES

ULLAPOOL
At 57°54′N 5°10′W

UT		Sunrise	Sunset
Jan	01	0905	1544
	15	0853	1608
Feb	01	0824	1646
	15	0751	1719
Mar	01	0715	1752
	15	0637	1824
BST			
Apr	01	0649	2002
	15	0610	2033
May	01	0529	2108
	15	0457	2139
Jun	01	0429	2210
	15	0418	2225
Jul	01	0424	2225
	15	0442	2210
Aug	01	0515	2138
	15	0544	2104
Sep	01	0621	2019
	15	0651	1940
Oct	01	0725	1854
	15	0756	1816
UT			
Nov	01	0735	1633
	15	0807	1603
Dec	01	0840	1539
	15	0900	1532

ULLAPOOL
LAT 57°54′N
LONG 5°10′W

TIMES AND HEIGHTS OF HIGH AND LOW WATER (Heights in Metres)

TIME ZONE UT
For Summer Time (area enclosed in shaded box) add 1 hour

2014

JULY

Date	Time	m
1 TU	0326 0915 1529 2116	1.1 4.5 1.3 4.6
2 W	0401 0953 1604 2153	1.3 4.3 1.5 4.5
3 TH	0438 1036 1643 2236	1.4 4.2 1.6 4.3
4 F	0518 1127 1726 2328	1.6 4.1 1.8 4.1
5 SA ☽	0605 1229 1819	1.8 4.0 2.0
6 SU	0035 0702 1336 1924	4.0 1.9 3.9 2.1
7 M	0149 0812 1440 2039	4.0 1.9 4.0 2.1
8 TU	0256 0923 1539 2149	4.0 1.8 4.2 1.9
9 W	0358 1025 1632 2249	4.2 1.6 4.5 1.6
10 TH	0454 1119 1720 2342	4.5 1.3 4.8 1.2
11 F	0545 1208 1806	4.7 1.0 5.1
12 SA ○	0032 0632 1256 1850	0.8 5.0 0.8 5.4
13 SU	0120 0719 1341 1935	0.5 5.2 0.6 5.5
14 M	0207 0806 1426 2021	0.3 5.2 0.5 5.5
15 TU	0253 0854 1512 2109	0.3 5.2 0.6 5.4
16 W	0339 0944 1558 2200	0.4 5.0 0.8 5.2
17 TH	0426 1038 1646 2257	0.7 4.7 1.1 4.9
18 F	0515 1138 1739	1.0 4.4 1.4
19 SA ☾	0002 0608 1246 1840	4.6 1.4 4.2 1.7
20 SU	0112 0710 1400 1954	4.3 1.7 4.1 1.9
21 M	0226 0824 1515 2116	4.1 1.9 4.1 2.0
22 TU	0338 0942 1618 2228	4.1 1.9 4.2 1.8
23 W	0438 1046 1707 2324	4.2 1.8 4.4 1.6
24 TH	0526 1136 1747	4.3 1.6 4.6
25 F	0009 0606 1218 1821	1.4 4.5 1.5 4.7
26 SA ●	0049 0641 1255 1852	1.2 4.6 1.3 4.8
27 SU	0125 0713 1329 1921	1.1 4.7 1.2 4.9
28 M	0158 0744 1402 1949	1.0 4.8 1.1 4.9
29 TU	0230 0814 1433 2018	1.0 4.7 1.1 4.9
30 W	0301 0845 1504 2047	1.0 4.7 1.2 4.8
31 TH	0332 0918 1537 2120	1.1 4.6 1.3 4.7

AUGUST

Date	Time	m
1 F	0405 0954 1611 2157	1.2 4.4 1.4 4.5
2 SA	0441 1038 1651 2242	1.4 4.3 1.6 4.3
3 SU	0522 1134 1737 2340	1.6 4.1 1.8 4.1
4 M ☽	0612 1245 1836	1.8 4.0 2.0
5 TU	0101 0719 1400 1953	4.0 2.0 4.0 2.1
6 W	0224 0842 1508 2118	4.0 2.0 4.2 2.0
7 TH	0338 1000 1610 2229	4.1 1.8 4.5 1.6
8 F	0441 1102 1703 2328	4.4 1.5 4.8 1.2
9 SA	0534 1153 1750	4.8 1.1 5.2
10 SU ○	0018 0620 1241 1834	0.8 5.1 0.8 5.5
11 M	0106 0704 1326 1917	0.4 5.3 0.5 5.7
12 TU	0151 0747 1410 2001	0.2 5.4 0.4 5.8
13 W	0235 0830 1453 2045	0.2 5.3 0.4 5.6
14 TH	0318 0915 1536 2133	0.3 5.1 0.6 5.3
15 F	0401 1003 1621 2225	0.6 4.8 1.0 4.9
16 SA	0445 1059 1710 2328	1.0 4.5 1.4 4.5
17 SU ☾	0533 1207 1806	1.4 4.2 1.8
18 M	0042 0629 1327 1918	4.2 1.9 4.0 2.1
19 TU	0202 0744 1450 2050	4.0 2.2 4.0 2.2
20 W	0320 0915 1558 2212	4.0 2.2 4.1 2.0
21 TH	0422 1028 1649 2308	4.1 2.0 4.3 1.8
22 F	0510 1118 1729 2351	4.2 1.8 4.5 1.5
23 SA	0548 1158 1802	4.4 1.6 4.7
24 SU	0028 0620 1234 1831	1.3 4.6 1.4 4.9
25 M ●	0102 0650 1307 1858	1.1 4.8 1.2 5.0
26 TU	0133 0718 1338 1924	1.0 4.9 1.1 5.0
27 W	0204 0746 1408 1950	0.9 4.9 1.0 5.0
28 TH	0233 0814 1438 2019	0.9 4.9 1.0 5.0
29 F	0303 0845 1509 2050	1.0 4.8 1.1 4.9
30 SA	0334 0919 1543 2126	1.1 4.7 1.3 4.7
31 SU	0408 0959 1621 2208	1.3 4.5 1.5 4.5

SEPTEMBER

Date	Time	m
1 M	0447 1050 1705 2305	1.5 4.3 1.7 4.2
2 TU ☽	0535 1203 1802	1.8 4.1 2.0
3 W	0032 0640 1329 1921	4.0 2.1 4.1 2.1
4 TH	0205 0814 1445 2057	4.0 2.1 4.2 2.0
5 F	0325 0943 1551 2215	4.2 1.9 4.5 1.6
6 SA	0430 1046 1646 2313	4.5 1.5 4.9 1.2
7 SU	0521 1138 1733	4.8 1.1 5.3
8 M	0002 0604 1224 1816	0.7 5.2 0.8 5.6
9 TU ○	0048 0645 1307 1857	0.4 5.4 0.5 5.8
10 W	0131 0725 1349 1939	0.2 5.5 0.4 5.8
11 TH	0212 0804 1431 2021	0.2 5.5 0.4 5.6
12 F	0253 0845 1512 2105	0.4 5.2 0.6 5.3
13 SA	0333 0928 1555 2154	0.7 4.9 1.0 4.9
14 SU	0414 1017 1641 2254	1.1 4.6 1.4 4.5
15 M	0458 1121 1733	1.6 4.2 1.8
16 TU ☾	0009 0550 1246 1841	4.1 2.0 4.0 2.2
17 W	0131 0700 1414 2017	3.9 2.3 3.9 2.3
18 TH	0252 0839 1528 2146	3.9 2.4 4.0 2.1
19 F	0357 1000 1622 2242	4.0 2.2 4.2 1.9
20 SA	0445 1052 1703 2324	4.2 2.0 4.4 1.6
21 SU	0523 1132 1736	4.4 1.7 4.6
22 M	0000 0554 1207 1804	1.4 4.7 1.4 4.8
23 TU	0033 0623 1240 1831	1.1 4.9 1.2 5.0
24 W ●	0104 0650 1311 1857	1.0 5.0 1.1 5.1
25 TH	0134 0717 1341 1924	0.9 5.1 1.0 5.1
26 F	0203 0746 1412 1953	0.9 5.1 1.0 5.1
27 SA	0234 0816 1444 2026	0.9 5.0 1.0 5.0
28 SU	0306 0851 1519 2103	1.0 4.9 1.2 4.8
29 M	0341 0931 1558 2148	1.2 4.7 1.4 4.5
30 TU	0421 1023 1643 2249	1.5 4.5 1.6 4.3

OCTOBER

Date	Time	m
1 W ☽	0510 1137 1742	1.8 4.3 1.9
2 TH	0021 0617 1306 1903	4.1 2.1 4.2 2.1
3 F	0152 0755 1424 2041	4.0 2.2 4.3 1.9
4 SA	0311 0925 1532 2158	4.2 2.0 4.6 1.6
5 SU	0415 1028 1628 2255	4.5 1.6 4.9 1.2
6 M	0505 1119 1714 2343	4.9 1.2 5.3 0.8
7 TU	0547 1204 1757	5.2 0.8 5.6
8 W ○	0027 0625 1247 1837	0.5 5.4 0.6 5.7
9 TH	0109 0702 1329 1918	0.4 5.5 0.5 5.7
10 F	0149 0740 1410 1959	0.4 5.5 0.6 5.5
11 SA	0227 0818 1450 2041	0.6 5.3 0.7 5.2
12 SU	0306 0858 1532 2127	0.9 5.0 1.1 4.8
13 M	0346 0940 1615 2221	1.3 4.7 1.4 4.4
14 TU	0427 1033 1704 2329	1.7 4.4 1.8 4.1
15 W ☾	0515 1150 1805	2.1 4.1 2.2
16 TH	0047 0615 1320 1928	3.9 2.4 3.9 2.3
17 F	0207 0745 1441 2059	3.8 2.5 4.0 2.3
18 SA	0317 0915 1543 2203	4.0 2.4 4.1 2.0
19 SU	0410 1015 1628 2248	4.2 2.2 4.3 1.8
20 M	0451 1058 1704 2326	4.4 1.9 4.6 1.5
21 TU	0524 1135 1734	4.6 1.6 4.8
22 W	0000 0554 1209 1802	1.3 4.9 1.4 4.9
23 TH ●	0032 0622 1242 1830	1.1 5.0 1.2 5.1
24 F	0104 0651 1315 1900	1.0 5.2 1.0 5.2
25 SA	0136 0721 1348 1932	0.9 5.2 1.0 5.2
26 SU	0208 0754 1423 2009	0.9 5.2 1.0 5.1
27 M	0243 0832 1501 2051	1.0 5.1 1.1 4.9
28 TU	0321 0915 1543 2141	1.2 4.9 1.3 4.6
29 W	0404 1009 1631 2248	1.5 4.7 1.5 4.4
30 TH	0455 1121 1731	1.8 4.5 1.8
31 F ☽	0012 0603 1244 1849	4.2 2.1 4.4 1.9

NOVEMBER

Date	Time	m
1 SA	0135 0733 1359 2018	4.2 2.2 4.4 1.8
2 SU	0251 0859 1508 2133	4.3 2.0 4.6 1.6
3 M	0355 1004 1606 2232	4.6 1.7 4.9 1.3
4 TU	0446 1057 1656 2321	4.9 1.4 5.2 1.0
5 W	0529 1145 1740	5.1 1.1 5.4
6 TH ○	0006 0607 1229 1821	0.8 5.3 0.9 5.5
7 F	0048 0644 1311 1901	0.7 5.4 0.8 5.5
8 SA	0127 0721 1352 1942	0.7 5.4 0.8 5.3
9 SU	0205 0758 1432 2023	0.9 5.3 0.9 5.1
10 M	0243 0835 1512 2106	1.1 5.1 1.2 4.8
11 TU	0321 0914 1554 2153	1.4 4.8 1.4 4.5
12 W	0401 0957 1638 2247	1.7 4.5 1.7 4.2
13 TH	0444 1050 1729 2352	2.0 4.3 2.0 4.0
14 F ☾	0535 1206 1832	2.3 4.1 2.2
15 SA	0104 0641 1329 1950	3.9 2.5 4.0 2.3
16 SU	0217 0806 1442 2105	3.9 2.5 4.1 2.2
17 M	0321 0921 1540 2201	4.1 2.4 4.2 2.0
18 TU	0410 1015 1624 2246	4.3 2.1 4.4 1.7
19 W	0449 1058 1700 2324	4.5 1.8 4.6 1.5
20 TH	0523 1137 1733	4.8 1.6 4.8
21 F	0000 0555 1214 1806	1.3 5.0 1.3 5.0
22 SA ●	0036 0627 1251 1841	1.1 5.2 1.1 5.1
23 SU	0112 0702 1329 1918	1.0 5.3 1.0 5.2
24 M	0149 0739 1408 2000	0.9 5.4 0.9 5.1
25 TU	0227 0820 1450 2046	1.0 5.3 1.0 5.0
26 W	0309 0907 1535 2139	1.1 5.2 1.1 4.8
27 TH	0354 1001 1625 2242	1.4 5.0 1.3 4.6
28 F	0446 1105 1722 2354	1.6 4.8 1.5 4.4
29 SA ☽	0549 1218 1830	1.9 4.6 1.7
30 SU	0108 0705 1331 1947	4.3 2.0 4.6 1.8

DECEMBER

Date	Time	m
1 M	0223 0825 1441 2101	4.4 2.0 4.6 1.7
2 TU	0331 0936 1545 2206	4.5 1.8 4.8 1.5
3 W	0427 1036 1640 2300	4.7 1.6 4.9 1.3
4 TH	0514 1128 1727 2347	4.9 1.4 5.1 1.2
5 F	0555 1214 1810	5.1 1.2 5.2
6 SA ○	0030 0632 1258 1851	1.1 5.2 1.1 5.2
7 SU	0110 0708 1339 1930	1.1 5.3 1.0 5.1
8 M	0148 0743 1418 2008	1.1 5.2 1.1 5.0
9 TU	0225 0818 1456 2047	1.2 5.1 1.2 4.8
10 W	0301 0852 1534 2126	1.4 5.0 1.4 4.6
11 TH	0338 0928 1613 2208	1.6 4.8 1.6 4.4
12 F	0416 1008 1654 2256	1.8 4.5 1.8 4.2
13 SA	0458 1057 1741 2356	2.0 4.3 2.0 4.1
14 SU ☾	0547 1203 1838	2.3 4.2 2.2
15 M	0106 0649 1322 1947	4.0 2.4 4.1 2.2
16 TU	0215 0805 1433 2058	4.0 2.5 4.1 2.2
17 W	0317 0917 1533 2158	4.2 2.3 4.2 2.0
18 TH	0409 1015 1622 2247	4.4 2.1 4.4 1.8
19 F	0451 1104 1705 2330	4.6 1.8 4.6 1.5
20 SA	0530 1148 1746	4.9 1.5 4.9
21 SU	0011 0608 1231 1826	1.3 5.2 1.2 5.1
22 M ●	0053 0647 1314 1909	1.1 5.4 1.0 5.2
23 TU	0134 0727 1357 1953	0.9 5.5 0.8 5.3
24 W	0216 0811 1441 2039	0.9 5.6 0.7 5.2
25 TH	0259 0857 1527 2129	0.9 5.5 0.8 5.1
26 F	0345 0947 1615 2224	1.1 5.3 1.0 4.8
27 SA	0434 1044 1706 2326	1.3 5.1 1.2 4.6
28 SU ☽	0529 1149 1804	1.6 4.8 1.5
29 M	0035 0632 1300 1910	4.4 1.9 4.6 1.7
30 TU	0150 0747 1412 2024	4.3 2.0 4.5 1.8
31 W	0305 0905 1524 2138	4.4 2.0 4.5 1.8

STORNOWAY
LAT 58°12'N
LONG 6°23'W

TIMES AND HEIGHTS OF HIGH AND LOW WATER (Heights in Metres)

TIME ZONE UT
For Summer Time (area enclosed in shaded box) add 1 hour

2014

JANUARY

Date	Day	Time	m	Time	m	Time	m	Time	m
1	W ●	0023	0.9	0621	5.1	1248	0.8	1847	5.0
2	TH	0109	0.7	0706	5.3	1335	0.6	1934	5.0
3	F	0154	0.6	0751	5.4	1422	0.5	2022	5.0
4	SA	0239	0.7	0837	5.4	1509	0.5	2110	4.8
5	SU	0324	0.8	0926	5.2	1556	0.7	2201	4.6
6	M	0411	1.1	1019	4.9	1644	1.0	2258	4.3
7	TU	0500	1.4	1118	4.6	1735	1.3		
8	W ☽	0004	4.0	0555	1.7	1227	4.3	1832	1.7
9	TH	0119	3.8	0701	2.0	1340	4.1	1939	1.9
10	F	0236	3.8	0821	2.1	1453	4.0	2058	2.0
11	SA	0346	3.9	0944	2.1	1559	4.0	2210	1.9
12	SU	0441	4.1	1048	1.9	1652	4.1	2304	1.8
13	M	0524	4.3	1138	1.7	1736	4.2	2347	1.6
14	TU	0559	4.5	1219	1.5	1813	4.3		
15	W	0025	1.4	0630	4.6	1257	1.3	1846	4.4
16	TH O	0100	1.3	0659	4.7	1331	1.2	1917	4.5
17	F	0132	1.2	0727	4.8	1403	1.1	1947	4.5
18	SA	0204	1.2	0754	4.8	1435	1.1	2017	4.5
19	SU	0235	1.2	0823	4.7	1506	1.1	2049	4.4
20	M	0306	1.2	0854	4.7	1539	1.2	2124	4.3
21	TU	0339	1.3	0928	4.5	1613	1.3	2203	4.2
22	W	0416	1.5	1008	4.4	1651	1.5	2251	4.0
23	TH	0457	1.7	1055	4.2	1736	1.7	2352	3.9
24	F ☾	0547	1.9	1159	4.0	1832	1.8		
25	SA	0108	3.8	0653	2.1	1323	3.9	1948	1.9
26	SU	0225	3.9	0818	2.1	1447	3.9	2113	1.9
27	M	0333	4.1	0943	1.9	1601	4.1	2224	1.6
28	TU	0433	4.4	1051	1.5	1702	4.4	2321	1.3
29	W	0523	4.7	1147	1.1	1752	4.7		
30	TH ●	0011	0.9	0609	5.1	1238	0.7	1838	4.9
31	F	0057	0.7	0652	5.4	1324	0.4	1921	5.1

FEBRUARY

Date	Day	Time	m	Time	m	Time	m	Time	m
1	SA	0141	0.5	0735	5.5	1409	0.3	2004	5.1
2	SU	0224	0.5	0818	5.5	1451	0.3	2046	4.9
3	M	0306	0.6	0902	5.3	1534	0.5	2130	4.7
4	TU	0348	0.8	0949	5.0	1616	0.8	2216	4.4
5	W	0432	1.1	1040	4.6	1659	1.2	2312	4.0
6	TH ☽	0520	1.5	1143	4.2	1747	1.6		
7	F	0026	3.8	0617	1.9	1300	3.9	1844	2.0
8	SA	0152	3.7	0734	2.2	1420	3.7	2005	2.2
9	SU	0312	3.7	0915	2.2	1534	3.7	2140	2.2
10	M	0417	3.9	1031	2.0	1634	3.8	2243	2.0
11	TU	0504	4.1	1122	1.8	1719	4.0	2329	1.7
12	W	0541	4.3	1202	1.5	1756	4.2		
13	TH	0006	1.5	0612	4.5	1238	1.3	1827	4.4
14	F O	0041	1.3	0640	4.6	1311	1.1	1856	4.5
15	SA	0113	1.1	0706	4.7	1341	0.9	1924	4.6
16	SU	0143	1.0	0732	4.8	1411	0.9	1952	4.6
17	M	0213	0.9	0759	4.8	1441	0.9	2022	4.6
18	TU	0244	0.9	0829	4.8	1511	0.9	2054	4.5
19	W	0316	1.0	0901	4.6	1544	1.0	2130	4.4
20	TH	0351	1.2	0939	4.5	1619	1.2	2213	4.2
21	F	0430	1.4	1024	4.2	1700	1.5	2309	4.0
22	SA ☾	0516	1.6	1125	4.0	1752	1.7		
23	SU	0026	3.8	0618	1.9	1256	3.8	1906	1.9
24	M	0153	3.8	0747	2.0	1431	3.8	2046	1.9
25	TU	0310	4.0	0926	1.8	1551	3.9	2209	1.7
26	W	0415	4.3	1040	1.4	1653	4.3	2308	1.3
27	TH	0508	4.7	1136	1.0	1741	4.6	2357	0.9
28	F	0553	5.0	1223	0.6	1824	4.8		

MARCH

Date	Day	Time	m	Time	m	Time	m	Time	m
1	SA ●	0041	0.6	0634	5.3	1308	0.3	1903	5.0
2	SU	0124	0.4	0715	5.4	1349	0.2	1941	5.0
3	M	0205	0.3	0756	5.4	1429	0.2	2020	4.9
4	TU	0245	0.4	0837	5.2	1507	0.4	2058	4.7
5	W	0325	0.6	0919	4.8	1546	0.8	2138	4.4
6	TH	0406	1.0	1006	4.4	1625	1.2	2223	4.1
7	F	0449	1.4	1102	4.0	1706	1.6	2325	3.8
8	SA ☽	0540	1.8	1217	3.7	1756	2.0		
9	SU	0058	3.6	0649	2.1	1341	3.5	1906	2.2
10	M	0226	3.5	0834	2.2	1500	3.5	2055	2.3
11	TU	0339	3.7	1033	2.0	1635	3.6	2214	2.1
12	W	0433	3.9	1056	1.8	1654	3.8	2302	1.8
13	TH	0513	4.1	1136	1.5	1731	4.0	2341	1.5
14	F	0545	4.3	1211	1.2	1802	4.3		
15	SA	0015	1.3	0612	4.5	1243	1.0	1830	4.4
16	SU O	0047	1.0	0639	4.6	1313	0.8	1857	4.6
17	M	0118	0.9	0705	4.7	1343	0.7	1925	4.7
18	TU	0149	0.8	0733	4.8	1413	0.7	1955	4.7
19	W	0220	0.7	0804	4.8	1444	0.7	2028	4.6
20	TH	0254	0.8	0839	4.6	1517	0.8	2105	4.5
21	F	0330	0.9	0919	4.4	1554	1.0	2149	4.3
22	SA	0410	1.2	1008	4.2	1635	1.3	2246	4.1
23	SU	0458	1.4	1116	3.9	1727	1.7		
24	M ☾	0003	3.9	0601	1.7	1250	3.7	1843	1.9
25	TU	0131	3.8	0733	1.8	1421	3.7	2027	1.9
26	W	0249	4.0	0913	1.6	1539	3.9	2151	1.7
27	TH	0355	4.2	1025	1.3	1639	4.2	2250	1.3
28	F	0448	4.6	1118	0.9	1725	4.5	2338	0.9
29	SA	0533	4.9	1204	0.6	1805	4.7		
30	SU ●	0022	0.6	0614	5.1	1247	0.3	1842	4.9
31	M	0104	0.4	0654	5.2	1326	0.3	1918	[illegible]

APRIL

Date	Day	Time	m	Time	m	Time	m	Time	m
1	TU	0144	0.4	0733	5.1	1404	0.3	1954	4.8
2	W	0223	0.5	0813	4.9	1440	0.5	2030	4.7
3	TH	0302	0.7	0854	4.6	1517	0.8	2107	4.4
4	F	0342	1.0	0938	4.3	1553	1.2	2147	4.1
5	SA	0423	1.3	1029	3.9	1632	1.5	2236	3.9
6	SU	0510	1.7	1137	3.6	1716	1.9	2353	3.6
7	M ☽	0610	2.0	1256	3.4	1816	2.2		
8	TU	0126	3.5	0738	2.1	1413	3.4	1949	2.3
9	W	0244	3.6	0915	2.0	1522	3.5	2125	2.2
10	TH	0346	3.7	1016	1.8	1616	3.7	2223	1.9
11	F	0432	3.9	1059	1.5	1657	3.9	2305	1.6
12	SA	0508	4.1	1135	1.2	1730	4.2	2342	1.3
13	SU	0539	4.3	1209	1.0	1800	4.4		
14	M	0016	1.1	0607	4.5	1241	0.8	1829	4.6
15	TU O	0050	0.9	0637	4.6	1313	0.7	1859	4.7
16	W	0124	0.7	0709	4.7	1346	0.6	1932	4.8
17	TH	0158	0.6	0744	4.7	1420	0.6	2008	4.7
18	F	0235	0.7	0824	4.6	1456	0.7	2048	4.6
19	SA	0315	0.8	0911	4.4	1535	1.0	2136	4.4
20	SU	0359	1.0	1007	4.1	1620	1.3	2236	4.2
21	M	0451	1.3	1121	3.9	1716	1.6	2351	4.0
22	TU ☾	0557	1.5	1246	3.7	1832	1.8		
23	W	0111	4.0	0723	1.6	1407	3.7	2006	1.9
24	TH	0225	4.0	0852	1.5	1520	3.9	2126	1.6
25	F	0331	4.2	1001	1.2	1619	4.1	2226	1.3
26	SA	0426	4.4	1055	0.9	1706	4.4	2317	1.1
27	SU	0513	4.7	1141	0.7	1746	4.6		
28	M	0002	0.8	0555	4.8	1224	0.6	1822	4.7
29	TU ●	0045	0.7	0635	4.8	1303	0.5	1858	4.8
30	W	0125	0.6	0714	4.8	1340	0.6	1933	4.7

MAY

Date	Day	Time	m	Time	m	Time	m	Time	m
1	TH	0204	0.6	0753	4.6	1416	0.7	2007	4.6
2	F	0243	0.8	0833	4.4	1451	0.9	2043	4.4
3	SA	0321	1.0	0916	4.1	1527	1.2	2120	4.2
4	SU	0402	1.3	1003	3.9	1605	1.5	2204	4.0
5	M	0445	1.5	1059	3.7	1647	1.8	2300	3.8
6	TU	0537	1.8	1207	3.5	1737	2.0		
7	W ☽	0018	3.6	0643	1.9	1318	3.4	1846	2.2
8	TH	0137	3.6	0804	1.9	1426	3.5	2014	2.2
9	F	0244	3.6	0916	1.8	1526	3.6	2127	2.0
10	SA	0339	3.8	1010	1.6	1614	3.8	2220	1.8
11	SU	0423	3.9	1052	1.3	1653	4.1	2303	1.5
12	M	0501	4.2	1131	1.1	1727	4.3	2343	1.2
13	TU	0536	4.4	1207	0.9	1801	4.5		
14	W O	0021	1.0	0611	4.5	1244	0.7	1835	4.7
15	TH	0100	0.8	0649	4.6	1322	0.6	1912	4.8
16	F	0140	0.6	0731	4.7	1400	0.6	1953	4.9
17	SA	0221	0.6	0817	4.6	1441	0.7	2038	4.8
18	SU	0306	0.7	0909	4.4	1524	0.9	2129	4.6
19	M	0354	0.8	1008	4.2	1613	1.2	2229	4.4
20	TU	0448	1.0	1117	4.0	1709	1.4	2338	4.2
21	W ☾	0551	1.3	1231	3.8	1818	1.7		
22	TH	0050	4.1	0704	1.4	1345	3.8	1937	1.7
23	F	0200	4.1	0821	1.4	1455	3.9	2054	1.7
24	SA	0306	4.2	0931	1.3	1556	4.0	2200	1.5
25	SU	0405	4.3	1029	1.2	1647	4.2	2255	1.3
26	M	0455	4.4	1118	1.0	1729	4.4	2344	1.1
27	TU	0540	4.5	1202	0.9	1807	4.5		
28	W ●	0028	0.9	0621	4.5	1242	0.9	1842	4.6
29	TH	0110	0.9	0700	4.5	1320	0.9	1916	4.6
30	F	0149	0.9	0738	4.4	1355	1.0	1950	4.6
31	SA	0227	0.9	0816	4.3	1430	1.1	[illegible]	[illegible]

JUNE

Date	Day	Time	m	Time	m	Time	m	Time	m
1	SU	0304	1.0	0855	4.1	1506	1.2	2059	4.3
2	M	0342	1.2	0937	4.0	1542	1.4	2137	4.2
3	TU	0422	1.4	1023	3.8	1621	1.6	2222	4.0
4	W	0505	1.5	1117	3.6	1705	1.8	2317	3.8
5	TH ☽	0556	1.7	1219	3.5	1757	2.0		
6	F	0025	3.7	0655	1.8	1326	3.5	1904	2.1
7	SA	0136	3.7	0804	1.8	1429	3.6	2018	2.0
8	SU	0239	3.7	0909	1.7	1525	3.8	2125	1.9
9	M	0334	3.8	1005	1.5	1613	4.0	2221	1.7
10	TU	0423	4.0	1053	1.3	1655	4.2	2310	1.4
11	W	0508	4.2	1137	1.1	1735	4.5	2356	1.1
12	TH	0552	4.4	1219	0.9	1816	4.7		
13	F O	0040	0.8	0636	4.6	1303	0.7	1857	4.9
14	SA	0126	0.6	0722	4.7	1346	0.6	1941	5.0
15	SU	0211	0.5	0811	4.7	1430	0.7	2028	5.0
16	M	0258	0.5	0902	4.6	1516	0.8	2119	4.9
17	TU	0347	0.6	0958	4.4	1604	1.0	2215	4.7
18	W	0439	0.8	1059	4.2	1657	1.2	2317	4.5
19	TH ☾	0534	1.0	1206	4.0	1757	1.5		
20	F	0024	4.3	0636	1.3	1316	3.8	1904	1.7
21	SA	0134	4.1	0744	1.4	1427	3.8	2019	1.7
22	SU	0242	4.1	0856	1.5	1533	3.9	2133	1.7
23	M	0346	4.1	1002	1.5	1629	4.1	2237	1.5
24	TU	0442	4.1	1057	1.4	1715	4.2	2330	1.4
25	W	0529	4.2	1144	1.3	1755	4.4		
26	TH	0016	1.2	0610	4.3	1226	1.2	1830	4.5
27	F ●	0058	1.1	0648	4.3	1303	1.1	1903	4.6
28	SA	0136	1.0	0724	4.3	1338	1.1	1934	4.6
29	SU	0211	1.0	0758	4.3	1412	1.1	2005	4.5
30	M	0246	1.0	0832	4.2	1446	1.2	2037	4.5

SUNRISE AND SUNSET TIMES

STORNOWAY
At 58°12'N 6°23'W

		Sunrise	Sunset
UT			
Jan	01	0912	1546
	15	0900	1610
Feb	01	0830	1649
	15	0757	1723
Mar	01	0720	1756
	15	0641	1829
BST			
Apr	01	0653	2007
	15	0614	2038
May	01	0532	2115
	15	0500	2145
Jun	01	0431	2217
	15	0420	2232
Jul	01	0426	2232
	15	0445	2217
Aug	01	0518	2145
	15	0548	2110
Sep	01	0625	2024
	15	0655	1945
Oct	01	0730	1859
	15	0801	1820
UT			
Nov	01	0741	1637
	15	0813	1606
Dec	01	0847	1542
	15	0907	1534

STORNOWAY
LAT 58°12′N
LONG 6°23′W

TIMES AND HEIGHTS OF HIGH AND LOW WATER (Heights in Metres)

TIME ZONE UT
For Summer Time (area enclosed in shaded box) add 1 hour

2014

JULY

Date	Time	m	Date	Time	m
1 TU	0321 0908 1520 2110	1.1 4.1 1.3 4.4	16 W	0333 0936 1549 2152	0.4 4.6 0.8 4.9
2 W	0356 0946 1556 2147	1.2 4.0 1.4 4.2	17 TH	0420 1031 1637 2249	0.6 4.3 1.0 4.6
3 TH	0433 1030 1634 2230	1.3 3.9 1.6 4.0	18 F	0509 1133 1730 2355	0.9 4.1 1.3 4.3
4 F	0514 1123 1717 2323	1.5 3.7 1.8 3.9	19 SA ☾	0602 1243 1831	1.3 3.9 1.6
5 SA ☽	0601 1226 1810	1.7 3.6 1.9	20 SU	0106 0704 1358 1944	4.1 1.6 3.8 1.9
6 SU	0029 0658 1333 1915	3.8 1.8 3.6 2.0	21 M	0219 0818 1511 2109	3.9 1.8 3.8 1.9
7 M	0142 0807 1437 2031	3.7 1.8 3.7 2.0	22 TU	0330 0936 1613 2223	3.8 1.8 3.9 1.8
8 TU	0250 0917 1536 2142	3.8 1.7 3.9 1.8	23 W	0430 1040 1702 2319	3.9 1.7 4.1 1.6
9 W	0352 1019 1628 2243	3.9 1.5 4.2 1.5	24 TH	0519 1128 1742	4.0 1.5 4.3
10 TH	0448 1112 1715 2336	4.1 1.2 4.5 1.2	25 F	0004 0558 1210 1816	1.4 4.1 1.4 4.5
11 F	0539 1201 1800	4.4 1.0 4.8	26 SA ●	0044 0633 1247 1846	1.2 4.3 1.2 4.6
12 SA ○	0026 0626 1248 1843	0.8 4.6 0.7 5.0	27 SU	0119 0705 1321 1915	1.1 4.4 1.1 4.6
13 SU	0114 0712 1333 1928	0.5 4.8 0.6 5.2	28 M	0153 0736 1353 1943	1.0 4.4 1.1 4.7
14 M	0201 0759 1418 2014	0.3 4.8 0.5 5.2	29 TU	0224 0806 1425 2011	0.9 4.4 1.1 4.6
15 TU	0247 0847 1503 2101	0.3 4.8 0.6 5.1	30 W	0256 0838 1456 2041	1.0 4.3 1.1 4.5
			31 TH	0327 0911 1529 2114	1.0 4.2 1.2 4.4

AUGUST

Date	Time	m	Date	Time	m
1 F	0400 0949 1604 2151	1.2 4.1 1.4 4.2	16 SA	0439 1052 1701 2322	0.9 4.2 1.3 4.3
2 SA	0436 1033 1642 2236	1.3 3.9 1.6 4.0	17 SU ☾	0526 1205 1757	1.4 3.9 1.7
3 SU	0517 1130 1728 2334	1.5 3.8 1.8 3.9	18 M	0038 0622 1327 1910	3.9 1.8 3.7 2.0
4 M ☽	0606 1242 1827	1.7 3.7 2.0	19 TU	0157 0735 1445 2046	3.7 2.0 3.7 2.1
5 TU	0053 0712 1357 1945	3.7 1.9 3.8 2.0	20 W	0312 0909 1553 2209	3.7 2.1 3.9 1.9
6 W	0218 0836 1505 2111	3.7 1.9 3.9 1.9	21 TH	0415 1021 1644 2304	3.8 1.9 4.0 1.7
7 TH	0333 0954 1606 2224	3.9 1.7 4.2 1.6	22 F	0503 1110 1723 2346	3.9 1.7 4.2 1.4
8 F	0436 1055 1658 2322	4.1 1.4 4.5 1.2	23 SA	0541 1150 1756	4.1 1.5 4.4
9 SA	0528 1146 1744	4.4 1.0 4.9	24 SU	0023 0613 1226 1824	1.2 4.3 1.3 4.6
10 SU ○	0013 0614 1233 1828	0.8 4.7 0.7 5.2	25 M ●	0057 0643 1259 1851	1.0 4.4 1.1 4.7
11 M	0100 0658 1318 1910	0.4 4.9 0.5 5.4	26 TU	0128 0711 1330 1917	0.9 4.5 1.0 4.7
12 TU	0145 0741 1401 1954	0.2 5.0 0.4 5.4	27 W	0158 0739 1400 1944	0.9 4.6 1.0 4.7
13 W	0229 0824 1444 2038	0.2 4.9 0.4 5.3	28 TH	0228 0807 1431 2012	0.9 4.5 1.0 4.7
14 TH	0312 0908 1528 2126	0.3 4.7 0.6 5.0	29 F	0257 0838 1502 2044	0.9 4.5 1.1 4.6
15 F	0354 0956 1613 2218	0.6 4.5 0.9 4.7	30 SA	0328 0913 1536 2119	1.0 4.3 1.2 4.4
			31 SU	0402 0954 1613 2202	1.2 4.2 1.4 4.2

SEPTEMBER

Date	Time	m	Date	Time	m
1 M	0441 1047 1657 2259	1.4 4.0 1.6 3.9	16 TU ☾	0006 0540 1248 1835	3.8 1.9 3.8 2.1
2 TU ☽	0527 1200 1753	1.7 3.8 1.9	17 W	0128 0649 1411 2014	3.6 2.2 3.7 2.2
3 W	0026 0632 1326 1913	3.7 1.9 3.8 2.0	18 TH	0245 0830 1522 2144	3.6 2.3 3.8 2.0
4 TH	0202 0807 1442 2052	3.7 2.0 3.9 1.9	19 F	0350 0953 1616 2239	3.7 2.1 4.0 1.8
5 F	0321 0936 1547 2210	3.9 1.8 4.2 1.5	20 SA	0439 1045 1657 2320	3.9 1.9 4.2 1.5
6 SA	0425 1039 1640 2308	4.1 1.5 4.6 1.1	21 SU	0517 1124 1729 2355	4.1 1.6 4.4 1.3
7 SU	0516 1130 1727 2357	4.5 1.1 5.0 0.7	22 M	0548 1159 1758	4.3 1.4 4.6
8 M	0559 1216 1809	4.8 0.7 5.3	23 TU	0028 0616 1232 1824	1.1 4.5 1.2 4.7
9 TU ○	0042 0639 1300 1850	0.4 5.0 0.5 5.5	24 W ●	0059 0643 1303 1850	0.9 4.6 1.0 4.8
10 W	0125 0719 1342 1932	0.2 5.1 0.4 5.5	25 TH	0128 0711 1334 1917	0.8 4.7 1.0 4.8
11 TH	0206 0758 1423 2014	0.2 5.1 0.4 5.3	26 F	0158 0739 1405 1946	0.8 4.7 0.9 4.8
12 F	0246 0839 1505 2058	0.3 4.9 0.6 5.0	27 SA	0228 0810 1437 2019	0.9 4.7 1.0 4.7
13 SA	0326 0921 1548 2147	0.6 4.6 0.9 4.6	28 SU	0300 0845 1512 2056	1.0 4.6 1.1 4.5
14 SU	0407 1010 1633 2247	1.1 4.2 1.3 4.2	29 M	0334 0926 1551 2142	1.2 4.4 1.3 4.2
15 M	0451 1117 1726	1.5 3.9 1.7	30 TU	0413 1019 1636 2245	1.4 4.2 1.6 4.0

OCTOBER

Date	Time	m	Date	Time	m
1 W ☽	0501 1133 1734	1.7 4.0 1.8	16 TH	0046 0603 1320 1924	3.6 2.3 3.7 2.2
2 TH	0017 0607 1302 1856	3.8 2.0 3.9 2.0	17 F	0202 0732 1434 2058	3.6 2.4 3.8 2.1
3 F	0150 0746 1419 2036	3.7 2.1 4.0 1.8	18 SA	0310 0906 1535 2200	3.7 2.3 3.9 1.9
4 SA	0308 0917 1525 2153	3.9 1.9 4.3 1.5	19 SU	0404 1007 1620 2244	3.9 2.1 4.1 1.7
5 SU	0410 1021 1621 2250	4.2 1.5 4.6 1.1	20 M	0445 1050 1656 2321	4.1 1.8 4.3 1.4
6 M	0500 1111 1707 2337	4.5 1.2 5.0 0.7	21 TU	0518 1128 1727 2355	4.3 1.5 4.5 1.2
7 TU	0541 1157 1750	4.8 0.8 5.2	22 W	0548 1202 1756	4.5 1.3 4.6
8 W ○	0021 0619 1240 1830	0.5 5.0 0.6 5.4	23 TH ●	0026 0616 1235 1823	1.0 4.7 1.1 4.8
9 TH	0103 0657 1322 1911	0.3 5.1 0.5 5.3	24 F	0058 0644 1308 1853	0.9 4.8 1.0 4.8
10 F	0142 0734 1403 1952	0.4 5.1 0.5 5.2	25 SA	0129 0715 1342 1926	0.8 4.9 0.9 4.8
11 SA	0221 0812 1443 2034	0.6 4.9 0.7 4.9	26 SU	0202 0748 1417 2002	0.9 4.9 0.9 4.7
12 SU	0259 0851 1525 2121	0.8 4.7 1.0 4.5	27 M	0236 0826 1455 2045	1.0 4.8 1.0 4.5
13 M	0338 0934 1609 2215	1.2 4.4 1.4 4.1	28 TU	0314 0910 1536 2136	1.2 4.6 1.2 4.3
14 TU	0419 1027 1658 2326	1.6 4.1 1.7 3.8	29 W	0356 1005 1625 2243	1.4 4.4 1.4 4.0
15 W ☾	0505 1151 1759	2.0 3.8 2.0	30 TH	0446 1116 1725	1.7 4.2 1.7
			31 F ☽	0008 0553 1238 1844	3.9 2.0 4.1 1.8

NOVEMBER

Date	Time	m	Date	Time	m
1 SA	0133 0724 1354 2014	3.9 2.1 4.2 1.7	16 SU	0213 0754 1435 2101	3.6 2.4 3.8 2.0
2 SU	0247 0850 1501 2129	4.0 1.9 4.4 1.5	17 M	0315 0910 1531 2157	3.8 2.3 4.0 1.8
3 M	0351 0956 1559 2227	4.2 1.6 4.6 1.2	18 TU	0404 1006 1616 2241	4.0 2.0 4.1 1.6
4 TU	0441 1050 1648 2316	4.5 1.3 4.8 0.9	19 W	0444 1050 1653 2319	4.2 1.8 4.3 1.4
5 W	0523 1137 1732	4.8 1.0 5.0	20 TH	0518 1130 1726 2354	4.5 1.5 4.5 1.2
6 TH ○	0000 0602 1222 1814	0.7 4.9 0.8 5.1	21 F	0550 1207 1759	4.7 1.3 4.7
7 F	0041 0638 1304 1854	0.7 5.0 0.7 5.1	22 SA ●	0029 0621 1244 1834	1.0 4.9 1.1 4.8
8 SA	0120 0715 1345 1935	0.7 5.0 0.8 5.0	23 SU	0105 0656 1322 1912	0.9 5.0 1.0 4.8
9 SU	0158 0751 1426 2016	0.8 4.9 0.9 4.7	24 M	0142 0733 1402 1953	0.9 5.0 0.9 4.8
10 M	0235 0829 1506 2059	1.0 4.7 1.1 4.4	25 TU	0220 0814 1443 2040	0.9 5.0 0.9 4.6
11 TU	0313 0907 1548 2146	1.3 4.5 1.4 4.2	26 W	0301 0901 1528 2133	1.1 4.9 1.0 4.5
12 W	0352 0951 1633 2241	1.6 4.3 1.7 3.9	27 TH	0346 0955 1618 2236	1.3 4.7 1.2 4.2
13 TH	0434 1045 1724 2349	1.9 4.0 1.9 3.7	28 F	0437 1059 1716 2349	1.6 4.5 1.4 4.1
14 F ☾	0524 1204 1828	2.2 3.9 2.1	29 SA ☽	0540 1211 1825	1.8 4.4 1.6
15 SA	0103 0629 1327 1946	3.6 2.4 3.8 2.1	30 SU	0106 0655 1325 1942	4.0 2.0 4.3 1.6

DECEMBER

Date	Time	m	Date	Time	m
1 M	0220 0816 1434 2056	4.0 1.9 4.4 1.6	16 TU	0213 0755 1428 2053	3.7 2.3 3.9 2.0
2 TU	0327 0928 1537 2201	4.2 1.8 4.5 1.4	17 W	0313 0908 1526 2153	3.9 2.2 4.0 1.9
3 W	0423 1028 1632 2254	4.4 1.5 4.6 1.2	18 TH	0404 1008 1616 2241	4.1 2.0 4.1 1.6
4 TH	0509 1120 1720 2341	4.6 1.3 4.7 1.1	19 F	0447 1057 1659 2324	4.3 1.7 4.3 1.4
5 F	0549 1208 1803	4.8 1.1 4.8	20 SA	0525 1141 1740	4.6 1.5 4.5
6 SA ○	0023 0626 1252 1843	1.0 4.9 1.0 4.8	21 SU	0005 0602 1225 1820	1.2 4.8 1.2 4.7
7 SU	0103 0702 1333 1923	1.0 4.9 1.0 4.8	22 M ●	0046 0641 1307 1902	1.0 5.0 0.9 4.8
8 M	0140 0737 1412 2001	1.1 4.9 1.0 4.6	23 TU	0127 0721 1350 1946	0.9 5.2 0.8 4.9
9 TU	0217 0812 1450 2039	1.2 4.8 1.1 4.5	24 W	0208 0804 1435 2033	0.8 5.2 0.7 4.8
10 W	0253 0846 1528 2119	1.3 4.7 1.3 4.3	25 TH	0251 0851 1520 2123	0.9 5.2 0.8 4.7
11 TH	0329 0922 1608 2201	1.5 4.5 1.5 4.1	26 F	0336 0941 1609 2218	1.0 5.0 0.9 4.5
12 F	0407 1003 1650 2251	1.7 4.3 1.7 3.9	27 SA	0425 1037 1701 2320	1.3 4.8 1.1 4.2
13 SA	0449 1052 1738 2352	1.9 4.1 1.9 3.7	28 SU ☽	0520 1142 1759	1.5 4.6 1.4
14 SU ☾	0537 1159 1835	2.1 3.9 2.0	29 M	0032 0623 1254 1904	4.0 1.8 4.4 1.6
15 M	0103 0639 1318 1943	3.7 2.3 3.8 2.1	30 TU	0147 0737 1407 2019	4.0 1.9 4.3 1.7
			31 W	0301 0857 1517 2133	4.0 1.9 4.2 1.7

OBAN

LAT 56°25′N
LONG 5°29′W

TIMES AND HEIGHTS OF HIGH AND LOW WATER (Heights in Metres)

TIME ZONE UT
For Summer Time (area enclosed in shaded box) add 1 hour

2014

Moon phases: ● new moon, ☽ first quarter, ○ full moon, ☾ last quarter.

JANUARY

Date	Day	Moon	Time	m	Time	m	Time	m	Time	m
1	W	●	0519	4.1	1133	0.7	1735	4.0	2355	0.6
2	TH		0603	4.2	1223	0.6	1818	4.1		
3	F		0040	0.5	0646	4.3	1311	0.6	1900	4.0
4	SA		0127	0.4	0729	4.2	1358	0.6	1943	3.9
5	SU		0214	0.5	0814	4.1	1445	0.8	2026	3.7
6	M		0301	0.7	0900	3.9	1533	1.0	2110	3.5
7	TU		0351	0.9	0949	3.6	1624	1.3	2159	3.2
8	W	☽	0445	1.2	1048	3.3	1719	1.5	2259	3.0
9	TH		0545	1.5	1213	3.1	1820	1.7		
10	F		0025	2.9	0657	1.7	1347	3.1	1928	1.8
11	SA		0152	2.9	0825	1.7	1500	3.1	2039	1.7
12	SU		0256	3.1	0941	1.7	1549	3.3	2138	1.6
13	M		0344	3.3	1034	1.6	1624	3.4	2224	1.4
14	TU		0426	3.5	1117	1.5	1658	3.6	2304	1.3
15	W		0505	3.7	1153	1.4	1733	3.8	2342	1.1
16	TH	○	0542	3.9	1226	1.3	1808	3.9		
17	F		0019	1.0	0617	4.0	1259	1.3	1842	3.9
18	SA		0055	1.0	0651	4.0	1331	1.3	1914	3.9
19	SU		0128	1.0	0722	4.0	1402	1.4	1944	3.8
20	M		0158	1.1	0752	3.9	1429	1.5	2012	3.7
21	TU		0226	1.2	0820	3.8	1449	1.6	2043	3.5
22	W		0258	1.3	0852	3.6	1519	1.7	2119	3.4
23	TH		0338	1.5	0931	3.5	1604	1.8	2203	3.2
24	F	☾	0429	1.6	1021	3.3	1710	1.9	2302	3.1
25	SA		0536	1.7	1131	3.2	1834	1.9		
26	SU		0033	3.0	0654	1.7	1324	3.1	1954	1.7
27	M		0231	3.2	0815	1.5	1501	3.3	2106	1.5
28	TU		0337	3.5	0930	1.3	1600	3.5	2206	1.1
29	W		0427	3.8	1033	1.0	1647	3.8	2258	0.8
30	TH	●	0512	4.1	1126	0.7	1729	4.0	2345	0.5
31	F		0554	4.3	1214	0.5	1809	4.1		

FEBRUARY

Date	Day	Moon	Time	m	Time	m	Time	m	Time	m
1	SA		0030	0.3	0635	4.4	1259	0.4	1848	4.1
2	SU		0115	0.3	0715	4.3	1342	0.5	1927	4.0
3	M		0158	0.3	0755	4.2	1424	0.6	2005	3.8
4	TU		0241	0.5	0835	3.9	1506	0.9	2042	3.6
5	W		0325	0.8	0915	3.6	1549	1.1	2120	3.4
6	TH	☽	0411	1.1	1000	3.3	1637	1.4	2203	3.1
7	F		0503	1.5	1056	3.0	1732	1.7	2303	2.9
8	SA		0607	1.7	1250	2.8	1836	1.8		
9	SU		0054	2.8	0742	1.9	1445	2.9	1952	1.8
10	M		0228	2.9	0932	1.8	1545	3.0	2112	1.7
11	TU		0328	3.1	1026	1.6	1616	3.2	2207	1.5
12	W		0410	3.3	1106	1.5	1645	3.5	2249	1.3
13	TH		0449	3.6	1140	1.3	1718	3.7	2325	1.1
14	F	○	0525	3.8	1210	1.2	1752	3.8	2359	0.9
15	SA		0600	3.9	1238	1.1	1825	3.9		
16	SU		0032	0.8	0632	4.0	1307	1.1	1854	3.9
17	M		0104	0.8	0701	4.0	1335	1.1	1920	3.9
18	TU		0131	0.9	0727	3.9	1358	1.2	1945	3.8
19	W		0158	0.9	0754	3.8	1417	1.2	2015	3.7
20	TH		0229	1.1	0825	3.7	1447	1.4	2050	3.5
21	F		0309	1.2	0902	3.5	1530	1.5	2132	3.3
22	SA	☾	0358	1.4	0948	3.3	1629	1.7	2228	3.1
23	SU		0506	1.6	1055	3.0	1757	1.7	2357	3.0
24	M		0634	1.6	1257	2.9	1928	1.7		
25	TU		0216	3.1	0803	1.5	1500	3.1	2048	1.4
26	W		0327	3.4	0923	1.2	1558	3.4	2153	1.1
27	TH		0417	3.8	1024	0.9	1641	3.6	2245	0.7
28	F		0500	4.1	1114	0.6	1718	3.9	2332	0.4

MARCH

Date	Day	Moon	Time	m	Time	m	Time	m	Time	m
1	SA	●	0540	4.3	1159	0.4	1754	4.0		
2	SU		0016	0.2	0618	4.3	1241	0.3	1830	4.1
3	M		0059	0.2	0656	4.3	1320	0.4	1906	4.0
4	TU		0140	0.3	0732	4.1	1358	0.5	1940	3.9
5	W		0220	0.5	0808	3.9	1437	0.8	2014	3.7
6	TH		0300	0.8	0843	3.6	1516	1.0	2048	3.5
7	F		0341	1.2	0921	3.3	1601	1.3	2125	3.2
8	SA	☽	0429	1.5	1006	3.0	1653	1.6	2213	3.0
9	SU		0527	1.8	1121	2.7	1755	1.8	2338	2.8
10	M		0650	2.0	1413	2.7	1908	1.8		
11	TU		0155	2.8	0914	1.9	1518	2.9	2033	1.7
12	W		0307	3.0	1007	1.7	1553	3.1	2139	1.5
13	TH		0349	3.2	1044	1.5	1622	3.3	2223	1.3
14	F		0426	3.5	1115	1.3	1654	3.6	2259	1.0
15	SA		0502	3.7	1143	1.1	1728	3.7	2332	0.9
16	SU	○	0536	3.8	1210	0.9	1800	3.9		
17	M		0004	0.7	0607	3.9	1238	0.9	1828	3.9
18	TU		0035	0.7	0635	4.0	1304	0.9	1853	3.9
19	W		0105	0.7	0701	3.9	1329	0.9	1919	3.8
20	TH		0135	0.7	0730	3.8	1355	1.0	1951	3.7
21	F		0210	0.9	0804	3.7	1429	1.1	2029	3.6
22	SA		0252	1.0	0843	3.4	1512	1.3	2114	3.4
23	SU		0345	1.2	0931	3.2	1612	1.4	2213	3.1
24	M	☾	0457	1.4	1041	2.9	1738	1.6	2343	3.0
25	TU		0625	1.5	1251	2.8	1907	1.5		
26	W		0158	3.1	0753	1.4	1448	3.0	2028	1.3
27	TH		0308	3.4	0910	1.2	1544	3.3	2134	1.0
28	F		0358	3.7	1008	0.9	1625	3.5	2227	0.7
29	SA		0441	4.0	1055	0.6	1700	3.8	2314	0.5
30	SU	●	0520	4.1	1138	0.5	1734	3.9	2357	0.3
31	M		0557	4.2	1217	0.4	1808	4.0		

APRIL

Date	Day	Moon	Time	m	Time	m	Time	m	Time	m
1	TU		0039	0.3	0633	4.2	1255	0.4	1842	4.0
2	W		0119	0.4	0707	4.0	1332	0.6	1916	3.9
3	TH		0158	0.6	0741	3.8	1409	0.8	1948	3.8
4	F		0236	0.9	0815	3.5	1447	1.0	2022	3.6
5	SA		0315	1.3	0852	3.3	1531	1.3	2059	3.3
6	SU		0401	1.6	0934	3.0	1620	1.5	2144	3.1
7	M	☽	0457	1.8	1034	2.7	1718	1.7	2248	2.9
8	TU		0610	2.0	1320	2.7	1825	1.8		
9	W		0051	2.8	0830	1.9	1434	2.8	1938	1.7
10	TH		0228	2.9	0932	1.7	1517	3.0	2050	1.6
11	F		0315	3.1	1009	1.5	1551	3.2	2142	1.3
12	SA		0354	3.4	1039	1.3	1624	3.4	2222	1.1
13	SU		0431	3.6	1107	1.1	1658	3.6	2257	0.9
14	M		0506	3.8	1135	0.9	1730	3.8	2331	0.7
15	TU	○	0539	3.9	1204	0.8	1800	3.9		
16	W		0005	0.6	0609	3.9	1234	0.7	1827	3.9
17	TH		0041	0.6	0639	3.9	1305	0.7	1858	3.9
18	F		0119	0.6	0712	3.8	1339	0.8	1935	3.8
19	SA		0200	0.7	0751	3.6	1420	0.9	2017	3.6
20	SU		0248	0.9	0835	3.4	1508	1.1	2106	3.4
21	M		0345	1.1	0928	3.1	1609	1.2	2208	3.2
22	TU	☾	0455	1.3	1039	2.9	1724	1.4	2335	3.1
23	W		0614	1.4	1238	2.8	1845	1.4		
24	TH		0132	3.2	0736	1.3	1421	2.9	2003	1.3
25	F		0241	3.4	0849	1.2	1519	3.2	2111	1.0
26	SA		0334	3.6	0945	1.0	1601	3.4	2206	0.8
27	SU		0418	3.8	1032	0.8	1636	3.6	2253	0.7
28	M		0458	3.9	1113	0.7	1710	3.8	2337	0.6
29	TU	●	0535	4.0	1152	0.6	1745	3.9		
30	W		0019	0.6	0610	4.0	1230	0.6	1819	3.9

MAY

Date	Day	Moon	Time	m	Time	m	Time	m	Time	m
1	TH		0059	0.7	0645	3.9	1306	0.7	1853	3.9
2	F		0138	0.9	0719	3.7	1343	0.9	1927	3.8
3	SA		0215	1.1	0754	3.5	1422	1.0	2002	3.6
4	SU		0254	1.4	0831	3.3	1504	1.3	2040	3.4
5	M		0338	1.6	0913	3.1	1550	1.5	2123	3.2
6	TU		0429	1.8	1005	2.9	1642	1.6	2216	3.0
7	W	☽	0533	2.0	1126	2.8	1740	1.7	2330	2.9
8	TH		0653	2.0	1330	2.8	1842	1.8		
9	F		0111	2.9	0821	1.8	1429	2.9	1945	1.7
10	SA		0224	3.1	0914	1.6	1511	3.1	2044	1.5
11	SU		0313	3.3	0952	1.4	1549	3.3	2133	1.3
12	M		0355	3.5	1026	1.2	1625	3.5	2216	1.0
13	TU		0434	3.7	1058	1.0	1700	3.7	2258	0.8
14	W	○	0510	3.8	1131	0.8	1733	3.8	2339	0.7
15	TH		0546	3.9	1207	0.7	1807	3.9		
16	F		0022	0.6	0622	3.9	1246	0.6	1844	3.9
17	SA		0107	0.6	0701	3.8	1328	0.6	1925	3.9
18	SU		0154	0.6	0744	3.6	1413	0.7	2011	3.7
19	M		0245	0.8	0831	3.4	1504	0.9	2102	3.6
20	TU		0342	1.0	0925	3.2	1601	1.0	2202	3.4
21	W	☾	0445	1.1	1031	3.0	1706	1.2	2319	3.2
22	TH		0556	1.3	1205	2.9	1819	1.3		
23	F		0058	3.2	0709	1.3	1342	2.9	1933	1.3
24	SA		0211	3.3	0820	1.2	1446	3.1	2044	1.2
25	SU		0309	3.4	0918	1.1	1533	3.3	2143	1.1
26	M		0356	3.6	1007	1.0	1611	3.5	2234	1.0
27	TU		0438	3.7	1049	0.9	1648	3.6	2319	0.9
28	W	●	0516	3.7	1128	0.9	1724	3.8		
29	TH		0001	0.9	0551	3.8	1206	0.9	1800	3.8
30	F		0042	1.0	0627	3.8	1244	0.9	1835	3.9
31	SA		0120	1.1	0702	3.7	1322	1.0		

JUNE

Date	Day	Moon	Time	m	Time	m	Time	m	Time	m
1	SU		0158	1.2	0738	3.6	1400	1.1	1946	3.7
2	M		0236	1.4	0815	3.4	1440	1.2	2023	3.6
3	TU		0316	1.6	0855	3.3	1521	1.4	2102	3.4
4	W		0401	1.8	0938	3.1	1605	1.6	2145	3.3
5	TH	☽	0452	1.9	1030	3.0	1653	1.7	2236	3.1
6	F		0551	1.9	1142	2.9	1747	1.7	2341	3.1
7	SA		0658	1.9	1314	2.9	1845	1.7		
8	SU		0107	3.1	0802	1.8	1421	3.0	1944	1.6
9	M		0221	3.2	0857	1.6	1510	3.2	2043	1.4
10	TU		0317	3.4	0943	1.3	1553	3.4	2138	1.2
11	W		0404	3.6	1025	1.1	1634	3.6	2230	0.9
12	TH		0448	3.7	1106	0.9	1714	3.8	2320	0.7
13	F	○	0530	3.8	1148	0.7	1755	3.9		
14	SA		0009	0.6	0611	3.9	1232	0.5	1836	4.0
15	SU		0058	0.5	0654	3.8	1317	0.5	1919	4.0
16	M		0147	0.5	0738	3.7	1404	0.5	2005	3.9
17	TU		0237	0.6	0824	3.5	1454	0.6	2055	3.7
18	W		0330	0.8	0915	3.3	1547	0.8	2149	3.5
19	TH	☾	0427	1.0	1012	3.1	1645	1.0	2253	3.3
20	F		0528	1.2	1124	2.9	1749	1.2		
21	SA		0017	3.2	0634	1.3	1252	2.9	1859	1.3
22	SU		0138	3.2	0743	1.4	1407	3.0	2013	1.4
23	M		0245	3.2	0848	1.4	1504	3.1	2123	1.3
24	TU		0339	3.3	0942	1.3	1549	3.3	2219	1.3
25	W		0423	3.4	1028	1.2	1629	3.5	2307	1.2
26	TH		0502	3.5	1108	1.1	1707	3.6	2349	1.2
27	F	●	0538	3.6	1147	1.0	1744	3.8		
28	SA		0027	1.2	0613	3.7	1225	1.0	1820	3.8
29	SU		0104	1.2	0649	3.7	1303	1.0	1856	3.9
30	M		0140	1.3	0724	3.7	1340	1.0	1931	3.8

SUNRISE AND SUNSET TIMES

OBAN
At 56°25′N 5°29′W

		Sunrise	Sunset
UT			
Jan	01	0856	1556
	15	0845	1618
Feb	01	0818	1654
	15	0748	1725
Mar	01	0714	1756
	15	0637	1825
BST			
Apr	01	0652	2001
	15	0615	2030
May	01	0536	2103
	15	0507	2131
Jun	01	0441	2200
	15	0432	2213
Jul	01	0437	2214
	15	0454	2201
Aug	01	0524	2131
	15	0551	2100
Sep	01	0625	2017
	15	0653	1940
Oct	01	0725	1857
	15	0754	1820
UT			
Nov	01	0731	1640
	15	0801	1612
Dec	01	0831	1550
	15	0850	1544

OBAN
LAT 56°25′N
LONG 5°29′W

TIMES AND HEIGHTS OF HIGH AND LOW WATER (Heights in Metres)

TIME ZONE UT
For Summer Time (area enclosed in shaded box) add 1 hour

2014

JULY

Day	Time	m	Day	Time	m
1 TU	0216 0759 1415 2005	1.4 3.6 1.1 3.7	16 W	0223 0811 1439 2040	0.5 3.7 0.4 3.9
2 W	0252 0833 1450 2039	1.5 3.5 1.3 3.6	17 TH	0311 0855 1528 2127	0.7 3.5 0.7 3.6
3 TH	0328 0908 1526 2113	1.6 3.3 1.4 3.5	18 F	0401 0943 1619 2220	0.9 3.2 0.9 3.4
4 F	0406 0947 1606 2152	1.7 3.2 1.6 3.3	19 SA ☾	0455 1040 1717 2329	1.2 3.0 1.2 3.1
5 SA ☽	0452 1033 1655 2240	1.8 3.0 1.7 3.2	20 SU	0554 1159 1822	1.4 2.9 1.4
6 SU	0551 1135 1753 2344	1.9 3.0 1.7 3.1	21 M	0102 0701 1328 1941	3.0 1.5 2.9 1.6
7 M	0658 1311 1858	1.8 3.0 1.7	22 TU	0226 0814 1440 2109	3.0 1.6 3.0 1.6
8 TU	0119 0805 1433 2005	3.1 1.7 3.1 1.5	23 W	0332 0920 1533 2213	3.1 1.5 3.1 1.5
9 W	0244 0907 1530 2111	3.3 1.4 3.3 1.3	24 TH	0415 1011 1614 2300	3.2 1.3 3.3 1.4
10 TH	0344 1000 1618 2213	3.4 1.2 3.6 1.0	25 F	0450 1053 1652 2339	3.4 1.2 3.6 1.3
11 F	0434 1049 1703 2308	3.6 0.9 3.8 0.8	26 SA ●	0524 1131 1730	3.6 1.0 3.7
12 SA O	0520 1135 1746 2359	3.8 0.6 4.0 0.5	27 SU	0014 0559 1208 1805	1.2 3.7 0.9 3.9
13 SU	0603 1220 1829	3.9 0.4 4.2	28 M	0047 0633 1244 1839	1.2 3.8 0.9 3.9
14 M	0048 0645 1306 1912	0.4 3.9 0.3 4.2	29 TU	0120 0706 1318 1912	1.2 3.8 0.9 3.9
15 TU	0136 0728 1352 1955	0.4 3.8 0.3 4.1	30 W	0153 0737 1350 1942	1.2 3.8 1.0 3.9
			31 TH	0224 0806 1419 2011	1.3 3.6 1.1 3.7

AUGUST

Day	Time	m	Day	Time	m
1 F	0251 0835 1449 2040	1.4 3.5 1.3 3.6	16 SA	0331 0910 1553 2143	0.9 3.4 1.0 3.4
2 SA	0315 0908 1524 2114	1.6 3.4 1.4 3.5	17 SU ☾	0420 0956 1645 2238	1.2 3.1 1.3 3.0
3 SU	0351 0949 1610 2157	1.7 3.2 1.6 3.3	18 M	0515 1100 1746	1.4 2.9 1.6
4 M ☽	0448 1042 1709 2254	1.8 3.0 1.7 3.1	19 TU	0016 0619 1249 1907	2.8 1.6 2.8 1.8
5 TU	0607 1202 1823	1.8 3.0 1.7	20 W	0213 0735 1424 2104	2.8 1.7 2.9 1.8
6 W	0025 0728 1410 1941	3.0 1.7 3.1 1.6	21 TH	0331 0856 1523 2206	2.9 1.6 3.1 1.6
7 TH	0228 0842 1519 2057	3.1 1.5 3.3 1.4	22 F	0406 0953 1559 2248	3.1 1.4 3.3 1.5
8 F	0337 0944 1609 2204	3.3 1.2 3.6 1.1	23 SA	0433 1036 1635 2323	3.3 1.2 3.5 1.3
9 SA	0427 1037 1653 2300	3.6 0.8 3.9 0.7	24 SU	0504 1113 1710 2354	3.6 1.0 3.8 1.2
10 SU O	0511 1124 1735 2349	3.8 0.5 4.2 0.5	25 M ●	0538 1147 1745	3.8 0.9 3.9
11 M	0551 1209 1816	3.9 0.3 4.3	26 TU	0023 0611 1220 1818	1.1 3.9 0.8 4.0
12 TU	0035 0631 1253 1856	0.3 4.0 0.2 4.3	27 W	0053 0642 1252 1848	1.0 3.9 0.8 4.0
13 W	0120 0710 1337 1937	0.3 4.0 0.2 4.2	28 TH	0124 0711 1322 1916	1.1 3.9 0.9 3.9
14 TH	0203 0749 1421 2017	0.4 3.8 0.4 4.0	29 F	0152 0736 1348 1942	1.1 3.8 1.0 3.8
15 F	0246 0829 1505 2058	0.6 3.6 0.6 3.7	30 SA	0214 0803 1417 2009	1.2 3.6 1.1 3.7
			31 SU	0236 0835 1452 2042	1.4 3.5 1.3 3.5

SEPTEMBER

Day	Time	m	Day	Time	m
1 M	0312 0915 1537 2123	1.5 3.3 1.5 3.3	16 TU ☾	0438 1009 1714 2304	1.5 3.0 1.8 2.8
2 TU ☽	0405 1007 1639 2220	1.7 3.1 1.7 3.1	17 W	0540 1152 1836	1.7 2.8 2.0
3 W	0530 1128 1802 2357	1.8 3.0 1.7 2.9	18 TH	0150 0654 1406 2051	2.7 1.8 2.9 1.9
4 TH	0701 1402 1929	1.7 3.1 1.7	19 F	0303 0820 1507 2148	2.9 1.7 3.1 1.7
5 F	0229 0822 1508 2050	3.0 1.5 3.4 1.4	20 SA	0340 0925 1539 2226	3.1 1.5 3.3 1.5
6 SA	0334 0929 1557 2155	3.3 1.2 3.7 1.1	21 SU	0408 1010 1611 2258	3.3 1.3 3.6 1.3
7 SU	0419 1022 1639 2248	3.6 0.8 4.0 0.7	22 M	0439 1047 1645 2326	3.6 1.1 3.8 1.2
8 M	0457 1109 1719 2333	3.8 0.5 4.3 0.5	23 TU	0512 1120 1719 2354	3.8 0.9 3.9 1.0
9 TU O	0534 1153 1757	4.0 0.3 4.4	24 W ●	0545 1152 1752	3.9 0.9 4.0
10 W	0016 0610 1236 1835	0.3 4.1 0.2 4.4	25 TH	0022 0615 1223 1821	1.0 4.0 0.8 4.1
11 TH	0058 0647 1318 1913	0.3 4.1 0.3 4.3	26 F	0052 0642 1253 1847	1.0 3.9 0.9 4.0
12 F	0138 0724 1400 1950	0.4 4.0 0.4 4.0	27 SA	0119 0707 1322 1914	1.0 3.9 0.9 3.9
13 SA	0218 0800 1442 2027	0.6 3.8 0.7 3.7	28 SU	0143 0736 1353 1944	1.1 3.8 1.1 3.8
14 SU	0300 0837 1526 2106	0.9 3.5 1.1 3.4	29 M	0212 0811 1431 2020	1.2 3.6 1.2 3.6
15 M	0346 0917 1615 2152	1.2 3.3 1.5 3.0	30 TU	0250 0852 1519 2102	1.4 3.4 1.4 3.3

OCTOBER

Day	Time	m	Day	Time	m
1 W ☽	0344 0947 1625 2202	1.6 3.2 1.6 3.0	16 TH	0503 1045 1800	1.7 3.0 2.1
2 TH	0506 1111 1752 2345	1.7 3.1 1.7 2.9	17 F	0105 0609 1319 2009	2.8 1.8 3.0 2.1
3 F	0637 1343 1920	1.7 3.2 1.6	18 SA	0219 0727 1431 2116	2.9 1.8 3.1 1.9
4 SA	0219 0800 1448 2038	3.0 1.5 3.5 1.4	19 SU	0304 0840 1509 2154	3.1 1.7 3.3 1.7
5 SU	0319 0908 1537 2139	3.3 1.2 3.8 1.1	20 M	0337 0932 1542 2225	3.3 1.5 3.5 1.5
6 M	0402 1002 1619 2228	3.6 0.9 4.1 0.8	21 TU	0409 1012 1616 2253	3.5 1.3 3.7 1.3
7 TU	0438 1050 1657 2312	3.8 0.6 4.3 0.6	22 W	0443 1047 1650 2321	3.7 1.1 3.9 1.1
8 W O	0512 1134 1735 2353	4.0 0.4 4.4 0.5	23 TH ●	0516 1120 1723 2350	3.9 1.0 4.0 1.0
9 TH	0548 1216 1811	4.1 0.4 4.4	24 F	0547 1153 1753	4.0 0.9 4.1
10 F	0032 0623 1258 1847	0.5 4.1 0.5 4.2	25 SA	0020 0614 1226 1822	0.9 4.0 0.9 4.0
11 SA	0111 0659 1339 1922	0.6 4.0 0.7 4.0	26 SU	0050 0643 1301 1853	0.9 4.0 0.9 4.0
12 SU	0150 0734 1420 1958	0.7 3.9 1.0 3.7	27 M	0122 0716 1338 1927	1.0 3.9 1.0 3.8
13 M	0230 0809 1502 2035	1.0 3.7 1.3 3.4	28 TU	0158 0755 1422 2007	1.1 3.8 1.2 3.6
14 TU	0315 0848 1548 2117	1.3 3.4 1.6 3.1	29 W	0241 0841 1514 2055	1.2 3.6 1.4 3.3
15 W ☾	0405 0935 1645 2215	1.5 3.2 1.9 2.9	30 TH	0336 0938 1621 2157	1.4 3.4 1.6 3.1
			31 F ☽	0448 1057 1740 2328	1.5 3.2 1.6 2.9

NOVEMBER

Day	Time	m	Day	Time	m
1 SA	0611 1311 1901	1.6 3.3 1.6	16 SU	0114 0627 1317 2011	2.9 1.9 3.1 2.1
2 SU	0149 0731 1421 2016	3.0 1.5 3.5 1.4	17 M	0217 0735 1423 2106	3.1 1.8 3.3 1.9
3 M	0254 0842 1513 2116	3.2 1.3 3.8 1.2	18 TU	0259 0836 1505 2143	3.2 1.7 3.5 1.7
4 TU	0339 0940 1557 2205	3.5 1.0 4.0 1.0	19 W	0336 0926 1543 2215	3.4 1.5 3.6 1.5
5 W	0415 1029 1636 2248	3.7 0.8 4.1 0.8	20 TH	0412 1008 1620 2246	3.6 1.3 3.8 1.2
6 TH O	0450 1115 1713 2329	3.9 0.7 4.2 0.7	21 F	0447 1047 1656 2318	3.8 1.1 4.0 1.1
7 F	0525 1158 1749	4.1 0.7 4.2	22 SA ●	0521 1125 1730 2352	3.9 1.0 4.0 0.9
8 SA	0008 0601 1240 1824	0.7 4.1 0.8 4.1	23 SU	0553 1204 1803	4.0 0.9 4.0
9 SU	0047 0637 1320 1900	0.8 4.1 1.0 4.0	24 M	0027 0627 1246 1838	0.9 4.0 0.9 4.0
10 M	0125 0712 1400 1935	0.9 4.0 1.2 3.8	25 TU	0106 0704 1329 1917	0.9 4.0 0.9 3.9
11 TU	0205 0748 1441 2012	1.1 3.8 1.5 3.5	26 W	0148 0746 1417 2001	0.9 3.9 1.0 3.7
12 W	0248 0827 1525 2053	1.3 3.6 1.7 3.3	27 TH	0234 0833 1510 2049	1.0 3.8 1.2 3.4
13 TH	0334 0910 1616 2142	1.5 3.4 2.0 3.1	28 F	0328 0928 1610 2147	1.2 3.6 1.4 3.2
14 F ☾	0426 1004 1718 2253	1.7 3.2 2.1 2.9	29 SA ☽	0430 1037 1718 2300	1.3 3.4 1.5 3.0
15 SA	0524 1121 1838	1.8 3.1 2.2	30 SU	0541 1222 1831	1.4 3.4 1.6

DECEMBER

Day	Time	m	Day	Time	m
1 M	0048 0657 1347 1943	3.0 1.5 3.5 1.5	16 TU	0041 0629 1257 1946	3.0 1.9 3.2 2.0
2 TU	0215 0812 1447 2047	3.2 1.4 3.6 1.4	17 W	0205 0730 1415 2045	3.1 1.9 3.3 1.9
3 W	0310 0916 1537 2140	3.4 1.2 3.8 1.2	18 TH	0258 0831 1509 2132	3.3 1.7 3.5 1.6
4 TH	0352 1011 1619 2226	3.6 1.1 3.9 1.1	19 F	0342 0926 1553 2212	3.5 1.5 3.6 1.4
5 F	0429 1059 1657 2307	3.8 1.0 4.0 1.0	20 SA	0422 1017 1634 2251	3.7 1.3 3.8 1.2
6 SA O	0506 1143 1733 2347	3.9 1.0 4.0 0.9	21 SU	0501 1103 1713 2330	3.9 1.1 3.9 0.9
7 SU	0544 1225 1809	4.0 1.1 4.0	22 M ●	0539 1149 1751	4.0 0.9 4.0
8 M	0026 0620 1305 1843	0.9 4.1 1.2 3.9	23 TU	0010 0617 1235 1829	0.8 4.1 0.8 4.0
9 TU	0105 0656 1344 1919	1.0 4.0 1.3 3.8	24 W	0053 0657 1321 1910	0.7 4.1 0.7 3.9
10 W	0144 0732 1422 1956	1.1 3.9 1.5 3.7	25 TH	0137 0739 1408 1953	0.7 4.1 0.8 3.8
11 TH	0224 0809 1502 2034	1.2 3.8 1.7 3.5	26 F	0224 0825 1458 2038	0.7 4.0 0.9 3.6
12 F	0305 0848 1545 2115	1.4 3.6 1.9 3.3	27 SA	0314 0915 1551 2129	0.9 3.8 1.1 3.4
13 SA	0349 0930 1634 2203	1.6 3.5 2.0 3.2	28 SU ☽	0409 1012 1649 2228	1.1 3.5 1.3 3.2
14 SU ☾	0437 1019 1731 2305	1.8 3.3 2.1 3.0	29 M	0512 1128 1754 2345	1.3 3.4 1.5 3.0
15 M	0531 1124 1837	1.9 3.2 2.1	30 TU	0622 1306 1903	1.4 3.3 1.6
			31 W	0122 0738 1422 2012	3.0 1.5 3.3 1.6

GREENOCK

LAT 55°57′N
LONG 4°46′W

TIMES AND HEIGHTS OF HIGH AND LOW WATER (Heights in Metres)

TIME ZONE UT
For Summer Time (area enclosed in shaded box) add 1 hour

2014

JANUARY

Day		Time	m	Time	m	Time	m	Time	m
1	W ●	0500	0.4	1207	3.7	1734	0.2		
2	TH	0026	3.6	0548	0.3	1253	3.8	1820	0.0
3	F	0118	3.6	0637	0.3	1338	3.9	1908	0.0
4	SA	0208	3.6	0725	0.3	1424	3.9	1957	0.0
5	SU	0256	3.6	0814	0.4	1509	3.9	2047	0.1
6	M	0342	3.5	0904	0.5	1555	3.8	2140	0.2
7	TU	0427	3.4	0956	0.6	1643	3.6	2238	0.4
8	W ☽	0513	3.3	1052	0.8	1734	3.4	2342	0.6
9	TH	0603	3.1	1157	0.9	1831	3.2		
10	F	0051	0.7	0700	3.0	1314	1.0	1943	3.0
11	SA	0157	0.8	0815	3.0	1425	1.0	2109	3.0
12	SU	0256	0.8	0934	3.1	1525	0.9	2219	3.1
13	M	0348	0.7	1033	3.2	1615	0.7	2312	3.2
14	TU	0434	0.6	1120	3.4	1658	0.6	2358	3.2
15	W	0516	0.6	1159	3.5	1735	0.6		
16	TH O	0037	3.3	0553	0.6	1234	3.6	1807	0.6
17	F	0112	3.3	0626	0.6	1306	3.6	1838	0.6
18	SA	0145	3.3	0658	0.6	1338	3.7	1908	0.5
19	SU	0217	3.3	0729	0.6	1410	3.7	1939	0.5
20	M	0250	3.3	0803	0.6	1445	3.7	2013	0.5
21	TU	0324	3.3	0840	0.6	1522	3.7	2052	0.5
22	W	0359	3.2	0922	0.7	1601	3.6	2136	0.6
23	TH	0437	3.2	1009	0.8	1642	3.4	2226	0.7
24	F ☾	0519	3.1	1102	0.9	1728	3.3	2323	0.8
25	SA	0609	2.9	1204	1.0	1825	3.1		
26	SU	0027	0.9	0719	2.9	1316	1.0	1939	3.0
27	M	0139	0.9	0853	2.9	1431	0.8	2107	3.1
28	TU	0252	0.8	1008	3.1	1537	0.6	2223	3.2
29	W	0354	0.6	1104	3.4	1632	0.3	2324	3.3
30	TH ●	0448	0.4	1153	3.6	1720	0.0		
31	F	0018	3.4	0536	0.2	1241	3.7	1806	-0.1

FEBRUARY

Day		Time	m	Time	m	Time	m	Time	m
1	SA	0109	3.5	0622	0.2	1326	3.8	1851	-0.2
2	SU	0156	3.5	0708	0.1	1411	3.9	1937	-0.1
3	M	0240	3.5	0753	0.2	1455	3.9	2022	0.0
4	TU	0321	3.5	0839	0.2	1537	3.8	2110	0.1
5	W	0400	3.4	0925	0.4	1619	3.6	2200	0.3
6	TH ☽	0439	3.3	1013	0.6	1702	3.4	2257	0.6
7	F	0520	3.2	1109	0.8	1749	3.1		
8	SA	0006	0.8	0607	3.0	1226	1.0	1845	2.9
9	SU	0124	0.9	0705	2.9	1354	1.0	2021	2.7
10	M	0230	0.9	0841	2.9	1501	0.9	2203	2.8
11	TU	0326	0.8	1008	3.0	1554	0.7	2257	3.0
12	W	0414	0.7	1059	3.2	1637	0.6	2340	3.1
13	TH	0456	0.5	1141	3.4	1715	0.5		
14	F O	0019	3.2	0533	0.5	1217	3.5	1747	0.5
15	SA	0054	3.2	0605	0.5	1248	3.5	1816	0.5
16	SU	0126	3.2	0635	0.5	1318	3.5	1843	0.4
17	M	0156	3.3	0703	0.5	1349	3.6	1911	0.4
18	TU	0225	3.3	0735	0.4	1423	3.6	1945	0.3
19	W	0256	3.3	0812	0.4	1459	3.6	2023	0.3
20	TH	0329	3.3	0853	0.4	1537	3.6	2107	0.4
21	F	0404	3.3	0939	0.5	1616	3.5	2156	0.5
22	SA ☾	0441	3.2	1032	0.6	1700	3.3	2252	0.7
23	SU	0525	3.0	1134	0.8	1751	3.1	2356	0.8
24	M	0626	2.8	1247	0.8	1902	2.9		
25	TU	0112	0.9	0816	2.8	1410	0.7	2049	2.9
26	W	0235	0.8	0949	3.0	1522	0.4	2216	3.1
27	TH	0342	0.6	1048	3.3	1617	0.1	2316	3.2
28	F	0436	0.4	1138	3.5	1705	-0.1		

MARCH

Day		Time	m	Time	m	Time	m	Time	m
1	SA ●	0006	3.4	0522	0.2	1225	3.7	1749	-0.2
2	SU	0053	3.4	0606	0.1	1311	3.8	1831	-0.2
3	M	0136	3.5	0648	0.0	1354	3.8	1913	-0.2
4	TU	0216	3.5	0729	0.1	1436	3.8	1955	0.0
5	W	0253	3.5	0810	0.1	1516	3.7	2038	0.1
6	TH	0329	3.4	0852	0.2	1554	3.5	2123	0.3
7	F	0406	3.4	0936	0.4	1634	3.3	2213	0.6
8	SA ☽	0445	3.2	1027	0.6	1717	3.0	2314	0.9
9	SU	0523	3.0	1131	0.9	1807	2.7		
10	M	0038	1.0	0620	2.9	1312	1.0	1918	2.6
11	TU	0157	1.0	0733	2.8	1429	0.9	2135	2.6
12	W	0258	0.9	0928	2.9	1524	0.7	2231	2.8
13	TH	0348	0.7	1029	3.1	1608	0.6	2313	3.0
14	F	0430	0.6	1112	3.2	1646	0.4	2351	3.1
15	SA	0507	0.5	1149	3.3	1719	0.4		
16	SU O	0027	3.2	0539	0.4	1222	3.4	1748	0.4
17	M	0100	3.2	0607	0.4	1252	3.4	1814	0.3
18	TU	0130	3.3	0636	0.3	1324	3.5	1843	0.3
19	W	0158	3.3	0708	0.3	1400	3.5	1919	0.2
20	TH	0229	3.4	0747	0.2	1438	3.6	2000	0.2
21	F	0302	3.4	0829	0.2	1517	3.5	2045	0.3
22	SA	0337	3.4	0917	0.3	1557	3.4	2135	0.4
23	SU	0415	3.3	1012	0.5	1641	3.3	2231	0.6
24	M ☾	0459	3.1	1115	0.6	1733	3.0	2337	0.8
25	TU	0559	2.9	1231	0.7	1843	2.8		
26	W	0056	0.9	0750	2.8	1355	0.5	2042	2.8
27	TH	0221	0.8	0928	3.0	1505	0.3	2205	3.0
28	F	0328	0.6	1028	3.3	1600	0.0	2300	3.2
29	SA	0421	0.3	1119	3.5	1646	-0.1	2348	3.3
30	SU ●	0506	0.2	1205	3.6	1729	-0.2		
31	M	0031	3.4	0547	0.1	1251	3.6	1810	-0.2

APRIL

Day		Time	m	Time	m	Time	m	Time	m
1	TU	0112	3.4	0627	0.0	1334	3.6	1849	-0.1
2	W	0149	3.5	0705	0.0	1414	3.6	1929	0.1
3	TH	0224	3.5	0743	0.1	1453	3.5	2009	0.2
4	F	0259	3.5	0822	0.2	1530	3.4	2052	0.4
5	SA	0335	3.4	0904	0.3	1609	3.2	2138	0.6
6	SU	0414	3.3	0952	0.5	1651	3.0	2232	0.8
7	M ☽	0456	3.1	1051	0.8	1740	2.7	2341	1.0
8	TU	0545	2.9	1212	0.9	1843	2.6		
9	W	0106	1.1	0648	2.8	1341	0.9	2027	2.6
10	TH	0218	1.0	0820	2.8	1442	0.7	2147	2.7
11	F	0312	0.8	0942	2.9	1530	0.6	2235	2.9
12	SA	0357	0.6	1031	3.1	1609	0.4	2316	3.1
13	SU	0435	0.5	1111	3.2	1644	0.4	2354	3.2
14	M	0508	0.4	1146	3.3	1715	0.3		
15	TU O	0029	3.2	0538	0.3	1221	3.3	1744	0.3
16	W	0101	3.3	0610	0.2	1258	3.4	1818	0.2
17	TH	0131	3.4	0646	0.2	1338	3.5	1858	0.2
18	F	0204	3.5	0727	0.1	1419	3.5	1942	0.2
19	SA	0240	3.5	0812	0.1	1501	3.5	2030	0.3
20	SU	0318	3.5	0903	0.2	1544	3.4	2122	0.4
21	M	0359	3.4	1000	0.3	1631	3.2	2220	0.6
22	TU ☾	0446	3.2	1106	0.4	1726	3.0	2326	0.8
23	W	0549	3.0	1221	0.5	1841	2.9		
24	TH	0043	0.9	0731	2.9	1337	0.4	2027	2.8
25	F	0202	0.8	0902	3.0	1443	0.2	2143	3.0
26	SA	0308	0.6	1004	3.2	1537	0.1	2237	3.2
27	SU	0402	0.4	1056	3.4	1625	0.0	2324	3.3
28	M	0448	0.2	1144	3.5	1708	0.0		
29	TU ●	0007	3.4	0529	0.1	1230	3.5	1748	0.0
30	W	0046	3.4	0607	0.1	1313	3.5	1827	0.1

MAY

Day		Time	m	Time	m	Time	m	Time	m
1	TH	0122	3.5	0643	0.1	1353	3.4	1905	0.2
2	F	0156	3.5	0719	0.2	1430	3.3	1944	0.3
3	SA	0232	3.5	0757	0.2	1508	3.2	2026	0.5
4	SU	0308	3.5	0838	0.3	1547	3.1	2111	0.6
5	M	0345	3.4	0924	0.5	1629	3.0	2200	0.8
6	TU	0426	3.2	1018	0.6	1717	2.8	2257	0.9
7	W ☽	0512	3.0	1124	0.8	1814	2.7		
8	TH	0004	1.1	0607	2.9	1238	0.8	1924	2.6
9	F	0116	1.1	0716	2.8	1345	0.8	2044	2.7
10	SA	0220	0.9	0833	2.9	1440	0.6	2146	2.9
11	SU	0313	0.8	0936	3.0	1525	0.5	2234	3.0
12	M	0356	0.6	1025	3.1	1604	0.4	2317	3.2
13	TU	0434	0.4	1107	3.2	1640	0.3	2355	3.2
14	W O	0510	0.3	1150	3.3	1717	0.2		
15	TH	0030	3.3	0547	0.2	1234	3.4	1757	0.2
16	F	0107	3.4	0628	0.1	1318	3.4	1841	0.2
17	SA	0144	3.5	0712	0.0	1404	3.4	1929	0.2
18	SU	0224	3.6	0800	0.0	1450	3.4	2019	0.3
19	M	0305	3.6	0852	0.1	1537	3.3	2113	0.4
20	TU	0349	3.5	0951	0.2	1627	3.2	2211	0.5
21	W ☾	0440	3.3	1055	0.3	1725	3.1	2313	0.7
22	TH	0543	3.1	1205	0.3	1835	3.0		
23	F	0022	0.8	0707	3.0	1314	0.3	1957	2.9
24	SA	0135	0.8	0831	3.1	1417	0.2	2110	3.0
25	SU	0242	0.7	0937	3.2	1513	0.2	2208	3.1
26	M	0340	0.5	1033	3.3	1602	0.2	2258	3.2
27	TU	0429	0.4	1123	3.3	1648	0.2	2342	3.3
28	W ●	0512	0.3	1209	3.3	1730	0.2		
29	TH	0021	3.4	0550	0.2	1253	3.3	1808	0.3
30	F	0058	3.4	0625	0.2	1333	3.2	1846	0.4
31	SA	0132	3.5	0700	0.3	1410	3.2	1924	0.4

JUNE

Day		Time	m	Time	m	Time	m	Time	m
1	SU	0207	3.5	0736	0.3	1447	3.1	2004	0.5
2	M	0243	3.5	0815	0.3	1525	3.1	2046	0.6
3	TU	0319	3.5	0858	0.4	1607	3.0	2131	0.7
4	W	0357	3.4	0945	0.5	1651	2.9	2220	0.8
5	TH ☽	0440	3.2	1039	0.7	1740	2.8	2313	0.9
6	F	0529	3.1	1139	0.7	1835	2.8		
7	SA	0012	1.0	0626	3.0	1243	0.7	1937	2.8
8	SU	0116	1.0	0731	2.9	1342	0.7	2045	2.8
9	M	0218	0.9	0838	3.0	1436	0.6	2146	3.0
10	TU	0313	0.7	0939	3.1	1524	0.5	2237	3.1
11	W	0401	0.5	1033	3.2	1609	0.3	2322	3.2
12	TH	0446	0.3	1123	3.3	1653	0.3		
13	F O	0004	3.4	0529	0.1	1213	3.3	1739	0.2
14	SA	0046	3.5	0613	0.0	1303	3.4	1827	0.2
15	SU	0129	3.6	0700	-0.1	1352	3.4	1917	0.2
16	M	0212	3.7	0748	-0.1	1442	3.4	2008	0.2
17	TU	0256	3.7	0840	-0.1	1532	3.3	2101	0.3
18	W	0342	3.6	0936	0.0	1622	3.3	2155	0.4
19	TH ☾	0432	3.5	1036	0.1	1715	3.2	2253	0.5
20	F	0529	3.3	1141	0.2	1812	3.1	2356	0.7
21	SA	0637	3.1	1246	0.3	1917	3.0		
22	SU	0104	0.7	0754	3.0	1350	0.4	2027	3.0
23	M	0214	0.7	0909	3.1	1448	0.4	2135	3.0
24	TU	0317	0.6	1012	3.1	1541	0.4	2232	3.1
25	W	0411	0.5	1106	3.2	1629	0.4	2320	3.2
26	TH	0456	0.4	1154	3.2	1713	0.4		
27	F ●	0002	3.3	0536	0.4	1239	3.2	1753	0.4
28	SA	0039	3.4	0612	0.3	1318	3.1	1830	0.4
29	SU	0113	3.5	0644	0.3	1353	3.1	1906	0.5
30	M	0146	3.5	0718	0.4	1427	3.1	1942	0.5

SUNRISE AND SUNSET TIMES

GREENOCK
At 55°57′N 4°46′W

UT		Sunrise	Sunset
Jan	01	0850	1556
	15	0840	1618
Feb	01	0813	1653
	15	0744	1723
Mar	01	0710	1754
	15	0634	1823
BST			
Apr	01	0650	1958
	15	0614	2026
May	01	0535	2058
	15	0506	2126
Jun	01	0441	2153
	15	0433	2207
Jul	01	0438	2208
	15	0454	2155
Aug	01	0523	2126
	15	0550	2055
Sep	01	0624	2013
	15	0651	1936
Oct	01	0722	1854
	15	0750	1818
UT			
Nov	01	0726	1638
	15	0756	1611
Dec	01	0826	1550
	15	0844	1544

GREENOCK

LAT 55°57′N
LONG 4°46′W

TIMES AND HEIGHTS OF HIGH AND LOW WATER (Heights in Metres)

TIME ZONE UT
For Summer Time (area enclosed in shaded box) add 1 hour

2014

JULY

Date	Day	Time	m
1	TU	0220 0753 1503 2020	3.5 0.4 3.1 0.5
2	W	0254 0830 1541 2100	3.5 0.4 3.1 0.6
3	TH	0330 0911 1620 2143	3.5 0.5 3.0 0.6
4	F	0409 0956 1702 2229	3.4 0.5 3.0 0.7
5	SA ☽	0453 1046 1748 2321	3.2 0.6 2.9 0.9
6	SU	0543 1144 1840	3.1 0.7 2.9
7	M	0020 0642 1246 1942	0.9 3.0 0.7 2.8
8	TU	0126 0751 1349 2053	0.9 2.9 0.7 2.9
9	W	0232 0901 1448 2200	0.8 3.0 0.6 3.0
10	TH	0332 1006 1543 2255	0.6 3.1 0.4 3.2
11	F	0425 1104 1634 2343	0.3 3.2 0.3 3.4
12	SA ○	0513 1158 1724	0.1 3.3 0.2
13	SU	0029 0559 1251 1812	3.5 -0.1 3.4 0.2
14	M	0115 0645 1342 1902	3.7 -0.2 3.4 0.1
15	TU	0200 0733 1432 1951	3.7 -0.2 3.4 0.2
16	W	0246 0822 1520 2041	3.8 -0.2 3.4 0.2
17	TH	0331 0914 1606 2132	3.7 -0.1 3.3 0.3
18	F	0417 1009 1652 2226	3.6 0.1 3.3 0.4
19	SA ☾	0506 1110 1739 2324	3.4 0.3 3.1 0.6
20	SU	0601 1217 1830	3.2 0.4 3.0
21	M	0032 0708 1324 1932	0.8 3.0 0.5 2.9
22	TU	0147 0838 1426 2055	0.8 2.9 0.6 2.9
23	W	0256 0956 1522 2207	0.8 2.9 0.6 3.0
24	TH	0353 1054 1612 2301	0.6 3.0 0.5 3.2
25	F	0441 1142 1657 2345	0.5 3.1 0.5 3.3
26	SA ●	0521 1224 1737	0.4 3.1 0.4
27	SU	0022 0556 1302 1812	3.4 0.4 3.1 0.5
28	M	0055 0627 1334 1845	3.5 0.4 3.1 0.5
29	TU	0125 0657 1405 1918	3.5 0.4 3.1 0.5
30	W	0156 0728 1437 1951	3.5 0.4 3.1 0.5
31	TH	0229 0800 1511 2027	3.6 0.4 3.2 0.5

AUGUST

Date	Day	Time	m
1	F	0304 0836 1545 2107	3.6 0.4 3.2 0.5
2	SA	0342 0917 1623 2151	3.5 0.4 3.1 0.6
3	SU	0421 1004 1704 2241	3.4 0.5 3.0 0.7
4	M ☽	0506 1059 1751 2338	3.2 0.7 2.9 0.9
5	TU	0600 1201 1850	3.0 0.8 2.9
6	W	0044 0708 1310 2007	0.9 2.9 0.8 2.9
7	TH	0159 0830 1420 2129	0.8 2.9 0.7 3.0
8	F	0309 0948 1524 2233	0.6 3.0 0.5 3.2
9	SA	0408 1052 1619 2326	0.3 3.2 0.4 3.4
10	SU ○	0457 1147 1709	0.0 3.3 0.2
11	M	0014 0543 1239 1756	3.6 -0.2 3.4 0.1
12	TU	0101 0628 1328 1843	3.7 -0.3 3.4 0.1
13	W	0146 0713 1415 1930	3.8 -0.3 3.4 0.1
14	TH	0231 0759 1458 2016	3.8 -0.2 3.4 0.2
15	F	0314 0846 1540 2104	3.8 0.0 3.4 0.2
16	SA	0356 0937 1620 2153	3.6 0.2 3.3 0.4
17	SU ☾	0439 1034 1701 2248	3.4 0.4 3.2 0.6
18	M	0526 1142 1747 2356	3.2 0.6 3.1 0.8
19	TU	0621 1256 1840	2.9 0.8 2.9
20	W	0121 0753 1403 1958	0.9 2.7 0.8 2.9
21	TH	0234 0943 1502 2140	0.9 2.8 0.7 3.0
22	F	0333 1039 1553 2239	0.7 2.9 0.6 3.2
23	SA	0420 1124 1637 2324	0.6 3.1 0.5 3.3
24	SU	0500 1203 1716	0.4 3.1 0.5
25	M ●	0001 0534 1239 1750	3.4 0.4 3.2 0.4
26	TU	0033 0605 1310 1821	3.5 0.4 3.2 0.5
27	W	0102 0632 1339 1850	3.5 0.4 3.2 0.5
28	TH	0132 0659 1408 1920	3.5 0.4 3.2 0.5
29	F	0204 0729 1438 1955	3.6 0.4 3.3 0.5
30	SA	0240 0804 1511 2034	3.6 0.4 3.3 0.5
31	SU	0317 0844 1547 2118	3.6 0.4 3.3 0.6

SEPTEMBER

Date	Day	Time	m
1	M	0355 0931 1625 2208	3.5 0.5 3.2 0.7
2	TU ☽	0437 1025 1709 2306	3.3 0.7 3.1 0.8
3	W	0526 1128 1806	3.1 0.9 2.9
4	TH	0014 0632 1242 1928	0.9 2.9 0.9 2.9
5	F	0135 0807 1401 2105	0.8 2.9 0.9 3.0
6	SA	0252 0939 1510 2215	0.6 3.0 0.7 3.3
7	SU	0351 1043 1606 2308	0.3 3.2 0.4 3.5
8	M	0440 1135 1654 2356	0.0 3.4 0.2 3.7
9	TU ○	0525 1222 1739	-0.2 3.4 0.1
10	W	0043 0608 1308 1823	3.8 -0.2 3.5 0.1
11	TH	0128 0650 1350 1906	3.8 -0.2 3.5 0.1
12	F	0212 0733 1430 1949	3.8 -0.1 3.5 0.2
13	SA	0253 0817 1508 2033	3.7 0.1 3.5 0.3
14	SU	0333 0903 1546 2119	3.6 0.3 3.4 0.4
15	M	0413 0954 1626 2210	3.4 0.6 3.3 0.7
16	TU ☾	0456 1058 1711 2315	3.1 0.9 3.2 0.9
17	W	0547 1222 1802	2.8 1.0 3.0
18	TH	0049 0659 1336 1908	1.0 2.6 1.0 2.9
19	F	0207 0919 1436 2057	1.0 2.7 0.9 3.0
20	SA	0305 1015 1528 2207	0.8 2.9 0.8 3.2
21	SU	0352 1057 1612 2253	0.6 3.1 0.6 3.3
22	M	0432 1134 1650 2331	0.5 3.2 0.5 3.4
23	TU	0507 1209 1724	0.4 3.3 0.5
24	W ●	0004 0537 1241 1753	3.5 0.4 3.3 0.5
25	TH	0034 0604 1311 1821	3.5 0.4 3.3 0.5
26	F	0105 0630 1338 1851	3.6 0.4 3.4 0.5
27	SA	0140 0701 1408 1927	3.6 0.4 3.4 0.5
28	SU	0217 0738 1441 2008	3.6 0.4 3.5 0.5
29	M	0255 0820 1517 2053	3.6 0.5 3.4 0.5
30	TU	0335 0907 1556 2145	3.5 0.6 3.4 0.7

OCTOBER

Date	Day	Time	m
1	W ☽	0416 1002 1640 2244	3.4 0.8 3.2 0.8
2	TH	0505 1106 1735 2356	3.2 1.0 3.1 0.9
3	F	0610 1222 1900	3.0 1.1 3.0
4	SA	0118 0753 1346 2043	0.8 2.9 1.0 3.1
5	SU	0234 0929 1456 2154	0.6 3.1 0.8 3.3
6	M	0333 1029 1551 2247	0.3 3.3 0.5 3.6
7	TU	0421 1117 1638 2336	0.1 3.4 0.3 3.7
8	W ○	0505 1202 1721	-0.1 3.5 0.2
9	TH	0023 0547 1244 1802	3.8 -0.1 3.6 0.2
10	F	0108 0628 1324 1843	3.8 0.0 3.6 0.2
11	SA	0151 0708 1401 1923	3.8 0.1 3.6 0.3
12	SU	0231 0749 1438 2004	3.7 0.3 3.6 0.4
13	M	0310 0833 1516 2048	3.5 0.5 3.6 0.5
14	TU	0350 0920 1556 2136	3.4 0.7 3.5 0.7
15	W ☾	0432 1015 1640 2235	3.1 1.0 3.3 0.9
16	TH	0522 1130 1729 2358	2.9 1.2 3.1 1.1
17	F	0626 1255 1830	2.7 1.2 3.0
18	SA	0125 0814 1402 1953	1.1 2.7 1.1 3.0
19	SU	0228 0933 1456 2118	0.9 2.9 1.0 3.1
20	M	0317 1019 1541 2212	0.8 3.1 0.8 3.3
21	TU	0358 1059 1620 2253	0.6 3.3 0.7 3.4
22	W	0434 1136 1655 2329	0.5 3.4 0.6 3.5
23	TH ●	0506 1210 1726	0.5 3.4 0.5
24	F	0003 0534 1242 1755	3.5 0.5 3.5 0.5
25	SA	0039 0604 1311 1828	3.6 0.5 3.5 0.5
26	SU	0117 0638 1343 1906	3.6 0.4 3.6 0.5
27	M	0157 0718 1419 1948	3.6 0.5 3.6 0.5
28	TU	0238 0803 1456 2036	3.6 0.5 3.6 0.5
29	W	0320 0852 1537 2129	3.6 0.7 3.6 0.6
30	TH	0404 0947 1623 2230	3.4 0.8 3.4 0.7
31	F ☽	0455 1051 1719 2342	3.2 1.0 3.3 0.8

NOVEMBER

Date	Day	Time	m
1	SA	0600 1205 1840	3.0 1.1 3.1
2	SU	0101 0737 1326 2016	0.7 3.0 1.1 3.2
3	M	0212 0907 1436 2128	0.6 3.1 0.9 3.4
4	TU	0311 1007 1533 2225	0.4 3.3 0.7 3.6
5	W	0401 1055 1621 2315	0.2 3.5 0.5 3.7
6	TH ○	0446 1139 1705	0.1 3.6 0.4
7	F	0002 0527 1221 1745	3.7 0.1 3.6 0.3
8	SA	0048 0608 1259 1824	3.7 0.2 3.7 0.3
9	SU	0131 0647 1336 1902	3.7 0.3 3.7 0.4
10	M	0211 0727 1413 1941	3.6 0.5 3.7 0.4
11	TU	0250 0808 1451 2023	3.5 0.6 3.7 0.6
12	W	0329 0853 1530 2108	3.3 0.8 3.6 0.7
13	TH	0412 0942 1612 2201	3.2 1.0 3.5 0.9
14	F ☾	0459 1039 1658 2305	3.0 1.2 3.3 1.0
15	SA	0555 1150 1752	2.9 1.3 3.2
16	SU	0021 0706 1306 1856	1.1 2.8 1.3 3.1
17	M	0134 0826 1410 2010	1.0 2.9 1.2 3.1
18	TU	0231 0930 1502 2117	0.9 3.1 1.0 3.2
19	W	0318 1019 1545 2208	0.8 3.3 0.9 3.3
20	TH	0358 1101 1623 2252	0.7 3.4 0.7 3.4
21	F	0434 1139 1658 2333	0.6 3.5 0.6 3.5
22	SA ●	0507 1214 1733	0.5 3.6 0.5
23	SU	0015 0542 1248 1809	3.6 0.5 3.6 0.4
24	M	0058 0621 1324 1850	3.6 0.5 3.7 0.4
25	TU	0142 0704 1402 1935	3.6 0.5 3.8 0.4
26	W	0226 0751 1443 2024	3.6 0.5 3.8 0.4
27	TH	0310 0841 1526 2118	3.6 0.6 3.7 0.5
28	F	0357 0936 1613 2217	3.5 0.8 3.6 0.6
29	SA ☽	0449 1036 1708 2325	3.3 0.9 3.4 0.6
30	SU	0550 1144 1819	3.2 1.0 3.3

DECEMBER

Date	Day	Time	m
1	M	0037 0710 1259 1944	0.6 3.1 1.1 3.3
2	TU	0146 0833 1411 2100	0.6 3.1 1.0 3.4
3	W	0247 0939 1512 2202	0.5 3.3 0.8 3.5
4	TH	0340 1032 1604 2256	0.4 3.4 0.6 3.5
5	F	0428 1119 1650 2346	0.3 3.5 0.5 3.6
6	SA ○	0512 1201 1732	0.3 3.6 0.4
7	SU	0033 0552 1240 1809	3.6 0.4 3.7 0.4
8	M	0116 0632 1317 1846	3.5 0.5 3.7 0.5
9	TU	0155 0710 1353 1922	3.4 0.6 3.8 0.5
10	W	0232 0748 1430 2001	3.4 0.6 3.7 0.6
11	TH	0310 0829 1507 2043	3.3 0.7 3.7 0.6
12	F	0351 0912 1546 2129	3.2 0.9 3.6 0.8
13	SA	0434 0959 1628 2219	3.1 1.0 3.5 0.9
14	SU ☾	0522 1052 1714 2318	3.0 1.1 3.3 1.0
15	M	0616 1153 1807	2.9 1.3 3.2
16	TU	0023 0719 1302 1908	1.1 2.9 1.3 3.1
17	W	0129 0829 1408 2014	1.0 3.0 1.2 3.1
18	TH	0228 0933 1503 2120	0.9 3.1 1.0 3.2
19	F	0317 1026 1550 2217	0.8 3.3 0.8 3.3
20	SA	0401 1110 1633 2307	0.7 3.4 0.6 3.4
21	SU	0442 1150 1713 2355	0.6 3.5 0.5 3.5
22	M ●	0523 1229 1754	0.5 3.7 0.3
23	TU	0043 0606 1309 1837	3.5 0.4 3.7 0.2
24	W	0130 0652 1350 1923	3.6 0.4 3.8 0.2
25	TH	0216 0739 1433 2012	3.6 0.4 3.9 0.2
26	F	0303 0829 1518 2103	3.6 0.5 3.8 0.3
27	SA	0350 0921 1605 2159	3.5 0.6 3.7 0.3
28	SU ☽	0438 1016 1656 2300	3.4 0.7 3.6 0.5
29	M	0531 1118 1755	3.3 0.8 3.4
30	TU	0008 0632 1228 1906	0.6 3.1 1.0 3.3
31	W	0118 0748 1343 2028	0.6 3.1 1.0 3.2

LIVERPOOL (GLADSTONE DOCK)
LAT 53°24'N
LONG 3°01'W

TIMES AND HEIGHTS OF HIGH AND LOW WATER (Heights in Metres)

TIME ZONE UT
For Summer Time (area enclosed in shaded box) add 1 hour

2014

JANUARY

Date	Day	Time	m
1	W ●	0511 1037 1739 2304	1.2 9.6 1.0 9.6
2	TH	0601 1125 1830 2354	0.9 9.9 0.7 9.7
3	F	0650 1214 1920	0.8 10.1 0.5
4	SA	0043 0736 1302 2006	9.7 0.9 10.0 0.6
5	SU	0131 0821 1350 2053	9.5 1.1 9.8 0.9
6	M	0219 0907 1439 2139	9.2 1.4 9.5 1.3
7	TU	0308 0954 1530 2227	8.8 1.9 9.0 1.8
8	W ☽	0401 1046 1626 2322	8.3 2.4 8.5 2.4
9	TH	0501 1147 1729	7.9 2.8 8.1
10	F	0025 0610 1259 1841	2.8 7.6 3.0 7.8
11	SA	0135 0725 1412 1952	2.9 7.7 3.0 7.8
12	SU	0242 0830 1517 2054	2.8 7.9 2.7 8.0
13	M	0338 0923 1611 2144	2.6 8.2 2.4 8.3
14	TU	0424 1006 1656 2226	2.4 8.6 2.1 8.5
15	W	0503 1043 1734 2302	2.2 8.8 1.9 8.7
16	TH O	0538 1117 1809 2335	2.0 9.0 1.8 8.8
17	F	0609 1149 1841	1.8 9.1 1.7
18	SA	0007 0640 1221 1911	8.9 1.7 9.1 1.6
19	SU	0040 0713 1253 1943	8.9 1.7 9.1 1.6
20	M	0112 0747 1324 2016	8.8 1.8 8.9 1.8
21	TU	0144 0822 1355 2050	8.6 2.0 8.8 2.0
22	W	0219 0858 1430 2126	8.4 2.3 8.5 2.3
23	TH	0258 0937 1512 2208	8.2 2.6 8.3 2.6
24	F ☾	0346 1026 1605 2303	8.0 2.9 8.0 2.9
25	SA	0448 1130 1716	7.7 3.1 7.8
26	SU	0020 0605 1255 1841	3.0 7.7 3.0 7.8
27	M	0146 0724 1418 1959	2.8 8.0 2.6 8.1
28	TU	0258 0833 1529 2106	2.3 8.5 2.0 8.6
29	W	0400 0932 1631 2203	1.8 9.1 1.4 9.1
30	TH ●	0457 1024 1728 2255	1.2 9.6 0.9 9.5
31	F	0549 1113 1819 2342	0.8 10.0 0.4 9.8

FEBRUARY

Date	Day	Time	m
1	SA	0637 1200 1906	0.6 10.2 0.2
2	SU	0028 0721 1246 1950	9.8 0.5 10.2 0.3
3	M	0112 0804 1330 2031	9.7 0.7 10.0 0.6
4	TU	0155 0845 1413 2111	9.4 1.1 9.6 1.1
5	W	0237 0926 1457 2152	8.9 1.6 9.1 1.8
6	TH ☽	0321 1010 1546 2236	8.4 2.2 8.5 2.4
7	F	0413 1103 1644 2332	7.9 2.8 7.8 3.0
8	SA	0519 1213 1756	7.4 3.2 7.4
9	SU	0047 0640 1336 1919	3.3 7.3 3.3 7.3
10	M	0207 0759 1451 2032	3.3 7.5 3.0 7.6
11	TU	0312 0900 1549 2126	3.0 7.9 2.6 8.0
12	W	0403 0945 1636 2208	2.6 8.3 2.2 8.3
13	TH	0444 1023 1714 2243	2.2 8.7 1.9 8.6
14	F O	0519 1057 1748 2315	1.9 8.9 1.6 8.8
15	SA	0551 1129 1820 2346	1.7 9.1 1.4 9.0
16	SU	0623 1200 1851	1.5 9.2 1.3
17	M	0017 0655 1230 1923	9.0 1.4 9.2 1.3
18	TU	0048 0729 1300 1955	9.0 1.4 9.1 1.4
19	W	0119 0802 1331 2027	8.9 1.6 9.0 1.6
20	TH	0152 0836 1405 2059	8.8 1.8 8.8 2.0
21	F	0229 0912 1445 2137	8.5 2.1 8.5 2.3
22	SA ☾	0314 0956 1535 2227	8.2 2.5 8.1 2.7
23	SU	0414 1057 1646 2341	7.9 2.8 7.7 3.0
24	M	0535 1223 1817	7.6 2.9 7.6
25	TU	0116 0701 1356 1944	2.9 7.8 2.6 7.9
26	W	0237 0816 1513 2055	2.4 8.3 2.0 8.5
27	TH	0344 0917 1617 2152	1.8 9.0 1.3 9.0
28	F	0442 1010 1713 2241	1.2 9.5 0.7 9.5

MARCH

Date	Day	Time	m
1	SA ●	0533 1057 1802 2326	0.8 9.9 0.3 9.8
2	SU	0620 1142 1846	0.5 10.1 0.2
3	M	0008 0702 1225 1927	9.8 0.4 10.1 0.2
4	TU	0049 0742 1306 2005	9.7 0.5 9.9 0.6
5	W	0128 0820 1346 2041	9.4 0.9 9.5 1.1
6	TH	0205 0857 1426 2115	9.0 1.5 9.0 1.8
7	F	0244 0936 1509 2152	8.5 2.1 8.4 2.5
8	SA ☽	0330 1021 1601 2238	7.9 2.7 7.7 3.1
9	SU	0430 1124 1711 2348	7.4 3.3 7.2 3.6
10	M	0550 1252 1838	7.1 3.4 7.0
11	TU	0121 0717 1415 1959	3.6 7.2 3.2 7.3
12	W	0237 0826 1517 2058	3.3 7.6 2.7 7.7
13	TH	0333 0915 1605 2141	2.8 8.1 2.2 8.2
14	F	0416 0955 1644 2216	2.3 8.5 1.8 8.5
15	SA	0452 1030 1720 2248	1.9 8.8 1.5 8.8
16	SU O	0527 1102 1753 2319	1.6 9.0 1.3 9.0
17	M	0601 1133 1826 2350	1.3 9.2 1.1 9.2
18	TU	0635 1204 1900	1.2 9.2 1.1
19	W	0022 0709 1236 1932	9.2 1.1 9.2 1.2
20	TH	0055 0743 1310 2005	9.2 1.3 9.1 1.4
21	F	0130 0818 1346 2038	9.0 1.5 8.9 1.7
22	SA	0209 0855 1429 2117	8.8 1.8 8.6 2.1
23	SU	0256 0940 1522 2207	8.4 2.2 8.2 2.6
24	M ☾	0357 1041 1634 2320	8.0 2.6 7.7 2.9
25	TU	0518 1207 1805	7.7 2.7 7.6
26	W	0054 0643 1339 1930	2.9 7.9 2.4 7.9
27	TH	0218 0758 1455 2040	2.4 8.3 1.9 8.4
28	F	0326 0859 1559 2135	1.9 8.9 1.3 9.0
29	SA	0424 0951 1653 2222	1.3 9.4 0.8 9.4
30	SU ●	0514 1037 1740 2305	0.9 9.7 0.5 9.6
31	M	0558 1121 1822 2345	0.6 9.9 0.4 9.7

APRIL

Date	Day	Time	m
1	TU	0639 1202 1901	0.5 9.9 0.5
2	W	0023 0718 1241 1936	9.6 0.6 9.6 0.8
3	TH	0100 0755 1319 2009	9.3 1.0 9.3 1.3
4	F	0136 0830 1357 2041	9.0 1.5 8.8 1.9
5	SA	0212 0906 1438 2113	8.5 2.0 8.3 2.5
6	SU	0255 0945 1526 2153	8.0 2.6 7.7 3.0
7	M ☽	0348 1038 1628 2250	7.5 3.1 7.2 3.5
8	TU	0501 1158 1748	7.1 3.4 6.9
9	W	0018 0624 1324 1910	3.7 7.1 3.2 7.1
10	TH	0145 0737 1430 2015	3.5 7.4 2.8 7.5
11	F	0247 0833 1522 2102	3.0 7.8 2.4 8.0
12	SA	0336 0917 1605 2141	2.5 8.2 1.9 8.4
13	SU	0417 0955 1645 2215	2.0 8.6 1.6 8.7
14	M	0456 1029 1722 2248	1.6 8.9 1.3 9.0
15	TU O	0534 1103 1759 2321	1.3 9.1 1.1 9.2
16	W	0612 1137 1836 2356	1.1 9.2 1.0 9.3
17	TH	0650 1214 1912	1.0 9.3 1.1
18	F	0033 0727 1253 1947	9.3 1.1 9.2 1.3
19	SA	0113 0805 1335 2024	9.2 1.3 9.0 1.6
20	SU	0157 0846 1422 2106	8.9 1.6 8.7 2.0
21	M	0248 0934 1519 2159	8.6 1.9 8.2 2.4
22	TU ☾	0351 1037 1631 2310	8.2 2.3 7.9 2.7
23	W	0507 1157 1752	8.0 2.4 7.8
24	TH	0035 0624 1320 1911	2.7 8.1 2.2 8.0
25	F	0155 0735 1433 2018	2.4 8.4 1.8 8.4
26	SA	0302 0837 1535 2113	1.9 8.8 1.4 8.8
27	SU	0400 0929 1629 2200	1.5 9.1 1.1 9.1
28	M	0450 1016 1715 2242	1.1 9.4 0.9 9.3
29	TU ●	0535 1059 1756 2321	0.9 9.5 0.9 9.4
30	W	0616 1139 1833 2359	0.9 9.4 1.0 9.3

MAY

Date	Day	Time	m
1	TH	0655 1218 1908	1.0 9.3 1.2
2	F	0035 0731 1256 1940	9.2 1.2 9.0 1.5
3	SA	0110 0806 1333 2011	8.9 1.6 8.6 2.0
4	SU	0146 0840 1411 2042	8.6 2.0 8.3 2.4
5	M	0226 0916 1455 2119	8.2 2.4 7.8 2.8
6	TU	0314 1000 1549 2208	7.8 2.8 7.4 3.2
7	W ☽	0414 1101 1655 2314	7.4 3.1 7.1 3.5
8	TH	0526 1217 1809	7.2 3.2 7.1
9	F	0034 0638 1330 1917	3.5 7.3 2.9 7.3
10	SA	0148 0740 1430 2012	3.1 7.6 2.6 7.7
11	SU	0246 0830 1520 2057	2.7 8.0 2.1 8.2
12	M	0336 0914 1606 2137	2.2 8.4 1.7 8.6
13	TU	0423 0954 1650 2215	1.8 8.7 1.4 9.0
14	W O	0507 1033 1732 2254	1.4 9.0 1.2 9.2
15	TH	0550 1114 1813 2334	1.1 9.2 1.0 9.4
16	F	0633 1156 1854	1.0 9.3 1.0
17	SA	0016 0715 1240 1934	9.5 0.9 9.3 1.1
18	SU	0101 0758 1327 2016	9.4 1.0 9.1 1.4
19	M	0149 0843 1418 2102	9.2 1.3 8.8 1.8
20	TU	0242 0935 1516 2156	8.9 1.6 8.5 2.1
21	W ☾	0343 1034 1621 2300	8.6 1.9 8.1 2.4
22	TH	0451 1143 1732	8.4 2.0 8.0
23	F	0013 0600 1256 1844	2.5 8.3 2.0 8.0
24	SA	0126 0709 1404 1951	2.4 8.4 1.9 8.2
25	SU	0234 0812 1507 2049	2.1 8.6 1.7 8.5
26	M	0334 0907 1602 2137	1.8 8.8 1.6 8.8
27	TU	0427 0955 1649 2221	1.6 8.9 1.5 9.0
28	W ●	0513 1039 1730 2300	1.4 9.0 1.4 9.1
29	TH	0555 1120 1807 2338	1.3 9.0 1.4 9.1
30	F	0634 1158 1842	1.3 8.9 1.5
31	SA	0013 0710 1235	9.0 1.5 8.8

JUNE

Date	Day	Time	m
1	SU	0049 0744 1311 1945	8.9 1.7 8.6 2.0
2	M	0124 0817 1348 2018	8.7 1.9 8.4 2.2
3	TU	0201 0851 1428 2054	8.4 2.2 8.1 2.5
4	W	0243 0930 1512 2137	8.1 2.5 7.7 2.8
5	TH ☽	0330 1017 1604 2229	7.8 2.7 7.5 3.1
6	F	0428 1115 1705 2332	7.5 2.9 7.3 3.3
7	SA	0533 1223 1811	7.4 2.9 7.3
8	SU	0043 0638 1332 1914	3.2 7.5 2.7 7.6
9	M	0153 0738 1433 2010	2.9 7.8 2.4 8.0
10	TU	0254 0832 1528 2100	2.4 8.2 2.0 8.5
11	W	0349 0921 1619 2146	2.0 8.6 1.6 8.9
12	TH	0441 1008 1707 2231	1.5 8.9 1.3 9.3
13	F O	0530 1055 1753 2316	1.2 9.2 1.1 9.5
14	SA	0618 1142 1839	0.9 9.4 1.0
15	SU	0002 0705 1230 1924	9.7 0.7 9.4 1.0
16	M	0051 0753 1320 2010	9.7 0.7 9.3 1.1
17	TU	0141 0840 1411 2057	9.5 0.9 9.1 1.4
18	W	0233 0930 1504 2147	9.3 1.2 8.8 1.7
19	TH ☾	0328 1023 1602 2243	9.0 1.5 8.4 2.1
20	F	0427 1121 1705 2346	8.7 1.8 8.1 2.3
21	SA	0532 1225 1813	8.4 2.1 8.0
22	SU	0055 0639 1333 1921	2.5 8.2 2.2 8.0
23	M	0205 0746 1438 2024	2.4 8.2 2.2 8.2
24	TU	0310 0846 1536 2117	2.2 8.3 2.1 8.4
25	W	0406 0938 1625 2203	2.0 8.5 2.0 8.6
26	TH	0455 1023 1708 2243	1.8 8.6 1.9 8.8
27	F ●	0538 1104 1746 2320	1.7 8.7 1.8 8.9
28	SA	0617 1141 1820 2355	1.6 8.8 1.8 8.9
29	SU	0652 1216 1852	1.6 8.7 1.8
30	M	0029 0724 1251 1923	8.9 1.6 8.7 1.9

SUNRISE AND SUNSET TIMES

LIVERPOOL
At 53°24'N 3°01'N

		Sunrise	Sunset
UT			
Jan	01	0828	1604
	15	0820	1624
Feb	01	0757	1655
	15	0730	1723
Mar	01	0700	1750
	15	0627	1816
BST			
Apr	01	0645	1948
	15	0612	2013
May	01	0538	2042
	15	0512	2106
Jun	01	0450	2130
	15	0443	2142
Jul	01	0448	2143
	15	0503	2133
Aug	01	0528	2107
	15	0552	2040
Sep	01	0621	2001
	15	0646	1928
Oct	01	0714	1849
	15	0739	1816
UT			
Nov	01	0711	1640
	15	0738	1615
Dec	01	0805	1557
	15	0821	1553

LIVERPOOL (GLADSTONE DOCK)
LAT 53°24′N
LONG 3°01′W

TIMES AND HEIGHTS OF HIGH AND LOW WATER (Heights in Metres)

TIME ZONE UT
For Summer Time (area enclosed in shaded box) add 1 hour

2014

JULY

Date	Day	Phase	Time	m	Time	m	Time	m	Time	m
1	TU		0103	8.8	0755	1.8	1325	8.5	1956	2.0
2	W		0138	8.7	0828	1.9	1401	8.3	2031	2.2
3	TH		0213	8.4	0903	2.1	1438	8.1	2110	2.5
4	F		0251	8.2	0942	2.4	1520	7.9	2153	2.7
5	SA	☽	0335	7.9	1028	2.7	1609	7.6	2244	3.0
6	SU		0430	7.7	1124	2.8	1710	7.5	2348	3.1
7	M		0536	7.6	1235	2.9	1819	7.6		
8	TU		0102	3.0	0647	7.7	1348	2.6	1927	7.9
9	W		0216	2.6	0755	8.0	1454	2.2	2028	8.4
10	TH		0320	2.1	0855	8.4	1552	1.8	2122	8.8
11	F		0419	1.6	0949	8.9	1646	1.4	2212	9.3
12	SA	○	0514	1.1	1040	9.2	1737	1.1	2301	9.7
13	SU		0606	0.7	1130	9.5	1827	0.8	2349	9.9
14	M		0656	0.5	1219	9.6	1914	0.7		
15	TU		0038	10.0	0743	0.4	1307	9.6	1959	0.8
16	W		0126	9.9	0829	0.5	1355	9.4	2044	1.0
17	TH		0215	9.6	0914	0.9	1443	9.0	2130	1.4
18	F		0305	9.2	1001	1.3	1534	8.6	2219	1.9
19	SA	☾	0358	8.8	1051	1.9	1630	8.2	2315	2.3
20	SU		0458	8.3	1150	2.4	1736	7.8		
21	M		0022	2.7	0606	7.9	1258	2.7	1848	7.7
22	TU		0137	2.8	0719	7.8	1409	2.7	1959	7.8
23	W		0248	2.6	0827	7.9	1513	2.6	2059	8.1
24	TH		0350	2.3	0923	8.1	1606	2.4	2147	8.4
25	F		0440	2.1	1009	8.4	1650	2.2	2227	8.7
26	SA	●	0522	1.8	1048	8.6	1727	2.0	2303	8.9
27	SU		0559	1.7	1123	8.7	1800	1.8	2336	9.0
28	M		0632	1.6	1156	8.8	1831	1.7		
29	TU		0009	9.0	0702	1.5	1228	8.8	1902	1.7
30	W		0041	9.0	0732	1.6	1300	8.8	1935	1.7
31	TH		0112	8.9	0804	1.7	1332	8.6	2009	1.9

AUGUST

Date	Day	Phase	Time	m	Time	m	Time	m	Time	m
1	F		0144	8.7	0836	1.9	1406	8.4	2044	2.1
2	SA		0216	8.5	0911	2.1	1442	8.2	2122	2.4
3	SU		0254	8.2	0950	2.5	1525	8.0	2206	2.7
4	M	☽	0342	7.9	1038	2.8	1621	7.7	2303	3.0
5	TU		0445	7.7	1145	2.9	1733	7.6		
6	W		0020	3.0	0606	7.6	1309	2.9	1852	7.8
7	TH		0144	2.8	0727	7.8	1425	2.5	2003	8.3
8	F		0257	2.2	0836	8.3	1530	2.0	2103	8.8
9	SA		0401	1.6	0935	8.9	1628	1.5	2157	9.4
10	SU	○	0459	1.0	1028	9.3	1722	1.0	2246	9.8
11	M		0553	0.6	1116	9.7	1812	0.7	2334	10.1
12	TU		0642	0.2	1203	9.8	1859	0.5		
13	W		0020	10.2	0727	0.2	1248	9.8	1942	0.6
14	TH		0106	10.1	0810	0.4	1333	9.5	2025	0.8
15	F		0151	9.8	0851	0.8	1416	9.2	2107	1.3
16	SA		0236	9.3	0932	1.4	1502	8.7	2152	1.9
17	SU	☾	0325	8.7	1017	2.1	1552	8.1	2243	2.5
18	M		0421	8.1	1110	2.7	1655	7.7	2348	2.9
19	TU		0531	7.6	1219	3.1	1813	7.4		
20	W		0109	3.1	0652	7.4	1340	3.2	1932	7.6
21	TH		0227	2.9	0808	7.6	1450	3.0	2038	7.9
22	F		0330	2.5	0907	7.9	1546	2.6	2127	8.3
23	SA		0420	2.2	0952	8.3	1630	2.3	2207	8.7
24	SU		0501	1.9	1028	8.6	1706	2.0	2242	8.9
25	M	●	0535	1.7	1101	8.8	1738	1.8	2314	9.1
26	TU		0607	1.5	1132	8.9	1809	1.6	2345	9.2
27	W		0637	1.4	1202	9.0	1840	1.5		
28	TH		0015	9.2	0707	1.4	1233	9.0	1913	1.5
29	F		0045	9.1	0738	1.5	1304	8.9	1946	1.7
30	SA		0115	8.9	0810	1.7	1336	8.7	2020	1.9
31	SU		0147	8.7	0843	2.0	1411	8.5	2056	2.2

SEPTEMBER

Date	Day	Phase	Time	m	Time	m	Time	m	Time	m
1	M		0224	8.5	0919	2.3	1452	8.2	2137	2.6
2	TU	☽	0310	8.1	1004	2.7	1546	7.9	2232	2.9
3	W		0413	7.7	1108	3.0	1701	7.7	2349	3.0
4	TH		0540	7.5	1237	3.0	1827	7.8		
5	F		0120	2.8	0709	7.8	1402	2.7	1943	8.2
6	SA		0238	2.2	0823	8.3	1511	2.1	2047	8.9
7	SU		0345	1.5	0922	8.9	1611	1.5	2141	9.5
8	M		0443	0.9	1013	9.4	1705	1.0	2229	9.9
9	TU	○	0535	0.5	1059	9.8	1754	0.6	2315	10.2
10	W		0622	0.2	1143	9.9	1839	0.5	2359	10.3
11	TH		0705	0.2	1225	9.8	1921	0.5		
12	F		0042	10.1	0745	0.5	1307	9.6	2002	0.8
13	SA		0125	9.7	0823	1.0	1347	9.2	2042	1.3
14	SU		0207	9.2	0901	1.6	1428	8.7	2124	2.0
15	M		0252	8.6	0940	2.3	1515	8.2	2211	2.6
16	TU	☾	0344	7.9	1028	3.0	1614	7.6	2313	3.1
17	W		0452	7.3	1135	3.5	1731	7.3		
18	TH		0036	3.3	0617	7.1	1303	3.6	1856	7.4
19	F		0157	3.1	0740	7.3	1420	3.3	2007	7.7
20	SA		0300	2.7	0841	7.8	1517	2.9	2059	8.2
21	SU		0350	2.3	0925	8.2	1601	2.5	2139	8.6
22	M		0430	1.9	1002	8.6	1637	2.1	2214	8.9
23	TU		0505	1.7	1034	8.9	1711	1.8	2246	9.1
24	W	●	0537	1.5	1104	9.0	1743	1.6	2317	9.2
25	TH		0609	1.3	1134	9.2	1817	1.4	2347	9.2
26	F		0641	1.3	1205	9.2	1851	1.4		
27	SA		0018	9.2	0714	1.4	1237	9.1	1925	1.5
28	SU		0050	9.1	0746	1.6	1310	9.0	2000	1.8
29	M		0125	8.9	0820	1.9	1347	8.8	2036	2.1
30	TU		0204	8.6	0856	2.3	1431	8.4	2118	2.4

OCTOBER

Date	Day	Phase	Time	m	Time	m	Time	m	Time	m
1	W	☽	0253	8.2	0942	2.7	1526	8.1	2214	2.8
2	TH		0358	7.8	1047	3.0	1642	7.8	2332	2.9
3	F		0526	7.6	1215	3.1	1808	7.9		
4	SA		0102	2.7	0654	7.8	1341	2.7	1924	8.3
5	SU		0220	2.1	0807	8.4	1451	2.1	2028	8.9
6	M		0326	1.5	0905	8.9	1551	1.6	2122	9.5
7	TU		0423	1.0	0954	9.4	1644	1.1	2210	9.9
8	W	○	0513	0.6	1039	9.7	1732	0.8	2254	10.1
9	TH		0558	0.5	1121	9.8	1817	0.6	2337	10.1
10	F		0639	0.5	1201	9.8	1858	0.7		
11	SA		0019	9.9	0718	0.8	1241	9.6	1938	1.0
12	SU		0100	9.5	0755	1.3	1319	9.2	2017	1.5
13	M		0140	9.0	0830	1.9	1357	8.8	2057	2.1
14	TU		0222	8.5	0906	2.5	1440	8.3	2140	2.7
15	W	☾	0310	7.9	0946	3.1	1534	7.8	2235	3.2
16	TH		0412	7.3	1044	3.6	1645	7.4	2352	3.4
17	F		0531	7.1	1208	3.8	1807	7.3		
18	SA		0112	3.3	0654	7.2	1333	3.6	1921	7.5
19	SU		0217	3.0	0801	7.6	1434	3.2	2019	8.0
20	M		0308	2.5	0849	8.0	1522	2.7	2103	8.4
21	TU		0351	2.1	0928	8.5	1602	2.3	2141	8.7
22	W		0429	1.8	1002	8.8	1639	1.9	2215	9.0
23	TH	●	0505	1.5	1034	9.1	1716	1.6	2248	9.2
24	F		0540	1.4	1106	9.2	1753	1.4	2321	9.3
25	SA		0616	1.3	1139	9.3	1830	1.4	2355	9.3
26	SU		0651	1.3	1214	9.3	1907	1.4		
27	M		0031	9.2	0726	1.5	1251	9.2	1945	1.6
28	TU		0110	9.0	0803	1.8	1332	9.0	2024	1.9
29	W		0154	8.7	0842	2.2	1419	8.7	2110	2.2
30	TH		0247	8.3	0931	2.6	1517	8.4	2207	2.5
31	F	☽	0352	8.0	1035	2.9	1629	8.1	2321	2.6

NOVEMBER

Date	Day	Phase	Time	m	Time	m	Time	m	Time	m
1	SA		0513	7.8	1156	3.0	1748	8.1		
2	SU		0043	2.5	0634	7.9	1318	2.7	1902	8.4
3	M		0158	2.1	0745	8.4	1428	2.3	2006	8.9
4	TU		0303	1.6	0844	8.8	1529	1.8	2101	9.3
5	W		0359	1.3	0934	9.2	1622	1.4	2150	9.6
6	TH	○	0449	1.0	1019	9.5	1711	1.1	2235	9.7
7	F		0533	0.9	1100	9.6	1755	1.0	2318	9.7
8	SA		0614	1.0	1140	9.6	1837	1.0	2359	9.6
9	SU		0652	1.2	1218	9.4	1917	1.3		
10	M		0038	9.3	0728	1.6	1255	9.2	1955	1.6
11	TU		0117	8.9	0801	2.0	1332	8.8	2033	2.1
12	W		0157	8.5	0835	2.5	1412	8.4	2111	2.6
13	TH		0240	8.0	0910	3.0	1459	8.0	2156	3.0
14	F	☾	0332	7.6	0956	3.4	1557	7.6	2254	3.3
15	SA		0437	7.2	1100	3.7	1709	7.4		
16	SU		0008	3.4	0551	7.2	1221	3.7	1822	7.4
17	M		0119	3.2	0703	7.4	1335	3.5	1926	7.7
18	TU		0217	2.8	0801	7.8	1432	3.0	2019	8.0
19	W		0306	2.4	0847	8.2	1521	2.6	2103	8.4
20	TH		0350	2.0	0926	8.6	1606	2.1	2142	8.7
21	F		0432	1.7	1003	9.0	1648	1.8	2219	9.0
22	SA	●	0512	1.5	1039	9.2	1730	1.5	2257	9.2
23	SU		0553	1.3	1117	9.4	1812	1.3	2336	9.3
24	M		0632	1.3	1156	9.5	1854	1.3		
25	TU		0017	9.3	0712	1.4	1238	9.5	1935	1.4
26	W		0101	9.2	0752	1.6	1323	9.3	2019	1.5
27	TH		0149	9.0	0836	1.9	1412	9.1	2107	1.8
28	F		0242	8.6	0925	2.3	1508	8.8	2202	2.1
29	SA	☽	0343	8.3	1024	2.6	1613	8.5	2307	2.3
30	SU		0453	8.1	1134	2.7	1724	8.4		

DECEMBER

Date	Day	Phase	Time	m	Time	m	Time	m	Time	m
1	M		0018	2.3	0607	8.0	1249	2.7	1834	8.4
2	TU		0130	2.2	0718	8.2	1400	2.4	1941	8.6
3	W		0236	2.0	0821	8.5	1505	2.1	2040	8.9
4	TH		0335	1.7	0914	8.9	1602	1.8	2132	9.1
5	F		0426	1.6	1001	9.1	1652	1.5	2219	9.2
6	SA	○	0511	1.5	1043	9.3	1738	1.4	2302	9.3
7	SU		0552	1.5	1123	9.3	1820	1.4	2343	9.2
8	M		0630	1.6	1200	9.3	1859	1.5		
9	TU		0021	9.1	0704	1.8	1236	9.2	1936	1.7
10	W		0058	8.9	0737	2.0	1311	9.0	2010	2.0
11	TH		0134	8.6	0809	2.3	1348	8.7	2044	2.3
12	F		0213	8.3	0842	2.7	1428	8.4	2120	2.6
13	SA		0256	7.9	0921	3.0	1513	8.0	2202	2.9
14	SU	☾	0345	7.6	1009	3.3	1608	7.7	2257	3.2
15	M		0444	7.3	1109	3.5	1712	7.5		
16	TU		0004	3.3	0552	7.3	1222	3.6	1821	7.5
17	W		0115	3.1	0659	7.5	1335	3.3	1925	7.7
18	TH		0218	2.8	0758	7.9	1438	2.9	2020	8.0
19	F		0312	2.4	0848	8.3	1532	2.4	2109	8.4
20	SA		0401	2.0	0933	8.8	1622	2.0	2154	8.8
21	SU		0448	1.6	1016	9.2	1711	1.6	2238	9.1
22	M	●	0533	1.4	1058	9.5	1757	1.2	2322	9.4
23	TU		0618	1.2	1142	9.7	1844	1.0		
24	W		0007	9.5	0701	1.1	1227	9.8	1929	1.0
25	TH		0053	9.5	0745	1.2	1314	9.7	2015	1.0
26	F		0141	9.3	0830	1.4	1403	9.5	2101	1.3
27	SA		0232	9.0	0917	1.8	1455	9.3	2151	1.6
28	SU	☽	0326	8.6	1008	2.1	1551	8.9	2245	1.9
29	M		0426	8.3	1108	2.5	1654	8.6	2348	2.3
30	TU		0534	8.0	1216	2.7	1803	8.3		
31	W		0057	2.4	0646	8.0	1331	2.7	1914	8.3

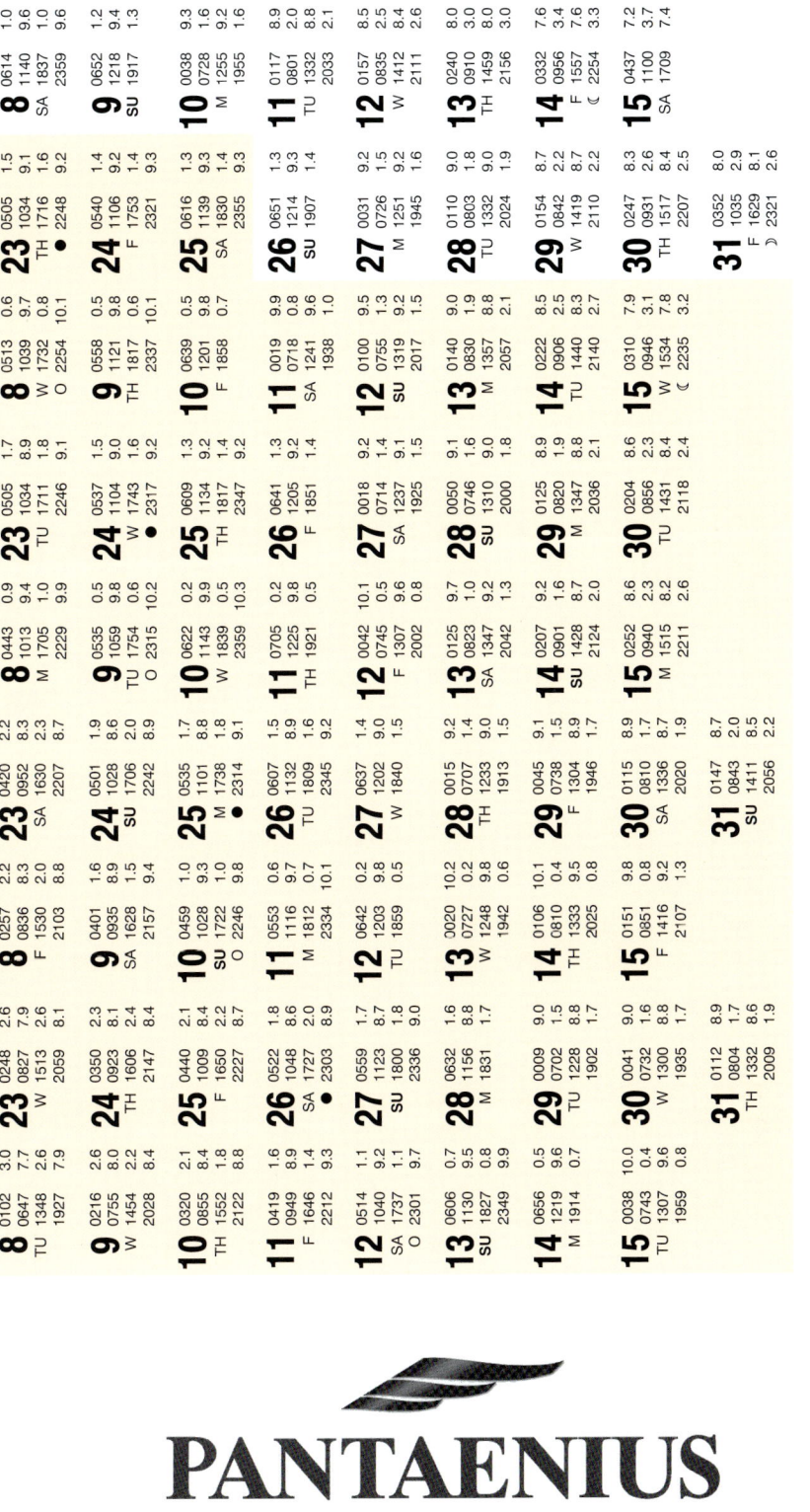

HOLYHEAD
LAT 53°19′N
LONG 4°37′W

TIMES AND HEIGHTS OF HIGH AND LOW WATER (Heights in Metres)

TIME ZONE UT
For Summer Time (area enclosed in shaded box) add 1 hour

2014

JANUARY

Date	Time	m
1 W	0335 0950 1600 ● 2217	0.8 5.9 0.6 5.8
2 TH	0422 1036 1649 2305	0.6 6.1 0.4 5.9
3 F	0509 1123 1738 2353	0.5 6.2 0.3 5.9
4 SA	0557 1211 1827	0.6 6.2 0.4
5 SU	0042 0644 1300 1917	5.7 0.7 6.0 0.6
6 M	0133 0735 1350 2009	5.5 1.0 5.8 0.9
7 TU	0226 0828 1444 2105	5.2 1.3 5.5 1.2
8 W	0323 0928 1544 ☽ 2207	4.9 1.6 5.2 1.6
9 TH	0430 1036 1652 2315	4.7 1.9 4.9 1.8
10 F	0544 1149 1807	4.6 2.0 4.7
11 SA	0025 0656 1301 1919	1.9 4.7 2.0 4.7
12 SU	0130 0756 1403 2017	1.9 4.9 1.8 4.8
13 M	0224 0844 1454 2103	1.7 5.1 1.6 5.0
14 TU	0307 0924 1535 2142	1.6 5.2 1.4 5.1
15 W	0344 0959 1611 2217	1.4 5.4 1.2 5.2
16 TH	0416 1031 1643 O 2249	1.3 5.5 1.1 5.3
17 F	0447 1102 1715 2320	1.2 5.6 1.1 5.3
18 SA	0519 1133 1747 2352	1.1 5.6 1.0 5.3
19 SU	0551 1205 1819	1.2 5.6 1.1
20 M	0025 0624 1239 1853	5.3 1.2 5.5 1.2
21 TU	0101 0659 1314 1928	5.2 1.3 5.4 1.3
22 W	0138 0737 1352 2008	5.0 1.5 5.2 1.5
23 TH	0219 0821 1435 2056	4.9 1.7 5.0 1.6
24 F	0309 0915 1530 ☾ 2156	4.7 1.9 4.8 1.8
25 SA	0414 1024 1642 2310	4.6 2.0 4.7 1.9
26 SU	0535 1143 1808	4.6 1.9 4.7
27 M	0027 0651 1259 1923	1.7 4.8 1.7 4.9
28 TU	0134 0754 1403 2025	1.5 5.1 1.3 5.2
29 W	0232 0848 1459 2118	1.1 5.5 0.9 5.5
30 TH	0323 0936 1549 ● 2206	0.8 5.8 0.5 5.7
31 F	0409 1022 1636 2252	0.5 6.1 0.3 5.9

FEBRUARY

Date	Time	m
1 SA	0455 1108 1722 2337	0.4 6.3 0.2 5.9
2 SU	0540 1153 1808	0.4 6.3 0.2
3 M	0022 0624 1239 1853	5.8 0.5 6.1 0.4
4 TU	0107 0710 1325 1939	5.6 0.7 5.9 0.8
5 W	0153 0757 1413 2028	5.3 1.1 5.5 1.2
6 TH	0242 0850 1505 ☽ 2122	5.0 1.4 5.1 1.6
7 F	0339 0953 1607 2228	4.7 1.8 4.7 1.9
8 SA	0450 1109 1726 2344	4.5 2.1 4.5 2.1
9 SU	0615 1229 1852	4.4 2.1 4.4
10 M	0059 0730 1341 1959	2.1 4.6 1.9 4.6
11 TU	0202 0824 1435 2048	1.9 4.8 1.7 4.8
12 W	0249 0905 1516 2126	1.7 5.1 1.4 5.0
13 TH	0326 0940 1551 2158	1.5 5.3 1.2 5.1
14 F	0357 1011 1622 O 2228	1.2 5.4 1.0 5.3
15 SA	0427 1040 1652 2258	1.1 5.5 0.9 5.4
16 SU	0457 1110 1722 2328	1.0 5.6 0.9 5.4
17 M	0528 1142 1753	0.9 5.6 0.9
18 TU	0000 0559 1215 1824	5.4 0.9 5.6 0.9
19 W	0034 0633 1249 1858	5.3 1.0 5.5 1.0
20 TH	0109 0709 1325 1936	5.2 1.2 5.3 1.2
21 F	0148 0751 1406 2021	5.1 1.4 5.1 1.4
22 SA	0235 0843 1458 ☾ 2119	4.9 1.6 4.9 1.7
23 SU	0336 0951 1610 2236	4.7 1.8 4.6 1.9
24 M	0459 1116 1745	4.6 1.8 4.6
25 TU	0003 0625 1240 1910	1.8 4.7 1.6 4.8
26 W	0118 0736 1349 2014	1.6 5.0 1.2 5.1
27 TH	0218 0832 1446 2106	1.2 5.4 0.8 5.4
28 F	0308 0920 1534 2151	0.8 5.8 0.4 5.7

MARCH

Date	Time	m
1 SA	0354 1005 1619 ● 2234	0.5 6.0 0.2 5.8
2 SU	0437 1049 1702 2316	0.3 6.2 0.1 5.9
3 M	0519 1133 1745 2358	0.2 6.2 0.2 5.8
4 TU	0602 1216 1827	0.3 6.0 0.4
5 W	0039 0644 1259 1908	5.6 0.6 5.7 0.8
6 TH	0121 0728 1343 1952	5.3 0.9 5.4 1.2
7 F	0204 0816 1429 2039	5.0 1.3 5.0 1.6
8 SA	0252 0912 1525 ☽ 2137	4.7 1.7 4.6 2.0
9 SU	0355 1024 1640 2255	4.4 2.1 4.3 2.3
10 M	0519 1149 1814	4.3 2.2 4.2
11 TU	0020 0648 1306 1930	2.3 4.4 2.0 4.4
12 W	0130 0751 1405 2022	2.1 4.6 1.7 4.6
13 TH	0221 0836 1448 2100	1.8 4.9 1.4 4.9
14 F	0259 0912 1523 2132	1.5 5.1 1.2 5.1
15 SA	0331 0943 1554 2202	1.2 5.3 1.0 5.3
16 SU	0401 1013 1623 O 2231	1.0 5.5 0.8 5.4
17 M	0431 1044 1653 2301	0.9 5.6 0.7 5.5
18 TU	0502 1116 1725 2334	0.8 5.6 0.7 5.5
19 W	0535 1150 1757	0.7 5.6 0.8
20 TH	0008 0610 1226 1832	5.5 0.8 5.5 0.9
21 F	0045 0648 1304 1912	5.4 0.9 5.3 1.1
22 SA	0126 0732 1348 1959	5.2 1.1 5.1 1.3
23 SU	0214 0826 1443 2058	5.0 1.4 4.8 1.6
24 M	0315 0935 1558 ☾ 2217	4.8 1.6 4.6 1.9
25 TU	0437 1101 1734 2345	4.6 1.7 4.5 1.8
26 W	0604 1224 1858	4.7 1.5 4.7
27 TH	0100 0716 1333 2000	1.6 5.0 1.1 5.1
28 F	0201 0813 1428 2050	1.2 5.4 0.8 5.3
29 SA	0251 0901 1516 2133	0.8 5.7 0.5 5.6
30 SU	0335 0946 1559 ● 2214	0.5 5.9 0.3 5.7
31 M	0417 1029 1640 2254	0.4 6.0 0.3 5.8

APRIL

Date	Time	m
1 TU	0459 1111 1720 2333	0.3 6.0 0.4 5.7
2 W	0540 1153 1800	0.4 5.8 0.6
3 TH	0013 0621 1235 1839	5.6 0.6 5.5 0.9
4 F	0052 0703 1316 1919	5.4 0.9 5.2 1.2
5 SA	0132 0747 1359 2002	5.1 1.3 4.9 1.6
6 SU	0215 0838 1449 2053	4.8 1.6 4.5 2.0
7 M	0308 0940 1555 ☽ 2200	4.5 1.9 4.3 2.3
8 TU	0421 1059 1720 2325	4.3 2.1 4.1 2.4
9 W	0547 1217 1843	4.3 2.0 4.3
10 TH	0042 0701 1320 1942	2.2 4.5 1.8 4.5
11 F	0139 0754 1407 2024	1.9 4.7 1.5 4.8
12 SA	0221 0834 1445 2058	1.6 5.0 1.2 5.0
13 SU	0257 0909 1519 2130	1.3 5.2 1.0 5.2
14 M	0330 0942 1551 2201	1.1 5.4 0.8 5.4
15 TU	0402 1015 1623 O 2234	0.9 5.5 0.7 5.5
16 W	0437 1050 1657 2309	0.7 5.6 0.7 5.6
17 TH	0513 1128 1734 2346	0.6 5.6 0.7 5.6
18 F	0552 1207 1813	0.7 5.5 0.8
19 SA	0027 0634 1251 1856	5.5 0.8 5.3 1.0
20 SU	0112 0722 1340 1947	5.4 1.0 5.1 1.3
21 M	0203 0819 1438 2048	5.2 1.2 4.9 1.6
22 TU	0305 0928 1554 ☾ 2205	4.9 1.4 4.6 1.8
23 W	0422 1048 1722 2326	4.8 1.4 4.6 1.7
24 TH	0543 1205 1839	4.9 1.3 4.8
25 F	0038 0653 1312 1940	1.5 5.1 1.1 5.0
26 SA	0139 0751 1407 2029	1.3 5.3 0.9 5.2
27 SU	0231 0841 1455 2113	1.0 5.5 0.7 5.4
28 M	0316 0926 1538 2153	0.7 5.6 0.6 5.6
29 TU	0358 1009 1618 ● 2232	0.6 5.7 0.6 5.6
30 W	0440 1051 1657 2311	0.5 5.7 0.6 5.6

MAY

Date	Time	m
1 TH	0520 1132 1735 2350	0.6 5.5 0.8 5.5
2 F	0601 1212 1813	0.8 5.3 1.0
3 SA	0027 0640 1252 1851	5.4 1.0 5.1 1.3
4 SU	0105 0722 1333 1932	5.2 1.3 4.9 1.6
5 M	0145 0808 1418 2018	4.9 1.5 4.6 1.9
6 TU	0231 0901 1513 2113	4.7 1.8 4.4 2.1
7 W	0330 1005 1623 ☽ 2222	4.5 1.9 4.2 2.3
8 TH	0442 1117 1739 2338	4.4 2.0 4.3 2.3
9 F	0556 1222 1845	4.4 1.8 4.4
10 SA	0042 0658 1317 1936	2.1 4.6 1.6 4.7
11 SU	0134 0748 1401 2018	1.8 4.8 1.4 4.9
12 M	0217 0830 1440 2055	1.5 5.0 1.1 5.2
13 TU	0256 0909 1518 2131	1.2 5.2 0.9 5.4
14 W	0334 0948 1555 O 2208	0.9 5.4 0.8 5.5
15 TH	0413 1028 1634 2247	0.7 5.5 0.7 5.7
16 F	0454 1110 1715 2329	0.6 5.6 0.7 5.7
17 SA	0538 1154 1759	0.6 5.5 0.7
18 SU	0014 0625 1243 1846	5.7 0.6 5.4 0.9
19 M	0102 0716 1335 1939	5.6 0.8 5.2 1.1
20 TU	0155 0814 1434 2040	5.4 1.0 5.0 1.4
21 W	0255 0919 1544 ☾ 2149	5.2 1.1 4.8 1.6
22 TH	0404 1030 1701 2303	5.0 1.3 4.7 1.6
23 F	0518 1142 1813	5.0 1.3 4.8
24 SA	0012 0627 1247 1915	1.6 5.0 1.2 4.9
25 SU	0115 0728 1345 2008	1.4 5.1 1.1 5.1
26 M	0210 0821 1434 2053	1.2 5.3 1.0 5.3
27 TU	0259 0909 1518 2134	1.0 5.3 0.9 5.4
28 W	0343 0952 1559 ● 2214	0.9 5.4 0.9 5.5
29 TH	0424 1034 1637 2252	0.8 5.4 0.9 5.5
30 F	0504 1114 1714 2329	0.8 5.3 1.0 5.4
31 SA	0543 1152 1751	0.9 5.2 1.1

JUNE

Date	Time	m
1 SU	0005 0620 1230 1827	5.4 1.0 5.1 1.3
2 M	0042 0659 1308 1905	5.2 1.2 4.9 1.5
3 TU	0119 0740 1348 1947	5.1 1.4 4.7 1.7
4 W	0200 0825 1434 2033	4.9 1.6 4.6 1.9
5 TH	0248 0916 1529 ☽ 2128	4.7 1.7 4.4 2.1
6 F	0345 1014 1633 2232	4.6 1.8 4.4 2.2
7 SA	0451 1118 1741 2339	4.5 1.8 4.4 2.1
8 SU	0559 1219 1842	4.6 1.7 4.6
9 M	0041 0659 1314 1935	1.9 4.7 1.5 4.8
10 TU	0136 0752 1403 2021	1.6 4.9 1.3 5.1
11 W	0224 0839 1448 2104	1.3 5.1 1.1 5.3
12 TH	0309 0924 1532 2146	1.0 5.3 0.8 5.6
13 F	0354 1009 1615 O 2230	0.7 5.5 0.7 5.7
14 SA	0440 1056 1701 2315	0.5 5.6 0.6 5.8
15 SU	0527 1143 1748	0.4 5.6 0.6
16 M	0002 0616 1234 1836	5.9 0.4 5.5 0.7
17 TU	0052 0708 1325 1928	5.8 0.5 5.4 0.9
18 W	0143 0802 1421 2024	5.6 0.7 5.2 1.2
19 TH	0239 0901 1523 ☾ 2126	5.4 0.9 4.9 1.4
20 F	0342 1005 1631 2234	5.2 1.2 4.8 1.6
21 SA	0450 1113 1742 2344	5.0 1.3 4.7 1.6
22 SU	0600 1219 1849	4.9 1.4 4.8
23 M	0051 0707 1322 1947	1.6 4.9 1.4 4.9
24 TU	0152 0805 1416 2037	1.4 5.0 1.3 5.1
25 W	0245 0856 1503 2120	1.3 5.1 1.3 5.2
26 TH	0331 0940 1544 2159	1.2 5.1 1.2 5.3
27 F	0412 1019 1621 ● 2236	1.1 5.2 1.1 5.4
28 SA	0449 1057 1656 2311	1.0 5.2 1.1 5.4
29 SU	0525 1132 1730 2345	1.0 5.2 1.2 5.4
30 M	0600 1207 1804	1.0 5.1 1.2

SUNRISE AND SUNSET TIMES

HOLYHEAD
At 53°19′N 4°37′W

UT		Sunrise	Sunset
Jan	01	0834	1611
	15	0826	1631
Feb	01	0803	1702
	15	0736	1730
Mar	01	0706	1757
	15	0633	1823
BST			
Apr	01	0652	1954
	15	0619	2019
May	01	0544	2048
	15	0519	2112
Jun	01	0457	2136
	15	0450	2148
Jul	01	0455	2149
	15	0510	2139
Aug	01	0535	2114
	15	0559	2046
Sep	01	0628	2008
	15	0652	1934
Oct	01	0720	1855
	15	0745	1822
UT			
Nov	01	0717	1646
	15	0744	1622
Dec	01	0811	1604
	15	0827	1600

HOLYHEAD
LAT 53°19′N
LONG 4°37′W

TIMES AND HEIGHTS OF HIGH AND LOW WATER (Heights in Metres)

TIME ZONE UT
For Summer Time (area enclosed in shaded box) add 1 hour

2014

JULY

Date	Day	Time	m	Time	m	Time	m	Time	m
1	TU	0018	5.3	0634	1.1	1242	5.0	1839	1.3
2	W	0054	5.2	0711	1.2	1319	4.9	1917	1.5
3	TH	0131	5.1	0750	1.4	1358	4.8	1957	1.7
4	F	0211	5.0	0832	1.5	1443	4.7	2043	1.8
5	SA	0257	4.8	0921	1.7	1535	4.5	☽ 2138	2.0
6	SU	0353	4.7	1019	1.8	1639	4.5	2242	2.0
7	M	0501	4.6	1125	1.8	1749	4.6	2352	1.9
8	TU	0613	4.6	1230	1.7	1855	4.7		
9	W	0058	1.7	0718	4.8	1331	1.5	1951	5.0
10	TH	0157	1.4	0815	5.0	1424	1.2	2041	5.3
11	F	0249	1.0	0907	5.3	1513	0.9	2128	5.6
12	SA	0338	0.7	0955	5.5	1600	0.7	O 2214	5.8
13	SU	0426	0.4	1043	5.7	1647	0.5	2300	6.0
14	M	0514	0.3	1130	5.7	1733	0.5	2347	6.1
15	TU	0603	0.2	1218	5.7	1821	0.5		
16	W	0035	6.0	0651	0.3	1308	5.5	1910	0.7
17	TH	0125	5.9	0742	0.6	1359	5.3	2002	1.0
18	F	0217	5.6	0836	0.9	1454	5.1	2058	1.3
19	SA	0314	5.3	0934	1.2	1555	4.8	☾ 2203	1.5
20	SU	0418	5.0	1040	1.5	1706	4.7	2314	1.7
21	M	0531	4.8	1150	1.7	1820	4.6		
22	TU	0027	1.8	0647	4.7	1259	1.7	1927	4.8
23	W	0136	1.7	0753	4.7	1359	1.7	2022	4.9
24	TH	0233	1.5	0845	4.9	1449	1.5	2106	5.1
25	F	0319	1.3	0928	5.0	1529	1.4	2144	5.3
26	SA	0358	1.2	1005	5.1	1604	1.2	● 2218	5.4
27	SU	0432	1.0	1038	5.2	1637	1.1	2250	5.4
28	M	0504	1.0	1110	5.2	1708	1.1	2322	5.5
29	TU	0536	1.0	1141	5.2	1740	1.1	2354	5.5
30	W	0608	1.0	1214	5.2	1813	1.2		
31	TH	0027	5.4	0641	1.1	1249	5.1	1847	1.3

AUGUST

Date	Day	Time	m	Time	m	Time	m	Time	m
1	F	0102	5.3	0715	1.2	1325	5.0	1923	1.4
2	SA	0138	5.1	0753	1.4	1404	4.9	2005	1.6
3	SU	0218	5.0	0836	1.6	1450	4.7	2054	1.8
4	M	0307	4.8	0930	1.7	1548	4.6	☽ 2156	1.9
5	TU	0412	4.6	1038	1.8	1702	4.6	2312	2.0
6	W	0535	4.6	1154	1.8	1820	4.7		
7	TH	0029	1.8	0653	4.7	1305	1.6	1926	5.0
8	F	0136	1.4	0759	5.0	1405	1.3	2022	5.3
9	SA	0233	1.0	0853	5.3	1457	0.9	2111	5.6
10	SU	0324	0.6	0941	5.6	1544	0.6	O 2157	5.9
11	M	0411	0.3	1027	5.8	1630	0.4	2243	6.2
12	TU	0457	0.1	1113	5.9	1715	0.3	2328	6.2
13	W	0543	0.1	1158	5.8	1801	0.4		
14	TH	0015	6.2	0629	0.3	1244	5.7	1847	0.6
15	F	0102	5.9	0716	0.6	1331	5.4	1935	0.9
16	SA	0151	5.6	0805	0.9	1421	5.1	2028	1.2
17	SU	0244	5.2	0859	1.4	1517	4.8	☾ 2130	1.6
18	M	0345	4.8	1003	1.7	1626	4.6	2243	1.9
19	TU	0501	4.6	1117	2.0	1747	4.5		
20	W	0002	2.0	0625	4.5	1233	2.0	1904	4.6
21	TH	0117	1.9	0738	4.6	1340	1.9	2003	4.8
22	F	0216	1.6	0831	4.8	1431	1.7	2048	5.1
23	SA	0301	1.4	0911	4.9	1510	1.5	2124	5.2
24	SU	0337	1.2	0945	5.1	1544	1.3	2156	5.4
25	M	0409	1.1	1015	5.2	1614	1.2	● 2226	5.5
26	TU	0439	1.0	1044	5.3	1643	1.0	2256	5.6
27	W	0508	0.9	1114	5.4	1713	1.0	2327	5.6
28	TH	0538	0.9	1145	5.4	1745	1.0	2359	5.5
29	F	0610	1.0	1218	5.3	1818	1.1		
30	SA	0032	5.4	0642	1.1	1254	5.2	1853	1.3
31	SU	0108	5.3	0718	1.3	1331	5.1	1933	1.5

SEPTEMBER

Date	Day	Time	m	Time	m	Time	m	Time	m
1	M	0147	5.1	0800	1.5	1415	4.9	2021	1.7
2	TU	0235	4.8	0853	1.7	1511	4.7	☽ 2124	1.9
3	W	0340	4.6	1003	1.9	1626	4.6	2244	1.9
4	TH	0510	4.5	1128	1.9	1753	4.7		
5	F	0008	1.8	0637	4.7	1246	1.7	1905	5.0
6	SA	0119	1.4	0745	5.0	1348	1.4	2003	5.4
7	SU	0217	1.0	0839	5.4	1440	1.0	2053	5.7
8	M	0307	0.6	0925	5.6	1527	0.6	2138	6.0
9	TU	0353	0.3	1008	5.8	1611	0.4	O 2222	6.2
10	W	0437	0.1	1051	5.9	1654	0.3	2307	6.3
11	TH	0520	0.2	1134	5.9	1738	0.4	2352	6.2
12	F	0604	0.4	1218	5.7	1823	0.6		
13	SA	0037	5.9	0647	0.7	1302	5.5	1909	0.9
14	SU	0124	5.5	0733	1.1	1348	5.2	1959	1.3
15	M	0213	5.1	0823	1.5	1439	4.9	2057	1.7
16	TU	0311	4.7	0922	2.0	1543	4.6	☾ 2209	2.0
17	W	0426	4.4	1037	2.2	1704	4.5	2331	2.1
18	TH	0556	4.3	1159	2.3	1830	4.5		
19	F	0047	2.0	0713	4.5	1311	2.2	1934	4.8
20	SA	0148	1.8	0806	4.7	1404	1.9	2020	5.0
21	SU	0233	1.5	0846	4.9	1444	1.6	2056	5.2
22	M	0309	1.3	0919	5.1	1517	1.4	2128	5.4
23	TU	0340	1.1	0948	5.3	1546	1.2	2158	5.5
24	W	0409	1.0	1016	5.4	1616	1.1	● 2228	5.6
25	TH	0438	0.9	1046	5.5	1646	1.0	2259	5.6
26	F	0508	0.9	1117	5.5	1718	1.0	2332	5.6
27	SA	0540	0.9	1151	5.5	1752	1.0		
28	SU	0006	5.5	0613	1.1	1227	5.4	1829	1.2
29	M	0044	5.4	0651	1.2	1306	5.3	1910	1.3
30	TU	0125	5.1	0734	1.5	1351	5.1	2000	1.6

OCTOBER

Date	Day	Time	m	Time	m	Time	m	Time	m
1	W	0216	4.9	0829	1.7	1448	4.9	☽ 2105	1.8
2	TH	0324	4.7	0941	2.0	1603	4.8	2226	1.9
3	F	0456	4.6	1108	2.0	1730	4.8	2350	1.7
4	SA	0623	4.8	1226	1.8	1844	5.1		
5	SU	0101	1.3	0729	5.1	1329	1.4	1943	5.4
6	M	0159	1.0	0821	5.4	1421	1.0	2033	5.8
7	TU	0248	0.6	0906	5.7	1507	0.7	2118	6.0
8	W	0332	0.4	0948	5.8	1551	0.5	O 2202	6.2
9	TH	0415	0.3	1029	5.9	1634	0.4	2246	6.2
10	F	0457	0.4	1111	5.9	1717	0.5	2330	6.0
11	SA	0538	0.6	1153	5.8	1801	0.7		
12	SU	0014	5.8	0620	0.9	1235	5.6	1845	1.0
13	M	0059	5.4	0703	1.3	1318	5.3	1932	1.4
14	TU	0145	5.1	0748	1.7	1404	5.0	2025	1.7
15	W	0238	4.7	0841	2.1	1500	4.7	☾ 2130	2.0
16	TH	0344	4.4	0948	2.4	1611	4.5	2247	2.2
17	F	0508	4.3	1110	2.5	1734	4.5		
18	SA	0003	2.1	0629	4.4	1226	2.4	1847	4.7
19	SU	0106	1.9	0728	4.6	1324	2.1	1940	4.9
20	M	0154	1.7	0811	4.9	1408	1.8	2020	5.1
21	TU	0233	1.4	0846	5.1	1443	1.6	2055	5.3
22	W	0306	1.2	0917	5.3	1516	1.3	2127	5.5
23	TH	0337	1.1	0947	5.5	1547	1.1	● 2159	5.6
24	F	0408	1.0	1018	5.6	1620	1.0	2233	5.6
25	SA	0440	0.9	1051	5.7	1655	0.9	2308	5.6
26	SU	0515	0.9	1127	5.7	1732	1.0	2346	5.6
27	M	0552	1.0	1206	5.6	1812	1.1		
28	TU	0026	5.4	0632	1.2	1248	5.5	1857	1.2
29	W	0113	5.2	0719	1.4	1336	5.3	1950	1.4
30	TH	0207	5.0	0816	1.7	1434	5.1	2054	1.6
31	F	0316	4.8	0926	1.9	1546	5.0	☽ 2211	1.7

NOVEMBER

Date	Day	Time	m	Time	m	Time	m	Time	m
1	SA	0442	4.7	1048	2.0	1707	5.0	2330	1.6
2	SU	0603	4.9	1203	1.8	1820	5.2		
3	M	0039	1.3	0709	5.1	1307	1.5	1920	5.4
4	TU	0138	1.1	0802	5.4	1401	1.2	2013	5.7
5	W	0228	0.8	0847	5.6	1449	0.9	2100	5.9
6	TH	0313	0.7	0929	5.8	1534	0.7	O 2144	6.0
7	F	0355	0.6	1010	5.9	1617	0.7	2228	5.9
8	SA	0436	0.7	1051	5.9	1700	0.7	2311	5.8
9	SU	0516	0.8	1131	5.8	1742	0.9	2354	5.6
10	M	0556	1.1	1212	5.6	1825	1.1		
11	TU	0036	5.3	0636	1.4	1252	5.4	1908	1.4
12	W	0119	5.1	0718	1.7	1333	5.2	1955	1.7
13	TH	0205	4.8	0804	2.0	1420	4.9	2048	1.9
14	F	0259	4.5	0858	2.3	1517	4.7	☾ 2152	2.1
15	SA	0407	4.4	1006	2.5	1628	4.6	2303	2.2
16	SU	0523	4.4	1122	2.5	1741	4.6		
17	M	0009	2.1	0632	4.5	1229	2.3	1845	4.8
18	TU	0105	1.9	0725	4.8	1322	2.1	1936	5.0
19	W	0150	1.6	0807	5.0	1405	1.8	2018	5.2
20	TH	0229	1.4	0844	5.3	1443	1.5	2056	5.3
21	F	0305	1.2	0918	5.5	1520	1.2	2133	5.5
22	SA	0340	1.1	0953	5.6	1557	1.1	● 2210	5.6
23	SU	0417	0.9	1030	5.8	1636	0.9	2249	5.7
24	M	0455	0.9	1109	5.8	1717	0.9	2331	5.6
25	TU	0536	0.9	1151	5.8	1801	0.9		
26	W	0016	5.5	0620	1.1	1236	5.7	1848	1.0
27	TH	0105	5.4	0709	1.3	1326	5.6	1942	1.2
28	F	0200	5.2	0805	1.5	1422	5.4	2043	1.3
29	SA	0304	5.0	0910	1.7	1526	5.2	☽ 2152	1.5
30	SU	0419	4.8	1022	1.8	1639	5.2	2305	1.5

DECEMBER

Date	Day	Time	m	Time	m	Time	m	Time	m
1	M	0535	4.9	1136	1.8	1752	5.2		
2	TU	0013	1.4	0643	5.0	1243	1.6	1857	5.3
3	W	0115	1.3	0741	5.2	1342	1.4	1955	5.4
4	TH	0209	1.1	0830	5.4	1434	1.2	2045	5.6
5	F	0256	1.0	0914	5.6	1521	1.0	2131	5.6
6	SA	0340	1.0	0955	5.7	1605	0.9	O 2215	5.6
7	SU	0420	1.0	1035	5.7	1647	0.9	2256	5.6
8	M	0459	1.0	1114	5.7	1727	1.0	2336	5.5
9	TU	0536	1.2	1152	5.6	1806	1.1		
10	W	0015	5.3	0613	1.3	1229	5.5	1845	1.3
11	TH	0053	5.1	0651	1.5	1306	5.3	1925	1.5
12	F	0133	4.9	0731	1.8	1345	5.1	2009	1.7
13	SA	0216	4.8	0815	2.0	1430	4.9	2058	1.9
14	SU	0308	4.6	0907	2.2	1524	4.8	☾ 2155	2.0
15	M	0411	4.5	1009	2.4	1629	4.6	2300	2.1
16	TU	0521	4.5	1119	2.4	1740	4.6		
17	W	0004	2.0	0627	4.6	1226	2.2	1844	4.8
18	TH	0102	1.8	0723	4.8	1322	2.0	1939	4.9
19	F	0151	1.6	0810	5.1	1411	1.7	2027	5.1
20	SA	0235	1.4	0851	5.3	1455	1.4	2110	5.4
21	SU	0317	1.1	0932	5.6	1538	1.1	2152	5.5
22	M	0358	0.9	1012	5.8	1621	0.8	● 2235	5.7
23	TU	0440	0.8	1054	5.9	1705	0.7	2319	5.7
24	W	0524	0.8	1138	6.0	1751	0.6		
25	TH	0006	5.7	0609	0.8	1225	6.0	1839	0.7
26	F	0055	5.6	0657	1.0	1313	5.9	1930	0.8
27	SA	0146	5.4	0750	1.2	1406	5.7	2025	1.0
28	SU	0243	5.2	0847	1.4	1503	5.4	☽ 2126	1.3
29	M	0348	4.9	0953	1.6	1609	5.2	2234	1.5
30	TU	0501	4.8	1105	1.8	1722	5.1	2345	1.6
31	W	0614	4.9	1217	1.8	1835	5.1		

MILFORD HAVEN
LAT 51°42′N
LONG 5°03′W

TIMES AND HEIGHTS OF HIGH AND LOW WATER (Heights in Metres)

TIME ZONE UT
For Summer Time (area enclosed in shaded box) add 1 hour

2014

JANUARY

Date	Day	Time	m
1	W ●	0540 1204 1807	7.2 0.7 7.2
2	TH	0028 0630 1255 1856	0.7 7.5 0.5 7.4
3	F	0116 0719 1343 1944	0.5 7.6 0.4 7.4
4	SA	0203 0807 1430 2031	0.5 7.6 0.4 7.2
5	SU	0249 0854 1517 2117	0.7 7.4 0.7 6.9
6	M	0334 0941 1603 2204	1.0 7.1 1.0 6.6
7	TU	0421 1029 1651 2253	1.3 6.7 1.5 6.2
8	W ☽	0512 1121 1744 2349	1.8 6.2 1.9 5.8
9	TH	0613 1222 1848	2.1 5.8 2.2
10	F	0056 0726 1332 2002	5.5 2.4 5.6 2.3
11	SA	0211 0844 1445 2113	5.5 2.4 5.6 2.2
12	SU	0322 0950 1551 2211	5.6 2.2 5.8 2.0
13	M	0420 1043 1644 2258	5.9 1.9 6.0 1.8
14	TU	0507 1126 1727 2339	6.2 1.7 6.3 1.5
15	W	0546 1204 1805	6.5 1.5 6.4
16	TH O	0015 0621 1240 1839	1.4 6.6 1.3 6.6
17	F	0049 0654 1312 1912	1.2 6.7 1.2 6.6
18	SA	0121 0725 1343 1943	1.2 6.8 1.2 6.6
19	SU	0152 0756 1414 2014	1.2 6.8 1.2 6.5
20	M	0224 0828 1445 2046	1.2 6.7 1.3 6.4
21	TU	0257 0900 1518 2119	1.4 6.5 1.5 6.2
22	W	0331 0935 1553 2156	1.6 6.3 1.7 6.0
23	TH	0409 1015 1634 2241	1.8 6.1 2.0 5.8
24	F ☾	0454 1105 1725 2339	2.1 5.8 2.2 5.5
25	SA	0556 1211 1837	2.3 5.6 2.4
26	SU	0055 0720 1332 2008	5.4 2.4 5.5 2.3
27	M	0218 0847 1453 2126	5.6 2.1 5.8 1.9
28	TU	0331 0959 1603 2230	6.1 1.6 6.2 1.4
29	W	0434 1059 1703 2325	6.6 1.1 6.7 0.9
30	TH ●	0529 1153 1756	7.1 0.6 7.1
31	F	0016 0619 1243 1844	0.5 7.5 0.3 7.4

FEBRUARY

Date	Day	Time	m
1	SA	0103 0706 1330 1930	0.3 7.7 0.1 7.5
2	SU	0148 0751 1414 2013	0.2 7.7 0.2 7.4
3	M	0231 0834 1456 2055	0.3 7.6 0.4 7.1
4	TU	0313 0917 1536 2136	0.6 7.2 0.8 6.7
5	W	0353 0959 1616 2218	1.1 6.7 1.3 6.3
6	TH ☽	0435 1043 1659 2304	1.6 6.2 1.8 5.8
7	F	0524 1135 1753	2.1 5.7 2.3
8	SA	0003 0630 1243 1907	5.4 2.5 5.3 2.6
9	SU	0124 0802 1407 2036	5.1 2.6 5.1 2.6
10	M	0250 0923 1525 2146	5.3 2.4 5.4 2.3
11	TU	0357 1022 1623 2237	5.6 2.1 5.7 1.9
12	W	0446 1107 1707 2319	6.0 1.7 6.1 1.6
13	TH	0526 1145 1745 2355	6.3 1.4 6.3 1.3
14	F O	0601 1219 1819	6.6 1.2 6.5
15	SA	0029 0633 1251 1850	1.1 6.7 1.1 6.7
16	SU	0101 0704 1322 1920	1.0 6.8 1.0 6.8
17	M	0132 0734 1352 1951	0.9 6.9 0.9 6.8
18	TU	0203 0804 1422 2022	0.9 6.9 1.0 6.7
19	W	0235 0836 1454 2054	1.0 6.7 1.2 6.5
20	TH	0308 0909 1527 2129	1.2 6.5 1.4 6.3
21	F	0344 0947 1604 2210	1.5 6.3 1.7 6.0
22	SA ☾	0426 1034 1651 2304	1.8 5.9 2.0 5.7
23	SU	0523 1137 1758	2.1 5.6 2.3
24	M	0020 0647 1304 1938	5.4 2.3 5.4 2.3
25	TU	0152 0826 1435 2108	5.5 2.1 5.6 2.0
26	W	0314 0944 1550 2215	5.9 1.6 6.1 1.5
27	TH	0420 1045 1650 2311	6.5 1.0 6.6 0.9
28	F	0515 1138 1741	7.0 0.6 7.1

MARCH

Date	Day	Time	m
1	SA ●	0000 0603 1226 1827	0.5 7.5 0.2 7.4
2	SU	0046 0648 1310 1910	0.2 7.7 0.1 7.5
3	M	0129 0730 1351 1950	0.1 7.7 0.1 7.4
4	TU	0209 0811 1430 2029	0.2 7.5 0.4 7.2
5	W	0247 0850 1507 2106	0.6 7.1 0.8 6.8
6	TH	0324 0928 1542 2144	1.0 6.7 1.3 6.3
7	F	0401 1007 1619 2224	1.5 6.1 1.8 5.8
8	SA ☽	0442 1052 1703 2314	2.0 5.6 2.3 5.4
9	SU	0536 1151 1809	2.5 5.1 2.7
10	M	0023 0707 1321 1946	5.0 2.7 4.9 2.8
11	TU	0207 0846 1450 2111	5.0 2.6 5.1 2.5
12	W	0324 0951 1554 2207	5.4 2.2 5.5 2.1
13	TH	0416 1038 1639 2251	5.8 1.8 5.9 1.7
14	F	0457 1117 1717 2328	6.2 1.5 6.2 1.3
15	SA	0533 1152 1751	6.5 1.2 6.5
16	SU O	0002 0605 1224 1822	1.1 6.7 1.0 6.7
17	M	0035 0637 1255 1854	0.9 6.9 0.8 6.9
18	TU	0108 0708 1327 1925	0.8 7.0 0.8 6.9
19	W	0140 0740 1359 1958	0.7 7.0 0.8 6.9
20	TH	0214 0813 1432 2031	0.8 6.9 1.0 6.8
21	F	0248 0849 1506 2108	1.0 6.7 1.2 6.5
22	SA	0326 0928 1545 2151	1.3 6.4 1.5 6.2
23	SU	0411 1017 1633 2247	1.6 6.0 1.9 5.8
24	M ☾	0509 1121 1741	2.0 5.6 2.2
25	TU	0003 0633 1248 1920	5.5 2.2 5.4 2.3
26	W	0135 0810 1420 2050	5.6 2.0 5.6 2.0
27	TH	0257 0927 1534 2158	5.9 1.6 6.0 1.5
28	F	0402 1028 1633 2253	6.5 1.0 6.5 1.0
29	SA	0456 1119 1722 2341	7.0 0.6 7.0 0.6
30	SU ●	0543 1204 1806	7.3 0.4 7.2
31	M	0025 0626 1247 1847	0.3 7.5 0.2 7.3

APRIL

Date	Day	Time	m
1	TU	0106 0707 1326 1925	0.3 7.4 0.3 7.3
2	W	0145 0746 1403 2002	0.4 7.3 0.5 7.1
3	TH	0221 0823 1438 2038	0.7 7.0 0.9 6.8
4	F	0257 0859 1512 2113	1.1 6.5 1.3 6.4
5	SA	0332 0936 1546 2151	1.5 6.1 1.8 5.9
6	SU	0409 1017 1625 2236	2.0 5.6 2.2 5.5
7	M ☽	0457 1109 1720 2337	2.4 5.2 2.6 5.1
8	TU	0612 1225 1847	2.7 4.9 2.8
9	W	0109 0748 1400 2018	5.0 2.7 4.9 2.6
10	TH	0234 0904 1510 2124	5.2 2.4 5.3 2.3
11	F	0333 0957 1600 2212	5.6 2.0 5.7 1.9
12	SA	0418 1039 1640 2253	6.0 1.6 6.1 1.5
13	SU	0456 1116 1717 2330	6.3 1.3 6.5 1.2
14	M	0532 1151 1751	6.6 1.0 6.7
15	TU O	0006 0606 1226 1825	0.9 6.8 0.8 6.9
16	W	0042 0641 1301 1900	0.8 7.0 0.7 7.0
17	TH	0118 0717 1337 1936	0.7 7.0 0.8 7.0
18	F	0155 0755 1414 2014	0.7 6.9 0.9 6.9
19	SA	0234 0835 1453 2056	0.9 6.7 1.1 6.7
20	SU	0316 0919 1536 2143	1.2 6.4 1.4 6.4
21	M	0405 1011 1627 2242	1.5 6.0 1.8 6.0
22	TU ☾	0505 1116 1736 2354	1.8 5.7 2.1 5.8
23	W	0625 1236 1906	2.0 5.5 2.1
24	TH	0116 0751 1359 2028	5.8 1.9 5.6 1.9
25	F	0234 0904 1511 2135	6.0 1.5 6.0 1.5
26	SA	0338 1004 1609 2230	6.4 1.2 6.4 1.1
27	SU	0432 1055 1659 2318	6.8 0.9 6.8 0.8
28	M	0520 1140 1743	7.0 0.7 7.0
29	TU ●	0002 0603 1221 1823	0.7 7.1 0.6 7.1
30	W	0043 0643 1300 1901	0.6 7.1 0.7 7.0

MAY

Date	Day	Time	m
1	TH	0121 0722 1337 1937	0.7 7.0 0.8 6.9
2	F	0158 0758 1412 2013	0.9 6.7 1.1 6.7
3	SA	0233 0834 1445 2048	1.2 6.4 1.4 6.4
4	SU	0307 0910 1519 2125	1.5 6.1 1.7 6.1
5	M	0344 0949 1556 2206	1.9 5.7 2.1 5.7
6	TU	0427 1035 1643 2257	2.2 5.4 2.4 5.4
7	W ☽	0525 1135 1750	2.5 5.1 2.6
8	TH	0004 0642 1253 1912	5.2 2.6 5.0 2.6
9	F	0127 0759 1410 2024	5.2 2.4 5.2 2.4
10	SA	0236 0902 1509 2122	5.4 2.1 5.5 2.1
11	SU	0329 0952 1556 2210	5.8 1.8 5.9 1.7
12	M	0414 1036 1638 2254	6.2 1.5 6.3 1.4
13	TU	0455 1117 1718 2335	6.5 1.2 6.7 1.1
14	W O	0536 1157 1757	6.8 0.9 6.9
15	TH	0016 0616 1238 1837	0.8 6.9 0.8 7.1
16	F	0058 0658 1319 1919	0.7 7.0 0.7 7.1
17	SA	0141 0741 1401 2003	0.7 7.0 0.8 7.1
18	SU	0225 0826 1444 2049	0.8 6.8 1.0 6.9
19	M	0312 0915 1531 2140	1.0 6.6 1.3 6.6
20	TU	0402 1008 1624 2237	1.2 6.2 1.6 6.3
21	W ☾	0501 1109 1728 2342	1.5 5.9 1.8 6.1
22	TH	0611 1218 1844	1.7 5.7 1.9
23	F	0053 0725 1332 1959	6.0 1.7 5.7 1.9
24	SA	0205 0835 1441 2107	6.0 1.6 5.9 1.7
25	SU	0310 0936 1542 2205	6.2 1.4 6.2 1.4
26	M	0407 1029 1634 2255	6.4 1.2 6.4 1.2
27	TU	0457 1115 1720 2340	6.6 1.1 6.6 1.1
28	W ●	0542 1157 1802	6.7 1.0 6.7
29	TH	0021 0623 1237 1840	1.0 6.7 1.0 6.8
30	F	0100 0701 1314 1917	1.0 6.7 1.1 6.7
31	SA	0137 0737 1349	1.1 6.5 1.2

JUNE

Date	Day	Time	m
1	SU	0212 0813 1423 2027	1.3 6.4 1.4 6.4
2	M	0246 0848 1456 2102	1.5 6.1 1.6 6.2
3	TU	0321 0925 1532 2140	1.7 5.9 1.9 6.0
4	W	0359 1005 1613 2224	1.9 5.6 2.1 5.7
5	TH ☽	0445 1053 1703 2315	2.2 5.4 2.3 5.5
6	F	0542 1150 1807	2.3 5.2 2.5
7	SA	0017 0651 1259 1919	5.4 2.4 5.2 2.4
8	SU	0127 0759 1408 2026	5.4 2.3 5.4 2.2
9	M	0233 0900 1507 2125	5.6 2.0 5.8 1.9
10	TU	0329 0954 1558 2218	6.0 1.7 6.2 1.5
11	W	0420 1044 1646 2307	6.3 1.3 6.6 1.2
12	TH	0508 1131 1733 2355	6.6 1.0 6.9 0.9
13	F O	0556 1217 1820	6.9 0.8 7.1
14	SA	0042 0643 1304 1906	0.7 7.1 0.7 7.3
15	SU	0130 0731 1350 1954	0.6 7.1 0.7 7.3
16	M	0217 0819 1437 2042	0.6 7.0 0.8 7.2
17	TU	0305 0908 1524 2132	0.7 6.8 1.0 6.9
18	W	0355 0958 1615 2225	0.9 6.5 1.3 6.6
19	TH ☾	0448 1052 1711 2321	1.2 6.2 1.6 6.3
20	F	0547 1152 1815	1.5 5.9 1.8
21	SA	0024 0652 1259 1926	6.1 1.8 5.7 1.9
22	SU	0132 0801 1408 2037	5.9 1.8 5.7 1.9
23	M	0239 0907 1514 2140	5.9 1.8 5.9 1.8
24	TU	0342 1004 1612 2235	6.0 1.7 6.1 1.6
25	W	0437 1054 1702 2322	6.2 1.5 6.3 1.4
26	TH	0524 1137 1745	6.3 1.4 6.5
27	F ●	0004 0605 1217 1823	1.3 6.4 1.3 6.6
28	SA	0043 0643 1254 1859	1.2 6.5 1.2 6.6
29	SU	0118 0719 1329 1933	1.2 6.5 1.2 6.6
30	M	0152 0753 1402 2007	1.3 6.4 1.3 6.5

SUNRISE AND SUNSET TIMES

MILFORD HAVEN
At 51°42′N 5°03′W

		Sunrise	Sunset
UT			
Jan	01	0827	1621
	15	0820	1640
Feb	01	0759	1709
	15	0734	1735
Mar	01	0705	1800
	15	0634	1825
BST			
Apr	01	0655	1954
	15	0624	2017
May	01	0551	2044
	15	0528	2107
Jun	01	0508	2129
	15	0501	2140
Jul	01	0506	2142
	15	0520	2132
Aug	01	0543	2109
	15	0605	2043
Sep	01	0633	2007
	15	0655	1935
Oct	01	0721	1858
	15	0745	1826
UT			
Nov	01	0714	1652
	15	0739	1630
Dec	01	0805	1614
	15	0820	1610

MILFORD HAVEN
LAT 51°42′N
LONG 5°03′W

TIMES AND HEIGHTS OF HIGH AND LOW WATER (Heights in Metres)

TIME ZONE UT
For Summer Time (area enclosed in shaded box) add 1 hour

2014

JULY

Date	Day	Time	m	Time	m	Time	m	Time	m
1	TU	0225	1.4	0826	6.3	1434	1.4	2040	6.4
2	W	0258	1.5	0900	6.1	1508	1.6	2114	6.2
3	TH	0332	1.7	0935	5.9	1544	1.8	2151	6.0
4	F	0410	1.9	1015	5.7	1625	2.0	2233	5.8
5	SA ☽	0453	2.1	1101	5.5	1713	2.2	2324	5.6
6	SU	0547	2.3	1158	5.4	1816	2.4		
7	M	0026	5.5	0656	2.3	1308	5.4	1931	2.3
8	TU	0138	5.5	0810	2.2	1420	5.6	2043	2.1
9	W	0248	5.8	0918	1.9	1524	6.0	2147	1.7
10	TH	0351	6.1	1017	1.5	1621	6.4	2244	1.3
11	F	0447	6.5	1111	1.1	1714	6.9	2337	0.9
12	SA ○	0540	6.9	1201	0.8	1805	7.2		
13	SU	0028	0.6	0630	7.1	1251	0.6	1854	7.4
14	M	0118	0.4	0719	7.3	1338	0.4	1942	7.5
15	TU	0206	0.3	0807	7.2	1425	0.5	2029	7.5
16	W	0252	0.4	0853	7.1	1511	0.7	2116	7.2
17	TH	0338	0.7	0940	6.8	1557	1.0	2204	6.9
18	F	0425	1.1	1028	6.4	1646	1.4	2254	6.4
19	SA ☾	0515	1.5	1120	6.0	1741	1.8	2350	6.0
20	SU	0614	1.9	1221	5.7	1848	2.1		
21	M	0056	5.7	0723	2.1	1333	5.5	2006	2.2
22	TU	0209	5.6	0838	2.2	1447	5.6	2119	2.1
23	W	0320	5.6	0943	2.0	1553	5.8	2218	1.9
24	TH	0420	5.9	1036	1.8	1646	6.1	2307	1.7
25	F	0508	6.1	1120	1.6	1729	6.4	2348	1.5
26	SA ●	0549	6.3	1159	1.4	1807	6.5		
27	SU	0024	1.3	0625	6.5	1235	1.2	1840	6.7
28	M	0059	1.2	0659	6.5	1308	1.2	1913	6.7
29	TU	0131	1.2	0731	6.5	1340	1.2	1944	6.7
30	W	0201	1.2	0802	6.5	1411	1.2	2015	6.6
31	TH	0232	1.3	0833	6.4	1443	1.3	2046	6.5

AUGUST

Date	Day	Time	m	Time	m	Time	m	Time	m
1	F	0304	1.4	0905	6.2	1516	1.5	2119	6.3
2	SA	0337	1.6	0940	6.0	1552	1.8	2156	6.1
3	SU	0414	1.9	1020	5.8	1634	2.0	2241	5.8
4	M ☽	0500	2.1	1111	5.5	1727	2.3	2338	5.5
5	TU	0601	2.3	1219	5.4	1842	2.4		
6	W	0054	5.4	0727	2.3	1341	5.5	2010	2.2
7	TH	0217	5.6	0850	2.1	1458	5.9	2125	1.8
8	F	0330	6.0	0957	1.6	1602	6.4	2228	1.3
9	SA	0432	6.5	1055	1.1	1659	6.9	2323	0.8
10	SU ○	0527	6.9	1146	0.7	1751	7.3		
11	M	0014	0.4	0616	7.3	1236	0.4	1839	7.6
12	TU	0103	0.2	0703	7.4	1322	0.3	1925	7.7
13	W	0149	0.1	0749	7.4	1407	0.3	2010	7.6
14	TH	0233	0.3	0832	7.3	1450	0.5	2054	7.4
15	F	0315	0.6	0915	6.9	1533	0.9	2138	6.9
16	SA	0357	1.1	0958	6.5	1616	1.4	2223	6.4
17	SU ☾	0440	1.6	1045	6.0	1705	1.9	2314	5.9
18	M	0532	2.1	1141	5.6	1807	2.3		
19	TU	0017	5.4	0640	2.5	1256	5.3	1933	2.5
20	W	0137	5.2	0807	2.5	1421	5.3	2058	2.4
21	TH	0258	5.3	0921	2.3	1533	5.6	2201	2.1
22	F	0402	5.7	1016	2.0	1627	6.0	2248	1.8
23	SA	0449	6.0	1100	1.7	1709	6.3	2328	1.5
24	SU	0528	6.3	1138	1.4	1745	6.6		
25	M ●	0003	1.3	0602	6.5	1212	1.2	1817	6.7
26	TU	0035	1.1	0635	6.7	1244	1.1	1848	6.8
27	W	0106	1.1	0705	6.7	1315	1.0	1918	6.9
28	TH	0135	1.0	0735	6.7	1346	1.1	1948	6.8
29	F	0205	1.1	0805	6.7	1417	1.2	2019	6.7
30	SA	0236	1.3	0836	6.5	1450	1.3	2050	6.5
31	SU	0308	1.5	0909	6.3	1524	1.6	2126	6.3

SEPTEMBER

Date	Day	Time	m	Time	m	Time	m	Time	m
1	M	0343	1.8	0948	6.0	1604	1.9	2208	5.9
2	TU ☽	0426	2.1	1037	5.7	1655	2.2	2305	5.6
3	W	0525	2.4	1145	5.5	1810	2.4		
4	TH	0024	5.4	0656	2.5	1314	5.5	1949	2.3
5	F	0157	5.5	0831	2.2	1439	5.8	2110	1.9
6	SA	0316	5.9	0942	1.7	1547	6.4	2213	1.3
7	SU	0418	6.5	1040	1.1	1644	7.0	2308	0.8
8	M	0511	7.0	1131	0.7	1734	7.4	2357	0.4
9	TU ○	0559	7.4	1218	0.4	1821	7.7		
10	W	0043	0.2	0644	7.5	1303	0.2	1905	7.8
11	TH	0127	0.1	0726	7.5	1345	0.3	1948	7.7
12	F	0208	0.3	0807	7.3	1426	0.5	2029	7.3
13	SA	0248	0.7	0847	7.0	1506	0.9	2110	6.9
14	SU	0326	1.2	0927	6.5	1546	1.5	2151	6.3
15	M	0405	1.7	1010	6.0	1630	2.0	2237	5.8
16	TU ☾	0451	2.3	1101	5.6	1726	2.5	2336	5.3
17	W	0555	2.7	1212	5.2	1853	2.8		
18	TH	0100	5.0	0728	2.8	1347	5.2	2029	2.7
19	F	0229	5.2	0853	2.6	1505	5.5	2134	2.3
20	SA	0335	5.5	0950	2.2	1559	5.9	2222	1.9
21	SU	0423	6.0	1034	1.8	1641	6.3	2301	1.6
22	M	0501	6.3	1111	1.5	1717	6.6	2335	1.3
23	TU	0535	6.6	1145	1.2	1750	6.8		
24	W ●	0007	1.1	0607	6.8	1218	1.1	1820	6.9
25	TH	0038	1.0	0637	6.9	1249	1.0	1851	7.0
26	F	0109	1.0	0708	6.9	1321	1.0	1922	7.0
27	SA	0140	1.0	0739	6.9	1354	1.1	1953	6.9
28	SU	0212	1.2	0811	6.8	1428	1.2	2027	6.7
29	M	0245	1.4	0846	6.5	1504	1.5	2104	6.4
30	TU	0322	1.7	0926	6.2	1546	1.8	2149	6.0

OCTOBER

Date	Day	Time	m	Time	m	Time	m	Time	m
1	W ☽	0407	2.0	1017	5.9	1639	2.2	2247	5.7
2	TH	0507	2.4	1127	5.6	1756	2.4		
3	F	0008	5.4	0639	2.5	1257	5.6	1934	2.3
4	SA	0141	5.5	0815	2.2	1422	5.9	2054	1.8
5	SU	0300	6.0	0926	1.7	1530	6.5	2157	1.3
6	M	0401	6.5	1022	1.2	1626	7.0	2250	0.8
7	TU	0453	7.0	1112	0.8	1715	7.4	2337	0.5
8	W ○	0539	7.3	1158	0.5	1801	7.6		
9	TH	0021	0.3	0622	7.5	1242	0.4	1843	7.6
10	F	0103	0.4	0703	7.5	1323	0.5	1924	7.5
11	SA	0143	0.6	0743	7.3	1402	0.7	2004	7.2
12	SU	0221	0.9	0821	7.0	1441	1.1	2043	6.8
13	M	0257	1.3	0859	6.6	1519	1.6	2122	6.3
14	TU	0334	1.8	0939	6.1	1559	2.1	2205	5.8
15	W ☾	0415	2.3	1025	5.7	1649	2.5	2257	5.3
16	TH	0510	2.7	1127	5.3	1804	2.8		
17	F	0012	5.0	0634	2.9	1255	5.2	1938	2.8
18	SA	0144	5.1	0805	2.8	1419	5.4	2053	2.5
19	SU	0255	5.4	0911	2.4	1519	5.7	2145	2.1
20	M	0346	5.8	0959	2.0	1605	6.1	2226	1.8
21	TU	0427	6.2	1039	1.7	1643	6.5	2303	1.5
22	W	0503	6.5	1115	1.4	1718	6.7	2336	1.2
23	TH ●	0536	6.8	1149	1.2	1751	6.9		
24	F	0009	1.1	0609	7.0	1224	1.0	1824	7.0
25	SA	0043	1.0	0642	7.1	1258	1.0	1858	7.0
26	SU	0117	1.0	0717	7.1	1334	1.0	1933	7.0
27	M	0152	1.1	0753	7.0	1412	1.2	2011	6.8
28	TU	0230	1.3	0832	6.8	1452	1.4	2052	6.5
29	W	0310	1.6	0916	6.5	1538	1.7	2141	6.2
30	TH	0358	1.9	1010	6.1	1634	2.0	2241	5.8
31	F ☽	0500	2.2	1119	5.9	1748	2.2	2358	5.6

NOVEMBER

Date	Day	Time	m	Time	m	Time	m	Time	m
1	SA	0626	2.4	1239	5.8	1916	2.1		
2	SU	0122	5.7	0754	2.2	1400	6.0	2032	1.8
3	M	0238	6.0	0904	1.8	1507	6.4	2135	1.4
4	TU	0340	6.4	1002	1.4	1604	6.8	2229	1.1
5	W	0432	6.8	1053	1.0	1654	7.1	2316	0.8
6	TH ○	0519	7.1	1138	0.8	1740	7.3	2359	0.7
7	F	0602	7.3	1221	0.7	1823	7.3		
8	SA	0040	0.7	0642	7.3	1302	0.8	1903	7.2
9	SU	0119	0.9	0721	7.2	1341	1.0	1942	7.0
10	M	0157	1.1	0759	6.9	1419	1.3	2020	6.7
11	TU	0233	1.4	0836	6.6	1456	1.6	2058	6.3
12	W	0309	1.8	0914	6.3	1534	2.0	2138	5.9
13	TH	0346	2.2	0955	5.9	1617	2.3	2223	5.5
14	F ☾	0431	2.5	1046	5.6	1713	2.6	2321	5.2
15	SA	0535	2.8	1151	5.3	1829	2.8		
16	SU	0037	5.1	0657	2.8	1313	5.3	1948	2.7
17	M	0157	5.2	0812	2.7	1424	5.5	2052	2.4
18	TU	0258	5.6	0912	2.3	1519	5.8	2143	2.0
19	W	0346	6.0	0959	2.0	1603	6.2	2225	1.7
20	TH	0427	6.3	1041	1.6	1643	6.5	2304	1.4
21	F	0505	6.7	1121	1.3	1722	6.8	2342	1.2
22	SA ●	0542	6.9	1200	1.1	1800	7.0		
23	SU	0020	1.0	0620	7.1	1240	1.0	1839	7.1
24	M	0059	1.0	0700	7.2	1320	0.9	1919	7.1
25	TU	0139	1.0	0741	7.2	1402	1.0	2002	6.9
26	W	0221	1.1	0825	7.0	1446	1.1	2048	6.7
27	TH	0305	1.4	0912	6.8	1534	1.4	2138	6.4
28	F	0354	1.7	1006	6.5	1629	1.7	2235	6.1
29	SA ☽	0453	1.9	1107	6.2	1734	1.9	2341	5.9
30	SU	0605	2.1	1217	6.1	1850	2.0		

DECEMBER

Date	Day	Time	m	Time	m	Time	m	Time	m
1	M	0055	5.8	0724	2.1	1330	6.1	2003	1.9
2	TU	0208	5.9	0837	1.9	1439	6.3	2109	1.7
3	W	0314	6.2	0939	1.6	1541	6.5	2206	1.4
4	TH	0411	6.5	1034	1.4	1635	6.7	2256	1.2
5	F	0500	6.8	1122	1.2	1723	6.9	2340	1.1
6	SA ○	0545	6.9	1205	1.1	1807	6.9		
7	SU	0021	1.0	0626	7.0	1246	1.1	1847	6.9
8	M	0101	1.1	0704	7.0	1325	1.1	1925	6.8
9	TU	0137	1.2	0741	6.9	1401	1.3	2002	6.6
10	W	0213	1.4	0817	6.7	1436	1.5	2037	6.4
11	TH	0247	1.6	0852	6.5	1511	1.8	2113	6.1
12	F	0321	1.9	0929	6.2	1548	2.0	2152	5.8
13	SA	0359	2.2	1010	5.9	1630	2.3	2236	5.5
14	SU ☾	0445	2.4	1058	5.6	1723	2.5	2330	5.3
15	M	0545	2.7	1157	5.4	1831	2.6		
16	TU	0038	5.2	0700	2.7	1309	5.4	1944	2.6
17	W	0153	5.3	0812	2.6	1419	5.5	2049	2.3
18	TH	0256	5.6	0913	2.3	1518	5.8	2144	2.0
19	F	0347	6.0	1006	1.9	1608	6.2	2232	1.6
20	SA	0434	6.4	1054	1.5	1655	6.5	2317	1.3
21	SU	0519	6.8	1139	1.2	1740	6.8		
22	M ●	0001	1.0	0602	7.1	1224	0.9	1824	7.1
23	TU	0045	0.9	0647	7.3	1309	0.7	1909	7.2
24	W	0129	0.8	0732	7.4	1354	0.7	1955	7.1
25	TH	0213	0.8	0818	7.3	1440	0.7	2042	7.0
26	F	0258	1.0	0905	7.1	1527	0.9	2130	6.7
27	SA	0346	1.2	0955	6.9	1617	1.2	2221	6.4
28	SU ☽	0437	1.5	1049	6.5	1712	1.5	2317	6.1
29	M	0537	1.8	1149	6.2	1816	1.8		
30	TU	0021	5.8	0648	2.1	1257	6.0	1927	2.0
31	W	0134	5.7	0805	2.1	1409	5.9	2040	2.0

SWANSEA
LAT 51°37′N
LONG 3°55′W

TIMES AND HEIGHTS OF HIGH AND LOW WATER (Heights in Metres)

TIME ZONE UT
For Summer Time (area enclosed in shaded box) add 1 hour

2014

JANUARY

Day	Time	m	Time	m	Time	m	Time	m
1 W ●	0548	9.6	1155	0.9	1812	9.6		
2 TH	0023	0.8	0637	9.9	1247	0.6	1901	9.8
3 F	0112	0.6	0725	10.1	1337	0.5	1950	9.9
4 SA	0159	0.6	0814	10.1	1425	0.5	2037	9.8
5 SU	0245	0.7	0901	9.9	1511	0.7	2124	9.5
6 M	0329	1.1	0949	9.5	1555	1.1	2210	9.0
7 TU	0414	1.5	1037	9.0	1641	1.6	2258	8.5
8 W ☽	0502	2.1	1127	8.5	1731	2.2	2351	7.9
9 TH	0559	2.6	1225	7.9	1831	2.7		
10 F	0053	7.5	0709	3.0	1333	7.5	1943	2.9
11 SA	0209	7.3	0829	3.0	1447	7.5	2100	2.8
12 SU	0323	7.5	0939	2.7	1553	7.8	2202	2.5
13 M	0421	8.0	1033	2.3	1646	8.1	2250	2.1
14 TU	0508	8.4	1115	1.9	1730	8.5	2329	1.7
15 W	0548	8.8	1153	1.6	1808	8.8		
16 TH ○	0006	1.4	0624	9.0	1229	1.4	1844	8.9
17 F	0041	1.3	0659	9.1	1303	1.4	1918	9.0
18 SA	0114	1.3	0732	9.1	1335	1.4	1951	8.9
19 SU	0145	1.3	0803	9.0	1404	1.5	2023	8.8
20 M	0214	1.5	0834	8.9	1431	1.6	2054	8.7
21 TU	0241	1.6	0905	8.7	1459	1.8	2125	8.4
22 W	0311	1.9	0938	8.5	1530	2.0	2159	8.2
23 TH	0346	2.1	1017	8.2	1610	2.3	2243	7.8
24 F ☾	0434	2.5	1109	7.9	1705	2.7	2343	7.5
25 SA	0544	2.8	1218	7.6	1828	2.9		
26 SU	0100	7.4	0718	2.9	1338	7.6	2002	2.8
27 M	0224	7.6	0841	2.5	1458	7.9	2120	2.3
28 TU	0340	8.2	0951	1.9	1608	8.5	2224	1.7
29 W	0442	8.9	1051	1.3	1707	9.1	2321	1.1
30 TH ●	0535	9.5	1145	0.8	1800	9.6		
31 F	0012	0.7	0625	10.0	1237	0.4	1849	9.9

FEBRUARY

Day	Time	m	Time	m	Time	m	Time	m
1 SA	0101	0.4	0712	10.3	1325	0.2	1936	10.1
2 SU	0147	0.3	0758	10.3	1410	0.2	2020	10.0
3 M	0229	0.4	0842	10.1	1451	0.4	2102	9.7
4 TU	0308	0.7	0925	9.8	1529	0.8	2142	9.3
5 W	0345	1.2	1006	9.2	1606	1.4	2223	8.7
6 TH ☽	0424	1.8	1049	8.5	1647	2.1	2306	8.0
7 F	0510	2.5	1138	7.8	1738	2.7		
8 SA	0000	7.3	0613	3.1	1242	7.2	1846	3.2
9 SU	0117	6.9	0737	3.3	1404	6.9	2012	3.3
10 M	0244	7.0	0906	3.1	1523	7.2	2131	2.9
11 TU	0354	7.5	1009	2.6	1622	7.7	2225	2.4
12 W	0445	8.1	1054	2.1	1707	8.2	2307	1.8
13 TH	0526	8.6	1132	1.7	1747	8.7	2344	1.4
14 F ○	0604	8.9	1207	1.4	1823	8.9		
15 SA	0019	1.2	0637	9.1	1241	1.2	1856	9.1
16 SU	0053	1.1	0709	9.2	1313	1.1	1928	9.1
17 M	0124	1.1	0741	9.2	1341	1.2	1959	9.1
18 TU	0152	1.1	0811	9.2	1408	1.2	2030	9.0
19 W	0220	1.2	0841	9.0	1434	1.4	2100	8.8
20 TH	0248	1.4	0912	8.8	1503	1.6	2131	8.5
21 F	0320	1.7	0947	8.5	1538	1.9	2210	8.2
22 SA ☾	0402	2.1	1035	8.0	1627	2.4	2306	7.7
23 SU	0506	2.6	1144	7.6	1747	2.9		
24 M	0027	7.3	0646	2.9	1311	7.4	1936	2.9
25 TU	0200	7.4	0821	2.6	1440	7.7	2103	2.5
26 W	0322	8.0	0938	2.0	1554	8.3	2211	1.7
27 TH	0427	8.8	1039	1.2	1653	9.0	2308	1.1
28 F	0521	9.5	1132	0.7	1745	9.6	2358	0.5

MARCH

Day	Time	m	Time	m	Time	m	Time	m
1 SA ●	0610	10.0	1221	0.3	1832	9.9		
2 SU	0044	0.2	0655	10.3	1307	0.1	1916	-0.1
3 M	0128	0.1	0738	10.3	1348	0.1	1957	10.0
4 TU	0207	0.3	0819	10.1	1425	0.4	2036	9.8
5 W	0242	0.6	0857	9.7	1459	0.8	2112	9.3
6 TH	0315	1.1	0934	9.2	1531	1.4	2148	8.8
7 F	0348	1.7	1012	8.5	1605	2.0	2225	8.1
8 SA ☽	0425	2.4	1053	7.7	1647	2.7	2313	7.4
9 SU	0521	3.0	1149	7.0	1753	3.3		
10 M	0017	6.8	0646	3.4	1316	6.6	1922	3.5
11 TU	0158	6.7	0820	3.3	1445	6.9	2049	3.2
12 W	0318	7.2	0934	2.8	1550	7.4	2151	2.6
13 TH	0414	7.8	1023	2.2	1638	8.0	2236	2.0
14 F	0458	8.4	1103	1.7	1718	8.6	2315	1.5
15 SA	0535	8.8	1139	1.3	1755	8.9	2352	1.2
16 SU ○	0610	9.1	1213	1.1	1829	9.2		
17 M	0026	1.0	0643	9.3	1246	1.0	1901	9.3
18 TU	0059	0.9	0715	9.4	1316	1.0	1934	9.3
19 W	0129	0.9	0748	9.3	1344	1.0	2006	9.3
20 TH	0159	1.0	0820	9.2	1413	1.1	2038	9.1
21 F	0230	1.1	0853	9.0	1443	1.4	2111	8.8
22 SA	0304	1.4	0930	8.6	1519	1.7	2152	8.4
23 SU	0348	1.9	1019	8.1	1610	2.3	2250	7.8
24 M ☾	0454	2.4	1128	7.6	1734	2.8		
25 TU	0010	7.4	0630	2.7	1256	7.3	1919	2.9
26 W	0143	7.5	0804	2.5	1424	7.6	2047	2.4
27 TH	0304	8.0	0921	1.9	1538	8.3	2155	1.7
28 F	0409	8.8	1022	1.2	1636	8.9	2249	1.1
29 SA	0502	9.4	1114	0.7	1726	9.5	2338	0.6
30 SU ●	0550	9.8	1200	0.4	1811	9.8		
31 M	0022	0.4	0634	10.0	1243	0.2	[illegible]	[illegible]

APRIL

Day	Time	m	Time	m	Time	m	Time	m
1 TU	0103	0.3	0715	10.0	1321	0.3	1931	9.9
2 W	0141	0.4	0754	9.9	1356	0.6	2008	9.6
3 TH	0215	0.7	0830	9.5	1428	0.9	2043	9.3
4 F	0246	1.2	0905	9.0	1458	1.4	2116	8.8
5 SA	0317	1.7	0940	8.4	1528	2.0	2152	8.2
6 SU	0350	2.3	1018	7.7	1605	2.6	2233	7.6
7 M ☽	0437	2.8	1107	7.1	1702	3.1	2330	7.0
8 TU	0554	3.3	1219	6.7	1831	3.4		
9 W	0059	6.8	0727	3.3	1354	6.7	1959	3.2
10 TH	0229	7.0	0845	2.9	1508	7.2	2106	2.7
11 F	0332	7.6	0941	2.4	1600	7.9	2157	2.2
12 SA	0419	8.2	1025	1.9	1643	8.4	2239	1.7
13 SU	0500	8.6	1104	1.5	1721	8.8	2318	1.3
14 M	0537	9.0	1140	1.2	1757	9.2	2354	1.0
15 TU ○	0613	9.2	1215	1.0	1833	9.4		
16 W	0030	0.9	0649	9.4	1250	0.9	1909	9.5
17 TH	0106	0.8	0725	9.4	1323	0.9	1944	9.4
18 F	0141	0.9	0802	9.4	1357	1.0	2021	9.3
19 SA	0218	1.0	0840	9.1	1433	1.3	2100	9.0
20 SU	0258	1.3	0923	8.8	1514	1.7	2147	8.6
21 M	0348	1.7	1015	8.3	1610	2.2	2247	8.1
22 TU ☾	0455	2.2	1122	7.8	1730	2.6		
23 W	0002	7.7	0617	2.4	1242	7.5	1901	2.7
24 TH	0124	7.7	0742	2.3	1403	7.7	2024	2.3
25 F	0241	8.1	0857	1.9	1515	8.2	2131	1.8
26 SA	0345	8.7	0959	1.4	1614	8.8	2226	1.3
27 SU	0439	9.1	1050	1.0	1703	9.2	2313	0.9
28 M	0527	9.5	1135	0.7	1747	9.5	2356	0.7
29 TU ●	0611	9.6	1216	0.6	1828	9.6		
30 W	0036	0.7	0651	9.6	1254	0.7	1906	9.6

MAY

Day	Time	m	Time	m	Time	m	Time	m
1 TH	0114	0.8	0729	9.5	1329	0.9	1942	9.4
2 F	0149	1.0	0805	9.2	1401	1.2	2017	9.1
3 SA	0221	1.3	0840	8.8	1431	1.5	2051	8.7
4 SU	0252	1.7	0915	8.4	1502	1.9	2126	8.3
5 M	0325	2.1	0952	7.9	1537	2.4	2206	7.8
6 TU	0407	2.6	1036	7.4	1625	2.8	2257	7.4
7 W ☽	0506	3.0	1133	7.0	1735	3.2		
8 TH	0002	7.1	0624	3.1	1249	6.9	1859	3.2
9 F	0123	7.1	0743	3.0	1409	7.1	2012	2.9
10 SA	0235	7.5	0847	2.6	1511	7.6	2109	2.4
11 SU	0331	7.9	0938	2.1	1601	8.2	2157	1.9
12 M	0418	8.4	1022	1.7	1644	8.7	2240	1.5
13 TU	0501	8.8	1104	1.4	1725	9.1	2321	1.2
14 W ○	0542	9.1	1145	1.1	1805	9.3		
15 TH	0003	1.0	0623	9.4	1226	0.9	1845	9.5
16 F	0045	0.8	0705	9.5	1306	0.9	1926	9.6
17 SA	0127	0.8	0748	9.4	1347	1.0	2008	9.5
18 SU	0210	0.9	0832	9.3	1429	1.1	2054	9.2
19 M	0257	1.1	0920	9.0	1516	1.5	2145	8.9
20 TU	0350	1.4	1013	8.6	1612	1.9	2243	8.5
21 W ☾	0451	1.8	1113	8.1	1720	2.2	2349	8.2
22 TH	0559	2.1	1221	7.8	1837	2.4		
23 F	0059	8.0	0712	2.2	1334	7.8	1954	2.3
24 SA	0211	8.1	0825	2.0	1445	8.1	2102	2.0
25 SU	0316	8.4	0929	1.8	1547	8.4	2159	1.7
26 M	0413	8.7	1023	1.5	1639	8.8	2248	1.4
27 TU	0504	8.9	1109	1.3	1724	9.0	2332	1.2
28 W ●	0548	9.1	1151	1.1	1805	9.2		
29 TH	0012	1.2	0629	9.1	1229	1.1	1843	9.2
30 F	0050	1.2	0707	9.1	1305	1.2	1920	9.2
31 SA	0126	1.3	0744	8.9	1338	1.3	[illegible]	[illegible]

JUNE

Day	Time	m	Time	m	Time	m	Time	m
1 SU	0200	1.5	0819	8.7	1410	1.5	2030	8.8
2 M	0232	1.7	0854	8.4	1441	1.8	2105	8.5
3 TU	0304	2.0	0930	8.1	1515	2.1	2142	8.1
4 W	0341	2.3	1009	7.8	1555	2.4	2225	7.8
5 TH ☽	0427	2.6	1055	7.5	1647	2.8	2317	7.5
6 F	0524	2.8	1151	7.2	1753	3.0		
7 SA	0018	7.4	0632	2.9	1258	7.2	1908	2.9
8 SU	0127	7.4	0742	2.7	1409	7.5	2015	2.6
9 M	0233	7.7	0845	2.4	1512	7.9	2113	2.2
10 TU	0332	8.2	0940	2.0	1606	8.4	2204	1.7
11 W	0424	8.6	1030	1.6	1654	8.9	2252	1.3
12 TH	0514	9.0	1119	1.2	1740	9.3	2340	1.0
13 F ○	0602	9.3	1206	1.0	1826	9.6		
14 SA	0028	0.8	0649	9.5	1253	0.8	1911	9.7
15 SU	0116	0.7	0736	9.6	1339	0.8	1958	9.7
16 M	0205	0.7	0824	9.5	1425	0.9	2047	9.6
17 TU	0254	0.8	0913	9.3	1513	1.1	2138	9.3
18 W	0344	1.1	1004	9.0	1604	1.4	2231	9.0
19 TH ☾	0437	1.4	1057	8.6	1700	1.8	2328	8.6
20 F	0534	1.8	1154	8.1	1804	2.2		
21 SA	0029	8.2	0636	2.1	1259	7.8	1915	2.4
22 SU	0136	8.0	0746	2.3	1408	7.8	2028	2.4
23 M	0244	8.0	0855	2.3	1517	8.0	2133	2.2
24 TU	0347	8.1	0956	2.0	1615	8.3	2227	1.9
25 W	0441	8.4	1047	1.8	1704	8.6	2312	1.7
26 TH	0528	8.6	1129	1.6	1746	8.8	2352	1.5
27 F ●	0610	8.8	1207	1.4	1825	9.0		
28 SA	0030	1.4	0648	8.8	1244	1.3	1902	9.0
29 SU	0106	1.4	0724	8.8	1318	1.3	1937	9.0
30 M	0140	1.5	0800	8.7	1351	1.4	2011	8.9

SUNRISE AND SUNSET TIMES

SWANSEA
At 51°37′N 3°55′W

UT		Sunrise	Sunset
Jan	01	0822	1617
	15	0815	1636
Feb	01	0754	1705
	15	0730	1731
Mar	01	0701	1756
	15	0630	1820
BST			
Apr	01	0651	1949
	15	0620	2013
May	01	0547	2040
	15	0523	2102
Jun	01	0504	2124
	15	0457	2135
Jul	01	0502	2137
	15	0516	2127
Aug	01	0539	2104
	15	0601	2038
Sep	01	0628	2002
	15	0651	1930
Oct	01	0716	1853
	15	0740	1822
UT			
Nov	01	0710	1648
	15	0734	1626
Dec	01	0800	1610
	15	0815	1606

SWANSEA
LAT 51°37′N
LONG 3°55′W

TIMES AND HEIGHTS OF HIGH AND LOW WATER (Heights in Metres)

TIME ZONE UT
For Summer Time (area enclosed in shaded box) add 1 hour

2014

JULY

Date	Day	Time	m	Time	m	Time	m	Time	m	Moon
1	TU	0212	1.6	0833	8.6	1421	1.6	2044	8.7	
2	W	0242	1.8	0906	8.4	1452	1.8	2117	8.4	
3	TH	0314	2.0	0941	8.1	1525	2.1	2153	8.2	
4	F	0350	2.2	1018	7.9	1605	2.4	2234	7.9	
5	SA	0434	2.4	1103	7.6	1656	2.7	2326	7.6	☽
6	SU	0530	2.7	1200	7.4	1803	2.9			
7	M	0029	7.5	0641	2.8	1308	7.4	1921	2.8	
8	TU	0140	7.6	0756	2.7	1422	7.7	2033	2.5	
9	W	0250	7.9	0904	2.3	1530	8.2	2135	2.0	
10	TH	0354	8.4	1004	1.8	1628	8.8	2231	1.5	
11	F	0451	8.9	1059	1.3	1720	9.3	2324	1.0	
12	SA	0544	9.3	1151	1.0	1810	9.7			○
13	SU	0015	0.7	0634	9.6	1242	0.7	1858	9.9	
14	M	0106	0.5	0724	9.7	1330	0.5	1947	10.0	
15	TU	0156	0.4	0812	9.8	1417	0.6	2035	10.0	
16	W	0243	0.5	0900	9.6	1502	0.7	2123	9.7	
17	TH	0329	0.7	0946	9.3	1547	1.1	2211	9.3	
18	F	0415	1.2	1033	8.9	1633	1.6	2301	8.8	
19	SA	0502	1.7	1123	8.3	1726	2.2	2355	8.2	☾
20	SU	0557	2.3	1220	7.8	1831	2.6			
21	M	0058	7.7	0702	2.7	1330	7.4	1949	2.9	
22	TU	0211	7.5	0819	2.8	1446	7.5	2109	2.7	
23	W	0323	7.6	0932	2.6	1553	7.8	2210	2.4	
24	TH	0422	7.9	1027	2.2	1646	8.2	2257	2.0	
25	F	0510	8.3	1110	1.8	1728	8.6	2335	1.7	
26	SA	0551	8.6	1147	1.5	1807	8.9			●
27	SU	0011	1.5	0628	8.8	1223	1.3	1843	9.1	
28	M	0046	1.3	0704	8.9	1258	1.3	1917	9.1	
29	TU	0119	1.3	0738	8.9	1330	1.3	1949	9.0	
30	W	0149	1.4	0810	8.8	1400	1.4	2020	8.9	
31	TH	0217	1.5	0841	8.7	1428	1.5	2050	8.7	

AUGUST

Date	Day	Time	m	Time	m	Time	m	Time	m	Moon
1	F	0245	1.7	0912	8.5	1457	1.7	2121	8.5	
2	SA	0315	1.9	0944	8.2	1530	2.0	2155	8.2	
3	SU	0351	2.1	1022	7.9	1611	2.3	2240	7.9	
4	M	0438	2.5	1113	7.6	1709	2.7	2342	7.6	☽
5	TU	0546	2.8	1222	7.4	1834	2.9			
6	W	0059	7.4	0717	2.9	1344	7.5	2004	2.7	
7	TH	0221	7.7	0839	2.5	1505	8.0	2117	2.2	
8	F	0335	8.2	0947	2.0	1610	8.7	2218	1.5	
9	SA	0436	8.8	1046	1.4	1705	9.3	2313	0.9	
10	SU	0530	9.3	1139	0.8	1756	9.8			○
11	M	0004	0.5	0620	9.7	1230	0.5	1844	10.2	
12	TU	0054	0.2	0708	10.0	1318	0.3	1931	10.3	
13	W	0141	0.2	0755	10.0	1402	0.3	2017	10.2	
14	TH	0226	0.3	0839	9.9	1444	0.5	2101	9.9	
15	F	0307	0.6	0922	9.5	1523	0.9	2145	9.4	
16	SA	0346	1.1	1004	9.0	1603	1.5	2229	8.8	
17	SU	0427	1.8	1048	8.3	1648	2.2	2318	8.0	☾
18	M	0516	2.5	1140	7.6	1747	2.9			
19	TU	0019	7.3	0618	3.0	1249	7.1	1907	3.3	
20	W	0138	7.0	0739	3.2	1415	7.1	2044	3.2	
21	TH	0258	7.1	0906	3.0	1531	7.4	2153	2.7	
22	F	0402	7.6	1006	2.5	1626	8.0	2239	2.2	
23	SA	0449	8.1	1048	2.0	1708	8.5	2316	1.7	
24	SU	0529	8.5	1125	1.6	1746	8.9	2350	1.4	
25	M	0606	8.8	1200	1.3	1821	9.1			●
26	TU	0023	1.2	0640	9.0	1235	1.1	1853	9.2	
27	W	0055	1.2	0712	9.1	1307	1.1	1925	9.2	
28	TH	0125	1.2	0744	9.0	1336	1.2	1955	9.1	
29	F	0152	1.3	0815	8.9	1404	1.3	2024	9.0	
30	SA	0219	1.5	0844	8.8	1432	1.5	2052	8.8	
31	SU	0246	1.7	0913	8.5	1502	1.8	2123	8.5	

SEPTEMBER

Date	Day	Time	m	Time	m	Time	m	Time	m	Moon
1	M	0317	2.0	0948	8.2	1539	2.2	2205	8.1	
2	TU	0400	2.4	1037	7.8	1633	2.6	2307	7.6	☽
3	W	0507	2.9	1150	7.4	1804	3.0			
4	TH	0031	7.3	0652	3.1	1320	7.4	1944	2.9	
5	F	0204	7.5	0823	2.7	1447	7.9	2104	2.2	
6	SA	0321	8.1	0935	2.0	1555	8.7	2207	1.5	
7	SU	0422	8.8	1034	1.3	1650	9.4	2301	0.9	
8	M	0515	9.4	1125	0.8	1740	10.0	2350	0.4	
9	TU	0603	9.9	1214	0.4	1827	10.3			○
10	W	0037	0.2	0649	10.1	1300	0.2	1912	10.4	
11	TH	0122	0.1	0733	10.1	1342	0.3	1955	10.3	
12	F	0202	0.3	0815	9.9	1421	0.6	2036	9.9	
13	SA	0240	0.7	0855	9.5	1457	1.0	2116	9.4	
14	SU	0315	1.3	0933	9.0	1533	1.6	2156	8.7	
15	M	0352	1.9	1013	8.3	1613	2.3	2240	7.9	
16	TU	0436	2.6	1100	7.6	1707	3.0	2336	7.2	☾
17	W	0536	3.2	1205	7.0	1825	3.5			
18	TH	0059	6.7	0659	3.5	1337	6.9	2004	3.5	
19	F	0228	6.9	0829	3.3	1500	7.3	2124	3.0	
20	SA	0335	7.4	0935	2.7	1558	7.9	2212	2.4	
21	SU	0423	8.0	1020	2.1	1642	8.4	2249	1.8	
22	M	0503	8.5	1058	1.7	1720	8.9	2324	1.4	
23	TU	0539	8.9	1134	1.3	1755	9.2	2357	1.2	
24	W	0613	9.1	1208	1.1	1828	9.3			●
25	TH	0029	1.1	0645	9.2	1242	1.1	1859	9.3	
26	F	0059	1.1	0718	9.2	1312	1.1	1930	9.3	
27	SA	0128	1.2	0749	9.2	1342	1.2	2001	9.2	
28	SU	0156	1.4	0820	9.0	1412	1.4	2031	8.9	
29	M	0224	1.6	0851	8.8	1443	1.7	2104	8.6	
30	TU	0256	1.9	0928	8.4	1522	2.1	2148	8.1	

OCTOBER

Date	Day	Time	m	Time	m	Time	m	Time	m	Moon
1	W	0340	2.4	1019	7.9	1619	2.6	2251	7.6	☽
2	TH	0451	2.9	1134	7.5	1751	3.0			
3	F	0016	7.3	0638	3.1	1305	7.5	1928	2.8	
4	SA	0149	7.5	0809	2.7	1430	8.0	2049	2.2	
5	SU	0307	8.1	0921	2.1	1538	8.7	2152	1.5	
6	M	0407	8.8	1018	1.4	1633	9.4	2245	0.9	
7	TU	0458	9.4	1108	0.9	1723	9.9	2333	0.5	
8	W	0545	9.8	1154	0.5	1809	10.2			○
9	TH	0017	0.3	0628	10.0	1238	0.4	1852	10.2	
10	F	0059	0.3	0710	10.0	1319	0.5	1933	10.1	
11	SA	0137	0.6	0750	9.8	1357	0.8	2012	9.7	
12	SU	0213	0.9	0828	9.4	1432	1.2	2049	9.2	
13	M	0247	1.4	0905	9.0	1507	1.8	2127	8.6	
14	TU	0321	2.0	0943	8.4	1544	2.4	2207	7.9	
15	W	0400	2.6	1026	7.7	1632	3.0	2257	7.2	☾
16	TH	0455	3.2	1124	7.2	1743	3.4			
17	F	0010	6.8	0614	3.5	1248	6.9	1912	3.5	
18	SA	0142	6.8	0741	3.4	1414	7.2	2035	3.2	
19	SU	0256	7.2	0852	3.0	1519	7.7	2132	2.6	
20	M	0349	7.9	0944	2.4	1607	8.3	2215	2.0	
21	TU	0431	8.4	1025	1.9	1648	8.7	2253	1.6	
22	W	0509	8.8	1103	1.5	1725	9.1	2328	1.3	
23	TH	0544	9.1	1140	1.3	1759	9.3			●
24	F	0001	1.2	0618	9.3	1215	1.2	1833	9.4	
25	SA	0035	1.1	0653	9.4	1249	1.1	1907	9.4	
26	SU	0107	1.2	0727	9.4	1323	1.2	1942	9.3	
27	M	0139	1.3	0801	9.2	1358	1.3	2017	9.1	
28	TU	0212	1.5	0838	9.0	1435	1.6	2056	8.8	
29	W	0249	1.9	0921	8.6	1520	2.0	2144	8.3	
30	TH	0338	2.3	1016	8.2	1621	2.4	2246	7.8	
31	F	0451	2.8	1127	7.8	1742	2.7			☽

NOVEMBER

Date	Day	Time	m	Time	m	Time	m	Time	m	Moon
1	SA	0004	7.5	0623	2.9	1248	7.8	1907	2.7	
2	SU	0129	7.6	0748	2.7	1407	8.1	2026	2.3	
3	M	0245	8.1	0900	2.2	1516	8.6	2131	1.7	
4	TU	0347	8.7	0958	1.6	1613	9.2	2225	1.2	
5	W	0439	9.2	1048	1.2	1703	9.6	2312	0.8	
6	TH	0526	9.6	1134	0.9	1749	9.8	2356	0.7	○
7	F	0609	9.8	1217	0.8	1832	9.9			
8	SA	0036	0.7	0649	9.8	1257	0.9	1912	9.7	
9	SU	0114	0.9	0727	9.6	1335	1.1	1950	9.4	
10	M	0149	1.2	0805	9.3	1410	1.4	2027	9.0	
11	TU	0223	1.5	0841	9.0	1445	1.8	2104	8.6	
12	W	0256	2.0	0919	8.5	1521	2.3	2142	8.0	
13	TH	0332	2.5	0959	8.0	1603	2.7	2226	7.5	
14	F	0418	2.9	1048	7.6	1659	3.1	2322	7.1	☾
15	SA	0523	3.3	1151	7.2	1813	3.4			
16	SU	0036	6.9	0643	3.4	1310	7.2	1933	3.3	
17	M	0158	7.1	0759	3.2	1424	7.5	2040	2.9	
18	TU	0303	7.5	0859	2.7	1522	7.9	2133	2.4	
19	W	0353	8.1	0948	2.3	1610	8.4	2217	2.0	
20	TH	0436	8.6	1030	1.8	1651	8.8	2256	1.6	
21	F	0515	9.0	1110	1.5	1731	9.1	2334	1.4	
22	SA	0553	9.3	1149	1.3	1809	9.3			●
23	SU	0012	1.2	0630	9.4	1229	1.2	1848	9.4	
24	M	0050	1.2	0709	9.5	1309	1.1	1927	9.4	
25	TU	0128	1.2	0748	9.5	1350	1.2	2009	9.3	
26	W	0208	1.4	0831	9.3	1434	1.3	2053	9.0	
27	TH	0251	1.6	0918	9.0	1522	1.6	2143	8.6	
28	F	0342	2.0	1013	8.6	1619	2.0	2240	8.2	
29	SA	0445	2.3	1115	8.3	1725	2.3	2346	7.9	☽
30	SU	0600	2.6	1224	8.1	1839	2.4			

DECEMBER

Date	Day	Time	m	Time	m	Time	m	Time	m	Moon
1	M	0059	7.8	0717	2.6	1337	8.1	1953	2.3	
2	TU	0214	8.0	0831	2.4	1447	8.4	2103	2.0	
3	W	0321	8.4	0935	2.0	1549	8.7	2202	1.7	
4	TH	0418	8.8	1029	1.6	1644	9.1	2253	1.4	
5	F	0507	9.1	1116	1.4	1732	9.3	2337	1.2	
6	SA	0551	9.3	1159	1.2	1815	9.4			○
7	SU	0017	1.1	0631	9.4	1240	1.2	1854	9.3	
8	M	0055	1.1	0709	9.4	1317	1.3	1932	9.2	
9	TU	0130	1.3	0746	9.3	1352	1.4	2008	9.0	
10	W	0204	1.5	0822	9.0	1427	1.7	2044	8.7	
11	TH	0236	1.8	0858	8.7	1500	2.0	2120	8.3	
12	F	0309	2.1	0935	8.4	1535	2.3	2157	7.9	
13	SA	0346	2.5	1015	8.0	1616	2.7	2240	7.5	
14	SU	0432	2.9	1102	7.6	1709	3.0	2333	7.2	☾
15	M	0534	3.2	1200	7.4	1817	3.2			
16	TU	0038	7.1	0650	3.3	1309	7.3	1931	3.2	
17	W	0155	7.2	0803	3.1	1421	7.5	2039	2.8	
18	TH	0303	7.6	0903	2.7	1523	7.9	2135	2.4	
19	F	0358	8.2	0955	2.2	1615	8.4	2224	2.0	
20	SA	0444	8.7	1042	1.7	1702	8.8	2309	1.6	
21	SU	0528	9.1	1127	1.4	1747	9.2	2353	1.2	
22	M	0611	9.5	1212	1.1	1831	9.4			●
23	TU	0036	1.0	0654	9.7	1258	0.9	1915	9.6	
24	W	0120	0.9	0738	9.8	1344	0.8	2001	9.6	
25	TH	0204	1.0	0824	9.7	1430	0.9	2047	9.4	
26	F	0249	1.1	0912	9.5	1517	1.1	2135	9.1	
27	SA	0337	1.4	1002	9.2	1608	1.4	2226	8.8	
28	SU	0429	1.8	1056	8.8	1702	1.8	2321	8.3	☽
29	M	0530	2.2	1155	8.4	1804	2.2			
30	TU	0023	7.9	0639	2.5	1301	8.1	1914	2.5	
31	W	0135	7.7	0756	2.6	1413	8.0	2029	2.5	

BRISTOL (AVONMOUTH)

LAT 51°30′N
LONG 2°44′W

TIMES AND HEIGHTS OF HIGH AND LOW WATER (Heights in Metres)

TIME ZONE UT
For Summer Time (area enclosed in shaded box) add 1 hour

2014

JANUARY

Date	Day	Time	m	Time	m	Time	m	Time	m
1	W ●	0104	1.4	0642	13.5	1330	1.1	1908	13.6
2	TH	0159	1.0	0731	14.0	1425	0.8	1958	13.9
3	F	0250	0.8	0820	14.2	1515	0.6	2046	14.0
4	SA	0336	0.7	0907	14.2	1600	0.6	2132	13.9
5	SU	0417	0.9	0952	13.9	1640	0.8	2216	13.4
6	M	0454	1.3	1036	13.4	1716	1.3	2258	12.8
7	TU	0527	1.8	1120	12.6	1750	1.8	2342	11.9
8	W ☽	0601	2.4	1209	11.7	1828	2.5		
9	TH	0031	11.1	0642	3.0	1311	10.9	1915	3.1
10	F	0139	10.4	0739	3.6	1425	10.4	2019	3.5
11	SA	0255	10.2	0902	3.8	1533	10.4	2145	3.5
12	SU	0400	10.5	1032	3.5	1633	10.8	2258	3.0
13	M	0458	11.1	1133	2.8	1727	11.4	2355	2.3
14	TU	0548	11.8	1224	2.2	1814	11.9		
15	W	0045	1.8	0631	12.3	1313	1.8	1857	12.3
16	TH O	0132	1.5	0712	12.6	1358	1.7	1936	12.5
17	F	0216	1.4	0750	12.7	1440	1.7	2013	12.4
18	SA	0255	1.6	0825	12.6	1516	1.9	2047	12.3
19	SU	0326	1.8	0858	12.5	1543	2.1	2117	12.2
20	M	0348	2.0	0927	12.3	1601	2.2	2146	12.0
21	TU	0408	2.0	0956	12.1	1623	2.2	2215	11.9
22	W	0437	2.1	1029	11.9	1654	2.2	2250	11.6
23	TH	0512	2.2	1109	11.6	1732	2.4	2333	11.2
24	F ☾	0554	2.6	1157	11.1	1817	2.8		
25	SA	0026	10.7	0646	3.2	1259	10.7	1915	3.4
26	SU	0135	10.3	0800	3.6	1416	10.5	2045	3.6
27	M	0305	10.5	0947	3.4	1548	10.8	2234	3.2
28	TU	0429	11.3	1111	2.6	1703	11.7	2348	2.3
29	W	0534	12.4	1218	1.8	1803	12.7		
30	TH ●	0050	1.5	0629	13.3	1318	1.0	1856	13.5
31	F	0147	0.9	0719	14.1	1414	0.5	1946	14.1

FEBRUARY

Date	Day	Time	m	Time	m	Time	m	Time	m
1	SA	0239	0.4	0807	14.5	1504	0.2	2032	14.3
2	SU	0325	0.2	0852	14.6	1548	0.1	2116	14.2
3	M	0406	0.4	0935	14.3	1625	0.4	2156	13.8
4	TU	0438	0.8	1015	13.7	1655	1.0	2233	13.1
5	W	0504	1.4	1052	12.9	1720	1.6	2308	12.2
6	TH ☽	0528	2.0	1129	11.8	1749	2.3	2344	11.3
7	F	0600	2.7	1212	10.8	1827	3.0		
8	SA	0031	10.3	0645	3.5	1319	9.9	1920	3.7
9	SU	0153	9.6	0751	4.1	1453	9.6	2037	4.0
10	M	0323	9.7	0927	4.1	1603	10.0	2214	3.6
11	TU	0429	10.4	1102	3.3	1702	10.7	2325	2.7
12	W	0523	11.3	1158	2.5	1751	11.5		
13	TH	0019	2.0	0609	12.0	1248	1.8	1834	12.1
14	F O	0108	1.5	0650	12.5	1336	1.5	1914	12.5
15	SA	0155	1.3	0728	12.7	1420	1.5	1951	12.6
16	SU	0237	1.3	0804	12.8	1500	1.6	2025	12.6
17	M	0313	1.5	0838	12.7	1531	1.8	2057	12.5
18	TU	0338	1.7	0907	12.6	1550	2.0	2125	12.4
19	W	0355	1.8	0936	12.5	1605	1.9	2154	12.3
20	TH	0418	1.7	1009	12.4	1632	1.9	2228	12.1
21	F	0450	1.8	1046	12.0	1706	2.0	2308	11.6
22	SA ☾	0528	2.2	1131	11.4	1747	2.5	2357	11.0
23	SU	0615	2.8	1228	10.7	1839	3.2		
24	M	0102	10.4	0721	3.5	1346	10.2	1958	3.8
25	TU	0235	10.2	0920	3.6	1528	10.5	2217	3.4
26	W	0412	11.0	1057	2.7	1650	11.4	2334	2.4
27	TH	0520	12.1	1205	1.7	1750	12.6		
28	F	0035	1.4	0615	13.3	1303	0.8	1842	13.5

MARCH

Date	Day	Time	m	Time	m	Time	m	Time	m
1	SA ●	0131	0.6	0704	14.1	1357	0.2	1929	14.1
2	SU	0222	0.1	0750	14.5	1445	-0.1	2013	14.4
3	M	0307	0.0	0833	14.6	1528	-0.1	2054	14.3
4	TU	0346	0.2	0913	14.3	1603	0.3	2132	13.9
5	W	0417	0.7	0950	13.7	1629	1.0	2205	13.2
6	TH	0438	1.3	1022	12.8	1649	1.6	2235	12.3
7	F	0456	1.9	1054	11.8	1712	2.2	2305	11.4
8	SA ☽	0524	2.5	1128	10.7	1745	2.9	2343	10.4
9	SU	0603	3.3	1217	9.7	1834	3.6		
10	M	0043	9.5	0704	4.0	1355	9.1	1948	4.2
11	TU	0239	9.3	0832	4.2	1529	9.4	2121	4.0
12	W	0355	9.9	1017	3.6	1631	10.3	2250	3.1
13	TH	0452	10.8	1127	2.7	1722	11.2	2349	2.2
14	F	0540	11.7	1219	1.9	1806	12.0		
15	SA	0040	1.6	0622	12.3	1308	1.5	1845	12.5
16	SU O	0127	1.3	0701	12.7	1353	1.4	1923	12.7
17	M	0211	1.2	0738	12.8	1434	1.4	1959	12.8
18	TU	0250	1.3	0813	12.9	1509	1.6	2032	12.8
19	W	0320	1.5	0845	12.9	1532	1.7	2102	12.7
20	TH	0341	1.5	0917	12.8	1549	1.7	2134	12.6
21	F	0403	1.5	0951	12.6	1613	1.7	2209	12.4
22	SA	0433	1.6	1029	12.2	1646	1.9	2249	11.9
23	SU	0510	2.0	1114	11.6	1726	2.4	2338	11.2
24	M ☾	0556	2.6	1210	10.7	1818	3.2		
25	TU	0043	10.4	0702	3.4	1329	10.1	1938	3.8
26	W	0221	10.2	0907	3.5	1515	10.4	2203	3.4
27	TH	0355	10.9	1039	2.6	1633	11.4	2315	2.3
28	F	0502	12.1	1144	1.6	1732	12.5		
29	SA	0013	1.3	0555	13.1	1240	0.8	1822	13.4
30	SU ●	0107	0.6	0644	13.8	1332	0.2	1907	14.0
31	M	0157	0.2	0728	14.2	1420	0.0	1950	14.1

APRIL

Date	Day	Time	m	Time	m	Time	m	Time	m
1	TU	0242	0.1	0810	14.2	1502	0.1	2029	14.0
2	W	0321	0.4	0849	13.9	1537	0.6	2105	13.6
3	TH	0352	0.9	0924	13.3	1602	1.2	2137	13.0
4	F	0412	1.5	0955	12.5	1620	1.7	2205	12.2
5	SA	0429	1.9	1024	11.7	1641	2.2	2234	11.4
6	SU	0455	2.4	1056	10.8	1712	2.7	2308	10.6
7	M ☽	0531	3.0	1137	9.9	1755	3.4	2357	9.7
8	TU	0625	3.7	1246	9.2	1904	4.0		
9	W	0133	9.2	0747	4.1	1438	9.2	2033	4.1
10	TH	0310	9.6	0914	3.8	1549	9.9	2157	3.4
11	F	0412	10.5	1037	3.0	1643	10.8	2307	2.6
12	SA	0502	11.3	1139	2.2	1730	11.7		
13	SU	0003	1.9	0547	12.0	1231	1.7	1812	12.3
14	M	0052	1.5	0628	12.5	1319	1.5	1852	12.7
15	TU O	0138	1.3	0708	12.8	1402	1.4	1929	12.9
16	W	0220	1.2	0746	13.0	1440	1.4	2006	13.0
17	TH	0256	1.3	0823	13.0	1511	1.5	2041	13.0
18	F	0326	1.3	0900	13.0	1537	1.5	2118	12.9
19	SA	0354	1.3	0938	12.8	1604	1.6	2156	12.6
20	SU	0425	1.5	1019	12.4	1637	1.9	2239	12.1
21	M	0504	1.9	1106	11.7	1718	2.4	2330	11.4
22	TU ☾	0552	2.5	1202	10.9	1812	3.1		
23	W	0036	10.7	0701	3.1	1321	10.4	1940	3.6
24	TH	0209	10.5	0849	3.1	1455	10.6	2137	3.1
25	F	0332	11.1	1011	2.4	1608	11.4	2247	2.3
26	SA	0436	12.0	1115	1.6	1706	12.3	2345	1.5
27	SU	0531	12.8	1211	1.0	1757	13.0		
28	M	0038	0.9	0619	13.3	1303	0.6	1842	13.5
29	TU ●	0128	0.6	0704	13.6	1350	0.5	1924	13.6
30	W	0214	0.6	0746	13.5	1433	0.6	2003	13.5

MAY

Date	Day	Time	m	Time	m	Time	m	Time	m
1	TH	0254	0.8	0825	13.3	1510	0.9	2040	13.1
2	F	0328	1.2	0900	12.8	1537	1.4	2112	12.7
3	SA	0351	1.7	0932	12.2	1557	1.9	2141	12.1
4	SU	0409	2.1	1002	11.6	1619	2.2	2210	11.5
5	M	0434	2.4	1033	10.9	1648	2.5	2244	10.8
6	TU	0509	2.8	1111	10.3	1727	3.0	2326	10.2
7	W ☽	0555	3.3	1203	9.7	1823	3.6		
8	TH	0031	9.7	0702	3.7	1323	9.4	1942	3.9
9	F	0203	9.7	0821	3.6	1449	9.8	2101	3.6
10	SA	0318	10.2	0935	3.2	1554	10.5	2212	2.9
11	SU	0416	10.9	1045	2.6	1647	11.3	2316	2.3
12	M	0507	11.7	1146	2.1	1735	12.0		
13	TU	0011	1.8	0553	12.3	1239	1.7	1819	12.6
14	W O	0102	1.4	0637	12.7	1328	1.4	1901	13.0
15	TH	0149	1.2	0720	13.0	1412	1.3	1942	13.2
16	F	0232	1.1	0803	13.2	1452	1.3	2024	13.3
17	SA	0313	1.1	0846	13.2	1529	1.3	2106	13.2
18	SU	0350	1.1	0930	13.0	1603	1.5	2149	12.9
19	M	0428	1.3	1015	12.6	1640	1.8	2235	12.5
20	TU	0509	1.7	1102	12.1	1722	2.2	2326	11.8
21	W ☾	0557	2.1	1157	11.4	1815	2.7		
22	TH	0029	11.2	0659	2.5	1306	10.9	1930	3.1
23	F	0149	11.0	0818	2.7	1426	10.9	2101	3.0
24	SA	0303	11.2	0935	2.5	1536	11.2	2212	2.5
25	SU	0406	11.7	1040	2.0	1636	11.8	2313	1.9
26	M	0503	12.2	1138	1.6	1729	12.3		
27	TU	0007	1.5	0553	12.6	1231	1.2	1815	12.8
28	W ●	0058	1.2	0639	12.8	1320	1.1	1859	13.0
29	TH	0145	1.1	0722	12.8	1405	1.1	1939	12.9
30	F	0229	1.3	0803	12.7	1445	1.3	2017	12.8
31	SA	0306	1.6	0840	12.4	1518	1.6	2051	12.4

JUNE

Date	Day	Time	m	Time	m	Time	m	Time	m
1	SU	0335	1.9	0914	12.0	1542	1.9	2123	12.0
2	M	0356	2.2	0945	11.6	1604	2.2	2154	11.6
3	TU	0420	2.3	1016	11.2	1632	2.3	2226	11.2
4	W	0451	2.5	1050	10.8	1707	2.6	2303	10.8
5	TH ☽	0531	2.8	1132	10.4	1751	3.0	2351	10.4
6	F	0622	3.1	1225	10.1	1850	3.4		
7	SA	0053	10.1	0726	3.3	1335	10.0	2003	3.5
8	SU	0208	10.2	0839	3.3	1450	10.3	2119	3.2
9	M	0320	10.7	0952	2.9	1558	10.9	2229	2.7
10	TU	0423	11.3	1101	2.4	1656	11.7	2332	2.1
11	W	0519	12.0	1202	1.9	1748	12.4		
12	TH	0028	1.6	0610	12.6	1257	1.5	1836	13.0
13	F O	0122	1.2	0659	13.1	1349	1.3	1923	13.4
14	SA	0213	1.0	0747	13.3	1438	1.1	2010	13.6
15	SU	0302	0.9	0835	13.4	1523	1.1	2056	13.6
16	M	0347	0.8	0922	13.4	1605	1.1	2142	13.4
17	TU	0430	0.9	1008	13.1	1645	1.4	2229	13.1
18	W	0511	1.2	1055	12.7	1725	1.7	2318	12.5
19	TH ☾	0554	1.6	1144	12.0	1809	2.2		
20	F	0013	11.8	0641	2.1	1242	11.4	1902	2.7
21	SA	0119	11.3	0739	2.5	1351	11.0	2013	3.0
22	SU	0230	11.0	0849	2.7	1500	10.9	2132	3.0
23	M	0334	11.1	1001	2.7	1603	11.1	2240	2.7
24	TU	0434	11.4	1105	2.3	1700	11.6	2338	2.2
25	W	0528	11.8	1201	1.9	1750	12.0		
26	TH	0030	1.8	0616	12.1	1252	1.6	1836	12.4
27	F ●	0120	1.6	0701	12.3	1340	1.4	1918	12.6
28	SA	0206	1.5	0742	12.4	1423	1.5	1957	12.6
29	SU	0247	1.7	0821	12.3	1502	1.6	2033	12.4
30	M	0323	1.9	0856	12.1	1532	1.9	2107	12.2

SUNRISE AND SUNSET TIMES

BRISTOL (AVONMOUTH)
At 51°30′N 2°44′W

		Sunrise	Sunset
UT			
Jan	01	0817	1613
	15	0810	1632
Feb	01	0749	1701
	15	0725	1726
Mar	01	0656	1751
	15	0625	1816
BST			
Apr	01	0646	1944
	15	0615	2008
May	01	0543	2034
	15	0519	2056
Jun	01	0459	2119
	15	0453	2130
Jul	01	0458	2131
	15	0511	2122
Aug	01	0535	2059
	15	0557	2033
Sep	01	0624	1957
	15	0646	1925
Oct	01	0712	1848
	15	0735	1817
UT			
Nov	01	0705	1644
	15	0729	1621
Dec	01	0754	1605
	15	0810	1602

BRISTOL (AVONMOUTH)
LAT 51°30′N
LONG 2°44′W

TIMES AND HEIGHTS OF HIGH AND LOW WATER (Heights in Metres)

TIME ZONE UT
For Summer Time (area enclosed in shaded box) add 1 hour

2014

JULY

Date	Time	m	Date	Time	m
1 TU	0350 0928 1555 2138	2.2 11.8 2.1 11.9	16 W	0424 0956 1640 2216	0.5 13.6 0.9 13.6
2 W	0410 0958 1618 2207	2.3 11.6 2.2 11.6	17 TH	0502 1039 1715 2300	0.8 13.2 1.3 13.0
3 TH	0435 1029 1647 2239	2.3 11.3 2.3 11.3	18 F	0537 1123 1749 2347	1.3 12.5 1.9 12.2
4 F	0507 1103 1724 2318	2.4 11.0 2.5 11.0	19 SA ☾	0614 1210 1827	1.9 11.6 2.5
5 SA ☽	0547 1146 1809	2.6 10.7 2.9	20 SU	0042 0656 1309 1917	11.3 2.6 10.8 3.2
6 SU	0008 0636 1241 1907	10.7 2.9 10.4 3.3	21 M	0152 0753 1422 2032	10.6 3.2 10.4 3.6
7 M	0111 0740 1349 2024	10.4 3.2 10.3 3.4	22 TU	0303 0911 1531 2205	10.4 3.4 10.4 3.5
8 TU	0225 0900 1508 2147	10.5 3.3 10.6 3.1	23 W	0407 1031 1633 2311	10.6 3.1 10.9 2.9
9 W	0342 1022 1622 2300	10.9 2.9 11.3 2.5	24 TH	0504 1133 1727	11.1 2.5 11.5
10 TH	0450 1133 1723	11.7 2.3 12.1	25 F	0006 0555 1227 1814	2.3 11.7 1.9 12.1
11 F	0004 0548 1235 1817	1.8 12.4 1.7 13.0	26 SA ●	0056 0640 1316 1857	1.8 12.1 1.5 12.5
12 SA ○	0104 0642 1333 1907	1.3 13.1 1.3 13.6	27 SU	0144 0722 1403 1937	1.5 12.3 1.4 12.6
13 SU	0200 0734 1427 1957	0.9 13.5 0.9 13.9	28 M	0228 0800 1445 2014	1.5 12.4 1.5 12.6
14 M	0253 0823 1517 2045	0.6 13.8 0.7 14.1	29 TU	0308 0836 1521 2048	1.7 12.3 1.7 12.4
15 TU	0341 0911 1601 2131	0.4 13.8 0.7 14.0	30 W	0340 0908 1547 2118	2.0 12.1 2.0 12.2
			31 TH	0401 0937 1604 2146	2.2 11.9 2.1 12.0

AUGUST

Date	Time	m	Date	Time	m
1 F	0416 1005 1626 2214	2.2 11.7 2.1 11.8	16 SA	0513 1055 1721 2315	1.3 12.6 1.9 12.2
2 SA	0442 1035 1657 2249	2.2 11.5 2.2 11.5	17 SU ☾	0540 1133 1750 2359	2.0 11.6 2.6 11.1
3 SU	0516 1113 1735 2333	2.3 11.2 2.6 11.1	18 M	0614 1220 1831	2.8 10.6 3.4
4 M ☽	0557 1202 1823	2.7 10.7 3.1	19 TU	0103 0703 1337 1932	10.1 3.5 9.9 4.1
5 TU	0029 0649 1304 1929	10.6 3.2 10.3 3.5	20 W	0232 0815 1502 2118	9.7 4.0 9.8 4.2
6 W	0141 0806 1426 2109	10.3 3.6 10.3 3.5	21 TH	0342 0956 1608 2248	10.0 3.7 10.4 3.4
7 TH	0309 0951 1555 2238	10.5 3.3 10.9 2.9	22 F	0441 1108 1704 2343	10.7 2.9 11.2 2.5
8 F	0429 1114 1704 2348	11.3 2.6 11.9 2.0	23 SA	0532 1202 1752	11.4 2.1 12.0
9 SA	0534 1220 1802	12.3 1.8 13.0	24 SU	0032 0617 1252 1834	1.8 12.1 1.5 12.5
10 SU ○	0050 0629 1320 1853	1.2 13.1 1.2 13.8	25 M ●	0120 0657 1339 1913	1.4 12.5 1.3 12.8
11 M	0148 0720 1415 1943	0.7 13.8 0.7 14.3	26 TU	0205 0735 1423 1950	1.3 12.6 1.3 12.8
12 TU	0241 0808 1505 2029	0.3 14.1 0.3 14.5	27 W	0247 0811 1502 2024	1.5 12.5 1.5 12.7
13 W	0329 0854 1549 2114	0.1 14.2 0.3 14.4	28 TH	0322 0843 1532 2054	1.8 12.4 1.8 12.5
14 TH	0410 0937 1626 2156	0.2 13.9 0.6 13.9	29 F	0345 0912 1549 2122	2.1 12.2 2.1 12.3
15 F	0444 1017 1656 2236	0.7 13.4 1.2 13.2	30 SA	0356 0939 1605 2150	2.2 12.0 2.1 12.1
			31 SU	0417 1009 1633 2224	2.2 11.8 2.1 11.9

SEPTEMBER

Date	Time	m	Date	Time	m
1 M	0447 1046 1707 2306	2.3 11.5 2.4 11.4	16 TU ☾	0535 1135 1751	3.0 10.5 3.5
2 TU ☽	0525 1132 1750 2359	2.6 10.9 3.0 10.7	17 W	0007 0619 1238 1847	9.8 3.7 9.6 4.2
3 W	0613 1232 1850	3.2 10.4 3.6	18 TH	0153 0729 1430 2017	9.2 4.3 9.4 4.5
4 TH	0110 0722 1357 2036	10.1 3.8 10.1 3.9	19 F	0313 0907 1539 2218	9.5 4.2 10.0 3.8
5 F	0248 0933 1537 2225	10.2 3.7 10.7 3.1	20 SA	0413 1038 1635 2316	10.3 3.3 10.9 2.8
6 SA	0416 1102 1649 2336	11.1 2.8 11.9 2.0	21 SU	0504 1134 1724	11.2 2.3 11.8
7 SU	0520 1206 1747	12.3 1.8 13.0	22 M	0005 0548 1224 1806	1.9 12.0 1.6 12.5
8 M	0036 0614 1304 1837	1.1 13.3 1.0 13.9	23 TU	0051 0628 1310 1845	1.4 12.5 1.3 12.8
9 TU ○	0131 0703 1357 1925	0.4 14.0 0.4 14.5	24 W ●	0136 0706 1355 1922	1.3 12.7 1.3 12.9
10 W	0222 0749 1445 2010	0.0 14.3 0.2 14.7	25 TH	0218 0742 1435 1957	1.4 12.8 1.4 12.9
11 TH	0308 0832 1528 2052	0.0 14.3 0.2 14.5	26 F	0255 0815 1508 2029	1.6 12.6 1.7 12.7
12 F	0347 0913 1604 2132	0.3 14.0 0.7 13.9	27 SA	0322 0846 1530 2058	2.0 12.5 2.0 12.6
13 SA	0420 0950 1632 2209	0.8 13.4 1.3 13.1	28 SU	0337 0915 1547 2130	2.1 12.4 2.0 12.4
14 SU	0443 1024 1651 2243	1.6 12.5 2.1 12.0	29 M	0356 0948 1614 2206	2.1 12.1 2.1 12.1
15 M	0505 1057 1715 2319	2.3 11.6 2.7 10.9	30 TU	0426 1026 1648 2248	2.2 11.7 2.4 11.5

OCTOBER

Date	Time	m	Date	Time	m
1 W ☽	0503 1112 1730 2340	2.6 11.1 2.9 10.8	16 TH	0543 1150 1810	3.7 9.8 4.1
2 TH	0550 1212 1828	3.3 10.5 3.6	17 F	0038 0645 1337 1929	9.2 4.3 9.3 4.5
3 F	0050 0657 1339 2018	10.1 3.9 10.2 3.9	18 SA	0232 0813 1501 2103	9.3 4.4 9.8 4.2
4 SA	0235 0922 1522 2210	10.2 3.8 10.8 3.1	19 SU	0336 0944 1559 2233	10.0 3.7 10.6 3.3
5 SU	0400 1045 1632 2317	11.1 2.8 11.9 2.0	20 M	0428 1054 1648 2328	10.9 2.8 11.5 2.4
6 M	0502 1146 1728	12.3 1.7 13.0	21 TU	0514 1147 1733	11.7 2.0 12.2
7 TU	0014 0554 1241 1817	1.0 13.3 0.9 13.9	22 W	0016 0556 1235 1813	1.8 12.4 1.6 12.7
8 W ○	0107 0641 1332 1904	0.4 13.9 0.5 14.4	23 TH ●	0102 0635 1320 1852	1.5 12.7 1.4 12.9
9 TH	0156 0726 1420 1947	0.1 14.2 0.3 14.5	24 F	0145 0712 1403 1929	1.4 12.9 1.5 13.0
10 F	0242 0808 1503 2029	0.2 14.2 0.5 14.2	25 SA	0224 0748 1440 2004	1.6 12.9 1.6 13.0
11 SA	0321 0847 1539 2108	0.5 13.8 0.9 13.7	26 SU	0256 0822 1510 2039	1.8 12.9 1.8 12.9
12 SU	0353 0923 1606 2143	1.1 13.2 1.6 12.9	27 M	0321 0857 1536 2115	1.9 12.7 1.9 12.7
13 M	0415 0956 1625 2215	1.8 12.4 2.2 11.9	28 TU	0345 0934 1605 2155	2.0 12.5 2.0 12.3
14 TU	0435 1026 1647 2247	2.4 11.6 2.8 10.9	29 W	0416 1015 1641 2238	2.2 12.1 2.3 11.8
15 W ☾	0503 1101 1720 2327	3.0 10.7 3.4 10.0	30 TH	0454 1102 1724 2330	2.6 11.5 2.8 11.1
			31 F ☽	0542 1202 1824	3.2 10.8 3.4

NOVEMBER

Date	Time	m	Date	Time	m
1 SA	0038 0649 1326 2002	10.5 3.8 10.5 3.6	16 SU	0106 0717 1355 2000	9.4 4.2 9.6 4.1
2 SU	0215 0858 1459 2141	10.4 3.7 11.0 3.0	17 M	0238 0838 1508 2117	9.6 4.0 10.1 3.7
3 M	0336 1017 1607 2249	11.1 2.8 11.8 2.1	18 TU	0341 0952 1604 2231	10.3 3.4 10.9 3.0
4 TU	0438 1118 1704 2346	12.1 1.9 12.7 1.3	19 W	0433 1058 1654 2331	11.2 2.7 11.6 2.3
5 W	0531 1213 1755	12.9 1.2 13.4	20 TH	0520 1153 1739	11.9 2.1 12.2
6 TH ○	0039 0618 1305 1841	0.8 13.5 0.8 13.9	21 F	0022 0602 1243 1821	1.9 12.5 1.7 12.7
7 F	0128 0702 1353 1925	0.5 13.8 0.7 13.9	22 SA ●	0109 0643 1329 1903	1.6 12.9 1.5 13.0
8 SA	0214 0744 1437 2007	0.6 13.8 0.8 13.7	23 SU	0153 0724 1413 1944	1.5 13.2 1.4 13.1
9 SU	0254 0823 1515 2046	0.9 13.5 1.2 13.3	24 M	0233 0803 1453 2025	1.5 13.2 1.5 13.2
10 M	0328 0900 1545 2121	1.4 13.0 1.8 12.6	25 TU	0310 0844 1530 2106	1.6 13.2 1.6 13.0
11 TU	0352 0932 1605 2153	1.9 12.4 2.3 11.9	26 W	0343 0926 1606 2149	1.8 13.0 1.7 12.7
12 W	0413 1003 1627 2224	2.4 11.7 2.7 11.2	27 TH	0417 1010 1644 2234	2.0 12.6 2.0 12.3
13 TH	0440 1036 1658 2300	2.8 11.0 3.1 10.4	28 F	0456 1058 1727 2324	2.3 12.1 2.3 11.7
14 F ☾	0515 1118 1741 2348	3.3 10.3 3.6 9.8	29 SA ☽	0542 1153 1822	2.8 11.5 2.8
15 SA	0605 1219 1842	3.8 9.7 4.0	30 SU	0024 0643 1305 1934	11.1 3.2 11.1 3.1

DECEMBER

Date	Time	m	Date	Time	m
1 M	0144 0815 1428 2102	10.8 3.4 11.1 3.0	16 TU	0108 0733 1346 2012	9.8 3.8 10.0 3.8
2 TU	0303 0941 1537 2214	11.0 3.0 11.5 2.5	17 W	0229 0850 1503 2128	9.9 3.7 10.3 3.5
3 W	0408 1047 1637 2315	11.6 2.4 12.1 2.0	18 TH	0341 1004 1607 2240	10.5 3.2 10.9 2.9
4 TH	0504 1144 1731	12.3 1.9 12.7	19 F	0440 1110 1703 2342	11.3 2.6 11.7 2.3
5 F	0010 0554 1237 1819	1.4 12.8 1.4 13.1	20 SA	0531 1207 1753	12.1 2.0 12.4
6 SA ○	0100 0639 1326 1904	1.1 13.2 1.2 13.2	21 SU	0036 0618 1300 1840	1.8 12.8 1.6 12.9
7 SU	0147 0722 1412 1947	1.0 13.3 1.2 13.2	22 M ●	0127 0703 1351 1927	1.5 13.3 1.3 13.3
8 M	0230 0803 1454 2027	1.2 13.2 1.5 12.9	23 TU	0216 0748 1440 2013	1.3 13.6 1.2 13.5
9 TU	0308 0840 1528 2103	1.5 12.9 1.9 12.5	24 W	0301 0833 1525 2058	1.3 13.7 1.1 13.5
10 W	0337 0915 1553 2136	1.9 12.5 2.3 12.0	25 TH	0343 0918 1607 2143	1.3 13.6 1.2 13.3
11 TH	0359 0946 1614 2206	2.2 12.0 2.5 11.5	26 F	0422 1003 1646 2227	1.5 13.4 1.3 13.0
12 F	0423 1017 1641 2238	2.5 11.5 2.7 11.0	27 SA	0459 1049 1726 2313	1.7 12.9 1.7 12.4
13 SA	0454 1052 1716 2315	2.7 11.0 3.0 10.5	28 SU ☽	0538 1138 1809	2.1 12.3 2.1
14 SU ☾	0533 1134 1800	3.1 10.5 3.3	29 M	0003 0624 1237 1900	11.7 2.6 11.6 2.6
15 M	0003 0624 1231 1858	10.1 3.5 10.1 3.6	30 TU	0107 0724 1350 2008	11.1 3.1 11.1 3.0
			31 W	0224 0852 1504 2132	10.8 3.4 11.0 3.1

COBH

LAT 51°51'N
LONG 8°18'W

TIMES AND HEIGHTS OF HIGH AND LOW WATER (Heights in Metres)

TIME ZONE UT
For Summer Time (area enclosed in shaded box) add 1 hour

2014

JANUARY

Date	Time	m
1 W ●	0454 1127 1717 2350	4.2 0.4 4.2 0.3
2 TH	0545 1215 1806	4.4 0.3 4.3
3 F	0037 0633 1303 1852	0.2 4.4 0.3 4.3
4 SA	0124 0720 1349 1939	0.2 4.4 0.3 4.2
5 SU	0211 0807 1436 2026	0.3 4.3 0.4 4.1
6 M	0259 0855 1524 2113	0.4 4.1 0.6 3.9
7 TU	0349 0944 1613 2202	0.6 3.9 0.8 3.7
8 W ☽	0442 1035 1707 2255	0.8 3.7 1.0 3.6
9 TH	0540 1133 1808 2358	1.0 3.6 1.1 3.4
10 F	0646 1238 1917	1.1 3.4 1.2
11 SA	0110 0756 1348 2026	3.4 1.2 3.4 1.2
12 SU	0221 0903 1450 2129	3.4 1.1 3.5 1.1
13 M	0321 1001 1545 2222	3.6 1.0 3.7 1.0
14 TU	0412 1049 1632 2304	3.8 0.9 3.8 0.8
15 W	0456 1128 1713 2339	3.9 0.8 3.9 0.7
16 TH O	0535 1200 1748	4.1 0.8 4.0
17 F	0009 0608 1230 1820	0.7 4.1 0.8 4.0
18 SA	0037 0640 1259 1851	0.7 4.1 0.8 4.0
19 SU	0107 0710 1331 1921	0.7 4.1 0.8 4.0
20 M	0140 0742 1406 1955	0.8 4.0 0.9 3.9
21 TU	0217 0817 1443 2031	0.9 4.0 1.0 3.9
22 W	0257 0855 1523 2112	1.0 3.9 1.1 3.8
23 TH	0341 0939 1608 2159	1.1 3.8 1.2 3.7
24 F ☾	0433 1030 1702 2256	1.2 3.7 1.3 3.6
25 SA	0535 1131 1813	1.3 3.6 1.4
26 SU	0004 0648 1242 1930	3.5 1.3 3.5 1.3
27 M	0119 0804 1356 2043	3.6 1.2 3.6 1.1
28 TU	0234 0916 1508 2149	3.7 0.9 3.7 0.8
29 W	0342 1020 1611 2246	3.9 0.6 4.0 0.5
30 TH ●	0440 1114 1705 2337	4.2 0.4 4.2 0.2
31 F	0531 1203 1753	4.4 0.2 4.3

FEBRUARY

Date	Time	m
1 SA	0023 0618 1249 1837	0.1 4.4 0.1 4.3
2 SU	0108 0702 1332 1921	0.0 4.4 0.1 4.3
3 M	0152 0746 1416 2003	0.1 4.3 0.2 4.2
4 TU	0237 0829 1459 2045	0.2 4.2 0.4 4.0
5 W	0321 0913 1542 2128	0.5 4.0 0.6 3.8
6 TH ☽	0407 0957 1629 2214	0.7 3.7 0.9 3.6
7 F	0458 1047 1722 2308	1.0 3.5 1.1 3.4
8 SA	0557 1148 1826	1.2 3.3 1.3
9 SU	0021 0708 1306 1941	3.2 1.3 3.2 1.3
10 M	0146 0825 1420 2057	3.2 1.3 3.3 1.2
11 TU	0255 0935 1521 2159	3.4 1.1 3.5 1.0
12 W	0350 1027 1611 2245	3.6 0.9 3.7 0.8
13 TH	0435 1108 1653 2321	3.8 0.8 3.9 0.7
14 F O	0514 1141 1730 2350	4.0 0.7 4.0 0.6
15 SA	0549 1209 1802	4.1 0.6 4.0
16 SU	0016 0619 1237 1831	0.6 4.1 0.6 4.0
17 M	0044 0647 1308 1900	0.6 4.1 0.7 4.0
18 TU	0116 0717 1341 1931	0.6 4.0 0.7 4.0
19 W	0152 0749 1416 2005	0.7 4.0 0.8 4.0
20 TH	0231 0826 1454 2043	0.8 3.9 0.9 3.9
21 F	0313 0908 1535 2127	0.9 3.8 1.0 3.8
22 SA ☾	0402 0957 1627 2222	1.0 3.7 1.2 3.6
23 SU	0501 1057 1735 2331	1.2 3.5 1.3 3.5
24 M	0616 1211 1858	1.3 3.3 1.3
25 TU	0051 0737 1334 2019	3.4 1.2 3.4 1.1
26 W	0215 0856 1452 2130	3.6 0.9 3.6 0.8
27 TH	0327 1004 1557 2230	3.8 0.6 3.9 0.4
28 F	0425 1059 1650 2321	4.1 0.3 4.1 0.2

MARCH

Date	Time	m
1 SA ●	0514 1146 1736	4.3 0.1 4.3
2 SU	0006 0559 1230 1819	0.0 4.4 0.0 4.3
3 M	0049 0641 1311 1859	0.0 4.4 0.0 4.3
4 TU	0131 0722 1352 1938	0.0 4.3 0.1 4.2
5 W	0212 0801 1432 2017	0.2 4.1 0.3 4.0
6 TH	0253 0841 1512 2055	0.4 3.9 0.6 3.8
7 F	0335 0921 1554 2137	0.6 3.7 0.8 3.6
8 SA ☽	0421 1005 1642 2225	0.9 3.4 1.1 3.3
9 SU	0513 1059 1743 2330	1.2 3.2 1.3 3.1
10 M	0623 1218 1857	1.3 3.0 1.4
11 TU	0135 0740 1346 2016	3.1 1.3 3.1 1.3
12 W	0224 0856 1452 2124	3.2 1.2 3.3 1.1
13 TH	0321 0954 1544 2215	3.5 0.9 3.5 0.8
14 F	0407 1038 1627 2253	3.7 0.7 3.7 0.7
15 SA	0447 1112 1704 2323	3.9 0.6 3.9 0.6
16 SU O	0521 1142 1737 2350	4.0 0.5 4.0 0.5
17 M	0552 1212 1807	4.0 0.5 4.0
18 TU	0019 0620 1243 1836	0.5 4.0 0.5 4.0
19 W	0053 0651 1317 1908	0.5 4.0 0.5 4.0
20 TH	0130 0725 1353 1943	0.5 4.0 0.6 4.0
21 F	0209 0803 1432 2022	0.6 3.9 0.7 3.9
22 SA	0253 0846 1516 2108	0.7 3.8 0.8 3.8
23 SU	0343 0936 1608 2203	0.9 3.6 1.0 3.6
24 M ☾	0442 1038 1715 2311	1.0 3.4 1.1 3.4
25 TU	0555 1152 1836	1.1 3.3 1.2
26 W	0034 0717 1317 1958	3.4 1.1 3.3 1.0
27 TH	0159 0837 1435 2111	3.5 0.8 3.5 0.7
28 F	0309 0945 1539 2211	3.8 0.5 3.8 0.4
29 SA	0406 1039 1631 2302	4.0 0.3 4.0 0.2
30 SU ●	0454 1126 1717 2347	4.2 0.1 4.2 0.0
31 M	0538 1209 1759	4.3 0.0 4.2

APRIL

Date	Time	m
1 TU	0028 0619 1249 1837	0.0 4.3 0.1 4.2
2 W	0109 0657 1328 1914	0.1 4.2 0.2 4.1
3 TH	0147 0734 1406 1950	0.2 4.0 0.4 4.0
4 F	0226 0811 1444 2027	0.4 3.8 0.6 3.8
5 SA	0306 0849 1524 2106	0.7 3.6 0.8 3.6
6 SU	0350 0930 1609 2151	0.9 3.4 1.0 3.4
7 M ☽	0441 1019 1705 2248	1.1 3.2 1.2 3.2
8 TU	0543 1126 1814	1.3 3.0 1.3
9 W	0010 0654 1256 1928	3.1 1.3 3.0 1.3
10 TH	0139 0805 1411 2034	3.2 1.2 3.2 1.1
11 F	0241 0905 1506 2128	3.4 1.0 3.4 0.9
12 SA	0329 0954 1551 2211	3.6 0.8 3.6 0.7
13 SU	0410 1034 1630 2248	3.8 0.6 3.8 0.6
14 M	0447 1110 1706 2321	3.9 0.5 3.9 0.5
15 TU O	0521 1145 1740 2355	4.0 0.5 4.0 0.4
16 W	0554 1220 1814	4.0 0.4 4.0
17 TH	0032 0628 1258 1849	0.4 4.0 0.4 4.0
18 F	0112 0707 1337 1927	0.4 4.0 0.5 4.0
19 SA	0154 0748 1420 2010	0.5 3.9 0.6 3.9
20 SU	0241 0835 1507 2059	0.6 3.8 0.7 3.8
21 M	0333 0927 1601 2155	0.7 3.6 0.8 3.6
22 TU ☾	0432 1028 1706 2302	0.9 3.4 1.0 3.5
23 W	0542 1140 1821	1.0 3.3 1.0
24 TH	0020 0659 1259 1939	3.4 0.9 3.4 0.9
25 F	0140 0816 1414 2050	3.5 0.8 3.5 0.7
26 SA	0246 0922 1516 2150	3.7 0.5 3.8 0.4
27 SU	0343 1017 1609 2241	3.9 0.4 3.9 0.3
28 M	0432 1105 1656 2327	4.1 0.2 4.1 0.2
29 TU ●	0516 1147 1738	4.1 0.2 4.1
30 W	0008 0556 1228 1816	0.2 4.1 0.2 4.1

MAY

Date	Time	m
1 TH	0047 0634 1305 1852	0.3 4.0 0.3 4.0
2 F	0124 0710 1342 1926	0.4 3.9 0.5 3.9
3 SA	0201 0745 1419 2002	0.6 3.8 0.6 3.8
4 SU	0239 0822 1457 2041	0.7 3.6 0.8 3.6
5 M	0320 0902 1539 2123	0.9 3.5 1.0 3.5
6 TU	0408 0947 1629 2213	1.1 3.3 1.1 3.3
7 W ☽	0504 1043 1730 2315	1.2 3.2 1.2 3.2
8 TH	0608 1152 1837	1.3 3.1 1.3
9 F	0032 0713 1309 1940	3.2 1.2 3.2 1.2
10 SA	0143 0812 1412 2036	3.3 1.1 3.4 1.0
11 SU	0238 0904 1503 2125	3.5 0.9 3.6 0.8
12 M	0325 0952 1549 2210	3.7 0.7 3.7 0.7
13 TU	0408 1037 1631 2252	3.8 0.6 3.9 0.5
14 W O	0449 1119 1712 2334	3.9 0.5 4.0 0.4
15 TH	0529 1200 1753	4.0 0.4 4.1
16 F	0015 0611 1243 1834	0.4 4.0 0.4 4.1
17 SA	0059 0654 1326 1917	0.3 4.0 0.4 4.1
18 SU	0145 0740 1412 2004	0.4 3.9 0.4 4.0
19 M	0234 0829 1502 2055	0.5 3.8 0.5 3.9
20 TU	0326 0922 1556 2150	0.6 3.7 0.6 3.8
21 W ☾	0424 1020 1656 2252	0.7 3.6 0.8 3.6
22 TH	0528 1125 1804	0.8 3.5 0.8
23 F	0002 0639 1236 1916	3.5 0.8 3.5 0.8
24 SA	0114 0751 1345 2025	3.6 0.8 3.5 0.7
25 SU	0219 0855 1448 2126	3.7 0.7 3.7 0.6
26 M	0316 0952 1544 2219	3.8 0.6 3.8 0.5
27 TU	0408 1042 1633 2307	3.9 0.5 3.9 0.4
28 W ●	0454 1127 1717 2348	3.9 0.4 4.0 0.4
29 TH	0536 1207 1756	4.0 0.4 4.0
30 F	0026 0613 1244 1832	0.5 3.9 0.5 4.0
31 SA	0102 0648 1319 1906	0.6 3.9 0.6 3.9

JUNE

Date	Time	m
1 SU	0136 0723 1354 1941	0.7 3.8 0.7 3.8
2 M	0212 0758 1430 2018	0.8 3.7 0.8 3.7
3 TU	0251 0837 1508 2058	0.9 3.6 0.9 3.6
4 W	0334 0919 1552 2142	1.0 3.5 1.1 3.5
5 TH ☽	0423 1007 1644 2233	1.1 3.4 1.2 3.4
6 F	0519 1102 1743 2331	1.2 3.3 1.2 3.4
7 SA	0621 1205 1846	1.2 3.3 1.2
8 SU	0035 0721 1310 1945	3.4 1.1 3.4 1.1
9 M	0139 0819 1411 2042	3.5 1.0 3.5 0.9
10 TU	0236 0914 1506 2135	3.6 0.9 3.7 0.8
11 W	0330 1006 1558 2227	3.8 0.7 3.9 0.6
12 TH	0420 1056 1648 2315	3.9 0.5 4.0 0.4
13 F O	0509 1143 1735	4.0 0.4 4.1
14 SA	0002 0556 1230 1821	0.3 4.1 0.3 4.2
15 SU	0049 0643 1316 1908	0.3 4.1 0.3 4.2
16 M	0136 0731 1404 1956	0.3 4.0 0.3 4.1
17 TU	0225 0821 1453 2047	0.3 4.0 0.3 4.0
18 W	0316 0912 1545 2139	0.4 3.8 0.5 3.9
19 TH ☾	0410 1005 1640 2234	0.6 3.7 0.6 3.7
20 F	0508 1102 1741 2335	0.7 3.6 0.7 3.6
21 SA	0612 1205 1848	0.8 3.5 0.8
22 SU	0041 0719 1313 1955	3.5 0.9 3.5 0.8
23 M	0148 0825 1418 2059	3.5 0.8 3.5 0.8
24 TU	0249 0926 1518 2157	3.6 0.8 3.6 0.7
25 W	0344 1021 1611 2247	3.7 0.7 3.8 0.6
26 TH	0433 1108 1657 2330	3.8 0.6 3.9 0.6
27 F ●	0516 1148 1738	3.8 0.6 3.9
28 SA	0007 0554 1224 1814	0.6 3.9 0.6 3.9
29 SU	0040 0629 1256 1848	0.7 3.9 0.6 3.9
30 M	0111 0703 1328 1921	0.7 3.8 0.7 3.9

SUNRISE AND SUNSET TIMES

COBH
At 51°51'N 8°18'W

		Sunrise	Sunset
UT			
Jan	01	0841	1633
	15	0834	1652
Feb	01	0812	1722
	15	0748	1748
Mar	01	0719	1813
	15	0647	1838
BST			
Apr	01	0708	2007
	15	0637	2031
May	01	0604	2058
	15	0540	2120
Jun	01	0520	2143
	15	0513	2154
Jul	01	0518	2155
	15	0532	2146
Aug	01	0556	2122
	15	0618	2056
Sep	01	0645	2020
	15	0708	1948
Oct	01	0734	1911
	15	0758	1839
UT			
Nov	01	0728	1705
	15	0753	1642
Dec	01	0818	1626
	15	0834	1622

COBH
LAT 51°51′N
LONG 8°18′W

TIMES AND HEIGHTS OF HIGH AND LOW WATER (Heights in Metres)

TIME ZONE UT
For Summer Time (area enclosed in shaded box) add 1 hour

2014

JULY

Date	Day	Time	m
1	TU	0144 0736 1401 1955	0.8 3.8 0.8 3.8
2	W	0220 0812 1436 2031	0.9 3.7 0.9 3.8
3	TH	0300 0851 1516 2111	1.0 3.7 1.0 3.7
4	F	0343 0933 1600 2155	1.0 3.6 1.0 3.6
5	SA ☽	0431 1021 1651 2245	1.1 3.5 1.1 3.5
6	SU	0527 1115 1751 2343	1.2 3.5 1.2 3.5
7	M	0631 1218 1857	1.2 3.5 1.2
8	TU	0048 0736 1325 2003	3.5 1.1 3.5 1.1
9	W	0154 0839 1430 2105	3.6 1.0 3.6 0.9
10	TH	0258 0939 1531 2204	3.7 0.8 3.8 0.6
11	F	0357 1035 1627 2258	3.9 0.6 4.0 0.4
12	SA ○	0451 1127 1719 2348	4.0 0.3 4.2 0.3
13	SU	0542 1215 1808	4.1 0.2 4.3
14	M	0036 0630 1302 1855	0.2 4.2 0.1 4.3
15	TU	0123 0718 1349 1942	0.1 4.1 0.1 4.2
16	W	0210 0805 1437 2030	0.2 4.1 0.2 4.1
17	TH	0259 0853 1525 2118	0.3 4.0 0.3 4.0
18	F	0348 0941 1616 2208	0.5 3.8 0.5 3.8
19	SA ☾	0440 1033 1710 2302	0.7 3.6 0.7 3.6
20	SU	0537 1130 1811	0.8 3.5 0.9
21	M	0005 0642 1237 1920	3.4 1.0 3.4 1.0
22	TU	0114 0752 1349 2030	3.4 1.0 3.4 1.0
23	W	0221 0901 1454 2135	3.4 1.0 3.5 0.9
24	TH	0321 1001 1550 2229	3.5 0.9 3.6 0.8
25	F	0412 1050 1638 2312	3.7 0.7 3.8 0.7
26	SA ●	0456 1130 1719 2348	3.8 0.6 3.9 0.7
27	SU	0535 1203 1755	3.9 0.6 4.0
28	M	0017 0609 1232 1827	0.7 3.9 0.6 4.0
29	TU	0046 0642 1300 1858	0.7 3.9 0.7 3.9
30	W	0116 0713 1330 1929	0.7 3.9 0.7 3.9
31	TH	0150 0745 1404 2001	0.8 3.8 0.8 3.9

AUGUST

Date	Day	Time	m
1	F	0226 0820 1442 2038	0.9 3.8 0.9 3.8
2	SA	0305 0859 1523 2118	1.0 3.7 1.0 3.8
3	SU	0348 0942 1609 2205	1.1 3.6 1.1 3.6
4	M ☽	0438 1034 1705 2301	1.2 3.6 1.2 3.5
5	TU	0542 1136 1813	1.2 3.5 1.2
6	W	0007 0656 1247 1927	3.4 1.2 3.5 1.2
7	TH	0121 0809 1401 2039	3.5 1.1 3.6 1.0
8	F	0233 0916 1510 2144	3.6 0.8 3.8 0.7
9	SA	0338 1016 1610 2242	3.8 0.5 4.0 0.4
10	SU ○	0435 1109 1703 2332	4.0 0.3 4.2 0.2
11	M	0526 1158 1751	4.2 0.1 4.3
12	TU	0019 0613 1244 1836	0.1 4.3 0.0 4.4
13	W	0105 0658 1329 1921	0.0 4.2 0.0 4.3
14	TH	0150 0743 1415 2006	0.1 4.2 0.1 4.2
15	F	0235 0828 1500 2050	0.2 4.0 0.3 4.0
16	SA	0321 0912 1546 2136	0.4 3.8 0.5 3.8
17	SU ☾	0408 0959 1636 2225	0.7 3.6 0.8 3.5
18	M	0501 1053 1733 2324	0.9 3.4 1.0 3.3
19	TU	0604 1200 1841	1.1 3.2 1.2
20	W	0038 0717 1321 1959	3.2 1.2 3.2 1.2
21	TH	0155 0834 1432 2111	3.2 1.1 3.3 1.1
22	F	0258 0940 1529 2207	3.4 1.0 3.5 0.9
23	SA	0350 1030 1616 2251	3.6 0.8 3.8 0.8
24	SU	0434 1109 1657 2325	3.8 0.7 3.9 0.7
25	M ●	0513 1140 1732 2353	3.9 0.6 4.0 0.6
26	TU	0547 1205 1804	3.9 0.6 4.0
27	W	0019 0617 1231 1832	0.6 3.9 0.6 4.0
28	TH	0048 0646 1300 1900	0.7 3.9 0.6 4.0
29	F	0120 0717 1334 1931	0.7 3.9 0.7 3.9
30	SA	0155 0749 1411 2006	0.8 3.9 0.8 3.9
31	SU	0233 0826 1451 2045	0.9 3.8 0.9 3.8

SEPTEMBER

Date	Day	Time	m
1	M	0315 0909 1537 2131	1.0 3.7 1.0 3.7
2	TU ☽	0403 1000 1631 2228	1.1 3.6 1.2 3.5
3	W	0506 1104 1740 2337	1.2 3.5 1.3 3.4
4	TH	0624 1219 1900	1.3 3.4 1.2
5	F	0055 0744 1341 2017	3.4 1.1 3.5 1.0
6	SA	0214 0855 1453 2126	3.6 0.8 3.8 0.7
7	SU	0321 0957 1553 2224	3.8 0.5 4.0 0.4
8	M	0418 1051 1645 2314	4.1 0.2 4.3 0.2
9	TU ○	0507 1139 1732	4.2 0.0 4.4
10	W	0000 0553 1224 1815	0.0 4.3 0.0 4.4
11	TH	0044 0636 1308 1858	0.0 4.3 0.0 4.3
12	F	0126 0718 1350 1939	0.1 4.2 0.1 4.2
13	SA	0209 0800 1433 2021	0.3 4.0 0.3 4.0
14	SU	0252 0842 1517 2103	0.5 3.8 0.6 3.8
15	M	0338 0926 1604 2148	0.7 3.6 0.9 3.5
16	TU ☾	0428 1016 1657 2242	1.0 3.4 1.1 3.3
17	W	0528 1121 1803 2356	1.2 3.2 1.3 3.1
18	TH	0641 1249 1922	1.3 3.1 1.3
19	F	0123 0801 1405 2038	3.1 1.2 3.3 1.2
20	SA	0231 0909 1502 2136	3.3 1.1 3.5 1.0
21	SU	0323 1000 1549 2220	3.6 0.9 3.7 0.8
22	M	0407 1039 1629 2255	3.8 0.7 3.9 0.7
23	TU	0446 1110 1705 2323	3.9 0.6 4.0 0.6
24	W ●	0520 1136 1736 2351	4.0 0.6 4.0 0.6
25	TH	0551 1203 1804	4.0 0.6 4.0
26	F	0020 0620 1234 1832	0.6 4.0 0.6 4.0
27	SA	0054 0650 1308 1903	0.7 4.0 0.7 4.0
28	SU	0130 0724 1346 1939	0.7 3.9 0.7 4.0
29	M	0208 0802 1428 2020	0.8 3.9 0.8 3.9
30	TU	0252 0846 1515 2108	0.9 3.8 1.0 3.7

OCTOBER

Date	Day	Time	m
1	W ☽	0343 0939 1611 2206	1.1 3.6 1.1 3.5
2	TH	0446 1043 1719 2316	1.2 3.5 1.2 3.4
3	F	0603 1201 1839	1.2 3.4 1.2
4	SA	0036 0723 1324 1958	3.4 1.1 3.6 1.0
5	SU	0157 0837 1436 2108	3.6 0.8 3.8 0.7
6	M	0304 0939 1535 2205	3.8 0.5 4.1 0.4
7	TU	0359 1032 1626 2255	4.1 0.3 4.3 0.2
8	W ○	0448 1120 1712 2340	4.3 0.1 4.4 0.1
9	TH	0533 1204 1755	4.3 0.1 4.4
10	F	0022 0615 1247 1835	0.1 4.3 0.1 4.3
11	SA	0104 0655 1327 1914	0.2 4.2 0.3 4.2
12	SU	0144 0734 1408 1952	0.4 4.1 0.5 4.0
13	M	0226 0814 1450 2031	0.6 3.9 0.7 3.8
14	TU	0309 0856 1534 2114	0.8 3.6 1.0 3.5
15	W ☾	0356 0942 1624 2202	1.1 3.4 1.2 3.3
16	TH	0453 1040 1725 2307	1.3 3.2 1.4 3.1
17	F	0601 1202 1838	1.4 3.1 1.4
18	SA	0035 0716 1325 1950	3.1 1.3 3.2 1.3
19	SU	0152 0823 1426 2050	3.3 1.2 3.4 1.1
20	M	0247 0916 1514 2138	3.5 1.0 3.7 1.0
21	TU	0333 0959 1556 2217	3.7 0.8 3.9 0.8
22	W	0413 1034 1632 2251	3.9 0.7 4.0 0.7
23	TH ●	0449 1106 1705 2324	4.0 0.6 4.1 0.6
24	F	0523 1138 1736 2357	4.1 0.6 4.1 0.6
25	SA	0555 1212 1808	4.1 0.6 4.1
26	SU	0033 0629 1250 1843	0.6 4.1 0.6 4.1
27	M	0111 0706 1330 1922	0.7 4.1 0.7 4.0
28	TU	0153 0747 1414 2005	0.8 4.0 0.8 3.9
29	W	0239 0834 1504 2055	0.9 3.9 0.9 3.8
30	TH	0332 0929 1600 2154	1.0 3.7 1.1 3.6
31	F ☽	0434 1032 1705 2301	1.1 3.6 1.2 3.5

NOVEMBER

Date	Day	Time	m
1	SA	0546 1146 1821	1.2 3.6 1.2
2	SU	0018 0704 1305 1939	3.5 1.1 3.6 1.0
3	M	0136 0817 1415 2048	3.6 0.9 3.8 0.8
4	TU	0243 0919 1514 2145	3.8 0.6 4.0 0.6
5	W	0339 1014 1605 2236	4.0 0.4 4.2 0.4
6	TH ○	0429 1102 1652 2321	4.2 0.3 4.3 0.3
7	F	0514 1146 1735	4.3 0.3 4.3
8	SA	0003 0556 1228 1814	0.3 4.3 0.4 4.2
9	SU	0043 0635 1307 1851	0.4 4.2 0.5 4.1
10	M	0122 0712 1346 1928	0.5 4.1 0.7 4.0
11	TU	0201 0750 1425 2004	0.7 3.9 0.9 3.8
12	W	0241 0830 1505 2044	0.9 3.7 1.1 3.6
13	TH	0324 0913 1551 2129	1.1 3.6 1.2 3.5
14	F ☾	0414 1003 1645 2222	1.3 3.4 1.4 3.3
15	SA	0515 1104 1749 2329	1.4 3.3 1.5 3.2
16	SU	0622 1220 1856	1.4 3.3 1.4
17	M	0048 0727 1332 1957	3.3 1.3 3.4 1.3
18	TU	0156 0824 1427 2050	3.5 1.2 3.6 1.1
19	W	0248 0913 1514 2137	3.7 1.0 3.8 0.9
20	TH	0334 0957 1555 2219	3.8 0.9 3.9 0.8
21	F	0416 1038 1634 2259	4.0 0.7 4.0 0.7
22	SA ●	0456 1118 1712 2338	4.1 0.7 4.1 0.6
23	SU	0535 1157 1750	4.2 0.6 4.2
24	M	0018 0614 1238 1829	0.6 4.2 0.6 4.1
25	TU	0100 0655 1321 1912	0.6 4.2 0.6 4.1
26	W	0144 0740 1407 1958	0.6 4.1 0.7 4.0
27	TH	0232 0829 1456 2048	0.7 4.0 0.8 3.9
28	F	0324 0922 1550 2144	0.8 3.9 0.9 3.7
29	SA ☽	0422 1021 1651 2246	0.9 3.8 1.0 3.6
30	SU	0527 1127 1800 2355	1.0 3.7 1.1 3.6

DECEMBER

Date	Day	Time	m
1	M	0640 1238 1914	1.0 3.7 1.1
2	TU	0108 0752 1348 2023	3.6 0.9 3.8 0.9
3	W	0217 0857 1449 2124	3.7 0.8 3.9 0.8
4	TH	0317 0955 1544 2217	3.9 0.7 4.0 0.6
5	F	0410 1046 1634 2304	4.1 0.6 4.1 0.6
6	SA ○	0458 1131 1718 2346	4.2 0.5 4.1 0.5
7	SU	0540 1212 1757	4.2 0.6 4.1
8	M	0025 0618 1249 1833	0.6 4.2 0.6 4.1
9	TU	0102 0655 1325 1907	0.6 4.1 0.8 4.0
10	W	0137 0730 1400 1942	0.8 4.0 0.9 3.9
11	TH	0213 0807 1437 2019	0.9 3.9 1.0 3.8
12	F	0251 0846 1517 2059	1.0 3.8 1.2 3.7
13	SA	0334 0929 1603 2145	1.2 3.6 1.3 3.5
14	SU ☾	0424 1017 1656 2237	1.3 3.5 1.4 3.4
15	M	0522 1113 1758 2339	1.4 3.5 1.4 3.4
16	TU	0627 1217 1902	1.4 3.4 1.4
17	W	0048 0730 1323 2002	3.4 1.3 3.5 1.3
18	TH	0154 0828 1423 2058	3.6 1.2 3.7 1.1
19	F	0252 0922 1517 2149	3.7 1.0 3.8 0.9
20	SA	0344 1013 1606 2238	3.9 0.8 4.0 0.7
21	SU	0432 1100 1652 2323	4.1 0.7 4.1 0.6
22	M ●	0518 1145 1736	4.2 0.6 4.2
23	TU	0006 0602 1229 1819	0.5 4.3 0.5 4.2
24	W	0050 0647 1313 1904	0.4 4.3 0.5 4.2
25	TH	0135 0732 1359 1950	0.4 4.3 0.5 4.1
26	F	0222 0820 1446 2039	0.5 4.2 0.6 4.0
27	SA	0312 0911 1537 2129	0.6 4.1 0.7 3.9
28	SU ☽	0404 1003 1631 2224	0.7 3.9 0.9 3.7
29	M	0503 1101 1731 2325	0.9 3.8 1.0 3.6
30	TU	0609 1205 1841	1.0 3.6 1.1
31	W	0033 0721 1315 1953	3.5 1.0 3.6 1.1

DUBLIN (NORTH WALL)
LAT 53°21′N
LONG 6°13′W

TIMES AND HEIGHTS OF HIGH AND LOW WATER (Heights in Metres)

TIME ZONE UT
For Summer Time (area enclosed in shaded box) add 1 hour

2014

JANUARY

Date	Day	Time	m	Time	m	Time	m	Time	m
1	W ●	0422	0.6	1101	4.3	1649	0.4	2332	4.2
2	TH	0508	0.5	1146	4.4	1736	0.3		
3	F	0020	4.2	0552	0.5	1233	4.5	1823	0.3
4	SA	0109	4.2	0639	0.5	1322	4.5	1913	0.3
5	SU	0200	4.1	0729	0.7	1413	4.4	2006	0.4
6	M	0255	4.0	0823	0.8	1508	4.2	2101	0.6
7	TU	0353	3.8	0920	1.0	1606	4.1	2158	0.9
8	W ☽	0455	3.7	1021	1.2	1709	3.9	2259	1.1
9	TH	0600	3.6	1127	1.4	1817	3.7		
10	F	0006	1.3	0705	3.6	1239	1.5	1924	3.6
11	SA	0121	1.4	0809	3.6	1353	1.4	2031	3.6
12	SU	0229	1.4	0909	3.7	1457	1.3	2132	3.6
13	M	0323	1.3	1001	3.8	1548	1.2	2222	3.6
14	TU	0407	1.2	1043	3.9	1630	1.0	2301	3.7
15	W	0443	1.1	1118	4.0	1706	0.9	2333	3.7
16	TH O	0515	1.0	1149	4.0	1740	0.9		
17	F	0003	3.7	0544	1.0	1219	4.0	1811	0.8
18	SA	0033	3.8	0611	0.9	1249	4.0	1841	0.8
19	SU	0105	3.8	0639	0.9	1322	4.0	1910	0.8
20	M	0141	3.8	0711	1.0	1400	3.9	1944	0.8
21	TU	0220	3.7	0748	1.0	1440	3.9	2023	0.9
22	W	0303	3.7	0831	1.1	1524	3.8	2107	1.0
23	TH	0350	3.6	0919	1.2	1612	3.7	2156	1.1
24	F ☾	0443	3.5	1014	1.3	1706	3.6	2255	1.2
25	SA	0544	3.4	1121	1.4	1811	3.5		
26	SU	0006	1.3	0654	3.5	1240	1.4	1926	3.5
27	M	0121	1.2	0804	3.6	1354	1.2	2038	3.6
28	TU	0227	1.1	0905	3.8	1456	0.9	2139	3.8
29	W	0323	0.8	0959	4.1	1551	0.6	2232	4.0
30	TH ●	0412	0.6	1047	4.3	1639	0.4	2320	4.1
31	F	0456	0.4	1133	4.4	1725	0.2		

FEBRUARY

Date	Day	Time	m	Time	m	Time	m	Time	m
1	SA	0006	4.2	0539	0.4	1218	4.5	1809	0.1
2	SU	0051	4.2	0622	0.4	1304	4.4	1854	0.2
3	M	0137	4.1	0708	0.5	1351	4.3	1942	0.3
4	TU	0224	4.0	0757	0.6	1441	4.2	2031	0.6
5	W	0315	3.8	0850	0.8	1533	4.0	2123	0.8
6	TH ☽	0410	3.6	0946	1.1	1632	3.7	2217	1.1
7	F	0514	3.5	1048	1.3	1739	3.5	2318	1.4
8	SA	0622	3.4	1157	1.4	1850	3.4		
9	SU	0032	1.5	0729	3.4	1321	1.5	1959	3.3
10	M	0201	1.5	0834	3.5	1436	1.3	2106	3.4
11	TU	0304	1.4	0932	3.7	1529	1.2	2200	3.5
12	W	0348	1.3	1018	3.8	1610	1.0	2240	3.6
13	TH	0424	1.1	1055	3.9	1645	0.9	2312	3.6
14	F O	0454	1.0	1127	3.9	1716	0.8	2341	3.7
15	SA	0522	0.9	1156	4.0	1744	0.7		
16	SU	0007	3.8	0546	0.8	1224	4.0	1809	0.7
17	M	0036	3.8	0611	0.7	1255	4.0	1837	0.6
18	TU	0110	3.8	0642	0.7	1331	4.0	1911	0.6
19	W	0148	3.8	0719	0.7	1412	3.9	1950	0.7
20	TH	0230	3.8	0801	0.8	1455	3.8	2034	0.8
21	F	0316	3.7	0848	0.9	1543	3.7	2123	0.9
22	SA ☾	0407	3.6	0943	1.1	1637	3.6	2221	1.1
23	SU	0507	3.5	1050	1.2	1743	3.4	2333	1.3
24	M	0620	3.4	1214	1.3	1905	3.4		
25	TU	0056	1.3	0738	3.5	1336	1.1	2023	3.5
26	W	0211	1.1	0847	3.7	1445	0.8	2127	3.7
27	TH	0311	0.9	0944	4.0	1541	0.5	2221	3.9
28	F	0400	0.6	1034	4.2	1628	0.3	2308	4.1

MARCH

Date	Day	Time	m	Time	m	Time	m	Time	m
1	SA ●	0444	0.4	1119	4.3	1711	0.1	2350	4.1
2	SU	0525	0.3	1202	4.4	1753	0.1		
3	M	0031	4.1	0605	0.3	1245	4.3	1834	0.2
4	TU	0111	4.0	0648	0.3	1328	4.2	1916	0.3
5	W	0153	3.9	0733	0.5	1414	4.1	2001	0.6
6	TH	0237	3.8	0822	0.7	1502	3.9	2048	0.8
7	F	0326	3.6	0916	0.9	1556	3.6	2140	1.1
8	SA ☽	0424	3.5	1014	1.1	1700	3.4	2237	1.4
9	SU	0535	3.3	1119	1.3	1813	3.2	2344	1.6
10	M	0648	3.3	1236	1.4	1925	3.2		
11	TU	0112	1.6	0756	3.3	1402	1.3	2032	3.2
12	W	0233	1.5	0857	3.5	1500	1.2	2129	3.4
13	TH	0321	1.3	0946	3.6	1541	1.0	2211	3.5
14	F	0357	1.1	1026	3.7	1615	0.8	2245	3.6
15	SA	0427	0.9	1100	3.8	1645	0.7	2314	3.7
16	SU O	0454	0.8	1129	3.9	1711	0.6	2339	3.8
17	M	0518	0.7	1156	3.9	1737	0.5		
18	TU	0006	3.9	0544	0.6	1228	4.0	1807	0.5
19	W	0040	3.9	0616	0.5	1305	4.0	1842	0.5
20	TH	0119	3.9	0655	0.5	1347	3.9	1923	0.6
21	F	0202	3.9	0739	0.6	1433	3.8	2009	0.7
22	SA	0249	3.8	0828	0.7	1522	3.7	2101	0.9
23	SU	0341	3.7	0927	0.9	1619	3.6	2202	1.1
24	M ☾	0442	3.5	1037	1.1	1729	3.4	2315	1.3
25	TU	0556	3.5	1200	1.1	1852	3.4		
26	W	0037	1.3	0717	3.5	1322	1.0	2009	3.5
27	TH	0153	1.1	0828	3.7	1430	0.7	2115	3.7
28	F	0255	0.9	0929	3.9	1525	0.5	2209	3.9
29	SA	0345	0.6	1021	4.1	1612	0.3	2255	4.0
30	SU ●	0429	0.4	1106	4.2	1655	0.2	2335	4.0
31	M	0509	0.3	1147	4.2	1734	0.2		

APRIL

Date	Day	Time	m	Time	m	Time	m	Time	m
1	TU	0011	4.0	0549	0.3	1227	4.2	1813	0.3
2	W	0047	4.0	0629	0.3	1308	4.1	1852	0.4
3	TH	0125	3.9	0712	0.4	1350	3.9	1933	0.6
4	F	0206	3.8	0759	0.6	1436	3.8	2018	0.9
5	SA	0252	3.7	0850	0.8	1527	3.5	2107	1.1
6	SU	0343	3.5	0946	1.0	1625	3.3	2202	1.4
7	M ☽	0448	3.3	1046	1.2	1735	3.2	2305	1.6
8	TU	0604	3.2	1153	1.3	1847	3.1		
9	W	0017	1.6	0714	3.3	1309	1.3	1952	3.2
10	TH	0138	1.5	0816	3.4	1414	1.2	2049	3.3
11	F	0239	1.4	0909	3.5	1501	1.0	2135	3.5
12	SA	0319	1.1	0952	3.6	1537	0.8	2212	3.6
13	SU	0352	0.9	1028	3.7	1608	0.7	2242	3.7
14	M	0420	0.8	1059	3.8	1637	0.6	2308	3.8
15	TU O	0447	0.6	1129	3.9	1707	0.5	2337	3.9
16	W	0518	0.5	1203	4.0	1740	0.4		
17	TH	0013	4.0	0554	0.4	1244	4.0	1818	0.5
18	F	0055	4.0	0636	0.5	1328	3.9	1902	0.6
19	SA	0140	4.0	0723	0.5	1417	3.9	1951	0.7
20	SU	0230	3.9	0818	0.6	1510	3.7	2047	0.9
21	M	0325	3.8	0921	0.8	1611	3.6	2150	1.1
22	TU ☾	0427	3.7	1031	0.9	1721	3.5	2301	1.2
23	W	0540	3.6	1148	0.9	1840	3.5		
24	TH	0017	1.2	0658	3.6	1303	0.9	1953	3.6
25	F	0130	1.1	0809	3.7	1409	0.7	2057	3.7
26	SA	0232	1.0	0911	3.9	1505	0.6	2152	3.8
27	SU	0325	0.8	1006	4.0	1553	0.5	2239	3.9
28	M	0411	0.6	1053	4.0	1637	0.4	2319	3.9
29	TU ●	0454	0.5	1134	4.0	1716	0.4	2353	3.9
30	W	0534	0.5	1211	4.0	1754	0.5		

MAY

Date	Day	Time	m	Time	m	Time	m	Time	m
1	TH	0026	3.9	0614	0.5	1250	3.9	1831	0.6
2	F	0102	3.9	0656	0.5	1330	3.8	1909	0.8
3	SA	0142	3.8	0740	0.6	1413	3.7	1951	0.9
4	SU	0224	3.7	0828	0.8	1500	3.5	2037	1.1
5	M	0311	3.6	0920	0.9	1552	3.4	2129	1.3
6	TU	0406	3.5	1015	1.1	1653	3.2	2228	1.5
7	W ☽	0513	3.3	1114	1.2	1801	3.2	2332	1.6
8	TH	0626	3.3	1216	1.2	1907	3.2		
9	F	0038	1.5	0729	3.3	1317	1.2	2004	3.3
10	SA	0139	1.4	0824	3.4	1409	1.1	2052	3.4
11	SU	0229	1.3	0911	3.6	1452	0.9	2132	3.6
12	M	0309	1.1	0951	3.7	1529	0.7	2206	3.7
13	TU	0344	0.8	1027	3.8	1604	0.6	2238	3.9
14	W O	0418	0.7	1103	3.9	1640	0.5	2313	4.0
15	TH	0456	0.5	1143	4.0	1718	0.5	2352	4.1
16	F	0537	0.4	1226	4.0	1800	0.5		
17	SA	0036	4.1	0622	0.4	1314	4.0	1846	0.6
18	SU	0124	4.1	0713	0.5	1405	3.9	1937	0.7
19	M	0216	4.1	0811	0.6	1501	3.8	2034	0.9
20	TU	0313	4.0	0914	0.7	1602	3.7	2137	1.0
21	W ☾	0415	3.9	1021	0.8	1710	3.6	2243	1.1
22	TH	0525	3.8	1130	0.8	1821	3.6	2353	1.2
23	F	0638	3.8	1239	0.9	1931	3.6		
24	SA	0102	1.2	0747	3.8	1344	0.8	2034	3.7
25	SU	0206	1.1	0851	3.8	1442	0.8	2131	3.8
26	M	0303	1.0	0948	3.9	1533	0.7	2220	3.8
27	TU	0353	0.8	1038	3.9	1619	0.7	2303	3.9
28	W ●	0439	0.7	1121	3.9	1659	0.7	2338	3.9
29	TH	0520	0.7	1157	3.9	1737	0.8		
30	F	0008	3.9	0600	0.7	1232	3.8	1812	0.8
31	SA	0042	3.9	0640	0.7	1309	3.7		

JUNE

Date	Day	Time	m	Time	m	Time	m	Time	m
1	SU	0119	3.9	0721	0.7	1349	3.7	1926	1.0
2	M	0159	3.8	0805	0.8	1432	3.6	2007	1.1
3	TU	0242	3.7	0851	0.9	1517	3.5	2053	1.2
4	W	0329	3.6	0940	1.0	1607	3.4	2144	1.4
5	TH ☽	0421	3.5	1033	1.1	1703	3.3	2242	1.5
6	F	0521	3.4	1128	1.2	1806	3.2	2343	1.5
7	SA	0627	3.4	1224	1.2	1908	3.3		
8	SU	0042	1.5	0729	3.4	1318	1.1	2002	3.4
9	M	0137	1.4	0824	3.5	1408	1.0	2049	3.6
10	TU	0226	1.2	0912	3.7	1453	0.9	2131	3.8
11	W	0310	0.9	0958	3.8	1536	0.7	2212	3.9
12	TH	0354	0.7	1042	3.9	1618	0.6	2253	4.1
13	F O	0437	0.5	1126	4.0	1700	0.5	2336	4.2
14	SA	0523	0.4	1212	4.1	1745	0.5		
15	SU	0021	4.3	0611	0.4	1301	4.1	1831	0.5
16	M	0110	4.3	0703	0.4	1353	4.0	1922	0.6
17	TU	0202	4.2	0759	0.4	1448	3.9	2017	0.8
18	W	0258	4.2	0859	0.6	1547	3.8	2117	0.9
19	TH ☾	0358	4.0	1002	0.7	1650	3.7	2219	1.1
20	F	0504	3.9	1105	0.8	1756	3.7	2324	1.2
21	SA	0614	3.8	1210	0.9	1903	3.6		
22	SU	0032	1.2	0723	3.8	1316	1.0	2007	3.7
23	M	0140	1.2	0828	3.8	1419	1.0	2106	3.7
24	TU	0243	1.2	0929	3.8	1514	1.0	2159	3.8
25	W	0337	1.0	1022	3.8	1601	1.0	2244	3.9
26	TH	0425	0.9	1106	3.8	1643	1.0	2321	3.9
27	F ●	0507	0.9	1142	3.7	1719	0.9	2351	3.9
28	SA	0545	0.8	1214	3.7	1753	0.9		
29	SU	0022	3.9	0622	0.8	1247	3.7	1825	0.9
30	M	0056	3.9	0659	0.8	1323	3.7	1858	1.0

SUNRISE AND SUNSET TIMES

DUBLIN
At 53°21′N 6°13′W

		Sunrise	Sunset
UT			
Jan	01	0840	1617
	15	0832	1637
Feb	01	0809	1708
	15	0743	1736
Mar	01	0712	1803
	15	0639	1829
BST			
Apr	01	0658	2000
	15	0625	2026
May	01	0551	2054
	15	0525	2118
Jun	01	0503	2143
	15	0456	2155
Jul	01	0501	2156
	15	0516	2145
Aug	01	0541	2120
	15	0605	2053
Sep	01	0634	2014
	15	0659	1940
Oct	01	0727	1901
	15	0752	1829
UT			
Nov	01	0724	1652
	15	0750	1628
Dec	01	0817	1610
	15	0834	1606

DUBLIN (NORTH WALL)
LAT 53°21'N
LONG 6°13'W

TIMES AND HEIGHTS OF HIGH AND LOW WATER (Heights in Metres)

TIME ZONE UT
For Summer Time (area enclosed in shaded box) add 1 hour

2014

JULY

Date	Day	Time	m	Time	m	Time	m	Time	m
1	TU	0133	3.9	0736	0.9	1401	3.6	1933	1.0
2	W	0212	3.8	0815	0.9	1441	3.6	2012	1.1
3	TH	0254	3.8	0856	1.0	1524	3.5	2054	1.2
4	F	0339	3.7	0941	1.1	1611	3.4	2142	1.3
5	SA ☽	0429	3.5	1032	1.1	1704	3.4	2238	1.4
6	SU	0526	3.5	1129	1.2	1804	3.4	2342	1.5
7	M	0631	3.4	1228	1.2	1909	3.4		
8	TU	0048	1.4	0738	3.5	1328	1.2	2008	3.5
9	W	0149	1.2	0840	3.6	1422	1.0	2102	3.7
10	TH	0244	1.0	0934	3.8	1513	0.8	2150	4.0
11	F	0335	0.8	1024	4.0	1600	0.6	2236	4.2
12	SA ○	0423	0.5	1111	4.1	1645	0.5	2321	4.3
13	SU	0510	0.3	1158	4.2	1730	0.4		
14	M	0006	4.4	0558	0.2	1246	4.2	1815	0.4
15	TU	0053	4.4	0647	0.2	1335	4.1	1903	0.5
16	W	0143	4.4	0740	0.3	1427	4.0	1955	0.7
17	TH	0236	4.3	0836	0.5	1522	3.9	2051	0.8
18	F	0334	4.1	0934	0.7	1620	3.8	2150	1.0
19	SA ☾	0436	3.9	1034	0.9	1724	3.6	2252	1.2
20	SU	0546	3.8	1137	1.1	1831	3.6		
21	M	0000	1.3	0656	3.7	1245	1.2	1936	3.6
22	TU	0113	1.4	0805	3.6	1355	1.3	2040	3.6
23	W	0225	1.3	0909	3.6	1455	1.3	2137	3.7
24	TH	0324	1.2	1005	3.6	1544	1.2	2224	3.8
25	F	0411	1.0	1050	3.7	1625	1.1	2301	3.9
26	SA ●	0451	0.9	1124	3.7	1700	1.0	2332	3.9
27	SU	0526	0.9	1153	3.7	1732	0.9		
28	M	0001	4.0	0559	0.8	1223	3.7	1801	0.9
29	TU	0032	4.0	0631	0.8	1255	3.7	1829	0.9
30	W	0104	4.0	0701	0.8	1329	3.7	1859	0.9
31	TH	0141	3.9	0733	0.8	1406	3.7	1935	1.0

AUGUST

Date	Day	Time	m	Time	m	Time	m	Time	m
1	F	0221	3.9	0810	0.9	1447	3.7	2015	1.0
2	SA	0304	3.8	0853	1.0	1532	3.6	2100	1.1
3	SU	0351	3.7	0941	1.1	1621	3.5	2151	1.3
4	M ☽	0444	3.5	1037	1.2	1717	3.4	2252	1.4
5	TU	0547	3.4	1143	1.3	1824	3.4		
6	W	0007	1.4	0703	3.4	1254	1.3	1935	3.5
7	TH	0121	1.3	0815	3.5	1359	1.1	2038	3.7
8	F	0226	1.0	0916	3.7	1456	0.9	2132	4.0
9	SA	0322	0.7	1009	3.9	1545	0.7	2220	4.2
10	SU ○	0411	0.4	1057	4.1	1631	0.5	2305	4.4
11	M	0458	0.2	1142	4.2	1714	0.4	2349	4.5
12	TU	0543	0.1	1227	4.2	1757	0.3		
13	W	0033	4.5	0628	0.1	1313	4.1	1842	0.4
14	TH	0120	4.4	0716	0.3	1400	4.0	1930	0.5
15	F	0210	4.3	0808	0.5	1450	3.9	2023	0.7
16	SA	0304	4.1	0902	0.7	1545	3.8	2120	1.0
17	SU ☾	0404	3.8	0958	1.0	1646	3.6	2221	1.2
18	M	0513	3.6	1059	1.3	1754	3.5	2327	1.4
19	TU	0627	3.5	1207	1.4	1903	3.5		
20	W	0045	1.4	0739	3.4	1327	1.5	2010	3.6
21	TH	0206	1.4	0849	3.5	1435	1.4	2110	3.7
22	F	0307	1.2	0946	3.6	1525	1.3	2159	3.8
23	SA	0352	1.0	1029	3.6	1605	1.1	2238	3.9
24	SU	0430	0.9	1102	3.7	1638	1.0	2309	4.0
25	M ●	0502	0.8	1131	3.7	1709	0.9	2338	4.0
26	TU	0532	0.8	1158	3.8	1735	0.9		
27	W	0006	4.0	0559	0.7	1226	3.8	1800	0.8
28	TH	0036	4.0	0625	0.7	1258	3.8	1829	0.8
29	F	0111	4.0	0655	0.7	1334	3.8	1903	0.8
30	SA	0150	3.9	0733	0.8	1415	3.8	1943	0.9
31	SU	0233	3.8	0815	0.9	1459	3.7	2028	1.0

SEPTEMBER

Date	Day	Time	m	Time	m	Time	m	Time	m
1	M	0320	3.7	0904	1.0	1547	3.6	2119	1.2
2	TU ☽	0413	3.6	1001	1.2	1643	3.5	2222	1.3
3	W	0517	3.4	1110	1.3	1750	3.4	2340	1.4
4	TH	0639	3.4	1228	1.4	1907	3.5		
5	F	0102	1.2	0757	3.5	1340	1.2	2016	3.7
6	SA	0213	1.0	0902	3.7	1441	1.0	2113	4.0
7	SU	0311	0.7	0956	3.9	1531	0.7	2203	4.2
8	M	0400	0.4	1043	4.1	1616	0.5	2249	4.4
9	TU ○	0444	0.2	1126	4.2	1658	0.3	2331	4.5
10	W	0526	0.1	1207	4.2	1740	0.3		
11	TH	0014	4.5	0608	0.1	1250	4.2	1822	0.3
12	F	0058	4.4	0652	0.3	1333	4.1	1907	0.5
13	SA	0145	4.2	0738	0.5	1419	3.9	1957	0.7
14	SU	0235	4.0	0828	0.8	1509	3.8	2052	0.9
15	M	0332	3.8	0923	1.1	1606	3.6	2151	1.1
16	TU ☾	0439	3.5	1022	1.4	1714	3.5	2256	1.3
17	W	0555	3.3	1127	1.6	1825	3.4		
18	TH	0011	1.4	0709	3.3	1249	1.6	1934	3.5
19	F	0138	1.4	0820	3.4	1406	1.5	2037	3.6
20	SA	0241	1.2	0918	3.5	1459	1.4	2128	3.8
21	SU	0326	1.0	1001	3.6	1539	1.2	2209	3.9
22	M	0402	0.9	1035	3.7	1612	1.0	2243	4.0
23	TU	0433	0.8	1105	3.8	1642	0.9	2313	4.0
24	W ●	0501	0.7	1132	3.8	1708	0.8	2340	4.0
25	TH	0526	0.7	1158	3.9	1733	0.8		
26	F	0009	4.0	0552	0.7	1229	3.9	1801	0.7
27	SA	0044	4.0	0624	0.7	1305	3.9	1837	0.7
28	SU	0124	4.0	0702	0.7	1347	3.9	1918	0.8
29	M	0208	3.9	0746	0.9	1432	3.8	2004	0.9
30	TU	0257	3.8	0837	1.0	1521	3.7	2059	1.1

OCTOBER

Date	Day	Time	m	Time	m	Time	m	Time	m
1	W ☽	0352	3.6	0936	1.2	1618	3.6	2205	1.2
2	TH	0459	3.5	1048	1.4	1725	3.6	2324	1.3
3	F	0622	3.4	1207	1.4	1842	3.6		
4	SA	0047	1.2	0741	3.5	1321	1.3	1954	3.8
5	SU	0158	0.9	0846	3.7	1423	1.0	2054	4.0
6	M	0256	0.6	0941	3.9	1515	0.8	2147	4.2
7	TU	0345	0.4	1028	4.1	1601	0.6	2233	4.3
8	W ○	0428	0.3	1111	4.2	1643	0.4	2316	4.4
9	TH	0509	0.2	1150	4.2	1724	0.4	2357	4.4
10	F	0549	0.3	1228	4.2	1805	0.4		
11	SA	0039	4.3	0629	0.4	1309	4.1	1849	0.5
12	SU	0124	4.1	0712	0.7	1352	4.0	1936	0.7
13	M	0212	3.9	0758	0.9	1439	3.9	2028	0.9
14	TU	0305	3.7	0850	1.2	1531	3.7	2124	1.1
15	W ☾	0407	3.5	0947	1.4	1634	3.6	2225	1.3
16	TH	0519	3.3	1050	1.6	1744	3.5	2333	1.4
17	F	0632	3.3	1202	1.7	1854	3.5		
18	SA	0051	1.4	0739	3.3	1322	1.6	1957	3.6
19	SU	0201	1.3	0838	3.5	1423	1.5	2051	3.7
20	M	0251	1.1	0924	3.6	1507	1.3	2136	3.8
21	TU	0328	0.9	1003	3.8	1542	1.1	2213	3.9
22	W	0400	0.8	1036	3.9	1612	1.0	2246	4.0
23	TH ●	0428	0.7	1104	3.9	1639	0.9	2314	4.0
24	F	0455	0.7	1130	4.0	1707	0.8	2345	4.0
25	SA	0525	0.6	1202	4.1	1739	0.7		
26	SU	0021	4.0	0559	0.7	1240	4.1	1816	0.7
27	M	0103	4.0	0639	0.7	1323	4.1	1900	0.7
28	TU	0149	3.9	0724	0.9	1410	4.0	1950	0.8
29	W	0241	3.8	0817	1.1	1502	3.9	2047	1.0
30	TH	0339	3.7	0919	1.2	1600	3.8	2154	1.1
31	F ☽	0447	3.6	1030	1.4	1705	3.7	2309	1.1

NOVEMBER

Date	Day	Time	m	Time	m	Time	m	Time	m
1	SA	0605	3.6	1146	1.4	1819	3.8		
2	SU	0027	1.1	0720	3.6	1258	1.3	1930	3.8
3	M	0137	0.9	0827	3.8	1402	1.1	2034	4.0
4	TU	0236	0.7	0923	4.0	1456	0.9	2130	4.1
5	W	0327	0.6	1013	4.1	1545	0.7	2220	4.2
6	TH ○	0412	0.5	1056	4.1	1629	0.6	2304	4.2
7	F	0454	0.5	1135	4.2	1711	0.6	2345	4.2
8	SA	0533	0.5	1212	4.2	1753	0.6		
9	SU	0025	4.1	0610	0.6	1249	4.1	1834	0.6
10	M	0107	4.0	0650	0.8	1329	4.0	1919	0.7
11	TU	0151	3.9	0733	1.0	1413	4.0	2007	0.9
12	W	0240	3.7	0820	1.2	1501	3.8	2058	1.0
13	TH	0334	3.5	0914	1.4	1555	3.7	2154	1.2
14	F ☾	0438	3.4	1013	1.6	1658	3.5	2253	1.3
15	SA	0546	3.3	1118	1.7	1806	3.5	2357	1.4
16	SU	0653	3.3	1225	1.7	1911	3.5		
17	M	0103	1.4	0752	3.4	1331	1.6	2007	3.6
18	TU	0201	1.2	0842	3.6	1423	1.4	2056	3.7
19	W	0246	1.1	0926	3.7	1504	1.3	2139	3.8
20	TH	0323	1.0	1002	3.9	1539	1.1	2216	3.9
21	F	0355	0.8	1034	4.0	1611	0.9	2249	4.0
22	SA ●	0427	0.7	1105	4.1	1645	0.8	2325	4.0
23	SU	0502	0.7	1140	4.2	1721	0.7		
24	M	0004	4.1	0539	0.7	1220	4.2	1802	0.6
25	TU	0048	4.1	0621	0.7	1305	4.2	1848	0.6
26	W	0136	4.0	0708	0.8	1353	4.2	1939	0.7
27	TH	0229	3.9	0802	1.0	1446	4.1	2037	0.8
28	F	0327	3.8	0902	1.1	1543	4.0	2140	0.9
29	SA ☽	0433	3.7	1009	1.3	1646	3.9	2249	1.0
30	SU	0544	3.7	1119	1.3	1755	3.9		

DECEMBER

Date	Day	Time	m	Time	m	Time	m	Time	m
1	M	0001	1.0	0655	3.7	1230	1.3	1905	3.9
2	TU	0111	1.0	0802	3.8	1337	1.2	2012	3.9
3	W	0214	0.9	0902	3.9	1437	1.1	2114	4.0
4	TH	0309	0.8	0955	4.0	1530	1.0	2209	4.0
5	F	0357	0.8	1042	4.1	1618	0.8	2256	4.1
6	SA ○	0440	0.8	1124	4.1	1701	0.7	2337	4.0
7	SU	0519	0.8	1159	4.1	1742	0.7		
8	M	0013	4.0	0555	0.8	1233	4.1	1822	0.7
9	TU	0051	3.9	0632	0.9	1310	4.1	1903	0.8
10	W	0131	3.8	0710	1.0	1349	4.0	1945	0.8
11	TH	0214	3.7	0751	1.1	1432	3.9	2030	1.0
12	F	0300	3.6	0837	1.3	1517	3.8	2118	1.1
13	SA	0350	3.5	0929	1.5	1607	3.6	2210	1.2
14	SU ☾	0448	3.4	1028	1.6	1704	3.5	2305	1.3
15	M	0554	3.3	1130	1.7	1809	3.4		
16	TU	0004	1.4	0657	3.4	1233	1.7	1913	3.4
17	W	0103	1.4	0754	3.5	1331	1.6	2010	3.5
18	TH	0157	1.3	0844	3.6	1421	1.4	2100	3.6
19	F	0243	1.1	0927	3.8	1505	1.2	2145	3.8
20	SA	0325	1.0	1005	4.0	1545	1.0	2227	3.9
21	SU	0404	0.8	1043	4.1	1625	0.8	2308	4.0
22	M ●	0443	0.7	1122	4.2	1706	0.6	2350	4.1
23	TU	0524	0.6	1203	4.3	1750	0.5		
24	W	0034	4.1	0607	0.6	1249	4.4	1836	0.4
25	TH	0123	4.1	0653	0.7	1337	4.3	1927	0.5
26	F	0214	4.0	0745	0.8	1429	4.3	2021	0.6
27	SA	0310	3.9	0842	1.0	1524	4.2	2120	0.7
28	SU ☽	0410	3.8	0943	1.1	1624	4.1	2222	0.9
29	M	0517	3.7	1049	1.2	1729	3.9	2329	1.0
30	TU	0626	3.7	1159	1.3	1840	3.8		
31	W	0040	1.1	0734	3.7	1310	1.3	1951	3.8

BELFAST
LAT 54°36′N
LONG 5°55′W

TIMES AND HEIGHTS OF HIGH AND LOW WATER (Heights in Metres)

TIME ZONE UT
For Summer Time (area enclosed in shaded box) add 1 hour

2014

JANUARY

Date	Day	Time	m	Time	m	Time	m	Time	m
1	W ●	0413	0.5	1033	3.7	1650	0.4	2300	3.6
2	TH	0500	0.5	1121	3.8	1736	0.3	2350	3.6
3	F	0547	0.5	1211	3.9	1823	0.3		
4	SA	0042	3.6	0634	0.5	1302	3.9	1911	0.3
5	SU	0136	3.5	0724	0.6	1353	3.9	2002	0.3
6	M	0229	3.4	0815	0.7	1445	3.8	2056	0.4
7	TU	0323	3.4	0908	0.8	1538	3.6	2155	0.6
8	W ☽	0419	3.3	1007	0.9	1634	3.5	2300	0.7
9	TH	0517	3.2	1113	1.0	1737	3.3		
10	F	0005	0.9	0622	3.1	1223	1.1	1851	3.2
11	SA	0108	0.9	0729	3.1	1331	1.1	2002	3.1
12	SU	0207	1.0	0830	3.2	1434	1.0	2102	3.1
13	M	0301	0.9	0923	3.3	1529	0.9	2152	3.2
14	TU	0347	0.9	1009	3.5	1612	0.8	2235	3.2
15	W	0425	0.8	1050	3.6	1647	0.7	2314	3.2
16	TH O	0459	0.8	1127	3.6	1720	0.7	2348	3.2
17	F	0532	0.8	1200	3.6	1752	0.6		
18	SA	0018	3.2	0605	0.8	1231	3.6	1824	0.6
19	SU	0043	3.2	0639	0.7	1258	3.6	1857	0.6
20	M	0108	3.2	0714	0.8	1328	3.6	1932	0.6
21	TU	0142	3.2	0751	0.8	1404	3.5	2010	0.6
22	W	0222	3.2	0831	0.8	1445	3.5	2052	0.7
23	TH	0306	3.1	0916	0.9	1532	3.4	2140	0.8
24	F ☾	0358	3.1	1008	1.0	1627	3.3	2236	0.9
25	SA	0500	3.0	1111	1.1	1734	3.2	2342	1.0
26	SU	0612	3.0	1237	1.1	1848	3.1		
27	M	0105	0.9	0724	3.1	1400	0.9	1957	3.2
28	TU	0218	0.8	0830	3.2	1500	0.7	2101	3.3
29	W	0314	0.7	0928	3.4	1552	0.5	2156	3.5
30	TH ●	0403	0.5	1019	3.6	1640	0.3	2246	3.5
31	F	0449	0.4	1107	3.8	1725	0.1	2335	3.6

FEBRUARY

Date	Day	Time	m	Time	m	Time	m	Time	m
1	SA	0534	0.4	1156	3.8	1810	0.1		
2	SU	0025	3.5	0618	0.4	1245	3.9	1855	0.1
3	M	0115	3.5	0704	0.4	1334	3.8	1941	0.2
4	TU	0205	3.4	0750	0.5	1423	3.7	2028	0.4
5	W	0253	3.4	0839	0.6	1511	3.6	2119	0.6
6	TH ☽	0341	3.3	0931	0.7	1600	3.4	2219	0.8
7	F	0431	3.2	1033	0.9	1653	3.2	2326	0.9
8	SA	0527	3.0	1147	1.0	1758	3.0		
9	SU	0032	1.1	0641	3.0	1259	1.1	1936	2.9
10	M	0136	1.1	0803	3.0	1405	1.0	2043	2.9
11	TU	0234	1.0	0901	3.2	1504	0.9	2134	3.0
12	W	0324	0.9	0948	3.3	1549	0.7	2217	3.1
13	TH	0403	0.8	1029	3.4	1624	0.6	2254	3.1
14	F O	0437	0.7	1106	3.5	1656	0.6	2328	3.2
15	SA	0510	0.6	1139	3.5	1728	0.5	2357	3.1
16	SU	0542	0.6	1205	3.5	1800	0.5		
17	M	0012	3.2	0615	0.6	1226	3.5	1832	0.5
18	TU	0034	3.2	0649	0.6	1257	3.5	1905	0.5
19	W	0110	3.2	0723	0.6	1335	3.5	1941	0.5
20	TH	0150	3.2	0801	0.6	1417	3.5	2021	0.5
21	F	0234	3.2	0844	0.7	1504	3.4	2108	0.6
22	SA ☾	0322	3.1	0935	0.8	1559	3.2	2202	0.8
23	SU	0421	3.0	1037	1.0	1707	3.1	2307	1.0
24	M	0536	2.9	1210	1.0	1823	3.0		
25	TU	0041	1.0	0656	3.0	1344	0.8	1939	3.0
26	W	0204	0.9	0812	3.1	1445	0.6	2048	3.2
27	TH	0301	0.7	0914	3.4	1538	0.3	2143	3.3
28	F	0351	0.5	1005	3.6	1625	0.1	2232	3.4

MARCH

Date	Day	Time	m	Time	m	Time	m	Time	m
1	SA ●	0436	0.4	1052	3.7	1709	0.1	2319	3.5
2	SU	0519	0.3	1139	3.8	1752	0.1		
3	M	0005	3.5	0600	0.3	1226	3.8	1833	0.1
4	TU	0052	3.5	0642	0.3	1313	3.7	1915	0.2
5	W	0138	3.4	0725	0.4	1358	3.6	1958	0.4
6	TH	0222	3.4	0809	0.5	1443	3.5	2043	0.6
7	F	0306	3.3	0856	0.6	1529	3.3	2134	0.8
8	SA ☽	0352	3.2	0952	0.8	1618	3.0	2240	1.0
9	SU	0443	3.0	1107	1.0	1714	2.8	2354	1.1
10	M	0542	2.9	1224	1.0	1841	2.7		
11	TU	0100	1.2	0712	2.9	1331	1.0	2019	2.7
12	W	0201	1.1	0831	3.0	1430	0.8	2110	2.9
13	TH	0254	0.9	0920	3.2	1517	0.7	2152	3.0
14	F	0336	0.8	1001	3.3	1554	0.6	2227	3.1
15	SA	0411	0.7	1037	3.4	1628	0.5	2259	3.1
16	SU O	0445	0.6	1108	3.4	1700	0.4	2326	3.2
17	M	0518	0.5	1131	3.4	1733	0.4	2340	3.2
18	TU	0551	0.5	1154	3.4	1805	0.4		
19	W	0006	3.3	0624	0.5	1229	3.5	1838	0.4
20	TH	0043	3.3	0659	0.5	1311	3.5	1915	0.4
21	F	0125	3.3	0737	0.5	1356	3.4	1957	0.5
22	SA	0210	3.3	0821	0.5	1446	3.3	2044	0.6
23	SU	0259	3.2	0914	0.7	1543	3.2	2139	0.8
24	M ☾	0358	3.1	1018	0.8	1652	3.0	2246	1.0
25	TU	0512	3.0	1201	0.8	1809	2.9		
26	W	0023	1.0	0636	3.0	1326	0.7	1928	3.0
27	TH	0146	0.9	0757	3.1	1428	0.5	2035	3.1
28	F	0245	0.7	0859	3.3	1520	0.2	2129	3.3
29	SA	0335	0.5	0950	3.5	1607	0.1	2216	3.4
30	SU ●	0420	0.4	1036	3.6	1650	0.1	2300	3.4
31	M	0502	0.3	1121	3.6	1731	0.1	2344	3.5

APRIL

Date	Day	Time	m	Time	m	Time	m	Time	m
1	TU	0542	0.3	1205	3.6	1811	0.2		
2	W	0028	3.5	0621	0.3	1250	3.6	1850	0.4
3	TH	0111	3.5	0701	0.4	1333	3.5	1929	0.5
4	F	0152	3.4	0742	0.4	1416	3.3	2010	0.7
5	SA	0234	3.4	0826	0.6	1500	3.2	2055	0.8
6	SU	0318	3.3	0915	0.7	1547	3.0	2151	1.0
7	M ☽	0407	3.1	1022	0.9	1641	2.8	2309	1.2
8	TU	0503	3.0	1145	1.0	1743	2.7		
9	W	0021	1.2	0605	2.9	1252	0.9	1931	2.7
10	TH	0123	1.1	0724	2.9	1350	0.8	2033	2.8
11	F	0217	1.0	0836	3.0	1439	0.7	2115	2.9
12	SA	0303	0.8	0920	3.2	1520	0.6	2150	3.1
13	SU	0342	0.7	0957	3.3	1555	0.5	2221	3.2
14	M	0417	0.6	1029	3.3	1629	0.4	2249	3.2
15	TU O	0451	0.5	1057	3.4	1703	0.4	2312	3.3
16	W	0526	0.5	1129	3.5	1738	0.4	2343	3.4
17	TH	0602	0.4	1207	3.5	1815	0.4		
18	F	0022	3.4	0639	0.4	1252	3.5	1855	0.5
19	SA	0107	3.4	0721	0.4	1341	3.4	1940	0.5
20	SU	0154	3.4	0809	0.5	1434	3.3	2030	0.7
21	M	0246	3.3	0904	0.6	1534	3.2	2127	0.8
22	TU ☾	0346	3.2	1013	0.7	1643	3.0	2236	1.0
23	W	0457	3.1	1146	0.7	1800	3.0		
24	TH	0003	1.0	0621	3.1	1304	0.6	1914	3.0
25	F	0121	0.9	0739	3.2	1406	0.4	2017	3.2
26	SA	0223	0.7	0840	3.3	1459	0.3	2110	3.3
27	SU	0316	0.6	0932	3.5	1546	0.2	2157	3.4
28	M	0402	0.5	1018	3.5	1629	0.2	2241	3.4
29	TU ●	0445	0.4	1103	3.5	1709	0.3	2324	3.5
30	W	0525	0.4	1146	3.5	1748	0.4		

MAY

Date	Day	Time	m	Time	m	Time	m	Time	m
1	TH	0005	3.5	0603	0.4	1228	3.4	1827	0.5
2	F	0045	3.5	0642	0.4	1308	3.3	1905	0.7
3	SA	0125	3.5	0720	0.5	1349	3.2	1943	0.8
4	SU	0206	3.5	0800	0.6	1432	3.1	2024	0.9
5	M	0249	3.4	0844	0.7	1519	3.0	2111	1.0
6	TU	0336	3.3	0937	0.8	1611	2.9	2211	1.1
7	W ☽	0429	3.1	1047	0.9	1708	2.8	2328	1.2
8	TH	0526	3.0	1204	0.9	1809	2.8		
9	F	0036	1.2	0626	3.0	1305	0.9	1913	2.8
10	SA	0133	1.1	0728	3.0	1356	0.7	2012	2.9
11	SU	0224	1.0	0825	3.1	1441	0.6	2059	3.1
12	M	0307	0.8	0911	3.2	1520	0.5	2139	3.2
13	TU	0347	0.7	0952	3.4	1558	0.5	2214	3.3
14	W O	0425	0.6	1030	3.4	1635	0.4	2248	3.4
15	TH	0504	0.5	1109	3.5	1714	0.4	2326	3.5
16	F	0543	0.4	1152	3.5	1756	0.4		
17	SA	0009	3.5	0625	0.3	1240	3.5	1840	0.5
18	SU	0056	3.6	0711	0.3	1332	3.4	1929	0.6
19	M	0145	3.5	0802	0.4	1427	3.3	2021	0.7
20	TU	0238	3.5	0859	0.4	1528	3.2	2119	0.8
21	W ☾	0337	3.4	1005	0.5	1635	3.1	2224	0.9
22	TH	0444	3.3	1124	0.6	1746	3.1	2338	0.9
23	F	0602	3.2	1237	0.5	1853	3.1		
24	SA	0050	0.9	0716	3.2	1339	0.5	1953	3.2
25	SU	0156	0.8	0818	3.3	1434	0.4	2047	3.3
26	M	0254	0.7	0912	3.4	1523	0.4	2137	3.4
27	TU	0344	0.6	1001	3.4	1608	0.5	2223	3.4
28	W ●	0429	0.6	1047	3.4	1649	0.5	2305	3.5
29	TH	0510	0.5	1129	3.3	1728	0.6	2345	3.5
30	F	0548	0.5	1208	3.3	1806	0.7		
31	SA	0023	3.5	0624	0.5	1245	3.2		

JUNE

Date	Day	Time	m	Time	m	Time	m	Time	m
1	SU	0101	3.5	0700	0.6	1323	3.2	1918	0.8
2	M	0140	3.5	0735	0.6	1405	3.1	1956	0.9
3	TU	0222	3.5	0815	0.6	1450	3.0	2038	0.9
4	W	0305	3.4	0859	0.7	1540	3.0	2126	1.0
5	TH ☽	0353	3.3	0950	0.8	1633	2.9	2221	1.1
6	F	0445	3.1	1050	0.9	1728	2.9	2326	1.2
7	SA	0542	3.1	1159	0.9	1825	2.9		
8	SU	0035	1.1	0640	3.1	1304	0.8	1919	3.0
9	M	0137	1.1	0737	3.1	1358	0.7	2012	3.1
10	TU	0230	0.9	0831	3.2	1445	0.6	2100	3.2
11	W	0318	0.7	0920	3.4	1529	0.5	2144	3.4
12	TH	0402	0.6	1006	3.5	1612	0.5	2227	3.5
13	F O	0446	0.4	1051	3.5	1655	0.4	2310	3.6
14	SA	0529	0.3	1138	3.5	1740	0.4	2356	3.6
15	SU	0614	0.3	1228	3.5	1827	0.5		
16	M	0045	3.7	0701	0.2	1321	3.4	1917	0.5
17	TU	0137	3.7	0752	0.3	1417	3.4	2009	0.6
18	W	0230	3.6	0847	0.3	1516	3.3	2105	0.7
19	TH ☾	0325	3.5	0948	0.4	1618	3.2	2205	0.8
20	F	0426	3.4	1058	0.5	1722	3.2	2311	0.9
21	SA	0535	3.3	1207	0.6	1825	3.1		
22	SU	0020	0.9	0648	3.2	1310	0.6	1926	3.2
23	M	0128	0.9	0755	3.2	1409	0.6	2024	3.2
24	TU	0231	0.8	0854	3.2	1502	0.6	2117	3.3
25	W	0327	0.7	0946	3.3	1548	0.7	2205	3.4
26	TH	0414	0.7	1032	3.3	1630	0.7	2248	3.5
27	F ●	0455	0.6	1114	3.2	1708	0.7	2328	3.5
28	SA	0531	0.6	1151	3.2	1745	0.7		
29	SU	0004	3.5	0605	0.6	1225	3.2	1819	0.8
30	M	0039	3.5	0637	0.6	1258	3.1	1852	0.8

SUNRISE AND SUNSET TIMES

BELFAST
At 54°36′N 5°55′ W

		Sunrise	Sunset
UT			
Jan	01	0846	1609
	15	0837	1630
Feb	01	0813	1703
	15	0745	1732
Mar	01	0713	1800
	15	0638	1828
BST			
Apr	01	0656	2000
	15	0621	2027
May	01	0545	2058
	15	0518	2123
Jun	01	0455	2149
	15	0447	2202
Jul	01	0452	2203
	15	0507	2151
Aug	01	0535	2124
	15	0600	2055
Sep	01	0631	2015
	15	0656	1940
Oct	01	0726	1900
	15	0753	1825
UT			
Nov	01	0726	1647
	15	0754	1622
Dec	01	0823	1603
	15	0840	1558

BELFAST
LAT 54°36′N
LONG 5°55′W

TIMES AND HEIGHTS OF HIGH AND LOW WATER (Heights in Metres)

TIME ZONE UT
For Summer Time (area enclosed in shaded box) add 1 hour

2014

JULY

Date	Day	Time	m
1	TU	0115 0710 1336 1928	3.5 0.6 3.1 0.8
2	W	0152 0746 1416 2007	3.5 0.6 3.1 0.8
3	TH	0230 0825 1500 2050	3.4 0.6 3.0 0.9
4	F	0309 0908 1547 2136	3.4 0.7 3.0 1.0
5	SA ☽	0353 0958 1640 2229	3.3 0.8 3.0 1.1
6	SU	0447 1054 1736 2331	3.1 0.8 2.9 1.1
7	M	0550 1200 1833	3.1 0.9 3.0
8	TU	0046 0654 1313 1930	1.1 3.1 0.8 3.1
9	W	0157 0756 1414 2026	1.0 3.2 0.7 3.2
10	TH	0254 0853 1506 2118	0.8 3.3 0.6 3.4
11	F	0345 0945 1554 2206	0.6 3.4 0.5 3.5
12	SA ○	0431 1034 1639 2253	0.4 3.5 0.4 3.6
13	SU	0516 1123 1725 2342	0.2 3.5 0.4 3.7
14	M	0601 1213 1812	0.2 3.5 0.4
15	TU	0032 0647 1306 1900	3.8 0.1 3.5 0.5
16	W	0123 0736 1400 1950	3.8 0.2 3.4 0.5
17	TH	0215 0827 1455 2043	3.7 0.3 3.3 0.6
18	F	0308 0923 1550 2139	3.6 0.4 3.3 0.7
19	SA ☾	0402 1026 1648 2241	3.5 0.5 3.2 0.8
20	SU	0502 1135 1749 2351	3.3 0.7 3.1 0.9
21	M	0614 1240 1856	3.1 0.8 3.1
22	TU	0101 0731 1342 2000	1.0 3.0 0.8 3.1
23	W	0208 0836 1440 2057	0.9 3.0 0.8 3.2
24	TH	0310 0931 1530 2147	0.8 3.1 0.8 3.4
25	F	0359 1017 1611 2230	0.7 3.1 0.8 3.4
26	SA ●	0438 1057 1647 2309	0.6 3.2 0.7 3.5
27	SU	0511 1133 1721 2344	0.6 3.1 0.7 3.5
28	M	0541 1205 1753	0.6 3.1 0.7
29	TU	0016 0611 1233 1825	3.5 0.6 3.1 0.7
30	W	0046 0643 1300 1859	3.5 0.6 3.1 0.7
31	TH	0116 0716 1332 1936	3.5 0.6 3.1 0.8

AUGUST

Date	Day	Time	m
1	F	0149 0752 1409 2015	3.5 0.6 3.1 0.8
2	SA	0227 0831 1451 2057	3.4 0.6 3.1 0.9
3	SU	0310 0916 1539 2146	3.3 0.7 3.1 1.0
4	M ☽	0401 1008 1638 2243	3.2 0.8 3.0 1.1
5	TU	0504 1109 1745 2356	3.1 0.9 3.0 1.1
6	W	0616 1226 1853	3.0 1.0 3.0
7	TH	0131 0726 1350 1957	1.0 3.1 0.9 3.2
8	F	0236 0831 1449 2055	0.8 3.2 0.7 3.4
9	SA	0329 0927 1539 2147	0.5 3.4 0.5 3.5
10	SU ○	0417 1018 1624 2236	0.3 3.5 0.4 3.7
11	M	0501 1106 1708 2325	0.1 3.5 0.4 3.8
12	TU	0545 1155 1753	0.1 3.5 0.4
13	W	0014 0629 1246 1838	3.8 0.1 3.5 0.4
14	TH	0105 0714 1337 1926	3.8 0.2 3.5 0.5
15	F	0155 0801 1428 2015	3.7 0.3 3.4 0.5
16	SA	0245 0851 1518 2108	3.6 0.5 3.3 0.7
17	SU ☾	0335 0949 1610 2208	3.4 0.7 3.2 0.8
18	M	0428 1058 1706 2320	3.2 0.9 3.1 0.9
19	TU	0530 1208 1813	3.0 1.0 3.1
20	W	0033 0705 1314 1933	1.0 2.9 1.1 3.1
21	TH	0143 0819 1415 2035	1.0 2.9 1.0 3.2
22	F	0247 0914 1507 2125	0.9 3.0 0.9 3.3
23	SA	0338 0958 1549 2208	0.7 3.1 0.8 3.4
24	SU	0414 1037 1624 2246	0.7 3.1 0.8 3.5
25	M ●	0444 1111 1655 2320	0.6 3.2 0.7 3.5
26	TU	0514 1142 1726 2349	0.6 3.2 0.7 3.5
27	W	0544 1204 1758	0.6 3.2 0.7
28	TH	0010 0614 1221 1831	3.5 0.5 3.2 0.7
29	F	0039 0646 1253 1905	3.5 0.5 3.2 0.7
30	SA	0115 0720 1331 1942	3.5 0.5 3.3 0.7
31	SU	0155 0758 1413 2023	3.5 0.6 3.2 0.8

SEPTEMBER

Date	Day	Time	m
1	M	0239 0842 1500 2111	3.4 0.7 3.2 0.9
2	TU ☽	0330 0933 1556 2208	3.2 0.8 3.1 1.0
3	W	0434 1034 1707 2321	3.1 1.0 3.0 1.1
4	TH	0549 1149 1822	3.0 1.1 3.0
5	F	0111 0704 1331 1933	1.0 3.0 1.0 3.2
6	SA	0218 0814 1433 2037	0.7 3.2 0.8 3.4
7	SU	0312 0912 1523 2131	0.5 3.4 0.6 3.6
8	M	0359 1002 1608 2220	0.2 3.5 0.5 3.7
9	TU ○	0443 1049 1650 2307	0.1 3.6 0.4 3.8
10	W	0525 1136 1732 2355	0.1 3.6 0.4 3.8
11	TH	0607 1223 1815	0.2 3.6 0.4
12	F	0044 0648 1312 1900	3.8 0.3 3.5 0.5
13	SA	0133 0732 1359 1946	3.7 0.4 3.5 0.6
14	SU	0220 0818 1446 2036	3.6 0.6 3.4 0.7
15	M	0307 0909 1534 2132	3.4 0.8 3.3 0.8
16	TU ☾	0357 1014 1625 2244	3.2 1.0 3.2 1.0
17	W	0453 1132 1724	2.9 1.2 3.1
18	TH	0002 0614 1240 1845	1.1 2.8 1.2 3.0
19	F	0110 0756 1342 2005	1.1 2.8 1.2 3.1
20	SA	0213 0850 1437 2058	0.9 2.9 1.1 3.3
21	SU	0304 0934 1521 2141	0.8 3.1 0.9 3.4
22	M	0342 1011 1556 2218	0.7 3.2 0.8 3.5
23	TU	0413 1043 1628 2250	0.6 3.2 0.8 3.5
24	W ●	0443 1112 1659 2316	0.6 3.3 0.7 3.5
25	TH	0514 1132 1731 2337	0.6 3.3 0.7 3.5
26	F	0546 1150 1804	0.6 3.3 0.7
27	SA	0008 0617 1224 1838	3.5 0.6 3.4 0.7
28	SU	0047 0652 1303 1915	3.5 0.6 3.4 0.7
29	M	0130 0731 1347 1957	3.5 0.6 3.4 0.7
30	TU	0217 0816 1434 2047	3.4 0.7 3.3 0.8

OCTOBER

Date	Day	Time	m
1	W ☽	0311 0908 1530 2146	3.3 0.9 3.2 1.0
2	TH	0416 1010 1640 2302	3.1 1.1 3.1 1.0
3	F	0531 1127 1758	3.0 1.2 3.1
4	SA	0050 0648 1308 1915	0.9 3.0 1.1 3.2
5	SU	0157 0759 1413 2022	0.7 3.2 0.9 3.4
6	M	0251 0857 1505 2116	0.5 3.4 0.7 3.6
7	TU	0339 0946 1550 2205	0.3 3.5 0.6 3.7
8	W ○	0423 1032 1632 2251	0.2 3.6 0.5 3.8
9	TH	0504 1117 1713 2337	0.3 3.7 0.5 3.8
10	F	0544 1202 1755	0.3 3.7 0.5
11	SA	0024 0624 1248 1837	3.7 0.5 3.6 0.5
12	SU	0110 0705 1332 1921	3.6 0.6 3.6 0.6
13	M	0155 0748 1416 2007	3.5 0.8 3.6 0.7
14	TU	0240 0835 1502 2058	3.3 1.0 3.5 0.9
15	W ☾	0328 0929 1551 2202	3.1 1.2 3.3 1.0
16	TH	0421 1045 1645 2322	2.9 1.3 3.2 1.1
17	F	0522 1200 1747	2.8 1.4 3.1
18	SA	0030 0708 1303 1903	1.1 2.8 1.3 3.1
19	SU	0131 0815 1359 2015	1.0 2.9 1.2 3.2
20	M	0222 0900 1446 2103	0.9 3.1 1.0 3.3
21	TU	0304 0936 1525 2142	0.8 3.2 0.9 3.4
22	W	0339 1009 1600 2216	0.7 3.3 0.8 3.5
23	TH ●	0412 1039 1633 2245	0.6 3.4 0.8 3.5
24	F	0445 1103 1707 2312	0.6 3.4 0.7 3.6
25	SA	0518 1127 1741 2346	0.6 3.5 0.7 3.6
26	SU	0553 1202 1818	0.6 3.6 0.7
27	M	0027 0631 1243 1857	3.6 0.6 3.6 0.7
28	TU	0113 0713 1329 1942	3.5 0.7 3.6 0.7
29	W	0203 0800 1418 2033	3.4 0.8 3.5 0.8
30	TH	0259 0853 1515 2134	3.3 1.0 3.4 0.9
31	F ☽	0403 0956 1621 2252	3.2 1.1 3.3 0.9

NOVEMBER

Date	Day	Time	m
1	SA	0517 1112 1738	3.1 1.2 3.2
2	SU	0023 0634 1239 1858	0.9 3.1 1.1 3.3
3	M	0131 0742 1348 2005	0.7 3.3 1.0 3.5
4	TU	0227 0840 1443 2101	0.6 3.4 0.8 3.6
5	W	0317 0929 1532 2150	0.5 3.5 0.7 3.7
6	TH ○	0401 1016 1616 2237	0.4 3.6 0.6 3.7
7	F	0443 1100 1658 2322	0.5 3.7 0.6 3.7
8	SA	0524 1143 1739	0.6 3.7 0.6
9	SU	0006 0603 1226 1820	3.6 0.7 3.7 0.6
10	M	0049 0643 1307 1901	3.5 0.8 3.7 0.7
11	TU	0131 0724 1349 1943	3.4 0.9 3.7 0.7
12	W	0214 0806 1433 2028	3.3 1.0 3.6 0.8
13	TH	0300 0852 1520 2119	3.2 1.2 3.5 1.0
14	F ☾	0351 0948 1611 2223	3.0 1.3 3.3 1.1
15	SA	0446 1103 1707 2338	2.9 1.4 3.2 1.1
16	SU	0547 1214 1807	2.9 1.4 3.2
17	M	0042 0653 1314 1909	1.1 2.9 1.3 3.2
18	TU	0136 0758 1406 2009	1.0 3.1 1.2 3.3
19	W	0223 0848 1451 2059	0.9 3.2 1.0 3.4
20	TH	0303 0930 1530 2141	0.8 3.3 0.9 3.5
21	F	0341 1007 1608 2218	0.7 3.5 0.8 3.5
22	SA ●	0418 1039 1645 2253	0.7 3.5 0.7 3.6
23	SU	0456 1111 1724 2331	0.6 3.6 0.6 3.6
24	M	0535 1147 1804	0.6 3.7 0.6
25	TU	0014 0616 1230 1847	3.6 0.7 3.7 0.6
26	W	0102 0701 1317 1934	3.6 0.7 3.7 0.6
27	TH	0153 0750 1408 2026	3.5 0.8 3.6 0.6
28	F	0249 0844 1503 2125	3.4 0.9 3.6 0.7
29	SA ☽	0352 0944 1605 2235	3.3 1.0 3.5 0.8
30	SU	0503 1053 1718 2353	3.2 1.1 3.4 0.8

DECEMBER

Date	Day	Time	m
1	M	0615 1208 1837	3.2 1.1 3.4
2	TU	0101 0720 1319 1945	0.7 3.3 1.0 3.4
3	W	0201 0819 1420 2044	0.7 3.4 0.9 3.5
4	TH	0254 0912 1515 2136	0.6 3.5 0.8 3.6
5	F	0342 1000 1603 2225	0.6 3.6 0.7 3.6
6	SA ○	0426 1045 1647 2310	0.7 3.7 0.7 3.5
7	SU	0507 1128 1728 2352	0.7 3.7 0.7 3.5
8	M	0547 1208 1807	0.8 3.7 0.7
9	TU	0031 0625 1247 1844	3.4 0.9 3.7 0.7
10	W	0110 0702 1326 1921	3.3 0.9 3.7 0.7
11	TH	0150 0739 1407 2000	3.3 1.0 3.7 0.8
12	F	0233 0820 1451 2042	3.2 1.1 3.6 0.9
13	SA	0320 0905 1538 2130	3.1 1.1 3.4 0.9
14	SU ☾	0411 0957 1629 2226	3.0 1.2 3.3 1.0
15	M	0506 1100 1724 2332	3.0 1.3 3.2 1.1
16	TU	0603 1213 1822	3.0 1.3 3.2
17	W	0040 0701 1318 1920	1.1 3.0 1.3 3.2
18	TH	0138 0758 1414 2017	1.0 3.1 1.1 3.3
19	F	0229 0851 1502 2108	0.9 3.3 1.0 3.4
20	SA	0314 0936 1546 2153	0.8 3.4 0.8 3.5
21	SU	0356 1016 1628 2235	0.7 3.5 0.7 3.6
22	M ●	0438 1055 1710 2317	0.6 3.7 0.5 3.6
23	TU	0520 1136 1753	0.6 3.7 0.5
24	W	0002 0603 1220 1837	3.6 0.6 3.8 0.4
25	TH	0051 0649 1308 1924	3.6 0.6 3.8 0.4
26	F	0143 0738 1358 2015	3.5 0.7 3.8 0.4
27	SA	0238 0830 1452 2110	3.4 0.8 3.7 0.5
28	SU ☽	0337 0926 1550 2213	3.3 0.8 3.6 0.6
29	M	0440 1028 1655 2323	3.2 0.9 3.5 0.7
30	TU	0547 1138 1809	3.2 1.0 3.4
31	W	0032 0653 1251 1922	0.8 3.2 1.0 3.3

GALWAY
LAT 53°16'N
LONG 9°03'W

TIMES AND HEIGHTS OF HIGH AND LOW WATER (Heights in Metres)

TIME ZONE UT
For Summer Time (area enclosed in shaded box) add 1 hour

2014

JANUARY

Date	Day	Time	m
1	W ●	0429 1036 1659 2255	5.5 0.6 5.4 0.7
2	TH	0518 1121 1748 2340	5.7 0.4 5.5 0.6
3	F	0606 1206 1836	5.8 0.4 5.5
4	SA	0025 0654 1252 1924	0.7 5.7 0.5 5.4
5	SU	0111 0742 1338 2013	0.8 5.5 0.6 5.2
6	M	0200 0832 1428 2104	1.1 5.3 0.9 4.9
7	TU	0253 0924 1522 2158	1.4 4.9 1.3 4.6
8	W ☽	0353 1021 1624 2300	1.6 4.6 1.6 4.3
9	TH	0505 1129 1735	1.9 4.3 1.9
10	F	0016 0619 1253 1846	4.2 2.0 4.1 2.0
11	SA	0133 0730 1403 1951	4.2 1.9 4.2 1.9
12	SU	0233 0832 1459 2045	4.3 1.8 4.3 1.8
13	M	0322 0921 1545 2128	4.5 1.6 4.5 1.7
14	TU	0403 0959 1626 2205	4.7 1.4 4.6 1.5
15	W	0440 1031 1703 2240	4.9 1.2 4.8 1.3
16	TH ○	0516 1104 1739 2315	5.0 1.1 4.9 1.2
17	F	0552 1137 1815 2349	5.1 1.0 4.9 1.1
18	SA	0628 1211 1850	5.1 1.0 4.9
19	SU	0022 0700 1245 1923	1.2 5.0 1.0 4.8
20	M	0056 0731 1319 1956	1.2 4.9 1.1 4.7
21	TU	0131 0801 1355 2030	1.3 4.8 1.2 4.6
22	W	0210 0838 1435 2111	1.5 4.6 1.4 4.4
23	TH	0254 0926 1521 2202	1.6 4.4 1.6 4.3
24	F ☾	0345 1023 1614 2300	1.8 4.3 1.8 4.2
25	SA	0444 1127 1718	2.0 4.2 1.9
26	SU	0005 0600 1238 1849	4.2 2.0 4.2 1.9
27	M	0117 0749 1355 2021	4.4 1.8 4.4 1.6
28	TU	0227 0852 1502 2115	4.7 1.4 4.7 1.3
29	W	0325 0942 1557 2202	5.1 0.9 5.1 0.9
30	TH ●	0417 1027 1646 2246	5.5 0.6 5.4 0.6
31	F	0505 1110 1733 2328	5.7 0.3 5.6 0.5

FEBRUARY

Date	Day	Time	m
1	SA	0552 1152 1819	5.9 0.2 5.6
2	SU	0010 0637 1234 1904	0.5 5.8 0.3 5.5
3	M	0052 0722 1315 1948	0.6 5.7 0.5 5.3
4	TU	0135 0807 1359 2034	0.8 5.4 0.8 5.0
5	W	0221 0854 1446 2120	1.2 5.0 1.2 4.7
6	TH ☽	0314 0943 1541 2210	1.5 4.6 1.6 4.3
7	F	0423 1038 1653 2308	1.9 4.2 2.0 4.1
8	SA	0541 1159 1809	2.1 3.9 2.1
9	SU	0055 0652 1341 1915	4.0 2.1 3.9 2.1
10	M	0213 0757 1443 2014	4.1 1.9 4.1 2.0
11	TU	0306 0852 1530 2103	4.3 1.7 4.3 1.8
12	W	0348 0934 1610 2144	4.5 1.5 4.5 1.5
13	TH	0425 1010 1645 2221	4.7 1.2 4.7 1.3
14	F ○	0500 1044 1720 2256	4.9 1.0 4.9 1.1
15	SA	0534 1116 1754 2328	5.0 0.9 5.0 1.0
16	SU	0607 1148 1827	5.1 0.8 5.0
17	M	0000 0638 1220 1857	0.9 5.1 0.8 5.0
18	TU	0033 0705 1253 1926	0.9 5.0 0.8 4.9
19	W	0108 0733 1329 1957	1.0 4.9 0.9 4.8
20	TH	0146 0809 1409 2037	1.1 4.7 1.1 4.6
21	F	0229 0855 1453 2126	1.3 4.5 1.4 4.4
22	SA ☾	0317 0952 1544 2226	1.6 4.3 1.7 4.2
23	SU	0414 1058 1647 2334	1.8 4.1 1.9 4.1
24	M	0528 1214 1817	1.9 4.0 2.0
25	TU	0053 0735 1341 2011	4.2 1.7 4.2 1.7
26	W	0213 0843 1452 2106	4.5 1.3 4.6 1.3
27	TH	0314 0932 1545 2151	5.0 0.8 5.0 0.9
28	F	0404 1015 1632 2232	5.4 0.5 5.4 0.5

MARCH

Date	Day	Time	m
1	SA ●	0450 1055 1716 2312	5.7 0.2 5.6 0.4
2	SU	0535 1133 1759 2350	5.8 0.2 5.6 0.3
3	M	0618 1210 1841	5.8 0.2 5.5
4	TU	0028 0700 1248 1921	0.4 5.6 0.5 5.3
5	W	0108 0742 1327 2003	0.7 5.3 0.8 5.0
6	TH	0150 0825 1410 2045	1.0 4.9 1.2 4.7
7	F	0237 0911 1459 2131	1.4 4.5 1.6 4.4
8	SA ☽	0340 1000 1610 2222	1.8 4.1 2.0 4.1
9	SU	0505 1053 1735 2322	2.0 3.8 2.2 3.8
10	M	0617 1311 1843	2.1 3.7 2.2
11	TU	0146 0720 1421 1942	3.8 2.0 3.9 2.0
12	W	0243 0816 1508 2034	4.1 1.7 4.1 1.8
13	TH	0326 0902 1547 2118	4.3 1.5 4.4 1.5
14	F	0402 0942 1622 2157	4.6 1.2 4.6 1.2
15	SA	0436 1018 1654 2232	4.8 0.9 4.8 1.0
16	SU ○	0509 1051 1726 2304	4.9 0.8 4.9 0.8
17	M	0541 1121 1758 2335	5.0 0.7 5.0 0.7
18	TU	0612 1152 1828	5.0 0.6 5.0
19	W	0008 0640 1227 1858	0.7 5.0 0.6 5.0
20	TH	0045 0711 1304 1931	0.7 4.9 0.8 4.9
21	F	0125 0750 1345 2012	0.8 4.8 1.0 4.7
22	SA	0208 0836 1430 2102	1.0 4.5 1.3 4.5
23	SU	0257 0933 1523 2201	1.3 4.3 1.6 4.2
24	M ☾	0356 1041 1628 2312	1.6 4.0 1.9 4.1
25	TU	0511 1200 1801	1.7 4.0 1.9
26	W	0035 0721 1330 1958	4.1 1.6 4.1 1.6
27	TH	0158 0830 1438 2052	4.4 1.2 4.5 1.2
28	F	0258 0917 1530 2136	4.8 0.8 4.9 0.8
29	SA	0348 0958 1614 2215	5.2 0.5 5.3 0.5
30	SU ●	0433 1035 1657 2252	5.5 0.3 5.4 0.4
31	M	0516 1110 1737 [illegible]	5.6 0.3 5.5 [illegible]

APRIL

Date	Day	Time	m
1	TU	0557 1145 1817	5.5 0.4 5.4
2	W	0004 0637 1221 1855	0.5 5.4 0.6 5.3
3	TH	0043 0718 1258 1935	0.7 5.1 0.9 5.0
4	F	0123 0800 1339 2016	1.0 4.8 1.3 4.7
5	SA	0208 0844 1424 2101	1.3 4.5 1.6 4.4
6	SU	0302 0931 1524 2149	1.7 4.1 2.0 4.1
7	M ☽	0426 1024 1700 2243	1.9 3.9 2.2 3.9
8	TU	0541 1126 1810 2349	2.0 3.7 2.2 3.7
9	W	0644 1343 1910	1.9 3.8 2.1
10	TH	0205 0740 1435 2002	3.9 1.7 4.0 1.8
11	F	0252 0829 1515 2048	4.1 1.5 4.3 1.5
12	SA	0331 0912 1549 2129	4.3 1.2 4.5 1.2
13	SU	0405 0949 1621 2205	4.6 1.0 4.7 1.0
14	M	0437 1023 1653 2237	4.8 0.8 4.9 0.8
15	TU ○	0510 1053 1725 2309	4.9 0.7 5.0 0.6
16	W	0543 1126 1759 2345	5.0 0.6 5.1 0.5
17	TH	0617 1202 1834	5.0 0.6 5.1
18	F	0024 0655 1243 1913	0.5 5.0 0.7 5.0
19	SA	0107 0738 1326 1957	0.7 4.8 0.9 4.8
20	SU	0153 0827 1414 2048	0.9 4.6 1.2 4.6
21	M	0245 0925 1510 2148	1.1 4.3 1.5 4.4
22	TU ☾	0345 1030 1618 2257	1.4 4.1 1.8 4.2
23	W	0458 1148 1746	1.5 4.0 1.8
24	TH	0018 0646 1312 1934	4.2 1.5 4.2 1.6
25	F	0138 0806 1418 2032	4.4 1.2 4.5 1.2
26	SA	0238 0856 1509 2117	4.7 0.9 4.8 0.9
27	SU	0328 0937 1554 2157	5.0 0.7 5.1 0.7
28	M	0414 1014 1635 2233	5.1 0.6 5.2 0.6
29	TU ●	0456 1047 1715 2308	5.2 0.6 5.3 0.5
30	W	0538 1120 1754 2343	5.2 0.7 5.2 0.6

MAY

Date	Day	Time	m
1	TH	0618 1156 1832	5.1 0.8 5.1
2	F	0020 0657 1234 1911	0.8 4.9 1.0 5.0
3	SA	0101 0738 1314 1951	1.0 4.7 1.3 4.7
4	SU	0143 0820 1356 2035	1.2 4.5 1.6 4.5
5	M	0231 0906 1444 2121	1.5 4.2 1.9 4.2
6	TU	0332 0955 1602 2211	1.8 4.0 2.1 4.0
7	W ☽	0456 1049 1730 2307	1.9 3.8 2.2 3.8
8	TH	0603 1151 1833	1.9 3.8 2.1
9	F	0012 0701 1331 1927	3.8 1.8 3.9 1.9
10	SA	0154 0753 1426 2016	3.9 1.6 4.1 1.7
11	SU	0244 0838 1504 2058	4.2 1.4 4.4 1.4
12	M	0322 0918 1539 2136	4.4 1.1 4.7 1.1
13	TU	0359 0952 1615 2210	4.7 0.9 4.9 0.9
14	W ○	0436 1026 1652 2245	4.9 0.8 5.1 0.7
15	TH	0515 1102 1732 2324	5.0 0.7 5.2 0.5
16	F	0557 1142 1815	5.1 0.6 5.2
17	SA	0007 0642 1226 1859	0.5 5.0 0.7 5.2
18	SU	0053 0729 1313 1947	0.5 4.9 0.9 5.0
19	M	0142 0820 1404 2039	0.7 4.7 1.1 4.8
20	TU	0235 0916 1501 2137	0.9 4.5 1.4 4.6
21	W ☾	0334 1018 1606 2242	1.2 4.3 1.6 4.4
22	TH	0442 1129 1724 2356	1.3 4.2 1.7 4.3
23	F	0603 1246 1855	1.4 4.3 1.6
24	SA	0112 0729 1352 2004	4.3 1.3 4.4 1.4
25	SU	0215 0829 1446 2055	4.5 1.2 4.7 1.2
26	M	0308 0915 1533 2139	4.7 1.1 4.9 1.0
27	TU	0355 0953 1615 2217	4.8 1.0 5.0 0.9
28	W ●	0439 1027 1655 2251	4.9 1.0 5.1 0.8
29	TH	0520 1100 1734 2325	4.9 1.0 5.1 0.8
30	F	0600 1136 1812	4.9 1.1 5.0
31	SA	0002 0639 1214	0.9 4.8 1.2

JUNE

Date	Day	Time	m
1	SU	0041 0718 1253 1930	1.0 4.7 1.3 4.8
2	M	0121 0758 1332 2011	1.2 4.5 1.5 4.6
3	TU	0202 0840 1412 2053	1.4 4.4 1.7 4.4
4	W	0245 0925 1455 2139	1.6 4.2 1.9 4.2
5	TH ☽	0334 1013 1551 2228	1.8 4.0 2.1 4.0
6	F	0442 1105 1732 2322	1.9 4.0 2.2 3.9
7	SA	0608 1202 1843	1.9 4.0 2.1
8	SU	0021 0709 1305 1937	4.0 1.8 4.1 1.8
9	M	0127 0800 1405 2024	4.1 1.6 4.3 1.6
10	TU	0229 0844 1455 2106	4.3 1.4 4.6 1.3
11	W	0319 0924 1540 2146	4.6 1.1 4.9 1.0
12	TH	0406 1003 1625 2227	4.9 0.9 5.2 0.7
13	F ○	0453 1044 1711 2310	5.1 0.8 5.3 0.5
14	SA	0540 1128 1758 2355	5.2 0.7 5.4 0.4
15	SU	0628 1214 1846	5.2 0.7 5.4
16	M	0041 0717 1302 1935	0.4 5.1 0.8 5.3
17	TU	0131 0808 1352 2026	0.5 5.0 1.0 5.1
18	W	0222 0901 1446 2121	0.7 4.8 1.2 4.8
19	TH ☾	0317 0959 1547 2221	1.0 4.6 1.4 4.6
20	F	0419 1103 1657 2329	1.3 4.4 1.6 4.4
21	SA	0528 1215 1815	1.4 4.3 1.7
22	SU	0044 0645 1325 1931	4.3 1.5 4.3 1.6
23	M	0153 0756 1424 2032	4.3 1.5 4.5 1.5
24	TU	0250 0851 1514 2122	4.4 1.4 4.6 1.3
25	W	0339 0935 1559 2203	4.5 1.4 4.8 1.2
26	TH	0424 1010 1639 2237	4.7 1.3 4.9 1.1
27	F ●	0505 1044 1718 2309	4.7 1.2 5.0 1.0
28	SA	0544 1118 1756 2343	4.8 1.2 5.0 1.0
29	SU	0622 1154 1833	4.8 1.2 4.9
30	M	0020 0659 1231 1910	1.0 4.8 1.2 4.9

SUNRISE AND SUNSET TIMES

GALWAY
At 53°16'N 9°03'W

		Sunrise	Sunset
UT			
Jan	01	0851	1629
	15	0843	1649
Feb	01	0820	1720
	15	0754	1747
Mar	01	0723	1814
	15	0651	1841
BST			
Apr	01	0710	2012
	15	0637	2037
May	01	0602	2106
	15	0537	2129
Jun	01	0515	2154
	15	0508	2206
Jul	01	0513	2207
	15	0528	2156
Aug	01	0553	2131
	15	0616	2104
Sep	01	0646	2025
	15	0710	1952
Oct	01	0738	1913
	15	0803	1840
UT			
Nov	01	0735	1704
	15	0801	1640
Dec	01	0828	1622
	15	0845	1618

GALWAY
LAT 53°16′N
LONG 9°03′W

TIMES AND HEIGHTS OF HIGH AND LOW WATER (Heights in Metres)

TIME ZONE UT
For Summer Time (area enclosed in shaded box) add 1 hour

2014

JULY

Date	Time	m
1 TU	0057 0736 1307 1947	1.1 4.7 1.4 4.7
2 W	0133 0814 1343 2024	1.2 4.5 1.5 4.5
3 TH	0210 0853 1421 2104	1.4 4.4 1.7 4.4
4 F	0250 0936 1505 2148	1.5 4.2 1.8 4.2
5 SA	0336 1024 1557 ☽ 2239	1.7 4.1 2.0 4.1
6 SU	0428 1117 1658 2336	1.8 4.1 2.0 4.0
7 M	0533 1215 1825	1.9 4.1 2.0
8 TU	0038 0706 1317 1948	4.1 1.8 4.3 1.7
9 W	0145 0813 1419 2042	4.3 1.6 4.6 1.4
10 TH	0249 0904 1514 2130	4.5 1.3 4.9 1.0
11 F	0344 0949 1605 2215	4.8 1.0 5.2 0.7
12 SA	0435 1033 1654 O 2259	5.1 0.8 5.5 0.4
13 SU	0524 1117 1742 2344	5.3 0.6 5.6 0.3
14 M	0613 1202 1831	5.4 0.5 5.7
15 TU	0029 0700 1248 1919	0.3 5.4 0.6 5.6
16 W	0115 0749 1335 2008	0.4 5.2 0.8 5.3
17 TH	0203 0839 1425 2059	0.6 5.0 1.0 5.0
18 F	0254 0931 1521 2154	0.9 4.7 1.3 4.7
19 SA	0351 1029 1627 ☾ 2257	1.3 4.4 1.6 4.4
20 SU	0456 1138 1742	1.6 4.2 1.8
21 M	0015 0609 1258 1857	4.1 1.8 4.2 1.8
22 TU	0132 0722 1406 2007	4.1 1.8 4.2 1.7
23 W	0235 0824 1500 2103	4.2 1.8 4.4 1.5
24 TH	0326 0914 1545 2146	4.3 1.6 4.6 1.3
25 F	0410 0952 1626 2219	4.5 1.4 4.8 1.2
26 SA	0449 1026 1703 ● 2250	4.6 1.3 4.9 1.0
27 SU	0526 1100 1739 2323	4.8 1.2 5.0 0.9
28 M	0602 1134 1815 2356	4.8 1.1 5.0 0.9
29 TU	0637 1208 1849	4.8 1.1 4.9
30 W	0030 0711 1242 1922	0.9 4.8 1.1 4.8
31 TH	0105 0744 1316 1952	1.0 4.7 1.2 4.7

AUGUST

Date	Time	m
1 F	0140 0818 1353 2026	1.1 4.5 1.4 4.5
2 SA	0218 0856 1434 2108	1.3 4.4 1.6 4.4
3 SU	0301 0942 1521 2200	1.5 4.3 1.7 4.2
4 M	0350 1037 1617 ☽ 2300	1.7 4.1 1.9 4.1
5 TU	0447 1137 1724	1.9 4.1 2.0
6 W	0005 0601 1244 1914	4.0 1.9 4.2 1.8
7 TH	0117 0751 1353 2026	4.2 1.7 4.5 1.4
8 F	0229 0850 1456 2118	4.5 1.4 4.9 1.0
9 SA	0329 0938 1550 2204	4.8 1.0 5.3 0.6
10 SU	0420 1022 1639 O 2247	5.2 0.7 5.6 0.3
11 M	0508 1105 1726 2329	5.4 0.4 5.8 0.1
12 TU	0555 1146 1813	5.5 0.4 5.8
13 W	0011 0640 1229 1859	0.1 5.5 0.4 5.7
14 TH	0054 0725 1313 1945	0.3 5.4 0.6 5.4
15 F	0137 0811 1359 2033	0.6 5.1 0.9 5.1
16 SA	0224 0859 1451 2123	1.0 4.8 1.3 4.7
17 SU	0318 0950 1555 ☾ 2220	1.4 4.4 1.6 4.3
18 M	0425 1049 1713 2337	1.7 4.1 1.9 4.0
19 TU	0540 1227 1827	2.0 4.0 1.9
20 W	0114 0650 1349 1935	3.9 2.0 4.1 1.9
21 TH	0221 0754 1445 2036	4.0 1.9 4.2 1.7
22 F	0312 0846 1530 2119	4.2 1.7 4.5 1.4
23 SA	0354 0928 1609 2154	4.4 1.5 4.7 1.2
24 SU	0431 1004 1644 2226	4.6 1.3 4.8 1.0
25 M	0505 1038 1719 ● 2259	4.8 1.1 4.9 0.8
26 TU	0539 1111 1752 2331	4.9 1.0 5.0 0.8
27 W	0612 1143 1825	4.9 0.9 5.0
28 TH	0003 0643 1216 1854	0.8 4.9 0.9 4.9
29 F	0036 0713 1250 1920	0.8 4.8 1.0 4.8
30 SA	0111 0743 1327 1952	0.9 4.7 1.1 4.6
31 SU	0149 0819 1408 2034	1.1 4.5 1.3 4.4

SEPTEMBER

Date	Time	m
1 M	0232 0905 1454 2128	1.4 4.4 1.5 4.2
2 TU	0320 1002 1548 ☽ 2231	1.6 4.2 1.8 4.0
3 W	0417 1106 1655 2341	1.9 4.1 1.9 4.0
4 TH	0533 1217 1853	2.0 4.1 1.8
5 F	0059 0738 1335 2014	4.1 1.8 4.4 1.4
6 SA	0219 0838 1443 2105	4.4 1.4 4.8 0.9
7 SU	0317 0925 1536 2149	4.8 0.9 5.2 0.5
8 M	0406 1007 1623 2230	5.2 0.6 5.6 0.2
9 TU	0451 1048 1708 O 2310	5.5 0.3 5.8 0.1
10 W	0534 1127 1753 2348	5.6 0.3 5.8 0.1
11 TH	0617 1207 1837	5.6 0.3 5.6
12 F	0027 0659 1248 1921	0.3 5.4 0.6 5.4
13 SA	0109 0742 1331 2006	0.6 5.1 0.9 5.0
14 SU	0153 0826 1420 2053	1.0 4.8 1.3 4.6
15 M	0243 0913 1522 2145	1.5 4.4 1.7 4.2
16 TU	0351 1005 1644 ☾ 2246	1.9 4.1 1.9 3.9
17 W	0512 1109 1757	2.1 3.9 2.0
18 TH	0052 0620 1325 1900	3.7 2.2 3.9 1.9
19 F	0201 0721 1423 1958	3.9 2.0 4.1 1.7
20 SA	0251 0815 1508 2044	4.1 1.8 4.3 1.5
21 SU	0331 0859 1546 2124	4.3 1.5 4.6 1.2
22 M	0407 0938 1620 2159	4.6 1.3 4.7 1.0
23 TU	0439 1014 1653 2233	4.7 1.0 4.9 0.8
24 W	0511 1047 1726 ● 2304	4.9 0.9 5.0 0.7
25 TH	0543 1118 1757 2335	4.9 0.8 5.0 0.7
26 F	0614 1150 1827	5.0 0.8 4.9
27 SA	0008 0642 1225 1854	0.7 4.9 0.8 4.8
28 SU	0045 0713 1304 1928	0.8 4.8 0.9 4.7
29 M	0124 0751 1345 2012	1.0 4.7 1.1 4.5
30 TU	0207 0838 1432 2106	1.3 4.5 1.4 4.2

OCTOBER

Date	Time	m
1 W	0257 0935 1528 ☽ 2211	1.6 4.3 1.6 4.0
2 TH	0357 1042 1637 2323	1.9 4.1 1.8 3.9
3 F	0517 1156 1830	2.0 4.1 1.7
4 SA	0047 0723 1319 1959	4.0 1.8 4.4 1.3
5 SU	0207 0823 1427 2049	4.4 1.4 4.8 0.9
6 M	0302 0909 1520 2131	4.8 0.9 5.2 0.5
7 TU	0349 0950 1606 2210	5.2 0.6 5.5 0.3
8 W	0432 1029 1650 O 2247	5.4 0.4 5.6 0.2
9 TH	0513 1106 1733 2324	5.5 0.3 5.6 0.3
10 F	0554 1144 1816	5.5 0.4 5.5
11 SA	0001 0634 1224 1858	0.5 5.4 0.6 5.2
12 SU	0041 0715 1306 1941	0.8 5.1 0.9 4.9
13 M	0123 0758 1352 2026	1.2 4.8 1.3 4.5
14 TU	0211 0843 1449 2115	1.6 4.5 1.6 4.2
15 W	0313 0932 1609 ☾ 2209	2.0 4.2 1.9 3.9
16 TH	0438 1027 1722 2319	2.2 4.0 2.0 3.7
17 F	0548 1138 1825	2.2 3.8 1.9
18 SA	0126 0648 1348 1920	3.8 2.1 4.0 1.8
19 SU	0220 0742 1436 2009	4.0 1.9 4.2 1.5
20 M	0301 0829 1515 2052	4.3 1.6 4.4 1.3
21 TU	0336 0911 1550 2131	4.5 1.4 4.6 1.1
22 W	0408 0948 1623 2206	4.7 1.1 4.8 0.9
23 TH	0439 1022 1655 ● 2237	4.9 0.9 4.9 0.8
24 F	0511 1053 1728 2309	5.0 0.8 5.0 0.7
25 SA	0543 1126 1801 2343	5.1 0.7 5.0 0.7
26 SU	0616 1203 1836	5.1 0.7 4.9
27 M	0022 0652 1245 1915	0.8 5.0 0.8 4.8
28 TU	0104 0733 1329 2001	1.0 4.9 1.0 4.6
29 W	0150 0821 1418 2055	1.3 4.7 1.2 4.4
30 TH	0242 0918 1515 2158	1.6 4.5 1.4 4.2
31 F	0344 1023 1623 ☽ 2308	1.8 4.3 1.6 4.1

NOVEMBER

Date	Time	m
1 SA	0502 1136 1754	1.9 4.2 1.6
2 SU	0031 0652 1259 1933	4.1 1.8 4.4 1.3
3 M	0147 0802 1407 2027	4.4 1.4 4.7 1.0
4 TU	0242 0850 1501 2111	4.8 1.1 5.0 0.8
5 W	0329 0932 1548 2150	5.1 0.8 5.2 0.6
6 TH	0412 1011 1632 O 2227	5.3 0.6 5.4 0.6
7 F	0453 1048 1715 2302	5.4 0.6 5.4 0.6
8 SA	0533 1126 1757 2339	5.4 0.6 5.3 0.8
9 SU	0613 1204 1839	5.3 0.8 5.1
10 M	0017 0652 1245 1920	1.0 5.1 1.0 4.9
11 TU	0059 0733 1328 2003	1.3 4.9 1.3 4.6
12 W	0143 0817 1417 2049	1.6 4.6 1.6 4.3
13 TH	0234 0903 1519 2138	1.9 4.4 1.8 4.1
14 F	0346 0953 1637 ☾ 2232	2.2 4.1 2.0 3.9
15 SA	0507 1049 1744 2337	2.3 4.0 2.0 3.8
16 SU	0611 1157 1842	2.2 3.9 1.9
17 M	0123 0707 1343 1934	3.9 2.1 4.0 1.7
18 TU	0216 0757 1433 2020	4.2 1.8 4.2 1.5
19 W	0255 0842 1512 2102	4.4 1.6 4.5 1.3
20 TH	0330 0922 1548 2139	4.7 1.3 4.7 1.1
21 F	0404 0957 1623 2212	4.9 1.1 4.9 1.0
22 SA	0439 1031 1700 ● 2246	5.1 0.9 5.0 0.9
23 SU	0516 1107 1739 2323	5.2 0.8 5.1 0.8
24 M	0555 1147 1821	5.3 0.7 5.1
25 TU	0005 0636 1230 1905	0.9 5.2 0.7 5.0
26 W	0049 0721 1316 1953	1.0 5.1 0.8 4.8
27 TH	0137 0810 1406 2045	1.2 5.0 1.0 4.6
28 F	0230 0904 1502 2143	1.4 4.7 1.2 4.4
29 SA	0331 1005 1605 ☽ 2249	1.6 4.5 1.4 4.3
30 SU	0441 1114 1719	1.8 4.4 1.5

DECEMBER

Date	Time	m
1 M	0005 0605 1233 1850	4.3 1.8 4.4 1.5
2 TU	0119 0732 1344 2000	4.4 1.6 4.5 1.3
3 W	0219 0830 1441 2050	4.7 1.3 4.8 1.2
4 TH	0309 0917 1531 2133	4.9 1.1 4.9 1.1
5 F	0354 0959 1617 2211	5.1 1.0 5.1 1.0
6 SA	0437 1036 1700 O 2246	5.2 0.9 5.1 1.0
7 SU	0517 1112 1742 2322	5.3 0.9 5.1 1.1
8 M	0556 1148 1823 2359	5.2 0.9 5.0 1.2
9 TU	0635 1226 1902	5.1 1.0 4.9
10 W	0038 0713 1306 1942	1.3 5.0 1.2 4.7
11 TH	0119 0754 1347 2024	1.5 4.8 1.4 4.6
12 F	0200 0836 1431 2108	1.7 4.6 1.6 4.4
13 SA	0244 0922 1521 2155	2.0 4.4 1.8 4.2
14 SU	0339 1011 1631 ☾ 2247	2.2 4.2 2.0 4.1
15 M	0512 1105 1752 2343	2.3 4.0 2.1 4.0
16 TU	0625 1204 1854	2.2 4.0 2.0
17 W	0048 0722 1315 1947	4.1 2.1 4.1 1.8
18 TH	0154 0812 1420 2033	4.3 1.8 4.3 1.6
19 F	0245 0856 1509 2115	4.5 1.6 4.6 1.4
20 SA	0328 0936 1553 2153	4.8 1.3 4.8 1.2
21 SU	0410 1015 1636 2230	5.1 1.0 5.0 1.0
22 M	0453 1054 1721 ● 2310	5.3 0.8 5.2 0.8
23 TU	0538 1135 1806 2353	5.4 0.6 5.3 0.8
24 W	0623 1219 1852	5.5 0.6 5.2
25 TH	0038 0709 1305 1940	0.8 5.4 0.6 5.1
26 F	0125 0757 1353 2030	1.0 5.3 0.8 5.0
27 SA	0216 0849 1445 2124	1.2 5.1 1.0 4.7
28 SU	0311 0945 1542 ☽ 2223	1.4 4.8 1.3 4.5
29 M	0414 1048 1647 2332	1.6 4.5 1.5 4.4
30 TU	0528 1202 1804	1.8 4.4 1.7
31 W	0048 0654 1319 1927	4.3 1.8 4.4 1.7

ESBJERG
LAT 55°28′N
LONG 8°27′E

TIMES AND HEIGHTS OF HIGH AND LOW WATER (Heights in Metres)

TIME ZONE –0100 (Danish Standard Time). **Subtract 1 hour for UT. For Danish Summer Time (area enclosed in shaded box) add 1 hour**

2014

JANUARY

Date	Time	m
1 W ●	0211 0806 1441 2028	1.9 0.2 1.9 0.3
2 TH	0302 0857 1533 2116	2.0 0.2 1.9 0.2
3 F	0350 0946 1622 2202	2.1 0.1 1.9 0.2
4 SA	0436 1033 1709 2248	2.1 0.1 1.9 0.2
5 SU	0521 1121 1754 2333	2.1 0.1 1.8 0.2
6 M	0606 1208 1841	2.1 0.1 1.8
7 TU	0021 0655 1257 1930	0.2 2.1 0.2 1.8
8 W ☽	0110 0748 1350 2024	0.3 2.0 0.3 1.7
9 TH	0205 0846 1448 2124	0.3 2.0 0.3 1.7
10 F	0306 0951 1552 2228	0.4 1.9 0.4 1.8
11 SA	0417 1057 1701 2331	0.4 1.9 0.4 1.8
12 SU	0530 1201 1805	0.4 1.9 0.4
13 M	0030 0634 1300 1900	1.8 0.3 1.8 0.4
14 TU	0125 0730 1352 1949	1.9 0.3 1.8 0.3
15 W	0214 0818 1439 2031	1.9 0.3 1.8 0.3
16 TH O	0257 0900 1521 2108	2.0 0.3 1.8 0.3
17 F	0335 0936 1555 2141	1.9 0.3 1.8 0.3
18 SA	0406 1008 1626 2211	1.9 0.3 1.7 0.3
19 SU	0434 1037 1653 2242	1.9 0.3 1.7 0.3
20 M	0500 1108 1720 2315	1.9 0.3 1.7 0.2
21 TU	0529 1142 1751 2353	2.0 0.2 1.8 0.2
22 W	0603 1221 1828	2.0 0.2 1.8
23 TH	0034 0644 1304 1912	0.2 2.0 0.2 1.8
24 F ☾	0120 0732 1352 2003	0.2 1.9 0.2 1.7
25 SA	0212 0828 1447 2103	0.3 1.9 0.3 1.7
26 SU	0312 0936 1550 2216	0.3 1.8 0.4 1.7
27 M	0422 1057 1702 2336	0.4 1.7 0.4 1.7
28 TU	0539 1218 1814	0.4 1.7 0.4
29 W	0048 0651 1327 1916	1.8 0.3 1.8 0.3
30 TH ●	0150 0750 1425 2010	1.9 0.2 1.8 0.2
31 F	0245 0842 1518	1.9 0.1 1.8

FEBRUARY

Date	Time	m
1 SA	0333 0931 1605 2145	2.0 0.0 1.8 0.1
2 SU	0420 1016 1649 2229	2.0 0.0 1.8 0.0
3 M	0503 1101 1731 2313	2.1 0.0 1.8 0.0
4 TU	0547 1145 1813 2358	2.0 0.0 1.8 0.1
5 W	0631 1230 1857	2.0 0.1 1.7
6 TH ☽	0044 0718 1317 1945	0.1 1.9 0.2 1.7
7 F	0134 0812 1409 2039	0.2 1.8 0.3 1.7
8 SA	0230 0912 1509 2143	0.3 1.7 0.4 1.7
9 SU	0339 1021 1621 2251	0.4 1.7 0.4 1.7
10 M	0501 1128 1734 2356	0.4 1.7 0.4 1.7
11 TU	0612 1230 1835	0.3 1.7 0.4
12 W	0054 0709 1325 1925	1.8 0.3 1.7 0.3
13 TH	0146 0757 1413 2009	1.8 0.2 1.7 0.3
14 F	0232 0838 1456 2045	1.9 0.2 1.7 0.2
15 SA O	0311 0912 1532 2118	1.9 0.2 1.7 0.2
16 SU	0345 0943 1604 2148	1.9 0.2 1.7 0.2
17 M	0414 1012 1633 2220	1.9 0.1 1.7 0.1
18 TU	0442 1043 1700 2254	1.9 0.1 1.7 0.1
19 W	0511 1118 1730 2330	1.9 0.1 1.7 0.0
20 TH	0544 1156 1804	1.9 0.1 1.7
21 F	0012 0623 1238 1845	0.0 1.9 0.1 1.7
22 SA ☾	0057 0709 1324 1932	0.1 1.8 0.1 1.7
23 SU	0147 0804 1418 2030	0.1 1.7 0.2 1.6
24 M	0246 0912 1520 2142	0.2 1.6 0.3 1.6
25 TU	0358 1039 1635 2310	0.3 1.6 0.4 1.6
26 W	0521 1202 1752	0.3 1.6 0.3
27 TH	0027 0634 1310 1857	1.7 0.2 1.6 0.2
28 F	0130 0733 1409 1951	1.8 0.0 1.7 0.1

MARCH

Date	Time	m
1 SA ●	0226 0825 1459 2040	1.9 -0.1 1.7 0.0
2 SU	0315 0912 1545 2125	1.9 -0.1 1.8 -0.1
3 M	0400 0955 1626 2209	2.0 -0.1 1.8 -0.1
4 TU	0443 1038 1705 2251	2.0 -0.1 1.7 -0.1
5 W	0524 1119 1743 2333	1.9 0.0 1.7 -0.1
6 TH	0605 1200 1822	1.8 0.1 1.7
7 F	0017 0648 1243 1904	0.0 1.8 0.2 1.7
8 SA ☽	0103 0735 1329 1952	0.1 1.7 0.3 1.6
9 SU	0155 0830 1421 2051	0.2 1.6 0.4 1.6
10 M	0258 0937 1529 2203	0.3 1.5 0.4 1.6
11 TU	0423 1048 1652 2314	0.4 1.5 0.4 1.6
12 W	0541 1154 1801	0.3 1.5 0.4
13 TH	0017 0639 1251 1854	1.6 0.2 1.6 0.3
14 F	0112 0727 1342 1938	1.7 0.2 1.6 0.2
15 SA	0159 0807 1426 2016	1.7 0.1 1.7 0.1
16 SU O	0241 0842 1504 2050	1.8 0.1 1.7 0.1
17 M	0318 0914 1539 2123	1.8 0.0 1.7 0.0
18 TU	0351 0945 1610 2157	1.8 0.0 1.7 0.0
19 W	0421 1018 1640 2232	1.8 0.0 1.7 0.0
20 TH	0454 1054 1711 2310	1.8 0.0 1.7 -0.1
21 F	0528 1133 1745 2352	1.8 0.0 1.7 -0.1
22 SA	0608 1215 1824	1.7 0.0 1.7
23 SU	0037 0654 1302 1911	0.0 1.7 0.1 1.6
24 M ☾	0129 0751 1355 2009	0.0 1.6 0.2 1.6
25 TU	0229 0902 1458 2124	0.1 1.5 0.3 1.6
26 W	0342 1028 1614 2251	0.2 1.5 0.3 1.6
27 TH	0505 1147 1732	0.2 1.5 0.3
28 F	0007 0616 1253 1836	1.7 0.1 1.6 0.2
29 SA	0110 0714 1348 1930	1.8 0.0 1.6 0.0
30 SU ●	0206 0804 1438 2019	1.8 -0.1 1.7 -0.1
31 M	0255 0850 1521	1.9 -0.2 1.7

APRIL

Date	Time	m
1 TU	0340 0933 1602 2148	1.9 -0.2 1.7 -0.2
2 W	0421 1013 1639 2230	1.8 -0.1 1.7 -0.2
3 TH	0500 1053 1715 2311	1.8 0.0 1.7 -0.1
4 F	0539 1131 1750 2351	1.7 0.0 1.7 0.0
5 SA	0617 1210 1827	1.6 0.1 1.6
6 SU	0034 0657 1251 1909	0.1 1.5 0.2 1.6
7 M ☽	0121 0746 1337 2000	0.2 1.5 0.3 1.6
8 TU	0216 0846 1433 2104	0.3 1.4 0.4 1.5
9 W	0328 0958 1548 2220	0.3 1.4 0.4 1.5
10 TH	0452 1108 1709 2329	0.3 1.4 0.4 1.6
11 F	0557 1209 1810	0.2 1.5 0.3
12 SA	0028 0647 1303 1859	1.6 0.1 1.5 0.2
13 SU	0120 0729 1351 1941	1.7 0.1 1.6 0.1
14 M	0206 0806 1433 2019	1.7 0.0 1.6 0.0
15 TU O	0247 0842 1511 2056	1.7 0.0 1.7 0.0
16 W	0325 0918 1546 2133	1.7 -0.1 1.7 -0.1
17 TH	0402 0954 1621 2212	1.7 -0.1 1.7 -0.1
18 F	0438 1032 1654 2253	1.7 -0.1 1.7 -0.1
19 SA	0517 1113 1731 2336	1.7 0.0 1.7 -0.1
20 SU	0559 1157 1812	1.6 0.0 1.7
21 M	0024 0648 1245 1900	-0.1 1.6 0.1 1.6
22 TU ☾	0116 0746 1338 1959	0.0 1.5 0.2 1.6
23 W	0218 0857 1441 2113	0.1 1.4 0.2 1.6
24 TH	0329 1016 1554 2233	0.1 1.4 0.3 1.6
25 F	0446 1128 1709 2345	0.1 1.5 0.2 1.7
26 SA	0554 1231 1813	0.0 1.5 0.1
27 SU	0048 0651 1326 1909	1.7 -0.1 1.6 0.0
28 M	0144 0742 1415 1959	1.8 -0.1 1.7 -0.1
29 TU ●	0234 0827 1459 2045	1.8 -0.1 1.7 -0.2
30 W	0320 0910 1539 2129	1.8 -0.1 1.7 -0.2

MAY

Date	Time	m
1 TH	0401 0950 1616 2210	1.7 -0.1 1.7 -0.1
2 F	0439 1028 1651 2250	1.6 0.0 1.7 -0.1
3 SA	0515 1105 1724 2329	1.6 0.1 1.7 0.0
4 SU	0548 1141 1756	1.5 0.1 1.6
5 M	0009 0624 1218 1832	0.1 1.4 0.2 1.6
6 TU	0051 0705 1300 1915	0.1 1.4 0.2 1.6
7 W ☽	0137 0756 1348 2009	0.2 1.4 0.3 1.6
8 TH	0233 0859 1446 2115	0.3 1.4 0.3 1.5
9 F	0340 1010 1557 2227	0.3 1.4 0.3 1.5
10 SA	0451 1118 1708 2335	0.2 1.4 0.3 1.6
11 SU	0552 1218 1809	0.2 1.5 0.2
12 M	0034 0643 1311 1900	1.6 0.1 1.6 0.1
13 TU	0127 0728 1358 1946	1.7 0.0 1.6 0.1
14 W O	0215 0810 1442 2029	1.7 0.0 1.7 0.0
15 TH	0300 0851 1523 2112	1.7 -0.1 1.7 -0.1
16 F	0343 0932 1602 2154	1.7 -0.1 1.7 -0.1
17 SA	0425 1013 1641 2238	1.7 -0.1 1.7 -0.1
18 SU	0509 1056 1721 2324	1.6 0.0 1.7 -0.1
19 M	0554 1142 1805	1.6 0.0 1.7
20 TU	0012 0644 1230 1854	-0.1 1.5 0.1 1.7
21 W ☾	0106 0741 1324 1952	0.0 1.5 0.1 1.7
22 TH	0205 0845 1423 2100	0.0 1.4 0.2 1.7
23 F	0311 0955 1531 2212	0.1 1.4 0.2 1.7
24 SA	0421 1103 1642 2322	0.1 1.5 0.2 1.7
25 SU	0528 1205 1748	0.0 1.6 0.1
26 M	0025 0627 1300 1847	1.7 0.0 1.6 0.0
27 TU	0122 0719 1351 1939	1.8 0.0 1.7 0.0
28 W ●	0214 0806 1438 2028	1.7 0.0 1.7 -0.1
29 TH	0301 0850 1520 2113	1.7 0.0 1.7 -0.1
30 F	0343 0930 1557 2154	1.7 0.0 1.7 0.0
31 SA	0421 1007 1632	1.6 0.1 1.7

JUNE

Date	Time	m
1 SU	0454 1042 1703 2309	1.5 0.1 1.7 0.1
2 M	0525 1115 1732 2345	1.5 0.2 1.7 0.1
3 TU	0556 1151 1803	1.4 0.2 1.7
4 W	0022 0631 1229 1841	0.1 1.4 0.2 1.7
5 TH ☽	0103 0714 1312 1927	0.2 1.4 0.2 1.7
6 F	0150 0806 1402 2021	0.2 1.4 0.3 1.6
7 SA	0243 0907 1500 2124	0.2 1.4 0.3 1.6
8 SU	0345 1016 1606 2235	0.2 1.5 0.3 1.6
9 M	0450 1125 1714 2345	0.2 1.5 0.3 1.6
10 TU	0553 1227 1817	0.2 1.6 0.2
11 W	0048 0649 1323 1913	1.6 0.1 1.6 0.1
12 TH	0145 0739 1414 2004	1.7 0.1 1.7 0.0
13 F O	0237 0827 1501 2053	1.7 0.0 1.7 0.0
14 SA	0327 0912 1545 2139	1.7 0.0 1.8 -0.1
15 SU	0413 0957 1629 2225	1.7 0.0 1.8 -0.1
16 M	0500 1042 1712 2312	1.7 0.0 1.8 -0.1
17 TU	0546 1127 1757	1.6 0.0 1.8
18 W	0000 0634 1215 1845	-0.1 1.6 0.0 1.8
19 TH ☾	0051 0727 1306 1940	0.0 1.5 0.1 1.8
20 F	0146 0824 1402 2041	0.0 1.5 0.1 1.8
21 SA	0246 0927 1503 2148	0.1 1.5 0.2 1.7
22 SU	0351 1032 1612 2256	0.1 1.5 0.2 1.7
23 M	0459 1135 1722	0.1 1.6 0.2
24 TU	0000 0602 1234 1826	1.7 0.1 1.7 0.1
25 W	0100 0657 1328 1923	1.7 0.1 1.7 0.1
26 TH	0154 0748 1417 2014	1.7 0.1 1.8 0.0
27 F ●	0243 0833 1501 2100	1.7 0.1 1.8 0.0
28 SA	0326 0912 1541 2140	1.7 0.1 1.8 0.1
29 SU	0404 0949 1615 2217	1.6 0.1 1.8 0.1
30 M	0436 1022 1645 2250	1.6 0.2 1.8 0.1

SUNRISE AND SUNSET TIMES

ESBJERG
At 55°28′N 8°27′E

		Sunrise	Sunset
European Standard Time (UT-1)			
Jan	01	0854	1606
	15	0844	1627
Feb	01	0819	1702
	15	0750	1732
Mar	01	0717	1801
	15	0641	1830
European Summer Time (UT-2)			
Apr	01	0657	2004
	15	0622	2032
May	01	0544	2104
	15	0516	2130
Jun	01	0452	2157
	15	0443	2210
Jul	01	0449	2211
	15	0505	2159
Aug	01	0533	2131
	15	0559	2101
Sep	01	0632	2019
	15	0658	1943
Oct	01	0729	1902
	15	0757	1826
European Standard Time (UT-1)			
Nov	01	0732	1647
	15	0800	1621

ESBJERG
LAT 55°28′N
LONG 8°27′E

TIMES AND HEIGHTS OF HIGH AND LOW WATER (Heights in Metres)

TIME ZONE –0100 (Danish Standard Time). **Subtract 1 hour for UT. For Danish Summer Time (area enclosed in shaded box) add 1 hour**

2014

JULY

Day	Time	m	Day	Time	m
1 TU	0505 1054 1712 2322	1.5 0.2 1.8 0.2	16 W	0530 1111 1744 2344	1.7 0.0 2.0 -0.1
2 W	0532 1127 1739 2355	1.5 0.2 1.8 0.2	17 TH	0615 1157 1830	1.7 0.0 1.9
3 TH	0603 1202 1812	1.6 0.2 1.8	18 F	0031 0703 1245 1921	0.0 1.7 0.1 1.9
4 F	0032 0639 1242 1853	0.2 1.6 0.2 1.8	19 SA	0121 0754 1336 ☾ 2016	0.1 1.6 0.1 1.9
5 SA	0114 0724 1327 ☽ 1941	0.2 1.6 0.2 1.8	20 SU	0215 0851 1434 2119	0.2 1.6 0.2 1.8
6 SU	0201 0817 1419 2036	0.2 1.6 0.2 1.7	21 M	0317 0955 1541 2227	0.3 1.6 0.3 1.8
7 M	0256 0918 1518 2142	0.2 1.6 0.3 1.7	22 TU	0426 1102 1656 2334	0.3 1.7 0.3 1.7
8 TU	0357 1029 1625 2257	0.3 1.6 0.3 1.7	23 W	0536 1205 1807	0.3 1.7 0.3
9 W	0506 1142 1737	0.3 1.6 0.3	24 TH	0036 0636 1303 1907	1.7 0.3 1.8 0.2
10 TH	0012 0613 1248 1845	1.7 0.2 1.7 0.2	25 F	0133 0729 1355 1959	1.7 0.2 1.8 0.2
11 F	0118 0712 1348 1943	1.7 0.2 1.7 0.1	26 SA	0223 0815 1442 ● 2044	1.7 0.2 1.9 0.1
12 SA	0218 0806 1440 ○ 2036	1.7 0.1 1.8 0.0	27 SU	0306 0854 1522 2124	1.7 0.2 1.9 0.2
13 SU	0311 0854 1529 2124	1.7 0.1 1.9 0.0	28 M	0345 0930 1557 2157	1.7 0.2 1.9 0.2
14 M	0400 0940 1615 2212	1.8 0.0 1.9 -0.1	29 TU	0417 1002 1627 2228	1.7 0.2 1.9 0.2
15 TU	0445 1026 1659 2257	1.7 0.0 2.0 -0.1	30 W	0445 1032 1653 2257	1.7 0.2 1.9 0.2
			31 TH	0510 1103 1718 2328	1.7 0.2 1.9 0.2

AUGUST

Day	Time	m	Day	Time	m
1 F	0537 1137 1748	1.7 0.2 1.9	16 SA	0006 0634 1221 1856	0.1 1.8 0.1 2.0
2 SA	0003 0610 1215 1825	0.2 1.7 0.2 1.9	17 SU	0053 0720 1310 ☾ 1948	0.2 1.8 0.2 1.9
3 SU	0043 0650 1259 1909	0.2 1.7 0.2 1.9	18 M	0142 0812 1404 2047	0.3 1.8 0.3 1.8
4 M	0127 0737 1347 ☽ 2001	0.2 1.7 0.2 1.8	19 TU	0239 0915 1509 2154	0.4 1.7 0.4 1.8
5 TU	0218 0833 1442 2103	0.3 1.7 0.3 1.8	20 W	0348 1024 1629 2305	0.5 1.7 0.4 1.7
6 W	0318 0939 1548 2219	0.3 1.7 0.4 1.7	21 TH	0506 1132 1746	0.5 1.8 0.4
7 TH	0427 1100 1705 2344	0.4 1.7 0.4 1.7	22 F	0009 0612 1233 1848	1.8 0.5 1.8 0.3
8 F	0542 1217 1821	0.4 1.7 0.3	23 SA	0107 0706 1328 1939	1.8 0.4 1.9 0.3
9 SA	0057 0649 1323 1924	1.7 0.3 1.8 0.2	24 SU	0157 0752 1416 2023	1.8 0.3 2.0 0.3
10 SU	0159 0745 1419 ○ 2018	1.8 0.2 1.9 0.1	25 M	0242 0833 1458 ● 2100	1.8 0.3 2.0 0.2
11 M	0253 0836 1510 2107	1.8 0.2 2.0 0.0	26 TU	0321 0907 1534 2133	1.8 0.3 2.0 0.3
12 TU	0342 0922 1557 2154	1.9 0.1 2.1 0.0	27 W	0353 0938 1604 2201	1.8 0.3 2.0 0.3
13 W	0427 1007 1642 2238	1.9 0.0 2.1 0.0	28 TH	0422 1008 1631 2230	1.8 0.3 2.0 0.3
14 TH	0509 1051 1725 2322	1.9 0.0 2.1 0.0	29 F	0448 1039 1658 2302	1.8 0.2 2.0 0.2
15 F	0551 1136 1809	1.8 0.0 2.1	30 SA	0515 1114 1727 2336	1.8 0.2 2.0 0.2
			31 SU	0545 1151 1803	1.9 0.2 2.0

SEPTEMBER

Day	Time	m	Day	Time	m
1 M	0015 0623 1234 1845	0.2 1.9 0.2 2.0	16 TU	0109 0733 1335 ☾ 2012	0.4 1.9 0.4 1.8
2 TU	0100 0706 1321 ☽ 1936	0.3 1.9 0.3 1.9	17 W	0200 0830 1436 2117	0.5 1.8 0.5 1.8
3 W	0149 0759 1416 2037	0.4 1.8 0.3 1.8	18 TH	0304 0939 1555 2228	0.6 1.8 0.6 1.7
4 TH	0247 0903 1522 2155	0.5 1.8 0.4 1.8	19 F	0425 1052 1717 2335	0.7 1.8 0.5 1.8
5 F	0357 1026 1642 2324	0.5 1.8 0.4 1.8	20 SA	0539 1157 1820	0.6 1.9 0.5
6 SA	0515 1151 1800	0.5 1.8 0.4	21 SU	0033 0636 1254 1910	1.8 0.5 2.0 0.4
7 SU	0038 0627 1300 1905	1.8 0.4 1.9 0.3	22 M	0126 0723 1344 1954	1.9 0.5 2.0 0.4
8 M	0140 0725 1358 1959	1.9 0.3 2.0 0.2	23 TU	0211 0804 1427 2030	1.9 0.4 2.0 0.3
9 TU	0233 0815 1450 ○ 2047	1.9 0.2 2.1 0.1	24 W	0251 0839 1505 ● 2103	1.9 0.4 2.0 0.3
10 W	0321 0902 1537 2133	2.0 0.1 2.2 0.1	25 TH	0327 0912 1539 2133	2.0 0.3 2.0 0.3
11 TH	0404 0947 1621 2215	2.0 0.1 2.2 0.1	26 F	0357 0943 1609 2203	2.0 0.3 2.0 0.3
12 F	0445 1030 1704 2257	2.0 0.1 2.1 0.1	27 SA	0427 1016 1639 2236	2.0 0.3 2.0 0.3
13 SA	0524 1113 1746 2340	2.0 0.1 2.1 0.2	28 SU	0455 1052 1710 2312	2.0 0.3 2.0 0.3
14 SU	0604 1157 1830	1.9 0.2 2.0	29 M	0526 1131 1747 2353	2.0 0.2 2.0 0.3
15 M	0023 0646 1244 1917	0.3 1.9 0.3 1.9	30 TU	0602 1215 1829	2.0 0.3 2.0

OCTOBER

Day	Time	m	Day	Time	m
1 W	0036 0645 1303 ☽ 1920	0.4 2.0 0.3 1.9	16 TH	0123 0746 1402 2033	0.6 1.9 0.6 1.7
2 TH	0127 0736 1358 2023	0.4 1.9 0.4 1.8	17 F	0218 0848 1511 2142	0.7 1.9 0.6 1.7
3 F	0224 0842 1505 2142	0.5 1.9 0.5 1.8	18 SA	0329 1001 1632 2251	0.7 1.9 0.6 1.8
4 SA	0334 1004 1624 2307	0.6 1.9 0.5 1.8	19 SU	0448 1110 1739 2352	0.7 1.9 0.6 1.8
5 SU	0452 1127 1740	0.6 1.9 0.4	20 M	0553 1210 1831	0.6 2.0 0.5
6 M	0018 0603 1236 1843	1.9 0.5 2.0 0.3	21 TU	0046 0645 1303 1915	1.9 0.6 2.0 0.4
7 TU	0118 0702 1336 1937	1.9 0.4 2.1 0.2	22 W	0135 0728 1351 1954	2.0 0.5 2.0 0.4
8 W	0211 0754 1428 ○ 2025	2.0 0.3 2.2 0.2	23 TH	0218 0807 1433 ● 2030	2.0 0.4 2.1 0.4
9 TH	0258 0841 1516 2109	2.0 0.2 2.2 0.2	24 F	0257 0843 1511 2103	2.0 0.4 2.1 0.3
10 F	0341 0926 1600 2152	2.1 0.1 2.2 0.2	25 SA	0333 0918 1547 2137	2.0 0.3 2.1 0.3
11 SA	0421 1009 1642 2233	2.1 0.1 2.1 0.2	26 SU	0406 0955 1621 2214	2.0 0.3 2.0 0.3
12 SU	0459 1052 1723 2314	2.0 0.2 2.1 0.3	27 M	0438 1034 1657 2252	2.0 0.3 2.0 0.3
13 M	0536 1135 1803 2354	2.0 0.3 2.0 0.4	28 TU	0512 1115 1737 2334	2.0 0.3 2.0 0.4
14 TU	0614 1219 1846	2.0 0.3 1.9	29 W	0549 1200 1821	2.0 0.3 1.9
15 W	0036 0657 1307 ☾ 1934	0.5 2.0 0.4 1.8	30 TH	0019 0633 1250 1914	0.4 2.0 0.3 1.9
			31 F	0110 0725 1346 ☽ 2017	0.5 2.0 0.4 1.8

NOVEMBER

Day	Time	m	Day	Time	m
1 SA	0207 0830 1451 2132	0.6 2.0 0.4 1.8	16 SU	0231 0900 1524 2152	0.7 1.9 0.6 1.7
2 SU	0315 0948 1604 2248	0.6 2.0 0.5 1.8	17 M	0338 1009 1634 2258	0.7 1.9 0.6 1.8
3 M	0428 1106 1717 2356	0.6 2.0 0.4 1.9	18 TU	0450 1116 1736 2359	0.7 1.9 0.6 1.8
4 TU	0538 1214 1819	0.5 2.1 0.3	19 W	0552 1216 1828	0.6 2.0 0.5
5 W	0055 0639 1314 1914	2.0 0.4 2.1 0.3	20 TH	0053 0645 1309 1913	1.9 0.5 2.0 0.4
6 TH	0148 0732 1407 ○ 2003	2.0 0.3 2.2 0.2	21 F	0142 0731 1358 1954	2.0 0.5 2.0 0.4
7 F	0235 0821 1457 2048	2.1 0.2 2.2 0.2	22 SA	0226 0814 1443 ● 2034	2.0 0.4 2.0 0.4
8 SA	0319 0907 1542 2130	2.1 0.2 2.1 0.3	23 SU	0307 0855 1526 2114	2.0 0.3 2.0 0.3
9 SU	0359 0951 1623 2211	2.1 0.2 2.0 0.3	24 M	0345 0936 1607 2154	2.1 0.3 2.0 0.3
10 M	0436 1034 1702 2250	2.1 0.3 2.0 0.4	25 TU	0423 1018 1648 2236	2.1 0.3 2.0 0.3
11 TU	0512 1115 1739 2328	2.1 0.3 1.9 0.5	26 W	0501 1103 1731 2319	2.1 0.2 1.9 0.3
12 W	0548 1157 1817	2.0 0.4 1.8	27 TH	0542 1149 1817	2.1 0.2 1.9
13 TH	0007 0624 1240 1858	0.5 2.0 0.5 1.8	28 F	0006 0627 1239 1909	0.4 2.1 0.3 1.8
14 F	0049 0707 1327 ☾ 1946	0.6 2.0 0.5 1.7	29 SA	0055 0719 1333 ☽ 2008	0.4 2.0 0.3 1.8
15 SA	0136 0758 1421 2045	0.6 1.9 0.6 1.7	30 SU	0151 0821 1434 2114	0.5 2.0 0.4 1.8

DECEMBER

Day	Time	m	Day	Time	m
1 M	0253 0930 1542 2224	0.5 2.0 0.4 1.8	16 TU	0240 0904 1523 2153	0.6 1.9 0.5 1.7
2 TU	0402 1042 1650 2330	0.5 2.0 0.4 1.9	17 W	0342 1012 1627 2301	0.6 1.9 0.5 1.8
3 W	0512 1151 1754	0.5 2.0 0.4	18 TH	0450 1121 1731	0.6 1.9 0.5
4 TH	0030 0615 1252 1851	1.9 0.4 2.1 0.3	19 F	0005 0556 1226 1829	1.8 0.5 1.9 0.4
5 F	0124 0712 1348 1942	2.0 0.3 2.1 0.3	20 SA	0103 0654 1324 1921	1.9 0.5 1.9 0.4
6 SA	0214 0804 1439 ○ 2028	2.0 0.3 2.0 0.3	21 SU	0155 0746 1418 2008	1.9 0.4 1.9 0.3
7 SU	0300 0852 1525 2112	2.1 0.2 2.0 0.3	22 M	0242 0834 1507 ● 2053	2.0 0.3 1.9 0.3
8 M	0342 0937 1606 2152	2.1 0.3 1.9 0.4	23 TU	0327 0920 1553 2136	2.0 0.2 1.9 0.3
9 TU	0419 1019 1644 2230	2.0 0.3 1.9 0.4	24 W	0409 1005 1638 2221	2.1 0.2 1.9 0.3
10 W	0454 1058 1718 2306	2.0 0.3 1.8 0.4	25 TH	0451 1050 1722 2305	2.1 0.1 1.9 0.2
11 TH	0526 1136 1751 2342	2.0 0.4 1.8 0.5	26 F	0534 1136 1808 2351	2.1 0.1 1.9 0.3
12 F	0557 1214 1824	2.0 0.4 1.7	27 SA	0619 1225 1857	2.1 0.2 1.8
13 SA	0018 0633 1253 1903	0.5 2.0 0.5 1.7	28 SU	0039 0709 1316 ☽ 1950	0.3 2.1 0.2 1.8
14 SU	0100 0715 1336 ☾ 1951	0.5 2.0 0.5 1.7	29 M	0132 0806 1412 2049	0.3 2.0 0.3 1.8
15 M	0146 0805 1426 2048	0.5 1.9 0.5 1.7	30 TU	0229 0909 1514 2154	0.4 2.0 0.3 1.8
			31 W	0334 1018 1621 2300	0.4 2.0 0.4 1.8

HELGOLAND
LAT 54°11′N
LONG 7°53′E

TIMES AND HEIGHTS OF HIGH AND LOW WATER (Heights in Metres)

TIME ZONE –0100 (German Standard Time). **Subtract 1 hour for UT. For German Summer Time (area enclosed in shaded box) add 1 hour**

2014

JANUARY

Date	Day	Time	m	Time	m	Time	m	Time	m
1	W ●	0542	0.5	1125	3.2	1807	0.5	2345	3.3
2	TH	0638	0.3	1221	3.2	1859	0.4		
3	F	0037	3.3	0729	0.2	1314	3.1	1947	0.4
4	SA	0127	3.3	0817	0.2	1402	3.1	2033	0.4
5	SU	0213	3.3	0904	0.2	1447	3.0	2117	0.4
6	M	0258	3.3	0949	0.2	1531	2.9	2200	0.4
7	TU	0345	3.3	1035	0.3	1617	2.9	2246	0.5
8	W ☽	0435	3.2	1124	0.4	1708	2.8	2337	0.6
9	TH	0531	3.1	1217	0.5	1806	2.8		
10	F	0037	0.7	0633	3.0	1319	0.6	1911	2.8
11	SA	0147	0.7	0742	2.9	1424	0.7	2020	2.8
12	SU	0258	0.7	0853	2.8	1529	0.7	2127	2.9
13	M	0404	0.7	0958	2.9	1628	0.7	2227	3.0
14	TU	0501	0.6	1054	2.9	1719	0.7	2316	3.1
15	W	0550	0.6	1140	3.0	1803	0.7	2358	3.2
16	TH ○	0632	0.6	1219	3.1	1841	0.7		
17	F	0033	3.3	0707	0.6	1254	3.1	1915	0.7
18	SA	0104	3.3	0740	0.7	1325	3.1	1946	0.7
19	SU	0133	3.4	0812	0.7	1356	3.1	2017	0.8
20	M	0202	3.4	0842	0.7	1425	3.1	2049	0.8
21	TU	0232	3.4	0914	0.8	1456	3.1	2122	0.8
22	W	0304	3.3	0948	0.8	1528	3.1	2158	0.8
23	TH	0341	3.3	1025	0.8	1607	3.0	2238	0.9
24	F ☾	0426	3.2	1109	0.9	1655	3.0	2326	0.9
25	SA	0522	3.1	1201	0.9	1754	3.0		
26	SU	0025	0.9	0627	3.1	1305	0.9	1901	3.0
27	M	0138	0.9	0740	3.0	1421	0.9	2013	3.0
28	TU	0301	0.8	0854	3.0	1541	0.8	2124	3.1
29	W	0420	0.7	1006	3.0	1652	0.7	2231	3.2
30	TH ●	0527	0.5	1112	3.1	1753	0.5	2332	3.2
31	F	0625	0.3	1210	3.1	1846	0.4		

FEBRUARY

Date	Day	Time	m	Time	m	Time	m	Time	m
1	SA	0026	3.3	0716	0.2	1301	3.1	1933	0.3
2	SU	0114	3.4	0802	0.1	1345	3.1	2016	0.3
3	M	0158	3.4	0845	0.2	1426	3.0	2057	0.3
4	TU	0239	3.3	0926	0.2	1505	3.0	2137	0.3
5	W	0321	3.3	1006	0.3	1546	3.0	2218	0.4
6	TH ☽	0406	3.2	1048	0.5	1632	2.9	2303	0.5
7	F	0457	3.0	1134	0.6	1725	2.9	2356	0.7
8	SA	0556	2.9	1230	0.8	1827	2.8		
9	SU	0103	0.8	0702	2.8	1339	0.9	1936	2.8
10	M	0221	0.9	0816	2.8	1452	0.9	2050	2.9
11	TU	0335	0.9	0927	2.8	1558	0.9	2156	3.0
12	W	0436	0.8	1028	2.9	1653	0.8	2251	3.1
13	TH	0527	0.7	1118	3.0	1739	0.8	2335	3.2
14	F	0609	0.7	1158	3.1	1819	0.7		
15	SA ○	0012	3.3	0646	0.6	1234	3.2	1854	0.7
16	SU	0045	3.4	0719	0.6	1305	3.2	1928	0.6
17	M	0115	3.4	0751	0.6	1334	3.2	2000	0.6
18	TU	0143	3.4	0822	0.6	1401	3.2	2031	0.6
19	W	0210	3.3	0853	0.7	1428	3.1	2103	0.7
20	TH	0239	3.3	0925	0.7	1457	3.1	2137	0.7
21	F	0314	3.2	1000	0.7	1534	3.1	2216	0.7
22	SA ☾	0358	3.2	1041	0.8	1622	3.0	2303	0.8
23	SU	0454	3.1	1132	0.8	1722	3.0		
24	M	0001	0.8	0602	3.0	1237	0.9	1834	3.0
25	TU	0117	0.9	0720	2.9	1359	1.0	1951	3.0
26	W	0245	0.8	0839	2.9	1524	0.9	2107	3.0
27	TH	0406	0.7	0954	3.0	1637	0.7	2219	3.2
28	F	0513	0.5	1101	3.1	1738	0.5	2320	3.3

MARCH

Date	Day	Time	m	Time	m	Time	m	Time	m
1	SA ●	0609	0.3	1156	3.1	1829	0.4		
2	SU	0013	3.3	0658	0.2	1244	3.2	1915	0.3
3	M	0059	3.4	0742	0.2	1325	3.1	1956	0.2
4	TU	0139	3.4	0822	0.2	1402	3.1	2035	0.3
5	W	0217	3.3	0859	0.3	1437	3.1	2112	0.3
6	TH	0256	3.2	0935	0.4	1515	3.1	2149	0.4
7	F	0337	3.1	1011	0.6	1557	3.0	2229	0.6
8	SA ☽	0424	3.0	1050	0.7	1645	3.0	2315	0.8
9	SU	0518	2.9	1137	0.9	1742	2.9		
10	M	0015	0.9	0621	2.8	1242	1.1	1850	2.9
11	TU	0135	1.1	0733	2.7	1404	1.2	2005	2.9
12	W	0258	1.1	0848	2.8	1520	1.1	2117	3.0
13	TH	0404	1.0	0954	2.9	1620	1.0	2217	3.2
14	F	0457	0.9	1048	3.0	1709	0.9	2305	3.3
15	SA	0540	0.8	1130	3.2	1752	0.7	2344	3.4
16	SU ○	0618	0.7	1207	3.2	1829	0.6		
17	M	0019	3.4	0653	0.6	1239	3.2	1904	0.6
18	TU	0050	3.4	0726	0.6	1308	3.2	1938	0.5
19	W	0120	3.3	0759	0.6	1335	3.2	2012	0.5
20	TH	0149	3.3	0831	0.6	1403	3.2	2045	0.5
21	F	0219	3.2	0904	0.6	1434	3.2	2121	0.6
22	SA	0256	3.2	0941	0.7	1513	3.1	2202	0.6
23	SU	0343	3.1	1023	0.7	1603	3.1	2251	0.7
24	M ☾	0441	3.0	1115	0.9	1705	3.0	2352	0.8
25	TU	0551	2.9	1222	1.0	1818	3.0		
26	W	0109	0.8	0708	2.9	1346	1.0	1936	3.0
27	TH	0235	0.8	0828	2.9	1509	0.9	2054	3.1
28	F	0352	0.6	0942	3.0	1619	0.7	2205	3.2
29	SA	0455	0.4	1046	3.1	1718	0.5	2305	3.3
30	SU ●	0549	0.3	1138	3.1	1809	0.4	2355	3.4
31	M	0637	0.2	1223	3.2	1854	0.3		

APRIL

Date	Day	Time	m	Time	m	Time	m	Time	m
1	TU	0039	3.4	0719	0.2	1302	3.2	1935	0.3
2	W	0119	3.3	0757	0.3	1337	3.2	2013	0.3
3	TH	0155	3.3	0832	0.4	1411	3.2	2048	0.4
4	F	0231	3.2	0904	0.6	1445	3.2	2122	0.5
5	SA	0309	3.1	0935	0.7	1524	3.2	2158	0.7
6	SU	0352	3.0	1009	0.9	1608	3.1	2239	0.9
7	M ☽	0442	2.9	1050	1.0	1702	3.1	2331	1.0
8	TU	0541	2.9	1145	1.2	1804	3.0		
9	W	0042	1.2	0648	2.8	1300	1.3	1915	3.0
10	TH	0208	1.2	0801	2.8	1426	1.3	2027	3.1
11	F	0320	1.1	0910	2.9	1536	1.2	2130	3.2
12	SA	0416	1.0	1007	3.1	1631	1.0	2223	3.3
13	SU	0503	0.8	1053	3.2	1717	0.8	2307	3.3
14	M	0544	0.7	1131	3.2	1759	0.7	2345	3.4
15	TU ○	0622	0.6	1206	3.3	1837	0.6		
16	W	0020	3.3	0658	0.5	1239	3.3	1914	0.5
17	TH	0055	3.3	0734	0.5	1311	3.2	1952	0.5
18	F	0129	3.3	0810	0.5	1343	3.2	2030	0.5
19	SA	0206	3.2	0847	0.6	1420	3.2	2110	0.5
20	SU	0248	3.1	0927	0.6	1503	3.2	2155	0.5
21	M	0338	3.0	1013	0.7	1554	3.2	2247	0.6
22	TU ☾	0437	2.9	1106	0.9	1656	3.1	2349	0.7
23	W	0544	2.9	1213	0.9	1806	3.1		
24	TH	0103	0.7	0657	2.8	1331	0.9	1921	3.1
25	F	0220	0.7	0812	2.9	1448	0.8	2036	3.1
26	SA	0330	0.6	0923	3.0	1556	0.7	2145	3.2
27	SU	0432	0.4	1024	3.1	1655	0.5	2244	3.3
28	M	0525	0.3	1117	3.1	1746	0.4	2335	3.3
29	TU ●	0612	0.3	1201	3.2	1833	0.3		
30	W	0019	3.3	0654	0.3	1241	3.2	1914	0.3

MAY

Date	Day	Time	m	Time	m	Time	m	Time	m
1	TH	0059	3.2	0732	0.4	1315	3.2	1951	0.4
2	F	0134	3.2	0805	0.5	1347	3.2	2026	0.5
3	SA	0209	3.1	0836	0.7	1419	3.3	2058	0.6
4	SU	0244	3.1	0904	0.8	1455	3.3	2131	0.8
5	M	0324	3.1	0936	0.9	1536	3.3	2208	0.9
6	TU	0410	3.0	1014	1.1	1625	3.2	2255	1.1
7	W ☽	0503	2.9	1103	1.2	1721	3.2	2354	1.2
8	TH	0603	2.9	1205	1.3	1824	3.2		
9	F	0105	1.2	0709	2.9	1321	1.4	1930	3.1
10	SA	0220	1.2	0814	2.9	1437	1.3	2035	3.2
11	SU	0323	1.1	0913	3.0	1541	1.1	2132	3.2
12	M	0416	0.9	1004	3.1	1635	0.9	2222	3.3
13	TU	0503	0.8	1049	3.2	1723	0.7	2307	3.3
14	W ○	0547	0.6	1130	3.2	1808	0.6	2349	3.3
15	TH	0629	0.5	1209	3.3	1851	0.5		
16	F	0030	3.3	0710	0.5	1248	3.3	1934	0.4
17	SA	0113	3.2	0752	0.5	1328	3.3	2017	0.4
18	SU	0157	3.1	0834	0.5	1410	3.3	2102	0.4
19	M	0244	3.1	0918	0.6	1456	3.3	2150	0.4
20	TU	0334	3.0	1005	0.7	1548	3.2	2242	0.5
21	W ☾	0430	2.9	1058	0.8	1646	3.2	2341	0.6
22	TH	0532	2.8	1200	0.8	1751	3.1		
23	F	0047	0.6	0638	2.8	1309	0.8	1900	3.1
24	SA	0156	0.6	0748	2.8	1420	0.7	2012	3.1
25	SU	0302	0.5	0856	2.9	1528	0.6	2120	3.1
26	M	0404	0.4	0958	3.0	1629	0.5	2221	3.1
27	TU	0458	0.4	1053	3.1	1724	0.4	2314	3.1
28	W ●	0547	0.4	1140	3.2	1812	0.4		
29	TH	0000	3.1	0630	0.4	1220	3.2	1854	0.4
30	F	0041	3.1	0709	0.5	1255	3.2	1932	0.5
31	SA	0116	3.1	0742	0.6	1327	3.3		

JUNE

Date	Day	Time	m	Time	m	Time	m	Time	m
1	SU	0149	3.1	0812	0.8	1358	3.3	2038	0.7
2	M	0223	3.1	0841	0.9	1431	3.3	2109	0.8
3	TU	0259	3.1	0911	1.0	1509	3.4	2144	0.9
4	W	0341	3.1	0948	1.0	1551	3.4	2225	1.0
5	TH ☽	0427	3.0	1031	1.2	1640	3.3	2314	1.1
6	F	0519	3.0	1123	1.2	1735	3.2		
7	SA	0010	1.1	0615	2.9	1224	1.3	1834	3.1
8	SU	0113	1.2	0715	2.9	1332	1.2	1936	3.1
9	M	0218	1.1	0814	3.0	1442	1.1	2037	3.1
10	TU	0321	1.0	0910	3.0	1547	1.0	2134	3.1
11	W	0419	0.8	1003	3.1	1646	0.8	2228	3.2
12	TH	0513	0.7	1054	3.2	1739	0.6	2320	3.2
13	F ○	0603	0.5	1142	3.3	1830	0.4		
14	SA	0011	3.2	0651	0.5	1229	3.3	1919	0.3
15	SU	0100	3.2	0737	0.4	1315	3.3	2006	0.3
16	M	0149	3.1	0823	0.4	1401	3.3	2053	0.3
17	TU	0236	3.1	0909	0.5	1448	3.3	2141	0.3
18	W	0325	3.0	0955	0.5	1537	3.3	2230	0.3
19	TH ☾	0415	2.9	1044	0.6	1631	3.2	2323	0.4
20	F	0510	2.8	1138	0.6	1729	3.1		
21	SA	0021	0.5	0609	2.8	1240	0.7	1833	3.1
22	SU	0124	0.5	0715	2.8	1349	0.7	1942	3.0
23	M	0230	0.5	0824	2.8	1458	0.6	2052	3.0
24	TU	0333	0.5	0929	2.9	1604	0.5	2157	3.0
25	W	0431	0.5	1028	3.0	1702	0.5	2254	3.0
26	TH	0524	0.5	1119	3.1	1753	0.5	2343	3.0
27	F ●	0609	0.5	1202	3.2	1837	0.5		
28	SA	0024	3.0	0649	0.6	1238	3.2	1915	0.6
29	SU	0100	3.1	0723	0.7	1310	3.3	1949	0.6
30	M	0132	3.1	0754	0.8	1340	3.3	2020	0.7

SUNRISE AND SUNSET TIMES

HELGOLAND
At 54°11′N 7°53′E

		Sunrise	Sunset
European Standard Time (UT-1)			
Jan	01	0848	1616
	15	0840	1637
Feb	01	0816	1709
	15	0749	1737
Mar	01	0717	1805
	15	0643	1833
European Summer Time (UT-2)			
Apr	01	0701	2005
	15	0627	2031
May	01	0551	2101
	15	0525	2126
Jun	01	0502	2151
	15	0455	2204
Jul	01	0500	2205
	15	0515	2153
Aug	01	0541	2127
	15	0606	2059
Sep	01	0636	2019
	15	0702	1945
Oct	01	0731	1905
	15	0757	1831
European Standard Time (UT-1)			
Nov	01	0730	1654
	15	0757	1629
Dec	01	0825	1610

HELGOLAND
LAT 54°11′N
LONG 7°53′E

TIMES AND HEIGHTS OF HIGH AND LOW WATER (Heights in Metres)

TIME ZONE –0100 (German Standard Time). **Subtract 1 hour for UT. For German Summer Time (area enclosed in shaded box) add 1 hour**

2014

JULY

Date	Day	Time	m	Date	Day	Time	m
1	TU	0204 0823 1411 2051	3.1 0.8 3.4 0.8	16	W	0223 0855 1435 2126	3.1 0.3 3.3 0.2
2	W	0237 0854 1445 2123	3.1 0.9 3.4 0.8	17	TH	0307 0939 1521 2211	3.0 0.4 3.3 0.2
3	TH	0313 0927 1521 2158	3.1 0.9 3.4 0.9	18	F	0352 1023 1610 2258	2.9 0.4 3.2 0.3
4	F	0351 1005 1602 2238	3.1 1.0 3.3 1.0	19	SA	0441 1112 1703 ☾ 2349	2.9 0.5 3.1 0.4
5	SA	0434 1049 1648 ☽ 2324	3.0 1.1 3.2 1.0	20	SU	0536 1208 1803	2.8 0.6 3.0
6	SU	0522 1138 1742	3.0 1.1 3.1	21	M	0047 0638 1314 1910	0.6 2.8 0.6 2.9
7	M	0016 0616 1237 1842	1.0 2.9 1.1 3.1	22	TU	0153 0747 1427 2022	0.6 2.8 0.7 2.8
8	TU	0118 0717 1345 1947	1.0 2.9 1.1 3.0	23	W	0301 0858 1538 2132	0.7 2.8 0.7 2.8
9	W	0226 0820 1459 2052	1.0 3.0 1.0 3.1	24	TH	0405 1003 1640 2234	0.7 2.9 0.6 2.9
10	TH	0337 0923 1611 2156	0.9 3.1 0.8 3.1	25	F	0501 1058 1733 2325	0.7 3.1 0.6 3.0
11	F	0442 1023 1715 2258	0.7 3.2 0.6 3.1	26	SA ●	0549 1144 1818	0.6 3.2 0.6
12	SA	0542 1120 1813 ○ 2355	0.6 3.3 0.4 3.2	27	SU	0007 0629 1222 1856	3.0 0.6 3.2 0.6
13	SU	0635 1213 1906	0.5 3.3 0.3	28	M	0043 0705 1254 1930	3.1 0.7 3.3 0.6
14	M	0048 0724 1303 1954	3.2 0.4 3.4 0.2	29	TU	0115 0737 1324 2002	3.1 0.7 3.4 0.7
15	TU	0137 0811 1350 2041	3.1 0.3 3.4 0.2	30	W	0145 0807 1353 2031	3.2 0.7 3.4 0.7
				31	TH	0215 0837 1423 2101	3.2 0.8 3.4 0.7

AUGUST

Date	Day	Time	m	Date	Day	Time	m
1	F	0245 0908 1454 2133	3.1 0.8 3.3 0.8	16	SA	0325 0959 1545 2228	3.0 0.3 3.2 0.4
2	SA	0316 0942 1527 2207	3.1 0.8 3.3 0.8	17	SU	0409 1043 1634 ☾ 2313	2.9 0.4 3.1 0.5
3	SU	0350 1019 1607 2246	3.1 0.9 3.2 0.9	18	M	0500 1134 1730	2.9 0.6 2.9
4	M	0432 1102 1657 ☽ 2333	3.0 0.9 3.1 0.9	19	TU	0005 0558 1237 1835	0.7 2.8 0.7 2.8
5	TU	0526 1155 1758	3.0 1.0 3.1	20	W	0111 0707 1353 1948	0.8 2.8 0.8 2.7
6	W	0031 0629 1302 1907	1.0 2.9 1.0 3.0	21	TH	0225 0822 1510 2103	0.9 2.8 0.8 2.8
7	TH	0143 0740 1422 2021	1.0 3.0 0.9 3.0	22	F	0336 0934 1616 2209	0.9 2.9 0.8 2.9
8	F	0304 0851 1545 2133	0.9 3.0 0.8 3.0	23	SA	0436 1034 1711 2303	0.8 3.1 0.7 3.0
9	SA	0420 1000 1657 2241	0.8 3.1 0.6 3.1	24	SU	0525 1122 1756 2346	0.7 3.2 0.7 3.1
10	SU	0525 1103 1758 ○ 2341	0.6 3.2 0.4 3.2	25	M ●	0607 1201 1834	0.7 3.3 0.6
11	M	0620 1200 1851	0.4 3.3 0.2	26	TU	0023 0643 1235 1908	3.2 0.6 3.4 0.6
12	TU	0034 0709 1250 1938	3.2 0.3 3.4 0.1	27	W	0055 0717 1305 1939	3.2 0.6 3.4 0.6
13	W	0121 0755 1336 2023	3.2 0.2 3.4 0.1	28	TH	0124 0748 1334 2009	3.2 0.6 3.4 0.6
14	TH	0204 0837 1419 2105	3.1 0.2 3.4 0.2	29	F	0151 0818 1401 2039	3.2 0.7 3.3 0.7
15	F	0244 0918 1501 2146	3.1 0.2 3.3 0.2	30	SA	0217 0849 1428 2109	3.2 0.7 3.3 0.7
				31	SU	0244 0920 1458 2141	3.1 0.7 3.3 0.8

SEPTEMBER

Date	Day	Time	m	Date	Day	Time	m
1	M	0315 0956 1536 2218	3.1 0.8 3.2 0.8	16	TU	0425 1100 1657 ☾ 2321	3.0 0.6 2.9 0.8
2	TU	0356 1037 1626 ☽ 2303	3.1 0.8 3.1 0.9	17	W	0520 1157 1758	2.9 0.8 2.8
3	W	0450 1130 1728	3.0 0.9 3.0	18	TH	0020 0625 1313 1909	1.0 2.9 1.0 2.7
4	TH	0000 0557 1237 1842	1.0 3.0 0.9 2.9	19	F	0139 0740 1435 2025	1.1 2.9 1.0 2.8
5	F	0115 0713 1401 2000	1.0 3.0 0.9 2.9	20	SA	0258 0855 1545 2136	1.1 3.0 1.0 2.9
6	SA	0242 0829 1527 2116	1.0 3.1 0.8 3.0	21	SU	0402 0959 1640 2232	1.0 3.1 0.8 3.0
7	SU	0402 0942 1640 2226	0.8 3.2 0.6 3.1	22	M	0454 1050 1726 2318	0.9 3.3 0.7 3.1
8	M	0507 1048 1741 2326	0.6 3.3 0.4 3.2	23	TU	0538 1132 1805 2356	0.7 3.4 0.6 3.2
9	TU ○	0603 1145 1833	0.4 3.4 0.2	24	W ●	0617 1208 1841	0.7 3.4 0.6
10	W	0017 0651 1234 1919	3.2 0.3 3.4 0.1	25	TH	0029 0652 1241 1913	3.3 0.6 3.4 0.6
11	TH	0102 0735 1318 2001	3.2 0.2 3.4 0.1	26	F	0058 0725 1310 1944	3.3 0.6 3.3 0.6
12	F	0142 0816 1359 2041	3.2 0.2 3.3 0.2	27	SA	0125 0757 1338 2015	3.2 0.6 3.3 0.6
13	SA	0219 0856 1439 2119	3.1 0.2 3.3 0.3	28	SU	0151 0829 1406 2046	3.2 0.6 3.2 0.7
14	SU	0257 0934 1520 2156	3.1 0.3 3.2 0.5	29	M	0219 0903 1438 2120	3.2 0.6 3.2 0.7
15	M	0338 1015 1606 2235	3.0 0.5 3.0 0.7	30	TU	0252 0940 1518 2158	3.2 0.7 3.1 0.8

OCTOBER

Date	Day	Time	m	Date	Day	Time	m
1	W	0335 1024 1610 ☽ 2244	3.2 0.7 3.1 0.9	16	TH	0443 1119 1721 2329	3.1 0.9 2.9 1.1
2	TH	0431 1118 1714 2343	3.1 0.8 3.0 1.0	17	F	0543 1225 1827	3.1 1.1 2.8
3	F	0539 1227 1828	3.1 0.9 2.9	18	SA	0040 0652 1347 1939	1.3 3.0 1.1 2.8
4	SA	0059 0654 1350 1945	1.0 3.1 0.8 2.9	19	SU	0205 0805 1501 2051	1.3 3.1 1.1 2.9
5	SU	0225 0812 1512 2101	1.0 3.1 0.7 3.0	20	M	0317 0912 1600 2152	1.2 3.2 1.0 3.0
6	M	0342 0925 1621 2209	0.8 3.2 0.5 3.1	21	TU	0415 1008 1648 2241	1.0 3.3 0.8 3.1
7	TU	0446 1030 1720 2307	0.6 3.3 0.4 3.2	22	W	0503 1055 1730 2321	0.9 3.3 0.7 3.2
8	W	0542 1126 1811 ○ 2357	0.4 3.4 0.2 3.2	23	TH	0545 1134 1808 ● 2356	0.7 3.4 0.6 3.3
9	TH	0630 1215 1857	0.3 3.4 0.2	24	F	0623 1210 1843	0.6 3.3 0.6
10	F	0040 0714 1259 1938	3.2 0.2 3.3 0.2	25	SA	0028 0659 1243 1918	3.3 0.6 3.3 0.6
11	SA	0119 0755 1338 2016	3.2 0.2 3.3 0.3	26	SU	0059 0735 1315 1952	3.3 0.5 3.2 0.6
12	SU	0155 0834 1416 2051	3.2 0.3 3.2 0.5	27	M	0129 0812 1349 2028	3.3 0.5 3.2 0.6
13	M	0231 0911 1455 2125	3.2 0.4 3.1 0.6	28	TU	0201 0850 1427 2105	3.2 0.6 3.1 0.7
14	TU	0309 0948 1537 2159	3.2 0.6 3.0 0.8	29	W	0239 0931 1511 2147	3.2 0.6 3.1 0.8
15	W	0352 1029 1625 ☾ 2238	3.1 0.8 2.9 1.0	30	TH	0325 1018 1605 2236	3.2 0.6 3.0 0.8
				31	F	0421 1114 1707 ☽ 2335	3.2 0.7 2.9 0.9

NOVEMBER

Date	Day	Time	m	Date	Day	Time	m
1	SA	0527 1221 1816	3.1 0.7 2.9	16	SU	0604 1247 1849	3.2 1.2 2.9
2	SU	0047 0639 1337 1929	1.0 3.1 0.7 2.9	17	M	0059 0710 1400 1955	1.3 3.1 1.2 2.9
3	M	0205 0753 1451 2041	0.9 3.1 0.6 2.9	18	TU	0216 0816 1505 2057	1.3 3.2 1.1 3.0
4	TU	0318 0904 1557 2147	0.8 3.2 0.5 3.0	19	W	0323 0916 1559 2151	1.1 3.2 0.9 3.1
5	W	0422 1009 1655 2246	0.6 3.2 0.4 3.1	20	TH	0419 1008 1647 2236	1.0 3.2 0.8 3.2
6	TH	0519 1106 1747 ○ 2336	0.4 3.3 0.3 3.2	21	F	0507 1054 1731 2317	0.8 3.2 0.7 3.2
7	F	0609 1156 1833	0.3 3.3 0.3	22	SA	0551 1135 1812 ● 2355	0.7 3.2 0.6 3.3
8	SA	0019 0654 1240 1914	3.2 0.3 3.2 0.4	23	SU	0634 1215 1852	0.6 3.2 0.5
9	SU	0058 0736 1319 1952	3.2 0.3 3.2 0.5	24	M	0032 0715 1255 1932	3.3 0.5 3.2 0.5
10	M	0133 0814 1356 2025	3.2 0.4 3.1 0.6	25	TU	0110 0757 1336 2013	3.3 0.4 3.2 0.5
11	TU	0207 0849 1432 2057	3.2 0.5 3.1 0.8	26	W	0149 0840 1420 2055	3.3 0.4 3.1 0.6
12	W	0242 0923 1511 2128	3.3 0.7 3.0 0.9	27	TH	0231 0925 1507 2140	3.3 0.5 3.0 0.7
13	TH	0322 1000 1555 2204	3.3 0.8 3.0 1.0	28	F	0319 1014 1559 2229	3.3 0.5 3.0 0.7
14	F	0408 1044 1646 ☾ 2249	3.3 1.0 2.9 1.2	29	SA	0413 1108 1656 ☽ 2325	3.2 0.5 2.9 0.8
15	SA	0502 1139 1744 2347	3.2 1.1 2.9 1.3	30	SU	0514 1209 1759	3.2 0.6 2.9

DECEMBER

Date	Day	Time	m	Date	Day	Time	m
1	M	0029 0620 1316 1906	0.8 3.1 0.6 2.9	16	TU	0003 0616 1252 1856	1.2 3.1 1.1 2.9
2	TU	0140 0730 1424 2015	0.8 3.1 0.5 2.9	17	W	0109 0717 1356 1956	1.2 3.1 1.1 2.9
3	W	0251 0840 1529 2122	0.7 3.1 0.5 3.0	18	TH	0219 0819 1500 2053	1.2 3.1 1.0 3.0
4	TH	0357 0947 1629 2222	0.5 3.1 0.4 3.0	19	F	0325 0917 1558 2146	1.1 3.1 0.9 3.1
5	F	0456 1046 1723 2315	0.4 3.1 0.4 3.1	20	SA	0425 1011 1652 2236	0.9 3.1 0.8 3.1
6	SA ○	0550 1138 1811	0.4 3.1 0.4	21	SU	0519 1102 1742 2323	0.7 3.2 0.6 3.2
7	SU	0000 0636 1224 1853	3.2 0.4 3.1 0.5	22	M ●	0609 1151 1830	0.5 3.2 0.5
8	M	0040 0718 1303 1931	3.2 0.4 3.1 0.6	23	TU	0009 0657 1239 1916	3.3 0.4 3.2 0.5
9	TU	0114 0756 1338 2004	3.2 0.5 3.1 0.7	24	W	0054 0744 1326 2001	3.3 0.3 3.1 0.5
10	W	0146 0830 1412 2034	3.3 0.6 3.1 0.8	25	TH	0138 0830 1412 2046	3.3 0.3 3.1 0.5
11	TH	0220 0902 1447 2104	3.3 0.7 3.1 0.9	26	F	0223 0916 1458 2131	3.3 0.3 3.0 0.5
12	F	0256 0936 1527 2138	3.4 0.8 3.1 1.0	27	SA	0310 1004 1546 2217	3.3 0.3 3.0 0.5
13	SA	0338 1014 1612 2218	3.4 0.9 3.0 1.1	28	SU	0401 1053 1638 ☽ 2308	3.3 0.4 2.9 0.6
14	SU	0425 1059 1702 ☾ 2306	3.3 1.0 3.0 1.2	29	M	0456 1148 1734	3.2 0.4 2.8
15	M	0518 1151 1757	3.2 1.1 2.9	30	TU	0005 0557 1248 1837	0.6 3.1 0.5 2.8
				31	W	0111 0704 1353 1944	0.6 3.0 0.5 2.8

CUXHAVEN
LAT 53°52'N
LONG 8°43'E

TIMES AND HEIGHTS OF HIGH AND LOW WATER (Heights in Metres)

TIME ZONE –0100 (German Standard Time). **Subtract 1 hour for UT. For German Summer Time (area enclosed in shaded box) add 1 hour**

2014

SUNRISE AND SUNSET TIMES

CUXHAVEN
At 53°52'N 8°43'E
European Standard Time (UT-1)

		Sunrise	Sunset
Jan	01	0843	1614
	15	0835	1635
Feb	01	0811	1707
	15	0745	1735
Mar	01	0713	1802
	15	0640	1829
European Summer Time (UT-2)			
Apr	01	0658	2001
	15	0625	2027
May	01	0549	2056
	15	0523	2121
Jun	01	0501	2146
	15	0453	2158
Jul	01	0458	2159
	15	0513	2148
Aug	01	0539	2123
	15	0603	2055
Sep	01	0634	2015
	15	0658	1941
Oct	01	0727	1901
	15	0753	1828
European Standard Time (UT-1)			
Nov	01	0725	1651
	15	0752	1626
Dec	01	0820	1608
	15	0837	1603

JANUARY

Date	Day	Time	m
1	W	0703	0.4
		1237	3.7
	●	1928	0.5
2	TH	0101	3.8
		0800	0.2
		1342	3.7
		2021	0.3
3	F	0200	3.8
		0852	0.1
		1437	3.7
		2110	0.3
4	SA	0251	3.9
		0940	0.1
		1525	3.6
		2156	0.3
5	SU	0337	3.8
		1026	0.1
		1610	3.5
		2240	0.3
6	M	0420	3.8
		1110	0.2
		1651	3.5
		2322	0.4
7	TU	0503	3.8
		1154	0.3
		1734	3.4
8	W	0005	0.5
		0548	3.7
		1240	0.4
	☽	1820	3.3
9	TH	0053	0.6
		0639	3.6
		1330	0.5
		1913	3.3
10	F	0148	0.7
		0737	3.5
		1428	0.6
		2014	3.3
11	SA	0257	0.7
		0842	3.4
		1535	0.7
		2121	3.3
12	SU	0412	0.7
		0952	3.4
		1642	0.7
		2230	3.4
13	M	0520	0.7
		1102	3.4
		1743	0.7
		2334	3.5
14	TU	0618	0.6
		1204	3.5
		1836	0.6
15	W	0027	3.7
		0707	0.6
		1254	3.5
		1920	0.6
16	TH	0111	3.8
		0750	0.6
		1335	3.6
	O	2000	0.6
17	F	0147	3.8
		0828	0.6
		1409	3.7
		2035	0.7
18	SA	0218	3.9
		0902	0.7
		1441	3.7
		2108	0.7
19	SU	0247	3.9
		0934	0.7
		1512	3.7
		2139	0.8
20	M	0314	3.9
		1006	0.7
		1541	3.6
		2211	0.8
21	TU	0337	3.9
		1038	0.8
		1604	3.6
		2244	0.8
22	W	0351	3.9
		1111	0.8
		1616	3.6
		2319	0.9
23	TH	0422	3.8
		1147	0.8
		1647	3.5
		2357	0.9
24	F	0511	3.7
		1228	0.9
	☾	1741	3.5
25	SA	0042	0.9
		0616	3.6
		1316	0.9
		1850	3.4
26	SU	0136	0.9
		0730	3.6
		1415	0.9
		2005	3.4
27	M	0245	0.9
		0844	3.5
		1530	0.9
		2118	3.5
28	TU	0412	0.8
		0958	3.5
		1655	0.8
		2229	3.6
29	W	0538	0.7
		1112	3.5
		1811	0.7
		2341	3.7
30	TH	0648	0.4
		1227	3.6
	●	1914	0.5
31	F	0050	3.8
		0746	0.2
		1332	3.7
		2008	0.3

FEBRUARY

Date	Day	Time	m
1	SA	0150	3.8
		0837	0.1
		1425	3.7
		2056	0.2
2	SU	0240	3.9
		0924	0.0
		1510	3.6
		2140	0.2
3	M	0323	3.9
		1007	0.1
		1550	3.6
		2221	0.2
4	TU	0402	3.8
		1048	0.2
		1627	3.5
		2300	0.3
5	W	0440	3.8
		1127	0.3
		1704	3.5
		2339	0.4
6	TH	0520	3.7
		1206	0.4
	☽	1745	3.4
7	F	0018	0.5
		0606	3.6
		1247	0.6
		1833	3.4
8	SA	0104	0.6
		0659	3.4
		1335	0.8
		1930	3.3
9	SU	0204	0.8
		0801	3.3
		1439	0.9
		2035	3.3
10	M	0328	0.9
		0910	3.3
		1600	1.0
		2146	3.3
11	TU	0449	0.9
		1025	3.3
		1712	0.9
		2257	3.5
12	W	0553	0.8
		1134	3.4
		1810	0.8
		2358	3.6
13	TH	0644	0.7
		1228	3.5
		1857	0.7
14	F	0045	3.8
		0728	0.6
		1312	3.7
		1938	0.6
15	SA	0125	3.9
		0806	0.6
		1349	3.7
	O	2015	0.6
16	SU	0159	3.9
		0841	0.6
		1422	3.7
		2050	0.6
17	M	0230	3.9
		0914	0.6
		1453	3.7
		2124	0.6
18	TU	0258	3.9
		0947	0.6
		1520	3.7
		2156	0.6
19	W	0319	3.8
		1019	0.6
		1530	3.6
		2229	0.7
20	TH	0314	3.8
		1052	0.7
		1521	3.6
		2303	0.7
21	F	0345	3.8
		1126	0.7
		1601	3.6
		2339	0.7
22	SA	0435	3.7
		1204	0.8
		1657	3.5
	☾		
23	SU	0021	0.7
		0544	3.6
		1250	0.8
		1812	3.5
24	M	0114	0.8
		0705	3.5
		1348	0.9
		1938	3.4
25	TU	0224	0.8
		0825	3.4
		1506	1.0
		2058	3.5
26	W	0357	0.8
		0944	3.4
		1638	0.9
		2215	3.5
27	TH	0524	0.7
		1102	3.5
		1756	0.7
		2330	3.7
28	F	0633	0.4
		1216	3.6
		1858	0.4

MARCH

Date	Day	Time	m
1	SA	0039	3.8
		0729	0.2
		1318	3.7
	●	1951	0.2
2	SU	0136	3.9
		0819	0.1
		1408	3.7
		2038	0.1
3	M	0224	3.9
		0904	0.0
		1450	3.7
		2120	0.1
4	TU	0304	3.9
		0944	0.1
		1527	3.6
		2159	0.1
5	W	0340	3.8
		1022	0.2
		1600	3.6
		2236	0.2
6	TH	0415	3.8
		1057	0.3
		1633	3.6
		2310	0.4
7	F	0451	3.7
		1129	0.5
		1709	3.5
		2344	0.5
8	SA	0534	3.6
		1202	0.7
		1754	3.5
	☽		
9	SU	0022	0.7
		0623	3.4
		1241	0.9
		1847	3.4
10	M	0111	0.9
		0722	3.3
		1332	1.1
		1950	3.4
11	TU	0223	1.1
		0827	3.3
		1448	1.2
		2039	3.4
12	W	0408	1.1
		0940	3.3
		1629	1.2
		2211	3.5
13	TH	0520	1.0
		1052	3.4
		1736	1.0
		2316	3.7
14	F	0614	0.8
		1152	3.6
		1827	0.8
15	SA	0009	3.8
		0658	0.7
		1240	3.7
		1910	0.7
16	SU	0054	3.9
		0737	0.6
		1320	3.8
	O	1950	0.6
17	M	0132	4.0
		0814	0.5
		1356	3.8
		2027	0.5
18	TU	0206	3.9
		0849	0.5
		1428	3.8
		2102	0.5
19	W	0238	3.9
		0924	0.5
		1457	3.7
		2137	0.5
20	TH	0303	3.8
		0958	0.5
		1505	3.6
		2212	0.5
21	F	0256	3.8
		1032	0.6
		1454	3.7
		2248	0.6
22	SA	0326	3.7
		1108	0.6
		1539	3.6
		2326	0.6
23	SU	0423	3.6
		1146	0.7
		1641	3.6
24	M	0010	0.7
		0539	3.5
		1233	0.8
	☾	1802	3.5
25	TU	0105	0.8
		0657	3.4
		1332	0.9
		1926	3.5
26	W	0219	0.8
		0814	3.4
		1454	1.0
		2045	3.5
27	TH	0350	0.8
		0933	3.4
		1624	0.9
		2203	3.6
28	F	0509	0.6
		1051	3.5
		1738	0.7
		2317	3.7
29	SA	0613	0.4
		1200	3.6
		1838	0.4
30	SU	0022	3.9
		0708	0.2
		1258	3.7
	●	1930	0.2
31	M	0117	3.9
		0756	0.1
		1346	3.8
		[illegible]	[illegible]

APRIL

Date	Day	Time	m
1	TU	0203	3.9
		0840	0.1
		1427	3.8
		2058	0.1
2	W	0242	3.9
		0919	0.2
		1502	3.7
		2136	0.2
3	TH	0317	3.8
		0954	0.3
		1533	3.7
		2211	0.3
4	F	0349	3.7
		1026	0.5
		1602	3.7
		2243	0.5
5	SA	0423	3.7
		1054	0.7
		1635	3.7
		2313	0.7
6	SU	0503	3.6
		1122	0.8
		1718	3.6
		2346	0.8
7	M	0550	3.5
		1157	1.0
		1809	3.6
	☽		
8	TU	0030	1.0
		0644	3.4
		1244	1.2
		1908	3.5
9	W	0129	1.2
		0746	3.3
		1345	1.3
		2014	3.6
10	TH	0258	1.3
		0854	3.4
		1511	1.4
		2121	3.6
11	F	0431	1.2
		1002	3.5
		1645	1.2
		2225	3.7
12	SA	0531	1.0
		1104	3.6
		1746	1.0
		2322	3.9
13	SU	0619	0.8
		1156	3.7
		1835	0.8
14	M	0011	3.9
		0702	0.7
		1242	3.8
		1918	0.6
15	TU	0056	4.0
		0742	0.5
		1321	3.8
	O	1959	0.5
16	W	0136	3.9
		0820	0.5
		1358	3.8
		2038	0.4
17	TH	0213	3.9
		0858	0.4
		1431	3.8
		2117	0.4
18	F	0247	3.8
		0936	0.5
		1459	3.7
		2155	0.4
19	SA	0319	3.7
		1013	0.5
		1456	3.7
		2235	0.5
20	SU	0355	3.6
		1052	0.6
		1544	3.7
		2318	0.5
21	M	0446	3.5
		1134	0.7
		1654	3.7
22	TU	0005	0.6
		0546	3.5
		1223	0.8
	☾	1804	3.6
23	W	0104	0.7
		0652	3.4
		1324	0.9
		1916	3.6
24	TH	0216	0.8
		0804	3.4
		1442	1.0
		2031	3.6
25	F	0335	0.7
		0918	3.4
		1603	0.8
		2145	3.7
26	SA	0447	0.5
		1031	3.5
		1713	0.6
		2256	3.8
27	SU	0548	0.4
		1137	3.6
		1814	0.4
		2359	3.8
28	M	0643	0.2
		1234	3.7
		1906	0.3
29	TU	0053	3.9
		0730	0.2
		1322	3.8
	●	1953	0.2
30	W	0140	3.8
		0814	0.2
		1403	3.8
		2035	0.2

MAY

Date	Day	Time	m
1	TH	0220	3.8
		0853	0.3
		1437	3.8
		2114	0.3
2	F	0254	3.7
		0927	0.5
		1506	3.8
		2148	0.5
3	SA	0325	3.7
		0957	0.7
		1533	3.8
		2218	0.6
4	SU	0357	3.7
		1022	0.8
		1605	3.8
		2246	0.8
5	M	0434	3.6
		1049	0.9
		1645	3.8
		2318	0.9
6	TU	0518	3.6
		1124	1.1
		1733	3.8
		2359	1.1
7	W	0610	3.5
		1209	1.2
		1829	3.7
	☽		
8	TH	0052	1.2
		0707	3.4
		1304	1.3
		1929	3.7
9	F	0158	1.3
		0810	3.4
		1411	1.4
		2032	3.7
10	SA	0317	1.3
		0912	3.5
		1532	1.3
		2133	3.7
11	SU	0430	1.1
		1011	3.6
		1650	1.2
		2230	3.8
12	M	0529	0.9
		1105	3.7
		1751	0.9
		2323	3.8
13	TU	0620	0.8
		1154	3.8
		1842	0.7
14	W	0013	3.9
		0706	0.6
		1241	3.8
	O	1929	0.5
15	TH	0101	3.9
		0751	0.5
		1325	3.8
		2014	0.4
16	F	0147	3.8
		0834	0.4
		1407	3.8
		2058	0.3
17	SA	0232	3.7
		0916	0.4
		1448	3.8
		2141	0.3
18	SU	0317	3.7
		0958	0.5
		1528	3.8
		2226	0.4
19	M	0403	3.6
		1041	0.6
		1612	3.8
		2312	0.4
20	TU	0451	3.5
		1126	0.7
		1702	3.7
21	W	0001	0.5
		0543	3.4
		1215	0.7
	☾	1758	3.7
22	TH	0058	0.6
		0642	3.4
		1313	0.8
		1901	3.7
23	F	0202	0.6
		0746	3.4
		1422	0.8
		2009	3.7
24	SA	0311	0.6
		0855	3.4
		1536	0.8
		2119	3.7
25	SU	0418	0.5
		1004	3.5
		1645	0.6
		2228	3.7
26	M	0519	0.4
		1109	3.6
		1747	0.5
		2332	3.7
27	TU	0615	0.3
		1207	3.7
		1842	0.3
28	W	0029	3.7
		0704	0.3
		1257	3.8
	●	1931	0.3
29	TH	0119	3.7
		0749	0.3
		1340	3.8
		2014	0.3
30	F	0200	3.7
		0829	0.5
		1415	3.8
		2053	0.5
31	SA	0234	3.6
		0903	0.6
		1444	3.8
		[illegible]	[illegible]

JUNE

Date	Day	Time	m
1	SU	0304	3.6
		0933	0.8
		1510	3.8
		2158	0.7
2	M	0335	3.6
		0958	0.9
		1539	3.9
		2226	0.8
3	TU	0409	3.6
		1026	1.0
		1616	3.9
		2258	0.9
4	W	0450	3.6
		1100	1.0
		1659	3.9
		2336	1.0
5	TH	0537	3.6
		1142	1.1
		1749	3.8
	☽		
6	F	0022	1.1
		0628	3.5
		1232	1.2
		1844	3.8
7	SA	0115	1.2
		0724	3.5
		1328	1.3
		1943	3.7
8	SU	0215	1.2
		0821	3.5
		1432	1.3
		2042	3.7
9	M	0321	1.1
		0918	3.5
		1545	1.2
		2140	3.7
10	TU	0430	1.0
		1013	3.6
		1658	1.0
		2236	3.7
11	W	0533	0.8
		1107	3.7
		1803	0.8
		2332	3.7
12	TH	0631	0.7
		1201	3.8
		1900	0.6
13	F	0029	3.7
		0723	0.5
		1255	3.8
	O	1952	0.4
14	SA	0127	3.7
		0813	0.4
		1347	3.9
		2042	0.3
15	SU	0221	3.7
		0900	0.4
		1437	3.9
		2129	0.2
16	M	0311	3.6
		0946	0.4
		1523	3.8
		2216	0.2
17	TU	0358	3.6
		1031	0.4
		1609	3.8
		2303	0.3
18	W	0445	3.5
		1116	0.5
		1655	3.8
		2351	0.3
19	TH	0532	3.4
		1203	0.6
		1745	3.8
	☾		
20	F	0041	0.4
		0622	3.4
		1255	0.6
		1840	3.7
21	SA	0137	0.5
		0719	3.3
		1354	0.7
		1941	3.6
22	SU	0238	0.5
		0822	3.3
		1502	0.7
		2047	3.5
23	M	0343	0.5
		0929	3.4
		1614	0.6
		2157	3.5
24	TU	0447	0.5
		1037	3.5
		1720	0.5
		2305	3.5
25	W	0547	0.4
		1139	3.6
		1819	0.4
26	TH	0007	3.5
		0639	0.4
		1234	3.7
		1910	0.4
27	F	0059	3.5
		0727	0.5
		1319	3.7
	●	1955	0.4
28	SA	0142	3.6
		0808	0.5
		1356	3.8
		2035	0.5
29	SU	0217	3.6
		0844	0.6
		1426	3.8
		2111	0.6
30	M	0248	3.6
		0915	0.8
		1453	3.9
		2142	0.7

CUXHAVEN
LAT 53°52'N
LONG 8°43'E

TIMES AND HEIGHTS OF HIGH AND LOW WATER (Heights in Metres)

TIME ZONE –0100 (German Standard Time). **Subtract 1 hour for UT. For German Summer Time (area enclosed in shaded box) add 1 hour**

2014

JULY

Date	Day	Time	m	Time	m	Time	m	Time	m
1	TU	0317	3.7	0943	0.8	1520	3.9	2211	0.8
2	W	0349	3.7	1012	0.9	1552	3.9	2242	0.9
3	TH	0424	3.6	1044	0.9	1627	3.9	2316	0.9
4	F	0502	3.6	1122	1.0	1707	3.8	2355	1.0
5	SA ☽	0544	3.5	1204	1.0	1755	3.7		
6	SU	0038	1.0	0631	3.5	1251	1.1	1850	3.6
7	M	0128	1.1	0726	3.4	1346	1.1	1950	3.6
8	TU	0226	1.1	0825	3.4	1450	1.1	2053	3.6
9	W	0333	1.0	0925	3.5	1606	1.0	2156	3.6
10	TH	0448	0.9	1026	3.6	1726	0.8	2300	3.6
11	F	0559	0.7	1128	3.7	1835	0.6		
12	SA O	0006	3.6	0701	0.6	1232	3.8	1934	0.4
13	SU	0112	3.7	0757	0.4	1332	3.8	2028	0.2
14	M	0210	3.7	0847	0.3	1426	3.9	2117	0.1
15	TU	0301	3.7	0934	0.2	1515	3.9	2203	0.1
16	W	0347	3.6	1019	0.3	1559	3.9	2248	0.1
17	TH	0430	3.5	1102	0.3	1642	3.8	2332	0.2
18	F	0512	3.4	1144	0.4	1726	3.7		
19	SA ☾	0017	0.3	0556	3.4	1230	0.4	1814	3.6
20	SU	0105	0.4	0646	3.3	1321	0.5	1910	3.5
21	M	0159	0.5	0744	3.3	1425	0.6	2013	3.4
22	TU	0303	0.6	0850	3.3	1540	0.7	2123	3.3
23	W	0413	0.7	1000	3.3	1653	0.7	2236	3.3
24	TH	0519	0.7	1110	3.5	1756	0.6	2344	3.4
25	F	0617	0.6	1210	3.6	1850	0.5		
26	SA ●	0039	3.5	0706	0.6	1259	3.7	1936	0.5
27	SU	0124	3.6	0749	0.6	1338	3.8	2017	0.5
28	M	0200	3.6	0826	0.6	1410	3.9	2052	0.6
29	TU	0232	3.7	0859	0.7	1438	3.9	2124	0.6
30	W	0302	3.7	0930	0.7	1506	3.9	2155	0.7
31	TH	0331	3.7	1000	0.8	1533	3.9	2225	0.7

AUGUST

Date	Day	Time	m	Time	m	Time	m	Time	m
1	F	0358	3.6	1031	0.8	1556	3.9	2256	0.8
2	SA	0421	3.6	1104	0.8	1618	3.8	2330	0.8
3	SU	0438	3.5	1140	0.9	1655	3.7		
4	M ☽	0007	0.9	0518	3.5	1221	0.9	1751	3.6
5	TU	0051	0.9	0620	3.4	1309	0.9	1901	3.5
6	W	0144	1.0	0733	3.4	1410	0.9	2014	3.5
7	TH	0250	1.0	0846	3.4	1527	0.9	2126	3.5
8	F	0412	1.0	0956	3.5	1659	0.8	2237	3.5
9	SA	0536	0.8	1106	3.6	1816	0.6	2350	3.6
10	SU O	0645	0.6	1216	3.8	1919	0.3		
11	M	0059	3.7	0742	0.4	1320	3.9	2013	0.1
12	TU	0157	3.7	0832	0.2	1415	3.9	2101	0.0
13	W	0246	3.7	0918	0.1	1502	3.9	2146	0.0
14	TH	0330	3.6	1001	0.1	1544	3.9	2228	0.0
15	F	0409	3.6	1042	0.1	1623	3.8	2308	0.2
16	SA	0447	3.5	1121	0.2	1703	3.7	2347	0.3
17	SU ☾	0526	3.4	1202	0.4	1747	3.6		
18	M	0028	0.5	0611	3.4	1247	0.5	1837	3.4
19	TU	0114	0.7	0705	3.3	1342	0.7	1936	3.3
20	W	0213	0.8	0808	3.3	1459	0.8	2045	3.2
21	TH	0333	0.9	0920	3.3	1624	0.9	2201	3.2
22	F	0450	0.9	1035	3.4	1732	0.8	2315	3.3
23	SA	0552	0.8	1141	3.6	1827	0.7		
24	SU	0014	3.5	0642	0.7	1234	3.8	1913	0.6
25	M ●	0101	3.6	0726	0.6	1315	3.9	1953	0.5
26	TU	0139	3.7	0804	0.5	1349	3.9	2029	0.5
27	W	0212	3.8	0839	0.5	1421	4.0	2102	0.5
28	TH	0243	3.8	0911	0.6	1450	3.9	2133	0.6
29	F	0311	3.7	0943	0.6	1516	3.9	2204	0.6
30	SA	0334	3.6	1014	0.7	1530	3.8	2235	0.7
31	SU	0316	3.6	1046	0.7	1531	3.8	2307	0.8

SEPTEMBER

Date	Day	Time	m	Time	m	Time	m	Time	m
1	M	0340	3.6	1120	0.7	1611	3.7	2342	0.8
2	TU ☽	0427	3.6	1158	0.8	1710	3.6		
3	W	0023	0.9	0533	3.5	1245	0.8	1827	3.5
4	TH	0115	1.0	0657	3.5	1346	0.9	1948	3.4
5	F	0222	1.0	0820	3.5	1507	0.9	2105	3.4
6	SA	0350	1.0	0936	3.5	1642	0.8	2221	3.5
7	SU	0518	0.8	1050	3.7	1800	0.6	2336	3.6
8	M	0628	0.6	1202	3.8	1901	0.3		
9	TU O	0044	3.7	0724	0.3	1306	3.9	1954	0.1
10	W	0140	3.8	0814	0.1	1358	4.0	2041	0.0
11	TH	0227	3.8	0859	0.0	1443	3.9	2124	0.0
12	F	0308	3.7	0940	0.0	1524	3.9	2204	0.1
13	SA	0345	3.6	1020	0.1	1601	3.8	2241	0.2
14	SU	0419	3.6	1057	0.3	1637	3.7	2316	0.4
15	M	0454	3.5	1133	0.4	1718	3.6	2350	0.6
16	TU ☾	0536	3.5	1211	0.6	1805	3.4		
17	W	0027	0.8	0626	3.4	1258	0.8	1900	3.3
18	TH	0115	1.0	0726	3.4	1405	1.0	2004	3.2
19	F	0227	1.2	0835	3.4	1545	1.1	2117	3.3
20	SA	0408	1.2	0949	3.5	1700	1.0	2233	3.4
21	SU	0518	1.0	1059	3.7	1757	0.8	2338	3.5
22	M	0612	0.8	1156	3.8	1844	0.7		
23	TU	0028	3.7	0657	0.7	1242	4.0	1924	0.6
24	W ●	0109	3.8	0736	0.6	1321	4.0	2000	0.5
25	TH	0145	3.9	0813	0.5	1355	4.0	2035	0.5
26	F	0217	3.8	0848	0.5	1427	3.9	2108	0.5
27	SA	0247	3.8	0922	0.5	1456	3.8	2141	0.6
28	SU	0310	3.7	0955	0.6	1514	3.8	2213	0.6
29	M	0242	3.7	1029	0.6	1507	3.7	2247	0.7
30	TU	0314	3.7	1105	0.7	1551	3.7	2323	0.8

OCTOBER

Date	Day	Time	m	Time	m	Time	m	Time	m
1	W ☽	0406	3.7	1145	0.7	1658	3.6		
2	TH	0005	0.9	0516	3.6	1234	0.8	1816	3.5
3	F	0057	1.0	0642	3.6	1337	0.9	1934	3.4
4	SA	0206	1.0	0803	3.6	1501	0.9	2051	3.4
5	SU	0335	1.0	0920	3.6	1628	0.7	2207	3.5
6	M	0459	0.8	1034	3.7	1739	0.5	2320	3.6
7	TU	0606	0.5	1144	3.9	1839	0.3		
8	W O	0024	3.7	0702	0.3	1246	3.9	1931	0.1
9	TH	0119	3.8	0752	0.1	1338	4.0	2017	0.1
10	F	0205	3.8	0837	0.1	1422	3.9	2059	0.1
11	SA	0245	3.8	0919	0.1	1502	3.8	2138	0.2
12	SU	0319	3.7	0957	0.2	1537	3.7	2213	0.4
13	M	0351	3.7	1032	0.4	1611	3.6	2245	0.6
14	TU	0423	3.7	1106	0.6	1649	3.6	2314	0.8
15	W ☾	0502	3.7	1139	0.8	1733	3.5	2346	0.9
16	TH	0550	3.6	1219	0.9	1825	3.4		
17	F	0027	1.1	0646	3.6	1315	1.1	1925	3.3
18	SA	0125	1.3	0750	3.6	1441	1.2	2032	3.3
19	SU	0248	1.3	0859	3.6	1612	1.1	2142	3.4
20	M	0426	1.2	1006	3.7	1714	1.0	2248	3.6
21	TU	0530	1.0	1106	3.8	1804	0.8	2343	3.7
22	W	0620	0.8	1158	3.9	1847	0.7		
23	TH ●	0029	3.8	0703	0.7	1243	3.9	1926	0.6
24	F	0109	3.9	0743	0.6	1322	3.9	2004	0.5
25	SA	0145	3.8	0822	0.5	1359	3.9	2041	0.5
26	SU	0219	3.8	0859	0.5	1434	3.8	2117	0.5
27	M	0248	3.8	0937	0.5	1505	3.7	2153	0.6
28	TU	0259	3.7	1015	0.6	1533	3.6	2231	0.7
29	W	0311	3.7	1055	0.6	1612	3.6	2310	0.7
30	TH	0408	3.7	1139	0.7	1710	3.5	2354	0.8
31	F ☽	0521	3.7	1231	0.7	1814	3.5		

NOVEMBER

Date	Day	Time	m	Time	m	Time	m	Time	m
1	SA	0047	0.9	0634	3.7	1335	0.8	1923	3.4
2	SU	0156	1.0	0748	3.7	1451	0.7	2035	3.4
3	M	0318	0.9	0901	3.7	1607	0.6	2148	3.5
4	TU	0435	0.8	1013	3.8	1714	0.5	2257	3.6
5	W	0541	0.5	1122	3.8	1813	0.3		
6	TH O	0000	3.7	0638	0.3	1223	3.9	1905	0.2
7	F	0055	3.8	0730	0.2	1316	3.8	1952	0.2
8	SA	0142	3.8	0816	0.2	1402	3.8	2035	0.2
9	SU	0222	3.8	0858	0.2	1441	3.7	2113	0.4
10	M	0255	3.8	0936	0.4	1515	3.6	2147	0.6
11	TU	0324	3.8	1010	0.5	1547	3.6	2216	0.8
12	W	0353	3.8	1041	0.7	1621	3.6	2242	0.9
13	TH	0430	3.8	1112	0.8	1703	3.6	2312	1.0
14	F ☾	0515	3.8	1149	1.0	1752	3.5	2353	1.1
15	SA	0609	3.8	1237	1.1	1847	3.5		
16	SU	0044	1.3	0708	3.7	1339	1.2	1948	3.4
17	M	0148	1.3	0810	3.7	1455	1.2	2052	3.5
18	TU	0308	1.3	0913	3.7	1610	1.1	2153	3.5
19	W	0429	1.2	1012	3.8	1711	1.0	2249	3.6
20	TH	0532	1.0	1107	3.8	1802	0.8	2340	3.7
21	F	0624	0.8	1158	3.8	1848	0.7		
22	SA ●	0026	3.8	0711	0.6	1245	3.8	1931	0.6
23	SU	0109	3.8	0755	0.5	1330	3.8	2014	0.5
24	M	0150	3.8	0838	0.4	1413	3.7	2055	0.5
25	TU	0229	3.8	0921	0.4	1456	3.7	2137	0.5
26	W	0307	3.8	1004	0.4	1539	3.6	2219	0.6
27	TH	0344	3.8	1048	0.5	1624	3.5	2302	0.6
28	F	0429	3.8	1135	0.5	1713	3.5	2348	0.7
29	SA ☽	0523	3.8	1226	0.5	1807	3.4		
30	SU	0040	0.8	0623	3.7	1325	0.6	1908	3.4

DECEMBER

Date	Day	Time	m	Time	m	Time	m	Time	m
1	M	0142	0.8	0729	3.7	1430	0.6	2014	3.4
2	TU	0253	0.8	0838	3.7	1539	0.5	2122	3.4
3	W	0407	0.7	0948	3.7	1645	0.4	2231	3.5
4	TH	0515	0.5	1056	3.7	1746	0.3	2335	3.6
5	F	0615	0.4	1200	3.7	1840	0.3		
6	SA O	0031	3.7	0708	0.3	1256	3.6	1929	0.3
7	SU	0120	3.7	0756	0.3	1343	3.6	2013	0.4
8	M	0201	3.8	0839	0.4	1423	3.6	2052	0.5
9	TU	0234	3.8	0917	0.5	1456	3.6	2126	0.7
10	W	0302	3.8	0952	0.6	1526	3.6	2154	0.8
11	TH	0329	3.8	1022	0.8	1558	3.6	2220	0.9
12	F	0403	3.9	1051	0.9	1636	3.6	2249	1.0
13	SA	0444	3.9	1125	0.9	1720	3.6	2328	1.1
14	SU ☾	0532	3.9	1207	1.0	1810	3.5		
15	M	0014	1.1	0625	3.8	1256	1.1	1904	3.5
16	TU	0108	1.2	0723	3.7	1353	1.1	2002	3.4
17	W	0209	1.3	0823	3.6	1456	1.2	2100	3.5
18	TH	0318	1.2	0922	3.6	1604	1.1	2155	3.5
19	F	0432	1.1	1018	3.6	1709	1.0	2249	3.6
20	SA	0539	0.9	1113	3.7	1807	0.8	2342	3.7
21	SU	0638	0.7	1209	3.7	1901	0.6		
22	M ●	0034	3.8	0730	0.5	1304	3.7	1950	0.5
23	TU	0125	3.8	0820	0.4	1357	3.7	2038	0.4
24	W	0214	3.9	0908	0.3	1447	3.7	2124	0.4
25	TH	0300	3.9	0954	0.3	1534	3.6	2209	0.4
26	F	0344	3.8	1040	0.3	1619	3.5	2253	0.4
27	SA	0429	3.8	1126	0.3	1705	3.5	2339	0.5
28	SU ☽	0516	3.8	1213	0.3	1753	3.4		
29	M	0026	0.5	0609	3.7	1305	0.4	1846	3.4
30	TU	0121	0.6	0707	3.6	1402	0.5	1946	3.3
31	W	0224	0.6	0811	3.6	1507	0.5	2052	3.3

WILHELMSHAVEN
LAT 53°31′N
LONG 8°09′E

TIMES AND HEIGHTS OF HIGH AND LOW WATER (Heights in Metres)

TIME ZONE –0100 (German Standard Time). **Subtract 1 hour for UT. For German Summer Time (area enclosed in shaded box) add 1 hour**

2014

SUNRISE AND SUNSET TIMES

WILHELMSHAVEN
At 53°31′N 8°09′E
European Standard Time (UT-1)

		Sunrise	Sunset
Jan	01	0844	1619
	15	0836	1639
Feb	01	0812	1710
	15	0746	1738
Mar	01	0715	1805
	15	0642	1832
European Summer Time (UT-2)			
Apr	01	0701	2003
	15	0628	2028
May	01	0553	2058
	15	0527	2122
Jun	01	0505	2146
	15	0458	2158
Jul	01	0503	2159
	15	0517	2149
Aug	01	0543	2123
	15	0607	2056
Sep	01	0637	2017
	15	0701	1943
Oct	01	0729	1904
	15	0755	1831
European Standard Time (UT-1)			
Nov	01	0727	1655
	15	0753	1630
Dec	01	0821	1612

JANUARY

Date	Day	Time	m	Time	m	Time	m	Time	m
1	W ●	0609	0.6	1223	4.6	1835	0.6		
2	TH	0048	4.7	0705	0.5	1318	4.6	1929	0.6
3	F	0139	4.8	0758	0.4	1413	4.6	2024	0.6
4	SA	0230	4.9	0852	0.4	1506	4.6	2115	0.5
5	SU	0319	5.0	0941	0.4	1555	4.5	2157	0.5
6	M	0405	5.0	1025	0.4	1638	4.5	2234	0.5
7	TU	0449	4.9	1108	0.5	1721	4.4	2314	0.7
8	W ☽	0535	4.7	1152	0.7	1806	4.3	2358	0.8
9	TH	0624	4.6	1238	0.9	1855	4.2		
10	F	0050	0.9	0722	4.4	1331	1.0	1955	4.2
11	SA	0156	1.1	0830	4.3	1437	1.1	2106	4.2
12	SU	0313	1.1	0944	4.3	1550	1.1	2216	4.4
13	M	0428	1.0	1052	4.4	1657	0.9	2318	4.5
14	TU	0531	0.8	1148	4.4	1751	0.8		
15	W	0009	4.6	0622	0.7	1235	4.4	1837	0.7
16	TH ○	0051	4.6	0705	0.6	1315	4.4	1916	0.7
17	F	0128	4.7	0743	0.6	1351	4.5	1953	0.7
18	SA	0203	4.8	0819	0.6	1423	4.5	2027	0.7
19	SU	0234	4.8	0852	0.7	1453	4.5	2057	0.7
20	M	0303	4.8	0920	0.7	1521	4.5	2125	0.7
21	TU	0332	4.7	0949	0.7	1553	4.4	2156	0.7
22	W	0406	4.7	1023	0.8	1628	4.4	2230	0.8
23	TH	0441	4.7	1055	0.8	1703	4.4	2303	0.8
24	F ☾	0517	4.6	1126	0.8	1741	4.3	2340	0.9
25	SA	0601	4.4	1207	0.9	1834	4.2		
26	SU	0035	1.1	0705	4.3	1311	1.0	1948	4.2
27	M	0154	1.1	0826	4.3	1433	1.0	2110	4.3
28	TU	0321	1.0	0950	4.3	1558	0.9	2229	4.4
29	W	0442	0.7	1108	4.4	1716	0.7	2338	4.6
30	TH ●	0552	0.5	1214	4.5	1823	0.6		
31	F	0036	4.7	0653	0.4	1310	4.6	[illegible]	[illegible]

FEBRUARY

Date	Day	Time	m	Time	m	Time	m	Time	m
1	SA	0128	4.8	0747	0.3	1402	4.6	2013	0.4
2	SU	0217	5.0	0839	0.3	1453	4.6	2101	0.4
3	M	0305	5.0	0926	0.3	1539	4.6	2142	0.3
4	TU	0349	5.0	1008	0.3	1618	4.5	2217	0.4
5	W	0430	4.9	1046	0.4	1655	4.5	2251	0.5
6	TH ☽	0509	4.7	1122	0.6	1731	4.4	2326	0.7
7	F	0549	4.5	1157	0.8	1810	4.3		
8	SA	0006	0.8	0636	4.3	1238	1.0	1902	4.2
9	SU	0102	1.0	0741	4.1	1340	1.1	2014	4.2
10	M	0222	1.1	0902	4.1	1502	1.2	2138	4.2
11	TU	0351	1.0	1024	4.2	1624	1.0	2253	4.4
12	W	0506	0.8	1129	4.3	1729	0.9	2349	4.5
13	TH	0601	0.7	1217	4.4	1817	0.7		
14	F	0032	4.6	0644	0.6	1256	4.4	1857	0.7
15	SA ○	0108	4.7	0722	0.6	1330	4.5	1934	0.6
16	SU	0142	4.7	0756	0.5	1401	4.5	2007	0.5
17	M	0213	4.7	0828	0.5	1430	4.5	2037	0.5
18	TU	0243	4.7	0857	0.5	1500	4.5	2106	0.5
19	W	0314	4.7	0928	0.5	1533	4.5	2139	0.5
20	TH	0349	4.7	1003	0.6	1609	4.5	2214	0.5
21	F	0425	4.7	1035	0.6	1642	4.5	2244	0.6
22	SA ☾	0457	4.6	1101	0.6	1713	4.4	2313	0.7
23	SU	0533	4.4	1132	0.8	1759	4.2		
24	M	0000	0.8	0633	4.2	1232	0.9	1912	4.2
25	TU	0119	0.9	0759	4.2	1402	1.0	2043	4.3
26	W	0256	0.9	0933	4.2	1538	0.9	2211	4.4
27	TH	0426	0.7	1057	4.4	1703	0.7	2324	4.6
28	F	0539	0.5	1205	4.5	1812	0.6		

MARCH

Date	Day	Time	m	Time	m	Time	m	Time	m
1	SA ●	0023	4.7	0640	0.3	1300	4.6	1908	0.4
2	SU	0114	4.9	0732	0.3	1348	4.6	1956	0.3
3	M	0201	4.9	0820	0.2	1433	4.6	2040	0.3
4	TU	0246	5.0	0904	0.2	1516	4.6	2120	0.3
5	W	0328	4.9	0944	0.3	1553	4.6	2156	0.3
6	TH	0407	4.8	1019	0.4	1627	4.6	2227	0.4
7	F	0443	4.7	1050	0.6	1656	4.5	2257	0.5
8	SA ☽	0517	4.5	1119	0.7	1731	4.4	2323	0.7
9	SU	0557	4.2	1152	0.9	1816	4.2		
10	M	0016	0.9	0654	4.0	1248	1.1	1924	4.1
11	TU	0130	1.0	0816	3.9	1411	1.2	2053	4.2
12	W	0305	1.0	0945	4.0	1542	1.1	2217	4.3
13	TH	0430	0.8	1059	4.2	1656	0.9	2320	4.5
14	F	0530	0.6	1149	4.4	1747	0.7		
15	SA	0004	4.6	0613	0.5	1227	4.5	1828	0.6
16	SU ○	0039	4.6	0649	0.5	1301	4.5	1906	0.5
17	M	0113	4.7	0725	0.4	1334	4.5	1941	0.4
18	TU	0147	4.7	0759	0.4	1406	4.6	2014	0.4
19	W	0220	4.7	0832	0.4	1439	4.6	2047	0.4
20	TH	0255	4.7	0907	0.4	1514	4.5	2122	0.3
21	F	0332	4.7	0942	0.4	1551	4.5	2158	0.3
22	SA	0410	4.6	1015	0.5	1625	4.5	2230	0.4
23	SU	0445	4.5	1044	0.5	1659	4.5	2301	0.5
24	M ☾	0524	4.3	1119	0.7	1745	4.3	2349	0.7
25	TU	0624	4.2	1219	0.9	1857	4.3		
26	W	0107	0.8	0750	4.1	1349	1.0	2029	4.3
27	TH	0244	0.8	0924	4.2	1527	0.9	2157	4.5
28	F	0414	0.6	1046	4.3	1649	0.7	2308	4.6
29	SA	0524	0.4	1149	4.5	1752	0.5		
30	SU ●	0005	4.7	0620	0.3	1241	4.5	1846	0.4
31	M	0056	4.8	0710	0.3	1328	4.6	[illegible]	[illegible]

APRIL

Date	Day	Time	m	Time	m	Time	m	Time	m
1	TU	0142	4.8	0756	0.2	1411	4.7	2016	0.3
2	W	0225	4.9	0837	0.3	1450	4.7	2055	0.3
3	TH	0305	4.8	0914	0.3	1526	4.7	2131	0.3
4	F	0343	4.7	0948	0.4	1558	4.6	2202	0.3
5	SA	0417	4.5	1018	0.5	1629	4.5	2231	0.4
6	SU	0450	4.4	1045	0.6	1700	4.4	2301	0.6
7	M ☽	0526	4.2	1117	0.8	1740	4.3	2342	0.8
8	TU	0616	4.0	1205	1.0	1840	4.2		
9	W	0046	0.9	0728	3.9	1320	1.1	2002	4.2
10	TH	0213	1.0	0855	3.9	1449	1.1	2127	4.2
11	F	0339	0.8	1012	4.1	1607	0.9	2235	4.4
12	SA	0443	0.6	1108	4.3	1703	0.7	2322	4.5
13	SU	0529	0.5	1149	4.4	1748	0.6		
14	M	0001	4.6	0609	0.4	1227	4.5	1831	0.5
15	TU ○	0039	4.6	0650	0.4	1304	4.6	1911	0.4
16	W	0118	4.7	0728	0.3	1341	4.6	1949	0.4
17	TH	0156	4.7	0806	0.3	1417	4.6	2026	0.3
18	F	0236	4.7	0845	0.3	1456	4.6	2105	0.3
19	SA	0317	4.6	0922	0.3	1535	4.6	2144	0.2
20	SU	0359	4.5	0959	0.4	1614	4.6	2221	0.3
21	M	0440	4.5	1037	0.5	1654	4.6	2301	0.4
22	TU ☾	0527	4.3	1120	0.7	1745	4.5	2354	0.6
23	W	0628	4.2	1222	0.8	1855	4.4		
24	TH	0108	0.7	0748	4.2	1344	0.9	2019	4.4
25	F	0237	0.7	0914	4.2	1512	0.8	2141	4.6
26	SA	0358	0.5	1028	4.3	1626	0.7	2247	4.7
27	SU	0501	0.4	1126	4.4	1724	0.5	2341	4.7
28	M	0553	0.3	1216	4.5	1818	0.4		
29	TU ●	0033	4.7	0643	0.3	1304	4.6	1908	0.3
30	W	0122	4.7	0730	0.3	1347	4.7	1952	0.2

MAY

Date	Day	Time	m	Time	m	Time	m	Time	m
1	TH	0205	4.7	0809	0.3	1425	4.7	2030	0.3
2	F	0243	4.6	0845	0.3	1459	4.7	2105	0.3
3	SA	0319	4.6	0918	0.4	1531	4.7	2137	0.4
4	SU	0354	4.5	0950	0.5	1603	4.6	2209	0.4
5	M	0427	4.3	1019	0.6	1636	4.6	2242	0.6
6	TU	0502	4.2	1052	0.8	1714	4.5	2320	0.7
7	W ☽	0545	4.1	1134	1.0	1803	4.3		
8	TH	0010	0.9	0643	4.0	1234	1.0	1909	4.3
9	F	0119	0.9	0756	4.0	1349	1.0	2026	4.3
10	SA	0236	0.8	0912	4.1	1505	0.9	2136	4.4
11	SU	0344	0.6	1014	4.3	1609	0.8	2232	4.5
12	M	0438	0.5	1104	4.4	1703	0.7	2320	4.6
13	TU	0527	0.5	1150	4.5	1753	0.6		
14	W ○	0005	4.6	0615	0.4	1234	4.6	1841	0.5
15	TH	0049	4.7	0659	0.4	1315	4.7	1924	0.4
16	F	0133	4.7	0741	0.3	1356	4.7	2007	0.3
17	SA	0219	4.7	0825	0.3	1439	4.7	2051	0.2
18	SU	0306	4.6	0909	0.4	1523	4.7	2135	0.2
19	M	0353	4.5	0951	0.4	1607	4.7	2219	0.3
20	TU	0440	4.4	1035	0.5	1654	4.7	2306	0.4
21	W ☾	0532	4.4	1124	0.7	1748	4.7		
22	TH	0002	0.5	0631	4.3	1223	0.7	1851	4.6
23	F	0107	0.6	0740	4.2	1332	0.8	2005	4.6
24	SA	0221	0.6	0853	4.2	1448	0.8	2118	4.6
25	SU	0332	0.5	1001	4.3	1557	0.7	2222	4.7
26	M	0433	0.5	1057	4.4	1655	0.6	2317	4.7
27	TU	0525	0.4	1149	4.5	1750	0.5		
28	W ●	0011	4.6	0616	0.4	1239	4.6	1844	0.4
29	TH	0102	4.6	0704	0.4	1324	4.6	1930	0.3
30	F	0146	4.6	0744	0.3	1402	4.7	2008	0.3
31	SA	0223	4.5	0820	0.4	1436	4.8		

JUNE

Date	Day	Time	m	Time	m	Time	m	Time	m
1	SU	0259	4.5	0854	0.5	1510	4.8	2119	0.5
2	M	0333	4.5	0928	0.5	1542	4.8	2153	0.5
3	TU	0406	4.4	1000	0.7	1615	4.7	2227	0.6
4	W	0440	4.3	1032	0.8	1651	4.6	2302	0.7
5	TH ☽	0517	4.2	1109	0.9	1731	4.5	2342	0.8
6	F	0602	4.1	1155	1.0	1822	4.4		
7	SA	0031	0.8	0659	4.1	1253	1.0	1924	4.4
8	SU	0133	0.8	0807	4.2	1402	1.0	2033	4.4
9	M	0241	0.8	0915	4.3	1511	0.9	2137	4.5
10	TU	0345	0.6	1016	4.4	1616	0.8	2237	4.5
11	W	0444	0.6	1111	4.5	1716	0.7	2332	4.6
12	TH	0540	0.5	1203	4.6	1811	0.5		
13	F ○	0025	4.7	0632	0.4	1252	4.7	1902	0.4
14	SA	0115	4.7	0721	0.4	1339	4.8	1951	0.3
15	SU	0206	4.7	0812	0.4	1427	4.9	2041	0.3
16	M	0259	4.6	0903	0.4	1515	4.9	2131	0.3
17	TU	0349	4.6	0948	0.4	1601	4.9	2217	0.3
18	W	0437	4.5	1031	0.5	1649	4.9	2305	0.4
19	TH ☾	0527	4.4	1119	0.6	1742	4.8	2358	0.5
20	F	0620	4.4	1212	0.7	1838	4.7		
21	SA	0054	0.6	0717	4.3	1309	0.7	1940	4.6
22	SU	0153	0.6	0820	4.3	1415	0.8	2047	4.6
23	M	0257	0.7	0925	4.3	1524	0.8	2154	4.6
24	TU	0401	0.6	1027	4.4	1630	0.7	2256	4.6
25	W	0500	0.6	1124	4.5	1729	0.6	2352	4.5
26	TH	0554	0.5	1216	4.6	1823	0.5		
27	F ●	0043	4.5	0642	0.5	1303	4.6	1911	0.4
28	SA	0128	4.5	0725	0.4	1342	4.7	1952	0.4
29	SU	0206	4.5	0802	0.5	1418	4.8	2029	0.5
30	M	0241	4.6	0838	0.6	1452	4.9	2105	0.5

WILHELMSHAVEN
LAT 53°31′N
LONG 8°09′E

TIMES AND HEIGHTS OF HIGH AND LOW WATER (Heights in Metres)

TIME ZONE –0100 (German Standard Time). **Subtract 1 hour for UT. For German Summer Time (area enclosed in shaded box) add 1 hour**

2014

JULY

Day	Time	m	Time	m	Time	m	Time	m
1 TU	0314	4.6	0912	0.6	1523	4.9	2137	0.6
2 W	0344	4.5	0942	0.7	1553	4.8	2208	0.7
3 TH	0416	4.4	1013	0.8	1627	4.7	2242	0.8
4 F	0451	4.4	1048	0.9	1704	4.7	2317	0.8
5 SA ☽	0528	4.3	1125	0.9	1744	4.6	2354	0.8
6 SU	0612	4.3	1208	0.9	1832	4.5		
7 M	0039	0.8	0707	4.3	1305	1.0	1934	4.4
8 TU	0141	0.9	0815	4.3	1415	1.0	2044	4.4
9 W	0251	0.8	0927	4.3	1530	0.9	2156	4.4
10 TH	0402	0.7	1034	4.5	1641	0.7	2304	4.5
11 F	0509	0.6	1136	4.6	1746	0.5		
12 SA ○	0006	4.6	0612	0.5	1232	4.8	1844	0.4
13 SU	0102	4.7	0709	0.4	1324	4.9	1939	0.3
14 M	0156	4.7	0804	0.4	1415	5.0	2033	0.3
15 TU	0250	4.7	0856	0.4	1504	5.1	2124	0.2
16 W	0340	4.6	0941	0.3	1551	5.0	2210	0.3
17 TH	0425	4.6	1021	0.4	1637	5.0	2254	0.4
18 F	0510	4.5	1104	0.5	1725	4.9	2341	0.5
19 SA ☾	0556	4.4	1150	0.6	1814	4.8		
20 SU	0027	0.7	0643	4.4	1238	0.7	1907	4.6
21 M	0116	0.8	0737	4.3	1336	0.8	2009	4.5
22 TU	0215	0.9	0843	4.3	1448	0.9	2122	4.4
23 W	0327	0.9	0956	4.4	1605	0.8	2235	4.4
24 TH	0438	0.8	1103	4.5	1713	0.7	2337	4.4
25 F	0537	0.7	1158	4.6	1808	0.6		
26 SA ●	0027	4.5	0626	0.6	1244	4.7	1855	0.5
27 SU	0110	4.5	0708	0.6	1324	4.8	1936	0.5
28 M	0148	4.5	0747	0.6	1359	4.8	2013	0.5
29 TU	0221	4.6	0823	0.6	1432	4.9	2047	0.6
30 W	0251	4.6	0854	0.6	1501	4.9	2116	0.6
31 TH	0319	4.6	0922	0.6	1530	4.8	2144	0.7

AUGUST

Day	Time	m	Time	m	Time	m	Time	m
1 F	0350	4.5	0952	0.7	1603	4.8	2218	0.8
2 SA	0425	4.5	1027	0.8	1639	4.8	2253	0.8
3 SU	0459	4.5	1101	0.8	1714	4.7	2323	0.8
4 M ☽	0533	4.4	1133	0.9	1751	4.5	2356	0.8
5 TU	0617	4.3	1218	0.9	1844	4.4		
6 W	0048	0.9	0722	4.3	1327	1.0	1958	4.3
7 TH	0204	1.0	0843	4.3	1451	0.9	2122	4.3
8 F	0329	0.9	1003	4.4	1614	0.7	2242	4.4
9 SA	0449	0.7	1114	4.6	1727	0.6	2352	4.5
10 SU ○	0559	0.6	1216	4.8	1831	0.4		
11 M	0051	4.7	0700	0.5	1309	4.9	1927	0.3
12 TU	0144	4.7	0754	0.4	1359	5.0	2020	0.3
13 W	0235	4.7	0843	0.4	1448	5.1	2109	0.3
14 TH	0322	4.7	0927	0.3	1534	5.1	2153	0.3
15 F	0404	4.6	1005	0.4	1618	5.0	2235	0.4
16 SA	0444	4.6	1043	0.5	1700	4.9	2315	0.6
17 SU ☾	0524	4.5	1122	0.6	1743	4.7	2353	0.8
18 M	0604	4.5	1203	0.8	1828	4.5		
19 TU	0033	1.0	0651	4.4	1254	0.9	1927	4.3
20 W	0129	1.1	0757	4.3	1407	1.1	2045	4.2
21 TH	0247	1.2	0920	4.3	1535	1.0	2209	4.2
22 F	0411	1.1	1039	4.5	1655	0.9	2319	4.3
23 SA	0520	0.9	1140	4.6	1753	0.7		
24 SU	0008	4.4	0609	0.7	1223	4.7	1835	0.6
25 M ●	0047	4.5	0648	0.7	1259	4.7	1913	0.6
26 TU	0122	4.5	0726	0.7	1333	4.8	1948	0.6
27 W	0154	4.6	0800	0.6	1405	4.8	2020	0.6
28 TH	0224	4.6	0831	0.6	1435	4.8	2050	0.6
29 F	0252	4.6	0900	0.6	1505	4.8	2119	0.7
30 SA	0323	4.6	0931	0.7	1538	4.8	2152	0.7
31 SU	0358	4.6	1006	0.7	1615	4.7	2226	0.8

SEPTEMBER

Day	Time	m	Time	m	Time	m	Time	m
1 M	0432	4.6	1038	0.7	1648	4.7	2255	0.8
2 TU ☽	0502	4.5	1106	0.8	1721	4.5	2323	0.9
3 W	0541	4.4	1145	0.9	1810	4.3		
4 TH	0012	1.0	0644	4.3	1253	1.0	1927	4.2
5 F	0132	1.1	0810	4.3	1425	1.0	2100	4.2
6 SA	0308	1.1	0940	4.4	1557	0.8	2227	4.4
7 SU	0436	0.9	1056	4.6	1714	0.6	2338	4.5
8 M	0547	0.7	1157	4.8	1816	0.4		
9 TU ○	0036	4.6	0646	0.6	1251	4.9	1911	0.4
10 W	0126	4.7	0737	0.5	1340	5.0	2001	0.3
11 TH	0213	4.7	0823	0.4	1426	5.1	2047	0.3
12 F	0257	4.8	0906	0.4	1511	5.0	2130	0.4
13 SA	0338	4.7	0945	0.4	1553	4.9	2209	0.5
14 SU	0414	4.7	1019	0.5	1632	4.8	2243	0.7
15 M	0449	4.6	1053	0.7	1710	4.6	2316	0.9
16 TU ☾	0524	4.5	1128	0.8	1750	4.4	2351	1.1
17 W	0607	4.4	1213	1.0	1845	4.1		
18 TH	0043	1.3	0711	4.3	1322	1.2	2001	4.0
19 F	0201	1.4	0836	4.3	1454	1.2	2130	4.1
20 SA	0332	1.3	1003	4.4	1622	1.1	2247	4.3
21 SU	0449	1.1	1109	4.5	1725	0.8	2339	4.4
22 M	0541	0.9	1152	4.6	1805	0.7		
23 TU	0015	4.5	0618	0.8	1226	4.7	1838	0.6
24 W ●	0047	4.5	0655	0.7	1259	4.7	1914	0.6
25 TH	0121	4.6	0731	0.6	1333	4.7	1949	0.6
26 F	0154	4.6	0805	0.6	1407	4.7	2022	0.6
27 SA	0225	4.7	0837	0.6	1440	4.7	2054	0.7
28 SU	0258	4.7	0910	0.6	1514	4.7	2126	0.7
29 M	0332	4.6	0944	0.6	1550	4.7	2158	0.7
30 TU	0406	4.6	1016	0.7	1625	4.6	2229	0.8

OCTOBER

Day	Time	m	Time	m	Time	m	Time	m
1 W ☽	0439	4.6	1047	0.8	1702	4.4	2302	1.0
2 TH	0520	4.4	1129	0.9	1754	4.2	2355	1.1
3 F	0623	4.3	1238	1.1	1911	4.2		
4 SA	0117	1.3	0749	4.4	1411	1.1	2044	4.2
5 SU	0254	1.2	0920	4.5	1543	0.9	2210	4.4
6 M	0420	1.0	1036	4.6	1657	0.7	2318	4.5
7 TU	0527	0.8	1135	4.8	1755	0.5		
8 W ○	0013	4.6	0623	0.7	1227	4.9	1848	0.4
9 TH	0102	4.6	0713	0.6	1317	4.9	1936	0.4
10 F	0147	4.7	0759	0.5	1403	4.9	2021	0.5
11 SA	0230	4.8	0841	0.5	1446	4.9	2101	0.5
12 SU	0308	4.8	0919	0.5	1526	4.8	2138	0.6
13 M	0343	4.7	0953	0.5	1603	4.6	2210	0.7
14 TU	0415	4.6	1024	0.7	1639	4.4	2240	0.9
15 W ☾	0449	4.5	1057	0.9	1717	4.3	2314	1.1
16 TH	0529	4.4	1139	1.1	1805	4.1		
17 F	0000	1.3	0625	4.3	1239	1.3	1913	4.0
18 SA	0110	1.5	0743	4.3	1402	1.3	2036	4.0
19 SU	0237	1.4	0908	4.3	1529	1.2	2155	4.2
20 M	0357	1.2	1019	4.4	1636	0.9	2253	4.3
21 TU	0456	1.0	1108	4.5	1721	0.8	2333	4.4
22 W	0538	0.9	1145	4.6	1758	0.7		
23 TH ●	0009	4.5	0618	0.8	1221	4.6	1837	0.7
24 F	0046	4.6	0659	0.7	1259	4.6	1916	0.7
25 SA	0123	4.6	0737	0.7	1337	4.7	1953	0.6
26 SU	0158	4.7	0814	0.6	1415	4.7	2030	0.7
27 M	0234	4.7	0850	0.6	1453	4.6	2104	0.7
28 TU	0310	4.7	0926	0.6	1531	4.6	2138	0.7
29 W	0346	4.7	1001	0.6	1611	4.5	2213	0.9
30 TH	0425	4.6	1039	0.8	1654	4.4	2254	1.0
31 F ☽	0511	4.6	1127	1.0	1749	4.3	2350	1.2

NOVEMBER

Day	Time	m	Time	m	Time	m	Time	m
1 SA	0613	4.5	1234	1.1	1902	4.2		
2 SU	0106	1.3	0733	4.5	1358	1.1	2027	4.2
3 M	0235	1.2	0858	4.6	1523	0.9	2147	4.3
4 TU	0355	1.1	1011	4.7	1633	0.8	2251	4.4
5 W	0459	0.9	1109	4.7	1729	0.6	2344	4.5
6 TH ○	0555	0.8	1202	4.8	1821	0.6		
7 F	0035	4.6	0647	0.7	1254	4.8	1910	0.6
8 SA	0121	4.7	0735	0.6	1340	4.7	1953	0.5
9 SU	0202	4.7	0815	0.5	1421	4.7	2031	0.6
10 M	0239	4.8	0852	0.6	1459	4.6	2107	0.7
11 TU	0313	4.8	0927	0.6	1537	4.5	2140	0.8
12 W	0346	4.7	1000	0.7	1612	4.4	2212	0.9
13 TH	0420	4.6	1034	0.9	1648	4.3	2244	1.1
14 F ☾	0457	4.5	1112	1.1	1729	4.1	2325	1.3
15 SA	0544	4.4	1200	1.2	1823	4.0		
16 SU	0020	1.4	0645	4.3	1303	1.3	1931	4.0
17 M	0131	1.5	0800	4.3	1418	1.3	2046	4.1
18 TU	0248	1.4	0913	4.4	1530	1.1	2153	4.3
19 W	0355	1.2	1012	4.5	1627	0.9	2245	4.4
20 TH	0450	1.1	1100	4.6	1715	0.8	2329	4.5
21 F	0540	1.0	1144	4.6	1800	0.8		
22 SA ●	0012	4.6	0626	0.8	1227	4.6	1844	0.7
23 SU	0053	4.6	0709	0.7	1309	4.6	1925	0.7
24 M	0132	4.7	0750	0.6	1353	4.6	2007	0.7
25 TU	0213	4.8	0832	0.6	1438	4.6	2049	0.7
26 W	0254	4.8	0914	0.6	1521	4.6	2128	0.7
27 TH	0335	4.8	0954	0.6	1605	4.5	2207	0.8
28 F	0417	4.8	1037	0.7	1652	4.4	2251	1.0
29 SA ☽	0507	4.7	1127	0.9	1746	4.3	2345	1.1
30 SU	0605	4.6	1227	1.0	1850	4.2		

DECEMBER

Day	Time	m	Time	m	Time	m	Time	m
1 M	0049	1.1	0714	4.6	1337	1.0	2002	4.2
2 TU	0205	1.2	0830	4.6	1452	1.0	2115	4.3
3 W	0321	1.1	0941	4.6	1601	0.9	2220	4.4
4 TH	0428	1.0	1044	4.7	1701	0.8	2316	4.5
5 F	0528	0.9	1140	4.7	1755	0.7		
6 SA ○	0009	4.6	0623	0.7	1233	4.6	1845	0.6
7 SU	0057	4.6	0712	0.6	1320	4.6	1928	0.6
8 M	0138	4.7	0752	0.5	1400	4.5	2005	0.6
9 TU	0215	4.8	0830	0.6	1437	4.5	2042	0.7
10 W	0250	4.8	0907	0.7	1514	4.5	2117	0.8
11 TH	0324	4.8	0943	0.7	1549	4.5	2150	0.9
12 F	0356	4.7	1015	0.8	1622	4.4	2220	1.0
13 SA	0430	4.7	1048	1.0	1657	4.3	2254	1.2
14 SU ☾	0508	4.6	1125	1.1	1738	4.1	2335	1.3
15 M	0554	4.4	1209	1.2	1829	4.1		
16 TU	0027	1.4	0652	4.4	1307	1.2	1934	4.1
17 W	0134	1.4	0801	4.4	1416	1.2	2044	4.2
18 TH	0247	1.3	0910	4.4	1525	1.1	2149	4.3
19 F	0356	1.2	1012	4.5	1626	0.9	2247	4.4
20 SA	0458	1.0	1108	4.5	1722	0.8	2338	4.6
21 SU	0553	0.9	1159	4.6	1813	0.8		
22 M ●	0026	4.6	0642	0.7	1248	4.6	1901	0.7
23 TU	0111	4.7	0729	0.6	1337	4.6	1950	0.7
24 W	0157	4.8	0818	0.6	1427	4.6	2039	0.6
25 TH	0243	4.9	0906	0.5	1516	4.6	2123	0.6
26 F	0327	4.9	0949	0.5	1601	4.5	2202	0.6
27 SA	0411	4.9	1033	0.5	1646	4.5	2244	0.7
28 SU ☽	0459	4.8	1121	0.7	1736	4.4	2332	0.8
29 M	0552	4.7	1212	0.8	1829	4.3		
30 TU	0025	0.9	0650	4.6	1308	0.9	1929	4.3
31 W	0128	1.0	0756	4.5	1412	1.0	2036	4.3

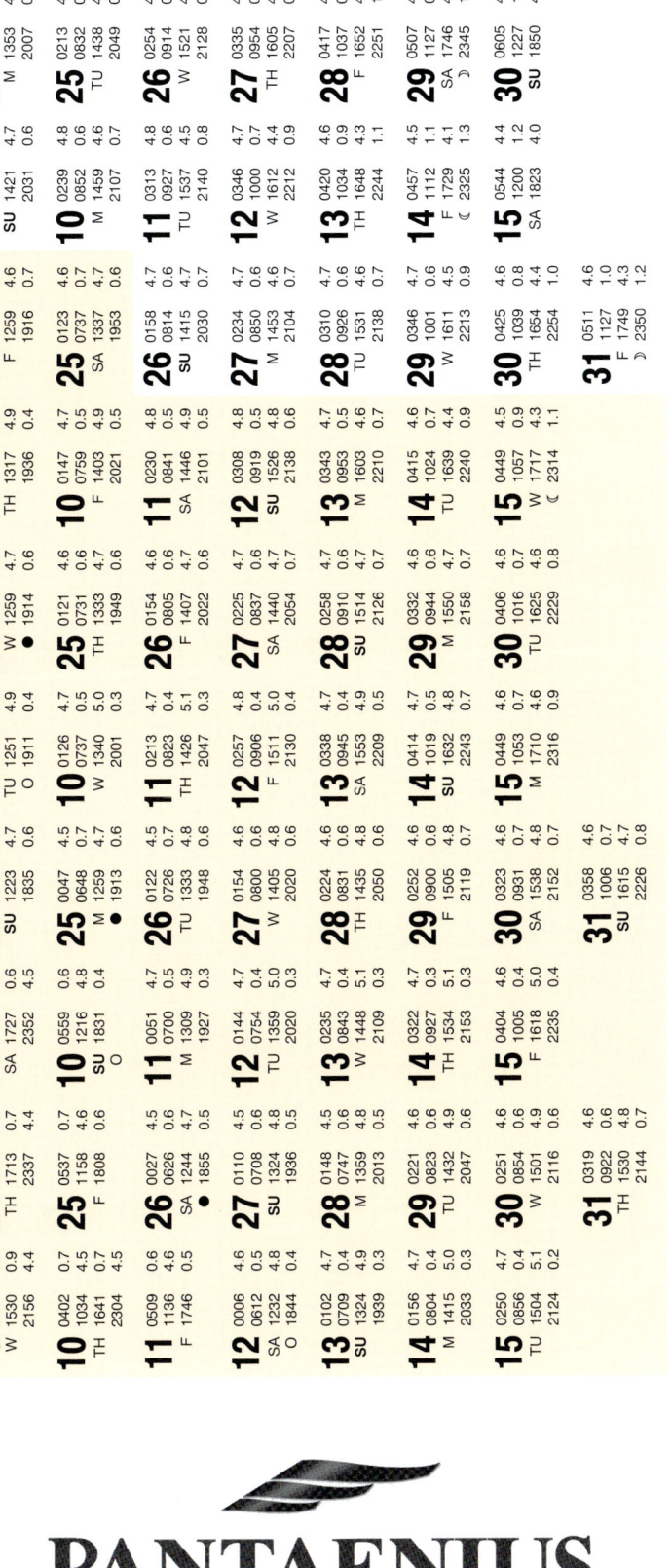

VLISSINGEN (FLUSHING)
LAT 51°27'N
LONG 3°36'E

TIMES AND HEIGHTS OF HIGH AND LOW WATER (Heights in Metres)

TIME ZONE –0100 (Dutch Standard Time). **Subtract 1 hour for UT. For Dutch Summer Time (area enclosed in shaded box) add 1 hour**

2014

SUNRISE AND SUNSET TIMES

VLISSINGEN (FLUSHING)
At 51°27'N 3°36'E

Date	Sunrise	Sunset
European Standard Time (UT-1)		
Jan 01	0851	1648
15	0844	1706
Feb 01	0824	1735
15	0759	1801
Mar 01	0731	1826
15	0700	1850
European Summer Time (UT-2)		
Apr 01	0721	2019
15	0650	2042
May 01	0618	2109
15	0554	2131
Jun 01	0534	2153
15	0528	2204
Jul 01	0533	2206
15	0546	2156
Aug 01	0610	2133
15	0631	2108
Sep 01	0658	2032
15	0721	2000
Oct 01	0746	1923
15	0810	1852
European Standard Time (UT-1)		
Nov 01	0739	1719
15	0804	1656
[illegible]	[illegible]	[illegible]

JANUARY

Date	Day	Time	m
1	W	0115 0746 1336 ● 2006	5.0 0.6 5.1 0.6
2	TH	0203 0833 1423 2052	5.1 0.4 5.2 0.6
3	F	0249 0923 1508 2138	5.1 0.3 5.3 0.6
4	SA	0336 1012 1557 2225	5.1 0.3 5.2 0.7
5	SU	0426 1056 1646 2308	5.0 0.3 5.1 0.7
6	M	0512 1145 1739 2355	5.0 0.3 5.0 0.8
7	TU	0605 1236 1835	4.8 0.4 4.8
8	W	0046 0702 1326 ☽ 1936	0.9 4.7 0.6 4.6
9	TH	0134 0759 1425 2039	1.1 4.5 0.8 4.4
10	F	0250 0905 1535 2156	1.2 4.3 1.0 4.2
11	SA	0416 1025 1706 2311	1.3 4.2 1.0 4.3
12	SU	0537 1135 1800	1.2 4.3 1.0
13	M	0005 0630 1232 1845	4.4 1.0 4.5 1.0
14	TU	0056 0716 1320 1925	4.5 0.9 4.6 1.0
15	W	0139 0749 1358 2006	4.6 0.8 4.7 0.9
16	TH	0215 0828 1429 O 2036	4.7 0.7 4.8 0.9
17	F	0245 0901 1501 2110	4.7 0.6 4.9 0.8
18	SA	0315 0940 1535 2146	4.8 0.6 4.9 0.8
19	SU	0349 1015 1606 2216	4.8 0.6 4.9 0.8
20	M	0421 1050 1637 2245	4.8 0.6 4.8 0.9
21	TU	0455 1120 1707 2319	4.7 0.7 4.8 0.9
22	W	0526 1156 1745 2356	4.6 0.7 4.7 0.9
23	TH	0605 1230 1829	4.6 0.7 4.6
24	F	0046 0656 1321 ☾ 1929	1.0 4.4 0.8 4.4
25	SA	0140 0806 1419 2048	1.0 4.3 0.9 4.3
26	SU	0256 0920 1538 2201	1.1 4.3 1.0 4.3
27	M	0415 1036 1650 2308	1.1 4.3 0.9 4.4
28	TU	0536 1138 1800	0.9 4.6 0.8
29	W	0012 0632 1236 1901	4.6 0.7 4.8 0.7
30	TH	0100 0732 1325 ● 1948	4.8 0.5 5.0 0.6
31	F	0146 0822 1409 [illegible]	5.0 0.3 5.2 [illegible]

FEBRUARY

Date	Day	Time	m
1	SA	0235 0907 1453 2122	5.1 0.2 5.3 0.6
2	SU	0316 0955 1540 2205	5.2 0.2 5.3 0.6
3	M	0405 1040 1626 2248	5.2 0.2 5.2 0.6
4	TU	0449 1126 1715 2329	5.1 0.2 5.0 0.7
5	W	0537 1206 1806	5.0 0.4 4.8
6	TH	0011 0628 1245 ☽ 1858	0.8 4.8 0.6 4.6
7	F	0102 0726 1340 1956	0.9 4.5 0.8 4.2
8	SA	0206 0825 1445 2115	1.1 4.2 1.0 4.0
9	SU	0314 0950 1604 2240	1.2 4.0 1.2 3.9
10	M	0450 1115 1725 2346	1.2 4.1 1.2 4.1
11	TU	0606 1216 1826	1.1 4.3 1.1
12	W	0039 0655 1259 1905	4.3 0.9 4.5 1.0
13	TH	0118 0738 1335 1939	4.5 0.8 4.6 0.9
14	F	0156 0810 1410 2016	4.6 0.7 4.7 0.9
15	SA	0226 0842 1439 O 2046	4.7 0.6 4.8 0.8
16	SU	0256 0919 1507 2119	4.8 0.5 4.9 0.7
17	M	0325 0952 1537 2158	4.9 0.5 5.0 0.7
18	TU	0353 1025 1609 2230	4.9 0.5 4.9 0.7
19	W	0425 1055 1643 2306	4.9 0.5 4.9 0.7
20	TH	0457 1130 1716 2338	4.8 0.6 4.8 0.8
21	F	0536 1208 1759	4.8 0.6 4.7
22	SA	0015 0619 1256 ☾ 1851	0.8 4.6 0.7 4.5
23	SU	0116 0721 1350 2005	0.9 4.4 0.9 4.3
24	M	0226 0848 1505 2130	1.0 4.2 1.0 4.1
25	TU	0345 1008 1625 2248	1.0 4.2 1.0 4.2
26	W	0510 1119 1745 2352	0.9 4.4 0.9 4.4
27	TH	0626 1217 1845	0.7 4.7 0.8
28	F	0045 0721 1308 1936	4.7 0.5 5.0 0.7

MARCH

Date	Day	Time	m
1	SA	0132 0807 1353 ● 2018	4.9 0.3 5.1 0.6
2	SU	0215 0852 1436 2103	5.1 0.2 5.2 0.5
3	M	0257 0936 1520 2146	5.2 0.1 5.2 0.5
4	TU	0342 1016 1603 2225	5.2 0.2 5.2 0.5
5	W	0425 1058 1646 2305	5.1 0.3 5.0 0.6
6	TH	0507 1135 1735 2345	5.0 0.4 4.8 0.7
7	F	0556 1215 1819	4.8 0.6 4.5
8	SA	0030 0639 1300 ☽ 1909	0.8 4.5 0.9 4.2
9	SU	0125 0740 1354 2009	1.0 4.2 1.1 3.8
10	M	0245 0906 1526 2200	1.2 3.9 1.3 3.7
11	TU	0416 1040 1645 2318	1.2 3.9 1.2 3.9
12	W	0525 1145 1744	1.1 4.1 1.1
13	TH	0015 0530 1236 1834	4.2 0.9 4.4 1.0
14	F	0056 0716 1309 1915	4.4 0.8 4.6 0.9
15	SA	0126 0745 1341 1950	4.5 0.7 4.7 0.8
16	SU	0156 0816 1408 O 2026	4.7 0.6 4.9 0.7
17	M	0222 0845 1438 2055	4.8 0.5 5.0 0.6
18	TU	0253 0925 1511 2136	5.0 0.4 5.0 0.6
19	W	0326 1000 1546 2210	5.0 0.4 5.0 0.6
20	TH	0359 1035 1618 2246	5.0 0.4 5.0 0.6
21	F	0435 1112 1655 2326	4.9 0.5 4.9 0.6
22	SA	0514 1150 1737	4.9 0.6 4.7
23	SU	0006 0558 1239 1828	0.7 4.7 0.7 4.4
24	M	0100 0702 1336 ☾ 1949	0.8 4.4 0.9 4.2
25	TU	0210 0831 1445 2111	0.9 4.2 1.0 4.0
26	W	0324 0950 1610 2230	0.9 4.2 1.1 4.1
27	TH	0500 1101 1730 2336	0.8 4.4 1.0 4.3
28	F	0609 1205 1835	0.6 4.7 0.8
29	SA	0027 0705 1250 1918	4.6 0.4 4.9 0.7
30	SU	0112 0748 1335 ● 2002	4.8 0.3 5.0 0.6
31	M	0155 0832 1416 [illegible]	5.0 0.2 5.1 [illegible]

APRIL

Date	Day	Time	m
1	TU	0236 0911 1459 2125	5.1 0.2 5.1 0.5
2	W	0318 0956 1543 2206	5.2 0.3 5.1 0.5
3	TH	0401 1032 1623 2245	5.1 0.4 4.9 0.5
4	F	0442 1106 1705 2326	5.0 0.5 4.7 0.6
5	SA	0526 1146 1750	4.7 0.7 4.4
6	SU	0006 0607 1226 1836	0.8 4.5 0.9 4.2
7	M	0056 0706 1326 ☽ 1926	0.9 4.2 1.2 3.9
8	TU	0205 0804 1450 2040	1.1 3.9 1.3 3.6
9	W	0325 0945 1554 2236	1.1 3.8 1.3 3.7
10	TH	0433 1102 1705 2336	1.1 4.0 1.1 4.0
11	F	0539 1157 1754	0.9 4.3 1.0
12	SA	0015 0629 1236 1845	4.2 0.8 4.5 0.9
13	SU	0049 0710 1305 1916	4.5 0.7 4.7 0.8
14	M	0118 0739 1336 1952	4.7 0.6 4.9 0.6
15	TU	0150 0818 1409 O 2028	4.8 0.5 5.0 0.5
16	W	0226 0856 1443 2108	5.0 0.4 5.1 0.5
17	TH	0259 0933 1519 2148	5.1 0.4 5.1 0.5
18	F	0335 1012 1556 2232	5.1 0.4 5.0 0.5
19	SA	0415 1056 1636 2312	5.0 0.5 4.8 0.5
20	SU	0458 1136 1726	4.9 0.6 4.6
21	M	0000 0547 1225 1819	0.5 4.7 0.7 4.4
22	TU	0056 0656 1319 ☾ 1935	0.6 4.5 0.9 4.2
23	W	0159 0816 1435 2049	0.7 4.3 1.0 4.1
24	TH	0320 0932 1555 2206	0.8 4.3 1.1 4.1
25	F	0446 1041 1716 2315	0.7 4.5 1.0 4.3
26	SA	0555 1145 1817	0.6 4.7 0.8
27	SU	0007 0646 1232 1900	4.6 0.4 4.8 0.7
28	M	0052 0728 1316 1946	4.8 0.4 4.9 0.6
29	TU	0135 0807 1359 ● 2026	4.9 0.3 5.0 0.5
30	W	0216 0847 1440 2105	5.0 0.3 5.0 0.5

MAY

Date	Day	Time	m
1	TH	0259 0928 1522 2146	5.1 0.4 4.9 0.5
2	F	0339 1007 1602 2226	5.0 0.5 4.8 0.5
3	SA	0421 1046 1645 2302	4.9 0.7 4.6 0.6
4	SU	0501 1118 1721 2339	4.7 0.8 4.4 0.7
5	M	0541 1155 1806	4.5 1.0 4.2
6	TU	0025 0636 1234 1856	0.8 4.3 1.1 4.0
7	W	0135 0724 1405 ☽ 1956	1.0 4.0 1.3 3.8
8	TH	0251 0835 1520 2105	1.0 3.9 1.2 3.8
9	F	0356 1006 1626 2236	1.0 4.0 1.2 3.9
10	SA	0444 1106 1711 2325	0.9 4.2 1.0 4.1
11	SU	0535 1150 1754	0.8 4.5 0.9
12	M	0008 0628 1226 1846	4.4 0.7 4.7 0.8
13	TU	0042 0705 1302 1919	4.6 0.6 4.9 0.6
14	W	0119 0746 1341 O 2006	4.8 0.5 5.0 0.5
15	TH	0156 0826 1419 2046	5.0 0.4 5.1 0.4
16	F	0236 0908 1458 2132	5.1 0.4 5.1 0.4
17	SA	0317 0952 1540 2215	5.1 0.5 5.0 0.4
18	SU	0400 1035 1626 2301	5.0 0.5 4.8 0.4
19	M	0446 1122 1716 2356	4.9 0.6 4.6 0.4
20	TU	0541 1209 1816	4.8 0.7 4.5
21	W	0050 0650 1305 ☾ 1922	0.5 4.6 0.9 4.3
22	TH	0149 0759 1411 2029	0.5 4.5 1.0 4.3
23	F	0300 0905 1523 2139	0.6 4.5 1.0 4.2
24	SA	0420 1019 1656 2248	0.6 4.5 1.0 4.4
25	SU	0530 1121 1756 2345	0.6 4.6 0.9 4.5
26	M	0622 1215 1846	0.5 4.7 0.8
27	TU	0036 0708 1301 1925	4.7 0.5 4.8 0.7
28	W	0117 0748 1346 ● 2005	4.8 0.5 4.8 0.6
29	TH	0202 0825 1427 2045	4.9 0.5 4.8 0.5
30	F	0246 0905 1507 2128	4.9 0.6 4.8 0.5
31	SA	0322 0942 1546	4.9 0.7 4.8

JUNE

Date	Day	Time	m
1	SU	0402 1018 1622 2245	4.9 0.8 4.7 0.6
2	M	0441 1057 1659 2326	4.7 0.9 4.5 0.7
3	TU	0521 1130 1740	4.6 1.0 4.4
4	W	0006 0605 1203 1826	0.8 4.4 1.1 4.2
5	TH	0045 0656 1255 ☽ 1917	0.9 4.2 1.2 4.1
6	F	0156 0750 1405 2012	0.9 4.2 1.2 4.0
7	SA	0256 0852 1536 2120	1.0 4.1 1.2 4.0
8	SU	0356 1000 1625 2225	0.9 4.2 1.1 4.1
9	M	0445 1100 1716 2319	0.8 4.4 0.9 4.4
10	TU	0540 1148 1805	0.7 4.7 0.8
11	W	0007 0625 1236 1856	4.6 0.6 4.8 0.7
12	TH	0053 0718 1317 1940	4.8 0.6 5.0 0.5
13	F	0136 0802 1359 O 2028	5.0 0.5 5.0 0.4
14	SA	0218 0848 1443 2117	5.1 0.5 5.0 0.3
15	SU	0303 0935 1528 2205	5.1 0.5 5.0 0.3
16	M	0348 1022 1616 2255	5.1 0.6 4.9 0.3
17	TU	0436 1108 1705 2346	5.0 0.6 4.8 0.3
18	W	0530 1158 1758	4.9 0.7 4.7
19	TH	0038 0636 1249 ☾ 1902	0.3 4.8 0.8 4.6
20	F	0136 0735 1350 2006	0.4 4.7 0.9 4.5
21	SA	0235 0839 1456 2110	0.5 4.5 1.0 4.4
22	SU	0340 0949 1610 2215	0.6 4.5 1.0 4.4
23	M	0506 1100 1731 2321	0.7 4.5 1.0 4.4
24	TU	0601 1155 1826	0.7 4.6 0.8
25	W	0019 0646 1247 1911	4.6 0.7 4.7 0.7
26	TH	0109 0728 1336 1949	4.7 0.7 4.7 0.6
27	F	0150 0805 1416 ● 2029	4.8 0.7 4.7 0.6
28	SA	0230 0846 1452 2109	4.8 0.8 4.8 0.5
29	SU	0308 0920 1527 2148	4.9 0.8 4.8 0.5
30	M	0346 0956 1605 2231	4.9 0.8 4.7 0.5

VLISSINGEN (FLUSHING)
LAT 51°27′N
LONG 3°36′E

TIMES AND HEIGHTS OF HIGH AND LOW WATER (Heights in Metres)

TIME ZONE –0100 (Dutch Standard Time). **Subtract 1 hour for UT. For Dutch Summer Time (area enclosed in shaded box) add 1 hour**

2014

JULY

Date	Day	Time	m	Time	m	Time	m	Time	m
1	TU	0421	4.8	1036	0.9	1640	4.7	2306	0.6
2	W	0458	4.7	1106	0.9	1715	4.5	2340	0.7
3	TH	0536	4.6	1140	1.0	1750	4.4		
4	F	0004	0.8	0612	4.5	1215	1.1	1829	4.3
5	SA ☽	0043	0.8	0654	4.4	1300	1.1	1926	4.2
6	SU	0133	0.9	0800	4.3	1355	1.1	2031	4.2
7	M	0256	0.9	0909	4.3	1526	1.1	2136	4.2
8	TU	0356	0.9	1009	4.4	1636	1.0	2240	4.3
9	W	0455	0.8	1111	4.6	1730	0.9	2336	4.5
10	TH	0556	0.7	1207	4.7	1826	0.7		
11	F	0029	4.8	0652	0.7	1257	4.9	1926	0.6
12	SA O	0116	5.0	0742	0.6	1346	5.0	2012	0.4
13	SU	0203	5.1	0830	0.6	1426	5.0	2102	0.3
14	M	0248	5.2	0917	0.6	1513	5.1	2149	0.2
15	TU	0333	5.2	1003	0.6	1559	5.0	2237	0.2
16	W	0423	5.2	1050	0.6	1648	5.0	2325	0.2
17	TH	0516	5.0	1138	0.7	1737	4.9		
18	F	0015	0.3	0609	4.9	1226	0.8	1835	4.8
19	SA ☾	0106	0.4	0708	4.7	1318	0.9	1936	4.6
20	SU	0155	0.6	0805	4.5	1415	1.0	2035	4.4
21	M	0259	0.8	0921	4.3	1530	1.1	2145	4.3
22	TU	0414	0.9	1036	4.3	1655	1.1	2306	4.3
23	W	0536	0.9	1146	4.4	1806	0.9		
24	TH	0005	4.5	0625	0.9	1235	4.5	1856	0.8
25	F	0059	4.6	0709	0.9	1326	4.6	1935	0.7
26	SA ●	0146	4.7	0748	0.9	1401	4.7	2015	0.7
27	SU	0219	4.8	0825	0.9	1436	4.8	2052	0.6
28	M	0251	4.9	0858	0.8	1506	4.8	2131	0.6
29	TU	0326	4.9	0935	0.8	1538	4.8	2205	0.5
30	W	0358	4.9	1011	0.8	1611	4.8	2240	0.6
31	TH	0427	4.8	1039	0.9	1642	4.7	2310	0.7

AUGUST

Date	Day	Time	m	Time	m	Time	m	Time	m
1	F	0458	4.7	1109	0.9	1716	4.6	2340	0.7
2	SA	0528	4.6	1146	1.0	1750	4.6		
3	SU	0009	0.8	0609	4.6	1226	1.0	1829	4.5
4	M ☽	0056	0.8	0659	4.5	1316	1.0	1930	4.3
5	TU	0156	0.9	0816	4.3	1419	1.1	2050	4.2
6	W	0311	1.0	0931	4.3	1545	1.1	2201	4.3
7	TH	0419	1.0	1046	4.4	1700	1.0	2311	4.5
8	F	0536	0.9	1146	4.6	1805	0.8		
9	SA	0011	4.7	0636	0.8	1237	4.8	1906	0.6
10	SU O	0100	5.0	0726	0.7	1326	5.0	1958	0.4
11	M	0146	5.2	0812	0.6	1410	5.1	2046	0.3
12	TU	0231	5.3	0858	0.6	1455	5.2	2133	0.2
13	W	0316	5.3	0946	0.6	1539	5.2	2218	0.2
14	TH	0401	5.2	1028	0.7	1626	5.2	2302	0.2
15	F	0449	5.1	1112	0.7	1710	5.1	2345	0.4
16	SA	0539	4.9	1156	0.8	1801	4.9		
17	SU ☾	0029	0.5	0636	4.7	1246	0.9	1856	4.7
18	M	0120	0.7	0732	4.4	1339	1.0	2000	4.4
19	TU	0214	1.0	0846	4.2	1455	1.2	2115	4.2
20	W	0334	1.1	1005	4.1	1625	1.2	2242	4.2
21	TH	0505	1.1	1126	4.2	1746	1.0	2349	4.4
22	F	0610	1.1	1219	4.4	1846	0.9		
23	SA	0045	4.6	0655	1.0	1308	4.6	1925	0.8
24	SU	0126	4.7	0724	1.0	1346	4.7	1955	0.7
25	M ●	0159	4.8	0806	0.9	1411	4.8	2032	0.7
26	TU	0227	4.9	0836	0.9	1441	4.9	2106	0.6
27	W	0257	5.0	0905	0.8	1511	4.9	2138	0.6
28	TH	0327	5.0	0946	0.8	1541	4.9	2209	0.6
29	F	0357	5.0	1015	0.8	1612	4.9	2242	0.7
30	SA	0427	4.9	1046	0.9	1642	4.8	2316	0.7
31	SU	0500	4.8	1116	0.9	1716	4.8	2346	0.8

SEPTEMBER

Date	Day	Time	m	Time	m	Time	m	Time	m
1	M	0537	4.7	1157	0.9	1755	4.7		
2	TU ☽	0026	0.8	0621	4.6	1246	1.0	1848	4.5
3	W	0120	1.0	0730	4.3	1350	1.1	2010	4.3
4	TH	0229	1.1	0855	4.2	1516	1.1	2137	4.3
5	F	0356	1.1	1015	4.2	1635	1.0	2249	4.4
6	SA	0510	1.1	1125	4.4	1756	0.8	2350	4.7
7	SU	0615	0.9	1218	4.7	1849	0.6		
8	M	0042	5.0	0708	0.8	1306	5.0	1942	0.4
9	TU O	0126	5.2	0756	0.7	1350	5.1	2027	0.3
10	W	0211	5.3	0840	0.6	1433	5.3	2109	0.3
11	TH	0255	5.3	0926	0.6	1516	5.3	2155	0.3
12	F	0339	5.3	1007	0.6	1559	5.3	2235	0.4
13	SA	0426	5.1	1048	0.7	1645	5.1	2317	0.5
14	SU	0511	4.9	1130	0.8	1729	4.9	2358	0.7
15	M	0559	4.6	1216	0.9	1818	4.7		
16	TU ☾	0039	0.9	0656	4.3	1305	1.1	1919	4.4
17	W	0147	1.2	0756	4.0	1419	1.2	2034	4.1
18	TH	0255	1.3	0935	3.9	1545	1.3	2215	4.1
19	F	0430	1.3	1056	4.0	1704	1.2	2325	4.3
20	SA	0546	1.2	1156	4.3	1816	1.0		
21	SU	0015	4.5	0624	1.1	1239	4.5	1900	0.8
22	M	0058	4.7	0706	1.0	1315	4.6	1932	0.8
23	TU	0129	4.8	0736	1.0	1342	4.8	2002	0.7
24	W ●	0159	4.9	0806	0.9	1408	4.9	2035	0.7
25	TH	0228	5.0	0840	0.8	1439	5.0	2106	0.6
26	F	0257	5.1	0916	0.7	1511	5.0	2140	0.6
27	SA	0327	5.1	0950	0.8	1543	5.0	2216	0.7
28	SU	0359	5.0	1022	0.8	1615	5.0	2246	0.7
29	M	0435	4.9	1101	0.8	1650	4.9	2322	0.8
30	TU	0513	4.8	1141	0.9	1733	4.8		

OCTOBER

Date	Day	Time	m	Time	m	Time	m	Time	m
1	W ☽	0006	0.9	0557	4.6	1226	0.9	1825	4.6
2	TH	0055	1.1	0706	4.3	1330	1.0	1946	4.3
3	F	0205	1.2	0831	4.1	1456	1.1	2109	4.3
4	SA	0330	1.3	0950	4.2	1613	1.0	2230	4.4
5	SU	0444	1.2	1102	4.4	1746	0.9	2331	4.7
6	M	0606	1.0	1157	4.6	1839	0.6		
7	TU	0026	5.0	0652	0.9	1245	4.9	1922	0.5
8	W O	0106	5.1	0736	0.8	1328	5.1	2007	0.4
9	TH	0152	5.2	0817	0.7	1412	5.2	2048	0.4
10	F	0235	5.3	0903	0.6	1453	5.3	2130	0.4
11	SA	0318	5.2	0946	0.6	1537	5.3	2210	0.5
12	SU	0401	5.1	1026	0.7	1621	5.1	2248	0.7
13	M	0447	4.8	1105	0.8	1706	4.9	2325	0.9
14	TU	0528	4.6	1146	0.9	1748	4.7		
15	W ☾	0008	1.1	0618	4.3	1236	1.1	1846	4.4
16	TH	0100	1.3	0709	4.0	1355	1.2	1955	4.1
17	F	0215	1.5	0820	3.8	1506	1.3	2125	3.9
18	SA	0333	1.5	1010	3.8	1620	1.2	2245	4.1
19	SU	0445	1.4	1117	4.1	1730	1.1	2339	4.4
20	M	0545	1.2	1159	4.3	1825	1.0		
21	TU	0026	4.6	0624	1.1	1236	4.5	1901	0.9
22	W	0055	4.8	0706	1.0	1305	4.7	1928	0.8
23	TH ●	0126	4.9	0738	0.9	1335	4.9	1955	0.7
24	F	0156	5.0	0809	0.8	1408	5.0	2035	0.7
25	SA	0226	5.1	0851	0.7	1443	5.1	2110	0.6
26	SU	0303	5.1	0928	0.7	1518	5.1	2148	0.7
27	M	0336	5.1	1007	0.7	1555	5.1	2229	0.7
28	TU	0416	5.0	1046	0.7	1633	5.0	2309	0.8
29	W	0456	4.8	1130	0.8	1717	4.9	2350	0.9
30	TH	0545	4.6	1220	0.8	1816	4.6		
31	F ☽	0045	1.1	0649	4.3	1326	0.9	1929	4.4

NOVEMBER

Date	Day	Time	m	Time	m	Time	m	Time	m
1	SA	0144	1.2	0810	4.2	1435	1.0	2049	4.4
2	SU	0305	1.3	0925	4.2	1555	1.0	2201	4.5
3	M	0430	1.3	1035	4.3	1721	0.8	2309	4.7
4	TU	0540	1.1	1132	4.6	1815	0.7		
5	W	0002	4.9	0636	1.0	1222	4.8	1902	0.6
6	TH O	0049	5.0	0716	0.8	1308	5.0	1945	0.5
7	F	0133	5.1	0802	0.7	1353	5.1	2027	0.5
8	SA	0216	5.1	0845	0.6	1436	5.2	2107	0.6
9	SU	0300	5.1	0926	0.6	1516	5.2	2146	0.7
10	M	0345	5.0	1006	0.6	1600	5.1	2226	0.8
11	TU	0425	4.8	1046	0.7	1642	4.9	2300	1.0
12	W	0506	4.6	1126	0.8	1727	4.7	2338	1.1
13	TH	0550	4.4	1210	1.0	1815	4.4		
14	F ☾	0025	1.3	0636	4.2	1305	1.1	1910	4.2
15	SA	0135	1.5	0730	4.0	1415	1.2	2015	4.0
16	SU	0250	1.5	0835	3.8	1526	1.2	2136	4.0
17	M	0356	1.4	1005	3.9	1630	1.2	2246	4.2
18	TU	0449	1.3	1105	4.1	1736	1.1	2336	4.4
19	W	0545	1.2	1149	4.4	1815	1.0		
20	TH	0016	4.6	0626	1.0	1229	4.6	1845	0.9
21	F	0052	4.8	0706	0.9	1306	4.8	1925	0.8
22	SA ●	0125	5.0	0742	0.8	1341	5.0	2005	0.7
23	SU	0202	5.1	0826	0.7	1419	5.1	2045	0.7
24	M	0241	5.1	0906	0.6	1456	5.1	2129	0.7
25	TU	0319	5.1	0949	0.6	1538	5.1	2210	0.7
26	W	0403	5.0	1038	0.6	1622	5.0	2256	0.8
27	TH	0446	4.8	1126	0.6	1711	4.9	2340	0.9
28	F	0537	4.6	1215	0.7	1806	4.7		
29	SA ☽	0036	1.0	0639	4.5	1315	0.7	1915	4.6
30	SU	0136	1.2	0745	4.3	1415	0.8	2028	4.5

DECEMBER

Date	Day	Time	m	Time	m	Time	m	Time	m
1	M	0240	1.2	0858	4.3	1525	0.9	2135	4.5
2	TU	0355	1.3	1005	4.3	1646	0.9	2246	4.5
3	W	0504	1.2	1109	4.5	1750	0.8	2342	4.7
4	TH	0616	1.0	1206	4.7	1842	0.7		
5	F	0036	4.8	0659	0.9	1255	4.8	1925	0.7
6	SA O	0121	4.9	0743	0.7	1337	4.9	2005	0.7
7	SU	0207	4.9	0828	0.6	1422	5.0	2045	0.7
8	M	0247	4.9	0908	0.6	1506	5.0	2121	0.8
9	TU	0329	4.9	0950	0.6	1545	5.0	2200	0.9
10	W	0407	4.8	1025	0.6	1625	4.9	2235	1.0
11	TH	0446	4.7	1106	0.7	1705	4.7	2316	1.1
12	F	0526	4.5	1146	0.8	1748	4.6	2356	1.2
13	SA	0606	4.4	1226	1.0	1832	4.4		
14	SU ☾	0030	1.3	0650	4.2	1315	1.1	1925	4.2
15	M	0125	1.4	0745	4.1	1414	1.2	2026	4.1
16	TU	0256	1.4	0850	4.0	1536	1.2	2130	4.1
17	W	0401	1.4	0955	4.0	1626	1.1	2235	4.3
18	TH	0456	1.2	1100	4.2	1720	1.0	2332	4.5
19	F	0546	1.1	1152	4.5	1804	0.9		
20	SA	0016	4.7	0632	0.9	1236	4.7	1857	0.8
21	SU	0102	4.9	0715	0.8	1318	4.9	1940	0.7
22	M ●	0143	5.0	0806	0.6	1359	5.1	2025	0.7
23	TU	0226	5.1	0856	0.5	1442	5.1	2111	0.7
24	W	0306	5.1	0940	0.4	1525	5.2	2155	0.7
25	TH	0350	5.0	1028	0.4	1613	5.1	2242	0.7
26	F	0436	4.9	1116	0.4	1659	5.0	2326	0.8
27	SA	0527	4.8	1205	0.4	1756	4.9		
28	SU ☽	0015	0.9	0626	4.7	1258	0.5	1855	4.7
29	M	0110	1.0	0725	4.5	1356	0.6	2002	4.6
30	TU	0204	1.1	0828	4.4	1455	0.8	2108	4.4
31	W	0315	1.2	0936	4.3	1605	0.9	2218	4.4

DUNKERQUE

LAT 51°03′N
LONG 2°22′E

TIMES AND HEIGHTS OF HIGH AND LOW WATER (Heights in Metres)

TIME ZONE −0100 (French Standard Time). **Subtract 1 hour for UT. For French Summer Time (area enclosed in shaded box) add 1 hour**

2014

JANUARY

Date	Day	Time	m
1	W ●	0001 0659 1222 1924	6.0 0.7 6.2 0.6
2	TH	0045 0749 1307 2013	6.1 0.4 6.3 0.5
3	F	0129 0837 1353 2100	6.2 0.3 6.4 0.5
4	SA	0214 0925 1441 2147	6.3 0.2 6.4 0.5
5	SU	0301 1013 1531 2233	6.2 0.3 6.2 0.7
6	M	0350 1100 1623 2320	6.0 0.4 6.0 0.9
7	TU	0441 1149 1718	5.8 0.7 5.7
8	W ☽	0010 0537 1246 1821	1.1 5.6 0.9 5.4
9	TH	0111 0643 1350 1934	1.3 5.3 1.2 5.2
10	F	0218 0800 1456 2044	1.5 5.2 1.4 5.1
11	SA	0325 0908 1604 2145	1.5 5.1 1.4 5.1
12	SU	0435 1008 1713 2240	1.4 5.2 1.3 5.2
13	M	0539 1101 1808 2328	1.3 5.3 1.2 5.4
14	TU	0628 1147 1850	1.1 5.5 1.1
15	W	0010 0706 1228 1923	5.6 0.9 5.7 1.0
16	TH ○	0047 0740 1304 1955	5.7 0.8 5.8 0.9
17	F	0121 0812 1338 2026	5.8 0.7 5.8 0.9
18	SA	0155 0845 1412 2057	5.9 0.7 5.9 0.9
19	SU	0229 0917 1447 2129	5.9 0.7 5.9 0.9
20	M	0302 0949 1520 2202	5.8 0.7 5.8 1.0
21	TU	0333 1023 1551 2236	5.7 0.8 5.7 1.1
22	W	0402 1059 1623 2314	5.6 0.9 5.6 1.2
23	TH	0437 1139 1704 2357	5.5 1.0 5.4 1.3
24	F ☾	0525 1226 1759	5.4 1.2 5.2
25	SA	0049 0626 1328 1905	1.5 5.2 1.4 5.0
26	SU	0203 0739 1452 2028	1.6 5.1 1.4 5.0
27	M	0331 0912 1610 2158	1.5 5.1 1.3 5.2
28	TU	0445 1029 1719 2301	1.2 5.5 1.0 5.5
29	W	0551 1125 1820 2351	0.9 5.8 0.8 5.9
30	TH ●	0647 1213 1912	0.6 6.1 0.6
31	F	0034 0737 1257 1959	6.1 0.3 6.3 0.4

FEBRUARY

Date	Day	Time	m
1	SA	0116 0824 1341 2044	6.2 0.1 6.4 0.4
2	SU	0158 0909 1425 2128	6.3 0.1 6.3 0.4
3	M	0241 0954 1510 2211	6.3 0.1 6.2 0.5
4	TU	0326 1037 1557 2252	6.1 0.3 6.0 0.7
5	W	0413 1118 1646 2333	6.0 0.6 5.7 0.9
6	TH ☽	0502 1203 1738	5.7 0.9 5.4
7	F	0021 0558 1259 1840	1.2 5.4 1.3 5.1
8	SA	0126 0708 1409 1959	1.5 5.0 1.5 4.8
9	SU	0240 0831 1521 2113	1.7 4.8 1.7 4.8
10	M	0355 0942 1640 2216	1.6 4.9 1.6 4.9
11	TU	0512 1041 1746 2310	1.4 5.1 1.4 5.1
12	W	0607 1131 1830 2353	1.1 5.3 1.1 5.4
13	TH	0647 1211 1904	0.9 5.5 1.0
14	F	0030 0720 1246 1934	5.6 0.8 5.7 0.9
15	SA ○	0102 0751 1318 2004	5.7 0.7 5.8 0.8
16	SU	0134 0822 1350 2035	5.9 0.6 5.9 0.8
17	M	0205 0854 1422 2107	5.9 0.6 5.9 0.8
18	TU	0236 0926 1451 2140	5.9 0.6 5.9 0.8
19	W	0303 1000 1519 2214	5.9 0.6 5.8 0.8
20	TH	0330 1035 1549 2249	5.8 0.7 5.7 1.0
21	F	0404 1113 1628 2330	5.7 0.9 5.6 1.1
22	SA ☾	0449 1157 1721	5.6 1.1 5.3
23	SU	0020 0550 1255 1830	1.3 5.3 1.3 5.0
24	M	0129 0708 1419 2000	1.5 5.0 1.4 4.8
25	TU	0304 0855 1548 2144	1.5 5.0 1.3 5.0
26	W	0427 1017 1704 2248	1.2 5.4 1.1 5.4
27	TH	0537 1113 1807 2337	0.9 5.8 0.8 5.8
28	F	0634 1201 1857	0.5 6.1 0.6

MARCH

Date	Day	Time	m
1	SA ●	0020 0721 1243 1941	6.0 0.3 6.3 0.4
2	SU	0059 0806 1324 2024	6.2 0.1 6.3 0.4
3	M	0138 0848 1404 2105	6.3 0.1 6.3 0.4
4	TU	0219 0930 1447 2145	6.2 0.1 6.1 0.4
5	W	0301 1009 1530 2223	6.2 0.3 6.0 0.6
6	TH	0345 1046 1614 2300	6.0 0.6 5.7 0.8
7	F	0431 1123 1700 2339	5.7 0.9 5.4 1.1
8	SA ☽	0520 1206 1751	5.4 1.3 5.0
9	SU	003[illegible] 0617 1313 1857	1.5 5.0 1.7 4.7
10	M	0152 0740 1436 2034	1.7 4.7 1.8 4.5
11	TU	0312 0911 1554 2146	1.8 4.6 1.8 4.7
12	W	0429 1015 1707 2242	1.6 4.9 1.5 4.9
13	TH	0532 1105 1757 2328	1.2 5.2 1.2 5.2
14	F	0615 1147 1834	1.0 5.4 1.0
15	SA	0005 0650 1222 1906	5.5 0.8 5.6 0.9
16	SU ○	0037 0722 1252 1937	5.7 0.7 5.8 0.8
17	M	0107 0754 1323 2009	5.8 0.6 5.9 0.7
18	TU	0137 0828 1353 2042	5.9 0.5 5.9 0.7
19	W	0206 0902 1422 2117	6.0 0.5 6.0 0.7
20	TH	0235 0938 1452 2153	6.0 0.5 5.9 0.7
21	F	0306 1015 1525 2231	5.9 0.6 5.8 0.8
22	SA	0343 1054 1607 2313	5.8 0.8 5.6 1.0
23	SU	0430 1139 1701	5.6 1.0 5.3
24	M ☾	0003 0534 1238 1813	1.2 5.3 1.3 5.0
25	TU	0113 0656 1403 1947	1.4 5.0 1.4 4.8
26	W	0248 0844 1532 2127	1.4 5.1 1.4 5.0
27	TH	0411 1001 1648 2230	1.1 5.4 1.1 5.4
28	F	0521 1057 1749 2319	0.8 5.8 0.8 5.7
29	SA	0616 1143 1838	0.5 6.0 0.6
30	SU ●	0000 0702 1225 1921	5.9 0.3 6.1 0.5
31	M	0038 0744 1303 2001	6.1 0.2 6.2 0.4

APRIL

Date	Day	Time	m
1	TU	0117 0825 1342 2041	6.2 0.2 6.1 0.4
2	W	0157 0904 1423 2119	6.2 0.3 6.0 0.5
3	TH	0238 0941 1504 2156	6.1 0.5 5.9 0.6
4	F	0320 1016 1545 2231	5.9 0.7 5.7 0.8
5	SA	0403 1050 1627 2307	5.7 1.0 5.4 1.1
6	SU	0449 1127 1713 2351	5.4 1.3 5.1 1.4
7	M ☽	0539 1218 1807	5.0 1.7 4.7
8	TU	0057 0640 1346 1920	1.7 4.7 1.9 4.5
9	W	0226 0820 1507 2103	1.8 4.5 1.9 4.5
10	TH	0339 0936 1615 2204	1.6 4.7 1.6 4.8
11	F	0442 1029 1711 2252	1.3 5.0 1.3 5.1
12	SA	0532 1112 1755 2331	1.0 5.3 1.1 5.4
13	SU	0613 1149 1832	0.8 5.5 0.9
14	M	0005 0649 1221 1907	5.6 0.7 5.7 0.8
15	TU ○	0037 0725 1252 1941	5.7 0.6 5.8 0.7
16	W	0107 0801 1323 2018	5.9 0.5 5.9 0.6
17	TH	0139 0839 1356 2057	6.0 0.5 6.0 0.6
18	F	0212 0919 1431 2137	6.0 0.5 5.9 0.6
19	SA	0250 0959 1511 2219	6.0 0.6 5.8 0.7
20	SU	0334 1043 1558 2305	5.8 0.8 5.6 0.9
21	M	0427 1131 1656 2358	5.6 1.0 5.3 1.0
22	TU ☾	0533 1231 1807	5.4 1.2 5.0
23	W	0108 0651 1354 1934	1.2 5.1 1.4 4.9
24	TH	0236 0828 1516 2105	1.2 5.2 1.3 5.1
25	F	0352 0940 1627 2206	1.0 5.4 1.1 5.4
26	SA	0459 1035 1727 2255	0.8 5.7 0.9 5.6
27	SU	0555 1121 1817 2337	0.6 5.9 0.8 5.8
28	M	0641 1202 1859	0.5 6.0 0.7
29	TU ●	0017 0722 1242 1938	5.9 0.5 6.0 0.6
30	W	0056 0801 1321 2017	6.0 0.5 6.0 0.5

MAY

Date	Day	Time	m
1	TH	0137 0839 1401 2055	6.0 0.5 5.9 0.5
2	F	0218 0915 1441 2132	6.0 0.6 5.8 0.6
3	SA	0300 0950 1521 2207	5.8 0.8 5.6 0.8
4	SU	0341 1023 1601 2242	5.6 1.1 5.4 1.0
5	M	0423 1058 1643 2322	5.4 1.3 5.2 1.3
6	TU	0509 1142 1731	5.2 1.6 4.9
7	W ☽	0012 0600 1244 1826	1.5 4.9 1.8 4.7
8	TH	0129 0702 1415 1938	1.6 4.7 1.8 4.6
9	F	0249 0831 1524 2109	1.6 4.7 1.7 4.7
10	SA	0351 0940 1622 2206	1.4 4.9 1.4 5.0
11	SU	0445 1029 1712 2250	1.1 5.2 1.2 5.2
12	M	0533 1110 1756 2329	0.9 5.4 1.0 5.5
13	TU	0615 1147 1836	0.8 5.6 0.9
14	W ○	0004 0655 1222 1916	5.7 0.7 5.8 0.8
15	TH	0039 0736 1258 1957	5.9 0.6 5.9 0.6
16	F	0116 0819 1336 2041	6.0 0.5 6.0 0.6
17	SA	0157 0903 1418 2126	6.1 0.5 6.0 0.5
18	SU	0242 0949 1504 2213	6.1 0.6 5.9 0.6
19	M	0331 1036 1556 2301	5.9 0.7 5.7 0.7
20	TU	0427 1126 1653 2355	5.8 0.9 5.5 0.8
21	W ☾	0529 1225 1756	5.5 1.1 5.3
22	TH	0102 0639 1339 1912	1.0 5.4 1.2 5.1
23	F	0218 0804 1453 2035	1.0 5.3 1.2 5.2
24	SA	0328 0914 1600 2138	0.9 5.4 1.2 5.4
25	SU	0433 1009 1701 2229	0.8 5.6 1.0 5.5
26	M	0531 1058 1754 2315	0.8 5.7 0.9 5.7
27	TU	0620 1141 1839 2358	0.7 5.7 0.8 5.8
28	W ●	0702 1222 1920	0.7 5.8 0.7
29	TH	0039 0740 1303 1958	5.8 0.7 5.8 0.7
30	F	0121 0817 1343 2036	5.9 0.8 5.8 0.6
31	SA	0202 0853 1422 2113	5.8 0.8 5.7 0.7

JUNE

Date	Day	Time	m
1	SU	0242 0928 1500 2148	5.8 0.9 5.6 0.8
2	M	0321 1001 1538 2222	5.6 1.1 5.5 0.9
3	TU	0400 1035 1618 2258	5.5 1.2 5.3 1.1
4	W	0442 1113 1701 2340	5.3 1.4 5.2 1.3
5	TH ☽	0527 1200 1749	5.1 1.6 5.0
6	F	0032 0618 1300 1842	1.4 5.0 1.7 4.9
7	SA	0144 0716 1423 1946	1.5 4.9 1.7 4.8
8	SU	0258 0825 1531 2100	1.4 4.9 1.6 4.9
9	M	0358 0935 1627 2203	1.2 5.1 1.4 5.1
10	TU	0452 1029 1719 2252	1.1 5.3 1.2 5.4
11	W	0542 1115 1807 2336	0.9 5.5 1.0 5.6
12	TH	0629 1157 1854	0.8 5.7 0.8
13	F ○	0017 0716 1239 1940	5.9 0.7 5.9 0.6
14	SA	0100 0803 1322 2028	6.0 0.6 6.0 0.5
15	SU	0145 0851 1407 2116	6.2 0.5 6.0 0.4
16	M	0233 0939 1455 2204	6.2 0.5 6.0 0.4
17	TU	0324 1027 1545 2253	6.1 0.6 5.9 0.4
18	W	0417 1116 1638 2345	5.9 0.8 5.7 0.6
19	TH ☾	0514 1209 1735	5.7 1.0 5.5
20	F	0044 0617 1313 1842	0.7 5.5 1.1 5.4
21	SA	0152 0732 1422 2000	0.9 5.4 1.2 5.3
22	SU	0259 0843 1528 2107	1.0 5.3 1.3 5.3
23	M	0404 0942 1633 2205	1.0 5.4 1.2 5.4
24	TU	0507 1035 1733 2256	1.0 5.4 1.1 5.5
25	W	0601 1123 1823 2342	1.0 5.5 1.0 5.6
26	TH	0646 1206 1906	0.9 5.6 0.9
27	F ●	0025 0724 1248 1944	5.7 0.9 5.7 0.8
28	SA	0107 0800 1326 2020	5.7 0.9 5.7 0.7
29	SU	0146 0834 1403 2055	5.8 0.9 5.7 0.7
30	M	0223 0908 1440 2129	5.8 0.9 5.7 0.8

SUNRISE AND SUNSET TIMES

DUNKERQUE
At 51°03′N 2°22′E

		Sunrise	Sunset
European Standard Time (UT-1)			
Jan	01	0854	1655
	15	0847	1713
Feb	01	0827	1742
	15	0803	1807
Mar	01	0735	1832
	15	0704	1855
European Summer Time (UT-2)			
Apr	01	0726	2023
	15	0656	2046
May	01	0624	2112
	15	0601	2134
Jun	01	0541	2156
	15	0535	2207
Jul	01	0540	2208
	15	0553	2159
Aug	01	0616	2137
	15	0637	2111
Sep	01	0704	2036
	15	0726	2005
Oct	01	0751	1928
	15	0814	1858
European Standard Time (UT-1)			
Nov	01	0743	1725
	15	0807	1703
Dec	01	0832	1647
	15	0848	1644

DUNKERQUE
LAT 51°03′N
LONG 2°22′E

TIMES AND HEIGHTS OF HIGH AND LOW WATER (Heights in Metres)

TIME ZONE –0100 (French Standard Time). **Subtract 1 hour for UT. For French Summer Time (area enclosed in shaded box) add 1 hour**

2014

JULY

Date	Time	m	Date	Time	m
1 TU	0300 0940 1516 2201	5.7 1.0 5.6 0.8	16 W	0307 1010 1525 2237	6.2 0.5 6.1 0.3
2 W	0337 1013 1552 2235	5.6 1.1 5.5 0.9	17 TH	0357 1056 1615 2325	6.1 0.7 5.9 0.4
3 TH	0414 1047 1629 2311	5.5 1.2 5.4 1.0	18 F	0450 1143 1708	5.9 0.9 5.7
4 F	0453 1126 1710 2353	5.4 1.3 5.3 1.2	19 SA ☾	0016 0548 1238 1808	0.7 5.6 1.1 5.5
5 SA ☽	0537 1211 1757	5.2 1.5 5.1	20 SU	0117 0654 1344 1920	0.9 5.4 1.3 5.3
6 SU	0043 0627 1308 1851	1.3 5.1 1.6 5.0	21 M	0224 0807 1453 2036	1.2 5.2 1.4 5.1
7 M	0150 0725 1426 1955	1.4 5.0 1.6 5.0	22 TU	0332 0915 1604 2142	1.3 5.1 1.4 5.2
8 TU	0307 0835 1541 2111	1.4 5.0 1.5 5.0	23 W	0442 1014 1714 2239	1.3 5.2 1.3 5.3
9 W	0412 0950 1644 2221	1.2 5.2 1.3 5.3	24 TH	0545 1107 1810 2329	1.2 5.3 1.1 5.4
10 TH	0512 1050 1742 2315	1.0 5.5 1.0 5.6	25 F	0632 1152 1853	1.1 5.5 0.9
11 F	0607 1139 1836	0.8 5.7 0.8	26 SA ●	0013 0709 1233 1929	5.6 1.0 5.6 0.8
12 SA ○	0003 0659 1225 1926	5.9 0.7 5.9 0.5	27 SU	0052 0742 1309 2002	5.7 1.0 5.7 0.7
13 SU	0048 0749 1308 2015	6.1 0.5 6.1 0.4	28 M	0128 0814 1343 2035	5.8 0.9 5.8 0.7
14 M	0133 0837 1352 2103	6.3 0.4 6.2 0.2	29 TU	0202 0846 1417 2106	5.8 0.9 5.8 0.7
15 TU	0219 0924 1438 2150	6.3 0.4 6.2 0.2	30 W	0236 0917 1451 2138	5.8 0.9 5.8 0.7
			31 TH	0310 0949 1523 2210	5.8 1.0 5.7 0.8

AUGUST

Date	Time	m	Date	Time	m
1 F	0343 1021 1554 2244	5.7 1.1 5.6 0.9	16 SA	0422 1113 1638 2342	5.9 0.8 5.9 0.8
2 SA	0415 1057 1626 2321	5.6 1.2 5.5 1.0	17 SU ☾	0515 1158 1734	5.6 1.1 5.6
3 SU	0451 1136 1707	5.4 1.3 5.3	18 M	0034 0614 1259 1840	1.1 5.3 1.4 5.2
4 M ☽	0004 0538 1224 1801	1.2 5.3 1.5 5.2	19 TU	0143 0727 1415 2003	1.4 5.0 1.6 5.0
5 TU	0059 0637 1328 1908	1.4 5.1 1.6 5.0	20 W	0257 0846 1532 2119	1.6 4.9 1.6 5.0
6 W	0216 0749 1456 2030	1.4 5.0 1.6 5.0	21 TH	0414 0953 1651 2222	1.6 5.0 1.4 5.1
7 TH	0338 0920 1614 2200	1.4 5.1 1.4 5.3	22 F	0525 1049 1751 2313	1.4 5.2 1.2 5.3
8 F	0447 1032 1721 2301	1.1 5.4 1.1 5.7	23 SA	0613 1135 1834 2356	1.2 5.4 1.0 5.5
9 SA	0550 1125 1820 2350	0.9 5.7 0.7 6.0	24 SU	0650 1213 1908	1.1 5.6 0.8
10 SU ○	0645 1210 1912	0.7 6.0 0.4	25 M ●	0032 0720 1248 1939	5.7 1.0 5.8 0.7
11 M	0034 0733 1252 1959	6.2 0.5 6.2 0.2	26 TU	0106 0750 1319 2009	5.8 0.9 5.9 0.7
12 TU	0117 0819 1333 2045	6.4 0.4 6.3 0.1	27 W	0137 0820 1351 2040	5.9 0.9 5.9 0.7
13 W	0200 0904 1416 2130	6.4 0.4 6.3 0.1	28 TH	0209 0851 1422 2111	5.9 0.9 5.9 0.7
14 TH	0245 0948 1500 2215	6.3 0.5 6.2 0.2	29 F	0240 0923 1451 2144	5.9 0.9 5.9 0.7
15 F	0332 1031 1548 2258	6.2 0.6 6.1 0.4	30 SA	0309 0956 1518 2217	5.8 0.9 5.8 0.8
			31 SU	0336 1030 1547 2253	5.7 1.1 5.7 1.0

SEPTEMBER

Date	Time	m	Date	Time	m
1 M	0410 1108 1626 2335	5.6 1.2 5.5 1.2	16 TU ☾	0536 1213 1802	5.3 1.4 5.2
2 TU ☽	0456 1154 1721	5.4 1.4 5.3	17 W	0053 0640 1331 1921	1.7 4.9 1.7 4.9
3 W	0027 0559 1256 1834	1.4 5.1 1.6 5.1	18 TH	0218 0809 1455 2051	1.9 4.7 1.8 4.8
4 TH	0141 0718 1424 2007	1.5 4.9 1.6 5.0	19 F	0337 0925 1614 2157	1.8 4.8 1.6 5.0
5 F	0312 0901 1551 2145	1.5 5.0 1.4 5.3	20 SA	0451 1022 1719 2249	1.6 5.1 1.3 5.3
6 SA	0429 1016 1704 2246	1.2 5.4 1.0 5.7	21 SU	0543 1109 1804 2332	1.3 5.4 1.0 5.5
7 SU	0534 1109 1805 2335	0.9 5.8 0.7 6.1	22 M	0620 1148 1839	1.1 5.6 0.9
8 M	0628 1153 1855	0.7 6.1 0.4	23 TU	0008 0652 1222 1909	5.7 1.0 5.8 0.8
9 TU ○	0017 0714 1232 1940	6.3 0.5 6.3 0.2	24 W ●	0039 0722 1252 1940	5.9 0.9 5.9 0.7
10 W	0058 0758 1311 2024	6.4 0.4 6.4 0.1	25 TH	0109 0753 1322 2011	6.0 0.9 6.0 0.7
11 TH	0138 0841 1352 2107	6.4 0.4 6.4 0.2	26 F	0139 0825 1352 2044	6.0 0.8 6.0 0.7
12 F	0221 0923 1435 2149	6.3 0.5 6.3 0.3	27 SA	0209 0858 1420 2119	6.0 0.8 6.0 0.7
13 SA	0305 1003 1521 2229	6.2 0.6 6.1 0.6	28 SU	0238 0933 1449 2154	6.0 0.9 5.9 0.8
14 SU	0352 1043 1610 2308	5.9 0.8 5.9 0.9	29 M	0308 1009 1522 2232	5.9 1.0 5.8 1.0
15 M	0442 1123 1702 2351	5.6 1.1 5.6 1.3	30 TU	0344 1049 1603 2315	5.7 1.1 5.7 1.2

OCTOBER

Date	Time	m	Date	Time	m
1 W ☽	0431 1136 1700	5.5 1.3 5.4	16 TH	0005 0555 1239 1829	1.8 5.0 1.7 4.9
2 TH	0008 0537 1238 1818	1.4 5.2 1.5 5.1	17 F	0129 0708 1411 2006	2.0 4.7 1.9 4.7
3 F	0122 0701 1405 1955	1.6 5.0 1.6 5.1	18 SA	0252 0844 1526 2121	2.0 4.7 1.7 4.9
4 SA	0253 0844 1534 2128	1.5 5.1 1.3 5.4	19 SU	0400 0946 1630 2215	1.8 5.0 1.5 5.2
5 SU	0411 0957 1647 2229	1.3 5.4 1.0 5.8	20 M	0457 1035 1721 2259	1.5 5.3 1.2 5.5
6 M	0516 1050 1747 2317	1.0 5.8 0.7 6.1	21 TU	0542 1116 1801 2336	1.2 5.5 1.0 5.7
7 TU	0609 1133 1836 2359	0.7 6.1 0.4 6.3	22 W	0619 1151 1837	1.0 5.7 0.8
8 W ○	0655 1211 1920	0.6 6.3 0.3	23 TH ●	0008 0652 1223 1910	5.8 0.9 5.9 0.8
9 TH	0037 0736 1250 2001	6.4 0.5 6.4 0.3	24 F	0039 0725 1253 1944	6.0 0.9 6.0 0.7
10 F	0117 0818 1331 2042	6.4 0.5 6.4 0.4	25 SA	0110 0800 1324 2019	6.1 0.8 6.1 0.7
11 SA	0158 0858 1413 2122	6.3 0.5 6.3 0.5	26 SU	0141 0836 1356 2057	6.1 0.8 6.1 0.7
12 SU	0241 0938 1458 2201	6.1 0.6 6.1 0.8	27 M	0214 0915 1430 2137	6.1 0.8 6.1 0.8
13 M	0325 1016 1544 2237	5.9 0.9 5.9 1.1	28 TU	0250 0956 1509 2218	6.0 0.9 6.0 1.0
14 TU	0411 1054 1633 2316	5.6 1.1 5.6 1.4	29 W	0332 1039 1556 2304	5.8 1.0 5.8 1.2
15 W ☾	0500 1137 1726	5.3 1.4 5.2	30 TH	0423 1129 1656 2358	5.5 1.2 5.5 1.4
			31 F ☽	0529 1229 1810	5.3 1.3 5.3

NOVEMBER

Date	Time	m	Date	Time	m
1 SA	0109 0646 1352 1940	1.5 5.1 1.4 5.2	16 SU	0157 0722 1433 2020	2.0 4.7 1.8 4.8
2 SU	0236 0821 1515 2107	1.5 5.2 1.2 5.4	17 M	0308 0853 1536 2128	1.9 4.8 1.6 5.0
3 M	0350 0933 1625 2207	1.3 5.5 1.0 5.8	18 TU	0406 0951 1632 2218	1.6 5.1 1.3 5.3
4 TU	0454 1027 1726 2256	1.1 5.8 0.7 6.0	19 W	0458 1037 1720 2259	1.4 5.3 1.1 5.5
5 W	0549 1111 1816 2339	0.9 6.0 0.6 6.2	20 TH	0542 1117 1802 2336	1.2 5.6 1.0 5.7
6 TH ○	0635 1152 1900	0.7 6.2 0.5	21 F	0622 1152 1841	1.0 5.8 0.9
7 F	0018 0716 1232 1940	6.2 0.7 6.3 0.5	22 SA ●	0010 0700 1227 1919	5.9 0.9 6.0 0.8
8 SA	0058 0757 1313 2020	6.2 0.6 6.3 0.6	23 SU	0045 0738 1301 1959	6.0 0.8 6.1 0.7
9 SU	0139 0837 1356 2059	6.2 0.6 6.2 0.7	24 M	0121 0819 1339 2041	6.1 0.7 6.2 0.7
10 M	0221 0916 1439 2136	6.1 0.7 6.1 0.9	25 TU	0159 0903 1419 2125	6.1 0.7 6.2 0.8
11 TU	0303 0954 1523 2212	5.9 0.8 5.9 1.1	26 W	0241 0948 1504 2211	6.1 0.7 6.1 0.9
12 W	0346 1030 1607 2247	5.6 1.1 5.6 1.4	27 TH	0327 1034 1554 2258	5.9 0.8 5.9 1.0
13 TH	0429 1108 1654 2328	5.4 1.3 5.3 1.7	28 F	0418 1124 1651 2350	5.7 0.9 5.7 1.2
14 F ☾	0517 1156 1746	5.1 1.6 5.0	29 SA ☽	0518 1221 1757	5.5 1.1 5.5
15 SA	0025 0611 1309 1847	1.9 4.9 1.8 4.8	30 SU	0054 0625 1335 1916	1.4 5.3 1.2 5.4

DECEMBER

Date	Time	m	Date	Time	m
1 M	0212 0749 1450 2039	1.4 5.3 1.1 5.4	16 TU	0202 0724 1439 2006	1.9 4.9 1.6 4.9
2 TU	0323 0904 1559 2142	1.3 5.4 1.0 5.6	17 W	0313 0842 1541 2122	1.8 4.9 1.5 5.0
3 W	0429 1002 1703 2234	1.2 5.6 0.9 5.8	18 TH	0411 0949 1637 2218	1.6 5.1 1.3 5.3
4 TH	0527 1051 1757 2321	1.0 5.8 0.8 5.9	19 F	0504 1041 1727 2305	1.3 5.4 1.1 5.5
5 F	0617 1136 1844	0.9 6.0 0.8	20 SA	0552 1125 1814 2346	1.1 5.6 0.9 5.7
6 SA ○	0003 0700 1219 1924	6.0 0.8 6.0 0.8	21 SU	0637 1205 1859	0.9 5.9 0.8
7 SU	0044 0741 1301 2003	6.0 0.7 6.1 0.8	22 M ●	0025 0721 1245 1943	6.0 0.7 6.1 0.7
8 M	0125 0821 1343 2041	6.0 0.7 6.1 0.8	23 TU	0105 0806 1326 2028	6.1 0.6 6.2 0.6
9 TU	0205 0859 1424 2117	6.0 0.7 6.0 0.9	24 W	0146 0852 1409 2115	6.2 0.5 6.3 0.6
10 W	0244 0935 1504 2151	5.9 0.8 5.8 1.1	25 TH	0230 0939 1455 2201	6.2 0.4 6.2 0.7
11 TH	0323 1010 1544 2224	5.7 1.0 5.7 1.3	26 F	0315 1026 1544 2248	6.1 0.5 6.1 0.8
12 F	0402 1044 1625 2259	5.5 1.1 5.5 1.5	27 SA	0404 1114 1636 2336	5.9 0.6 5.9 1.0
13 SA	0443 1123 1709 2342	5.3 1.3 5.3 1.7	28 SU ☽	0458 1206 1735	5.7 0.8 5.7
14 SU ☾	0530 1210 1758	5.1 1.5 5.1	29 M	0031 0558 1309 1845	1.1 5.5 1.0 5.4
15 M	0037 0622 1318 1855	1.8 5.0 1.6 4.9	30 TU	0140 0712 1420 2006	1.3 5.4 1.1 5.3
			31 W	0251 0832 1530 2115	1.4 5.3 1.2 5.4

CALAIS

LAT 50°58′N
LONG 1°51′E

TIMES AND HEIGHTS OF HIGH AND LOW WATER (Heights in Metres)

TIME ZONE –0100 (French Standard Time). **Subtract 1 hour for UT. For Summer Time (area enclosed in shaded box) add 1 hour**

2014

SUNRISE AND SUNSET TIMES

CALAIS
At 50°58′N 1°51′E

		Sunrise	Sunset
European Standard Time (UT-1)			
Jan	01	0856	1657
	15	0849	1715
Feb	01	0829	1744
	15	0805	1809
Mar	01	0737	1834
	15	0706	1857
European Summer Time (UT-2)			
Apr	01	0728	2026
	15	0658	2048
May	01	0626	2114
	15	0603	2136
Jun	01	0544	2158
	15	0538	2209
Jul	01	0543	2210
	15	0556	2201
Aug	01	0618	2138
	15	0640	2113
Sep	01	0706	2038
	15	0728	2007
Oct	01	0753	1930
	15	0816	1900
European Standard Time (UT-1)			
Nov	01	0745	1727
	15	0809	1705
Dec	01	0834	1649

JANUARY

Date	Day	Time	m	Time	m	Time	m	Time	m
1	W ●	0651	1.0	1153	7.4	1920	0.9		
2	TH	0018	7.4	0741	0.8	1240	7.6	2009	0.7
3	F	0104	7.5	0830	0.7	1326	7.6	2057	0.7
4	SA	0150	7.6	0918	0.6	1415	7.6	2143	0.7
5	SU	0237	7.5	1005	0.7	1505	7.4	2228	0.9
6	M	0327	7.4	1051	0.8	1559	7.2	2312	1.1
7	TU	0420	7.1	1139	1.1	1657	6.9	2359	1.4
8	W ☽	0519	6.9	1231	1.4	1758	6.6		
9	TH	0054	1.7	0622	6.6	1333	1.8	1902	6.3
10	F	0159	2.0	0728	6.4	1442	1.9	2009	6.2
11	SA	0310	2.1	0836	6.3	1554	1.9	2114	6.2
12	SU	0421	2.0	0939	6.3	1700	1.8	2213	6.3
13	M	0521	1.8	1034	6.5	1753	1.6	2304	6.5
14	TU	0609	1.6	1121	6.7	1836	1.5	2346	6.7
15	W	0649	1.4	1201	6.8	1913	1.4		
16	TH ○	0023	6.8	0724	1.2	1236	7.0	1947	1.3
17	F	0056	7.0	0759	1.1	1309	7.1	2021	1.2
18	SA	0128	7.1	0833	1.1	1343	7.2	2054	1.2
19	SU	0201	7.2	0906	1.1	1417	7.2	2126	1.3
20	M	0235	7.2	0939	1.1	1451	7.1	2157	1.3
21	TU	0307	7.1	1013	1.2	1524	7.0	2231	1.4
22	W	0338	6.9	1049	1.4	1557	6.8	2308	1.6
23	TH	0413	6.8	1129	1.6	1636	6.6	2351	1.8
24	F ☾	0458	6.5	1218	1.8	1728	6.4		
25	SA	0042	2.0	0557	6.3	1316	1.9	1835	6.1
26	SU	0146	2.1	0714	6.1	1426	2.0	2002	6.0
27	M	0304	2.1	0845	6.2	1552	1.8	2128	6.3
28	TU	0431	1.8	0959	6.6	1711	1.5	2231	6.7
29	W	0542	1.4	1054	7.0	1814	1.1	2321	7.0
30	TH ●	0639	1.0	1143	7.4	1909	0.8		
31	F	0007	7.3	0732	0.7	1229	7.6	2000	0.6

FEBRUARY

Date	Day	Time	m	Time	m	Time	m	Time	m
1	SA	0051	7.5	0822	0.5	1314	7.7	2048	0.5
2	SU	0135	7.6	0910	0.4	1401	7.6	2132	0.5
3	M	0221	7.6	0953	0.4	1449	7.5	2211	0.7
4	TU	0308	7.5	1033	0.6	1538	7.3	2248	0.9
5	W	0355	7.3	1112	0.9	1628	7.0	2326	1.3
6	TH ☽	0446	7.0	1155	1.4	1720	6.6		
7	F	0011	1.7	0541	6.6	1246	1.8	1818	6.2
8	SA	0108	2.1	0644	6.2	1351	2.2	1926	5.8
9	SU	0220	2.4	0756	5.9	1508	2.3	2041	5.7
10	M	0341	2.3	0910	5.9	1627	2.1	2151	5.9
11	TU	0452	2.1	1014	6.1	1728	1.9	2246	6.2
12	W	0546	1.7	1104	6.4	1814	1.6	2330	6.5
13	TH	0628	1.4	1144	6.7	1853	1.4		
14	F	0004	6.7	0705	1.2	1217	6.9	1928	1.2
15	SA ○	0035	7.0	0740	1.1	1248	7.1	2001	1.1
16	SU	0105	7.1	0814	1.0	1319	7.2	2034	1.1
17	M	0137	7.3	0847	0.9	1353	7.3	2105	1.0
18	TU	0209	7.3	0920	0.9	1425	7.3	2137	1.1
19	W	0239	7.2	0952	1.0	1454	7.2	2209	1.2
20	TH	0307	7.1	1026	1.1	1523	7.0	2243	1.3
21	F	0338	6.9	1104	1.3	1559	6.8	2322	1.6
22	SA ☾	0420	6.7	1148	1.6	1648	6.4		
23	SU	0012	1.8	0517	6.3	1245	1.8	1756	6.0
24	M	0115	2.0	0640	6.0	1356	2.0	1937	5.8
25	TU	0234	2.1	0827	6.1	1527	1.9	2112	6.1
26	W	0410	1.8	0944	6.5	1655	1.5	2216	6.6
27	TH	0526	1.3	1041	7.0	1800	1.1	2307	7.0
28	F	0626	0.9	1130	7.3	1856	0.8	2352	7.3

MARCH

Date	Day	Time	m	Time	m	Time	m	Time	m
1	SA ●	0720	0.6	1215	7.5	1947	0.6		
2	SU	0035	7.5	0809	0.4	1300	7.6	2030	0.5
3	M	0118	7.6	0853	0.3	1345	7.6	2109	0.5
4	TU	0202	7.6	0932	0.4	1430	7.4	2144	0.6
5	W	0246	7.5	1007	0.6	1515	7.2	2218	0.8
6	TH	0329	7.2	1041	0.9	1559	6.9	2252	1.2
7	F	0413	6.9	1117	1.4	1643	6.5	2330	1.7
8	SA ☽	0501	6.5	1159	1.8	1734	6.1		
9	SU	0018	2.1	0557	6.0	1257	2.3	1837	5.6
10	M	0126	2.5	0708	5.7	1414	2.5	1938	5.4
11	TU	0250	2.6	0833	5.6	1542	2.4	2119	5.6
12	W	0411	2.3	0945	5.9	1651	2.1	2219	6.0
13	TH	0511	1.9	1039	6.3	1742	1.7	2304	6.4
14	F	0557	1.5	1120	6.6	1823	1.4	2339	6.7
15	SA	0637	1.2	1152	6.9	1900	1.2		
16	SU ○	0008	6.9	0714	1.1	1222	7.1	1935	1.1
17	M	0037	7.1	0749	0.9	1253	7.2	2008	1.0
18	TU	0108	7.3	0823	0.8	1325	7.3	2041	0.9
19	W	0141	7.3	0858	0.8	1357	7.3	2114	0.9
20	TH	0211	7.3	0932	0.9	1427	7.2	2148	1.0
21	F	0241	7.2	1007	1.0	1458	7.0	2223	1.2
22	SA	0314	7.0	1046	1.2	1536	6.8	2304	1.4
23	SU	0358	6.7	1131	1.5	1626	6.4	2354	1.7
24	M ☾	0458	6.4	1226	1.8	1738	6.0		
25	TU	0056	1.9	0627	6.0	1338	2.0	1924	5.8
26	W	0218	2.0	0813	6.1	1510	1.9	2055	6.1
27	TH	0353	1.8	0928	6.5	1637	1.5	2158	6.6
28	F	0509	1.3	1024	6.9	1743	1.1	2248	7.0
29	SA	0610	0.9	1113	7.2	1837	0.8	2333	7.2
30	SU ●	0702	0.6	1158	7.4	1924	0.7		
31	M	0015	7.4	0748	0.5	1242	7.4	2003	0.6

APRIL

Date	Day	Time	m	Time	m	Time	m	Time	m
1	TU	0058	7.5	0827	0.5	1326	7.4	2039	0.6
2	W	0141	7.4	0903	0.5	1410	7.3	2114	0.7
3	TH	0223	7.3	0937	0.7	1451	7.1	2148	0.9
4	F	0304	7.1	1010	1.0	1531	6.8	2220	1.3
5	SA	0343	6.8	1042	1.4	1609	6.5	2254	1.7
6	SU	0424	6.5	1118	1.9	1652	6.1	2336	2.1
7	M ☽	0512	6.1	1208	2.3	1745	5.7		
8	TU	0037	2.5	0612	5.7	1319	2.6	1856	5.4
9	W	0154	2.6	0733	5.6	1441	2.6	2026	5.5
10	TH	0315	2.4	0858	5.7	1558	2.2	2135	5.8
11	F	0423	2.0	0959	6.1	1656	1.8	2225	6.3
12	SA	0516	1.6	1044	6.5	1743	1.5	2303	6.6
13	SU	0600	1.3	1119	6.7	1824	1.3	2335	6.9
14	M	0641	1.1	1151	7.0	1903	1.1		
15	TU ○	0006	7.1	0720	1.0	1223	7.1	1939	1.0
16	W	0039	7.2	0758	0.9	1257	7.2	2016	0.9
17	TH	0112	7.3	0835	0.8	1332	7.3	2052	0.9
18	F	0147	7.3	0913	0.8	1407	7.2	2130	1.0
19	SA	0223	7.2	0952	0.9	1444	7.0	2210	1.1
20	SU	0304	7.0	1034	1.1	1527	6.8	2253	1.3
21	M	0353	6.7	1120	1.4	1622	6.4	2344	1.6
22	TU ☾	0457	6.4	1216	1.7	1736	6.1		
23	W	0047	1.8	0623	6.2	1326	1.9	1909	6.0
24	TH	0206	1.8	0754	6.3	1453	1.8	2032	6.2
25	F	0334	1.6	0906	6.6	1614	1.5	2135	6.6
26	SA	0447	1.3	1003	6.9	1719	1.2	2226	6.9
27	SU	0547	1.0	1052	7.1	1812	1.0	2311	7.1
28	M	0639	0.8	1138	7.2	1857	0.9	2354	7.2
29	TU ●	0722	0.7	1221	7.2	1935	0.8		
30	W	0036	7.3	0759	0.7	1305	7.2	2010	0.8

MAY

Date	Day	Time	m	Time	m	Time	m	Time	m
1	TH	0119	7.2	0835	0.8	1348	7.1	2047	0.9
2	F	0201	7.1	0910	0.9	1428	6.9	2122	1.0
3	SA	0240	7.0	0943	1.1	1505	6.7	2155	1.3
4	SU	0317	6.7	1015	1.5	1540	6.5	2227	1.6
5	M	0354	6.5	1049	1.8	1617	6.2	2306	2.0
6	TU	0437	6.2	1132	2.1	1702	6.0	2358	2.2
7	W ☽	0528	6.0	1232	2.4	1759	5.7		
8	TH	0104	2.4	0630	5.8	1342	2.4	1909	5.7
9	F	0215	2.3	0746	5.8	1454	2.3	2028	5.8
10	SA	0325	2.1	0859	6.0	1601	2.0	2131	6.1
11	SU	0427	1.7	0955	6.3	1657	1.7	2218	6.5
12	M	0519	1.4	1039	6.6	1746	1.4	2258	6.7
13	TU	0606	1.2	1117	6.8	1830	1.2	2334	6.9
14	W ○	0650	1.1	1154	7.0	1911	1.1		
15	TH	0011	7.1	0732	1.0	1232	7.1	1952	1.0
16	F	0050	7.2	0815	0.9	1312	7.2	2033	0.9
17	SA	0131	7.3	0857	0.8	1354	7.2	2116	0.9
18	SU	0214	7.2	0940	0.9	1438	7.1	2200	1.0
19	M	0301	7.1	1025	1.0	1526	6.9	2246	1.1
20	TU	0354	6.9	1113	1.2	1622	6.6	2338	1.3
21	W ☾	0456	6.6	1207	1.5	1728	6.4		
22	TH	0038	1.5	0611	6.5	1314	1.6	1847	6.3
23	F	0152	1.6	0730	6.4	1431	1.7	2003	6.4
24	SA	0310	1.5	0839	6.6	1546	1.5	2107	6.6
25	SU	0420	1.3	0938	6.7	1650	1.3	2201	6.8
26	M	0522	1.2	1030	6.9	1746	1.2	2249	6.9
27	TU	0614	1.1	1117	6.9	1832	1.1	2334	7.0
28	W ●	0657	1.0	1202	7.0	1910	1.1		
29	TH	0017	7.0	0734	1.0	1245	7.0	1947	1.0
30	F	0100	7.0	0810	1.0	1326	6.9	2024	1.0
31	SA	0140	7.0	0847	1.1	1405	6.9	2100	1.1

JUNE

Date	Day	Time	m	Time	m	Time	m	Time	m
1	SU	0218	6.9	0922	1.2	1441	6.8	2135	1.3
2	M	0254	6.8	0955	1.4	1514	6.6	2207	1.5
3	TU	0330	6.6	1028	1.7	1550	6.5	2243	1.7
4	W	0409	6.5	1106	1.9	1630	6.3	2328	1.9
5	TH ☽	0453	6.3	1154	2.1	1717	6.2		
6	F	0022	2.0	0544	6.1	1252	2.2	1813	6.0
7	SA	0123	2.1	0644	6.0	1355	2.2	1917	6.0
8	SU	0227	2.0	0751	6.0	1502	2.1	2026	6.1
9	M	0333	1.8	0859	6.2	1608	1.8	2129	6.3
10	TU	0435	1.6	0957	6.4	1707	1.6	2221	6.6
11	W	0531	1.4	1046	6.7	1759	1.4	2307	6.8
12	TH	0622	1.2	1130	6.9	1846	1.2	2349	7.1
13	F ○	0710	1.0	1214	7.1	1932	1.0		
14	SA	0033	7.3	0757	0.9	1258	7.2	2018	0.9
15	SU	0118	7.4	0844	0.8	1343	7.3	2105	0.8
16	M	0205	7.4	0931	0.8	1430	7.3	2151	0.8
17	TU	0255	7.3	1017	0.8	1519	7.1	2239	0.9
18	W	0347	7.1	1105	1.0	1612	7.0	2330	1.0
19	TH ☾	0446	6.9	1156	1.2	1712	6.8		
20	F	0026	1.3	0550	6.7	1255	1.5	1819	6.6
21	SA	0131	1.4	0659	6.5	1402	1.6	1929	6.5
22	SU	0241	1.5	0808	6.5	1513	1.7	2036	6.5
23	M	0350	1.5	0911	6.5	1620	1.6	2136	6.6
24	TU	0455	1.4	1008	6.6	1721	1.5	2229	6.7
25	W	0551	1.4	1059	6.7	1811	1.4	2317	6.7
26	TH	0636	1.3	1145	6.7	1851	1.3		
27	F ●	0000	6.8	0714	1.3	1227	6.8	1928	1.2
28	SA	0041	6.9	0751	1.2	1306	6.8	2005	1.2
29	SU	0119	6.9	0827	1.2	1342	6.9	2041	1.2
30	M	0156	6.9	0903	1.3	1416	6.9	2116	1.2

CALAIS
LAT 50°58′N
LONG 1°51′E

TIMES AND HEIGHTS OF HIGH AND LOW WATER (Heights in Metres)

TIME ZONE –0100 (French Standard Time). **Subtract 1 hour for UT. For Summer Time (area enclosed in shaded box) add 1 hour**

2014

JULY

Date	Day	Time	m	Time	m	Time	m	Time	m
1	TU	0231	6.9	0936	1.4	1450	6.8	2149	1.3
2	W	0306	6.9	1008	1.5	1524	6.8	2223	1.4
3	TH	0342	6.8	1042	1.6	1600	6.7	2301	1.6
4	F	0421	6.6	1122	1.8	1640	6.5	2345	1.7
5	SA ☽	0505	6.5	1208	1.9	1727	6.3		
6	SU	0036	1.9	0555	6.3	1303	2.1	1822	6.1
7	M	0134	2.0	0655	6.1	1405	2.1	1928	6.1
8	TU	0240	1.9	0805	6.1	1517	2.0	2043	6.1
9	W	0352	1.8	0919	6.2	1630	1.8	2151	6.4
10	TH	0500	1.5	1021	6.5	1732	1.5	2246	6.8
11	F	0559	1.2	1113	6.8	1826	1.2	2333	7.1
12	SA O	0651	1.0	1159	7.1	1916	0.9		
13	SU	0019	7.3	0742	0.8	1244	7.3	2005	0.7
14	M	0105	7.5	0832	0.7	1329	7.4	2054	0.6
15	TU	0152	7.6	0921	0.6	1415	7.5	2143	0.6
16	W	0241	7.5	1007	0.7	1503	7.4	2230	0.7
17	TH	0333	7.3	1051	0.8	1554	7.3	2317	0.8
18	F	0427	7.1	1137	1.1	1649	7.0		
19	SA ☾	0006	1.1	0525	6.8	1228	1.4	1748	6.7
20	SU	0103	1.4	0627	6.5	1328	1.7	1854	6.5
21	M	0207	1.7	0734	6.3	1436	1.9	2004	6.3
22	TU	0318	1.8	0843	6.2	1550	1.9	2112	6.3
23	W	0429	1.8	0948	6.3	1658	1.8	2212	6.4
24	TH	0530	1.6	1043	6.4	1752	1.6	2302	6.5
25	F	0618	1.5	1130	6.6	1834	1.4	2345	6.7
26	SA ●	0657	1.4	1209	6.7	1911	1.3		
27	SU	0023	6.8	0732	1.3	1245	6.9	1946	1.2
28	M	0058	7.0	0807	1.2	1318	7.0	2021	1.1
29	TU	0132	7.1	0841	1.2	1351	7.1	2055	1.1
30	W	0206	7.1	0914	1.2	1424	7.1	2128	1.1
31	TH	0240	7.1	0946	1.3	1457	7.0	2200	1.2

AUGUST

Date	Day	Time	m	Time	m	Time	m	Time	m
1	F	0314	7.0	1017	1.4	1529	6.9	2234	1.4
2	SA	0347	6.9	1052	1.6	1602	6.7	2312	1.5
3	SU	0423	6.7	1131	1.8	1641	6.5	2356	1.7
4	M ☽	0508	6.4	1219	2.0	1732	6.3		
5	TU	0050	1.9	0605	6.2	1319	2.1	1839	6.1
6	W	0155	2.0	0721	6.0	1432	2.2	2005	6.0
7	TH	0314	1.9	0850	6.1	1557	1.9	2129	6.3
8	F	0434	1.6	1002	6.5	1710	1.5	2229	6.8
9	SA	0539	1.3	1057	6.9	1808	1.2	2319	7.2
10	SU O	0635	1.0	1143	7.2	1901	0.8		
11	M	0004	7.5	0726	0.7	1227	7.5	1951	0.6
12	TU	0049	7.6	0817	0.6	1311	7.6	2042	0.5
13	W	0135	7.7	0905	0.5	1356	7.7	2130	0.5
14	TH	0223	7.6	0949	0.6	1443	7.6	2213	0.6
15	F	0313	7.4	1028	0.8	1532	7.4	2254	0.8
16	SA	0404	7.2	1108	1.1	1623	7.1	2337	1.2
17	SU ☾	0457	6.9	1153	1.5	1718	6.8		
18	M	0026	1.6	0553	6.5	1248	1.9	1818	6.4
19	TU	0127	2.0	0658	6.1	1357	2.2	1929	6.1
20	W	0241	2.2	0813	5.9	1517	2.3	2046	6.0
21	TH	0401	2.2	0927	6.0	1633	2.1	2154	6.2
22	F	0506	1.9	1026	6.2	1730	1.8	2246	6.4
23	SA	0555	1.7	1112	6.5	1813	1.5	2328	6.7
24	SU	0635	1.5	1150	6.8	1850	1.3		
25	M ●	0003	6.9	0709	1.3	1222	7.0	1924	1.2
26	TU	0035	7.1	0743	1.2	1252	7.1	1957	1.1
27	W	0106	7.2	0816	1.1	1323	7.2	2031	1.0
28	TH	0138	7.3	0849	1.1	1355	7.3	2103	1.0
29	F	0211	7.3	0920	1.2	1427	7.2	2135	1.1
30	SA	0242	7.2	0952	1.3	1455	7.1	2208	1.3
31	SU	0311	7.0	1024	1.4	1523	6.9	2243	1.5

SEPTEMBER

Date	Day	Time	m	Time	m	Time	m	Time	m
1	M	0342	6.8	1101	1.7	1559	6.7	2325	1.7
2	TU ☽	0425	6.6	1147	1.9	1649	6.4		
3	W	0017	1.9	0524	6.2	1246	2.1	1801	6.1
4	TH	0124	2.1	0649	6.0	1401	2.2	1942	6.0
5	F	0246	2.1	0831	6.1	1533	2.0	2111	6.4
6	SA	0414	1.7	0945	6.5	1651	1.6	2213	6.9
7	SU	0522	1.3	1039	7.0	1752	1.1	2303	7.3
8	M	0619	0.9	1125	7.4	1845	0.8	2348	7.6
9	TU O	0710	0.7	1207	7.6	1936	0.5		
10	W	0031	7.7	0757	0.6	1250	7.7	2023	0.5
11	TH	0116	7.7	0841	0.6	1335	7.7	2107	0.5
12	F	0203	7.6	0921	0.6	1421	7.6	2146	0.6
13	SA	0251	7.4	0958	0.8	1508	7.4	2224	0.9
14	SU	0339	7.2	1036	1.2	1556	7.1	2302	1.3
15	M	0427	6.8	1116	1.6	1646	6.7	2345	1.8
16	TU ☾	0519	6.4	1205	2.1	1742	6.3		
17	W	0042	2.3	0619	6.0	1312	2.5	1849	5.9
18	TH	0157	2.6	0735	5.7	1436	2.6	2013	5.8
19	F	0324	2.5	0857	5.8	1600	2.4	2127	6.0
20	SA	0434	2.2	0959	6.1	1659	2.0	2222	6.3
21	SU	0524	1.8	1046	6.5	1744	1.6	2304	6.7
22	M	0605	1.5	1123	6.8	1822	1.3	2338	6.9
23	TU	0641	1.3	1154	7.0	1857	1.2		
24	W ●	0008	7.1	0715	1.2	1223	7.2	1931	1.1
25	TH	0037	7.3	0748	1.1	1252	7.3	2004	1.0
26	F	0108	7.4	0821	1.1	1324	7.4	2038	1.0
27	SA	0140	7.4	0854	1.1	1355	7.3	2111	1.1
28	SU	0211	7.3	0927	1.2	1424	7.2	2145	1.2
29	M	0241	7.1	1002	1.4	1454	7.0	2222	1.4
30	TU	0314	6.9	1041	1.6	1532	6.8	2305	1.7

OCTOBER

Date	Day	Time	m	Time	m	Time	m	Time	m
1	W ☽	0358	6.6	1127	1.9	1625	6.5	2357	1.9
2	TH	0501	6.3	1226	2.1	1744	6.1		
3	F	0102	2.1	0634	6.0	1341	2.2	1928	6.1
4	SA	0226	2.1	0813	6.2	1513	2.0	2053	6.5
5	SU	0356	1.8	0924	6.6	1633	1.5	2155	7.0
6	M	0505	1.3	1018	7.1	1735	1.1	2245	7.3
7	TU	0601	1.0	1104	7.4	1828	0.8	2330	7.6
8	W O	0650	0.8	1147	7.6	1916	0.6		
9	TH	0013	7.7	0733	0.7	1230	7.7	1959	0.6
10	F	0057	7.7	0813	0.7	1313	7.7	2039	0.6
11	SA	0143	7.5	0851	0.8	1358	7.5	2117	0.8
12	SU	0229	7.4	0929	1.0	1444	7.3	2153	1.1
13	M	0313	7.1	1006	1.3	1529	7.0	2229	1.5
14	TU	0357	6.7	1043	1.7	1614	6.6	2307	1.9
15	W ☾	0442	6.4	1126	2.2	1703	6.2	2356	2.4
16	TH	0535	6.0	1225	2.6	1803	5.9		
17	F	0103	2.7	0642	5.7	1342	2.7	1921	5.7
18	SA	0228	2.7	0806	5.7	1508	2.6	2043	5.9
19	SU	0347	2.4	0916	6.0	1615	2.1	2143	6.2
20	M	0443	2.0	1007	6.4	1706	1.7	2230	6.6
21	TU	0528	1.6	1048	6.8	1748	1.4	2306	6.9
22	W	0608	1.4	1121	7.0	1827	1.2	2337	7.1
23	TH ●	0646	1.3	1151	7.2	1903	1.1		
24	F	0007	7.3	0721	1.2	1222	7.3	1938	1.1
25	SA	0040	7.4	0755	1.1	1255	7.4	2014	1.1
26	SU	0113	7.4	0831	1.1	1329	7.3	2050	1.1
27	M	0148	7.4	0907	1.2	1403	7.2	2128	1.2
28	TU	0222	7.2	0946	1.3	1439	7.1	2208	1.4
29	W	0301	7.0	1028	1.5	1523	6.8	2252	1.6
30	TH	0349	6.7	1116	1.7	1620	6.5	2344	1.8
31	F ☽	0454	6.4	1214	1.9	1740	6.3		

NOVEMBER

Date	Day	Time	m	Time	m	Time	m	Time	m
1	SA	0048	2.0	0621	6.2	1326	2.0	1912	6.3
2	SU	0208	2.0	0749	6.4	1453	1.9	2031	6.6
3	M	0333	1.8	0859	6.7	1612	1.5	2133	7.0
4	TU	0443	1.4	0955	7.1	1715	1.1	2225	7.3
5	W	0540	1.1	1043	7.4	1810	0.9	2311	7.4
6	TH O	0629	1.0	1127	7.5	1857	0.8	2355	7.5
7	F	0711	0.9	1211	7.5	1938	0.8		
8	SA	0039	7.5	0749	0.9	1255	7.5	2015	0.8
9	SU	0123	7.4	0827	0.9	1339	7.4	2052	1.0
10	M	0207	7.2	0905	1.1	1422	7.2	2128	1.2
11	TU	0248	7.0	0942	1.4	1503	6.9	2203	1.6
12	W	0327	6.8	1017	1.7	1543	6.6	2238	1.9
13	TH	0407	6.5	1055	2.0	1626	6.3	2319	2.3
14	F ☾	0451	6.2	1144	2.4	1716	6.1		
15	SA	0014	2.6	0545	6.0	1247	2.6	1818	5.9
16	SU	0122	2.7	0653	5.9	1359	2.5	1933	5.9
17	M	0238	2.6	0809	6.0	1514	2.3	2046	6.1
18	TU	0349	2.2	0914	6.3	1617	1.9	2143	6.4
19	W	0445	1.9	1004	6.6	1709	1.6	2227	6.7
20	TH	0533	1.6	1045	6.8	1754	1.4	2305	6.9
21	F	0615	1.4	1120	7.0	1836	1.3	2340	7.1
22	SA ●	0655	1.3	1155	7.2	1915	1.2		
23	SU	0015	7.3	0733	1.2	1232	7.3	1953	1.1
24	M	0053	7.4	0812	1.1	1311	7.4	2033	1.1
25	TU	0132	7.4	0852	1.1	1351	7.3	2115	1.1
26	W	0213	7.3	0935	1.1	1434	7.2	2158	1.2
27	TH	0257	7.1	1019	1.2	1522	7.0	2244	1.4
28	F	0347	6.9	1108	1.4	1619	6.8	2334	1.6
29	SA ☽	0448	6.7	1203	1.6	1730	6.6		
30	SU	0034	1.8	0602	6.5	1310	1.7	1849	6.5

DECEMBER

Date	Day	Time	m	Time	m	Time	m	Time	m
1	M	0146	1.9	0720	6.5	1428	1.7	2004	6.6
2	TU	0305	1.8	0831	6.7	1546	1.5	2108	6.8
3	W	0417	1.6	0931	6.9	1653	1.3	2204	7.0
4	TH	0519	1.3	1023	7.1	1751	1.1	2253	7.1
5	F	0611	1.2	1111	7.2	1840	1.0	2339	7.2
6	SA O	0654	1.1	1155	7.3	1920	1.0		
7	SU	0023	7.2	0732	1.1	1239	7.3	1956	1.1
8	M	0106	7.2	0809	1.1	1321	7.2	2032	1.1
9	TU	0146	7.1	0846	1.1	1402	7.1	2109	1.3
10	W	0224	7.0	0923	1.3	1440	6.9	2143	1.5
11	TH	0300	6.9	0957	1.5	1516	6.8	2216	1.8
12	F	0335	6.7	1032	1.8	1554	6.6	2251	2.0
13	SA	0414	6.5	1112	2.0	1637	6.4	2335	2.2
14	SU ☾	0459	6.3	1201	2.2	1727	6.2		
15	M	0028	2.4	0553	6.2	1300	2.3	1826	6.0
16	TU	0131	2.4	0656	6.1	1405	2.3	1934	6.0
17	W	0239	2.4	0807	6.1	1515	2.1	2044	6.1
18	TH	0350	2.1	0913	6.3	1622	1.9	2144	6.4
19	F	0452	1.8	1008	6.6	1719	1.6	2233	6.6
20	SA	0544	1.6	1054	6.8	1808	1.4	2316	6.9
21	SU	0631	1.3	1135	7.1	1854	1.2	2357	7.1
22	M ●	0714	1.1	1215	7.3	1937	1.0		
23	TU	0038	7.3	0757	1.0	1258	7.4	2021	0.9
24	W	0120	7.4	0841	0.9	1341	7.5	2105	0.9
25	TH	0204	7.5	0926	0.8	1427	7.4	2150	0.9
26	F	0249	7.4	1012	0.9	1515	7.3	2235	1.0
27	SA	0337	7.2	1059	1.0	1609	7.1	2323	1.2
28	SU ☽	0433	7.0	1151	1.2	1711	6.8		
29	M	0016	1.5	0537	6.8	1250	1.4	1821	6.6
30	TU	0119	1.7	0648	6.6	1359	1.6	1932	6.5
31	W	0230	1.8	0800	6.6	1514	1.7	2041	6.5

DIEPPE
LAT 49°56′N
LONG 1°05′E

TIMES AND HEIGHTS OF HIGH AND LOW WATER (Heights in Metres)

TIME ZONE –0100 (French Standard Time). **Subtract 1 hour for UT. For French Summer Time (area enclosed in shaded box) add 1 hour**

2014

SUNRISE AND SUNSET TIMES

DIEPPE
At 49°56′N 1°05′E

European Standard Time (UT-1)

		Sunrise	Sunset
Jan	01	0854	1705
	15	0848	1723
Feb	01	0829	1750
	15	0806	1814
Mar	01	0739	1838
	15	0709	1901
European Summer Time (UT-2)			
Apr	01	0732	2028
	15	0703	2049
May	01	0632	2114
	15	0610	2135
Jun	01	0552	2156
	15	0546	2206
Jul	01	0551	2208
	15	0504	2159
Aug	01	0625	2138
	15	0646	2114
Sep	01	0711	2039
	15	0732	2010
Oct	01	0756	1934
	15	0818	1905
European Standard Time (UT-1)			
Nov	01	0745	1733
	15	0808	1712
Dec	01	0832	1657
	15	0847	1654

JANUARY

Date	Day	Time	m	Time	m	Time	m	Time	m
1	W ●	0556	1.0	1120	9.4	1828	0.7	2347	9.5
2	TH	0653	0.8	1208	9.7	1922	0.4		
3	F	0036	9.7	0744	0.6	1257	9.8	2011	0.3
4	SA	0124	9.7	0832	0.6	1344	9.7	2057	0.3
5	SU	0211	9.6	0916	0.7	1431	9.5	2139	0.5
6	M	0257	9.3	0958	1.0	1519	9.1	2219	0.9
7	TU	0345	8.9	1039	1.4	1608	8.6	2300	1.4
8	W ☽	0435	8.4	1124	1.9	1702	8.1	2347	1.9
9	TH	0532	7.9	1219	2.3	1805	7.6		
10	F	0047	2.4	0638	7.6	1332	2.6	1916	7.3
11	SA	0204	2.6	0750	7.5	1452	2.5	2029	7.4
12	SU	0319	2.4	0857	7.6	1558	2.2	2130	7.7
13	M	0418	2.1	0952	7.9	1649	1.9	2221	8.0
14	TU	0505	1.9	1038	8.2	1732	1.6	2303	8.3
15	W	0545	1.6	1118	8.5	1810	1.4	2341	8.6
16	TH ○	0622	1.4	1154	8.7	1847	1.3		
17	F	0016	8.8	0658	1.3	1228	8.8	1922	1.2
18	SA	0050	8.9	0733	1.3	1301	8.9	1956	1.2
19	SU	0122	8.9	0806	1.4	1333	8.9	2027	1.3
20	M	0154	8.8	0837	1.5	1405	8.8	2057	1.4
21	TU	0225	8.7	0907	1.6	1436	8.6	2127	1.6
22	W	0257	8.5	0941	1.8	1509	8.4	2201	1.8
23	TH	0332	8.3	1020	2.0	1547	8.1	2243	2.1
24	F ☾	0413	8.0	1109	2.3	1635	7.7	2336	2.3
25	SA	0508	7.6	1209	2.5	1741	7.4		
26	SU	0042	2.5	0626	7.4	1324	2.5	1913	7.3
27	M	0203	2.4	0757	7.6	1447	2.2	2040	7.8
28	TU	0324	2.0	0912	8.2	1605	1.7	2147	8.4
29	W	0437	1.5	1013	8.8	1714	1.2	2244	9.0
30	TH ●	0543	1.1	1106	9.3	1816	0.7	2335	9.5
31	F	0641	0.7	1156	9.7	1910	0.3		

FEBRUARY

Date	Day	Time	m	Time	m	Time	m	Time	m
1	SA	0022	9.8	0732	0.4	1243	9.9	1958	0.0
2	SU	0108	9.9	0818	0.3	1328	9.9	2041	0.1
3	M	0153	9.8	0859	0.4	1412	9.8	2120	0.3
4	TU	0235	9.6	0937	0.7	1455	9.4	2155	0.7
5	W	0317	9.1	1012	1.2	1538	8.8	2228	1.3
6	TH ☽	0359	8.5	1048	1.7	1623	8.1	2305	1.9
7	F	0445	7.9	1132	2.3	1716	7.5	2354	2.5
8	SA	0544	7.3	1234	2.8	1825	7.0		
9	SU	0107	3.0	0659	7.0	1402	2.9	1947	6.9
10	M	0236	2.9	0819	7.1	1521	2.6	2101	7.2
11	TU	0346	2.5	0926	7.5	1620	2.2	2158	7.7
12	W	0439	2.0	1017	7.9	1708	1.7	2243	8.2
13	TH	0524	1.7	1058	8.4	1750	1.4	2321	8.5
14	F	0604	1.4	1135	8.7	1829	1.2	2356	8.8
15	SA ○	0641	1.2	1209	8.9	1905	1.1		
16	SU	0029	9.0	0715	1.2	1242	9.0	1938	1.0
17	M	0100	9.1	0748	1.1	1312	9.1	2008	1.0
18	TU	0131	9.1	0818	1.1	1343	9.1	2037	1.1
19	W	0202	9.1	0848	1.2	1415	9.0	2107	1.2
20	TH	0233	8.9	0920	1.4	1448	8.7	2139	1.4
21	F	0307	8.6	0957	1.6	1524	8.4	2218	1.8
22	SA ☾	0345	8.3	1042	1.9	1608	7.9	2307	2.1
23	SU	0437	7.8	1139	2.3	1711	7.4		
24	M	0011	2.5	0553	7.4	1253	2.5	1846	7.2
25	TU	0135	2.5	0734	7.4	1423	2.3	2023	7.6
26	W	0305	2.2	0857	8.0	1548	1.8	2134	8.3
27	TH	0423	1.6	0959	8.7	1701	1.1	2230	9.0
28	F	0530	1.0	1052	9.3	1802	0.6	2319	9.5

MARCH

Date	Day	Time	m	Time	m	Time	m	Time	m
1	SA ●	0626	0.5	1140	9.7	1854	0.2		
2	SU	0005	9.8	0714	0.3	1225	9.9	1939	0.0
3	M	0049	9.9	0758	0.2	1309	10.0	2019	0.0
4	TU	0130	9.8	0836	0.3	1350	9.8	2055	0.3
5	W	0210	9.6	0911	0.6	1430	9.4	2126	0.8
6	TH	0247	9.1	0941	1.1	1508	8.8	2154	1.3
7	F	0324	8.6	1012	1.6	1547	8.2	2226	1.9
8	SA ☽	0403	7.9	1049	2.2	1632	7.5	2308	2.6
9	SU	0453	7.3	1141	2.8	1735	6.9		
10	M	0013	3.1	0606	6.8	1307	3.1	1853	6.7
11	TU	0150	3.2	0733	6.8	1439	2.9	2023	6.9
12	W	0310	2.7	0851	7.1	1546	2.4	2127	7.5
13	TH	0408	2.2	0948	7.7	1638	1.8	2215	8.0
14	F	0456	1.7	1032	8.2	1722	1.4	2254	8.5
15	SA	0538	1.4	1110	8.6	1803	1.2	2330	8.8
16	SU ○	0616	1.2	1144	8.9	1840	1.0		
17	M	0003	9.0	0652	1.0	1217	9.1	1914	0.9
18	TU	0035	9.2	0726	1.0	1249	9.2	1946	0.9
19	W	0107	9.3	0759	0.9	1322	9.3	2018	0.9
20	TH	0139	9.3	0832	0.9	1356	9.2	2050	1.0
21	F	0213	9.1	0906	1.1	1431	8.9	2124	1.3
22	SA	0249	8.8	0943	1.3	1509	8.5	2204	1.6
23	SU	0329	8.3	1028	1.7	1555	8.0	2253	2.0
24	M ☾	0421	7.8	1123	2.1	1659	7.4	2356	2.4
25	TU	0539	7.4	1235	2.3	1835	7.2		
26	W	0118	2.5	0719	7.4	1406	2.2	2010	7.7
27	TH	0249	2.1	0841	8.0	1533	1.7	2117	8.4
28	F	0408	1.5	0942	8.7	1645	1.1	2212	9.0
29	SA	0512	1.0	1034	9.3	1743	0.6	2300	9.5
30	SU ●	0606	0.6	1121	9.6	1832	0.3	2344	9.7
31	M	0653	0.3	1205	9.7	1915	0.2		

APRIL

Date	Day	Time	m	Time	m	Time	m	Time	m
1	TU	0026	9.8	0734	0.3	1247	9.7	1953	0.3
2	W	0106	9.7	0810	0.4	1326	9.5	2026	0.5
3	TH	0143	9.4	0842	0.7	1403	9.2	2055	0.9
4	F	0218	9.1	0911	1.1	1439	8.7	2124	1.4
5	SA	0253	8.6	0941	1.6	1516	8.2	2155	1.9
6	SU	0330	8.0	1015	2.1	1557	7.6	2234	2.5
7	M ☽	0415	7.4	1101	2.7	1653	7.0	2330	3.0
8	TU	0519	6.9	1212	3.1	1810	6.7		
9	W	0058	3.2	0643	6.7	1348	3.0	1933	6.8
10	TH	0224	2.9	0804	6.9	1501	2.6	2044	7.3
11	F	0326	2.3	0908	7.5	1556	2.0	2137	7.9
12	SA	0416	1.9	0957	8.0	1643	1.6	2220	8.3
13	SU	0500	1.5	1038	8.4	1726	1.3	2258	8.7
14	M	0542	1.2	1114	8.8	1807	1.1	2333	9.0
15	TU ○	0623	1.0	1150	9.0	1846	1.0		
16	W	0008	9.2	0702	0.9	1225	9.2	1923	0.9
17	TH	0043	9.4	0740	0.8	1302	9.3	2000	0.8
18	F	0119	9.4	0818	0.8	1339	9.2	2037	0.9
19	SA	0157	9.2	0856	0.9	1419	9.0	2115	1.2
20	SU	0237	8.9	0936	1.2	1501	8.6	2157	1.5
21	M	0321	8.4	1022	1.5	1551	8.1	2247	1.9
22	TU ☾	0417	7.9	1117	1.9	1657	7.6	2349	2.2
23	W	0533	7.5	1226	2.1	1826	7.5		
24	TH	0106	2.3	0703	7.6	1349	2.0	1949	7.9
25	F	0231	2.0	0819	8.1	1512	1.6	2055	8.4
26	SA	0347	1.5	0920	8.6	1622	1.2	2149	8.9
27	SU	0450	1.0	1013	9.0	1719	0.8	2237	9.2
28	M	0543	0.8	1100	9.2	1807	0.7	2321	9.4
29	TU ●	0629	0.6	1143	9.3	1848	0.6		
30	W	0002	9.4	0707	0.6	1224	9.3	1924	0.7

MAY

Date	Day	Time	m	Time	m	Time	m	Time	m
1	TH	0041	9.3	0742	0.7	1302	9.2	1956	0.9
2	F	0117	9.2	0814	0.9	1339	9.0	2027	1.1
3	SA	0152	8.9	0845	1.2	1415	8.6	2058	1.5
4	SU	0227	8.5	0916	1.5	1451	8.2	2131	1.9
5	M	0304	8.1	0951	2.0	1531	7.8	2209	2.4
6	TU	0345	7.6	1032	2.4	1618	7.3	2258	2.8
7	W ☽	0438	7.1	1128	2.8	1720	7.0		
8	TH	0004	3.0	0547	6.8	1245	2.9	1834	6.9
9	F	0124	2.9	0703	6.9	1401	2.7	1947	7.1
10	SA	0230	2.6	0814	7.2	1502	2.3	2049	7.6
11	SU	0325	2.1	0911	7.7	1554	1.9	2138	8.1
12	M	0415	1.7	0959	8.2	1642	1.6	2221	8.5
13	TU	0503	1.4	1041	8.6	1730	1.3	2302	8.9
14	W ○	0551	1.1	1122	8.9	1816	1.1	2341	9.1
15	TH	0638	0.9	1202	9.1	1902	0.9		
16	F	0021	9.3	0723	0.8	1244	9.3	1945	0.9
17	SA	0102	9.4	0807	0.7	1326	9.3	2028	0.9
18	SU	0145	9.3	0850	0.8	1410	9.1	2110	1.1
19	M	0229	9.0	0933	1.0	1457	8.8	2154	1.3
20	TU	0318	8.6	1020	1.2	1550	8.4	2244	1.6
21	W ☾	0414	8.2	1112	1.5	1652	8.0	2341	1.9
22	TH	0522	7.9	1213	1.8	1805	7.9		
23	F	0049	2.0	0638	7.8	1326	1.9	1920	8.0
24	SA	0205	1.9	0751	8.0	1443	1.7	2027	8.3
25	SU	0320	1.6	0855	8.3	1554	1.5	2124	8.6
26	M	0425	1.3	0950	8.6	1652	1.3	2214	8.8
27	TU	0518	1.1	1039	8.7	1740	1.2	2259	8.9
28	W ●	0603	1.0	1123	8.8	1821	1.1	2340	8.9
29	TH	0641	1.0	1203	8.8	1856	1.1		
30	F	0018	8.9	0715	1.0	1241	8.8	1929	1.2
31	SA	0054	8.9	0749	1.1	1317	8.7	2002	1.3

JUNE

Date	Day	Time	m	Time	m	Time	m	Time	m
1	SU	0129	8.8	0822	1.2	1353	8.6	2036	1.5
2	M	0205	8.5	0856	1.5	1430	8.3	2110	1.8
3	TU	0241	8.2	0930	1.8	1507	8.0	2146	2.1
4	W	0319	7.9	1007	2.2	1546	7.7	2227	2.5
5	TH ☽	0401	7.5	1051	2.5	1632	7.3	2317	2.7
6	F	0451	7.2	1145	2.7	1728	7.1		
7	SA	0018	2.8	0552	7.0	1250	2.7	1835	7.1
8	SU	0125	2.6	0704	7.1	1357	2.5	1946	7.4
9	M	0228	2.3	0814	7.4	1500	2.2	2049	7.8
10	TU	0327	1.9	0915	7.9	1558	1.8	2143	8.3
11	W	0424	1.5	1007	8.3	1654	1.5	2231	8.7
12	TH	0520	1.2	1056	8.7	1749	1.2	2317	9.1
13	F ○	0616	1.0	1142	9.1	1842	1.0		
14	SA	0002	9.3	0708	0.7	1229	9.3	1933	0.8
15	SU	0048	9.4	0758	0.6	1315	9.4	2021	0.8
16	M	0135	9.4	0846	0.5	1402	9.3	2106	0.8
17	TU	0222	9.3	0931	0.6	1450	9.1	2151	1.0
18	W	0311	9.0	1015	0.9	1540	8.8	2237	1.3
19	TH ☾	0403	8.6	1101	1.2	1635	8.4	2326	1.6
20	F	0501	8.2	1153	1.6	1736	8.1		
21	SA	0024	1.8	0606	7.9	1255	1.9	1844	7.9
22	SU	0133	2.0	0717	7.8	1407	2.0	1954	7.9
23	M	0248	1.9	0826	7.9	1522	1.9	2057	8.1
24	TU	0356	1.7	0927	8.0	1624	1.8	2152	8.3
25	W	0452	1.5	1019	8.2	1714	1.6	2239	8.4
26	TH	0538	1.4	1105	8.4	1755	1.5	2321	8.6
27	F ●	0617	1.3	1145	8.5	1832	1.4	2359	8.7
28	SA	0653	1.2	1223	8.6	1907	1.4		
29	SU	0035	8.7	0727	1.2	1259	8.7	1942	1.4
30	M	0110	8.7	0803	1.3	1334	8.6	2016	1.5

DIEPPE
LAT 49°56′N
LONG 1°05′E

TIMES AND HEIGHTS OF HIGH AND LOW WATER (Heights in Metres)

TIME ZONE –0100 (French Standard Time). **Subtract 1 hour for UT. For French Summer Time (area enclosed in shaded box) add 1 hour**

2014

JULY

Date	Day	Phase	Time	m	Time	m	Time	m	Time	m
1	TU		0145	8.6	0837	1.4	1408	8.5	2050	1.6
2	W		0219	8.5	0909	1.6	1442	8.3	2122	1.9
3	TH		0253	8.2	0941	1.9	1515	8.1	2157	2.1
4	F		0328	8.0	1016	2.1	1551	7.8	2237	2.3
5	SA	☽	0407	7.7	1059	2.4	1633	7.6	2327	2.5
6	SU		0454	7.4	1152	2.5	1728	7.4		
7	M		0026	2.6	0556	7.2	1257	2.6	1838	7.3
8	TU		0135	2.4	0714	7.3	1409	2.4	1958	7.6
9	W		0245	2.1	0833	7.6	1519	2.1	2107	8.0
10	TH		0351	1.7	0938	8.1	1624	1.7	2205	8.6
11	F		0455	1.3	1034	8.7	1726	1.3	2257	9.0
12	SA	○	0557	1.0	1125	9.1	1826	1.0	2346	9.4
13	SU		0656	0.6	1214	9.4	1922	0.7		
14	M		0034	9.6	0748	0.4	1302	9.6	2011	0.6
15	TU		0122	9.7	0836	0.3	1349	9.6	2057	0.5
16	W		0209	9.6	0920	0.3	1435	9.5	2140	0.7
17	TH		0255	9.4	1001	0.6	1522	9.1	2221	1.0
18	F		0343	9.0	1041	1.0	1610	8.7	2303	1.4
19	SA	☾	0434	8.5	1124	1.5	1702	8.2	2352	1.8
20	SU		0531	7.9	1217	2.0	1804	7.8		
21	M		0054	2.2	0639	7.5	1326	2.4	1916	7.5
22	TU		0212	2.4	0754	7.4	1447	2.5	2027	7.6
23	W		0326	2.2	0903	7.6	1555	2.2	2129	7.8
24	TH		0426	1.9	1000	7.9	1649	1.9	2221	8.1
25	F		0514	1.6	1048	8.2	1732	1.7	2304	8.4
26	SA	●	0555	1.4	1128	8.4	1811	1.5	2342	8.6
27	SU		0633	1.3	1205	8.6	1848	1.4		
28	M		0017	8.8	0708	1.2	1239	8.7	1922	1.3
29	TU		0051	8.8	0743	1.2	1312	8.8	1956	1.3
30	W		0124	8.8	0816	1.3	1344	8.8	2028	1.4
31	TH		0155	8.8	0845	1.4	1415	8.7	2057	1.6

AUGUST

Date	Day	Phase	Time	m	Time	m	Time	m	Time	m
1	F		0226	8.6	0914	1.6	1445	8.5	2128	1.7
2	SA		0258	8.4	0944	1.8	1517	8.3	2203	1.9
3	SU		0332	8.1	1022	2.0	1554	8.0	2247	2.2
4	M	☽	0414	7.8	1109	2.3	1641	7.7	2342	2.4
5	TU		0510	7.4	1211	2.6	1747	7.4		
6	W		0051	2.5	0629	7.2	1327	2.6	1916	7.4
7	TH		0210	2.3	0801	7.5	1449	2.3	2040	7.9
8	F		0326	1.8	0916	8.1	1602	1.8	2145	8.5
9	SA		0435	1.3	1017	8.7	1709	1.3	2240	9.1
10	SU	○	0542	0.9	1109	9.2	1811	0.9	2331	9.6
11	M		0641	0.5	1158	9.6	1907	0.5		
12	TU		0018	9.9	0733	0.2	1245	9.8	1955	0.3
13	W		0105	10.0	0819	0.1	1330	9.9	2040	0.3
14	TH		0150	9.9	0901	0.2	1414	9.7	2120	0.5
15	F		0234	9.6	0939	0.5	1457	9.3	2157	0.9
16	SA		0318	9.1	1014	1.0	1540	8.8	2234	1.4
17	SU	☾	0403	8.5	1050	1.7	1626	8.2	2316	2.0
18	M		0454	7.8	1136	2.3	1722	7.6		
19	TU		0012	2.5	0559	7.3	1242	2.8	1833	7.2
20	W		0131	2.8	0718	7.1	1410	2.9	1954	7.2
21	TH		0255	2.6	0836	7.2	1526	2.6	2105	7.5
22	F		0359	2.1	0938	7.7	1623	2.1	2159	7.9
23	SA		0449	1.7	1027	8.1	1709	1.7	2243	8.4
24	SU		0532	1.4	1107	8.5	1750	1.5	2321	8.7
25	M	●	0611	1.2	1143	8.8	1827	1.3	2356	8.9
26	TU		0647	1.1	1216	8.9	1901	1.2		
27	W		0028	9.0	0721	1.1	1247	9.0	1933	1.2
28	TH		0059	9.1	0752	1.1	1318	9.0	2004	1.2
29	F		0130	9.0	0820	1.2	1347	9.0	2033	1.3
30	SA		0200	8.9	0848	1.3	1418	8.8	2103	1.4
31	SU		0232	8.7	0919	1.6	1450	8.6	2138	1.7

SEPTEMBER

Date	Day	Phase	Time	m	Time	m	Time	m	Time	m
1	M		0307	8.4	0955	1.9	1525	8.3	2220	2.0
2	TU	☽	0347	8.0	1041	2.2	1611	7.8	2313	2.3
3	W		0442	7.5	1140	2.6	1716	7.4		
4	TH		0021	2.5	0602	7.2	1259	2.7	1850	7.3
5	F		0144	2.4	0741	7.5	1427	2.4	2021	7.8
6	SA		0307	1.9	0900	8.1	1545	1.8	2129	8.6
7	SU		0420	1.3	1000	8.9	1654	1.2	2224	9.3
8	M		0526	0.8	1052	9.4	1755	0.8	2313	9.7
9	TU	○	0623	0.4	1139	9.8	1848	0.4		
10	W		0000	10.0	0712	0.1	1224	10.0	1935	0.2
11	TH		0045	10.1	0757	0.1	1308	10.0	2017	0.3
12	F		0128	10.0	0836	0.3	1349	9.8	2055	0.5
13	SA		0210	9.7	0911	0.6	1430	9.4	2129	0.9
14	SU		0251	9.1	0943	1.2	1509	8.8	2202	1.5
15	M		0332	8.5	1015	1.8	1551	8.2	2239	2.1
16	TU	☾	0419	7.8	1057	2.5	1641	7.5	2330	2.6
17	W		0519	7.2	1158	3.0	1751	7.0		
18	TH		0047	3.0	0638	6.9	1331	3.2	1914	6.9
19	F		0218	2.9	0800	7.1	1454	2.8	2032	7.3
20	SA		0326	2.4	0908	7.6	1553	2.2	2131	7.8
21	SU		0419	1.8	0958	8.1	1641	1.8	2216	8.3
22	M		0503	1.5	1039	8.5	1722	1.4	2255	8.7
23	TU		0543	1.2	1115	8.9	1800	1.3	2330	8.9
24	W	●	0620	1.1	1148	9.0	1835	1.2		
25	TH		0002	9.1	0653	1.1	1220	9.2	1908	1.1
26	F		0034	9.2	0725	1.1	1251	9.2	1940	1.1
27	SA		0105	9.2	0756	1.1	1322	9.2	2012	1.1
28	SU		0138	9.2	0827	1.2	1354	9.1	2045	1.3
29	M		0212	9.0	0900	1.5	1429	8.8	2121	1.5
30	TU		0249	8.6	0938	1.8	1506	8.4	2204	1.8

OCTOBER

Date	Day	Phase	Time	m	Time	m	Time	m	Time	m
1	W	☽	0331	8.1	1025	2.2	1553	7.9	2256	2.2
2	TH		0427	7.6	1124	2.5	1700	7.5		
3	F		0002	2.4	0549	7.3	1241	2.7	1835	7.4
4	SA		0126	2.3	0727	7.6	1410	2.4	2004	7.9
5	SU		0250	1.9	0843	8.3	1529	1.8	2110	8.7
6	M		0404	1.3	0941	9.0	1637	1.2	2205	9.3
7	TU		0507	0.8	1031	9.5	1735	0.7	2254	9.7
8	W	○	0601	0.4	1118	9.8	1827	0.4	2339	10.0
9	TH		0649	0.3	1201	9.9	1912	0.3		
10	F		0023	10.0	0731	0.3	1244	9.9	1952	0.4
11	SA		0105	9.8	0808	0.5	1324	9.7	2028	0.7
12	SU		0145	9.5	0841	0.9	1402	9.3	2100	1.0
13	M		0224	9.0	0912	1.4	1440	8.8	2132	1.5
14	TU		0304	8.5	0944	1.9	1519	8.2	2207	2.1
15	W	☾	0347	7.9	1023	2.5	1605	7.6	2252	2.6
16	TH		0442	7.3	1118	3.1	1708	7.1		
17	F		0000	3.0	0554	6.9	1244	3.3	1827	6.8
18	SA		0132	3.0	0713	7.0	1412	3.0	1946	7.1
19	SU		0245	2.6	0825	7.4	1515	2.5	2051	7.5
20	M		0341	2.1	0920	7.9	1604	2.0	2141	8.1
21	TU		0427	1.7	1004	8.4	1647	1.6	2223	8.5
22	W		0508	1.4	1042	8.8	1727	1.3	2259	8.9
23	TH	●	0547	1.2	1118	9.0	1805	1.2	2334	9.1
24	F		0624	1.1	1151	9.2	1842	1.1		
25	SA		0008	9.2	0659	1.1	1225	9.3	1918	1.0
26	SU		0043	9.3	0735	1.1	1259	9.3	1955	1.0
27	M		0119	9.3	0812	1.2	1336	9.2	2032	1.1
28	TU		0157	9.1	0849	1.4	1414	9.0	2112	1.3
29	W		0237	8.7	0930	1.7	1456	8.5	2155	1.7
30	TH		0323	8.3	1017	2.1	1545	8.1	2247	2.0
31	F	☽	0421	7.8	1115	2.4	1652	7.7	2351	2.2

NOVEMBER

Date	Day	Phase	Time	m	Time	m	Time	m	Time	m
1	SA		0540	7.6	1227	2.5	1820	7.6		
2	SU		0108	2.2	0707	7.8	1351	2.3	1942	8.0
3	M		0229	1.8	0820	8.4	1509	1.8	2049	8.6
4	TU		0343	1.4	0919	8.9	1617	1.3	2144	9.1
5	W		0445	1.0	1010	9.3	1715	0.9	2233	9.5
6	TH	○	0538	0.7	1056	9.6	1804	0.7	2319	9.6
7	F		0625	0.6	1139	9.6	1848	0.6		
8	SA		0002	9.6	0704	0.7	1221	9.6	1926	0.7
9	SU		0043	9.5	0740	0.9	1259	9.4	2001	0.9
10	M		0122	9.3	0813	1.1	1337	9.1	2034	1.1
11	TU		0200	8.9	0845	1.5	1414	8.8	2106	1.5
12	W		0239	8.5	0919	1.9	1452	8.3	2141	2.0
13	TH		0319	8.0	0956	2.4	1535	7.8	2222	2.5
14	F	☾	0407	7.6	1043	2.9	1626	7.3	2315	2.9
15	SA		0506	7.2	1148	3.2	1733	6.9		
16	SU		0028	3.1	0616	7.0	1310	3.2	1847	6.9
17	M		0147	2.9	0728	7.2	1421	2.8	1958	7.2
18	TU		0249	2.5	0831	7.6	1517	2.4	2057	7.7
19	W		0341	2.1	0922	8.1	1605	1.9	2145	8.2
20	TH		0427	1.7	1006	8.5	1649	1.6	2227	8.6
21	F		0511	1.4	1046	8.9	1733	1.3	2306	8.9
22	SA	●	0554	1.2	1124	9.1	1817	1.1	2344	9.2
23	SU		0637	1.1	1202	9.3	1900	1.0		
24	M		0023	9.3	0719	1.1	1241	9.4	1943	0.9
25	TU		0104	9.4	0801	1.1	1322	9.4	2025	0.9
26	W		0146	9.2	0843	1.2	1404	9.1	2108	1.1
27	TH		0230	9.0	0926	1.5	1450	8.8	2152	1.3
28	F		0319	8.6	1013	1.7	1541	8.4	2241	1.6
29	SA	☽	0415	8.2	1107	2.0	1642	8.0	2338	1.8
30	SU		0522	8.0	1210	2.2	1756	7.9		

DECEMBER

Date	Day	Phase	Time	m	Time	m	Time	m	Time	m
1	M		0044	2.0	0638	8.0	1324	2.2	1914	8.0
2	TU		0200	1.9	0751	8.2	1443	1.9	2023	8.3
3	W		0316	1.7	0854	8.6	1554	1.6	2122	8.7
4	TH		0422	1.4	0948	8.9	1654	1.2	2214	8.9
5	F		0516	1.2	1036	9.1	1743	1.0	2301	9.1
6	SA	○	0601	1.1	1120	9.2	1826	1.0	2344	9.1
7	SU		0641	1.1	1201	9.2	1904	1.0		
8	M		0024	9.1	0715	1.1	1239	9.1	1938	1.0
9	TU		0103	9.0	0749	1.3	1316	9.0	2011	1.2
10	W		0140	8.9	0823	1.5	1352	8.8	2045	1.4
11	TH		0217	8.6	0857	1.8	1429	8.5	2119	1.8
12	F		0254	8.3	0932	2.1	1507	8.1	2154	2.1
13	SA		0333	7.9	1010	2.5	1547	7.7	2234	2.5
14	SU	☾	0416	7.5	1056	2.8	1634	7.3	2324	2.8
15	M		0508	7.2	1154	3.0	1733	7.0		
16	TU		0026	2.9	0613	7.1	1303	3.0	1844	7.0
17	W		0137	2.8	0726	7.2	1413	2.7	1958	7.2
18	TH		0243	2.5	0832	7.6	1514	2.3	2101	7.7
19	F		0341	2.1	0927	8.1	1610	1.9	2153	8.2
20	SA		0434	1.7	1015	8.6	1702	1.5	2239	8.7
21	SU		0526	1.4	1059	9.0	1754	1.2	2324	9.0
22	M	●	0617	1.2	1143	9.3	1845	0.9		
23	TU		0007	9.3	0706	1.0	1227	9.5	1934	0.7
24	W		0052	9.5	0754	0.9	1311	9.5	2021	0.6
25	TH		0137	9.5	0840	0.9	1356	9.5	2105	0.7
26	F		0222	9.3	0924	1.0	1442	9.2	2148	0.9
27	SA		0310	9.1	1007	1.3	1531	8.9	2232	1.1
28	SU	☽	0400	8.7	1054	1.6	1625	8.4	2319	1.5
29	M		0457	8.3	1147	1.9	1727	8.1		
30	TU		0015	1.8	0603	8.0	1251	2.1	1840	7.8
31	W		0124	2.1	0717	7.9	1410	2.2	1955	7.8

LE HAVRE

LAT 49°29′N
LONG 0°07′E

TIMES AND HEIGHTS OF HIGH AND LOW WATER (Heights in Metres)

TIME ZONE –0100 (French Standard Time). **Subtract 1 hour for UT. For French Summer Time (area enclosed in shaded box) add 1 hour**

2014

SUNRISE AND SUNSET TIMES

LE HAVRE
At 49°29′N 0°07′E
European Standard Time (UT-1)

		Sunrise	Sunset
Jan	01	0856	1711
	15	0850	1728
Feb	01	0831	1756
	15	0809	1819
Mar	01	0742	1842
	15	0713	1905
European Summer Time (UT-2)			
Apr	01	0737	2031
	15	0708	2052
May	01	0637	2117
	15	0616	2137
Jun	01	0558	2158
	15	0552	2208
Jul	01	0557	2209
	15	0609	2201
Aug	01	0631	2140
	15	0651	2116
Sep	01	0715	2043
	15	0736	2013
Oct	01	0759	1938
	15	0821	1909
European Standard Time (UT-1)			
Nov	01	0748	1738
	15	0811	1717
Dec	01	0834	1703

JANUARY

Date	Day	Time	m
1	W ●	0502 1020 1732 2250	1.4 8.1 1.1 8.1
2	TH	0557 1109 1827 2338	1.1 8.3 0.8 8.2
3	F	0650 1156 1918	1.0 8.4 0.7
4	SA	0026 0740 1244 2006	8.3 1.0 8.4 0.7
5	SU	0113 0826 1330 2050	8.2 1.1 8.2 1.0
6	M	0200 0910 1417 2132	8.0 1.4 7.9 1.4
7	TU	0248 0953 1505 2214	7.7 1.9 7.5 1.9
8	W ☽	0338 1038 1559 2300	7.3 2.3 7.1 2.4
9	TH	0436 1131 1705 2356	7.0 2.7 6.8 2.8
10	F	0545 1236 1820	6.8 2.9 6.7
11	SA	0104 0658 1349 1937	2.9 6.8 2.9 6.7
12	SU	0217 0807 1458 2042	2.9 6.9 2.6 6.9
13	M	0322 0901 1557 2131	2.6 7.1 2.3 7.2
14	TU	0416 0944 1644 2211	2.3 7.4 2.0 7.4
15	W	0500 1020 1726 2245	2.1 7.5 1.8 7.5
16	TH O	0540 1053 1804 2318	1.9 7.7 1.6 7.6
17	F	0617 1125 1839 2350	1.8 7.7 1.5 7.6
18	SA	0651 1157 1911	1.7 7.8 1.5
19	SU	0022 0723 1229 1942	7.6 1.7 7.8 1.6
20	M	0055 0754 1302 2012	7.6 1.8 7.7 1.7
21	TU	0128 0826 1337 2043	7.5 1.9 7.5 1.9
22	W	0204 0858 1414 2116	7.4 2.1 7.3 2.1
23	TH	0243 0935 1456 2154	7.1 2.4 7.0 2.4
24	F ☾	0327 1019 1547 2242	6.9 2.7 6.8 2.7
25	SA	0425 1114 1655 2345	6.8 2.8 6.7 2.9
26	SU	0542 1226 1821	6.7 2.9 6.7
27	M	0112 0705 1402 1946	2.8 6.9 2.6 7.0
28	TU	0241 0817 1517 2052	2.4 7.3 2.0 7.4
29	W	0347 0916 1620 2147	1.9 7.7 1.5 7.8
30	TH ●	0449 1007 1722 2237	1.4 8.1 1.0 8.1
31	F	0550 1055 1819 2324	1.0 8.3 0.7 8.3

FEBRUARY

Date	Day	Time	m
1	SA	0643 1142 1909	0.8 8.4 0.5
2	SU	0010 0730 1227 1954	8.3 0.7 8.4 0.5
3	M	0055 0812 1312 2033	8.3 0.8 8.3 0.7
4	TU	0138 0850 1354 2109	8.1 1.1 8.0 1.2
5	W	0220 0926 1436 2143	7.8 1.6 7.6 1.8
6	TH ☽	0301 1002 1521 2219	7.4 2.1 7.1 2.4
7	F	0348 1045 1618 2306	7.0 2.7 6.7 2.9
8	SA	0451 1143 1737	6.6 3.1 6.4
9	SU	0013 0613 1301 1907	3.3 6.5 3.2 6.4
10	M	0136 0739 1424 2024	3.3 6.5 3.0 6.6
11	TU	0254 0843 1532 2115	3.0 6.8 2.6 6.9
12	W	0355 0927 1625 2153	2.5 7.1 2.1 7.2
13	TH	0443 1002 1708 2226	2.1 7.4 1.8 7.5
14	F	0524 1034 1746 2257	1.8 7.6 1.5 7.6
15	SA O	0600 1105 1821 2328	1.6 7.7 1.4 7.7
16	SU	0633 1137 1852	1.5 7.8 1.3
17	M	0000 0704 1210 1922	7.7 1.5 7.8 1.3
18	TU	0033 0734 1243 1952	7.8 1.4 7.8 1.4
19	W	0106 0806 1318 2024	7.7 1.5 7.7 1.6
20	TH	0141 0839 1355 2056	7.6 1.7 7.5 1.9
21	F	0217 0913 1434 2131	7.3 2.0 7.2 2.2
22	SA ☾	0258 0953 1521 2214	7.0 2.4 6.9 2.6
23	SU	0351 1043 1627 2314	6.8 2.7 6.6 2.9
24	M	0509 1154 1759	6.6 2.9 6.6
25	TU	0045 0643 1339 1932	2.9 6.8 2.6 6.9
26	W	0221 0802 1458 2040	2.5 7.2 2.1 7.3
27	TH	0332 0901 1606 2134	1.9 7.6 1.5 7.8
28	F	0438 0952 1711 2222	1.4 8.0 1.0 8.0

MARCH

Date	Day	Time	m
1	SA ●	0539 1039 1806 2307	1.0 8.2 0.6 8.2
2	SU	0629 1124 1852 2350	0.7 8.3 0.4 8.3
3	M	0712 1207 1933	0.6 8.4 0.5
4	TU	0032 0750 1249 2009	8.2 0.7 8.2 0.8
5	W	0112 0825 1329 2041	8.1 1.0 8.0 1.2
6	TH	0149 0857 1407 2111	7.8 1.5 7.6 1.8
7	F	0226 0928 1447 2141	7.4 2.1 7.1 2.4
8	SA ☽	0305 1003 1536 2222	7.0 2.6 6.6 3.0
9	SU	0359 1055 1652 2325	6.5 3.1 6.3 3.4
10	M	0523 1210 1825	6.2 3.4 6.2
11	TU	0048 0654 1339 1952	3.5 6.3 3.2 6.4
12	W	0218 0811 1457 2047	3.2 6.5 2.8 6.8
13	TH	0325 0859 1554 2125	2.7 6.9 2.3 7.1
14	F	0415 0935 1640 2158	2.2 7.2 1.9 7.4
15	SA	0458 1008 1720 2230	1.9 7.5 1.6 7.6
16	SU O	0535 1041 1755 2302	1.6 7.7 1.4 7.7
17	M	0609 1114 1827 2335	1.4 7.8 1.3 7.8
18	TU	0640 1148 1858	1.3 7.8 1.2
19	W	0009 0712 1223 1930	7.9 1.2 7.9 1.2
20	TH	0043 0746 1259 2003	7.8 1.3 7.8 1.4
21	F	0119 0820 1338 2037	7.7 1.5 7.6 1.7
22	SA	0157 0855 1419 2112	7.5 1.8 7.3 2.1
23	SU	0239 0934 1508 2156	7.2 2.2 7.0 2.5
24	M ☾	0333 1023 1614 2256	6.9 2.5 6.7 2.9
25	TU	0450 1136 1748	6.7 2.8 6.6
26	W	0033 0627 1322 1918	2.9 6.8 2.6 6.9
27	TH	0204 0744 1440 2023	2.5 7.1 2.1 7.3
28	F	0315 0843 1550 2115	1.9 7.5 1.5 7.7
29	SA	0423 0933 1654 2202	1.4 7.8 1.1 7.9
30	SU ●	0520 1019 1746 2245	1.1 8.0 0.8 8.1
31	M	0608 1103 1829 2327	0.8 8.1 0.7 8.1

APRIL

Date	Day	Time	m
1	TU	0648 1145 1907	0.8 8.1 0.8
2	W	0006 0724 1225 1940	8.1 0.9 8.0 1.0
3	TH	0044 0757 1303 2011	7.9 1.1 7.8 1.4
4	F	0119 0827 1340 2040	7.7 1.5 7.5 1.9
5	SA	0154 0857 1418 2110	7.4 2.0 7.1 2.4
6	SU	0229 0929 1501 2147	7.0 2.5 6.7 2.9
7	M ☽	0314 1014 1605 2244	6.6 3.0 6.3 3.4
8	TU	0427 1122 1734 2359	6.2 3.3 6.2 3.6
9	W	0558 1242 1854	6.1 3.3 6.3
10	TH	0123 0714 1404 1959	3.4 6.3 3.0 6.6
11	F	0237 0813 1508 2044	2.9 6.7 2.5 7.0
12	SA	0333 0857 1559 2122	2.4 7.0 2.1 7.3
13	SU	0420 0935 1643 2157	2.0 7.3 1.8 7.6
14	M	0501 1011 1721 2232	1.7 7.6 1.5 7.7
15	TU O	0538 1048 1757 2308	1.5 7.7 1.3 7.8
16	W	0614 1124 1832 2344	1.3 7.8 1.2 7.9
17	TH	0650 1202 1908	1.2 7.9 1.2
18	F	0021 0727 1242 1945	7.9 1.2 7.8 1.4
19	SA	0101 0804 1324 2021	7.8 1.3 7.7 1.6
20	SU	0142 0841 1410 2059	7.6 1.6 7.4 2.0
21	M	0228 0921 1501 2145	7.3 2.0 7.1 2.4
22	TU ☾	0323 1013 1607 2249	7.0 2.3 6.9 2.7
23	W	0438 1129 1735	6.8 2.6 6.8
24	TH	0023 0606 1303 1856	2.8 6.8 2.4 7.0
25	F	0144 0720 1417 2000	2.4 7.1 2.1 7.3
26	SA	0253 0820 1525 2053	2.0 7.4 1.7 7.6
27	SU	0359 0912 1627 2139	1.6 7.6 1.4 7.8
28	M	0455 0958 1719 2222	1.3 7.8 1.2 7.9
29	TU ●	0542 1041 1801 2302	1.2 7.8 1.2 7.9
30	W	0621 1122 1837 2340	1.1 7.9 1.2 7.9

MAY

Date	Day	Time	m
1	TH	0656 1202 1911	1.2 7.8 1.4
2	F	0016 0729 1239 1943	7.8 1.3 7.6 1.6
3	SA	0051 0801 1316 2014	7.6 1.6 7.4 2.0
4	SU	0126 0831 1353 2045	7.4 2.0 7.1 2.4
5	M	0201 0903 1432 2119	7.1 2.4 6.8 2.8
6	TU	0239 0941 1521 2207	6.8 2.8 6.5 3.2
7	W ☽	0331 1037 1635 2310	6.4 3.1 6.3 3.4
8	TH	0452 1144 1752	6.2 3.2 6.3
9	F	0021 0611 1255 1856	3.3 6.3 3.1 6.5
10	SA	0132 0714 1405 1952	3.1 6.5 2.8 6.9
11	SU	0236 0808 1505 2039	2.6 6.8 2.4 7.2
12	M	0331 0855 1556 2121	2.2 7.2 2.0 7.5
13	TU	0419 0938 1642 2201	1.9 7.4 1.7 7.7
14	W O	0504 1020 1725 2240	1.6 7.6 1.5 7.8
15	TH	0547 1101 1807 2320	1.3 7.8 1.3 7.9
16	F	0629 1144 1849	1.1 7.9 1.3
17	SA	0002 0711 1228 1930	8.0 1.1 7.9 1.3
18	SU	0046 0752 1314 2012	7.9 1.2 7.8 1.5
19	M	0132 0834 1402 2054	7.8 1.4 7.6 1.8
20	TU	0220 0918 1454 2144	7.6 1.7 7.3 2.2
21	W ☾	0315 1011 1557 2248	7.3 2.0 7.1 2.4
22	TH	0421 1122 1712	7.0 2.3 7.0
23	F	0005 0538 1238 1826	2.5 7.0 2.3 7.1
24	SA	0116 0650 1347 1930	2.4 7.0 2.2 7.2
25	SU	0222 0753 1452 2026	2.2 7.2 2.0 7.4
26	M	0327 0849 1554 2115	1.9 7.4 1.8 7.5
27	TU	0425 0938 1647 2159	1.7 7.5 1.7 7.6
28	W ●	0513 1022 1730 2239	1.6 7.6 1.7 7.7
29	TH	0553 1103 1808 2317	1.5 7.6 1.6 7.7
30	F	0630 1141 1844 2352	1.5 7.6 1.7 7.7
31	SA	0704 1218 1918	1.5 7.5 1.8

JUNE

Date	Day	Time	m
1	SU	0027 0738 1254 1952	7.6 1.7 7.4 2.0
2	M	0101 0810 1330 2023	7.4 1.9 7.2 2.3
3	TU	0135 0841 1406 2057	7.2 2.2 7.0 2.5
4	W	0211 0915 1445 2134	7.0 2.5 6.8 2.8
5	TH ☽	0252 0955 1533 2223	6.8 2.7 6.6 3.0
6	F	0345 1048 1638 2321	6.5 2.9 6.5 3.1
7	SA	0455 1149 1749	6.4 3.0 6.6
8	SU	0024 0608 1255 1852	3.1 6.5 2.9 6.8
9	M	0132 0713 1404 1950	2.8 6.7 2.6 7.0
10	TU	0239 0812 1509 2042	2.4 7.0 2.3 7.3
11	W	0338 0905 1605 2130	2.0 7.3 1.9 7.6
12	TH	0431 0954 1656 2215	1.7 7.5 1.6 7.8
13	F O	0522 1042 1746 2301	1.4 7.8 1.4 8.0
14	SA	0611 1129 1834 2347	1.1 7.9 1.3 8.1
15	SU	0700 1216 1922	1.0 8.0 1.2
16	M	0034 0748 1304 2009	8.1 1.0 7.9 1.3
17	TU	0121 0834 1352 2056	8.0 1.1 7.8 1.5
18	W	0210 0921 1443 2145	7.8 1.4 7.6 1.8
19	TH ☾	0301 1010 1537 2238	7.5 1.7 7.3 2.1
20	F	0358 1104 1639 2338	7.2 2.1 7.1 2.4
21	SA	0504 1206 1748	7.0 2.3 7.0
22	SU	0043 0616 1311 1857	2.5 6.9 2.4 7.0
23	M	0148 0725 1416 1959	2.4 6.9 2.4 7.1
24	TU	0253 0828 1519 2053	2.3 7.1 2.3 7.3
25	W	0353 0921 1615 2140	2.1 7.2 2.2 7.4
26	TH	0445 1006 1702 2221	1.9 7.3 2.0 7.5
27	F ●	0528 1047 1743 2257	1.8 7.4 1.9 7.6
28	SA	0607 1123 1821 2331	1.7 7.5 1.8 7.6
29	SU	0644 1158 1858	1.6 7.5 1.8
30	M	0005 0718 1232 1931	7.6 1.6 7.4 1.9

LE HAVRE
LAT 49°29′N
LONG 0°07′E

TIMES AND HEIGHTS OF HIGH AND LOW WATER (Heights in Metres)

TIME ZONE –0100 (French Standard Time). **Subtract 1 hour for UT. For French Summer Time (area enclosed in shaded box) add 1 hour**

2014

JULY

Date	Day	Time	m	Time	m	Time	m	Time	m
1	TU	0039	7.6	0751	1.8	1306	7.4	2003	2.0
2	W	0112	7.5	0821	1.9	1340	7.3	2034	2.2
3	TH	0145	7.3	0851	2.1	1414	7.1	2106	2.4
4	F	0222	7.1	0923	2.4	1453	7.0	2144	2.6
5	SA ☽	0305	6.9	1003	2.6	1541	6.8	2230	2.8
6	SU	0358	6.7	1053	2.8	1640	6.7	2327	2.9
7	M	0504	6.6	1155	2.9	1750	6.7		
8	TU	0034	2.9	0618	6.6	1309	2.8	1900	6.9
9	W	0153	2.6	0730	6.8	1429	2.5	2006	7.2
10	TH	0305	2.2	0837	7.2	1535	2.1	2104	7.5
11	F	0405	1.7	0934	7.5	1633	1.7	2156	7.8
12	SA O	0502	1.3	1025	7.8	1729	1.4	2245	8.1
13	SU	0558	1.0	1114	8.0	1824	1.2	2333	8.2
14	M	0652	0.8	1202	8.1	1916	1.0		
15	TU	0020	8.3	0742	0.7	1250	8.1	2004	1.0
16	W	0107	8.2	0828	0.8	1337	8.0	2049	1.2
17	TH	0153	8.0	0911	1.1	1423	7.8	2132	1.5
18	F	0240	7.7	0953	1.5	1510	7.5	2215	1.9
19	SA ☾	0329	7.4	1036	2.0	1602	7.2	2305	2.3
20	SU	0427	7.0	1128	2.5	1705	6.9		
21	M	0005	2.6	0539	6.7	1232	2.8	1819	6.8
22	TU	0113	2.8	0658	6.7	1342	2.8	1932	6.9
23	W	0221	2.6	0810	6.8	1449	2.7	2035	7.0
24	TH	0325	2.4	0908	7.0	1549	2.5	2124	7.2
25	F	0422	2.1	0953	7.2	1641	2.2	2204	7.4
26	SA ●	0508	1.9	1031	7.4	1724	2.0	2239	7.6
27	SU	0548	1.7	1104	7.5	1803	1.9	2311	7.7
28	M	0625	1.6	1136	7.5	1838	1.8	2343	7.7
29	TU	0658	1.6	1209	7.6	1911	1.8		
30	W	0016	7.7	0729	1.6	1241	7.5	1941	1.8
31	TH	0048	7.7	0758	1.7	1313	7.5	2011	1.9

AUGUST

Date	Day	Time	m	Time	m	Time	m	Time	m
1	F	0121	7.5	0827	1.9	1346	7.4	2042	2.1
2	SA	0156	7.3	0857	2.1	1422	7.2	2115	2.3
3	SU	0235	7.1	0931	2.4	1503	7.0	2154	2.6
4	M ☽	0321	6.9	1014	2.7	1554	6.8	2244	2.8
5	TU	0420	6.7	1110	2.9	1701	6.7	2348	2.9
6	W	0537	6.6	1224	3.0	1822	6.8		
7	TH	0115	2.8	0701	6.7	1401	2.7	1939	7.1
8	F	0241	2.3	0817	7.1	1513	2.2	2045	7.5
9	SA	0345	1.7	0918	7.6	1615	1.7	2139	7.9
10	SU O	0446	1.3	1010	7.9	1716	1.3	2229	8.2
11	M	0546	0.9	1058	8.1	1814	1.0	2316	8.4
12	TU	0641	0.6	1145	8.3	1905	0.8		
13	W	0002	8.4	0729	0.6	1231	8.3	1949	0.8
14	TH	0048	8.4	0812	0.7	1315	8.2	2030	1.0
15	F	0132	8.2	0850	1.0	1358	7.9	2109	1.4
16	SA	0215	7.8	0926	1.5	1440	7.6	2146	1.9
17	SU ☾	0259	7.4	1002	2.1	1524	7.2	2227	2.4
18	M	0351	6.9	1046	2.7	1621	6.8	2323	2.9
19	TU	0502	6.5	1149	3.1	1739	6.6		
20	W	0035	3.1	0629	6.4	1307	3.2	1904	6.6
21	TH	0152	3.0	0753	6.6	1423	3.0	2016	6.8
22	F	0301	2.6	0852	6.9	1528	2.7	2107	7.1
23	SA	0400	2.3	0935	7.2	1621	2.3	2145	7.4
24	SU	0447	1.9	1010	7.4	1704	2.0	2218	7.6
25	M ●	0527	1.7	1041	7.6	1742	1.8	2248	7.7
26	TU	0603	1.6	1111	7.7	1817	1.7	2320	7.8
27	W	0635	1.5	1143	7.7	1847	1.6	2352	7.8
28	TH	0704	1.5	1214	7.7	1917	1.6		
29	F	0024	7.8	0733	1.5	1246	7.7	1947	1.7
30	SA	0057	7.7	0803	1.7	1320	7.6	2019	1.8
31	SU	0133	7.5	0834	1.9	1355	7.4	2052	2.1

SEPTEMBER

Date	Day	Time	m	Time	m	Time	m	Time	m
1	M	0211	7.2	0907	2.3	1434	7.1	2128	2.4
2	TU ☽	0255	7.0	0947	2.6	1522	6.9	2214	2.7
3	W	0353	6.7	1039	2.9	1629	6.7	2316	2.9
4	TH	0513	6.6	1154	3.1	1756	6.7		
5	F	0050	2.9	0646	6.8	1342	2.8	1922	7.1
6	SA	0222	2.3	0804	7.2	1456	2.2	2029	7.5
7	SU	0328	1.7	0902	7.7	1559	1.6	2123	7.9
8	M	0430	1.2	0953	8.0	1701	1.2	2211	8.2
9	TU O	0531	0.8	1039	8.2	1757	0.9	2257	8.4
10	W	0623	0.6	1124	8.3	1845	0.7	2342	8.5
11	TH	0708	0.6	1208	8.3	1928	0.8		
12	F	0025	8.4	0748	0.8	1250	8.2	2006	1.0
13	SA	0108	8.1	0823	1.2	1330	7.9	2041	1.4
14	SU	0148	7.8	0856	1.7	1408	7.6	2114	2.0
15	M	0230	7.4	0927	2.3	1448	7.2	2150	2.5
16	TU ☾	0317	6.9	1006	2.9	1539	6.8	2240	3.0
17	W	0425	6.5	1106	3.4	1657	6.4	2352	3.3
18	TH	0555	6.3	1228	3.5	1826	6.4		
19	F	0116	3.2	0722	6.5	1352	3.3	1946	6.6
20	SA	0231	2.9	0826	6.8	1500	2.8	2040	7.0
21	SU	0330	2.4	0908	7.2	1553	2.4	2118	7.3
22	M	0417	2.0	0941	7.5	1637	2.0	2151	7.6
23	TU	0458	1.7	1012	7.6	1716	1.8	2222	7.8
24	W ●	0535	1.6	1043	7.8	1750	1.6	2255	7.9
25	TH	0607	1.5	1115	7.8	1821	1.5	2327	7.9
26	F	0637	1.4	1147	7.8	1852	1.5		
27	SA	0000	7.9	0708	1.5	1220	7.8	1924	1.5
28	SU	0036	7.8	0741	1.6	1255	7.7	1958	1.7
29	M	0113	7.6	0814	1.9	1333	7.5	2033	1.9
30	TU	0154	7.4	0848	2.2	1414	7.3	2110	2.3

OCTOBER

Date	Day	Time	m	Time	m	Time	m	Time	m
1	W ☽	0240	7.1	0928	2.6	1503	7.0	2154	2.6
2	TH	0339	6.8	1021	2.9	1611	6.8	2255	2.9
3	F	0500	6.7	1138	3.1	1740	6.8		
4	SA	0034	2.8	0634	6.9	1327	2.8	1906	7.1
5	SU	0205	2.3	0747	7.3	1439	2.2	2010	7.5
6	M	0310	1.7	0844	7.7	1542	1.6	2104	7.9
7	TU	0412	1.3	0933	8.1	1643	1.2	2152	8.2
8	W O	0510	1.0	1018	8.2	1736	1.0	2237	8.3
9	TH	0600	0.8	1101	8.3	1823	0.9	2320	8.3
10	F	0642	0.9	1143	8.3	1903	0.9		
11	SA	0003	8.3	0720	1.1	1223	8.1	1939	1.2
12	SU	0044	8.0	0755	1.4	1301	7.9	2013	1.5
13	M	0123	7.7	0826	1.9	1339	7.6	2045	2.0
14	TU	0203	7.3	0857	2.4	1416	7.2	2118	2.5
15	W ☾	0247	6.9	0933	2.9	1502	6.8	2202	3.0
16	TH	0348	6.5	1027	3.4	1611	6.4	2307	3.4
17	F	0512	6.3	1142	3.6	1738	6.3		
18	SA	0025	3.4	0630	6.4	1305	3.5	1854	6.5
19	SU	0145	3.1	0738	6.7	1419	3.0	1956	6.8
20	M	0249	2.6	0827	7.1	1515	2.6	2041	7.1
21	TU	0340	2.2	0905	7.4	1602	2.2	2118	7.4
22	W	0423	1.9	0939	7.6	1643	1.9	2154	7.7
23	TH ●	0501	1.7	1013	7.8	1719	1.7	2229	7.8
24	F	0537	1.6	1047	7.9	1754	1.5	2304	7.9
25	SA	0610	1.5	1122	7.9	1828	1.4	2340	7.9
26	SU	0645	1.5	1157	7.9	1904	1.4		
27	M	0017	7.9	0721	1.6	1235	7.9	1941	1.5
28	TU	0058	7.7	0758	1.8	1316	7.7	2018	1.8
29	W	0143	7.5	0835	2.1	1401	7.5	2057	2.1
30	TH	0232	7.3	0917	2.5	1453	7.2	2142	2.4
31	F ☽	0331	7.0	1010	2.8	1559	7.0	2244	2.7

NOVEMBER

Date	Day	Time	m	Time	m	Time	m	Time	m
1	SA	0449	6.9	1130	3.0	1722	6.9		
2	SU	0019	2.7	0615	7.0	1307	2.7	1843	7.1
3	M	0142	2.3	0725	7.4	1418	2.2	1948	7.5
4	TU	0248	1.8	0822	7.7	1521	1.8	2043	7.8
5	W	0349	1.5	0911	8.0	1620	1.4	2132	8.0
6	TH O	0445	1.3	0956	8.1	1713	1.2	2217	8.1
7	F	0534	1.2	1039	8.1	1758	1.1	2301	8.1
8	SA	0615	1.2	1120	8.1	1837	1.2	2342	8.1
9	SU	0653	1.4	1158	8.0	1914	1.3		
10	M	0022	7.9	0727	1.6	1236	7.8	1947	1.6
11	TU	0101	7.7	0800	2.0	1312	7.6	2021	2.0
12	W	0139	7.4	0833	2.4	1349	7.3	2054	2.4
13	TH	0220	7.0	0908	2.8	1429	7.0	2132	2.8
14	F ☾	0309	6.7	0953	3.2	1520	6.6	2223	3.2
15	SA	0419	6.5	1053	3.5	1639	6.4	2326	3.3
16	SU	0533	6.5	1201	3.5	1755	6.4		
17	M	0037	3.3	0638	6.6	1315	3.3	1859	6.6
18	TU	0150	3.0	0735	6.9	1424	2.9	1955	6.9
19	W	0252	2.6	0822	7.2	1519	2.4	2041	7.2
20	TH	0342	2.2	0904	7.5	1605	2.1	2123	7.5
21	F	0425	1.9	0943	7.7	1647	1.8	2203	7.7
22	SA ●	0506	1.7	1021	7.9	1727	1.5	2242	7.8
23	SU	0546	1.5	1059	8.0	1808	1.4	2322	7.9
24	M	0626	1.5	1139	8.0	1848	1.3		
25	TU	0004	7.9	0707	1.5	1221	8.0	1929	1.3
26	W	0048	7.9	0747	1.6	1305	7.9	2010	1.5
27	TH	0135	7.7	0828	1.9	1353	7.7	2051	1.8
28	F	0225	7.5	0913	2.2	1444	7.5	2138	2.1
29	SA ☽	0321	7.3	1006	2.5	1545	7.2	2237	2.3
30	SU	0430	7.1	1118	2.7	1658	7.1	2356	2.5

DECEMBER

Date	Day	Time	m	Time	m	Time	m	Time	m
1	M	0547	7.1	1239	2.6	1815	7.1		
2	TU	0113	2.4	0657	7.3	1351	2.3	1923	7.3
3	W	0221	2.1	0757	7.5	1456	2.0	2022	7.5
4	TH	0323	1.9	0850	7.7	1557	1.8	2114	7.7
5	F	0420	1.7	0937	7.8	1650	1.6	2201	7.8
6	SA O	0509	1.6	1020	7.9	1735	1.4	2245	7.9
7	SU	0551	1.6	1100	7.9	1815	1.4	2325	7.9
8	M	0629	1.6	1138	7.9	1852	1.4		
9	TU	0004	7.8	0705	1.7	1214	7.8	1927	1.6
10	W	0041	7.7	0740	1.9	1249	7.7	2001	1.8
11	TH	0118	7.5	0813	2.2	1325	7.5	2034	2.1
12	F	0154	7.2	0847	2.5	1400	7.2	2107	2.5
13	SA	0233	7.0	0923	2.8	1438	6.9	2144	2.8
14	SU ☾	0318	6.7	1006	3.1	1527	6.6	2231	3.0
15	M	0421	6.6	1059	3.3	1637	6.5	2328	3.2
16	TU	0532	6.6	1200	3.3	1754	6.5		
17	W	0032	3.2	0636	6.7	1309	3.1	1900	6.6
18	TH	0144	2.9	0735	7.0	1424	2.8	2000	6.9
19	F	0254	2.6	0827	7.3	1525	2.3	2052	7.2
20	SA	0349	2.2	0914	7.6	1617	1.9	2139	7.5
21	SU	0438	1.8	0958	7.8	1704	1.6	2224	7.8
22	M ●	0525	1.6	1041	8.0	1751	1.3	2308	8.0
23	TU	0612	1.4	1125	8.1	1838	1.1	2353	8.1
24	W	0658	1.3	1210	8.2	1923	1.0		
25	TH	0039	8.1	0744	1.3	1256	8.1	2008	1.1
26	F	0126	8.0	0828	1.5	1344	8.0	2052	1.3
27	SA	0214	7.8	0913	1.7	1432	7.8	2137	1.6
28	SU ☽	0305	7.5	1001	2.1	1525	7.5	2226	2.0
29	M	0403	7.3	1057	2.4	1627	7.2	2326	2.3
30	TU	0511	7.1	1205	2.6	1741	7.0		
31	W	0037	2.5	0624	7.1	1318	2.6	1856	7.0

CHERBOURG
LAT 49°39′N
LONG 1°38′W

TIMES AND HEIGHTS OF HIGH AND LOW WATER (Heights in Metres)

TIME ZONE –0100 (French Standard Time). **Subtract 1 hour for UT. For French Summer Time (area enclosed in shaded box) add 1 hour**

2014

SUNRISE AND SUNSET TIMES

CHERBOURG
At 49°39′N 1°38′W

		Sunrise	Sunset
European Standard Time (UT-1)			
Jan	01	0903	1717
	15	0858	1735
Feb	01	0839	1802
	15	0816	1826
Mar	01	0749	1849
	15	0720	1912
European Summer Time (UT-2)			
Apr	01	0744	2038
	15	0714	2100
May	01	0644	2124
	15	0622	2145
Jun	01	0604	2205
	15	0559	2216
Jul	01	0603	2217
	15	0616	2209
Aug	01	0637	2148
	15	0657	2124
Sep	01	0722	2050
	15	0743	2020
Oct	01	0806	1945
	15	0828	1916
European Standard Time (UT-1)			
Nov	01	0755	1744
	15	0818	1724
Dec	01	0842	1709

JANUARY

Date	Day		Time	m	Time	m	Time	m	Time	m
1	W	●	0249	1.3	0825	6.5	1517	0.9	2054	6.5
2	TH		0341	1.0	0914	6.8	1607	0.7	2143	6.6
3	F		0430	0.9	1001	6.8	1655	0.6	2230	6.6
4	SA		0517	0.9	1048	6.8	1742	0.7	2317	6.5
5	SU		0604	1.1	1134	6.6	1827	0.9		
6	M		0003	6.2	0649	1.4	1222	6.3	1912	1.3
7	TU		0050	5.9	0736	1.7	1310	5.9	1959	1.7
8	W	☽	0141	5.6	0828	2.1	1405	5.5	2053	2.1
9	TH		0239	5.3	0931	2.4	1508	5.2	2158	2.4
10	F		0345	5.1	1046	2.6	1619	5.1	2314	2.5
11	SA		0456	5.2	1201	2.5	1730	5.1		
12	SU		0024	2.5	0600	5.3	1303	2.3	1833	5.3
13	M		0122	2.3	0656	5.5	1354	2.0	1926	5.5
14	TU		0209	2.1	0743	5.7	1436	1.8	2010	5.7
15	W		0250	1.9	0823	5.9	1514	1.6	2048	5.9
16	TH	○	0326	1.7	0900	6.1	1549	1.5	2123	6.0
17	F		0401	1.6	0933	6.1	1623	1.4	2155	6.0
18	SA		0434	1.6	1005	6.2	1655	1.4	2227	6.0
19	SU		0506	1.6	1037	6.2	1726	1.4	2258	6.0
20	M		0538	1.6	1108	6.1	1757	1.5	2329	5.8
21	TU		0610	1.8	1139	5.9	1830	1.7		
22	W		0000	5.7	0645	1.9	1210	5.7	1905	1.9
23	TH		0033	5.5	0726	2.1	1246	5.5	1948	2.1
24	F	☾	0114	5.3	0815	2.3	1333	5.2	2041	2.3
25	SA		0211	5.1	0917	2.5	1443	5.0	2150	2.5
26	SU		0335	5.0	1036	2.5	1618	5.0	2314	2.4
27	M		0508	5.2	1158	2.2	1747	5.3		
28	TU		0032	2.1	0620	5.6	1309	1.8	1854	5.7
29	W		0139	1.7	0719	6.1	1410	1.3	1951	6.1
30	TH	●	0237	1.3	0812	6.5	1505	0.9	2042	6.5
31	F		0329	1.0	0902	6.8	1555	0.6	2131	6.6

FEBRUARY

Date	Day		Time	m	Time	m	Time	m	Time	m
1	SA		0418	0.8	0949	6.9	1642	0.4	2217	6.7
2	SU		0503	0.7	1034	6.9	1725	0.5	2300	6.6
3	M		0546	0.8	1118	6.7	1807	0.7	2341	6.4
4	TU		0627	1.1	1159	6.4	1847	1.1		
5	W		0021	6.1	0707	1.5	1241	6.0	1926	1.6
6	TH	☽	0102	5.7	0750	2.0	1326	5.5	2008	2.1
7	F		0148	5.3	0840	2.4	1420	5.1	2102	2.6
8	SA		0248	5.0	0949	2.7	1531	4.8	2219	2.8
9	SU		0406	4.8	1117	2.8	1654	4.8	2347	2.8
10	M		0526	4.9	1233	2.5	1810	4.9		
11	TU		0057	2.6	0632	5.2	1331	2.2	1907	5.2
12	W		0149	2.2	0724	5.5	1416	1.9	1951	5.5
13	TH		0232	1.9	0805	5.8	1455	1.6	2029	5.8
14	F		0309	1.7	0842	6.0	1530	1.4	2104	6.0
15	SA	○	0343	1.5	0915	6.2	1603	1.3	2135	6.1
16	SU		0415	1.4	0946	6.3	1634	1.2	2206	6.1
17	M		0446	1.3	1016	6.3	1704	1.2	2235	6.1
18	TU		0516	1.3	1046	6.2	1734	1.2	2305	6.1
19	W		0547	1.4	1115	6.1	1805	1.4	2333	5.9
20	TH		0621	1.6	1145	5.9	1839	1.6		
21	F		0003	5.7	0659	1.8	1218	5.6	1919	1.9
22	SA	☾	0040	5.5	0745	2.1	1302	5.3	2010	2.2
23	SU		0133	5.2	0845	2.3	1410	5.0	2117	2.5
24	M		0259	5.0	1004	2.4	1556	4.9	2247	2.5
25	TU		0445	5.1	1135	2.2	1734	5.2		
26	W		0014	2.2	0604	5.5	1253	1.8	1842	5.6
27	TH		0125	1.8	0704	6.0	1356	1.3	1937	6.1
28	F		0224	1.3	0757	6.4	1451	0.9	2027	6.4

MARCH

Date	Day		Time	m	Time	m	Time	m	Time	m
1	SA	●	0315	0.9	0847	6.7	1539	0.6	2114	6.6
2	SU		0401	0.7	0933	6.9	1623	0.4	2158	6.7
3	M		0444	0.6	1016	6.9	1704	0.5	2238	6.6
4	TU		0523	0.7	1057	6.7	1742	0.7	2315	6.4
5	W		0601	1.0	1135	6.4	1817	1.1	2350	6.1
6	TH		0637	1.4	1211	6.0	1852	1.6		
7	F		0025	5.8	0713	1.8	1250	5.5	1928	2.1
8	SA	☽	0103	5.4	0754	2.3	1335	5.1	2012	2.6
9	SU		0154	5.0	0852	2.7	1441	4.7	2121	2.9
10	M		0310	4.7	1021	2.9	1612	4.6	2301	3.0
11	TU		0443	4.7	1153	2.7	1739	4.8		
12	W		0023	2.7	0601	4.9	1258	2.4	1840	5.1
13	TH		0120	2.4	0656	5.3	1346	2.0	1924	5.5
14	F		0204	2.0	0739	5.6	1426	1.7	2002	5.8
15	SA		0242	1.7	0816	5.9	1502	1.4	2037	6.0
16	SU	○	0316	1.4	0850	6.1	1535	1.2	2109	6.2
17	M		0349	1.3	0922	6.3	1607	1.1	2140	6.3
18	TU		0421	1.2	0953	6.4	1639	1.1	2211	6.3
19	W		0454	1.1	1024	6.3	1711	1.1	2241	6.3
20	TH		0526	1.2	1056	6.2	1743	1.2	2312	6.1
21	F		0602	1.3	1128	6.0	1820	1.5	2344	5.9
22	SA		0642	1.5	1204	5.7	1902	1.8		
23	SU		0024	5.6	0728	1.8	1252	5.4	1953	2.2
24	M	☾	0119	5.3	0827	2.1	1403	5.0	2102	2.5
25	TU		0244	5.0	0946	2.3	1548	4.9	2231	2.5
26	W		0427	5.1	1117	2.2	1720	5.2	2359	2.2
27	TH		0546	5.5	1235	1.8	1825	5.6		
28	F		0109	1.8	0645	5.9	1339	1.3	1918	6.1
29	SA		0207	1.3	0738	6.3	1432	0.9	2007	6.4
30	SU	●	0257	1.0	0827	6.6	1519	0.7	2053	6.5
31	M		0341	0.8	0913	6.7	1600	0.6	2135	6.6

APRIL

Date	Day		Time	m	Time	m	Time	m	Time	m
1	TU		0421	0.7	0955	6.7	1639	0.7	2213	6.5
2	W		0459	0.8	1034	6.5	1714	0.9	2248	6.4
3	TH		0534	1.0	1109	6.3	1748	1.2	2320	6.1
4	F		0608	1.3	1144	5.9	1821	1.7	2353	5.8
5	SA		0643	1.8	1219	5.5	1855	2.1		
6	SU		0028	5.4	0720	2.2	1300	5.1	1936	2.6
7	M	☽	0111	5.0	0809	2.6	1356	4.8	2036	2.9
8	TU		0216	4.7	0925	2.8	1521	4.6	2206	3.0
9	W		0348	4.6	1057	2.7	1653	4.7	2334	2.8
10	TH		0514	4.8	1209	2.5	1759	5.0		
11	F		0036	2.5	0615	5.1	1303	2.1	1847	5.3
12	SA		0124	2.1	0701	5.5	1346	1.8	1927	5.7
13	SU		0205	1.8	0741	5.8	1425	1.5	2003	6.0
14	M		0243	1.5	0818	6.0	1502	1.3	2038	6.2
15	TU	○	0319	1.3	0854	6.2	1538	1.1	2112	6.3
16	W		0356	1.1	0929	6.3	1614	1.1	2146	6.4
17	TH		0432	1.0	1004	6.3	1650	1.1	2221	6.4
18	F		0510	1.0	1041	6.3	1727	1.2	2257	6.2
19	SA		0549	1.1	1120	6.1	1807	1.4	2336	6.0
20	SU		0632	1.4	1203	5.8	1853	1.7		
21	M		0021	5.7	0720	1.6	1255	5.4	1947	2.1
22	TU	☾	0119	5.4	0820	1.9	1405	5.2	2055	2.4
23	W		0237	5.2	0935	2.1	1537	5.1	2218	2.4
24	TH		0407	5.2	1058	2.0	1659	5.3	2340	2.2
25	F		0522	5.5	1213	1.8	1802	5.6		
26	SA		0048	1.8	0622	5.8	1316	1.4	1855	6.0
27	SU		0146	1.5	0716	6.1	1409	1.2	1943	6.2
28	M		0236	1.2	0806	6.3	1455	1.0	2029	6.4
29	TU	●	0319	1.0	0851	6.4	1536	1.0	2110	6.4
30	W		0359	1.0	0933	6.4	1613	1.0	2147	6.4

MAY

Date	Day		Time	m	Time	m	Time	m	Time	m
1	TH		0435	1.0	1011	6.3	1648	1.2	2221	6.3
2	F		0510	1.2	1046	6.1	1722	1.4	2254	6.1
3	SA		0544	1.4	1120	5.8	1755	1.7	2327	5.8
4	SU		0618	1.7	1155	5.5	1830	2.1		
5	M		0002	5.5	0655	2.0	1235	5.2	1910	2.4
6	TU		0043	5.2	0740	2.3	1323	4.9	2004	2.7
7	W	☽	0135	4.9	0840	2.6	1428	4.7	2114	2.9
8	TH		0245	4.7	0954	2.6	1549	4.7	2231	2.8
9	F		0407	4.8	1107	2.5	1702	4.9	2338	2.6
10	SA		0517	5.0	1207	2.2	1758	5.2		
11	SU		0033	2.3	0612	5.3	1257	2.0	1843	5.5
12	M		0121	1.9	0659	5.6	1343	1.7	1925	5.8
13	TU		0206	1.6	0743	5.9	1426	1.4	2005	6.1
14	W	○	0249	1.3	0825	6.1	1509	1.2	2045	6.3
15	TH		0332	1.1	0906	6.2	1551	1.1	2125	6.4
16	F		0414	1.0	0948	6.3	1633	1.1	2205	6.4
17	SA		0457	0.9	1031	6.3	1716	1.2	2247	6.4
18	SU		0541	1.0	1115	6.2	1801	1.3	2332	6.2
19	M		0627	1.1	1203	5.9	1849	1.6		
20	TU		0020	5.9	0717	1.4	1256	5.6	1943	1.9
21	W	☾	0116	5.6	0814	1.7	1359	5.4	2047	2.1
22	TH		0224	5.4	0920	1.9	1515	5.3	2200	2.3
23	F		0340	5.3	1034	2.0	1629	5.3	2315	2.2
24	SA		0452	5.4	1145	1.9	1733	5.5		
25	SU		0023	1.9	0554	5.6	1250	1.7	1827	5.8
26	M		0122	1.7	0651	5.8	1344	1.5	1918	6.0
27	TU		0213	1.5	0743	6.0	1431	1.4	2004	6.1
28	W	●	0258	1.3	0830	6.1	1512	1.4	2046	6.2
29	TH		0337	1.3	0912	6.1	1549	1.4	2124	6.2
30	F		0414	1.3	0950	6.0	1625	1.5	2159	6.1
31	SA		0449	1.3	1025	5.9	1700	1.6	[illegible]	[illegible]

JUNE

Date	Day		Time	m	Time	m	Time	m	Time	m
1	SU		0524	1.5	1100	5.8	1735	1.8	2307	5.8
2	M		0559	1.6	1135	5.6	1810	2.0	2342	5.6
3	TU		0635	1.9	1212	5.4	1849	2.2		
4	W		0020	5.4	0715	2.1	1253	5.2	1933	2.5
5	TH	☽	0103	5.2	0802	2.3	1341	5.0	2027	2.6
6	F		0153	5.0	0857	2.4	1439	4.9	2129	2.7
7	SA		0254	4.9	1001	2.5	1547	4.9	2235	2.6
8	SU		0404	4.9	1105	2.4	1655	5.1	2338	2.4
9	M		0513	5.1	1206	2.2	1754	5.4		
10	TU		0036	2.1	0614	5.3	1301	1.9	1846	5.7
11	W		0130	1.8	0708	5.7	1353	1.6	1934	6.0
12	TH		0221	1.4	0759	5.9	1443	1.4	2021	6.2
13	F	○	0310	1.1	0848	6.2	1532	1.2	2107	6.4
14	SA		0358	0.9	0935	6.3	1619	1.1	2152	6.5
15	SU		0446	0.8	1022	6.4	1707	1.1	2238	6.5
16	M		0533	0.8	1109	6.3	1754	1.2	2325	6.4
17	TU		0620	0.9	1156	6.1	1843	1.4		
18	W		0013	6.2	0708	1.1	1247	5.9	1933	1.6
19	TH	☾	0105	5.9	0800	1.4	1342	5.6	2029	1.9
20	F		0203	5.6	0858	1.8	1444	5.4	2133	2.2
21	SA		0309	5.4	1003	2.0	1552	5.3	2244	2.2
22	SU		0419	5.3	1113	2.1	1659	5.4	2354	2.2
23	M		0526	5.3	1220	2.0	1759	5.5		
24	TU		0057	2.0	0627	5.5	1319	1.9	1853	5.7
25	W		0152	1.8	0722	5.6	1408	1.8	1942	5.9
26	TH		0238	1.6	0811	5.7	1451	1.7	2025	6.0
27	F	●	0318	1.5	0854	5.8	1530	1.6	2104	6.0
28	SA		0355	1.5	0932	5.9	1606	1.6	2140	6.0
29	SU		0431	1.4	1007	5.9	1641	1.6	2214	6.0
30	M		0505	1.4	1041	5.8	1716	1.7	2248	5.9

CHERBOURG
LAT 49°39'N
LONG 1°38'W

TIMES AND HEIGHTS OF HIGH AND LOW WATER (Heights in Metres)

TIME ZONE –0100 (French Standard Time). **Subtract 1 hour for UT. For French Summer Time (area enclosed in shaded box) add 1 hour**

2014

JULY

Date	Time	m
1 TU	0539 1115 1750 2322	1.5 5.7 1.8 5.8
2 W	0613 1148 1825 2356	1.7 5.6 2.0 5.7
3 TH	0647 1223 1902	1.8 5.4 2.1
4 F	0031 0724 1300 1944	5.5 2.0 5.3 2.3
5 SA	0110 0808 1343 ☽ 2036	5.3 2.2 5.1 2.5
6 SU	0157 0902 1438 2137	5.1 2.4 5.0 2.6
7 M	0259 1006 1548 2246	4.9 2.4 5.0 2.5
8 TU	0415 1118 1705 2355	4.9 2.3 5.2 2.3
9 W	0533 1225 1812	5.2 2.1 5.5
10 TH	0058 0641 1326 1909	1.9 5.5 1.8 5.9
11 F	0157 0739 1422 2001	1.5 5.9 1.5 6.2
12 SA	0252 0832 1515 ○ 2051	1.1 6.2 1.2 6.5
13 SU	0344 0922 1606 2139	0.8 6.4 1.0 6.7
14 M	0433 1010 1655 2226	0.6 6.5 0.9 6.8
15 TU	0521 1057 1742 2313	0.6 6.5 0.9 6.7
16 W	0607 1142 1828 2359	0.7 6.4 1.1 6.4
17 TH	0652 1228 1914	0.9 6.1 1.4
18 F	0046 0737 1316 2003	6.1 1.3 5.8 1.8
19 SA	0137 0827 1409 ☾ 2100	5.7 1.7 5.5 2.1
20 SU	0235 0926 1511 2208	5.4 2.1 5.2 2.4
21 M	0343 1037 1621 2324	5.1 2.4 5.2 2.4
22 TU	0456 1150 1729	5.1 2.4 5.2
23 W	0033 0605 1255 1830	2.3 5.2 2.3 5.4
24 TH	0131 0705 1349 1922	2.0 5.4 2.1 5.6
25 F	0219 0754 1434 2007	1.8 5.6 1.9 5.8
26 SA	0300 0836 1513 ● 2046	1.7 5.7 1.7 6.0
27 SU	0337 0913 1548 2122	1.5 5.9 1.6 6.1
28 M	0412 0947 1622 2155	1.4 5.9 1.6 6.1
29 TU	0445 1019 1655 2227	1.4 6.0 1.6 6.1
30 W	0516 1050 1726 2258	1.4 5.9 1.6 6.0
31 TH	0546 1121 1757 2329	1.5 5.8 1.7 5.9

AUGUST

Date	Time	m
1 F	0617 1152 1830 2359	1.6 5.7 1.9 5.7
2 SA	0650 1223 1908	1.8 5.5 2.1
3 SU	0032 0728 1259 1952	5.5 2.0 5.3 2.3
4 M	0113 0815 1346 ☽ 2049	5.2 2.3 5.2 2.5
5 TU	0209 0918 1455 2202	5.0 2.5 5.0 2.5
6 W	0331 1038 1626 2322	4.9 2.5 5.1 2.4
7 TH	0506 1157 1747	5.1 2.3 5.4
8 F	0035 0623 1306 1850	2.0 5.4 1.9 5.9
9 SA	0138 0723 1405 1944	1.5 5.9 1.5 6.3
10 SU	0235 0816 1500 ○ 2035	1.1 6.3 1.1 6.6
11 M	0328 0906 1551 2123	0.7 6.5 0.8 6.9
12 TU	0417 0953 1638 2210	0.5 6.7 0.7 6.9
13 W	0503 1038 1723 2255	0.4 6.7 0.7 6.8
14 TH	0546 1121 1806 2339	0.6 6.5 0.9 6.6
15 F	0628 1203 1848	0.9 6.3 1.3
16 SA	0022 0708 1245 1932	6.2 1.3 5.9 1.7
17 SU	0107 0752 1331 ☾ 2021	5.8 1.9 5.5 2.2
18 M	0159 0844 1427 2127	5.3 2.3 5.2 2.5
19 TU	0305 0956 1539 2250	5.0 2.7 5.0 2.7
20 W	0426 1121 1659	4.8 2.7 5.0
21 TH	0007 0544 1233 1808	2.5 4.9 2.6 5.2
22 F	0109 0646 1329 1902	2.2 5.2 2.3 5.5
23 SA	0158 0734 1414 1947	2.0 5.5 2.0 5.8
24 SU	0238 0814 1452 2025	1.7 5.8 1.8 6.0
25 M	0314 0850 1526 ● 2100	1.5 6.0 1.6 6.1
26 TU	0347 0923 1559 2132	1.4 6.1 1.5 6.2
27 W	0419 0953 1630 2202	1.3 6.1 1.4 6.3
28 TH	0449 1023 1700 2232	1.3 6.1 1.4 6.2
29 F	0518 1052 1730 2301	1.3 6.1 1.5 6.1
30 SA	0548 1121 1802 2330	1.5 6.0 1.6 5.9
31 SU	0620 1150 1838	1.7 5.8 1.8

SEPTEMBER

Date	Time	m
1 M	0002 0657 1224 1921	5.7 1.9 5.5 2.1
2 TU	0041 0743 1310 ☽ 2016	5.4 2.2 5.3 2.4
3 W	0138 0845 1420 2130	5.1 2.5 5.0 2.5
4 TH	0308 1010 1602 2258	4.9 2.6 5.1 2.4
5 F	0454 1138 1730	5.1 2.4 5.4
6 SA	0016 0609 1250 1833	2.0 5.5 1.9 5.9
7 SU	0122 0707 1350 1927	1.5 6.0 1.5 6.4
8 M	0218 0758 1444 2017	1.0 6.4 1.1 6.7
9 TU	0309 0847 1532 ○ 2105	0.7 6.7 0.8 6.9
10 W	0356 0932 1618 2150	0.5 6.8 0.7 7.0
11 TH	0440 1015 1700 2234	0.5 6.8 0.7 6.9
12 F	0521 1056 1740 2315	0.6 6.6 0.9 6.6
13 SA	0600 1134 1820 2355	1.0 6.3 1.3 6.2
14 SU	0637 1212 1859	1.5 6.0 1.7
15 M	0036 0716 1253 1942	5.7 2.0 5.6 2.2
16 TU	0124 0801 1344 ☾ 2040	5.3 2.5 5.2 2.6
17 W	0227 0910 1456 2208	4.9 2.9 4.9 2.9
18 TH	0352 1046 1623 2336	4.7 3.0 4.8 2.7
19 F	0518 1205 1740	4.8 2.8 5.1
20 SA	0039 0620 1302 1836	2.4 5.2 2.4 5.4
21 SU	0128 0707 1346 1920	2.1 5.5 2.1 5.7
22 M	0209 0746 1424 1958	1.7 5.8 1.8 6.0
23 TU	0244 0821 1458 2033	1.5 6.0 1.5 6.2
24 W	0318 0854 1531 ● 2104	1.4 6.2 1.4 6.3
25 TH	0350 0924 1603 2135	1.3 6.3 1.3 6.4
26 F	0421 0954 1634 2205	1.2 6.3 1.3 6.3
27 SA	0451 1024 1706 2236	1.3 6.3 1.4 6.2
28 SU	0523 1055 1739 2308	1.4 6.2 1.5 6.0
29 M	0557 1126 1817 2343	1.6 6.0 1.7 5.8
30 TU	0637 1203 1902	1.9 5.7 2.0

OCTOBER

Date	Time	m
1 W	0026 0724 1252 ☽ 1957	5.5 2.2 5.4 2.3
2 TH	0127 0828 1406 2111	5.1 2.5 5.1 2.4
3 F	0301 0954 1546 2240	5.0 2.6 5.1 2.3
4 SA	0443 1123 1712 2359	5.2 2.4 5.5 2.0
5 SU	0554 1234 1815	5.6 2.0 5.9
6 M	0104 0648 1334 1907	1.5 6.1 1.5 6.4
7 TU	0200 0738 1426 1957	1.1 6.4 1.1 6.7
8 W	0249 0825 1513 ○ 2044	0.8 6.7 0.9 6.9
9 TH	0334 0909 1556 2129	0.7 6.8 0.7 6.9
10 F	0415 0950 1636 2211	0.7 6.8 0.8 6.8
11 SA	0454 1029 1715 2250	0.9 6.6 1.0 6.5
12 SU	0531 1105 1752 2328	1.2 6.4 1.3 6.1
13 M	0607 1141 1829	1.6 6.0 1.8
14 TU	0007 0643 1220 1908	5.7 2.1 5.6 2.2
15 W	0052 0725 1306 ☾ 1959	5.3 2.6 5.2 2.6
16 TH	0149 0826 1410 2115	4.9 3.0 4.9 2.9
17 F	0308 0958 1536 2248	4.7 3.1 4.8 2.8
18 SA	0436 1124 1658 2358	4.8 2.9 4.9 2.6
19 SU	0543 1224 1759	5.1 2.6 5.3
20 M	0049 0631 1311 1845	2.2 5.4 2.2 5.6
21 TU	0132 0711 1350 1925	1.9 5.8 1.9 5.9
22 W	0209 0748 1426 2001	1.6 6.0 1.6 6.1
23 TH	0245 0822 1501 ● 2035	1.5 6.2 1.4 6.3
24 F	0319 0854 1536 2109	1.3 6.4 1.3 6.4
25 SA	0354 0927 1611 2142	1.3 6.4 1.2 6.4
26 SU	0428 1001 1647 2218	1.3 6.4 1.3 6.3
27 M	0504 1036 1724 2255	1.4 6.3 1.3 6.2
28 TU	0542 1113 1805 2336	1.6 6.1 1.5 5.9
29 W	0625 1155 1852	1.9 5.9 1.8
30 TH	0024 0716 1248 1947	5.6 2.2 5.6 2.1
31 F	0127 0819 1359 ☽ 2057	5.3 2.4 5.3 2.2

NOVEMBER

Date	Time	m
1 SA	0252 0939 1528 2220	5.1 2.5 5.3 2.2
2 SU	0423 1103 1649 2338	5.3 2.4 5.5 2.0
3 M	0531 1215 1752	5.6 2.0 5.9
4 TU	0043 0626 1315 1846	1.6 6.0 1.6 6.2
5 W	0139 0715 1407 1937	1.3 6.3 1.3 6.5
6 TH	0228 0802 1453 ○ 2024	1.1 6.5 1.1 6.6
7 F	0312 0846 1535 2109	1.0 6.6 1.0 6.6
8 SA	0352 0926 1615 2149	1.0 6.6 1.0 6.5
9 SU	0430 1004 1652 2228	1.2 6.5 1.2 6.3
10 M	0506 1039 1728 2304	1.4 6.3 1.4 6.1
11 TU	0542 1115 1804 2342	1.8 6.0 1.7 5.7
12 W	0618 1152 1842	2.1 5.7 2.1
13 TH	0023 0658 1235 1926	5.4 2.5 5.4 2.4
14 F	0112 0749 1327 ☾ 2024	5.1 2.8 5.1 2.7
15 SA	0215 0858 1436 2140	4.9 3.0 4.9 2.8
16 SU	0333 1020 1555 2257	4.8 3.0 4.9 2.7
17 M	0447 1130 1705 2358	5.0 2.7 5.1 2.4
18 TU	0544 1224 1800	5.3 2.4 5.3
19 W	0047 0630 1310 1846	2.2 5.6 2.1 5.6
20 TH	0130 0711 1352 1927	1.9 5.9 1.8 5.9
21 F	0211 0749 1432 2007	1.6 6.1 1.5 6.1
22 SA	0251 0827 1512 ● 2045	1.5 6.3 1.3 6.3
23 SU	0331 0904 1552 2125	1.4 6.5 1.2 6.4
24 M	0411 0943 1633 2205	1.3 6.5 1.1 6.4
25 TU	0452 1023 1715 2247	1.3 6.5 1.2 6.3
26 W	0534 1105 1759 2332	1.5 6.3 1.3 6.1
27 TH	0620 1151 1846	1.7 6.1 1.5
28 F	0022 0711 1243 1939	5.8 1.9 5.8 1.7
29 SA	0121 0810 1346 ☽ 2042	5.5 2.2 5.6 2.0
30 SU	0233 0919 1502 2154	5.4 2.4 5.4 2.1

DECEMBER

Date	Time	m
1 M	0352 1037 1619 2310	5.4 2.3 5.5 2.0
2 TU	0502 1151 1726	5.6 2.1 5.7
3 W	0019 0601 1254 1824	1.9 5.8 1.8 5.9
4 TH	0118 0653 1349 1918	1.6 6.1 1.5 6.1
5 F	0209 0742 1436 2007	1.5 6.3 1.3 6.3
6 SA	0253 0826 1518 ○ 2051	1.4 6.4 1.2 6.3
7 SU	0333 0907 1557 2132	1.4 6.4 1.2 6.3
8 M	0410 0944 1633 2209	1.4 6.4 1.3 6.2
9 TU	0446 1019 1709 2245	1.6 6.2 1.4 6.0
10 W	0522 1054 1745 2320	1.8 6.1 1.6 5.8
11 TH	0558 1130 1821 2357	2.0 5.9 1.9 5.6
12 F	0635 1207 1859	2.2 5.6 2.1
13 SA	0037 0716 1249 1942	5.3 2.5 5.3 2.4
14 SU	0123 0806 1337 ☾ 2035	5.1 2.7 5.1 2.6
15 M	0219 0907 1437 2139	4.9 2.8 4.9 2.7
16 TU	0327 1017 1548 2248	4.9 2.8 4.9 2.6
17 W	0438 1125 1700 2352	5.0 2.6 5.0 2.4
18 TH	0540 1224 1801	5.3 2.4 5.3
19 F	0048 0632 1316 1854	2.2 5.6 2.0 5.6
20 SA	0138 0719 1404 1941	1.9 5.9 1.7 5.9
21 SU	0225 0803 1451 2027	1.6 6.2 1.4 6.2
22 M	0312 0847 1537 ● 2111	1.4 6.4 1.1 6.4
23 TU	0357 0930 1622 2155	1.2 6.6 0.9 6.5
24 W	0442 1013 1707 2240	1.2 6.7 0.9 6.4
25 TH	0528 1058 1752 2326	1.2 6.6 0.9 6.3
26 F	0614 1144 1838	1.3 6.4 1.1
27 SA	0013 0701 1233 1927	6.1 1.6 6.1 1.4
28 SU	0105 0753 1327 ☽ 2020	5.8 1.9 5.8 1.7
29 M	0204 0853 1431 2123	5.5 2.2 5.5 2.0
30 TU	0314 1004 1545 2236	5.4 2.3 5.4 2.2
31 W	0427 1121 1657 2351	5.4 2.3 5.4 2.2

ST PETER PORT

LAT 49°27′N
LONG 2°31′W

TIMES AND HEIGHTS OF HIGH AND LOW WATER (Heights in Metres)

TIME ZONE UT
For Summer Time (area enclosed in shaded box) add 1 hour

2014

JANUARY

Date	Time	m	Time	m	Time	m	Time	m
1 W ●	0004	1.6	0603	9.4	1233	1.2	1831	9.3
2 TH	0056	1.2	0653	9.8	1324	0.8	1920	9.6
3 F	0144	0.9	0741	10.0	1412	0.6	2008	9.7
4 SA	0231	0.9	0827	10.0	1458	0.7	2053	9.6
5 SU	0315	1.1	0912	9.7	1542	1.0	2136	9.2
6 M	0359	1.5	0956	9.3	1626	1.5	2220	8.7
7 TU	0443	2.1	1042	8.6	1711	2.1	2307	8.1
8 W ☽	0531	2.7	1133	8.0	1801	2.8		
9 TH	0000	7.6	0628	3.3	1234	7.4	1901	3.3
10 F	0108	7.2	0741	3.6	1351	7.1	2014	3.6
11 SA	0230	7.1	0904	3.6	1508	7.1	2130	3.5
12 SU	0339	7.3	1011	3.3	1610	7.4	2230	3.2
13 M	0432	7.7	1103	2.9	1659	7.7	2319	2.8
14 TU	0517	8.2	1147	2.5	1743	8.1		
15 W	0001	2.4	0557	8.5	1228	2.2	1822	8.4
16 TH O	0039	2.1	0635	8.8	1304	2.0	1859	8.6
17 F	0114	2.0	0710	8.9	1338	1.8	1934	8.7
18 SA	0147	1.9	0744	9.0	1410	1.8	2006	8.7
19 SU	0218	1.9	0816	8.9	1440	1.9	2037	8.6
20 M	0248	2.1	0846	8.7	1509	2.1	2106	8.4
21 TU	0318	2.3	0917	8.5	1538	2.3	2137	8.1
22 W	0350	2.6	0950	8.2	1611	2.6	2211	7.9
23 TH	0426	2.9	1030	7.9	1650	2.9	2254	7.6
24 F ☾	0512	3.2	1119	7.5	1741	3.2	2351	7.3
25 SA	0615	3.4	1225	7.3	1850	3.4		
26 SU	0107	7.2	0741	3.5	1349	7.2	2021	3.4
27 M	0237	7.4	0910	3.1	1516	7.5	2145	2.9
28 TU	0354	7.9	1024	2.5	1627	8.1	2254	2.3
29 W	0457	8.6	1126	1.8	1727	8.7	2352	1.6
30 TH ●	0552	9.3	1222	1.1	1821	9.3		
31 F	0045	1.0	0642	9.8	1312	0.6	1909	9.7

FEBRUARY

Date	Time	m	Time	m	Time	m	Time	m
1 SA	0133	0.6	0729	10.1	1359	0.3	1954	9.9
2 SU	0218	0.5	0813	10.2	1442	0.3	2036	9.9
3 M	0300	0.6	0855	10.0	1523	0.6	2116	9.5
4 TU	0339	1.0	0935	9.5	1602	1.1	2154	9.0
5 W	0417	1.6	1013	8.8	1639	1.9	2231	8.3
6 TH ☽	0455	2.4	1054	8.0	1719	2.7	2312	7.6
7 F	0539	3.1	1141	7.3	1807	3.4		
8 SA	0004	7.0	0639	3.7	1251	6.7	1912	3.9
9 SU	0128	6.7	0806	4.0	1430	6.6	2042	4.0
10 M	0305	6.8	0941	3.7	1546	6.9	2203	3.6
11 TU	0409	7.3	1041	3.2	1639	7.4	2257	3.1
12 W	0456	7.8	1126	2.7	1722	7.8	2340	2.6
13 TH	0537	8.3	1206	2.3	1801	8.3		
14 F O	0019	2.1	0615	8.7	1243	1.9	1838	8.6
15 SA	0055	1.8	0651	8.9	1318	1.6	1913	8.8
16 SU	0128	1.6	0725	9.1	1350	1.5	1946	8.9
17 M	0200	1.5	0757	9.1	1419	1.5	2016	8.9
18 TU	0230	1.6	0827	9.0	1448	1.7	2045	8.7
19 W	0259	1.8	0856	8.8	1516	1.9	2114	8.5
20 TH	0329	2.1	0928	8.5	1547	2.2	2146	8.2
21 F	0402	2.4	1005	8.1	1623	2.6	2226	7.9
22 SA ☾	0444	2.8	1051	7.7	1709	3.0	2318	7.5
23 SU	0542	3.2	1154	7.2	1815	3.4		
24 M	0031	7.1	0707	3.4	1321	7.0	1951	3.5
25 TU	0210	7.2	0850	3.2	1500	7.3	2129	3.1
26 W	0338	7.7	1011	2.5	1616	7.9	2242	2.4
27 TH	0444	8.5	1113	1.7	1715	8.6	2339	1.6
28 F	0538	9.2	1206	1.0	1806	9.3		

MARCH

Date	Time	m	Time	m	Time	m	Time	m
1 SA ●	0030	0.9	0626	9.8	1255	0.5	1852	9.7
2 SU	0116	0.5	0711	10.1	1340	0.2	1935	10.0
3 M	0159	0.3	0754	10.2	1421	0.2	2015	9.9
4 TU	0239	0.4	0833	10.0	1459	0.5	2051	9.6
5 W	0315	0.8	0910	9.5	1534	1.1	2125	9.1
6 TH	0349	1.5	0944	8.8	1607	1.8	2157	8.4
7 F	0422	2.2	1018	8.0	1640	2.6	2231	7.7
8 SA ☽	0458	3.0	1058	7.3	1719	3.4	2313	7.1
9 SU	0549	3.7	1153	6.6	1818	4.0		
10 M	0019	6.6	0707	4.1	1332	6.3	1943	4.2
11 TU	0211	6.5	0852	4.0	1512	6.6	2121	3.9
12 W	0335	6.9	1008	3.5	1610	7.1	2225	3.3
13 TH	0427	7.5	1056	2.9	1654	7.7	2311	2.7
14 F	0509	8.0	1136	2.3	1734	8.2	2350	2.2
15 SA	0548	8.5	1214	1.9	1812	8.6		
16 SU O	0027	1.8	0625	8.9	1250	1.5	1847	8.9
17 M	0103	1.5	0700	9.1	1323	1.3	1921	9.1
18 TU	0137	1.3	0733	9.2	1355	1.3	1952	9.1
19 W	0208	1.3	0805	9.2	1425	1.4	2022	9.0
20 TH	0239	1.4	0836	9.0	1455	1.6	2053	8.8
21 F	0310	1.7	0910	8.7	1527	1.9	2127	8.5
22 SA	0345	2.1	0948	8.3	1604	2.4	2207	8.1
23 SU	0428	2.5	1035	7.8	1651	2.9	2300	7.6
24 M ☾	0526	3.0	1138	7.3	1757	3.4		
25 TU	0013	7.2	0651	3.3	1307	7.0	1935	3.5
26 W	0152	7.2	0835	3.1	1446	7.3	2115	3.1
27 TH	0321	7.7	0954	2.4	1600	7.9	2224	2.3
28 F	0425	8.4	1054	1.7	1656	8.6	2320	1.6
29 SA	0518	9.1	1145	1.1	1745	9.2		
30 SU ●	0009	1.0	0605	9.6	1233	0.6	1829	9.6
31 M	0055	0.6	0650	9.9	1316	0.4	1911	9.8

APRIL

Date	Time	m	Time	m	Time	m	Time	m
1 TU	0136	0.5	0731	9.9	1356	0.5	1950	9.8
2 W	0215	0.6	0809	9.7	1433	0.8	2025	9.5
3 TH	0250	1.0	0845	9.3	1506	1.3	2057	9.0
4 F	0322	1.6	0917	8.7	1537	2.0	2128	8.5
5 SA	0353	2.2	0950	8.0	1607	2.7	2200	7.8
6 SU	0426	2.9	1026	7.3	1642	3.3	2238	7.2
7 M ☽	0510	3.5	1115	6.7	1733	3.9	2332	6.7
8 TU	0621	3.9	1233	6.4	1853	4.1		
9 W	0102	6.5	0749	4.0	1415	6.5	2020	4.0
10 TH	0239	6.7	0912	3.6	1525	6.9	2135	3.5
11 F	0343	7.2	1011	3.1	1615	7.5	2229	2.9
12 SA	0431	7.8	1056	2.5	1658	8.0	2313	2.4
13 SU	0513	8.3	1137	2.0	1738	8.5	2354	1.9
14 M	0553	8.7	1216	1.6	1816	8.9		
15 TU O	0032	1.5	0631	9.0	1253	1.4	1851	9.1
16 W	0110	1.3	0707	9.2	1329	1.2	1926	9.2
17 TH	0146	1.2	0743	9.2	1403	1.3	2000	9.2
18 F	0221	1.2	0819	9.1	1438	1.4	2036	9.1
19 SA	0257	1.4	0857	8.8	1514	1.8	2114	8.8
20 SU	0336	1.8	0939	8.4	1554	2.2	2158	8.3
21 M	0422	2.3	1029	7.9	1644	2.8	2253	7.8
22 TU ☾	0523	2.8	1132	7.4	1752	3.2		
23 W	0004	7.5	0644	3.0	1255	7.2	1923	3.3
24 TH	0133	7.4	0815	2.9	1424	7.4	2053	3.0
25 F	0256	7.8	0930	2.4	1535	7.9	2201	2.4
26 SA	0400	8.3	1029	1.9	1631	8.5	2256	1.8
27 SU	0454	8.8	1120	1.4	1720	9.0	2345	1.4
28 M	0542	9.2	1207	1.1	1805	9.3		
29 TU ●	0030	1.1	0626	9.4	1251	1.0	1846	9.5
30 W	0112	1.0	0708	9.4	1330	1.0	1924	9.4

MAY

Date	Time	m	Time	m	Time	m	Time	m
1 TH	0151	1.1	0746	9.3	1407	1.2	2000	9.2
2 F	0226	1.3	0821	8.9	1440	1.6	2032	8.9
3 SA	0258	1.7	0854	8.5	1511	2.1	2103	8.5
4 SU	0329	2.2	0927	8.0	1541	2.6	2136	8.0
5 M	0402	2.8	1003	7.5	1615	3.2	2213	7.5
6 TU	0442	3.3	1047	7.0	1659	3.6	2259	7.1
7 W ☽	0538	3.6	1147	6.7	1805	3.9		
8 TH	0005	6.8	0653	3.8	1307	6.6	1923	3.9
9 F	0129	6.8	0808	3.6	1423	6.9	2035	3.6
10 SA	0243	7.1	0913	3.2	1524	7.3	2137	3.2
11 SU	0341	7.5	1007	2.8	1614	7.8	2229	2.6
12 M	0431	8.0	1055	2.3	1659	8.3	2316	2.1
13 TU	0516	8.4	1139	1.9	1741	8.7		
14 W O	0000	1.7	0559	8.8	1223	1.5	1822	9.1
15 TH	0044	1.3	0642	9.1	1304	1.3	1902	9.3
16 F	0126	1.1	0724	9.2	1345	1.2	1943	9.4
17 SA	0207	1.1	0806	9.2	1425	1.3	2024	9.3
18 SU	0249	1.2	0849	9.0	1507	1.6	2107	9.0
19 M	0333	1.5	0935	8.6	1552	2.0	2154	8.7
20 TU	0423	1.9	1026	8.2	1644	2.4	2248	8.2
21 W ☾	0521	2.4	1125	7.8	1747	2.9	2352	7.8
22 TH	0631	2.7	1236	7.6	1903	3.0		
23 F	0108	7.7	0747	2.7	1353	7.6	2023	2.9
24 SA	0225	7.8	0859	2.5	1504	7.8	2132	2.6
25 SU	0332	8.0	1000	2.2	1603	8.2	2230	2.2
26 M	0428	8.3	1054	2.0	1653	8.5	2320	1.9
27 TU	0518	8.6	1141	1.7	1739	8.8		
28 W ●	0007	1.7	0604	8.8	1226	1.6	1821	9.0
29 TH	0050	1.5	0646	8.9	1307	1.6	1901	9.1
30 F	0129	1.5	0725	8.8	1344	1.7	1937	9.0
31 SA	0205	1.7	0801	8.7	1417	1.9	2011	8.8

JUNE

Date	Time	m	Time	m	Time	m	Time	m
1 SU	0238	1.9	0835	8.4	1449	2.2	2044	8.5
2 M	0310	2.2	0909	8.1	1520	2.5	2116	8.2
3 TU	0342	2.6	0943	7.7	1553	2.9	2151	7.8
4 W	0417	2.9	1021	7.4	1631	3.3	2231	7.4
5 TH ☽	0500	3.3	1107	7.1	1720	3.6	2321	7.2
6 F	0556	3.5	1204	6.9	1824	3.7		
7 SA	0023	7.0	0704	3.5	1314	6.9	1935	3.6
8 SU	0135	7.1	0813	3.4	1423	7.2	2043	3.3
9 M	0245	7.3	0916	3.0	1524	7.6	2144	2.9
10 TU	0346	7.7	1013	2.6	1618	8.1	2239	2.4
11 W	0440	8.2	1106	2.2	1708	8.5	2331	1.9
12 TH	0532	8.6	1156	1.7	1757	9.0		
13 F O	0021	1.4	0621	9.0	1245	1.4	1843	9.3
14 SA	0110	1.1	0709	9.2	1332	1.2	1929	9.5
15 SU	0157	0.9	0756	9.3	1417	1.1	2015	9.6
16 M	0243	0.9	0842	9.3	1503	1.3	2101	9.4
17 TU	0330	1.1	0929	9.0	1549	1.6	2148	9.1
18 W	0418	1.5	1017	8.7	1638	2.0	2238	8.7
19 TH ☾	0510	1.9	1110	8.2	1732	2.4	2333	8.2
20 F	0607	2.4	1209	7.8	1834	2.8		
21 SA	0037	7.8	0712	2.7	1317	7.6	1946	3.0
22 SU	0150	7.6	0823	2.9	1429	7.6	2100	3.0
23 M	0302	7.6	0930	2.8	1534	7.7	2204	2.8
24 TU	0404	7.8	1028	2.6	1629	8.0	2258	2.5
25 W	0457	8.0	1119	2.4	1717	8.3	2346	2.2
26 TH	0544	8.3	1204	2.1	1801	8.6		
27 F ●	0029	2.0	0627	8.5	1246	2.0	1840	8.8
28 SA	0110	1.8	0706	8.6	1324	1.9	1918	8.8
29 SU	0146	1.8	0743	8.6	1358	2.0	1953	8.8
30 M	0219	1.9	0817	8.5	1430	2.1	2026	8.6

SUNRISE AND SUNSET TIMES

ST PETER PORT (GUERNSEY)
At 49°27′N 2°31′W

			Sunrise	Sunset
UT				
Jan	01		0806	1622
	15		0800	1639
Feb	01		0742	1706
	15		0719	1730
Mar	01		0653	1753
	15		0624	1815
BST (UT-1)				
Apr	01		0547	1942
	15		0518	2003
May	01		0548	2027
	15		0526	2048
Jun	01		0508	2108
	15		0503	2118
Jul	01		0508	2120
	15		0520	2111
Aug	01		0541	2051
	15		0601	2027
Sep	01		0626	1953
	15		0646	1923
Oct	01		0710	1849
	15		0731	1820
UT				
Nov	01		0659	1648
	15		0721	1628
Dec	01		0745	1613
	15		0800	1611

ST PETER PORT
LAT 49°27′N
LONG 2°31′W

TIMES AND HEIGHTS OF HIGH AND LOW WATER (Heights in Metres)

TIME ZONE UT
For Summer Time (area enclosed in shaded box) add 1 hour

2014

JULY

Day	Time	m
1 TU	0251 0850 1501 2057	2.1 8.3 2.3 8.4
2 W	0321 0922 1532 2129	2.3 8.1 2.6 8.1
3 TH	0352 0955 1605 2203	2.6 7.8 2.9 7.8
4 F	0426 1031 1642 2243	2.9 7.5 3.2 7.6
5 SA ☽	0507 1115 1730 2333	3.2 7.3 3.4 7.3
6 SU	0601 1211 1833	3.4 7.1 3.5
7 M	0036 0711 1321 1949	7.2 3.4 7.2 3.4
8 TU	0150 0827 1436 2103	7.2 3.3 7.4 3.1
9 W	0305 0936 1543 2209	7.5 2.9 7.8 2.6
10 TH	0411 1039 1643 2309	8.0 2.4 8.4 2.0
11 F	0511 1136 1737	8.4 1.9 8.9
12 SA ○	0004 0605 1230 1828	1.4 8.9 1.4 9.4
13 SU	0058 0657 1321 1918	1.0 9.3 1.0 9.7
14 M	0147 0745 1409 2005	0.6 9.6 0.8 9.9
15 TU	0234 0832 1454 2050	0.5 9.6 0.8 9.8
16 W	0319 0916 1538 2134	0.7 9.5 1.1 9.5
17 TH	0404 1001 1622 2219	1.0 9.1 1.5 9.0
18 F	0449 1046 1708 2307	1.6 8.5 2.1 8.4
19 SA ☾	0537 1136 1800	2.3 7.9 2.8
20 SU	0002 0633 1236 1904	7.7 2.9 7.4 3.3
21 M	0112 0741 1350 2024	7.2 3.3 7.2 3.5
22 TU	0233 0859 1507 2141	7.1 3.4 7.3 3.3
23 W	0344 1006 1608 2240	7.3 3.2 7.6 3.0
24 TH	0440 1100 1658 2329	7.6 2.8 8.0 2.6
25 F	0527 1146 1742	8.0 2.5 8.3
26 SA ●	0012 0608 1227 1821	2.2 8.3 2.2 8.6
27 SU	0051 0647 1304 1858	2.0 8.5 2.0 8.8
28 M	0126 0723 1339 1933	1.8 8.7 1.9 8.9
29 TU	0159 0757 1410 2006	1.8 8.7 1.9 8.8
30 W	0229 0828 1440 2036	1.8 8.6 2.0 8.7
31 TH	0258 0858 1509 2105	2.0 8.4 2.2 8.5

AUGUST

Day	Time	m
1 F	0325 0926 1538 2136	2.3 8.2 2.5 8.2
2 SA	0355 0958 1611 2211	2.6 7.9 2.8 7.9
3 SU	0430 1036 1650 2254	2.9 7.6 3.1 7.6
4 M ☽	0515 1125 1744 2351	3.2 7.3 3.4 7.3
5 TU	0617 1231 1900	3.5 7.2 3.5
6 W	0107 0743 1356 2030	7.1 3.5 7.2 3.3
7 TH	0235 0909 1517 2148	7.3 3.2 7.7 2.8
8 F	0353 1021 1625 2253	7.8 2.6 8.3 2.1
9 SA	0457 1122 1723 2351	8.4 1.9 9.0 1.4
10 SU ○	0553 1217 1815	9.0 1.3 9.6
11 M	0044 0643 1308 1903	0.8 9.5 0.8 10.0
12 TU	0133 0730 1355 1949	0.4 9.8 0.5 10.2
13 W	0218 0815 1439 2033	0.3 9.9 0.5 10.1
14 TH	0301 0857 1520 2114	0.4 9.8 0.8 9.8
15 F	0342 0937 1600 2155	0.9 9.3 1.3 9.2
16 SA	0422 1017 1640 2236	1.6 8.7 2.0 8.4
17 SU ☾	0503 1059 1724 2323	2.4 8.0 2.8 7.6
18 M	0552 1150 1821	3.1 7.3 3.5
19 TU	0027 0656 1306 1941	6.9 3.7 6.9 3.9
20 W	0203 0823 1439 2117	6.7 3.9 6.9 3.7
21 TH	0326 0944 1548 2222	6.9 3.6 7.2 3.3
22 F	0422 1040 1638 2310	7.3 3.2 7.7 2.8
23 SA	0506 1125 1720 2350	7.8 2.7 8.2 2.4
24 SU	0546 1205 1759	8.3 2.3 8.6
25 M ●	0027 0623 1241 1835	2.0 8.6 1.9 8.9
26 TU	0102 0658 1315 1910	1.7 8.8 1.7 9.1
27 W	0134 0732 1347 1942	1.6 8.9 1.7 9.1
28 TH	0204 0803 1417 2012	1.7 8.9 1.7 9.0
29 F	0232 0831 1445 2041	1.8 8.7 1.9 8.8
30 SA	0259 0859 1513 2110	2.0 8.5 2.2 8.5
31 SU	0327 0929 1544 2143	2.3 8.2 2.5 8.2

SEPTEMBER

Day	Time	m
1 M	0400 1005 1621 2225	2.7 7.9 2.9 7.8
2 TU ☽	0442 1052 1712 2320	3.1 7.5 3.3 7.3
3 W	0542 1158 1826	3.5 7.2 3.6
4 TH	0039 0712 1329 2008	7.1 3.7 7.2 3.4
5 F	0218 0852 1501 2134	7.2 3.3 7.6 2.8
6 SA	0341 1008 1611 2240	7.8 2.7 8.3 2.1
7 SU	0444 1108 1708 2336	8.5 1.9 9.0 1.3
8 M	0537 1201 1759	9.2 1.2 9.7
9 TU ○	0026 0625 1250 1845	0.7 9.7 0.7 10.1
10 W	0114 0710 1336 1930	0.3 10.0 0.4 10.3
11 TH	0157 0753 1418 2012	0.3 10.1 0.4 10.2
12 F	0238 0832 1457 2051	0.5 9.9 0.8 9.8
13 SA	0316 0910 1534 2128	1.0 9.4 1.3 9.1
14 SU	0352 0946 1611 2205	1.7 8.7 2.1 8.3
15 M	0429 1022 1649 2245	2.5 8.0 2.9 7.5
16 TU ☾	0511 1106 1739 2340	3.3 7.3 3.6 6.8
17 W	0611 1214 1855	4.0 6.7 4.1
18 TH	0119 0738 1401 2041	6.5 4.2 6.6 4.1
19 F	0259 0914 1519 2154	6.7 4.0 7.0 3.6
20 SA	0356 1013 1611 2242	7.2 3.4 7.6 3.0
21 SU	0439 1057 1653 2321	7.8 2.9 8.1 2.5
22 M	0518 1136 1731 2358	8.3 2.4 8.6 2.1
23 TU	0554 1212 1808	8.7 2.0 8.9
24 W ●	0032 0629 1247 1843	1.8 8.9 1.7 9.1
25 TH	0105 0703 1320 1916	1.6 9.1 1.6 9.2
26 F	0136 0735 1351 1947	1.6 9.1 1.6 9.2
27 SA	0206 0804 1422 2017	1.7 9.0 1.7 9.0
28 SU	0235 0834 1452 2048	1.9 8.8 2.0 8.7
29 M	0305 0906 1524 2123	2.2 8.5 2.3 8.4
30 TU	0339 0943 1603 2206	2.6 8.1 2.7 7.9

OCTOBER

Day	Time	m
1 W ☽	0422 1032 1654 2303	3.1 7.7 3.2 7.4
2 TH	0523 1139 1810	3.5 7.3 3.5
3 F	0023 0656 1312 1953	7.1 3.7 7.2 3.4
4 SA	0205 0839 1445 2119	7.3 3.4 7.7 2.8
5 SU	0326 0953 1553 2223	7.9 2.7 8.4 2.1
6 M	0426 1051 1649 2317	8.6 1.9 9.1 1.4
7 TU	0517 1142 1738	9.2 1.3 9.6
8 W ○	0005 0603 1229 1824	0.9 9.7 0.8 10.0
9 TH	0051 0647 1314 1908	0.6 10.0 0.6 10.1
10 F	0134 0728 1355 1949	0.6 10.0 0.7 10.0
11 SA	0213 0807 1434 2027	0.8 9.8 1.0 9.6
12 SU	0250 0843 1509 2102	1.3 9.3 1.5 9.0
13 M	0324 0916 1544 2137	1.9 8.7 2.2 8.3
14 TU	0357 0951 1619 2214	2.7 8.1 2.9 7.6
15 W ☾	0434 1030 1703 2301	3.4 7.4 3.6 6.9
16 TH	0526 1126 1810	4.0 6.9 4.1
17 F	0020 0645 1259 1938	6.5 4.3 6.6 4.2
18 SA	0207 0818 1431 2105	6.6 4.2 6.9 3.8
19 SU	0316 0930 1531 2200	7.0 3.7 7.3 3.3
20 M	0403 1019 1617 2244	7.6 3.1 7.9 2.8
21 TU	0443 1100 1657 2322	8.1 2.6 8.4 2.3
22 W	0521 1139 1736 2359	8.6 2.2 8.8 1.9
23 TH ●	0558 1216 1813	8.9 1.8 9.0
24 F	0034 0633 1252 1848	1.7 9.1 1.6 9.2
25 SA	0109 0707 1327 1923	1.6 9.2 1.5 9.2
26 SU	0142 0740 1402 1957	1.6 9.2 1.6 9.1
27 M	0215 0814 1436 2033	1.8 9.1 1.8 8.9
28 TU	0250 0850 1513 2112	2.1 8.8 2.1 8.5
29 W	0328 0932 1555 2158	2.5 8.4 2.5 8.1
30 TH	0414 1023 1649 2255	2.9 8.0 3.0 7.6
31 F ☽	0515 1129 1802	3.4 7.6 3.3

NOVEMBER

Day	Time	m
1 SA	0012 0642 1255 1934	7.3 3.6 7.5 3.2
2 SU	0145 0818 1421 2056	7.4 3.3 7.8 2.8
3 M	0303 0931 1530 2200	7.9 2.8 8.3 2.2
4 TU	0403 1029 1626 2254	8.5 2.1 8.8 1.7
5 W	0454 1120 1716 2342	9.0 1.6 9.3 1.3
6 TH ○	0541 1207 1803	9.4 1.2 9.6
7 F	0028 0624 1252 1846	1.1 9.7 1.1 9.6
8 SA	0110 0705 1333 1927	1.1 9.7 1.1 9.5
9 SU	0149 0743 1412 2005	1.3 9.5 1.3 9.2
10 M	0226 0819 1448 2041	1.6 9.2 1.7 8.8
11 TU	0259 0852 1521 2114	2.1 8.7 2.3 8.3
12 W	0331 0926 1555 2150	2.7 8.2 2.8 7.7
13 TH	0405 1003 1634 2231	3.2 7.7 3.4 7.2
14 F ☾	0448 1049 1725 2328	3.8 7.2 3.8 6.8
15 SA	0551 1155 1835	4.1 6.9 4.0
16 SU	0049 0709 1319 1951	6.7 4.2 6.8 3.9
17 M	0211 0825 1432 2100	6.9 3.9 7.1 3.6
18 TU	0313 0927 1529 2154	7.3 3.5 7.5 3.1
19 W	0401 1017 1617 2241	7.8 3.0 8.0 2.7
20 TH	0444 1102 1701 2323	8.3 2.5 8.4 2.2
21 F	0525 1144 1743	8.7 2.0 8.8
22 SA ●	0004 0604 1226 1823	1.9 9.1 1.7 9.0
23 SU	0044 0643 1307 1903	1.7 9.3 1.5 9.2
24 M	0123 0721 1347 1943	1.6 9.4 1.4 9.2
25 TU	0202 0801 1427 2024	1.6 9.3 1.5 9.1
26 W	0242 0842 1509 2107	1.8 9.1 1.7 8.8
27 TH	0324 0927 1554 2154	2.1 8.8 2.1 8.4
28 F	0412 1018 1647 2249	2.5 8.4 2.5 8.0
29 SA ☽	0510 1118 1751 2355	3.0 8.0 2.8 7.7
30 SU	0623 1231 1906	3.2 7.8 3.0

DECEMBER

Day	Time	m
1 M	0113 0746 1350 2024	7.6 3.2 7.8 2.9
2 TU	0232 0903 1502 2132	7.8 2.9 8.0 2.6
3 W	0337 1005 1603 2230	8.2 2.5 8.4 2.2
4 TH	0431 1059 1656 2321	8.6 2.1 8.7 1.9
5 F	0519 1148 1744	9.0 1.8 9.0
6 SA ○	0007 0603 1233 1828	1.7 9.2 1.6 9.1
7 SU	0050 0645 1315 1909	1.6 9.3 1.5 9.1
8 M	0130 0724 1354 1948	1.6 9.3 1.6 9.0
9 TU	0206 0759 1429 2023	1.8 9.1 1.8 8.7
10 W	0239 0833 1502 2056	2.1 8.8 2.2 8.4
11 TH	0310 0906 1534 2130	2.5 8.4 2.5 8.0
12 F	0342 0940 1607 2205	2.9 8.0 3.0 7.6
13 SA	0417 1018 1645 2247	3.3 7.6 3.3 7.2
14 SU ☾	0501 1104 1734 2340	3.7 7.2 3.7 7.0
15 M	0601 1204 1839	3.9 7.0 3.8
16 TU	0050 0715 1319 1950	6.9 4.0 7.0 3.8
17 W	0207 0826 1431 2057	7.0 3.7 7.2 3.5
18 TH	0311 0929 1532 2156	7.4 3.3 7.6 3.0
19 F	0405 1025 1626 2249	7.9 2.8 8.0 2.6
20 SA	0454 1115 1715 2338	8.4 2.3 8.5 2.1
21 SU	0539 1203 1802	8.9 1.8 8.8
22 M ●	0024 0624 1251 1848	1.7 9.2 1.4 9.1
23 TU	0110 0708 1336 1933	1.4 9.5 1.2 9.3
24 W	0154 0752 1421 2017	1.3 9.6 1.1 9.3
25 TH	0238 0836 1506 2102	1.3 9.6 1.2 9.2
26 F	0322 0921 1551 2147	1.5 9.3 1.4 8.9
27 SA	0407 1009 1638 2236	1.9 8.9 1.8 8.5
28 SU ☽	0457 1101 1731 2331	2.4 8.4 2.3 8.0
29 M	0556 1201 1832	2.8 8.0 2.8
30 TU	0036 0707 1314 1944	7.6 3.2 7.6 3.0
31 W	0154 0828 1432 2100	7.5 3.2 7.6 3.0

ST HELIER
LAT 49°11′N
LONG 2°07′W

TIMES AND HEIGHTS OF HIGH AND LOW WATER (Heights in Metres)

TIME ZONE UT
For Summer Time (area enclosed in shaded box) add 1 hour

2014

JANUARY

Date	Day	Time	m	Time	m	Time	m	Time	m
1	W ●	0011	1.6	0553	11.0	1239	1.2	1821	11.1
2	TH	0104	1.2	0644	11.5	1333	0.8	1911	11.4
3	F	0155	1.0	0733	11.7	1423	0.6	1959	11.5
4	SA	0243	0.9	0820	11.7	1509	0.7	2045	11.3
5	SU	0328	1.1	0904	11.4	1554	1.0	2128	10.9
6	M	0411	1.6	0947	10.9	1636	1.6	2211	10.2
7	TU	0453	2.2	1031	10.1	1719	2.3	2254	9.5
8	W ☽	0538	2.9	1118	9.3	1805	3.0	2344	8.9
9	TH	0631	3.5	1215	8.7	1903	3.6		
10	F	0049	8.4	0740	3.9	1331	8.3	2015	3.9
11	SA	0209	8.3	0858	3.9	1452	8.3	2129	3.7
12	SU	0323	8.6	1009	3.6	1559	8.7	2233	3.4
13	M	0422	9.1	1107	3.1	1652	9.1	2325	2.9
14	TU	0509	9.6	1153	2.7	1736	9.6		
15	W	0008	2.6	0550	10.0	1234	2.4	1815	9.9
16	TH O	0046	2.3	0626	10.2	1310	2.1	1850	10.1
17	F	0121	2.1	0700	10.4	1343	2.0	1922	10.2
18	SA	0154	2.0	0732	10.5	1415	1.9	1954	10.3
19	SU	0225	2.0	0803	10.5	1445	2.0	2024	10.2
20	M	0256	2.1	0834	10.4	1515	2.1	2054	10.0
21	TU	0326	2.3	0904	10.1	1545	2.4	2125	9.7
22	W	0358	2.7	0936	9.7	1617	2.8	2157	9.3
23	TH	0433	3.1	1012	9.3	1653	3.2	2237	8.8
24	F ☾	0516	3.5	1058	8.8	1740	3.6	2332	8.4
25	SA	0615	3.9	1204	8.4	1850	3.9		
26	SU	0050	8.3	0738	3.9	1331	8.3	2020	3.8
27	M	0221	8.6	0906	3.4	1459	8.8	2145	3.2
28	TU	0340	9.3	1022	2.7	1614	9.5	2255	2.4
29	W	0445	10.1	1128	1.8	1716	10.3	2357	1.7
30	TH ●	0542	10.9	1228	1.1	1811	11.0		
31	F	0053	1.1	0633	11.6	1322	0.6	1900	11.5

FEBRUARY

Date	Day	Time	m	Time	m	Time	m	Time	m
1	SA	0145	0.7	0721	11.9	1411	0.3	1946	11.7
2	SU	0231	0.5	0805	12.0	1456	0.3	2028	11.6
3	M	0313	0.7	0847	11.7	1536	0.6	2107	11.2
4	TU	0352	1.1	0926	11.1	1613	1.3	2144	10.6
5	W	0427	1.8	1003	10.3	1647	2.1	2220	9.8
6	TH ☽	0503	2.6	1041	9.4	1723	3.0	2259	9.0
7	F	0543	3.5	1127	8.5	1807	3.7	2352	8.2
8	SA	0640	4.1	1235	7.9	1916	4.3		
9	SU	0114	7.8	0808	4.4	1413	7.7	2047	4.3
10	M	0249	8.0	0937	4.1	1535	8.1	2205	3.9
11	TU	0358	8.5	1043	3.5	1632	8.7	2302	3.2
12	W	0449	9.2	1132	2.9	1717	9.3	2347	2.7
13	TH	0530	9.7	1213	2.4	1756	9.8		
14	F O	0027	2.3	0607	10.1	1251	2.0	1830	10.1
15	SA	0103	2.0	0641	10.4	1325	1.8	1902	10.4
16	SU	0137	1.8	0713	10.7	1357	1.6	1933	10.5
17	M	0208	1.6	0744	10.8	1427	1.6	2003	10.6
18	TU	0239	1.6	0814	10.7	1456	1.7	2033	10.5
19	W	0309	1.8	0845	10.5	1525	1.9	2103	10.2
20	TH	0339	2.1	0915	10.2	1555	2.3	2133	9.8
21	F	0412	2.6	0949	9.6	1628	2.8	2209	9.2
22	SA ☾	0450	3.1	1031	9.0	1710	3.4	2258	8.7
23	SU	0544	3.6	1131	8.4	1814	3.8		
24	M	0014	8.3	0704	3.8	1302	8.2	1950	3.9
25	TU	0155	8.3	0843	3.5	1443	8.5	2126	3.4
26	W	0325	9.0	1006	2.7	1603	9.3	2241	2.5
27	TH	0433	10.0	1115	1.8	1705	10.2	2344	1.6
28	F	0529	10.9	1214	1.0	1757	11.0		

MARCH

Date	Day	Time	m	Time	m	Time	m	Time	m
1	SA ●	0039	1.0	0618	11.5	1307	0.5	1844	11.5
2	SU	0129	0.5	0704	11.9	1353	0.2	1926	11.8
3	M	0213	0.4	0746	12.0	1435	0.3	2006	11.7
4	TU	0252	0.5	0825	11.7	1511	0.6	2042	11.3
5	W	0327	1.0	0901	11.1	1544	1.3	2115	10.7
6	TH	0359	1.7	0934	10.3	1614	2.1	2147	9.9
7	F	0429	2.5	1007	9.4	1644	3.0	2220	9.1
8	SA ☽	0501	3.4	1045	8.5	1720	3.8	2303	8.3
9	SU	0547	4.1	1143	7.7	1817	4.4		
10	M	0016	7.6	0706	4.6	1329	7.4	1954	4.6
11	TU	0207	7.6	0854	4.4	1503	7.8	2128	4.2
12	W	0326	8.2	1009	3.8	1604	8.4	2231	3.5
13	TH	0420	8.9	1101	3.1	1349	9.1	2318	2.8
14	F	0503	9.5	1143	2.5	1728	9.7	2359	2.3
15	SA	0541	10.0	1223	2.0	1804	10.1		
16	SU O	0038	1.9	0615	10.4	1300	1.7	1836	10.5
17	M	0114	1.6	0648	10.7	1334	1.5	1908	10.7
18	TU	0147	1.4	0721	10.9	1406	1.4	1940	10.8
19	W	0219	1.3	0753	10.9	1436	1.4	2011	10.8
20	TH	0251	1.4	0825	10.8	1506	1.6	2043	10.6
21	F	0323	1.7	0859	10.4	1538	2.0	2116	10.1
22	SA	0357	2.2	0934	9.8	1613	2.6	2153	9.5
23	SU	0437	2.8	1018	9.1	1656	3.2	2243	8.9
24	M ☾	0530	3.3	1119	8.5	1800	3.7	2358	8.4
25	TU	0650	3.6	1250	8.2	1935	3.9		
26	W	0140	8.4	0827	3.4	1431	8.5	2110	3.3
27	TH	0310	9.0	0949	2.7	1548	9.3	2224	2.5
28	F	0416	9.9	1056	1.8	1647	10.2	2326	1.7
29	SA	0511	10.7	1154	1.2	1737	10.9		
30	SU ●	0019	1.1	0558	11.3	1245	0.7	1822	11.3
31	M	0107	0.7	0642	11.6	1330	0.6	1903	11.5

APRIL

Date	Day	Time	m	Time	m	Time	m	Time	m
1	TU	0149	0.6	0723	11.6	1409	0.6	1941	11.5
2	W	0227	0.8	0800	11.4	1444	1.0	2015	11.2
3	TH	0300	1.2	0835	10.9	1515	1.5	2047	10.6
4	F	0330	1.8	0907	10.2	1543	2.2	2117	9.9
5	SA	0359	2.5	0939	9.3	1612	3.0	2148	9.2
6	SU	0429	3.3	1014	8.5	1645	3.7	2226	8.4
7	M ☽	0510	3.9	1104	7.8	1734	4.3	2327	7.8
8	TU	0614	4.4	1234	7.4	1854	4.7		
9	W	0109	7.5	0750	4.5	1415	7.6	2033	4.4
10	TH	0239	7.9	0917	4.0	1522	8.2	2145	3.8
11	F	0339	8.6	1016	3.3	1610	8.9	2238	3.1
12	SA	0425	9.2	1103	2.7	1652	9.5	2323	2.5
13	SU	0505	9.8	1146	2.2	1729	10.0		
14	M	0005	2.0	0542	10.3	1227	1.8	1805	10.5
15	TU O	0045	1.6	0619	10.6	1305	1.5	1840	10.8
16	W	0122	1.4	0655	10.9	1341	1.3	1915	11.0
17	TH	0158	1.2	0732	11.0	1416	1.3	1951	11.0
18	F	0233	1.3	0809	10.9	1450	1.5	2027	10.8
19	SA	0309	1.5	0847	10.5	1526	1.9	2105	10.4
20	SU	0348	1.9	0929	10.0	1605	2.4	2148	9.8
21	M	0432	2.5	1017	9.3	1653	3.0	2242	9.1
22	TU ☾	0528	3.0	1120	8.7	1758	3.5	2354	8.7
23	W	0643	3.3	1242	8.4	1923	3.6		
24	TH	0124	8.7	0809	3.1	1411	8.7	2049	3.2
25	F	0246	9.1	0926	2.6	1524	9.3	2200	2.6
26	SA	0352	9.8	1031	2.0	1623	10.0	2301	1.9
27	SU	0447	10.4	1128	1.5	1713	10.6	2354	1.5
28	M	0535	10.8	1218	1.3	1757	10.9		
29	TU ●	0042	1.2	0619	11.0	1302	1.2	1837	11.1
30	W	0124	1.2	0659	11.0	1341	1.2	1914	11.1

MAY

Date	Day	Time	m	Time	m	Time	m	Time	m
1	TH	0201	1.3	0736	10.9	1415	1.5	1949	10.9
2	F	0234	1.6	0811	10.5	1447	1.8	2021	10.5
3	SA	0305	2.0	0844	10.0	1516	2.3	2052	10.0
4	SU	0334	2.5	0916	9.4	1546	2.9	2124	9.4
5	M	0406	3.1	0951	8.7	1620	3.5	2201	8.7
6	TU	0444	3.6	1035	8.2	1703	4.0	2250	8.2
7	W ☽	0535	4.1	1139	7.7	1805	4.4		
8	TH	0004	7.8	0645	4.3	1308	7.7	1924	4.4
9	F	0133	7.9	0807	4.1	1423	8.0	2043	4.1
10	SA	0243	8.3	0917	3.6	1520	8.6	2146	3.5
11	SU	0336	8.9	1014	3.1	1607	9.2	2238	2.8
12	M	0422	9.5	1103	2.5	1649	9.8	2326	2.3
13	TU	0506	10.0	1150	2.0	1731	10.3		
14	W O	0012	1.8	0548	10.5	1235	1.7	1811	10.8
15	TH	0056	1.4	0630	10.8	1317	1.4	1852	11.0
16	F	0138	1.2	0713	11.0	1357	1.3	1934	11.1
17	SA	0219	1.2	0756	10.9	1438	1.4	2016	11.0
18	SU	0301	1.3	0841	10.7	1519	1.7	2101	10.7
19	M	0345	1.6	0927	10.2	1604	2.1	2148	10.2
20	TU	0433	2.0	1018	9.7	1654	2.6	2241	9.6
21	W ☾	0527	2.5	1115	9.2	1753	3.0	2344	9.2
22	TH	0631	2.9	1223	8.9	1904	3.3		
23	F	0058	9.0	0743	2.9	1340	8.9	2020	3.2
24	SA	0214	9.1	0855	2.8	1451	9.2	2130	2.8
25	SU	0322	9.4	1000	2.4	1553	9.6	2232	2.4
26	M	0420	9.8	1058	2.1	1645	10.0	2328	2.1
27	TU	0511	10.2	1150	1.9	1732	10.4		
28	W ●	0017	1.9	0555	10.4	1235	1.8	1813	10.6
29	TH	0100	1.8	0636	10.4	1315	1.8	1851	10.6
30	F	0137	1.8	0714	10.4	1350	1.9	1926	10.6
31	SA	0211	1.9	0750	10.2	1423	2.1	2000	10.4

JUNE

Date	Day	Time	m	Time	m	Time	m	Time	m
1	SU	0243	2.1	0824	9.9	1454	2.4	2032	10.0
2	M	0314	2.4	0857	9.6	1526	2.7	2105	9.6
3	TU	0346	2.8	0931	9.1	1559	3.1	2140	9.2
4	W	0421	3.2	1008	8.7	1637	3.6	2220	8.7
5	TH ☽	0503	3.6	1055	8.3	1725	3.9	2311	8.3
6	F	0555	3.9	1155	8.0	1825	4.1		
7	SA	0018	8.1	0659	4.0	1309	8.0	1936	4.1
8	SU	0133	8.2	0811	3.8	1418	8.4	2047	3.7
9	M	0239	8.6	0919	3.4	1516	8.9	2150	3.2
10	TU	0337	9.2	1019	2.9	1608	9.5	2247	2.6
11	W	0430	9.8	1113	2.3	1658	10.2	2340	2.0
12	TH	0521	10.3	1205	1.8	1746	10.7		
13	F O	0031	1.5	0610	10.7	1255	1.5	1834	11.1
14	SA	0121	1.2	0659	11.0	1343	1.3	1921	11.3
15	SU	0209	1.0	0747	11.1	1430	1.2	2008	11.3
16	M	0256	1.0	0835	11.0	1515	1.3	2055	11.1
17	TU	0342	1.1	0922	10.7	1601	1.6	2142	10.7
18	W	0429	1.5	1009	10.2	1649	2.1	2231	10.2
19	TH ☾	0518	2.0	1059	9.7	1740	2.6	2324	9.6
20	F	0611	2.5	1155	9.2	1838	3.0		
21	SA	0025	9.1	0711	2.9	1301	8.9	1945	3.3
22	SU	0136	8.9	0819	3.1	1413	8.8	2056	3.2
23	M	0248	8.9	0927	3.0	1520	9.1	2203	3.0
24	TU	0353	9.2	1030	2.8	1619	9.5	2303	2.7
25	W	0448	9.5	1125	2.6	1709	9.8	2354	2.4
26	TH	0536	9.8	1212	2.4	1752	10.1		
27	F ●	0038	2.2	0618	10.0	1253	2.2	1831	10.3
28	SA	0117	2.1	0656	10.1	1329	2.2	1907	10.4
29	SU	0152	2.0	0731	10.1	1403	2.2	1941	10.4
30	M	0224	2.1	0805	10.0	1435	2.2	2013	10.2

SUNRISE AND SUNSET TIMES

ST HELIER
At 49°N 2°W

		Sunrise	Sunset
UT			
Jan	01	0803	1621
	15	0758	1639
Feb	01	0739	1705
	15	0717	1729
Mar	01	0651	1752
	15	0622	1814
BST (UT-1)			
Apr	01	0646	1940
	15	0617	2001
May	01	0547	2025
	15	0526	2045
Jun	01	0508	2105
	15	0503	2115
Jul	01	0508	2117
	15	0520	2109
Aug	01	0541	2048
	15	0600	2025
Sep	01	0625	1951
	15	0645	1921
Oct	01	0708	1847
	15	0729	1818
UT			
Nov	01	0656	1647
	15	0719	1627
Dec	01	0742	1613
	15	0757	1611

ST HELIER
LAT 49°11′N
LONG 2°07′W

TIMES AND HEIGHTS OF HIGH AND LOW WATER (Heights in Metres)

TIME ZONE UT
For Summer Time (area enclosed in shaded box) add 1 hour

2014

JULY

Date	Day	Time	m	Time	m	Time	m	Time	m
1	TU	0255	2.2	0837	9.9	1506	2.4	2045	10.0
2	W	0326	2.4	0908	9.6	1538	2.7	2117	9.7
3	TH	0358	2.7	0941	9.2	1612	3.0	2151	9.3
4	F	0433	3.1	1017	8.8	1651	3.4	2230	8.8
5	SA ☽	0513	3.5	1100	8.5	1737	3.8	2319	8.5
6	SU	0604	3.8	1158	8.2	1837	4.0		
7	M	0025	8.3	0709	3.9	1311	8.2	1950	3.9
8	TU	0141	8.4	0825	3.7	1426	8.6	2105	3.5
9	W	0255	8.8	0939	3.2	1532	9.2	2213	2.8
10	TH	0400	9.4	1043	2.6	1632	9.9	2314	2.1
11	F	0500	10.1	1142	2.0	1727	10.6		
12	SA ○	0012	1.5	0555	10.7	1239	1.5	1820	11.2
13	SU	0108	1.0	0647	11.1	1331	1.1	1910	11.5
14	M	0159	0.7	0737	11.4	1421	0.9	1958	11.7
15	TU	0248	0.6	0824	11.4	1507	0.9	2044	11.6
16	W	0333	0.7	0908	11.2	1552	1.1	2128	11.2
17	TH	0416	1.1	0952	10.7	1634	1.6	2212	10.6
18	F	0459	1.7	1035	10.0	1718	2.3	2257	9.8
19	SA ☾	0543	2.4	1121	9.3	1806	3.0	2348	9.1
20	SU	0634	3.1	1218	8.7	1907	3.5		
21	M	0055	8.5	0739	3.6	1331	8.4	2021	3.7
22	TU	0215	8.3	0854	3.7	1450	8.5	2137	3.6
23	W	0330	8.5	1005	3.4	1556	8.9	2243	3.2
24	TH	0430	9.0	1103	3.0	1649	9.4	2335	2.7
25	F	0519	9.4	1152	2.6	1734	9.8		
26	SA ●	0020	2.4	0600	9.8	1233	2.4	1812	10.2
27	SU	0058	2.2	0637	10.0	1310	2.2	1848	10.4
28	M	0133	2.0	0711	10.2	1344	2.1	1921	10.5
29	TU	0205	1.9	0743	10.3	1415	2.0	1953	10.5
30	W	0235	1.9	0814	10.2	1446	2.1	2023	10.4
31	TH	0305	2.1	0844	10.1	1517	2.2	2053	10.1

AUGUST

Date	Day	Time	m	Time	m	Time	m	Time	m
1	F	0335	2.3	0913	9.8	1548	2.6	2124	9.8
2	SA	0405	2.7	0944	9.4	1621	3.0	2156	9.3
3	SU	0439	3.1	1018	8.9	1700	3.4	2236	8.8
4	M ☽	0520	3.6	1105	8.5	1751	3.8	2333	8.4
5	TU	0619	3.9	1215	8.2	1903	4.0		
6	W	0053	8.2	0741	3.9	1344	8.4	2029	3.7
7	TH	0223	8.5	0908	3.5	1506	9.0	2148	3.0
8	F	0341	9.2	1022	2.8	1614	9.8	2255	2.2
9	SA	0446	10.0	1126	2.0	1713	10.6	2357	1.4
10	SU ○	0543	10.7	1224	1.3	1807	11.3		
11	M	0054	0.8	0634	11.3	1318	0.9	1856	11.8
12	TU	0146	0.4	0722	11.7	1407	0.6	1942	12.0
13	W	0233	0.3	0806	11.7	1452	0.6	2026	11.9
14	TH	0316	0.4	0848	11.5	1534	0.9	2107	11.5
15	F	0356	0.9	0927	10.9	1613	1.5	2147	10.7
16	SA	0433	1.7	1005	10.2	1650	2.3	2226	9.8
17	SU ☾	0511	2.6	1044	9.3	1731	3.1	2310	8.9
18	M	0554	3.4	1133	8.5	1824	3.9		
19	TU	0012	8.1	0655	4.1	1247	8.0	1943	4.2
20	W	0144	7.8	0820	4.3	1421	8.0	2112	4.1
21	TH	0311	8.1	0941	3.9	1536	8.5	2222	3.5
22	F	0412	8.7	1043	3.3	1630	9.2	2314	2.9
23	SA	0500	9.3	1130	2.8	1714	9.7	2357	2.5
24	SU	0540	9.8	1211	2.4	1752	10.2		
25	M ●	0035	2.1	0615	10.1	1248	2.1	1826	10.5
26	TU	0110	1.9	0648	10.4	1322	1.9	1858	10.6
27	W	0142	1.8	0719	10.5	1353	1.8	1929	10.7
28	TH	0213	1.7	0749	10.5	1424	1.8	1959	10.7
29	F	0242	1.8	0818	10.5	1454	1.9	2029	10.5
30	SA	0311	2.0	0846	10.2	1524	2.2	2058	10.1
31	SU	0340	2.4	0915	9.8	1556	2.7	2129	9.6

SEPTEMBER

Date	Day	Time	m	Time	m	Time	m	Time	m
1	M	0411	2.9	0947	9.3	1632	3.2	2206	9.1
2	TU ☽	0449	3.5	1030	8.7	1720	3.7	2259	8.5
3	W	0546	3.9	1137	8.3	1832	4.0		
4	TH	0023	8.1	0711	4.1	1316	8.2	2006	3.8
5	F	0205	8.3	0849	3.7	1451	8.8	2131	3.1
6	SA	0329	9.1	1006	2.8	1601	9.8	2240	2.2
7	SU	0434	10.0	1111	2.0	1659	10.7	2341	1.3
8	M	0528	10.9	1208	1.2	1751	11.5		
9	TU ○	0036	0.7	0617	11.5	1300	0.7	1838	11.9
10	W	0127	0.4	0702	11.8	1348	0.5	1922	12.1
11	TH	0212	0.3	0744	11.8	1431	0.6	2004	11.9
12	F	0252	0.6	0823	11.6	1510	0.9	2043	11.4
13	SA	0329	1.1	0859	11.0	1546	1.6	2119	10.6
14	SU	0403	1.9	0934	10.2	1620	2.4	2155	9.7
15	M	0436	2.8	1008	9.3	1655	3.3	2234	8.7
16	TU ☾	0513	3.7	1051	8.5	1741	4.1	2329	7.9
17	W	0609	4.4	1159	7.8	1858	4.6		
18	TH	0107	7.5	0739	4.7	1347	7.7	2039	4.4
19	F	0245	7.8	0911	4.3	1509	8.2	2153	3.8
20	SA	0347	8.5	1014	3.6	1604	9.0	2245	3.2
21	SU	0433	9.2	1102	3.0	1647	9.6	2327	2.6
22	M	0513	9.8	1142	2.4	1725	10.1		
23	TU	0005	2.2	0547	10.2	1220	2.1	1759	10.5
24	W ●	0042	1.9	0620	10.5	1255	1.8	1832	10.7
25	TH	0116	1.7	0651	10.7	1329	1.7	1903	10.9
26	F	0147	1.6	0722	10.8	1400	1.6	1934	10.9
27	SA	0218	1.7	0752	10.8	1432	1.7	2005	10.7
28	SU	0247	1.9	0822	10.5	1503	2.0	2037	10.4
29	M	0318	2.2	0853	10.1	1536	2.4	2110	9.9
30	TU	0351	2.8	0928	9.6	1614	3.0	2150	9.2

OCTOBER

Date	Day	Time	m	Time	m	Time	m	Time	m
1	W ☽	0431	3.4	1012	9.0	1703	3.5	2245	8.6
2	TH	0529	3.9	1120	8.4	1816	3.9		
3	F	0009	8.2	0656	4.1	1300	8.3	1950	3.7
4	SA	0153	8.4	0833	3.7	1435	8.9	2115	3.0
5	SU	0315	9.1	0950	2.9	1545	9.8	2223	2.2
6	M	0417	10.1	1052	2.0	1641	10.7	2321	1.4
7	TU	0509	10.8	1148	1.3	1732	11.3		
8	W ○	0014	0.9	0556	11.4	1238	0.9	1817	11.7
9	TH	0103	0.7	0639	11.7	1324	0.7	1900	11.8
10	F	0146	0.7	0719	11.7	1406	0.8	1940	11.6
11	SA	0225	1.0	0757	11.4	1444	1.2	2018	11.2
12	SU	0300	1.5	0832	10.9	1518	1.8	2053	10.5
13	M	0332	2.2	0904	10.2	1550	2.5	2127	9.6
14	TU	0404	3.0	0937	9.4	1623	3.3	2203	8.7
15	W ☾	0438	3.8	1015	8.6	1704	4.1	2252	8.0
16	TH	0526	4.4	1113	7.9	1807	4.6		
17	F	0016	7.5	0644	4.8	1253	7.6	1943	4.6
18	SA	0200	7.7	0822	4.6	1426	8.0	2106	4.2
19	SU	0309	8.3	0932	4.0	1526	8.6	2204	3.5
20	M	0358	9.0	1023	3.3	1612	9.3	2249	2.9
21	TU	0438	9.6	1106	2.7	1651	9.9	2329	2.4
22	W	0515	10.1	1146	2.2	1728	10.3		
23	TH ●	0008	2.0	0549	10.5	1225	1.9	1802	10.6
24	F	0046	1.8	0622	10.7	1302	1.7	1836	10.8
25	SA	0121	1.7	0655	10.9	1337	1.6	1911	10.9
26	SU	0155	1.7	0729	11.0	1412	1.6	1946	10.8
27	M	0228	1.8	0804	10.8	1446	1.8	2023	10.6
28	TU	0302	2.1	0840	10.4	1523	2.2	2102	10.1
29	W	0340	2.6	0920	9.9	1605	2.7	2146	9.5
30	TH	0424	3.1	1009	9.3	1657	3.2	2244	8.8
31	F ☽	0523	3.6	1115	8.8	1807	3.5		

NOVEMBER

Date	Day	Time	m	Time	m	Time	m	Time	m
1	SA	0001	8.5	0643	3.9	1243	8.6	1931	3.5
2	SU	0132	8.6	0812	3.6	1411	9.0	2052	3.0
3	M	0251	9.2	0927	2.9	1521	9.7	2159	2.4
4	TU	0353	9.9	1029	2.2	1619	10.4	2257	1.8
5	W	0446	10.6	1125	1.7	1710	10.9	2350	1.4
6	TH ○	0533	11.0	1215	1.3	1756	11.2		
7	F	0037	1.2	0615	11.3	1301	1.2	1838	11.3
8	SA	0120	1.2	0655	11.3	1342	1.3	1918	11.2
9	SU	0159	1.4	0732	11.1	1419	1.5	1955	10.8
10	M	0233	1.8	0807	10.8	1453	2.0	2030	10.3
11	TU	0305	2.3	0840	10.2	1525	2.5	2104	9.7
12	W	0337	2.9	0913	9.6	1557	3.1	2139	9.0
13	TH	0410	3.6	0949	8.9	1633	3.7	2221	8.3
14	F ☾	0451	4.1	1035	8.3	1722	4.2	2320	7.9
15	SA	0550	4.5	1144	7.9	1832	4.5		
16	SU	0048	7.7	0709	4.6	1317	7.8	1955	4.4
17	M	0211	8.0	0830	4.3	1432	8.2	2107	4.0
18	TU	0310	8.5	0934	3.8	1526	8.8	2202	3.4
19	W	0356	9.1	1024	3.2	1611	9.4	2249	2.8
20	TH	0437	9.7	1110	2.6	1652	9.9	2333	2.4
21	F	0516	10.2	1153	2.1	1732	10.4		
22	SA ●	0015	2.0	0553	10.7	1236	1.8	1811	10.7
23	SU	0056	1.7	0632	10.9	1316	1.6	1851	10.9
24	M	0135	1.6	0711	11.1	1356	1.5	1932	10.9
25	TU	0214	1.7	0752	11.0	1436	1.5	2015	10.8
26	W	0253	1.9	0834	10.8	1518	1.8	2059	10.4
27	TH	0336	2.2	0919	10.4	1603	2.2	2147	9.9
28	F	0423	2.7	1009	9.8	1655	2.6	2240	9.4
29	SA ☽	0518	3.1	1107	9.3	1755	3.0	2344	9.0
30	SU	0626	3.4	1217	9.0	1906	3.2		

DECEMBER

Date	Day	Time	m	Time	m	Time	m	Time	m
1	M	0059	8.8	0742	3.4	1336	9.0	2021	3.1
2	TU	0217	9.0	0857	3.1	1450	9.3	2130	2.7
3	W	0324	9.5	1003	2.7	1553	9.8	2231	2.3
4	TH	0421	10.0	1102	2.2	1648	10.2	2326	2.0
5	F	0511	10.4	1154	1.9	1736	10.5		
6	SA ○	0015	1.8	0555	10.7	1241	1.7	1819	10.7
7	SU	0059	1.8	0635	10.9	1322	1.7	1900	10.7
8	M	0137	1.8	0713	10.8	1359	1.8	1937	10.5
9	TU	0212	2.0	0748	10.7	1433	2.0	2012	10.2
10	W	0244	2.3	0821	10.3	1505	2.4	2045	9.8
11	TH	0315	2.7	0854	9.9	1536	2.8	2119	9.4
12	F	0347	3.1	0927	9.4	1608	3.2	2154	8.9
13	SA	0422	3.6	1004	8.9	1646	3.7	2235	8.4
14	SU ☾	0505	4.0	1050	8.4	1734	4.1	2330	8.0
15	M	0602	4.3	1152	8.0	1837	4.3		
16	TU	0044	7.9	0713	4.4	1311	8.0	1952	4.2
17	W	0202	8.1	0830	4.2	1425	8.3	2104	3.9
18	TH	0304	8.6	0936	3.7	1523	8.8	2204	3.3
19	F	0355	9.2	1032	3.0	1615	9.4	2257	2.7
20	SA	0442	9.9	1123	2.4	1703	10.0	2347	2.2
21	SU	0528	10.4	1212	1.9	1750	10.5		
22	M ●	0034	1.8	0613	10.9	1259	1.5	1837	10.9
23	TU	0120	1.5	0658	11.2	1345	1.2	1923	11.1
24	W	0205	1.4	0744	11.4	1430	1.1	2009	11.1
25	TH	0249	1.4	0829	11.3	1515	1.2	2055	10.9
26	F	0333	1.6	0915	11.0	1600	1.5	2140	10.5
27	SA	0418	2.0	1001	10.5	1646	1.9	2228	10.0
28	SU ☽	0506	2.5	1050	9.9	1737	2.5	2319	9.4
29	M	0601	3.0	1147	9.3	1835	2.9		
30	TU	0020	8.9	0706	3.4	1256	8.9	1943	3.3
31	W	0134	8.7	0821	3.5	1414	8.8	2056	3.3

ST-MALO
LAT 48°38′N
LONG 2°02′W

TIMES AND HEIGHTS OF HIGH AND LOW WATER (Heights in Metres)

TIME ZONE –0100 (French Standard Time). **Subtract 1 hour for UT. For French Summer Time (area enclosed in shaded box) add 1 hour**

2014

SUNRISE AND SUNSET TIMES

ST MALO
At 48°38′N 2°02′W
European Standard Time (UT-1)

		Sunrise	Sunset
Jan	01	0901	1723
	15	0855	1740
Feb	01	0838	1807
	15	0816	1829
Mar	01	0750	1852
	15	0721	1913
European Summer Time (UT-2)			
Apr	01	0746	2039
	15	0718	2100
May	01	0648	2123
	15	0627	2143
Jun	01	0610	2202
	15	0605	2212
Jul	01	0610	2214
	15	0622	2206
Aug	01	0642	2146
	15	0701	2123
Sep	01	0725	2050
	15	0745	2021
Oct	01	0808	1947
	15	0828	1919
European Standard Time (UT-1)			
Nov	01	0755	1748
	15	0816	1728
Dec	01	0839	1715
	15	0854	1712

JANUARY

Date	Day	Time	m	Time	m	Time	m	Time	m
1	W ●	0114	1.8	0642	12.2	1343	1.3	1908	12.2
2	TH	0209	1.2	0731	12.7	1437	0.8	1957	12.6
3	F	0300	0.9	0818	13.0	1526	0.6	2044	12.7
4	SA	0347	0.9	0904	12.9	1612	0.7	2130	12.5
5	SU	0431	1.1	0949	12.6	1656	1.1	2214	12.0
6	M	0513	1.7	1034	12.0	1737	1.8	2258	11.3
7	TU	0554	2.4	1121	11.2	1819	2.6	2345	10.6
8	W ☽	0637	3.2	1212	10.4	1904	3.4		
9	TH	0039	9.9	0730	3.9	1314	9.7	2002	4.0
10	F	0146	9.4	0840	4.2	1427	9.3	2115	4.2
11	SA	0302	9.4	0957	4.2	1542	9.4	2227	4.0
12	SU	0412	9.7	1103	3.8	1647	9.7	2327	3.6
13	M	0510	10.2	1158	3.3	1740	10.2		
14	TU	0018	3.1	0556	10.6	1245	2.9	1823	10.6
15	W	0102	2.8	0637	11.0	1326	2.5	1902	10.9
16	TH ○	0141	2.5	0714	11.3	1404	2.3	1938	11.2
17	F	0218	2.3	0748	11.5	1439	2.2	2011	11.3
18	SA	0252	2.2	0821	11.6	1513	2.1	2043	11.3
19	SU	0326	2.2	0852	11.6	1546	2.2	2114	11.3
20	M	0358	2.3	0923	11.5	1617	2.3	2144	11.1
21	TU	0429	2.5	0954	11.2	1648	2.6	2214	10.7
22	W	0502	2.9	1025	10.8	1721	3.0	2245	10.3
23	TH	0539	3.3	1059	10.3	1800	3.4	2321	9.8
24	F ☾	0624	3.7	1142	9.8	1848	3.8		
25	SA	0012	9.4	0721	4.0	1245	9.3	1952	4.1
26	SU	0133	9.1	0835	4.1	1419	9.1	2114	4.0
27	M	0317	9.4	1000	3.7	1555	9.6	2241	3.5
28	TU	0436	10.2	1120	2.9	1707	10.5	2356	2.7
29	W	0537	11.2	1230	2.0	1806	11.4		
30	TH ●	0101	1.8	0630	12.1	1331	1.2	1858	12.1
31	F	0158	1.0	0720	12.8	1426	0.6	1946	12.6

FEBRUARY

Date	Day	Time	m	Time	m	Time	m	Time	m
1	SA	0249	0.6	0807	13.1	1515	0.2	2032	12.8
2	SU	0335	0.4	0851	13.2	1559	0.3	2114	12.7
3	M	0416	0.6	0933	12.9	1639	0.7	2155	12.3
4	TU	0454	1.2	1014	12.2	1715	1.4	2233	11.6
5	W	0530	2.0	1053	11.4	1749	2.3	2312	10.9
6	TH ☽	0604	2.9	1135	10.5	1824	3.3	2355	10.0
7	F	0644	3.8	1224	9.6	1909	4.1		
8	SA	0049	9.3	0742	4.4	1332	8.9	2017	4.6
9	SU	0207	8.9	0907	4.7	1501	8.7	2144	4.6
10	M	0336	9.0	1028	4.3	1622	9.0	2257	4.2
11	TU	0446	9.5	1131	3.7	1721	9.6	2354	3.5
12	W	0538	10.1	1222	3.2	1806	10.3		
13	TH	0041	3.0	0619	10.7	1306	2.7	1844	10.8
14	F	0123	2.5	0656	11.2	1346	2.3	1920	11.2
15	SA ○	0201	2.2	0730	11.5	1423	2.0	1952	11.5
16	SU	0237	1.9	0802	11.8	1458	1.8	2024	11.6
17	M	0310	1.8	0834	11.9	1530	1.7	2053	11.7
18	TU	0342	1.8	0904	11.9	1600	1.8	2123	11.6
19	W	0413	2.0	0933	11.7	1630	2.1	2151	11.3
20	TH	0444	2.3	1003	11.3	1701	2.5	2220	10.8
21	F	0518	2.8	1035	10.7	1735	3.0	2254	10.3
22	SA ☾	0558	3.3	1115	10.1	1819	3.6	2340	9.7
23	SU	0651	3.8	1212	9.4	1920	4.1		
24	M	0054	9.1	0804	4.1	1351	8.9	2044	4.2
25	TU	0254	9.2	0936	3.9	1541	9.4	2222	3.7
26	W	0420	10.0	1104	3.1	1654	10.3	2343	2.8
27	TH	0523	11.1	1216	2.1	1752	11.3		
28	F	0048	1.8	0616	12.0	1317	1.2	1843	12.1

MARCH

Date	Day	Time	m	Time	m	Time	m	Time	m
1	SA ●	0144	1.0	0705	12.7	1410	0.5	1930	12.6
2	SU	0233	0.5	0750	13.1	1457	0.2	2013	12.8
3	M	0317	0.4	0833	13.1	1538	0.3	2054	12.8
4	TU	0355	0.6	0913	12.8	1614	0.7	2131	12.4
5	W	0430	1.1	0950	12.2	1646	1.4	2206	11.8
6	TH	0501	1.9	1025	11.4	1715	2.3	2239	11.0
7	F	0529	2.8	1100	10.5	1744	3.2	2315	10.2
8	SA ☽	0600	3.7	1140	9.6	1819	4.1	2358	9.4
9	SU	0645	4.5	1235	8.8	1917	4.9		
10	M	0106	8.7	0807	5.0	1407	8.3	2055	5.1
11	TU	0247	8.5	0947	4.8	1548	8.6	2222	4.7
12	W	0413	9.0	1059	4.2	1654	9.3	2324	3.9
13	TH	0510	9.7	1152	3.5	1740	10.0		
14	F	0012	3.2	0553	10.4	1238	2.8	1818	10.7
15	SA	0056	2.6	0630	11.1	1319	2.3	1854	11.2
16	SU ○	0136	2.2	0705	11.5	1358	1.9	1927	11.6
17	M	0213	1.8	0738	11.9	1434	1.7	1958	11.9
18	TU	0249	1.6	0810	12.1	1508	1.6	2029	12.0
19	W	0322	1.5	0842	12.2	1540	1.6	2100	12.0
20	TH	0355	1.7	0913	12.0	1611	1.9	2130	11.7
21	F	0428	2.0	0945	11.6	1643	2.3	2202	11.3
22	SA	0503	2.5	1019	11.0	1719	2.9	2238	10.6
23	SU	0543	3.1	1101	10.2	1802	3.5	2326	9.9
24	M ☾	0635	3.7	1201	9.4	1902	4.1		
25	TU	0044	9.3	0746	4.0	1344	9.0	2027	4.3
26	W	0239	9.3	0919	3.9	1526	9.5	2207	3.8
27	TH	0401	10.1	1049	3.1	1636	10.4	2326	2.9
28	F	0503	11.0	1159	2.2	1733	11.3		
29	SA	0029	2.0	0556	11.9	1258	1.4	1822	12.0
30	SU ●	0124	1.2	0644	12.5	1349	0.8	1908	12.4
31	M	0211	0.8	0729	12.8	1433	0.6	1950	12.6

APRIL

Date	Day	Time	m	Time	m	Time	m	Time	m
1	TU	0253	0.7	0811	12.8	1512	0.7	2029	12.6
2	W	0330	0.9	0849	12.5	1545	1.1	2104	12.3
3	TH	0402	1.3	0924	12.0	1615	1.7	2137	11.8
4	F	0430	2.0	0957	11.3	1641	2.4	2208	11.2
5	SA	0457	2.7	1029	10.6	1708	3.3	2241	10.4
6	SU	0525	3.6	1104	9.7	1739	4.1	2319	9.6
7	M ☽	0603	4.3	1151	8.9	1827	4.8		
8	TU	0015	8.9	0706	4.9	1307	8.4	1955	5.3
9	W	0144	8.5	0850	5.0	1451	8.4	2134	5.0
10	TH	0320	8.7	1012	4.5	1610	9.0	2240	4.3
11	F	0427	9.4	1109	3.8	1702	9.8	2331	3.6
12	SA	0515	10.1	1157	3.1	1743	10.5		
13	SU	0017	2.9	0555	10.8	1242	2.5	1820	11.1
14	M	0101	2.3	0633	11.4	1324	2.1	1855	11.6
15	TU ○	0143	1.9	0709	11.9	1405	1.8	1930	12.0
16	W	0223	1.6	0745	12.1	1443	1.6	2004	12.2
17	TH	0301	1.5	0820	12.2	1519	1.6	2038	12.2
18	F	0338	1.5	0855	12.1	1555	1.8	2113	12.0
19	SA	0415	1.8	0932	11.8	1631	2.2	2150	11.6
20	SU	0454	2.2	1013	11.2	1710	2.8	2233	10.9
21	M	0537	2.8	1101	10.4	1756	3.4	2327	10.2
22	TU ☾	0628	3.4	1205	9.7	1855	3.9		
23	W	0045	9.7	0736	3.8	1335	9.4	2015	4.2
24	TH	0219	9.7	0902	3.7	1502	9.7	2147	3.8
25	F	0336	10.2	1026	3.2	1611	10.4	2303	3.0
26	SA	0438	10.9	1134	2.5	1708	11.1		
27	SU	0005	2.3	0532	11.5	1232	1.8	1757	11.7
28	M	0059	1.7	0621	12.0	1322	1.5	1843	12.1
29	TU ●	0145	1.4	0706	12.2	1405	1.3	1924	12.2
30	W	0226	1.4	0747	12.2	1442	1.4	2002	12.2

MAY

Date	Day	Time	m	Time	m	Time	m	Time	m
1	TH	0301	1.5	0825	12.0	1514	1.7	2037	12.0
2	F	0332	1.7	0859	11.7	1543	2.1	2110	11.7
3	SA	0402	2.2	0932	11.2	1612	2.6	2142	11.2
4	SU	0430	2.8	1004	10.6	1641	3.2	2214	10.6
5	M	0500	3.4	1038	9.9	1713	3.9	2251	9.9
6	TU	0535	4.1	1120	9.3	1755	4.6	2338	9.2
7	W ☽	0626	4.6	1218	8.8	1900	5.0		
8	TH	0045	8.8	0742	4.9	1340	8.6	2027	5.0
9	F	0209	8.8	0906	4.7	1504	8.9	2141	4.6
10	SA	0325	9.2	1012	4.1	1608	9.5	2239	3.9
11	SU	0424	9.8	1107	3.5	1657	10.2	2331	3.2
12	M	0513	10.5	1157	2.9	1741	10.9		
13	TU	0020	2.6	0557	11.1	1247	2.4	1821	11.5
14	W ○	0109	2.1	0639	11.6	1334	2.0	1901	11.9
15	TH	0156	1.8	0720	12.0	1419	1.7	1940	12.2
16	F	0241	1.5	0801	12.2	1502	1.6	2020	12.4
17	SA	0325	1.4	0842	12.2	1543	1.7	2101	12.3
18	SU	0407	1.6	0925	11.9	1624	2.0	2145	11.9
19	M	0450	1.9	1011	11.5	1707	2.5	2233	11.4
20	TU	0535	2.4	1102	10.9	1754	3.0	2328	10.8
21	W ☾	0625	2.9	1202	10.3	1850	3.6		
22	TH	0035	10.3	0725	3.4	1315	9.9	1959	3.8
23	F	0152	10.1	0839	3.5	1431	9.9	2119	3.7
24	SA	0305	10.2	0956	3.3	1540	10.3	2233	3.3
25	SU	0409	10.6	1104	2.9	1639	10.7	2336	2.8
26	M	0506	11.0	1202	2.5	1732	11.2		
27	TU	0030	2.4	0557	11.3	1252	2.2	1818	11.5
28	W ●	0117	2.1	0643	11.5	1335	2.1	1900	11.7
29	TH	0158	2.0	0725	11.6	1412	2.1	1938	11.8
30	F	0234	2.0	0803	11.5	1446	2.2	2014	11.7
31	SA	0306	2.1	0838	11.4	1517	2.3	2048	11.6

JUNE

Date	Day	Time	m	Time	m	Time	m	Time	m
1	SU	0338	2.3	0912	11.1	1549	2.7	2120	11.2
2	M	0409	2.7	0945	10.7	1621	3.1	2153	10.8
3	TU	0441	3.1	1018	10.3	1654	3.6	2229	10.3
4	W	0516	3.6	1055	9.8	1733	4.1	2309	9.8
5	TH ☽	0558	4.1	1139	9.3	1821	4.5	2358	9.3
6	F	0651	4.4	1236	9.0	1924	4.7		
7	SA	0100	9.1	0756	4.5	1348	9.0	2034	4.6
8	SU	0214	9.1	0907	4.2	1502	9.3	2142	4.1
9	M	0325	9.5	1012	3.8	1606	9.8	2243	3.6
10	TU	0426	10.1	1112	3.2	1700	10.5	2341	2.9
11	W	0521	10.8	1210	2.7	1750	11.2		
12	TH	0038	2.3	0611	11.4	1306	2.2	1836	11.8
13	F ○	0133	1.8	0659	11.9	1358	1.8	1922	12.3
14	SA	0225	1.4	0746	12.2	1448	1.5	2007	12.5
15	SU	0314	1.2	0833	12.3	1535	1.4	2053	12.6
16	M	0401	1.2	0919	12.2	1620	1.6	2139	12.4
17	TU	0446	1.4	1006	11.9	1704	1.9	2227	11.9
18	W	0531	1.8	1055	11.4	1749	2.5	2318	11.4
19	TH ☾	0617	2.4	1147	10.8	1838	3.1		
20	F	0014	10.7	0708	3.0	1246	10.3	1936	3.6
21	SA	0119	10.2	0809	3.5	1354	10.0	2046	3.8
22	SU	0230	10.0	0919	3.6	1504	10.0	2159	3.7
23	M	0339	10.1	1029	3.5	1609	10.2	2305	3.3
24	TU	0441	10.4	1130	3.1	1707	10.6		
25	W	0002	2.9	0535	10.7	1223	2.8	1755	11.0
26	TH	0051	2.6	0623	10.9	1308	2.6	1839	11.3
27	F ●	0133	2.4	0706	11.1	1348	2.5	1919	11.4
28	SA	0211	2.3	0744	11.2	1424	2.4	1955	11.5
29	SU	0246	2.3	0820	11.2	1458	2.4	2029	11.5
30	M	0320	2.3	0854	11.2	1532	2.5	2102	11.4

ST-MALO
LAT 48°38′N
LONG 2°02′W

TIMES AND HEIGHTS OF HIGH AND LOW WATER (Heights in Metres)

TIME ZONE –0100 (French Standard Time). **Subtract 1 hour for UT. For French Summer Time (area enclosed in shaded box) add 1 hour**

2014

JULY

Date	Time	m	Date	Time	m
1 TU	0353 0927 1605 2135	2.5 11.0 2.8 11.1	16 W	0437 0954 1654 2214	0.8 12.4 1.4 12.4
2 W	0425 0959 1637 2207	2.8 10.7 3.1 10.8	17 TH	0519 1038 1736 2259	1.3 11.9 2.0 11.8
3 TH	0457 1031 1711 2241	3.1 10.3 3.5 10.3	18 F	0600 1123 1818 2348	2.1 11.2 2.7 11.0
4 F	0532 1106 1750 2319	3.5 9.9 3.9 9.9	19 SA ☾	0643 1213 1906	2.9 10.5 3.5
5 SA ☽	0613 1146 1837	3.8 9.5 4.2	20 SU	0043 0733 1313 2007	10.2 3.6 9.9 4.0
6 SU	0005 0703 1240 1936	9.5 4.1 9.2 4.4	21 M	0151 0839 1425 2123	9.7 4.0 9.6 4.2
7 M	0108 0806 1352 2046	9.3 4.2 9.2 4.3	22 TU	0307 0953 1539 2236	9.5 4.1 9.7 3.9
8 TU	0226 0919 1514 2159	9.3 4.0 9.5 3.8	23 W	0418 1101 1644 2337	9.7 3.7 10.1 3.4
9 W	0344 1032 1625 2308	9.7 3.6 10.1 3.2	24 TH	0517 1157 1738	10.1 3.3 10.5
10 TH	0452 1140 1725	10.4 3.0 11.0	25 F	0027 0606 1246 1822	3.0 10.5 2.9 11.0
11 F	0013 0550 1244 1818	2.5 11.1 2.3 11.7	26 SA ●	0112 0648 1328 1901	2.7 10.9 2.7 11.3
12 SA O	0114 0644 1342 1908	1.8 11.8 1.7 12.4	27 SU	0152 0726 1406 1937	2.4 11.1 2.5 11.5
13 SU	0211 0735 1436 1956	1.2 12.3 1.2 12.8	28 M	0229 0802 1442 2011	2.3 11.3 2.3 11.6
14 M	0304 0823 1525 2043	0.8 12.6 1.0 13.0	29 TU	0303 0834 1515 2043	2.2 11.4 2.3 11.6
15 TU	0352 0909 1611 2128	0.7 12.6 1.0 12.9	30 W	0336 0906 1547 2114	2.2 11.3 2.4 11.5
			31 TH	0406 0936 1618 2144	2.3 11.2 2.6 11.3

AUGUST

Date	Time	m	Date	Time	m
1 F	0436 1005 1648 2214	2.6 10.9 2.9 10.9	16 SA	0534 1055 1751 2318	2.0 11.4 2.6 11.0
2 SA	0507 1034 1722 2245	3.0 10.5 3.3 10.4	17 SU ☾	0611 1138 1830	2.9 10.6 3.5
3 SU	0541 1107 1801 2323	3.4 10.0 3.8 9.9	18 M	0006 0652 1231 1922	10.1 3.8 9.8 4.3
4 M ☽	0624 1149 1853	3.8 9.6 4.2	19 TU	0110 0753 1341 2042	9.3 4.5 9.2 4.7
5 TU	0015 0720 1254 2001	9.4 4.2 9.2 4.3	20 W	0233 0917 1507 2207	9.0 4.7 9.2 4.5
6 W	0136 0835 1431 2123	9.1 4.3 9.2 4.1	21 TH	0356 1035 1623 2313	9.2 4.3 9.6 3.9
7 TH	0314 1000 1600 2243	9.4 3.9 9.9 3.4	22 F	0459 1135 1718	9.7 3.7 10.2
8 F	0433 1118 1707 2355	10.2 3.2 10.8 2.5	23 SA	0005 0547 1224 1802	3.3 10.3 3.1 10.8
9 SA	0536 1227 1803	11.1 2.3 11.8	24 SU	0050 0628 1307 1841	2.8 10.9 2.7 11.2
10 SU O	0059 0630 1328 1854	1.7 11.9 1.5 12.6	25 M ●	0130 0705 1345 1916	2.4 11.2 2.4 11.6
11 M	0158 0720 1422 1942	0.9 12.5 0.9 13.1	26 TU	0207 0739 1421 1949	2.2 11.5 2.2 11.8
12 TU	0250 0807 1511 2028	0.5 12.9 0.6 13.3	27 W	0242 0810 1454 2020	2.0 11.7 2.1 11.9
13 W	0337 0852 1556 2112	0.3 12.9 0.6 13.2	28 TH	0314 0840 1526 2050	2.0 11.7 2.1 11.9
14 TH	0419 0934 1637 2154	0.5 12.7 1.0 12.7	29 F	0344 0909 1556 2119	2.0 11.6 2.2 11.7
15 F	0458 1015 1714 2235	1.1 12.1 1.7 11.9	30 SA	0412 0937 1626 2147	2.3 11.4 2.5 11.3
			31 SU	0442 1005 1657 2217	2.7 11.0 3.0 10.8

SEPTEMBER

Date	Time	m	Date	Time	m
1 M	0514 1035 1735 2252	3.2 10.4 3.5 10.2	16 TU ☾	0610 1148 1835	4.0 9.7 4.5
2 TU ☽	0554 1115 1823 2341	3.7 9.9 4.0 9.6	17 W	0025 0703 1254 1952	9.1 4.8 9.0 5.0
3 W	0649 1216 1929	4.2 9.3 4.4	18 TH	0152 0836 1427 2133	8.7 5.2 8.8 4.9
4 TH	0104 0804 1405 2057	9.0 4.5 9.1 4.2	19 F	0326 1005 1553 2245	8.8 4.8 9.2 4.3
5 F	0259 0939 1544 2226	9.3 4.1 9.8 3.5	20 SA	0434 1107 1652 2337	9.5 4.1 9.9 3.6
6 SA	0420 1103 1651 2340	10.1 3.3 10.9 2.5	21 SU	0522 1156 1736	10.2 3.4 10.6
7 SU	0521 1212 1746	11.2 2.3 11.9	22 M	0021 0601 1238 1814	3.0 10.8 2.8 11.2
8 M	0044 0613 1312 1836	1.6 12.1 1.4 12.7	23 TU	0102 0637 1317 1849	2.5 11.4 2.4 11.6
9 TU O	0140 0702 1405 1924	0.8 12.7 0.8 13.2	24 W ●	0139 0710 1354 1922	2.1 11.7 2.1 12.0
10 W	0230 0747 1452 2008	0.4 13.0 0.5 13.4	25 TH	0214 0742 1429 1953	1.9 12.0 1.9 12.1
11 TH	0315 0830 1534 2050	0.3 13.1 0.6 13.2	26 F	0247 0812 1502 2024	1.9 12.1 1.9 12.2
12 F	0355 0910 1613 2130	0.6 12.8 1.0 12.7	27 SA	0319 0842 1534 2054	1.9 12.0 2.0 12.0
13 SA	0431 0948 1647 2208	1.3 12.2 1.8 11.9	28 SU	0349 0911 1605 2125	2.1 11.8 2.3 11.7
14 SU	0503 1025 1719 2246	2.1 11.5 2.7 11.0	29 M	0420 0941 1639 2157	2.5 11.4 2.7 11.1
15 M	0534 1103 1752 2329	3.1 10.6 3.6 10.0	30 TU	0454 1014 1717 2234	3.1 10.8 3.3 10.4

OCTOBER

Date	Time	m	Date	Time	m
1 W ☽	0536 1057 1806 2326	3.7 10.1 3.9 9.7	16 TH	0618 1206 1856	4.9 9.1 5.1
2 TH	0630 1201 1911	4.2 9.5 4.3	17 F	0059 0740 1333 2039	8.6 5.4 8.7 5.2
3 F	0054 0746 1353 2038	9.1 4.5 9.3 4.2	18 SA	0237 0920 1505 2202	8.6 5.1 8.9 4.7
4 SA	0247 0923 1526 2210	9.4 4.2 10.0 3.6	19 SU	0354 1028 1612 2258	9.2 4.5 9.5 4.0
5 SU	0403 1047 1631 2323	10.3 3.3 10.9 2.6	20 M	0446 1118 1700 2343	9.9 3.7 10.3 3.3
6 M	0501 1154 1726	11.2 2.3 11.9	21 TU	0527 1201 1741	10.6 3.1 10.9
7 TU	0025 0552 1252 1816	1.7 12.1 1.5 12.6	22 W	0025 0604 1242 1817	2.7 11.2 2.5 11.5
8 W O	0119 0639 1343 1902	1.0 12.7 1.0 13.0	23 TH ●	0105 0638 1322 1852	2.3 11.7 2.2 11.9
9 TH	0207 0724 1429 1946	0.7 12.9 0.8 13.1	24 F	0143 0711 1400 1926	2.0 12.0 1.9 12.1
10 F	0249 0805 1509 2027	0.7 12.9 0.9 12.9	25 SA	0220 0744 1438 1959	1.9 12.2 1.8 12.2
11 SA	0327 0844 1545 2105	1.0 12.7 1.3 12.4	26 SU	0256 0817 1514 2033	1.9 12.3 1.9 12.1
12 SU	0400 0920 1617 2141	1.6 12.2 1.9 11.7	27 M	0330 0851 1551 2109	2.0 12.1 2.1 11.9
13 M	0430 0954 1647 2217	2.3 11.5 2.7 10.9	28 TU	0406 0926 1628 2147	2.4 11.7 2.5 11.3
14 TU	0459 1030 1717 2255	3.2 10.7 3.6 10.0	29 W	0444 1005 1710 2230	2.9 11.2 3.0 10.7
15 W ☾	0532 1110 1755 2343	4.1 9.9 4.4 9.2	30 TH	0528 1053 1758 2326	3.4 10.5 3.5 10.0
			31 F ☽	0622 1201 1900	4.0 9.9 3.9

NOVEMBER

Date	Time	m	Date	Time	m
1 SA	0049 0734 1336 2020	9.5 4.3 9.7 4.0	16 SU	0126 0811 1354 2054	8.6 5.2 8.8 4.9
2 SU	0225 0903 1501 2148	9.7 4.1 10.1 3.5	17 M	0251 0929 1512 2202	8.9 4.8 9.1 4.4
3 M	0338 1025 1607 2301	10.3 3.4 10.8 2.8	18 TU	0356 1027 1612 2255	9.5 4.1 9.7 3.7
4 TU	0437 1131 1703	11.1 2.6 11.6	19 W	0445 1117 1700 2343	10.2 3.5 10.4 3.1
5 W	0001 0529 1229 1753	2.0 11.8 1.9 12.1	20 TH	0527 1203 1742	10.8 2.9 11.0
6 TH O	0055 0616 1320 1841	1.5 12.3 1.5 12.5	21 F	0028 0605 1249 1822	2.6 11.4 2.4 11.5
7 F	0141 0700 1404 1924	1.3 12.5 1.3 12.5	22 SA ●	0112 0643 1333 1901	2.2 11.9 2.0 11.9
8 SA	0222 0741 1443 2005	1.3 12.6 1.4 12.4	23 SU	0155 0720 1417 1939	1.9 12.2 1.8 12.1
9 SU	0258 0819 1518 2042	1.5 12.4 1.6 12.1	24 M	0237 0758 1500 2019	1.8 12.4 1.7 12.2
10 M	0331 0854 1550 2118	1.9 12.1 2.1 11.5	25 TU	0318 0837 1542 2100	1.8 12.4 1.7 12.0
11 TU	0401 0928 1620 2152	2.5 11.5 2.7 10.9	26 W	0359 0919 1624 2143	2.0 12.1 2.0 11.7
12 W	0431 1003 1651 2227	3.1 10.9 3.4 10.2	27 TH	0441 1003 1708 2230	2.4 11.6 2.4 11.1
13 TH	0504 1040 1726 2309	3.9 10.1 4.1 9.5	28 F	0526 1053 1755 2325	2.9 11.0 2.9 10.5
14 F ☾	0544 1125 1813	4.6 9.4 4.7	29 SA ☽	0617 1154 1851	3.4 10.4 3.4
15 SA	0004 0644 1230 1926	8.9 5.1 8.9 5.0	30 SU	0032 0719 1310 1959	10.0 3.8 10.1 3.6

DECEMBER

Date	Time	m	Date	Time	m
1 M	0152 0836 1429 2117	9.8 3.9 10.1 3.6	16 TU	0126 0812 1353 2047	8.8 4.8 8.9 4.6
2 TU	0307 0956 1539 2232	10.1 3.6 10.5 3.1	17 W	0246 0923 1509 2156	9.0 4.5 9.2 4.1
3 W	0411 1105 1639 2335	10.6 3.0 11.0 2.6	18 TH	0353 1026 1613 2256	9.5 3.9 9.7 3.6
4 TH	0506 1204 1733	11.2 2.4 11.4	19 F	0447 1122 1706 2351	10.2 3.3 10.4 3.0
5 F	0029 0555 1256 1821	2.1 11.7 2.0 11.7	20 SA	0535 1216 1755	10.9 2.6 11.1
6 SA O	0117 0640 1341 1906	1.9 12.0 1.8 11.8	21 SU	0044 0619 1310 1840	2.4 11.6 2.1 11.6
7 SU	0158 0721 1420 1946	1.8 12.1 1.8 11.8	22 M ●	0135 0702 1401 1925	1.9 12.1 1.6 12.1
8 M	0234 0759 1455 2024	1.9 12.0 1.9 11.7	23 TU	0223 0745 1449 2009	1.6 12.5 1.3 12.3
9 TU	0307 0834 1528 2059	2.1 11.9 2.1 11.4	24 W	0310 0829 1536 2054	1.4 12.7 1.2 12.3
10 W	0339 0909 1559 2133	2.4 11.5 2.5 11.0	25 TH	0355 0913 1621 2138	1.4 12.6 1.3 12.1
11 TH	0411 0942 1631 2206	2.8 11.1 3.0 10.5	26 F	0439 0958 1705 2224	1.7 12.2 1.6 11.7
12 F	0444 1016 1704 2241	3.4 10.5 3.5 10.0	27 SA	0522 1046 1749 2313	2.1 11.7 2.2 11.1
13 SA	0519 1054 1742 2322	3.9 9.9 4.0 9.4	28 SU ☽	0608 1138 1837	2.7 11.0 2.8
14 SU ☾	0603 1139 1830	4.4 9.4 4.5	29 M	0008 0659 1239 1932	10.4 3.3 10.3 3.3
15 M	0014 0700 1238 1933	9.0 4.7 9.0 4.7	30 TU	0114 0803 1352 2041	9.9 3.7 9.9 3.7
			31 W	0230 0921 1508 2158	9.8 3.8 9.9 3.6

BREST
LAT 48°23′N
LONG 4°30′W

TIMES AND HEIGHTS OF HIGH AND LOW WATER (Heights in Metres)

TIME ZONE –0100 (French Standard Time). **Subtract 1 hour for UT. For French Summer Time (area enclosed in shaded box) add 1 hour**

2014

SUNRISE AND SUNSET TIMES

BREST
At 48°23′N 4°30′W

		Sunrise	Sunset
European Standard Time (UT-1)			
Jan	01	0910	1735
	15	0905	1752
Feb	01	0847	1818
	15	0826	1841
Mar	01	0800	1903
	15	0732	1924
European Summer Time (UT-2)			
Apr	01	0757	2049
	15	0729	2110
May	01	0700	2133
	15	0639	2152
Jun	01	0622	2212
	15	0617	2222
Jul	01	0622	2223
	15	0633	2215
Aug	01	0654	2156
	15	0713	2133
Sep	01	0736	2100
	15	0756	2031
Oct	01	0818	1958
	15	0839	1930
European Standard Time (UT-1)			
Nov	01	0805	1759
	15	0826	1740
Dec	01	0849	1726

JANUARY

Date	Day	Moon	Time	m	Time	m	Time	m	Time	m
1	W	●	0429	7.3	1051	1.0	1654	7.2	2315	1.0
2	TH		0518	7.5	1141	0.7	1743	7.4		
3	F		0004	0.8	0606	7.7	1230	0.6	1830	7.4
4	SA		0052	0.8	0653	7.6	1318	0.7	1917	7.2
5	SU		0140	1.0	0740	7.4	1405	0.9	2005	6.9
6	M		0228	1.3	0828	7.0	1454	1.3	2054	6.5
7	TU		0318	1.7	0919	6.6	1545	1.8	2147	6.1
8	W	☽	0412	2.1	1015	6.1	1641	2.2	2246	5.8
9	TH		0512	2.5	1117	5.8	1743	2.5	2353	5.6
10	F		0620	2.7	1227	5.6	1852	2.7		
11	SA		0104	5.6	0732	2.7	1340	5.6	2001	2.6
12	SU		0212	5.8	0839	2.5	1442	5.8	2059	2.4
13	M		0307	6.0	0932	2.2	1531	6.0	2147	2.2
14	TU		0352	6.2	1015	2.0	1613	6.2	2227	2.0
15	W		0431	6.5	1053	1.8	1650	6.4	2304	1.8
16	TH	O	0506	6.6	1128	1.7	1724	6.5	2338	1.7
17	F		0539	6.7	1201	1.6	1757	6.6		
18	SA		0011	1.6	0611	6.8	1233	1.5	1828	6.6
19	SU		0044	1.6	0641	6.8	1305	1.6	1859	6.5
20	M		0116	1.7	0712	6.7	1336	1.7	1931	6.4
21	TU		0149	1.8	0744	6.5	1410	1.9	2005	6.2
22	W		0225	2.0	0820	6.3	1447	2.1	2044	6.0
23	TH		0307	2.2	0901	6.0	1532	2.4	2131	5.8
24	F	☾	0356	2.5	0952	5.8	1627	2.6	2232	5.6
25	SA		0458	2.7	1101	5.6	1738	2.7	2351	5.5
26	SU		0614	2.7	1227	5.6	1857	2.6		
27	M		0111	5.8	0732	2.4	1348	5.9	2010	2.2
28	TU		0223	6.2	0843	1.9	1455	6.3	2114	1.8
29	W		0323	6.7	0944	1.4	1552	6.8	2210	1.3
30	TH	●	0416	7.2	1038	0.9	1642	7.2	2302	0.9
31	F		0506	7.6	1128	0.6	1730	7.4	2350	0.6

FEBRUARY

Date	Day	Moon	Time	m	Time	m	Time	m	Time	m
1	SA		0553	7.8	1215	0.4	1815	7.5		
2	SU		0036	0.6	0637	7.8	1301	0.5	1859	7.4
3	M		0122	0.7	0721	7.5	1345	0.8	1942	7.1
4	TU		0206	1.0	0805	7.2	1428	1.2	2025	6.7
5	W		0251	1.5	0848	6.6	1513	1.7	2109	6.2
6	TH	☽	0338	2.0	0935	6.1	1601	2.2	2200	5.8
7	F		0430	2.5	1030	5.6	1657	2.7	2303	5.4
8	SA		0534	2.8	1139	5.3	1805	2.9		
9	SU		0018	5.3	0650	2.9	1302	5.2	1924	2.9
10	M		0140	5.4	0811	2.8	1419	5.4	2035	2.7
11	TU		0246	5.7	0911	2.5	1513	5.8	2126	2.4
12	W		0333	6.0	0956	2.1	1555	6.1	2208	2.1
13	TH		0412	6.3	1034	1.8	1631	6.4	2244	1.8
14	F		0447	6.6	1108	1.6	1705	6.6	2318	1.6
15	SA	O	0520	6.8	1140	1.4	1736	6.7	2350	1.4
16	SU		0550	6.9	1211	1.4	1806	6.8		
17	M		0021	1.4	0619	6.9	1241	1.3	1835	6.8
18	TU		0053	1.4	0649	6.9	1311	1.4	1905	6.7
19	W		0125	1.5	0720	6.8	1344	1.6	1938	6.6
20	TH		0201	1.7	0755	6.6	1421	1.8	2015	6.3
21	F		0242	1.9	0834	6.2	1504	2.1	2100	6.0
22	SA	☾	0330	2.2	0922	5.9	1557	2.5	2159	5.7
23	SU		0430	2.5	1029	5.6	1706	2.7	2319	5.5
24	M		0546	2.6	1201	5.4	1830	2.7		
25	TU		0048	5.7	0710	2.4	1331	5.7	1951	2.3
26	W		0205	6.1	0827	2.0	1442	6.2	2059	1.8
27	TH		0308	6.7	0930	1.4	1538	6.7	2156	1.3
28	F		0401	7.2	1023	0.9	1628	7.2	2246	0.9

MARCH

Date	Day	Moon	Time	m	Time	m	Time	m	Time	m
1	SA	●	0450	7.5	1112	0.6	1713	7.4	2333	0.6
2	SU		0535	7.7	1157	0.4	1756	7.5		
3	M		0018	0.5	0618	7.7	1240	0.5	1837	7.4
4	TU		0101	0.7	0659	7.5	1321	0.8	1916	7.1
5	W		0142	1.0	0738	7.1	1400	1.2	1953	6.7
6	TH		0222	1.4	0816	6.6	1439	1.7	2032	6.3
7	F		0304	1.9	0857	6.1	1521	2.3	2115	5.8
8	SA	☽	0350	2.4	0944	5.6	1610	2.7	2211	5.4
9	SU		0448	2.9	1050	5.2	1716	3.1	2328	5.1
10	M		0603	3.1	1216	5.0	1839	3.1		
11	TU		0057	5.2	0731	3.0	1345	5.2	2001	2.9
12	W		0213	5.4	0840	2.6	1446	5.6	2057	2.5
13	TH		0304	5.8	0927	2.2	1528	6.0	2140	2.1
14	F		0344	6.2	1005	1.9	1604	6.3	2216	1.8
15	SA		0419	6.5	1040	1.6	1637	6.6	2251	1.5
16	SU	O	0452	6.8	1112	1.4	1709	6.8	2324	1.3
17	M		0524	6.9	1144	1.3	1740	6.9	2356	1.2
18	TU		0555	7.0	1215	1.2	1810	7.0		
19	W		0029	1.2	0626	7.0	1248	1.3	1842	6.9
20	TH		0104	1.3	0659	6.9	1322	1.4	1916	6.8
21	F		0142	1.5	0735	6.7	1401	1.7	1955	6.5
22	SA		0224	1.7	0817	6.3	1445	2.0	2042	6.2
23	SU		0314	2.1	0907	5.9	1539	2.4	2142	5.8
24	M	☾	0414	2.4	1016	5.6	1649	2.6	2303	5.6
25	TU		0529	2.5	1146	5.5	1813	2.6		
26	W		0030	5.7	0653	2.4	1315	5.7	1934	2.3
27	TH		0147	6.1	0809	1.9	1425	6.2	2043	1.8
28	F		0250	6.6	0912	1.4	1521	6.7	2139	1.3
29	SA		0343	7.0	1005	1.0	1609	7.1	2228	0.9
30	SU	●	0431	7.4	1052	0.7	1653	7.3	2314	0.7
31	M		0515	7.5	1136	0.6	1735	7.4	2357	0.7

APRIL

Date	Day	Moon	Time	m	Time	m	Time	m	Time	m
1	TU		0556	7.5	1216	0.7	1813	7.3		
2	W		0037	0.8	0634	7.3	1254	1.0	1849	7.1
3	TH		0116	1.1	0711	6.9	1331	1.3	1923	6.7
4	F		0154	1.5	0747	6.5	1407	1.8	1959	6.3
5	SA		0233	1.9	0824	6.0	1445	2.3	2038	5.9
6	SU		0315	2.4	0908	5.6	1530	2.7	2128	5.5
7	M	☽	0408	2.8	1008	5.2	1630	3.1	2240	5.2
8	TU		0517	3.0	1127	5.0	1749	3.2		
9	W		0004	5.1	0637	3.0	1252	5.1	1910	3.0
10	TH		0121	5.3	0750	2.8	1401	5.4	2013	2.7
11	F		0220	5.7	0844	2.4	1449	5.8	2100	2.3
12	SA		0304	6.0	0926	2.0	1528	6.2	2140	1.9
13	SU		0343	6.4	1004	1.7	1604	6.5	2217	1.6
14	M		0419	6.7	1040	1.4	1638	6.8	2254	1.4
15	TU	O	0455	6.9	1115	1.3	1713	7.0	2330	1.2
16	W		0530	7.0	1150	1.2	1747	7.1		
17	TH		0007	1.1	0605	7.0	1227	1.2	1823	7.1
18	F		0047	1.2	0642	6.9	1306	1.3	1901	6.9
19	SA		0128	1.3	0723	6.7	1348	1.6	1944	6.7
20	SU		0214	1.6	0808	6.4	1436	1.9	2034	6.3
21	M		0306	1.9	0903	6.0	1531	2.2	2136	6.0
22	TU	☾	0406	2.1	1012	5.7	1639	2.5	2252	5.8
23	W		0518	2.3	1134	5.6	1757	2.5		
24	TH		0012	5.9	0635	2.2	1254	5.8	1914	2.3
25	F		0125	6.1	0748	1.9	1403	6.1	2022	1.9
26	SA		0228	6.5	0850	1.6	1459	6.5	2118	1.5
27	SU		0322	6.8	0943	1.3	1548	6.8	2208	1.2
28	M		0409	7.0	1030	1.1	1632	7.0	2253	1.0
29	TU	●	0453	7.1	1113	1.0	1712	7.1	2335	1.0
30	W		0533	7.1	1152	1.1	1749	7.1		

MAY

Date	Day	Moon	Time	m	Time	m	Time	m	Time	m
1	TH		0014	1.1	0610	6.9	1229	1.3	1823	6.9
2	F		0051	1.3	0646	6.7	1304	1.5	1858	6.7
3	SA		0128	1.6	0721	6.4	1339	1.8	1933	6.3
4	SU		0206	1.9	0759	6.0	1417	2.2	2012	6.0
5	M		0246	2.3	0841	5.7	1459	2.6	2057	5.6
6	TU		0334	2.6	0933	5.4	1551	2.9	2156	5.4
7	W	☽	0433	2.9	1039	5.2	1658	3.0	2308	5.2
8	TH		0541	2.9	1152	5.2	1811	3.0		
9	F		0019	5.3	0649	2.8	1300	5.4	1915	2.8
10	SA		0122	5.5	0748	2.5	1356	5.7	2010	2.4
11	SU		0215	5.8	0838	2.2	1444	6.0	2057	2.1
12	M		0301	6.2	0922	1.9	1526	6.4	2141	1.7
13	TU		0344	6.5	1005	1.6	1607	6.7	2224	1.4
14	W	O	0425	6.7	1046	1.4	1647	6.9	2306	1.2
15	TH		0507	6.9	1127	1.2	1727	7.1	2348	1.1
16	F		0548	7.0	1209	1.2	1808	7.2		
17	SA		0032	1.0	0630	7.0	1253	1.2	1851	7.1
18	SU		0118	1.1	0716	6.8	1339	1.4	1938	6.9
19	M		0207	1.3	0805	6.5	1429	1.7	2030	6.6
20	TU		0259	1.6	0900	6.2	1524	2.0	2130	6.3
21	W	☾	0358	1.8	1004	5.9	1628	2.2	2238	6.1
22	TH		0503	2.1	1115	5.8	1738	2.3	2349	6.0
23	F		0612	2.1	1227	5.8	1849	2.2		
24	SA		0058	6.1	0721	2.0	1335	6.0	1956	2.0
25	SU		0202	6.3	0824	1.8	1434	6.3	2055	1.8
26	M		0258	6.5	0919	1.6	1525	6.5	2147	1.5
27	TU		0348	6.6	1007	1.5	1610	6.7	2233	1.4
28	W	●	0432	6.7	1050	1.4	1651	6.8	2314	1.3
29	TH		0512	6.7	1129	1.4	1728	6.8	2352	1.4
30	F		0549	6.6	1205	1.5	1803	6.7		
31	SA		0029	1.5	0624	6.5	1241	1.7	1837	6.6

JUNE

Date	Day	Moon	Time	m	Time	m	Time	m	Time	m
1	SU		0105	1.7	0700	6.3	1316	1.8	1913	6.4
2	M		0142	1.9	0737	6.1	1353	2.1	1950	6.1
3	TU		0220	2.1	0816	5.8	1432	2.3	2030	5.9
4	W		0302	2.4	0900	5.6	1516	2.6	2116	5.6
5	TH	☽	0349	2.6	0951	5.4	1608	2.8	2212	5.5
6	F		0445	2.7	1051	5.3	1710	2.8	2315	5.4
7	SA		0547	2.7	1156	5.4	1816	2.8		
8	SU		0021	5.5	0649	2.6	1259	5.5	1917	2.6
9	M		0123	5.7	0747	2.4	1357	5.8	2013	2.3
10	TU		0219	6.0	0841	2.1	1449	6.2	2106	1.9
11	W		0311	6.3	0932	1.7	1537	6.6	2156	1.5
12	TH		0400	6.6	1020	1.4	1624	6.9	2244	1.2
13	F	O	0447	6.9	1108	1.2	1710	7.1	2332	1.0
14	SA		0534	7.0	1155	1.1	1756	7.3		
15	SU		0020	0.8	0620	7.1	1242	1.0	1842	7.3
16	M		0108	0.8	0708	7.0	1330	1.1	1930	7.2
17	TU		0157	1.0	0757	6.8	1420	1.3	2021	6.9
18	W		0248	1.2	0849	6.5	1512	1.6	2116	6.6
19	TH	☾	0343	1.6	0946	6.2	1610	1.9	2216	6.3
20	F		0441	1.9	1049	5.9	1713	2.2	2320	6.0
21	SA		0545	2.1	1155	5.8	1820	2.3		
22	SU		0027	5.9	0650	2.2	1303	5.8	1928	2.2
23	M		0134	5.9	0756	2.1	1407	6.0	2032	2.1
24	TU		0235	6.1	0855	2.0	1503	6.2	2127	1.9
25	W		0328	6.2	0946	1.9	1551	6.4	2215	1.7
26	TH		0413	6.3	1030	1.8	1633	6.5	2256	1.6
27	F	●	0454	6.4	1109	1.7	1710	6.6	2334	1.6
28	SA		0531	6.4	1145	1.7	1746	6.6		
29	SU		0010	1.6	0606	6.4	1220	1.7	1819	6.6
30	M		0045	1.6	0640	6.4	1255	1.8	1853	6.5

BREST
LAT 48°23′N
LONG 4°30′W

TIMES AND HEIGHTS OF HIGH AND LOW WATER (Heights in Metres)

TIME ZONE –0100 (French Standard Time). **Subtract 1 hour for UT. For French Summer Time (area enclosed in shaded box) add 1 hour**

2014

JULY

Date	Day	Time	m	Time	m	Time	m	Time	m
1	TU	0119	1.7	0714	6.3	1330	1.9	1927	6.4
2	W	0154	1.9	0749	6.1	1405	2.0	2002	6.2
3	TH	0230	2.1	0826	5.9	1443	2.2	2040	6.0
4	F	0308	2.3	0906	5.7	1525	2.4	2123	5.7
5	SA	0353	2.5	0955	5.5	1615	2.6	☽ 2215	5.6
6	SU	0448	2.6	1055	5.4	1717	2.7	2320	5.5
7	M	0553	2.7	1203	5.5	1826	2.7		
8	TU	0032	5.5	0700	2.5	1313	5.7	1933	2.4
9	W	0142	5.8	0805	2.2	1416	6.0	2035	2.0
10	TH	0244	6.1	0904	1.9	1513	6.5	2133	1.6
11	F	0339	6.5	0959	1.5	1605	6.9	2226	1.2
12	SA	0431	6.9	1050	1.1	1654	7.3	○ 2317	0.8
13	SU	0520	7.1	1140	0.9	1743	7.5		
14	M	0006	0.6	0607	7.3	1229	0.8	1829	7.6
15	TU	0054	0.6	0654	7.2	1316	0.8	1917	7.4
16	W	0142	0.7	0742	7.0	1404	1.0	2005	7.2
17	TH	0230	1.0	0830	6.7	1454	1.3	2055	6.8
18	F	0320	1.4	0921	6.3	1546	1.7	2148	6.3
19	SA	0414	1.9	1017	6.0	1643	2.1	☾ 2248	5.9
20	SU	0513	2.2	1120	5.7	1748	2.4	2354	5.7
21	M	0618	2.5	1229	5.6	1858	2.5		
22	TU	0105	5.6	0727	2.5	1341	5.7	2009	2.4
23	W	0214	5.7	0833	2.4	1443	5.9	2109	2.2
24	TH	0310	5.9	0927	2.2	1533	6.1	2158	2.0
25	F	0357	6.1	1012	2.0	1616	6.3	2239	1.8
26	SA	0437	6.3	1050	1.8	1653	6.5	● 2316	1.6
27	SU	0513	6.4	1126	1.7	1727	6.6	2350	1.5
28	M	0546	6.5	1159	1.6	1800	6.7		
29	TU	0022	1.5	0617	6.5	1232	1.6	1830	6.7
30	W	0054	1.5	0649	6.5	1304	1.6	1901	6.6
31	TH	0125	1.7	0720	6.4	1337	1.8	1932	6.5

AUGUST

Date	Day	Time	m	Time	m	Time	m	Time	m
1	F	0157	1.8	0752	6.2	1411	1.9	2006	6.3
2	SA	0232	2.0	0828	6.0	1449	2.2	2044	6.0
3	SU	0312	2.3	0911	5.8	1534	2.4	2130	5.7
4	M	0402	2.5	1005	5.6	1631	2.6	☽ 2231	5.5
5	TU	0506	2.7	1116	5.5	1742	2.7	2351	5.4
6	W	0622	2.7	1237	5.6	1900	2.5		
7	TH	0113	5.6	0736	2.4	1350	6.0	2011	2.1
8	F	0223	6.0	0843	2.0	1453	6.5	2114	1.6
9	SA	0323	6.5	0941	1.5	1548	7.0	2210	1.1
10	SU	0415	7.0	1034	1.0	1638	7.4	○ 2301	0.7
11	M	0504	7.3	1124	0.7	1726	7.7	2349	0.4
12	TU	0551	7.5	1211	0.6	1813	7.8		
13	W	0036	0.4	0635	7.4	1258	0.6	1858	7.6
14	TH	0122	0.6	0720	7.2	1344	0.8	1943	7.3
15	F	0207	0.9	0804	6.9	1430	1.2	2028	6.9
16	SA	0253	1.4	0850	6.4	1518	1.7	2117	6.3
17	SU	0341	1.9	0941	6.0	1611	2.2	☾ 2212	5.8
18	M	0436	2.4	1042	5.6	1713	2.6	2318	5.4
19	TU	0541	2.7	1154	5.4	1826	2.8		
20	W	0035	5.3	0656	2.8	1313	5.5	1945	2.7
21	TH	0152	5.4	0810	2.7	1423	5.7	2049	2.4
22	F	0252	5.7	0907	2.4	1514	6.0	2138	2.1
23	SA	0338	6.0	0951	2.1	1555	6.3	2218	1.8
24	SU	0416	6.3	1029	1.8	1631	6.5	2253	1.6
25	M	0450	6.5	1103	1.6	1704	6.7	● 2326	1.5
26	TU	0522	6.6	1135	1.5	1735	6.8	2356	1.4
27	W	0552	6.7	1206	1.5	1805	6.9		
28	TH	0026	1.4	0621	6.7	1237	1.5	1834	6.8
29	F	0056	1.5	0650	6.7	1309	1.6	1904	6.7
30	SA	0127	1.6	0722	6.5	1342	1.7	1936	6.5
31	SU	0202	1.9	0757	6.3	1421	2.0	2013	6.2

SEPTEMBER

Date	Day	Time	m	Time	m	Time	m	Time	m
1	M	0242	2.2	0838	6.0	1506	2.3	2058	5.9
2	TU	0330	2.5	0931	5.7	1601	2.5	☽ 2158	5.6
3	W	0433	2.7	1044	5.5	1713	2.7	2323	5.4
4	TH	0554	2.7	1212	5.6	1835	2.6		
5	F	0053	5.6	0715	2.5	1331	6.0	1952	2.1
6	SA	0207	6.0	0825	2.0	1436	6.5	2057	1.6
7	SU	0307	6.6	0924	1.5	1530	7.1	2153	1.1
8	M	0358	7.1	1017	1.0	1620	7.5	2243	0.6
9	TU	0446	7.4	1105	0.7	1707	7.7	○ 2330	0.4
10	W	0531	7.6	1152	0.5	1752	7.8		
11	TH	0015	0.4	0613	7.5	1237	0.6	1835	7.6
12	F	0059	0.6	0655	7.3	1320	0.8	1917	7.3
13	SA	0141	1.0	0736	7.0	1403	1.3	1959	6.8
14	SU	0223	1.5	0817	6.5	1448	1.8	2043	6.3
15	M	0307	2.1	0903	6.0	1537	2.3	2134	5.7
16	TU	0357	2.6	1001	5.6	1635	2.8	☾ 2239	5.3
17	W	0501	3.0	1115	5.3	1749	3.0	2359	5.1
18	TH	0621	3.1	1239	5.3	1913	2.9		
19	F	0123	5.3	0740	2.9	1354	5.6	2022	2.6
20	SA	0226	5.6	0839	2.5	1447	5.9	2110	2.3
21	SU	0311	6.0	0923	2.2	1527	6.2	2149	1.9
22	M	0348	6.3	1001	1.9	1603	6.5	2224	1.7
23	TU	0422	6.6	1035	1.6	1636	6.8	2256	1.5
24	W	0453	6.8	1107	1.5	1707	6.9	● 2328	1.4
25	TH	0524	6.9	1139	1.4	1737	7.0	2358	1.4
26	F	0554	6.9	1211	1.4	1808	6.9		
27	SA	0029	1.4	0624	6.9	1244	1.5	1839	6.8
28	SU	0102	1.6	0657	6.7	1320	1.6	1913	6.6
29	M	0139	1.8	0733	6.5	1400	1.9	1952	6.3
30	TU	0220	2.1	0816	6.2	1447	2.2	2039	6.0

OCTOBER

Date	Day	Time	m	Time	m	Time	m	Time	m
1	W	0311	2.4	0911	5.9	1544	2.4	☽ 2142	5.6
2	TH	0414	2.7	1025	5.7	1655	2.6	2307	5.5
3	F	0534	2.7	1154	5.7	1817	2.5		
4	SA	0037	5.7	0657	2.5	1313	6.1	1934	2.1
5	SU	0150	6.1	0808	2.0	1417	6.6	2039	1.6
6	M	0249	6.6	0907	1.5	1512	7.1	2134	1.1
7	TU	0339	7.1	0958	1.1	1601	7.4	2223	0.8
8	W	0426	7.4	1046	0.8	1647	7.6	○ 2309	0.6
9	TH	0509	7.5	1131	0.7	1731	7.7	2352	0.7
10	F	0550	7.5	1214	0.7	1812	7.5		
11	SA	0033	0.9	0629	7.3	1256	1.0	1852	7.2
12	SU	0114	1.2	0707	7.0	1337	1.4	1931	6.7
13	M	0153	1.7	0746	6.5	1418	1.9	2011	6.2
14	TU	0234	2.2	0828	6.1	1503	2.4	2058	5.7
15	W	0320	2.7	0919	5.6	1557	2.8	☾ 2159	5.3
16	TH	0418	3.0	1030	5.3	1706	3.1	2316	5.1
17	F	0534	3.2	1151	5.3	1826	3.1		
18	SA	0037	5.2	0654	3.1	1308	5.4	1938	2.8
19	SU	0145	5.5	0758	2.7	1406	5.8	2030	2.5
20	M	0234	5.9	0846	2.4	1450	6.1	2112	2.1
21	TU	0313	6.2	0926	2.0	1528	6.4	2149	1.8
22	W	0349	6.6	1002	1.7	1603	6.7	2224	1.6
23	TH	0423	6.8	1037	1.5	1637	6.9	● 2258	1.4
24	F	0456	7.0	1112	1.4	1711	7.0	2332	1.4
25	SA	0529	7.0	1147	1.3	1745	7.0		
26	SU	0006	1.4	0603	7.0	1225	1.4	1820	6.9
27	M	0043	1.5	0639	6.9	1304	1.5	1858	6.7
28	TU	0123	1.7	0719	6.7	1347	1.7	1941	6.5
29	W	0208	2.0	0805	6.5	1436	2.0	2031	6.1
30	TH	0300	2.3	0901	6.1	1533	2.2	2134	5.8
31	F	0402	2.5	1013	5.9	1641	2.4	☽ 2254	5.7

NOVEMBER

Date	Day	Time	m	Time	m	Time	m	Time	m
1	SA	0518	2.6	1134	5.9	1758	2.4		
2	SU	0016	5.8	0636	2.5	1250	6.1	1912	2.1
3	M	0128	6.1	0746	2.1	1355	6.5	2017	1.7
4	TU	0228	6.5	0847	1.7	1452	6.9	2113	1.4
5	W	0319	6.9	0940	1.3	1542	7.2	2203	1.1
6	TH	0406	7.2	1028	1.1	1628	7.3	○ 2249	1.0
7	F	0449	7.3	1112	1.0	1710	7.3	2331	1.0
8	SA	0529	7.3	1154	1.0	1751	7.2		
9	SU	0010	1.2	0607	7.2	1234	1.2	1828	7.0
10	M	0049	1.4	0644	6.9	1313	1.5	1906	6.6
11	TU	0126	1.8	0720	6.6	1352	1.9	1945	6.2
12	W	0205	2.2	0800	6.2	1433	2.3	2028	5.8
13	TH	0247	2.5	0845	5.8	1521	2.7	2119	5.5
14	F	0337	2.9	0942	5.5	1618	2.9	☾ 2224	5.3
15	SA	0441	3.1	1052	5.3	1727	3.0	2337	5.2
16	SU	0554	3.1	1205	5.4	1837	2.9		
17	M	0045	5.4	0701	2.9	1310	5.6	1937	2.7
18	TU	0144	5.7	0758	2.6	1403	5.9	2026	2.4
19	W	0231	6.0	0845	2.3	1449	6.2	2109	2.1
20	TH	0313	6.4	0927	2.0	1530	6.5	2150	1.8
21	F	0352	6.7	1008	1.7	1609	6.7	2229	1.6
22	SA	0430	6.9	1048	1.4	1648	6.9	● 2308	1.4
23	SU	0508	7.1	1128	1.3	1727	7.0	2348	1.3
24	M	0548	7.2	1209	1.2	1807	7.0		
25	TU	0029	1.4	0628	7.1	1253	1.3	1849	6.9
26	W	0113	1.5	0711	7.0	1339	1.4	1935	6.7
27	TH	0200	1.7	0759	6.8	1428	1.6	2026	6.4
28	F	0252	2.0	0853	6.5	1523	1.9	2125	6.1
29	SA	0350	2.2	0957	6.2	1626	2.1	☽ 2235	5.9
30	SU	0458	2.4	1109	6.1	1735	2.2	2349	5.9

DECEMBER

Date	Day	Time	m	Time	m	Time	m	Time	m
1	M	0611	2.4	1222	6.1	1846	2.2		
2	TU	0100	6.0	0721	2.2	1331	6.3	1952	2.0
3	W	0204	6.3	0826	1.9	1431	6.5	2052	1.7
4	TH	0259	6.6	0922	1.6	1524	6.8	2144	1.5
5	F	0348	6.8	1011	1.4	1611	6.9	2230	1.4
6	SA	0432	7.0	1055	1.3	1653	6.9	○ 2312	1.4
7	SU	0512	7.0	1136	1.3	1733	6.9	2350	1.4
8	M	0550	7.0	1215	1.4	1810	6.8		
9	TU	0027	1.6	0625	6.9	1252	1.6	1846	6.6
10	W	0104	1.8	0701	6.6	1329	1.8	1923	6.3
11	TH	0141	2.0	0737	6.4	1406	2.1	2001	6.0
12	F	0219	2.3	0815	6.1	1447	2.4	2043	5.8
13	SA	0301	2.6	0858	5.8	1531	2.6	2131	5.5
14	SU	0349	2.8	0950	5.6	1625	2.8	☾ 2230	5.4
15	M	0448	3.0	1053	5.4	1728	2.9	2336	5.3
16	TU	0554	3.0	1202	5.4	1833	2.9		
17	W	0042	5.5	0659	2.8	1307	5.6	1933	2.6
18	TH	0142	5.7	0758	2.6	1406	5.8	2027	2.3
19	F	0235	6.1	0852	2.2	1457	6.2	2117	2.0
20	SA	0322	6.5	0940	1.8	1544	6.5	2203	1.7
21	SU	0407	6.8	1027	1.5	1629	6.8	2248	1.4
22	M	0451	7.1	1112	1.2	1713	7.0	● 2333	1.2
23	TU	0535	7.3	1157	1.0	1757	7.2		
24	W	0018	1.1	0618	7.4	1243	0.9	1841	7.1
25	TH	0104	1.1	0704	7.4	1329	1.0	1927	7.0
26	F	0151	1.3	0751	7.2	1417	1.2	2016	6.7
27	SA	0241	1.5	0841	6.8	1509	1.5	2109	6.4
28	SU	0334	1.9	0937	6.5	1605	1.9	☽ 2210	6.1
29	M	0434	2.2	1041	6.2	1708	2.2	2317	5.9
30	TU	0541	2.4	1151	6.0	1816	2.3		
31	W	0028	5.8	0652	2.4	1303	5.9	1925	2.3

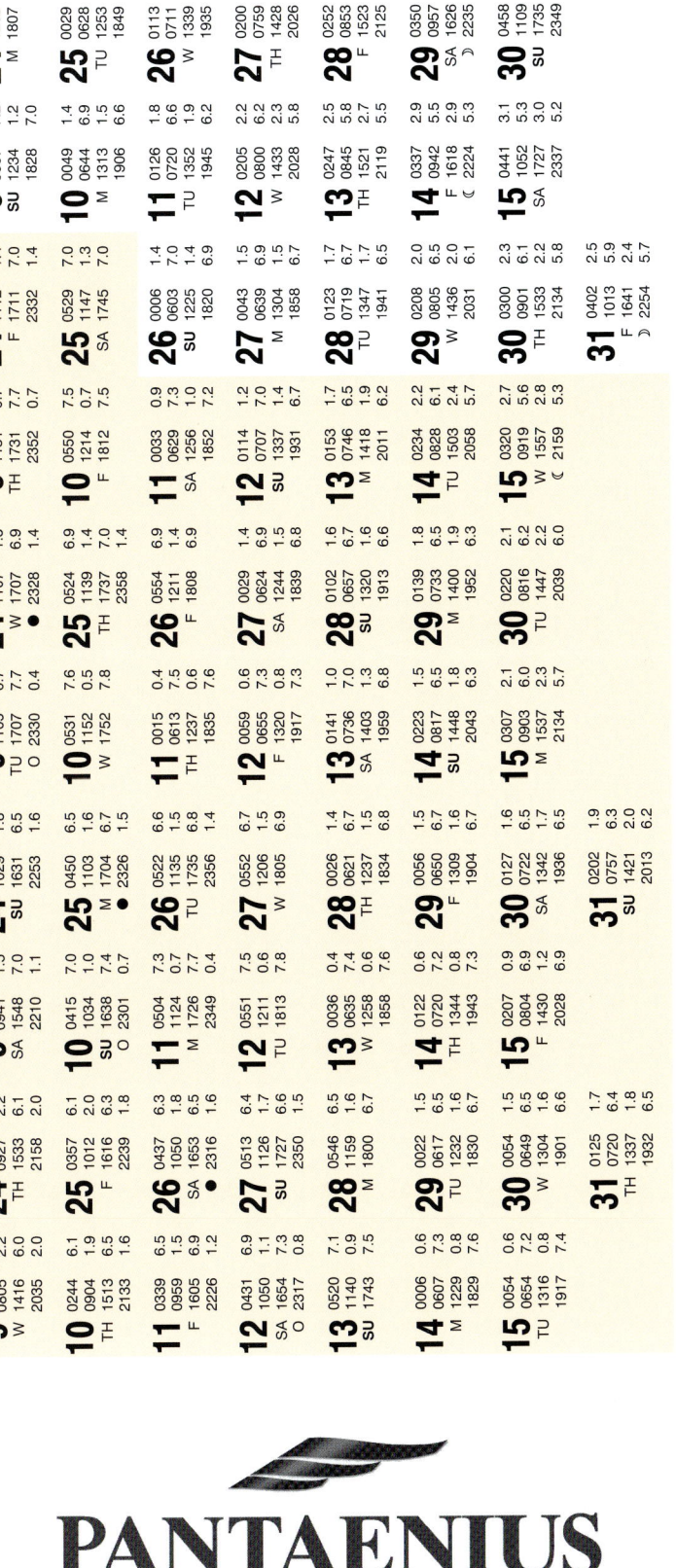

POINTE DE GRAVE

LAT 45°34′N
LONG 1°04′W

TIMES AND HEIGHTS OF HIGH AND LOW WATER (Heights in Metres)

TIME ZONE –0100 (French Standard Time). **Subtract 1 hour for UT. For French Summer Time (area enclosed in shaded box) add 1 hour**

2014

SUNRISE AND SUNSET TIMES

POINTE DE GRAVE
At 45°34′N 1°04′W

European Standard Time (UT-1)

		Sunrise	Sunset
Jan	01	0845	1731
	15	0841	1747
Feb	01	0825	1811
	15	0806	1831
Mar	01	0743	1851
	15	0717	1910
European Summer Time (UT-2)			
Apr	01	0745	2033
	15	0719	2051
May	01	0652	2111
	15	0634	2128
Jun	01	0619	2146
	15	0615	2155
Jul	01	0619	2157
	15	0630	2150
Aug	01	0648	2132
	15	0705	2112
Sep	01	0726	2042
	15	0743	2015
Oct	01	0803	1945
	15	0821	1919
European Standard Time (UT-1)			
Nov	01	0744	1751
	15	0804	1734
Dec	01	0824	1722

JANUARY

Date	Day	Time	m
1	W ●	0438	5.7
		1040	1.0
		1709	5.6
		2303	1.0
2	TH	0529	5.8
		1131	0.9
		1759	5.6
		2352	0.9
3	F	0618	5.9
		1219	0.8
		1847	5.6
4	SA	0039	0.9
		0707	5.8
		1306	0.9
		1935	5.5
5	SU	0126	1.1
		0755	5.7
		1353	1.0
		2022	5.2
6	M	0213	1.2
		0843	5.4
		1440	1.3
		2112	5.0
7	TU	0303	1.5
		0934	5.1
		1530	1.6
		2208	4.7
8	W ☽	0358	1.7
		1032	4.8
		1627	1.9
		2316	4.5
9	TH	0501	2.0
		1142	4.6
		1732	2.1
10	F	0033	4.5
		0610	2.1
		1300	4.5
		1842	2.1
11	SA	0144	4.5
		0721	2.1
		1410	4.5
		1949	2.1
12	SU	0242	4.7
		0824	2.0
		1505	4.6
		2046	1.9
13	M	0327	4.8
		0917	1.8
		1548	4.8
		2134	1.8
14	TU	0404	5.0
		1003	1.7
		1624	4.9
		2215	1.7
15	W	0437	5.1
		1042	1.6
		1657	5.0
		2251	1.5
16	TH O	0509	5.2
		1118	1.5
		1728	5.1
		2325	1.5
17	F	0540	5.2
		1151	1.4
		1759	5.1
		2358	1.4
18	SA	0610	5.2
		1223	1.4
		1828	5.1
19	SU	0030	1.4
		0639	5.2
		1255	1.4
		1857	5.0
20	M	0103	1.4
		0709	5.1
		1326	1.5
		1928	4.9
21	TU	0136	1.5
		0741	5.0
		1358	1.5
		2003	4.8
22	W	0211	1.6
		0818	4.9
		1435	1.7
		2045	4.6
23	TH	0252	1.7
		0903	4.7
		1518	1.8
		2141	4.5
24	F ☾	0342	1.9
		1006	4.5
		1613	2.0
		2257	4.4
25	SA	0445	2.0
		1128	4.4
		1722	2.1
26	SU	0019	4.5
		0559	2.0
		1253	4.5
		1842	2.0
27	M	0132	4.7
		0717	1.9
		1407	4.7
		1958	1.8
28	TU	0237	5.0
		0830	1.6
		1512	5.0
		2103	1.5
29	W	0334	5.3
		0932	1.3
		1608	5.3
		2159	1.2
30	TH ●	0427	5.7
		1027	1.0
		1659	5.6
		2250	1.0
31	F	0517	5.9
		1117	0.8
		1746	5.7
		2338	0.8

FEBRUARY

Date	Day	Time	m
1	SA	0605	6.0
		1204	0.7
		1832	5.7
2	SU	0024	0.8
		0650	5.9
		1250	0.7
		1915	5.6
3	M	0109	0.8
		0734	5.8
		1333	0.9
		1956	5.4
4	TU	0152	1.0
		0816	5.5
		1415	1.2
		2035	5.1
5	W	0237	1.3
		0858	5.1
		1459	1.5
		2117	4.8
6	TH ☽	0325	1.6
		0944	4.8
		1547	1.8
		2210	4.5
7	F	0420	1.9
		1045	4.4
		1646	2.1
		2330	4.3
8	SA	0528	2.2
		1212	4.2
		1759	2.3
9	SU	0104	4.3
		0645	2.3
		1339	4.3
		1916	2.3
10	M	0215	4.4
		0758	2.2
		1443	4.4
		2022	2.1
11	TU	0306	4.6
		0856	2.0
		1529	4.6
		2113	1.9
12	W	0346	4.8
		0942	1.8
		1606	4.8
		2154	1.7
13	TH	0420	5.0
		1021	1.6
		1638	5.0
		2231	1.5
14	F	0451	5.2
		1056	1.4
		1709	5.1
		2306	1.4
15	SA O	0521	5.3
		1130	1.3
		1738	5.2
		2339	1.3
16	SU	0549	5.3
		1202	1.2
		1806	5.2
17	M	0011	1.2
		0617	5.3
		1233	1.2
		1834	5.2
18	TU	0042	1.2
		0647	5.3
		1303	1.3
		1904	5.1
19	W	0113	1.2
		0718	5.2
		1333	1.3
		1938	5.0
20	TH	0147	1.3
		0754	5.0
		1408	1.5
		2017	4.8
21	F	0226	1.5
		0837	4.8
		1449	1.6
		2108	4.6
22	SA ☾	0313	1.7
		0937	4.6
		1540	1.9
		2221	4.5
23	SU	0413	1.9
		1101	4.4
		1648	2.1
		2349	4.5
24	M	0530	2.0
		1233	4.4
		1815	2.1
25	TU	0111	4.6
		0658	1.9
		1354	4.7
		1941	1.9
26	W	0221	5.0
		0817	1.6
		1500	5.0
		2049	1.5
27	TH	0321	5.3
		0919	1.2
		1555	5.3
		2145	1.2
28	F	0413	5.6
		1012	0.9
		1644	5.5
		2235	0.9

MARCH

Date	Day	Time	m
1	SA ●	0501	5.9
		1100	0.7
		1729	5.7
		2322	0.7
2	SU	0547	6.0
		1145	0.6
		1811	5.7
3	M	0006	0.7
		0629	5.9
		1228	0.7
		1850	5.6
4	TU	0048	0.7
		0709	5.7
		1309	0.9
		1927	5.4
5	W	0129	0.9
		0746	5.5
		1347	1.1
		2000	5.2
6	TH	0209	1.2
		0823	5.1
		1426	1.4
		2034	4.9
7	F	0251	1.5
		0902	4.7
		1509	1.8
		2116	4.6
8	SA ☽	0341	1.9
		0953	4.4
		1602	2.1
		2219	4.3
9	SU	0444	2.2
		1117	4.1
		1711	2.4
10	M	0009	4.1
		0603	2.4
		1300	4.1
		1834	2.5
11	TU	0137	4.3
		0724	2.3
		1410	4.3
		1948	2.3
12	W	0235	4.5
		0826	2.1
		1459	4.5
		2043	2.0
13	TH	0318	4.7
		0912	1.8
		1538	4.8
		2126	1.8
14	F	0354	5.0
		0952	1.6
		1611	5.0
		2204	1.5
15	SA	0426	5.2
		1028	1.4
		1642	5.1
		2240	1.3
16	SU O	0456	5.3
		1102	1.2
		1712	5.3
		2314	1.2
17	M	0525	5.4
		1136	1.2
		1741	5.3
		2348	1.1
18	TU	0555	5.4
		1208	1.1
		1812	5.3
19	W	0020	1.1
		0626	5.4
		1240	1.2
		1844	5.3
20	TH	0054	1.1
		0701	5.3
		1312	1.2
		1920	5.2
21	F	0128	1.2
		0739	5.1
		1348	1.4
		2001	5.0
22	SA	0208	1.3
		0826	4.9
		1429	1.6
		2054	4.8
23	SU	0255	1.5
		0928	4.6
		1521	1.8
		2205	4.6
24	M ☾	0355	1.8
		1051	4.4
		1629	2.0
		2330	4.5
25	TU	0514	1.9
		1221	4.5
		1759	2.1
26	W	0053	4.7
		0645	1.8
		1340	4.7
		1926	1.9
27	TH	0204	5.0
		0802	1.6
		1445	5.0
		2033	1.5
28	F	0305	5.3
		0902	1.2
		1538	5.3
		2127	1.2
29	SA	0356	5.6
		0953	1.0
		1625	5.5
		2216	0.9
30	SU ●	0443	5.7
		1040	0.8
		1708	5.6
		2302	0.8
31	M	0526	5.8
		1123	0.8
		1747	5.6
		2345	0.7

APRIL

Date	Day	Time	m
1	TU	0606	5.8
		1204	0.8
		1824	5.6
2	W	0025	0.8
		0643	5.6
		1242	1.0
		1858	5.4
3	TH	0104	1.0
		0718	5.4
		1319	1.2
		1930	5.2
4	F	0142	1.2
		0753	5.1
		1355	1.5
		2003	4.9
5	SA	0221	1.5
		0829	4.7
		1435	1.8
		2041	4.7
6	SU	0305	1.9
		0915	4.4
		1523	2.1
		2132	4.4
7	M ☽	0402	2.2
		1025	4.1
		1625	2.4
		2301	4.2
8	TU	0515	2.3
		1210	4.1
		1744	2.5
9	W	0044	4.2
		0635	2.3
		1325	4.2
		1900	2.4
10	TH	0150	4.4
		0742	2.1
		1418	4.5
		2000	2.1
11	F	0238	4.6
		0832	1.9
		1501	4.7
		2047	1.9
12	SA	0318	4.9
		0915	1.6
		1537	5.0
		2129	1.6
13	SU	0353	5.1
		0953	1.4
		1610	5.1
		2208	1.4
14	M	0426	5.2
		1030	1.3
		1643	5.3
		2246	1.2
15	TU O	0459	5.4
		1107	1.2
		1716	5.4
		2323	1.1
16	W	0534	5.4
		1142	1.1
		1752	5.4
		2359	1.0
17	TH	0611	5.4
		1218	1.1
		1829	5.4
18	F	0036	1.0
		0650	5.3
		1255	1.2
		1910	5.3
19	SA	0115	1.1
		0734	5.1
		1334	1.3
		1956	5.2
20	SU	0157	1.2
		0825	4.9
		1419	1.5
		2051	5.0
21	M	0246	1.4
		0927	4.7
		1512	1.8
		2157	4.8
22	TU ☾	0347	1.7
		1044	4.5
		1621	2.0
		2315	4.7
23	W	0504	1.8
		1207	4.6
		1745	2.0
24	TH	0033	4.8
		0628	1.8
		1322	4.7
		1905	1.8
25	F	0144	5.0
		0741	1.6
		1425	4.9
		2010	1.6
26	SA	0245	5.2
		0840	1.3
		1518	5.2
		2106	1.3
27	SU	0337	5.4
		0931	1.1
		1604	5.3
		2155	1.1
28	M	0423	5.5
		1017	1.0
		1645	5.4
		2241	1.0
29	TU ●	0504	5.5
		1059	1.0
		1723	5.5
		2323	0.9
30	W	0543	5.5
		1139	1.0
		1759	5.4

MAY

Date	Day	Time	m
1	TH	0003	1.0
		0618	5.4
		1217	1.1
		1832	5.3
2	F	0041	1.1
		0653	5.2
		1252	1.3
		1906	5.2
3	SA	0117	1.3
		0728	5.0
		1327	1.5
		1939	5.0
4	SU	0154	1.5
		0804	4.7
		1405	1.7
		2016	4.8
5	M	0235	1.8
		0846	4.5
		1450	2.0
		2101	4.5
6	TU	0325	2.0
		0942	4.3
		1544	2.2
		2203	4.3
7	W ☽	0426	2.2
		1105	4.1
		1651	2.3
		2332	4.2
8	TH	0538	2.2
		1227	4.2
		1802	2.3
9	F	0049	4.3
		0645	2.1
		1327	4.4
		1905	2.2
10	SA	0147	4.5
		0742	2.0
		1415	4.6
		1959	1.9
11	SU	0234	4.7
		0830	1.7
		1456	4.8
		2047	1.7
12	M	0315	4.9
		0914	1.5
		1535	5.1
		2132	1.5
13	TU	0355	5.1
		0956	1.3
		1613	5.2
		2215	1.3
14	W O	0434	5.3
		1038	1.2
		1652	5.4
		2258	1.1
15	TH	0515	5.4
		1119	1.1
		1734	5.5
		2340	1.0
16	F	0558	5.4
		1200	1.1
		1818	5.5
17	SA	0022	0.9
		0643	5.4
		1242	1.1
		1904	5.5
18	SU	0106	1.0
		0731	5.2
		1326	1.2
		1953	5.3
19	M	0152	1.1
		0824	5.0
		1413	1.4
		2047	5.2
20	TU	0242	1.3
		0923	4.8
		1507	1.6
		2148	5.0
21	W ☾	0340	1.5
		1031	4.7
		1612	1.8
		2257	4.9
22	TH	0449	1.6
		1146	4.6
		1725	1.8
23	F	0009	4.8
		0603	1.7
		1258	4.7
		1838	1.8
24	SA	0120	4.9
		0713	1.6
		1402	4.8
		1944	1.6
25	SU	0223	5.0
		0813	1.5
		1456	5.0
		2042	1.4
26	M	0317	5.1
		0906	1.3
		1543	5.1
		2133	1.3
27	TU	0403	5.2
		0954	1.2
		1623	5.2
		2220	1.2
28	W ●	0444	5.2
		1037	1.2
		1700	5.3
		2303	1.1
29	TH	0521	5.2
		1116	1.2
		1736	5.3
		2343	1.2
30	F	0557	5.2
		1153	1.3
		1810	5.2
31	SA	0019	1.2
		0632	5.1
		1228	1.4
		[illegible]	[illegible]

JUNE

Date	Day	Time	m
1	SU	0055	1.3
		0706	4.9
		1303	1.5
		1918	5.0
2	M	0130	1.5
		0741	4.8
		1340	1.6
		1953	4.8
3	TU	0209	1.6
		0819	4.6
		1420	1.8
		2033	4.7
4	W	0251	1.8
		0904	4.4
		1507	2.0
		2120	4.5
5	TH ☽	0341	1.9
		1002	4.3
		1600	2.1
		2221	4.4
6	F	0439	2.1
		1114	4.2
		1702	2.2
		2334	4.3
7	SA	0542	2.1
		1223	4.3
		1805	2.1
8	SU	0042	4.4
		0643	2.0
		1321	4.5
		1905	2.0
9	M	0142	4.6
		0741	1.8
		1412	4.7
		2002	1.8
10	TU	0234	4.8
		0833	1.6
		1500	4.9
		2055	1.5
11	W	0324	5.0
		0923	1.4
		1546	5.2
		2146	1.3
12	TH	0412	5.2
		1011	1.2
		1632	5.4
		2235	1.1
13	F O	0500	5.3
		1058	1.1
		1719	5.5
		2323	0.9
14	SA	0548	5.4
		1144	1.0
		1807	5.6
15	SU	0010	0.8
		0636	5.4
		1231	1.0
		1855	5.6
16	M	0057	0.8
		0725	5.4
		1317	1.0
		1945	5.5
17	TU	0144	0.9
		0816	5.2
		1405	1.2
		2037	5.4
18	W	0233	1.1
		0909	5.0
		1457	1.4
		2133	5.2
19	TH ☾	0327	1.3
		1009	4.8
		1554	1.5
		2233	5.0
20	F	0426	1.5
		1116	4.7
		1659	1.7
		2340	4.8
21	SA	0532	1.6
		1226	4.6
		1808	1.7
22	SU	0050	4.7
		0640	1.7
		1335	4.7
		1916	1.7
23	M	0158	4.7
		0745	1.6
		1434	4.8
		2018	1.6
24	TU	0257	4.8
		0842	1.6
		1523	4.9
		2112	1.5
25	W	0345	4.9
		0932	1.5
		1604	5.0
		2201	1.4
26	TH	0426	4.9
		1017	1.4
		1641	5.1
		2245	1.3
27	F ●	0502	5.0
		1057	1.3
		1716	5.1
		2324	1.3
28	SA	0537	5.0
		1133	1.3
		1750	5.2
29	SU	0000	1.3
		0611	5.0
		1208	1.4
		1823	5.1
30	M	0034	1.3
		0644	4.9
		1241	1.4
		1855	5.1

POINTE DE GRAVE
LAT 45°34′N
LONG 1°04′W

TIMES AND HEIGHTS OF HIGH AND LOW WATER (Heights in Metres)

TIME ZONE –0100 (French Standard Time). **Subtract 1 hour for UT. For French Summer Time (area enclosed in shaded box) add 1 hour**

2014

JULY

Date	Day	Time	m	Time	m	Time	m	Time	m	Moon
1	TU	0108	1.4	0717	4.9	1316	1.5	1928	4.9	
2	W	0143	1.4	0751	4.7	1352	1.6	2003	4.8	
3	TH	0219	1.5	0828	4.6	1431	1.7	2042	4.7	
4	F	0259	1.7	0913	4.4	1515	1.8	2130	4.5	
5	SA	0345	1.8	1010	4.3	1606	1.9	2230	4.4	☽
6	SU	0440	1.9	1118	4.3	1707	2.0	2342	4.3	
7	M	0544	2.0	1228	4.4	1814	2.0			
8	TU	0053	4.4	0651	1.9	1332	4.6	1919	1.8	
9	W	0158	4.6	0755	1.7	1429	4.8	2022	1.6	
10	TH	0258	4.9	0854	1.5	1522	5.1	2121	1.3	
11	F	0353	5.1	0949	1.2	1614	5.4	2216	1.0	
12	SA	0445	5.3	1040	1.0	1704	5.6	2307	0.8	○
13	SU	0535	5.5	1129	0.8	1753	5.8	2356	0.6	
14	M	0624	5.6	1217	0.8	1843	5.8			
15	TU	0044	0.6	0711	5.5	1304	0.8	1931	5.7	
16	W	0130	0.7	0759	5.3	1350	0.9	2020	5.5	
17	TH	0217	0.9	0847	5.1	1438	1.1	2110	5.3	
18	F	0305	1.2	0938	4.9	1530	1.4	2204	5.0	
19	SA	0358	1.4	1037	4.6	1629	1.6	2305	4.7	☾
20	SU	0458	1.7	1148	4.5	1736	1.8			
21	M	0017	4.5	0606	1.8	1305	4.5	1847	1.9	
22	TU	0133	4.5	0716	1.9	1412	4.6	1955	1.8	
23	W	0237	4.5	0819	1.8	1506	4.7	2053	1.7	
24	TH	0328	4.7	0913	1.6	1548	4.9	2143	1.5	
25	F	0409	4.8	0958	1.5	1623	5.0	2226	1.4	
26	SA	0444	4.9	1038	1.4	1656	5.1	2304	1.3	●
27	SU	0517	5.0	1114	1.3	1728	5.2	2339	1.2	
28	M	0549	5.0	1147	1.3	1800	5.2			
29	TU	0012	1.2	0619	5.0	1220	1.3	1830	5.1	
30	W	0045	1.2	0650	5.0	1252	1.3	1900	5.1	
31	TH	0116	1.3	0721	4.9	1325	1.3	1931	5.0	

AUGUST

Date	Day	Time	m	Time	m	Time	m	Time	m	Moon
1	F	0148	1.4	0754	4.8	1359	1.4	2006	4.8	
2	SA	0223	1.5	0832	4.6	1437	1.6	2049	4.6	
3	SU	0302	1.6	0922	4.5	1522	1.7	2144	4.4	
4	M	0351	1.8	1027	4.3	1619	1.9	2257	4.3	☽
5	TU	0454	1.9	1145	4.4	1729	1.9			
6	W	0017	4.4	0608	1.9	1300	4.5	1845	1.8	
7	TH	0133	4.5	0724	1.8	1405	4.8	1958	1.6	
8	F	0238	4.8	0832	1.5	1503	5.1	2102	1.3	
9	SA	0336	5.1	0931	1.2	1557	5.5	2159	0.9	
10	SU	0429	5.4	1024	0.9	1648	5.7	2251	0.7	○
11	M	0519	5.6	1113	0.7	1737	5.9	2339	0.5	
12	TU	0606	5.7	1200	0.6	1825	5.9			
13	W	0025	0.5	0651	5.6	1246	0.6	1910	5.8	
14	TH	0110	0.6	0736	5.4	1330	0.8	1956	5.6	
15	F	0154	0.8	0819	5.2	1415	1.0	2041	5.3	
16	SA	0238	1.1	0903	4.9	1503	1.3	2129	4.9	
17	SU	0326	1.5	0954	4.6	1557	1.7	2227	4.6	☾
18	M	0422	1.8	1102	4.4	1702	1.9	2342	4.3	
19	TU	0530	2.0	1231	4.3	1818	2.1			
20	W	0107	4.3	0646	2.1	1349	4.4	1932	2.0	
21	TH	0217	4.4	0756	2.0	1445	4.6	2033	1.8	
22	F	0308	4.6	0851	1.8	1528	4.8	2122	1.6	
23	SA	0347	4.7	0936	1.6	1603	5.0	2203	1.4	
24	SU	0421	4.9	1015	1.4	1634	5.1	2240	1.3	
25	M	0453	5.0	1050	1.3	1705	5.2	2314	1.2	●
26	TU	0523	5.1	1124	1.2	1734	5.3	2347	1.2	
27	W	0552	5.1	1156	1.2	1803	5.2			
28	TH	0018	1.2	0621	5.1	1227	1.2	1831	5.2	
29	F	0049	1.2	0651	5.1	1258	1.2	1902	5.1	
30	SA	0119	1.3	0723	5.0	1331	1.3	1936	4.9	
31	SU	0152	1.4	0800	4.8	1407	1.4	2016	4.7	

SEPTEMBER

Date	Day	Time	m	Time	m	Time	m	Time	m	Moon
1	M	0230	1.6	0847	4.6	1450	1.6	2112	4.5	
2	TU	0317	1.8	0952	4.4	1545	1.8	2229	4.4	☽
3	W	0418	1.9	1114	4.4	1656	1.9	2356	4.4	
4	TH	0537	2.0	1235	4.6	1821	1.9			
5	F	0115	4.6	0702	1.9	1346	4.9	1941	1.6	
6	SA	0222	4.9	0814	1.6	1446	5.2	2046	1.3	
7	SU	0320	5.2	0914	1.2	1540	5.5	2142	0.9	
8	M	0412	5.5	1006	0.9	1630	5.8	2232	0.7	
9	TU	0459	5.6	1054	0.7	1718	5.9	2319	0.6	○
10	W	0545	5.7	1140	0.6	1803	5.9			
11	TH	0003	0.6	0628	5.7	1225	0.6	1847	5.8	
12	F	0047	0.7	0709	5.5	1307	0.8	1929	5.6	
13	SA	0128	0.9	0748	5.3	1350	1.1	2010	5.2	
14	SU	0209	1.3	0827	5.0	1434	1.4	2053	4.8	
15	M	0253	1.6	0912	4.7	1523	1.8	2146	4.5	
16	TU	0345	1.9	1013	4.4	1625	2.1	2303	4.2	☾
17	W	0452	2.2	1149	4.3	1743	2.2			
18	TH	0037	4.2	0611	2.3	1317	4.3	1903	2.2	
19	F	0148	4.3	0725	2.2	1417	4.5	2006	2.0	
20	SA	0239	4.5	0823	2.0	1501	4.8	2054	1.7	
21	SU	0319	4.8	0908	1.7	1536	5.0	2135	1.5	
22	M	0353	5.0	0947	1.5	1608	5.1	2211	1.4	
23	TU	0424	5.1	1023	1.4	1638	5.3	2245	1.2	
24	W	0454	5.2	1057	1.2	1707	5.3	2318	1.2	●
25	TH	0523	5.3	1130	1.2	1736	5.3	2350	1.2	
26	F	0553	5.3	1202	1.2	1806	5.3			
27	SA	0021	1.2	0625	5.2	1235	1.2	1837	5.2	
28	SU	0053	1.3	0659	5.1	1308	1.3	1913	5.0	
29	M	0127	1.4	0738	5.0	1345	1.4	1957	4.8	
30	TU	0207	1.6	0827	4.8	1429	1.6	2055	4.6	

OCTOBER

Date	Day	Time	m	Time	m	Time	m	Time	m	Moon
1	W	0254	1.8	0933	4.6	1524	1.8	2215	4.4	☽
2	TH	0356	2.0	1055	4.5	1636	2.0	2342	4.4	
3	F	0518	2.1	1216	4.7	1804	1.9			
4	SA	0100	4.6	0644	1.9	1328	4.9	1925	1.7	
5	SU	0206	4.9	0756	1.6	1429	5.3	2028	1.3	
6	M	0302	5.2	0855	1.3	1523	5.5	2122	1.0	
7	TU	0352	5.5	0946	1.0	1612	5.8	2211	0.8	
8	W	0438	5.6	1034	0.8	1658	5.9	2257	0.7	○
9	TH	0522	5.7	1119	0.7	1741	5.8	2340	0.8	
10	F	0603	5.7	1202	0.8	1823	5.7			
11	SA	0021	0.9	0641	5.5	1244	0.9	1901	5.5	
12	SU	0101	1.1	0718	5.3	1324	1.2	1940	5.2	
13	M	0140	1.4	0754	5.0	1405	1.5	2019	4.8	
14	TU	0221	1.7	0835	4.8	1450	1.9	2107	4.5	
15	W	0309	2.0	0928	4.5	1546	2.2	2217	4.2	☾
16	TH	0410	2.3	1052	4.3	1659	2.4	2354	4.2	
17	F	0526	2.4	1229	4.3	1820	2.3			
18	SA	0108	4.3	0641	2.4	1335	4.5	1926	2.2	
19	SU	0201	4.5	0742	2.2	1423	4.7	2017	1.9	
20	M	0243	4.8	0831	1.9	1503	4.9	2059	1.7	
21	TU	0319	5.0	0912	1.7	1537	5.1	2137	1.5	
22	W	0352	5.1	0950	1.5	1609	5.2	2213	1.4	
23	TH	0424	5.3	1027	1.4	1640	5.3	2248	1.3	●
24	F	0456	5.3	1103	1.3	1712	5.4	2323	1.2	
25	SA	0529	5.4	1139	1.2	1745	5.4	2358	1.3	
26	SU	0605	5.4	1215	1.2	1822	5.3			
27	M	0033	1.3	0643	5.3	1252	1.3	1902	5.1	
28	TU	0110	1.4	0727	5.2	1332	1.4	1950	4.9	
29	W	0152	1.6	0819	5.0	1417	1.6	2050	4.7	
30	TH	0242	1.8	0923	4.8	1512	1.8	2206	4.6	
31	F	0344	2.0	1038	4.7	1622	1.9	2328	4.6	☽

NOVEMBER

Date	Day	Time	m	Time	m	Time	m	Time	m	Moon
1	SA	0502	2.1	1156	4.8	1746	1.9			
2	SU	0043	4.7	0624	1.9	1307	5.0	1903	1.7	
3	M	0148	5.0	0734	1.7	1410	5.2	2007	1.5	
4	TU	0244	5.2	0833	1.4	1505	5.4	2101	1.2	
5	W	0333	5.4	0926	1.2	1554	5.6	2149	1.1	
6	TH	0418	5.5	1014	1.0	1639	5.6	2235	1.0	○
7	F	0500	5.6	1100	1.0	1721	5.6	2317	1.0	
8	SA	0540	5.6	1142	1.0	1800	5.5	2357	1.1	
9	SU	0617	5.5	1222	1.1	1838	5.3			
10	M	0035	1.3	0652	5.3	1301	1.4	1913	5.1	
11	TU	0113	1.5	0727	5.1	1339	1.6	1950	4.8	
12	W	0152	1.8	0804	4.9	1421	1.9	2032	4.6	
13	TH	0236	2.0	0849	4.6	1509	2.1	2128	4.3	
14	F	0329	2.3	0949	4.4	1609	2.3	2250	4.2	☾
15	SA	0433	2.4	1118	4.3	1721	2.4			
16	SU	0012	4.2	0544	2.4	1237	4.4	1830	2.3	
17	M	0113	4.4	0648	2.3	1335	4.5	1928	2.1	
18	TU	0201	4.6	0743	2.1	1421	4.7	2016	1.9	
19	W	0242	4.9	0831	1.9	1502	4.9	2059	1.7	
20	TH	0320	5.1	0915	1.7	1539	5.1	2140	1.5	
21	F	0356	5.2	0957	1.5	1615	5.2	2219	1.4	
22	SA	0432	5.4	1038	1.3	1652	5.3	2259	1.3	●
23	SU	0510	5.5	1119	1.2	1732	5.4	2338	1.3	
24	M	0551	5.5	1200	1.2	1814	5.4			
25	TU	0018	1.3	0634	5.5	1241	1.2	1858	5.3	
26	W	0100	1.4	0721	5.4	1324	1.3	1948	5.1	
27	TH	0145	1.5	0813	5.2	1411	1.4	2045	4.9	
28	F	0235	1.7	0912	5.1	1505	1.6	2152	4.7	
29	SA	0334	1.8	1019	4.9	1608	1.8	2306	4.7	☽
30	SU	0443	2.0	1131	4.9	1722	1.9			

DECEMBER

Date	Day	Time	m	Time	m	Time	m	Time	m	Moon
1	M	0019	4.7	0558	1.9	1243	4.9	1836	1.8	
2	TU	0126	4.9	0708	1.8	1349	5.0	1942	1.7	
3	W	0225	5.0	0811	1.6	1448	5.2	2039	1.5	
4	TH	0317	5.2	0907	1.4	1539	5.3	2129	1.4	
5	F	0402	5.3	0957	1.3	1624	5.3	2216	1.3	
6	SA	0443	5.4	1043	1.2	1704	5.4	2258	1.3	○
7	SU	0521	5.4	1125	1.2	1742	5.3	2337	1.3	
8	M	0557	5.4	1204	1.3	1818	5.2			
9	TU	0014	1.4	0631	5.3	1241	1.4	1851	5.1	
10	W	0050	1.6	0704	5.2	1317	1.6	1925	4.9	
11	TH	0126	1.7	0739	5.0	1354	1.7	2001	4.7	
12	F	0206	1.9	0815	4.8	1435	1.9	2043	4.5	
13	SA	0250	2.1	0858	4.6	1522	2.1	2137	4.3	
14	SU	0341	2.2	0955	4.4	1617	2.3	2251	4.2	☾
15	M	0441	2.3	1112	4.3	1722	2.3			
16	TU	0007	4.3	0545	2.4	1229	4.4	1826	2.3	
17	W	0109	4.4	0647	2.3	1330	4.5	1925	2.1	
18	TH	0200	4.6	0745	2.1	1423	4.7	2018	1.9	
19	F	0246	4.9	0838	1.9	1509	4.9	2107	1.7	
20	SA	0330	5.1	0928	1.6	1554	5.1	2153	1.5	
21	SU	0412	5.3	1015	1.4	1637	5.3	2238	1.3	
22	M	0456	5.5	1102	1.2	1722	5.4	2322	1.2	●
23	TU	0541	5.6	1147	1.1	1807	5.5			
24	W	0007	1.1	0626	5.7	1233	1.0	1853	5.4	
25	TH	0052	1.2	0714	5.6	1317	1.1	1942	5.3	
26	F	0137	1.3	0804	5.5	1404	1.2	2033	5.1	
27	SA	0225	1.4	0857	5.3	1453	1.4	2130	4.9	
28	SU	0319	1.6	0956	5.1	1548	1.6	2236	4.7	☽
29	M	0420	1.8	1102	4.9	1653	1.8	2348	4.7	
30	TU	0529	1.9	1214	4.8	1804	1.9			
31	W	0101	4.7	0641	1.9	1328	4.8	1914	1.9	

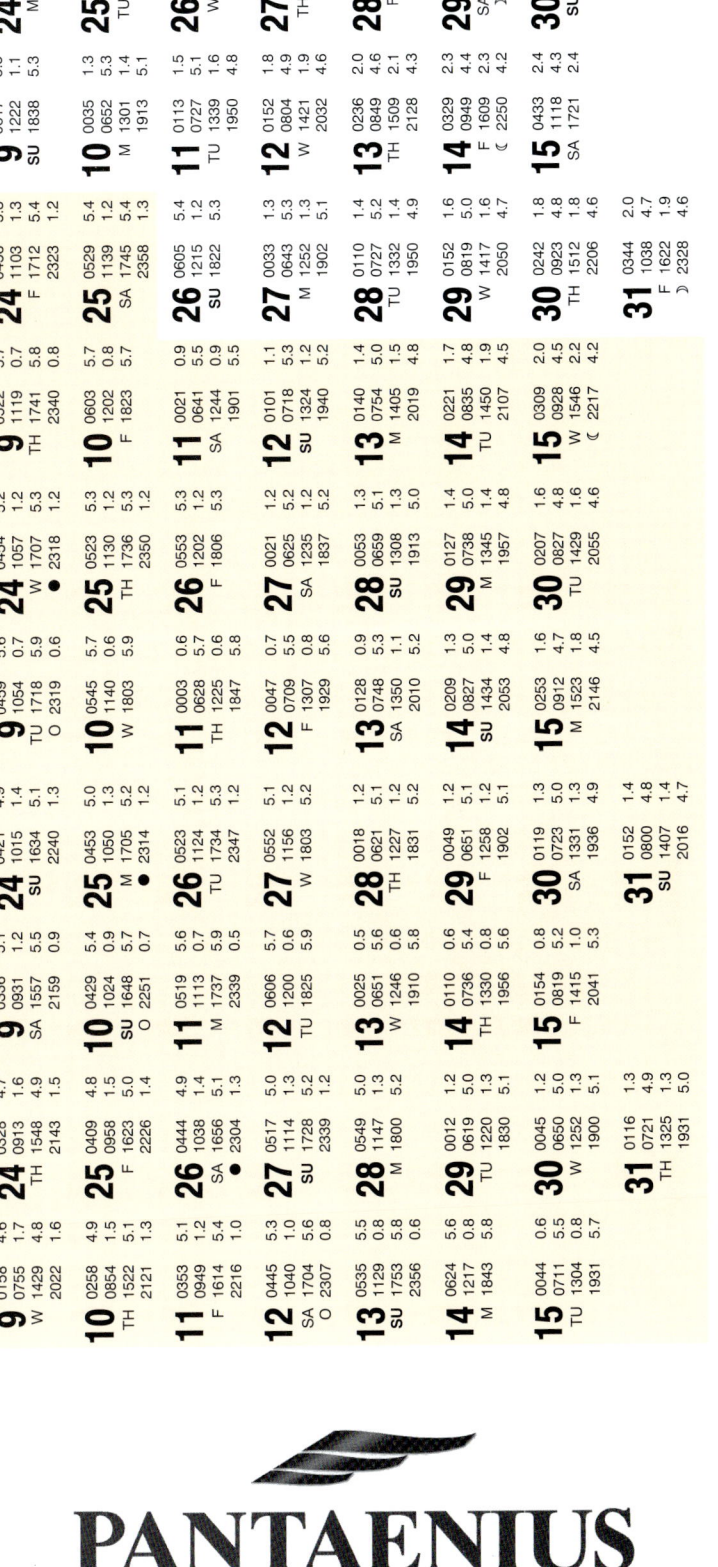

LISBON
LAT 38°42'N
LONG 9°08'W

TIMES AND HEIGHTS OF HIGH AND LOW WATER (Heights in Metres)

TIME ZONE UT (Portuguese Standard Time) **For Portuguese Summer Time (area enclosed in shaded box) add 1 hour**

2014

JANUARY

Day	Time	m
1 W ●	0244 0839 1512 2057	3.8 0.2 3.7 0.3
2 TH	0334 0927 1602 2145	3.9 0.1 3.8 0.2
3 F	0422 1015 1650 2232	4.0 0.1 3.8 0.2
4 SA	0510 1102 1737 2318	4.0 0.1 3.7 0.3
5 SU	0557 1149 1825	3.8 0.3 3.5
6 M	0006 0645 1238 1914	0.5 3.6 0.5 3.3
7 TU	0056 0736 1329 2008	0.7 3.4 0.7 3.1
8 W ☽	0153 0834 1428 2111	0.9 3.1 1.0 2.9
9 TH	0259 0941 1536 2221	1.1 2.9 1.1 2.9
10 F	0416 1053 1649 2331	1.2 2.8 1.1 2.9
11 SA	0531 1201 1755	1.1 2.8 1.1
12 SU	0031 0633 1259 1849	3.0 1.0 2.9 1.0
13 M	0122 0722 1346 1933	3.1 0.9 3.0 0.9
14 TU	0205 0803 1427 2011	3.3 0.8 3.1 0.8
15 W	0243 0838 1503 2045	3.3 0.7 3.2 0.7
16 TH O	0317 0911 1537 2118	3.4 0.6 3.2 0.6
17 F	0350 0943 1609 2150	3.5 0.5 3.3 0.6
18 SA	0421 1015 1640 2222	3.5 0.5 3.3 0.6
19 SU	0453 1046 1713 2254	3.5 0.6 3.3 0.6
20 M	0526 1119 1747 2328	3.4 0.6 3.2 0.7
21 TU	0601 1154 1823	3.3 0.7 3.1
22 W	0005 0639 1232 1905	0.8 3.2 0.8 3.0
23 TH	0048 0724 1319 1956	0.9 3.0 1.0 2.9
24 F ☾	0142 0819 1418 2100	1.1 2.9 1.1 2.8
25 SA	0252 0931 1533 2216	1.1 2.8 1.1 2.8
26 SU	0414 1052 1652 2332	1.1 2.8 1.0 3.0
27 M	0532 1208 1803	0.9 3.0 0.8
28 TU	0039 0639 1312 1903	3.3 0.7 3.3 0.6
29 W	0138 0736 1409 1956	3.5 0.4 3.5 0.4
30 TH ●	0231 0827 1500 2046	3.8 0.2 3.7 0.2
31 F	0321 0915 1548 2132	4.0 0.0 3.8 0.1

FEBRUARY

Day	Time	m
1 SA	0408 1000 1633 2216	4.1 0.0 3.8 0.1
2 SU	0453 1044 1717 2259	4.1 0.0 3.8 0.2
3 M	0536 1126 1800 2342	3.9 0.2 3.6 0.3
4 TU	0620 1208 1843	3.7 0.4 3.4
5 W	0027 0704 1253 1929	0.6 3.4 0.7 3.2
6 TH ☽	0116 0753 1342 2023	0.8 3.1 1.0 2.9
7 F	0215 0854 1445 2132	1.1 2.8 1.2 2.8
8 SA	0332 1011 1605 2253	1.3 2.6 1.3 2.7
9 SU	0500 1133 1726	1.3 2.6 1.3
10 M	0005 0612 1238 1828	2.8 1.2 2.8 1.1
11 TU	0100 0704 1327 1914	3.0 1.0 2.9 1.0
12 W	0144 0744 1407 1952	3.2 0.8 3.1 0.8
13 TH	0222 0818 1442 2026	3.3 0.7 3.2 0.7
14 F O	0256 0850 1515 2058	3.4 0.6 3.3 0.6
15 SA	0328 0921 1547 2129	3.5 0.5 3.4 0.5
16 SU	0400 0952 1618 2201	3.6 0.4 3.4 0.5
17 M	0433 1023 1651 2233	3.6 0.4 3.4 0.5
18 TU	0506 1054 1724 2305	3.5 0.5 3.4 0.6
19 W	0540 1127 1759 2341	3.4 0.6 3.3 0.7
20 TH	0616 1203 1838	3.3 0.7 3.2
21 F	0021 0657 1246 1924	0.8 3.1 0.9 3.0
22 SA ☾	0111 0749 1341 2025	1.0 3.0 1.0 2.9
23 SU	0219 0900 1458 2144	1.1 2.8 1.2 2.9
24 M	0347 1030 1627 2310	1.1 2.8 1.1 3.0
25 TU	0514 1154 1746	1.0 3.0 0.9
26 W	0024 0625 1301 1850	3.3 0.7 3.3 0.7
27 TH	0124 0723 1356 1943	3.6 0.4 3.5 0.4
28 F	0217 0812 1445 2030	3.8 0.2 3.8 0.2

MARCH

Day	Time	m
1 SA ●	0304 0858 1530 2115	4.0 0.1 3.9 0.1
2 SU	0349 0940 1613 2157	4.1 0.0 3.9 0.1
3 M	0432 1020 1653 2237	4.1 0.1 3.9 0.2
4 TU	0513 1059 1733 2317	3.9 0.3 3.7 0.3
5 W	0553 1133 1812 2358	3.7 0.5 3.5 0.6
6 TH	0633 1217 1852	3.4 0.8 3.3
7 F	0042 07[illegible]5 1301 1937	0.9 3.1 1.1 3.0
8 SA ☽	0134 0807 1356 2037	1.2 2.8 1.3 2.8
9 SU	0246 0921 1515 2202	1.4 2.6 1.5 2.7
10 M	0419 1055 1647 2327	1.4 2.6 1.5 2.8
11 TU	0539 1208 1757	1.3 2.7 1.3
12 W	0029 0634 1259 1846	2.9 1.1 2.9 1.1
13 TH	0114 0715 1339 1925	3.1 0.9 3.1 0.9
14 F	0153 0750 1414 2000	3.3 0.8 3.3 0.8
15 SA	0228 0823 1448 2033	3.5 0.6 3.4 0.6
16 SU O	0302 0854 1521 2105	3.6 0.5 3.5 0.5
17 M	0336 0926 1554 2138	3.7 0.5 3.6 0.5
18 TU	0410 0957 1627 2211	3.7 0.5 3.6 0.5
19 W	0444 1030 1702 2245	3.7 0.5 3.6 0.5
20 TH	0520 1104 1738 2322	3.6 0.6 3.5 0.6
21 F	0558 1141 1818	3.4 0.7 3.4
22 SA	0004 0641 1225 1905	0.8 3.3 0.9 3.2
23 SU	0056 0735 1322 2006	0.9 3.1 1.1 3.1
24 M ☾	0204 0847 1439 2126	1.1 2.9 1.3 3.0
25 TU	0332 1019 1611 2254	1.2 2.9 1.2 3.1
26 W	0500 1141 1731	1.0 3.1 1.1
27 TH	0007 0610 1245 1834	3.3 0.8 3.3 0.8
28 F	0107 0705 1338 1926	3.6 0.6 3.6 0.6
29 SA	0158 0753 1425 2012	3.8 0.3 3.8 0.4
30 SU ●	0245 0836 1508 2055	4.0 0.2 3.9 0.3
31 M	0328 0917 1549 2135	4.0 0.2 4.0 0.2

APRIL

Day	Time	m
1 TU	0410 0955 1629 2215	4.0 0.3 3.9 0.3
2 W	0449 1032 1706 2253	3.8 0.4 3.8 0.5
3 TH	0527 1109 1743 2332	3.6 0.6 3.6 0.7
4 F	0604 1145 1819	3.3 0.9 3.3
5 SA	0013 0642 1225 1858	0.9 3.1 1.1 3.1
6 SU	0100 0726 1314 1947	1.2 2.8 1.4 2.9
7 M ☽	0202 0829 1423 2058	1.4 2.7 1.5 2.8
8 TU	0325 0959 1553 2229	1.5 2.6 1.6 2.8
9 W	0448 1121 1711 2341	1.4 2.7 1.5 2.9
10 TH	0550 1218 1806	1.3 2.9 1.3
11 F	0034 0636 1302 1850	3.1 1.1 3.1 1.1
12 SA	0116 0715 1340 1928	3.3 0.9 3.3 0.9
13 SU	0155 0750 1416 2003	3.5 0.7 3.5 0.7
14 M	0232 0824 1451 2038	3.6 0.6 3.6 0.6
15 TU O	0309 0858 1527 2114	3.7 0.5 3.7 0.5
16 W	0346 0932 1604 2150	3.7 0.5 3.8 0.5
17 TH	0424 1007 1642 2228	3.7 0.5 3.8 0.5
18 F	0503 1045 1722 2309	3.6 0.6 3.7 0.6
19 SA	0546 1126 1806 2355	3.5 0.7 3.6 0.7
20 SU	0633 1214 1856	3.3 0.9 3.4
21 M	0050 0730 1314 1958	0.9 3.2 1.1 3.3
22 TU ☾	0159 0842 1429 2114	1.1 3.0 1.3 3.2
23 W	0320 1006 1555 2236	1.1 3.0 1.2 3.2
24 TH	0441 1122 1711 2346	1.0 3.2 1.1 3.4
25 F	0548 1224 1813	0.9 3.4 0.9
26 SA	0045 0643 1316 1905	3.6 0.7 3.6 0.7
27 SU	0136 0730 1402 1951	3.7 0.5 3.8 0.5
28 M	0223 0813 1445 2034	3.8 0.5 3.8 0.4
29 TU ●	0306 0853 1526 2115	3.8 0.5 3.9 0.4
30 W	0347 0930 1605 2154	3.8 0.5 3.8 0.5

MAY

Day	Time	m
1 TH	0426 1007 1642 2232	3.6 0.6 3.7 0.6
2 F	0503 1042 1717 2309	3.5 0.8 3.5 0.8
3 SA	0539 1118 1751 2347	3.3 0.9 3.4 1.0
4 SU	0614 1156 1827	3.1 1.1 3.2
5 M	0030 0654 1240 1909	1.1 2.9 1.3 3.0
6 TU	0123 0746 1337 2005	1.3 2.8 1.5 2.9
7 W ☽	0230 0856 1452 2120	1.4 2.7 1.6 2.8
8 TH	0345 1017 1610 2238	1.4 2.7 1.5 2.9
9 F	0453 1124 1715 2341	1.3 2.9 1.4 3.0
10 SA	0547 1216 1806	1.1 3.1 1.2
11 SU	0032 0632 1300 1850	3.2 1.0 3.3 1.0
12 M	0117 0713 1341 1931	3.4 0.8 3.5 0.8
13 TU	0159 0751 1421 2010	3.5 0.7 3.6 0.6
14 W O	0241 0829 1501 2051	3.6 0.6 3.7 0.5
15 TH	0323 0908 1543 2132	3.7 0.5 3.8 0.4
16 F	0406 0949 1626 2215	3.7 0.5 3.8 0.4
17 SA	0450 1032 1710 2300	3.7 0.6 3.8 0.5
18 SU	0537 1117 1758 2350	3.6 0.7 3.7 0.6
19 M	0628 1208 1850	3.4 0.8 3.6
20 TU	0046 0725 1307 1949	0.8 3.3 1.0 3.4
21 W ☾	0149 0831 1415 2058	0.9 3.1 1.1 3.3
22 TH	0301 0944 1531 2211	1.0 3.1 1.2 3.3
23 F	0414 1055 1644 2320	1.0 3.2 1.1 3.3
24 SA	0520 1157 1748	0.9 3.3 1.0
25 SU	0020 0616 1251 1843	3.4 0.8 3.5 0.8
26 M	0113 0706 1339 1931	3.5 0.7 3.6 0.7
27 TU	0202 0750 1424 2016	3.5 0.7 3.7 0.6
28 W ●	0246 0830 1506 2057	3.5 0.6 3.7 0.6
29 TH	0327 0908 1545 2135	3.5 0.7 3.7 0.6
30 F	0406 0945 1621 2212	3.4 0.7 3.6 0.7
31 SA	0442 1020 1655 [illegible]	3.3 0.8 3.5 [illegible]

JUNE

Day	Time	m
1 SU	0516 1054 1727 2324	3.2 0.9 3.4 0.9
2 M	0550 1130 1801	3.1 1.0 3.3
3 TU	0003 0627 1210 1839	1.0 3.0 1.1 3.1
4 W	0047 0710 1258 1926	1.1 2.9 1.3 3.0
5 TH ☽	0140 0805 1356 2024	1.2 2.8 1.4 2.9
6 F	0242 0911 1505 2133	1.3 2.8 1.4 2.9
7 SA	0349 1021 1614 2242	1.3 2.8 1.4 2.9
8 SU	0452 1123 1716 2343	1.2 3.0 1.2 3.0
9 M	0546 1217 1809	1.0 3.1 1.0
10 TU	0037 0634 1305 1858	3.2 0.9 3.3 0.8
11 W	0127 0719 1352 1945	3.3 0.7 3.5 0.6
12 TH	0215 0804 1438 2031	3.5 0.6 3.7 0.5
13 F O	0303 0849 1525 2117	3.6 0.4 3.8 0.4
14 SA	0351 0934 1612 2204	3.7 0.4 3.9 0.3
15 SU	0440 1021 1700 2252	3.7 0.4 3.9 0.3
16 M	0528 1109 1749 2342	3.6 0.5 3.8 0.4
17 TU	0618 1159 1839	3.5 0.6 3.7
18 W	0034 0711 1253 1934	0.5 3.4 0.8 3.5
19 TH ☾	0130 0810 1353 2034	0.7 3.2 0.9 3.3
20 F	0233 0914 1500 2141	0.9 3.1 1.0 3.2
21 SA	0340 1022 1612 2250	1.0 3.1 1.1 3.2
22 SU	0448 1128 1722 2355	1.0 3.2 1.0 3.2
23 M	0550 1227 1823	0.9 3.3 0.9
24 TU	0052 0643 1319 1915	3.2 0.9 3.3 0.8
25 W	0143 0730 1405 2001	3.2 0.8 3.4 0.8
26 TH	0229 0812 1448 2041	3.3 0.8 3.5 0.7
27 F ●	0310 0850 1526 2119	3.3 0.7 3.5 0.7
28 SA	0347 0925 1601 2153	3.3 0.7 3.5 0.7
29 SU	0421 0959 1634 2227	3.3 0.8 3.5 0.7
30 M	0454 1032 1705 2300	3.2 0.8 3.4 0.7

SUNRISE AND SUNSET TIMES

LISBON
At 38°42'N 9°08'W

Portuguese Time UT		Sunrise	Sunset
Jan	01	0755	1726
	15	0753	1739
Feb	01	0742	1758
	15	0727	1814
Mar	01	0709	1829
	15	0648	1844
Portuguese Summer Time (UT-1)			
Apr	01	0721	2000
	15	0700	2013
May	01	0639	2029
	15	0624	2042
Jun	01	0614	2055
	15	0611	2103
Jul	01	0616	2105
	15	0624	2101
Aug	01	0638	2047
	15	0650	2031
Sep	01	0706	2007
	15	0718	1945
Oct	01	0732	1919
	15	0746	1858
Portuguese Standard Time (UT)			
Nov	01	0703	1736
	15	0719	1723
Dec	01	0736	1715
	15	0747	1716

LISBON
LAT 38°42′N
LONG 9°08′W

TIMES AND HEIGHTS OF HIGH AND LOW WATER (Heights in Metres)

TIME ZONE UT (Portuguese Standard Time) **For Portuguese Summer Time (area enclosed in shaded box) add 1 hour**

2014

JULY

Day	Time	m	Time	m	Time	m	Time	m
1 TU	0526	3.2	1107	0.9	1738	3.3	2335	0.8
2 W	0601	3.1	1143	0.9	1813	3.3		
3 TH	0013	0.9	0639	3.0	1223	1.0	1853	3.1
4 F	0056	1.0	0724	2.9	1309	1.2	1940	3.0
5 SA	0146	1.1	0817	2.8	1406	1.3	☽ 2038	2.9
6 SU	0246	1.2	0922	2.8	1514	1.3	2145	2.9
7 M	0354	1.2	1030	2.9	1625	1.2	2255	2.9
8 TU	0459	1.1	1134	3.0	1731	1.1		
9 W	0000	3.0	0559	0.9	1233	3.2	1830	0.9
10 TH	0100	3.2	0653	0.7	1327	3.5	1924	0.6
11 F	0155	3.4	0744	0.5	1419	3.7	2015	0.4
12 SA	0248	3.6	0833	0.4	1510	3.9	○ 2104	0.2
13 SU	0338	3.7	0921	0.3	1559	4.0	2152	0.1
14 M	0426	3.8	1008	0.3	1647	4.0	2239	0.1
15 TU	0514	3.7	1055	0.3	1734	4.0	2326	0.2
16 W	0601	3.6	1142	0.4	1821	3.8		
17 TH	0013	0.4	0649	3.5	1231	0.6	1911	3.6
18 F	0104	0.6	0741	3.3	1325	0.8	2005	3.3
19 SA	0159	0.9	0839	3.1	1427	1.0	☾ 2108	3.1
20 SU	0303	1.0	0946	3.0	1539	1.1	2218	3.0
21 M	0414	1.1	1058	3.0	1657	1.1	2330	2.9
22 TU	0525	1.1	1204	3.1	1806	1.1		
23 W	0034	3.0	0625	1.0	1300	3.2	1902	1.0
24 TH	0127	3.1	0714	0.9	1348	3.3	1947	0.8
25 F	0212	3.1	0755	0.9	1429	3.4	2025	0.7
26 SA	0251	3.2	0832	0.8	1506	3.5	● 2059	0.7
27 SU	0326	3.3	0906	0.7	1539	3.5	2132	0.6
28 M	0358	3.3	0938	0.7	1611	3.5	2203	0.6
29 TU	0430	3.3	1010	0.7	1642	3.5	2235	0.6
30 W	0501	3.3	1042	0.7	1714	3.5	2307	0.7
31 TH	0534	3.3	1116	0.8	1748	3.4	2341	0.8

AUGUST

Day	Time	m	Time	m	Time	m	Time	m
1 F	0609	3.2	1151	0.9	1824	3.3		
2 SA	0017	0.9	0648	3.0	1231	1.0	1905	3.1
3 SU	0100	1.0	0735	2.9	1320	1.1	1955	3.0
4 M	0153	1.1	0833	2.9	1423	1.2	☽ 2059	2.9
5 TU	0302	1.2	0944	2.9	1541	1.3	2216	2.9
6 W	0419	1.2	1059	3.0	1700	1.1	2333	3.0
7 TH	0531	1.0	1208	3.2	1809	0.9		
8 F	0041	3.2	0633	0.8	1309	3.5	1908	0.6
9 SA	0140	3.4	0728	0.6	1404	3.7	2000	0.4
10 SU	0233	3.7	0819	0.3	1454	4.0	○ 2049	0.2
11 M	0322	3.8	0906	0.2	1543	4.1	2135	0.1
12 TU	0409	3.9	0952	0.1	1629	4.2	2220	0.1
13 W	0454	3.9	1036	0.2	1714	4.1	2304	0.2
14 TH	0538	3.8	1120	0.3	1759	3.9	2347	0.4
15 F	0622	3.6	1206	0.5	1845	3.6		
16 SA	0033	0.6	0709	3.4	1255	0.8	1934	3.3
17 SU	0122	0.9	0802	3.1	1353	1.1	☾ 2033	3.0
18 M	0223	1.2	0908	3.0	1506	1.3	2146	2.8
19 TU	0339	1.3	1026	2.9	1633	1.3	2307	2.8
20 W	0501	1.3	1141	3.0	1749	1.2		
21 TH	0016	2.9	0607	1.2	1240	3.1	1845	1.1
22 F	0108	3.0	0656	1.1	1327	3.3	1927	0.9
23 SA	0151	3.2	0736	0.9	1407	3.4	2003	0.8
24 SU	0227	3.3	0811	0.8	1442	3.5	2036	0.7
25 M	0301	3.4	0843	0.7	1514	3.6	● 2107	0.6
26 TU	0333	3.5	0915	0.6	1546	3.6	2137	0.6
27 W	0404	3.5	0946	0.6	1618	3.6	2208	0.6
28 TH	0435	3.5	1017	0.6	1650	3.6	2239	0.6
29 F	0508	3.4	1049	0.7	1723	3.5	2311	0.7
30 SA	0542	3.4	1123	0.8	1758	3.4	2345	0.8
31 SU	0619	3.3	1201	0.9	1837	3.2		

SEPTEMBER

Day	Time	m	Time	m	Time	m	Time	m
1 M	0024	1.0	0702	3.1	1247	1.1	1925	3.0
2 TU	0115	1.1	0758	3.0	1349	1.2	☽ 2028	2.9
3 W	0224	1.3	0910	3.0	1511	1.3	2151	2.9
4 TH	0351	1.3	1034	3.0	1639	1.2	2317	3.0
5 F	0512	1.1	1150	3.3	1753	0.9		
6 SA	0027	3.3	0618	0.9	1253	3.6	1852	0.6
7 SU	0125	3.5	0713	0.6	1347	3.8	1944	0.4
8 M	0216	3.8	0802	0.4	1437	4.1	2031	0.2
9 TU	0303	4.0	0848	0.2	1523	4.2	○ 2115	0.1
10 W	0347	4.0	0932	0.2	1608	4.2	2157	0.1
11 TH	0430	4.0	1015	0.2	1651	4.1	2238	0.3
12 F	0512	3.9	1057	0.3	1734	3.9	2319	0.5
13 SA	0554	3.7	1140	0.6	1817	3.6		
14 SU	0001	0.8	0637	3.5	1226	0.9	1903	3.3
15 M	0046	1.1	0726	3.2	1319	1.2	1957	3.0
16 TU	0142	1.4	0826	3.0	1430	1.4	☾ 2109	2.8
17 W	0259	1.5	0947	2.9	1601	1.5	2237	2.7
18 TH	0429	1.5	1109	2.9	1721	1.4	2350	2.8
19 F	0540	1.4	1212	3.1	1817	1.2		
20 SA	0042	3.0	0630	1.2	1259	3.3	1859	1.0
21 SU	0123	3.2	0710	1.0	1338	3.4	1935	0.9
22 M	0159	3.4	0745	0.9	1413	3.6	2007	0.7
23 TU	0232	3.5	0817	0.8	1446	3.7	2039	0.6
24 W	0304	3.6	0849	0.7	1519	3.7	● 2109	0.6
25 TH	0336	3.7	0921	0.6	1552	3.7	2140	0.6
26 F	0409	3.7	0953	0.6	1625	3.7	2212	0.6
27 SA	0443	3.6	1026	0.7	1700	3.6	2244	0.7
28 SU	0518	3.5	1101	0.8	1736	3.5	2319	0.8
29 M	0556	3.4	1140	0.9	1817	3.3		
30 TU	0000	1.0	0640	3.3	1228	1.1	1907	3.1

OCTOBER

Day	Time	m	Time	m	Time	m	Time	m
1 W	0052	1.2	0736	3.2	1331	1.2	☽ 2012	3.0
2 TH	0203	1.3	0850	3.1	1454	1.3	2138	3.0
3 F	0332	1.4	1016	3.2	1623	1.2	2304	3.1
4 SA	0455	1.2	1133	3.4	1736	1.0		
5 SU	0012	3.4	0601	0.9	1235	3.6	1834	0.7
6 M	0107	3.6	0656	0.7	1328	3.9	1924	0.5
7 TU	0156	3.9	0744	0.4	1417	4.1	2010	0.3
8 W	0242	4.0	0829	0.3	1502	4.2	○ 2052	0.3
9 TH	0325	4.1	0911	0.3	1546	4.1	2133	0.3
10 F	0407	4.0	0953	0.3	1629	4.0	2213	0.4
11 SA	0448	3.9	1034	0.5	1710	3.8	2252	0.6
12 SU	0528	3.7	1116	0.7	1751	3.5	2331	0.9
13 M	0608	3.5	1159	0.9	1833	3.2		
14 TU	0013	1.2	0650	3.3	1248	1.2	1920	3.0
15 W	0103	1.4	0742	3.0	1350	1.4	☾ 2024	2.8
16 TH	0211	1.6	0853	2.9	1512	1.5	2149	2.7
17 F	0339	1.6	1018	2.9	1634	1.5	2307	2.8
18 SA	0457	1.5	1128	3.0	1735	1.3		
19 SU	0004	3.0	0553	1.4	1220	3.2	1822	1.1
20 M	0047	3.2	0636	1.2	1302	3.3	1900	1.0
21 TU	0125	3.4	0714	1.0	1340	3.5	1935	0.8
22 W	0200	3.5	0749	0.8	1415	3.6	2008	0.7
23 TH	0234	3.6	0822	0.7	1451	3.7	● 2041	0.6
24 F	0309	3.7	0856	0.6	1526	3.7	2114	0.6
25 SA	0344	3.8	0931	0.6	1603	3.7	2148	0.6
26 SU	0421	3.7	1007	0.6	1641	3.6	2223	0.7
27 M	0459	3.7	1046	0.7	1721	3.5	2302	0.8
28 TU	0541	3.6	1128	0.8	1806	3.4	2346	0.9
29 W	0628	3.5	1219	1.0	1858	3.2		
30 TH	0040	1.1	0725	3.3	1322	1.1	2004	3.1
31 F	0150	1.3	0836	3.2	1440	1.2	☽ 2125	3.0

NOVEMBER

Day	Time	m	Time	m	Time	m	Time	m
1 SA	0313	1.3	0957	3.2	1602	1.1	2245	3.2
2 SU	0434	1.2	1111	3.4	1714	0.9	2351	3.4
3 M	0540	1.0	1214	3.6	1812	0.8		
4 TU	0046	3.6	0636	0.8	1307	3.8	1903	0.6
5 W	0135	3.8	0725	0.6	1356	3.9	1948	0.5
6 TH	0220	3.9	0810	0.4	1442	3.9	○ 2030	0.4
7 F	0304	4.0	0853	0.4	1526	3.9	2111	0.5
8 SA	0346	3.9	0934	0.4	1608	3.8	2150	0.6
9 SU	0426	3.8	1015	0.6	1648	3.6	2227	0.7
10 M	0504	3.7	1054	0.7	1727	3.4	2305	0.9
11 TU	0541	3.5	1134	0.9	1805	3.2	2343	1.1
12 W	0618	3.3	1217	1.1	1846	3.0		
13 TH	0027	1.3	0700	3.1	1308	1.3	1935	2.8
14 F	0122	1.5	0754	2.9	1412	1.4	☾ 2042	2.7
15 SA	0235	1.6	0906	2.8	1528	1.4	2202	2.7
16 SU	0354	1.5	1024	2.9	1638	1.4	2310	2.9
17 M	0501	1.4	1128	3.0	1734	1.2		
18 TU	0002	3.0	0554	1.3	1219	3.2	1820	1.0
19 W	0046	3.2	0638	1.1	1303	3.3	1900	0.9
20 TH	0126	3.4	0717	0.9	1343	3.5	1937	0.8
21 F	0204	3.5	0755	0.7	1423	3.5	2013	0.6
22 SA	0243	3.7	0833	0.6	1503	3.6	● 2050	0.6
23 SU	0323	3.8	0912	0.5	1544	3.6	2128	0.5
24 M	0403	3.8	0953	0.5	1627	3.6	2208	0.6
25 TU	0446	3.8	1035	0.5	1711	3.5	2251	0.6
26 W	0531	3.7	1122	0.6	1759	3.4	2338	0.8
27 TH	0620	3.6	1213	0.7	1852	3.3		
28 F	0032	0.9	0715	3.4	1311	0.9	1953	3.2
29 SA	0135	1.1	0819	3.3	1419	1.0	☽ 2103	3.1
30 SU	0249	1.1	0932	3.3	1534	1.0	2217	3.1

DECEMBER

Day	Time	m	Time	m	Time	m	Time	m
1 M	0405	1.1	1044	3.3	1645	0.9	2324	3.2
2 TU	0515	1.0	1149	3.4	1747	0.8		
3 W	0022	3.4	0615	0.8	1247	3.5	1841	0.7
4 TH	0114	3.5	0707	0.7	1338	3.6	1928	0.6
5 F	0202	3.7	0755	0.6	1425	3.6	2012	0.6
6 SA	0246	3.7	0838	0.5	1510	3.6	○ 2053	0.6
7 SU	0328	3.7	0919	0.5	1551	3.5	2131	0.6
8 M	0407	3.7	0958	0.6	1629	3.4	2207	0.7
9 TU	0444	3.6	1035	0.6	1705	3.3	2243	0.8
10 W	0518	3.4	1111	0.8	1739	3.2	2318	0.9
11 TH	0551	3.3	1149	0.9	1814	3.0	2356	1.1
12 F	0626	3.2	1230	1.0	1854	2.9		
13 SA	0040	1.2	0708	3.0	1318	1.2	1944	2.8
14 SU	0134	1.3	0802	2.9	1418	1.3	☾ 2047	2.7
15 M	0241	1.4	0909	2.8	1527	1.3	2200	2.7
16 TU	0354	1.4	1023	2.8	1635	1.2	2306	2.8
17 W	0501	1.3	1128	2.9	1732	1.1		
18 TH	0002	3.0	0557	1.1	1222	3.0	1821	0.9
19 F	0050	3.2	0645	0.9	1311	3.2	1906	0.8
20 SA	0135	3.4	0730	0.7	1358	3.4	1948	0.6
21 SU	0220	3.6	0813	0.5	1444	3.5	2031	0.5
22 M	0305	3.7	0857	0.4	1529	3.6	● 2114	0.4
23 TU	0350	3.8	0941	0.3	1615	3.6	2157	0.3
24 W	0435	3.8	1027	0.3	1702	3.6	2243	0.4
25 TH	0522	3.8	1113	0.3	1749	3.5	2330	0.5
26 F	0610	3.7	1202	0.4	1839	3.4		
27 SA	0020	0.6	0701	3.6	1254	0.6	1933	3.3
28 SU	0115	0.8	0757	3.4	1353	0.8	☽ 2034	3.1
29 M	0219	0.9	0902	3.2	1459	0.9	2143	3.0
30 TU	0332	1.0	1014	3.1	1611	1.0	2254	3.0
31 W	0447	1.0	1124	3.1	1721	0.9	2359	3.2

GIBRALTAR

LAT 36°08′N
LONG 5°21′W

TIMES AND HEIGHTS OF HIGH AND LOW WATER (Heights in Metres)

TIME ZONE –0100

Subtract 1 hour for UT. Summer Time (area enclosed in shaded box) add 1 hour

2014

SUNRISE AND SUNSET TIMES

GIBRALTAR
At 36°08′N 5°21′W

		Sunrise	Sunset
European Standard Time (UT-1)			
Jan	01	0832	1818
	15	0832	1830
Feb	01	0822	1848
	15	0809	1903
Mar	01	0752	1916
	15	0732	1929
European Summer Time (UT-2)			
Apr	01	0808	2043
	15	0748	2055
May	01	0729	2109
	15	0715	2121
Jun	01	0706	2133
	15	0704	2140
Jul	01	0708	2142
	15	0716	2139
Aug	01	0729	2126
	15	0740	2111
Sep	01	0753	2049
	15	0804	2029
Oct	01	0816	2005
	15	0828	1945
European Standard Time (UT-1)			
Nov	01	0744	1825
	15	0758	1814
Dec	01	0814	1807

JANUARY

Date	Day	Time	m	Time	m	Time	m	Time	m
1	W ●	0240	1.0	0818	0.1	1502	1.0	2051	0.0
2	TH	0329	1.0	0906	0.0	1551	1.0	2137	0.0
3	F	0416	1.0	0953	0.0	1639	1.0	2222	0.0
4	SA	0502	1.0	1041	0.0	1727	1.0	2307	0.0
5	SU	0550	1.0	1128	0.1	1817	0.9	2353	0.1
6	M	0640	1.0	1219	0.1	1909	0.9		
7	TU	0042	0.1	0734	0.9	1316	0.2	2005	0.8
8	W ☽	0140	0.2	0831	0.8	1421	0.2	2106	0.8
9	TH	0249	0.3	0935	0.8	1537	0.3	2218	0.7
10	F	0410	0.3	1046	0.8	1702	0.3	2337	0.7
11	SA	0527	0.3	1155	0.8	1807	0.2		
12	SU	0042	0.7	0622	0.2	1251	0.8	1854	0.2
13	M	0132	0.8	0706	0.2	1337	0.8	1933	0.2
14	TU	0214	0.8	0744	0.2	1418	0.8	2009	0.1
15	W	0251	0.8	0821	0.1	1456	0.9	2044	0.1
16	TH O	0324	0.9	0856	0.1	1532	0.9	2117	0.1
17	F	0355	0.9	0929	0.1	1605	0.9	2148	0.1
18	SA	0425	0.9	1002	0.1	1637	0.9	2218	0.1
19	SU	0455	0.9	1034	0.1	1709	0.9	2247	0.1
20	M	0526	0.9	1106	0.1	1743	0.8	2317	0.1
21	TU	0601	0.8	1141	0.2	1820	0.8	2349	0.2
22	W	0641	0.8	1221	0.2	1903	0.8		
23	TH	0029	0.2	0728	0.8	1313	0.2	1955	0.7
24	F ☾	0122	0.2	0826	0.7	1423	0.2	2057	0.7
25	SA	0238	0.3	0935	0.7	1551	0.2	2214	0.7
26	SU	0418	0.3	1055	0.7	1717	0.2	2336	0.7
27	M	0539	0.2	1207	0.8	1820	0.1		
28	TU	0044	0.8	0636	0.1	1308	0.9	1911	0.0
29	W	0139	0.9	0726	0.1	1401	0.9	1959	0.0
30	TH ●	0230	0.9	0813	0.0	1452	1.0	2044	-0.1
31	F	0318	1.0	0900	0.0	1541	1.0		

FEBRUARY

Date	Day	Time	m	Time	m	Time	m	Time	m
1	SA	0404	1.0	0945	-0.1	1627	1.0	2211	-0.1
2	SU	0448	1.0	1029	0.0	1713	1.0	2251	0.0
3	M	0533	1.0	1112	0.0	1759	0.9	2331	0.0
4	TU	0618	0.9	1155	0.1	1847	0.9		
5	W	0013	0.1	0706	0.9	1242	0.1	1937	0.8
6	TH ☽	0101	0.2	0758	0.8	1336	0.2	2031	0.7
7	F	0158	0.2	0856	0.7	1446	0.3	2136	0.7
8	SA	0319	0.3	1005	0.7	1626	0.3	2259	0.6
9	SU	0459	0.3	1126	0.7	1751	0.3		
10	M	0020	0.7	0606	0.3	1234	0.7	1840	0.2
11	TU	0116	0.7	0652	0.2	1323	0.7	1919	0.2
12	W	0158	0.8	0730	0.2	1403	0.8	1954	0.1
13	TH	0233	0.8	0805	0.1	1439	0.8	2027	0.1
14	F	0305	0.8	0838	0.1	1513	0.9	2058	0.1
15	SA O	0334	0.9	0911	0.1	1546	0.9	2128	0.1
16	SU	0403	0.9	0942	0.1	1617	0.9	2157	0.1
17	M	0433	0.9	1013	0.1	1649	0.9	2225	0.1
18	TU	0504	0.9	1044	0.1	1722	0.9	2255	0.1
19	W	0537	0.9	1117	0.1	1759	0.8	2327	0.1
20	TH	0616	0.8	1154	0.1	1841	0.8		
21	F	0004	0.2	0700	0.8	1241	0.2	1930	0.7
22	SA ☾	0051	0.2	0756	0.7	1345	0.2	2031	0.7
23	SU	0202	0.3	0905	0.7	1522	0.2	2147	0.7
24	M	0353	0.3	1031	0.7	1704	0.2	2316	0.7
25	TU	0529	0.2	1154	0.7	1811	0.1		
26	W	0030	0.8	0630	0.1	1258	0.8	1902	0.0
27	TH	0127	0.8	0720	0.0	1351	0.9	1948	0.0
28	F	0216	0.9	0806	0.0	1440	0.9	2032	-0.1

MARCH

Date	Day	Time	m	Time	m	Time	m	Time	m
1	SA ●	0302	1.0	0850	-0.1	1526	1.0	2113	-0.1
2	SU	0346	1.0	0932	-0.1	1611	1.0	2153	-0.1
3	M	0429	1.0	1012	-0.1	1655	1.0	2230	-0.1
4	TU	0511	1.0	1051	0.0	1738	0.9	2307	0.0
5	W	0553	0.9	1129	0.0	1822	0.9	2345	0.1
6	TH	0637	0.9	1209	0.1	1909	0.8		
7	F	0026	0.1	0724	0.8	1254	0.2	1959	0.7
8	SA ☽	0116	0.2	0813	0.7	1354	0.3	2057	0.7
9	SU	0229	0.3	0922	0.6	1531	0.3	2212	0.6
10	M	0418	0.3	1045	0.6	1716	0.3	2342	0.6
11	TU	0541	0.3	1205	0.7	1813	0.3		
12	W	0044	0.7	0629	0.2	1258	0.7	1852	0.2
13	TH	0128	0.7	0707	0.2	1338	0.8	1927	0.2
14	F	0202	0.8	0741	0.1	1414	0.8	1959	0.1
15	SA	0234	0.8	0814	0.1	1448	0.9	2030	0.1
16	SU O	0305	0.9	0846	0.1	1521	0.9	2101	0.1
17	M	0336	0.9	0918	0.0	1554	0.9	2131	0.1
18	TU	0408	0.9	0950	0.0	1628	0.9	2201	0.1
19	W	0442	0.9	1023	0.0	1703	0.9	2233	0.1
20	TH	0517	0.9	1057	0.1	1741	0.9	2308	0.1
21	F	0556	0.9	1135	0.1	1825	0.8	2347	0.2
22	SA	0642	0.8	1220	0.2	1915	0.8		
23	SU	0036	0.2	0738	0.8	1325	0.2	2016	0.7
24	M ☾	0149	0.3	0848	0.7	1504	0.2	2130	0.7
25	TU	0339	0.3	1015	0.7	1646	0.2	2257	0.7
26	W	0517	0.2	1141	0.7	1754	0.2		
27	TH	0012	0.8	0619	0.1	1245	0.8	1845	0.1
28	F	0108	0.9	0707	0.1	1336	0.9	1929	0.0
29	SA	0156	0.9	0751	0.0	1423	0.9	2011	0.0
30	SU ●	0241	1.0	0833	0.0	1508	1.0	2051	0.0
31	M	0324	1.0	0913	-0.1	1551	1.0		

APRIL

Date	Day	Time	m	Time	m	Time	m	Time	m
1	TU	0406	1.0	0951	0.0	1633	1.0	2206	0.0
2	W	0447	1.0	1028	0.0	1715	0.9	2242	0.0
3	TH	0527	0.9	1103	0.0	1757	0.9	2318	0.1
4	F	0608	0.8	1139	0.1	1842	0.8	2357	0.2
5	SA	0653	0.8	1220	0.2	1930	0.7		
6	SU	0043	0.2	0743	0.7	1313	0.3	2023	0.7
7	M ☽	0147	0.3	0842	0.6	1434	0.3	2125	0.7
8	TU	0321	0.3	0954	0.6	1616	0.3	2242	0.7
9	W	0454	0.3	1116	0.6	1726	0.3	2353	0.7
10	TH	0552	0.3	1217	0.7	1813	0.2		
11	F	0042	0.7	0633	0.2	1302	0.8	1849	0.2
12	SA	0120	0.8	0709	0.2	1340	0.8	1923	0.2
13	SU	0155	0.9	0743	0.1	1415	0.9	1955	0.1
14	M	0230	0.9	0817	0.1	1451	0.9	2028	0.1
15	TU O	0306	0.9	0852	0.1	1528	0.9	2102	0.1
16	W	0343	1.0	0927	0.0	1606	1.0	2137	0.1
17	TH	0420	1.0	1003	0.1	1645	1.0	2213	0.1
18	F	0500	0.9	1040	0.1	1726	0.9	2253	0.1
19	SA	0542	0.9	1121	0.1	1812	0.9	2336	0.2
20	SU	0630	0.9	1210	0.2	1904	0.8		
21	M	0030	0.2	0727	0.8	1316	0.2	2005	0.8
22	TU ☾	0144	0.3	0836	0.7	1446	0.3	2115	0.8
23	W	0321	0.3	0958	0.7	1616	0.2	2234	0.8
24	TH	0453	0.2	1120	0.8	1726	0.2	2347	0.8
25	F	0558	0.2	1224	0.8	1820	0.1		
26	SA	0043	0.9	0648	0.1	1316	0.9	1904	0.1
27	SU	0132	0.9	0732	0.0	1402	0.9	1946	0.1
28	M	0217	0.9	0813	0.0	1447	0.9	2026	0.0
29	TU ●	0300	1.0	0852	0.0	1530	0.9	2104	0.0
30	W	0341	0.9	0929	0.0	1611	0.9	2142	0.1

MAY

Date	Day	Time	m	Time	m	Time	m	Time	m
1	TH	0422	0.9	1005	0.0	1652	0.9	2218	0.1
2	F	0502	0.9	1040	0.1	1733	0.9	2255	0.1
3	SA	0542	0.8	1116	0.1	1815	0.8	2333	0.2
4	SU	0624	0.8	1154	0.2	1900	0.8		
5	M	0017	0.2	0711	0.7	1240	0.3	1949	0.7
6	TU	0112	0.3	0803	0.7	1344	0.3	2042	0.7
7	W ☽	0225	0.3	0903	0.7	1505	0.3	2141	0.7
8	TH	0346	0.3	1011	0.7	1621	0.3	2246	0.7
9	F	0457	0.3	1120	0.7	1720	0.3	2344	0.7
10	SA	0550	0.2	1215	0.7	1804	0.2		
11	SU	0031	0.8	0631	0.2	1259	0.8	1842	0.2
12	M	0113	0.9	0709	0.1	1340	0.9	1918	0.2
13	TU	0154	0.9	0746	0.1	1420	0.9	1955	0.1
14	W O	0235	0.9	0825	0.1	1502	0.9	2034	0.1
15	TH	0317	1.0	0904	0.1	1544	1.0	2115	0.1
16	F	0401	1.0	0945	0.1	1628	1.0	2157	0.1
17	SA	0445	1.0	1027	0.1	1713	1.0	2241	0.1
18	SU	0531	1.0	1112	0.1	1801	0.9	2329	0.2
19	M	0621	0.9	1203	0.2	1854	0.9		
20	TU	0025	0.2	0718	0.8	1305	0.2	1952	0.9
21	W ☾	0133	0.2	0823	0.8	1420	0.2	2057	0.8
22	TH	0253	0.3	0935	0.8	1537	0.2	2207	0.8
23	F	0417	0.2	1052	0.8	1649	0.2	2316	0.8
24	SA	0530	0.2	1159	0.8	1749	0.2		
25	SU	0016	0.9	0625	0.2	1254	0.8	1838	0.2
26	M	0107	0.9	0712	0.1	1342	0.9	1921	0.1
27	TU	0153	0.9	0753	0.1	1427	0.9	2002	0.1
28	W ●	0236	0.9	0832	0.1	1510	0.9	2042	0.1
29	TH	0319	0.9	0910	0.1	1552	0.9	2120	0.1
30	F	0400	0.9	0946	0.1	1631	0.9	2158	0.1
31	SA	0439	0.9	1021	0.1	1710	0.9		

JUNE

Date	Day	Time	m	Time	m	Time	m	Time	m
1	SU	0517	0.8	1055	0.1	1748	0.8	2312	0.2
2	M	0556	0.8	1130	0.2	1828	0.8	2351	0.2
3	TU	0638	0.8	1209	0.2	1910	0.8		
4	W	0036	0.3	0723	0.7	1257	0.3	1956	0.7
5	TH ☽	0131	0.3	0814	0.7	1356	0.3	2046	0.7
6	F	0236	0.3	0910	0.7	1503	0.3	2141	0.7
7	SA	0346	0.3	1014	0.7	1612	0.3	2242	0.7
8	SU	0453	0.3	1120	0.7	1712	0.3	2341	0.8
9	M	0549	0.2	1216	0.8	1801	0.2		
10	TU	0032	0.8	0635	0.2	1306	0.8	1845	0.2
11	W	0121	0.9	0719	0.1	1352	0.9	1928	0.2
12	TH	0208	0.9	0802	0.1	1439	0.9	2012	0.1
13	F O	0255	1.0	0846	0.0	1525	1.0	2057	0.1
14	SA	0343	1.0	0931	0.0	1612	1.0	2144	0.1
15	SU	0431	1.0	1016	0.0	1659	1.0	2232	0.1
16	M	0519	1.0	1102	0.1	1747	1.0	2320	0.1
17	TU	0610	1.0	1150	0.1	1838	1.0		
18	W	0013	0.2	0704	0.9	1245	0.2	1933	0.9
19	TH ☾	0113	0.2	0804	0.8	1347	0.2	2032	0.9
20	F	0220	0.2	0909	0.8	1455	0.2	2135	0.9
21	SA	0336	0.3	1019	0.8	1608	0.3	2243	0.8
22	SU	0457	0.2	1131	0.8	1718	0.2	2347	0.8
23	M	0604	0.2	1232	0.8	1815	0.2		
24	TU	0043	0.8	0654	0.2	1325	0.8	1902	0.2
25	W	0133	0.9	0737	0.1	1411	0.9	1944	0.2
26	TH	0217	0.9	0815	0.1	1454	0.9	2023	0.1
27	F ●	0300	0.9	0852	0.1	1534	0.9	2101	0.1
28	SA	0339	0.9	0927	0.1	1611	0.9	2138	0.1
29	SU	0417	0.9	1000	0.1	1645	0.9	2214	0.1
30	M	0452	0.9	1033	0.1	1719	0.9	2249	0.2

GIBRALTAR
LAT 36°08'N
LONG 5°21'W

TIMES AND HEIGHTS OF HIGH AND LOW WATER (Heights in Metres)

TIME ZONE
–0100
Subtract 1 hour for UT. Summer Time (area enclosed in shaded box) add 1 hour

2014

JULY

Day	Time	m	Day	Time	m
1 TU	0527 1104 1752 2324	0.8 0.2 0.8 0.2	16 W	0554 1131 1818 2354	1.0 0.1 1.0 0.1
2 W	0603 1137 1828	0.8 0.2 0.8	17 TH	0645 1218 1909	0.9 0.1 1.0
3 TH	0001 0641 1213 1907	0.2 0.8 0.2 0.8	18 F	0046 0740 1311 2003	0.2 0.9 0.2 0.9
4 F	0044 0725 1256 1952	0.3 0.7 0.3 0.8	19 SA	0144 0840 1412 ☾ 2102	0.2 0.8 0.3 0.9
5 SA	0135 0817 1351 ☽ 2044	0.3 0.7 0.3 0.8	20 SU	0253 0947 1525 2207	0.3 0.8 0.3 0.8
6 SU	0238 0917 1459 2144	0.3 0.7 0.3 0.8	21 M	0420 1102 1648 2319	0.3 0.8 0.3 0.8
7 M	0352 1026 1616 2251	0.3 0.7 0.3 0.8	22 TU	0544 1213 1756	0.3 0.8 0.3
8 TU	0508 1136 1725 2356	0.2 0.7 0.3 0.8	23 W	0023 0639 1310 1845	0.8 0.2 0.8 0.3
9 W	0608 1236 1821	0.2 0.8 0.2	24 TH	0117 0720 1357 1927	0.8 0.2 0.8 0.2
10 TH	0053 0657 1330 1909	0.9 0.1 0.9 0.2	25 F	0201 0757 1437 2005	0.9 0.2 0.9 0.2
11 F	0147 0744 1420 1957	0.9 0.1 1.0 0.1	26 SA	0242 0831 1513 ● 2041	0.9 0.1 0.9 0.2
12 SA	0238 0830 1508 O 2045	1.0 0.0 1.0 0.1	27 SU	0318 0904 1546 2116	0.9 0.1 0.9 0.1
13 SU	0328 0916 1556 2133	1.0 0.0 1.1 0.0	28 M	0352 0935 1617 2150	0.9 0.1 0.9 0.1
14 M	0417 1002 1643 2220	1.0 0.0 1.1 0.0	29 TU	0425 1005 1647 2223	0.9 0.1 0.9 0.1
15 TU	0505 1046 1730 2307	1.0 0.0 1.1 0.1	30 W	0456 1035 1716 2255	0.9 0.1 0.9 0.2
			31 TH	0529 1104 1748 2327	0.9 0.2 0.9 0.2

AUGUST

Day	Time	m	Day	Time	m
1 F	0604 1136 1823	0.8 0.2 0.9	16 SA	0015 0712 1235 1930	0.2 0.9 0.2 0.9
2 SA	0004 0644 1212 1905	0.2 0.8 0.2 0.8	17 SU	0105 0808 1329 ☾ 2026	0.2 0.8 0.3 0.8
3 SU	0047 0734 1258 1956	0.2 0.8 0.3 0.8	18 M	0208 0912 1441 2129	0.3 0.8 0.4 0.8
4 M	0145 0833 1403 ☽ 2057	0.3 0.7 0.3 0.8	19 TU	0336 1030 1615 2247	0.4 0.7 0.4 0.8
5 TU	0303 0943 1531 2209	0.3 0.7 0.3 0.8	20 W	0520 1151 1735	0.3 0.8 0.4
6 W	0435 1103 1700 2328	0.3 0.8 0.3 0.8	21 TH	0004 0618 1252 1826	0.8 0.3 0.8 0.3
7 TH	0549 1214 1805	0.2 0.8 0.2	22 F	0100 0658 1337 1906	0.8 0.3 0.9 0.3
8 F	0034 0642 1312 1857	0.9 0.1 0.9 0.2	23 SA	0142 0732 1413 1942	0.9 0.2 0.9 0.2
9 SA	0131 0729 1403 1945	0.9 0.1 1.0 0.1	24 SU	0219 0804 1446 2016	0.9 0.2 0.9 0.2
10 SU	0222 0815 1451 O 2032	1.0 0.0 1.1 0.0	25 M	0252 0835 1516 ● 2050	0.9 0.2 1.0 0.1
11 M	0312 0859 1538 2118	1.1 0.0 1.1 0.0	26 TU	0324 0905 1545 2123	1.0 0.1 1.0 0.1
12 TU	0400 0943 1623 2203	1.1 0.0 1.1 0.0	27 W	0355 0935 1614 2154	1.0 0.1 1.0 0.1
13 W	0446 1025 1708 2247	1.1 0.0 1.1 0.0	28 TH	0426 1004 1644 2225	1.0 0.1 1.0 0.1
14 TH	0533 1106 1753 2330	1.0 0.1 1.1 0.1	29 F	0458 1033 1715 2257	1.0 0.2 1.0 0.2
15 F	0621 1148 1840	1.0 0.1 1.0	30 SA	0533 1105 1750 2331	0.9 0.2 0.9 0.2
			31 SU	0613 1139 1830	0.9 0.2 0.9

SEPTEMBER

Day	Time	m	Day	Time	m
1 M	0011 0701 1223 1920	0.2 0.8 0.3 0.8	16 TU	0121 0835 1358 ☾ 2050	0.3 0.8 0.4 0.8
2 TU	0105 0801 1326 ☽ 2023	0.3 0.8 0.4 0.8	17 W	0246 0950 1535 2208	0.4 0.8 0.4 0.7
3 W	0228 0912 1503 2139	0.3 0.8 0.4 0.8	18 TH	0439 1116 1704 2335	0.4 0.8 0.4 0.8
4 TH	0415 1037 1644 2307	0.3 0.8 0.3 0.8	19 F	0546 1221 1759	0.4 0.8 0.3
5 F	0534 1155 1753	0.2 0.9 0.2	20 SA	0034 0627 1305 1838	0.8 0.3 0.9 0.3
6 SA	0020 0627 1254 1844	0.9 0.2 0.9 0.2	21 SU	0116 0701 1340 1914	0.9 0.3 0.9 0.2
7 SU	0117 0713 1344 1931	1.0 0.1 1.0 0.1	22 M	0151 0733 1412 1947	0.9 0.2 1.0 0.2
8 M	0206 0756 1431 2015	1.0 0.0 1.1 0.0	23 TU	0223 0803 1442 2020	1.0 0.2 1.0 0.2
9 TU	0254 0838 1516 O 2059	1.1 0.0 1.1 0.0	24 W	0254 0834 1512 ● 2053	1.0 0.2 1.0 0.1
10 W	0339 0920 1600 2142	1.1 0.0 1.1 0.0	25 TH	0326 0904 1543 2125	1.0 0.2 1.0 0.1
11 TH	0424 0959 1643 2222	1.1 0.0 1.1 0.0	26 F	0358 0935 1615 2158	1.0 0.2 1.0 0.1
12 F	0508 1039 1725 2302	1.1 0.1 1.1 0.1	27 SA	0432 1006 1649 2230	1.0 0.2 1.0 0.2
13 SA	0553 1118 1809 2342	1.0 0.2 1.0 0.2	28 SU	0509 1039 1725 2305	1.0 0.2 1.0 0.2
14 SU	0641 1159 1856	0.9 0.2 0.9	29 M	0550 1116 1807 2346	1.0 0.3 0.9 0.3
15 M	0026 0734 1249 1949	0.3 0.8 0.3 0.8	30 TU	0638 1201 1857	0.9 0.3 0.9

OCTOBER

Day	Time	m	Day	Time	m
1 W	0039 0737 1306 ☽ 2000	0.3 0.8 0.4 0.8	16 TH	0154 0903 1449 2121	0.4 0.8 0.4 0.7
2 TH	0205 0849 1448 2119	0.4 0.8 0.4 0.8	17 F	0339 1021 1618 2245	0.4 0.8 0.4 0.7
3 F	0357 1014 1628 2250	0.3 0.8 0.3 0.8	18 SA	0459 1133 1720 2355	0.4 0.8 0.4 0.8
4 SA	0515 1134 1737	0.3 0.9 0.3	19 SU	0549 1222 1805	0.3 0.9 0.3
5 SU	0005 0609 1234 1828	0.9 0.2 1.0 0.2	20 M	0041 0627 1301 1842	0.9 0.3 0.9 0.3
6 M	0101 0654 1323 1913	1.0 0.1 1.0 0.1	21 TU	0117 0700 1334 1917	0.9 0.3 1.0 0.2
7 TU	0149 0735 1408 1956	1.0 0.1 1.1 0.1	22 W	0151 0732 1407 1950	1.0 0.2 1.0 0.2
8 W	0234 0815 1452 O 2037	1.1 0.1 1.1 0.0	23 TH	0224 0803 1441 ● 2024	1.0 0.2 1.0 0.1
9 TH	0318 0855 1535 2118	1.1 0.1 1.1 0.0	24 F	0258 0835 1516 2058	1.0 0.2 1.1 0.1
10 F	0400 0934 1617 2157	1.1 0.1 1.1 0.1	25 SA	0334 0908 1552 2133	1.1 0.2 1.1 0.1
11 SA	0443 1012 1658 2234	1.0 0.1 1.0 0.1	26 SU	0411 0943 1629 2209	1.1 0.2 1.0 0.2
12 SU	0525 1050 1740 2312	1.0 0.2 1.0 0.2	27 M	0450 1021 1709 2247	1.0 0.2 1.0 0.2
13 M	0610 1130 1824 2351	0.9 0.3 0.9 0.3	28 TU	0533 1101 1753 2330	1.0 0.3 1.0 0.3
14 TU	0659 1216 1914	0.9 0.3 0.8	29 W	0622 1150 1844	0.9 0.3 0.9
15 W	0040 0756 1320 ☾ 2011	0.4 0.8 0.4 0.8	30 TH	0024 0720 1257 1947	0.3 0.9 0.4 0.9
			31 F	0148 0830 1432 ☽ 2103	0.4 0.9 0.4 0.8

NOVEMBER

Day	Time	m	Day	Time	m
1 SA	0329 0949 1604 2230	0.3 0.9 0.3 0.8	16 SU	0359 1027 1631 2255	0.4 0.8 0.4 0.8
2 SU	0448 1108 1714 2346	0.3 0.9 0.3 0.9	17 M	0503 1128 1725 2355	0.4 0.8 0.3 0.8
3 M	0546 1210 1809	0.2 1.0 0.2	18 TU	0550 1216 1809	0.3 0.9 0.3
4 TU	0042 0632 1300 1854	0.9 0.2 1.0 0.1	19 W	0040 0627 1256 1846	0.9 0.3 0.9 0.2
5 W	0130 0714 1346 1936	1.0 0.1 1.1 0.1	20 TH	0119 0702 1334 1923	0.9 0.2 1.0 0.2
6 TH	0214 0754 1429 O 2017	1.0 0.1 1.1 0.1	21 F	0156 0736 1412 1959	1.0 0.2 1.0 0.1
7 F	0257 0833 1512 2057	1.0 0.1 1.1 0.1	22 SA	0235 0811 1452 ● 2036	1.0 0.2 1.0 0.1
8 SA	0339 0912 1554 2135	1.0 0.1 1.0 0.1	23 SU	0314 0848 1533 2115	1.0 0.2 1.0 0.1
9 SU	0420 0950 1635 2212	1.0 0.1 1.0 0.1	24 M	0355 0927 1615 2155	1.0 0.2 1.0 0.1
10 M	0501 1028 1715 2248	1.0 0.2 0.9 0.2	25 TU	0438 1009 1659 2237	1.0 0.2 1.0 0.2
11 TU	0542 1108 1757 2326	0.9 0.2 0.9 0.2	26 W	0522 1054 1745 2322	1.0 0.2 1.0 0.2
12 W	0627 1152 1843	0.9 0.3 0.8	27 TH	0611 1145 1837	1.0 0.3 0.9
13 TH	0009 0717 1246 1934	0.3 0.8 0.4 0.8	28 F	0016 0707 1250 1936	0.2 0.9 0.3 0.9
14 F	0108 0814 1400 ☾ 2033	0.4 0.8 0.4 0.7	29 SA	0128 0811 1409 ☽ 2044	0.3 0.9 0.3 0.8
15 SA	0233 0918 1521 2141	0.4 0.8 0.4 0.7	30 SU	0252 0923 1532 2202	0.3 0.9 0.3 0.8

DECEMBER

Day	Time	m	Day	Time	m
1 M	0412 1038 1647 2320	0.3 0.9 0.3 0.8	16 TU	0358 1023 1636 2254	0.3 0.7 0.3 0.7
2 TU	0519 1144 1749	0.2 0.9 0.2	17 W	0503 1125 1733 2357	0.3 0.8 0.3 0.8
3 W	0022 0612 1239 1838	0.9 0.2 0.9 0.1	18 TH	0553 1218 1819	0.3 0.8 0.2
4 TH	0114 0657 1326 1922	0.9 0.2 1.0 0.1	19 F	0047 0634 1304 1900	0.8 0.2 0.9 0.1
5 F	0159 0738 1411 2003	0.9 0.1 1.0 0.1	20 SA	0132 0713 1349 1940	0.9 0.2 0.9 0.1
6 SA	0242 0818 1454 O 2043	1.0 0.1 1.0 0.1	21 SU	0216 0752 1434 2021	0.9 0.1 1.0 0.1
7 SU	0324 0857 1536 2121	1.0 0.1 1.0 0.1	22 M	0300 0834 1519 ● 2104	1.0 0.1 1.0 0.0
8 M	0404 0935 1617 2157	0.9 0.1 0.9 0.1	23 TU	0344 0917 1605 2147	1.0 0.1 1.0 0.0
9 TU	0443 1013 1656 2232	0.9 0.2 0.9 0.1	24 W	0428 1002 1651 2231	1.0 0.1 1.0 0.1
10 W	0521 1051 1735 2308	0.9 0.2 0.9 0.2	25 TH	0513 1049 1737 2316	1.0 0.1 1.0 0.1
11 TH	0559 1131 1816 2345	0.8 0.2 0.8 0.2	26 F	0601 1139 1828	1.0 0.1 0.9
12 F	0641 1215 1859	0.8 0.3 0.8	27 SA	0006 0653 1236 1922	0.1 1.0 0.2 0.9
13 SA	0029 0728 1310 1947	0.3 0.8 0.3 0.7	28 SU	0104 0751 1343 ☽ 2023	0.2 0.9 0.2 0.8
14 SU	0126 0821 1417 ☾ 2041	0.3 0.7 0.3 0.7	29 M	0213 0855 1457 2133	0.2 0.9 0.2 0.8
15 M	0240 0919 1529 2144	0.4 0.7 0.3 0.7	30 TU	0331 1006 1618 2251	0.3 0.8 0.2 0.8
			31 W	0450 1118 1732	0.3 0.8 0.2

BREST — TIDAL COEFFICIENTS 2014

The tidal co-efficients for Brest are used in many marinas in N Brittany to denote the time of opening of lock gates.
Spring tides may have a co-efficient of 100 and neaps of say 45.
Tidal streams and heights vary in proportion to the co-efficient.

Day	January am	January pm	February am	February pm	March am	March pm	April am	April pm	May am	May pm	June am	June pm
1	96	100	113	114	108	112	108	106	94	91	76	72
2	104	107	113	110	114	115	102	98	86	82	69	65
3	108	108	106	101	114	112	92	86	77	71	61	57
4	106	103	94	87	108	102	79	72	66	60	53	49
5	99	94	79	71	96	89	64	57	54	49	46	43
6	88	82	63	55	80	72	50	44	44	40	42	41
7	74	68	48	42	64	56	38	34	37	36	42	–
8	61	55	38	–	48	41	32	–	36	–	44	47
9	50	47	36	37	35	32	32	35	38	42	52	57
10	45	–	40	45	32	–	39	45	46	52	62	68
11	45	48	50	55	34	38	51	57	57	63	73	79
12	50	54	60	65	43	50	62	68	68	74	84	89
13	58	62	70	74	55	61	74	79	79	84	93	96
14	66	70	78	81	67	72	83	87	88	91	98	100
15	73	75	84	86	77	81	91	93	94	96	100	99
16	78	79	87	88	85	88	95	96	97	97	98	95
17	81	82	89	88	91	93	96	95	96	94	92	87
18	82	82	87	86	94	94	93	90	91	87	83	78
19	81	80	83	80	93	92	87	82	83	78	73	68
20	78	76	76	72	90	87	77	71	73	68	54	60
21	73	70	67	62	83	78	66	60	64	61	58	–
22	66	62	57	52	73	67	56	53	59	59	57	58
23	59	54	48	46	61	55	53	–	60	–	59	61
24	51	48	46	–	51	48	54	58	62	65	64	67
25	46	46	49	54	47	–	63	69	69	72	70	72
26	47	–	61	70	50	55	75	81	76	79	75	77
27	51	57	79	87	62	70	86	91	82	84	78	79
28	64	72	95	102	78	85	94	97	86	86	80	80
29	80	88			93	99	98	99	87	86	79	79
30	95	101			104	107	98	96	85	84	77	76
31	107	111			109	109			81	79		

Day	July am	July pm	August am	August pm	September am	September pm	October am	October pm	November am	November pm	December am	December pm
1	73	71	70	67	60	55	53	49	51	–	59	–
2	68	65	63	59	50	46	45	44	54	59	62	66
3	62	58	55	51	43	43	46	–	65	72	70	74
4	55	52	48	45	44	–	50	57	78	84	78	82
5	48	46	44	44	49	56	65	73	90	94	85	88
6	44	44	47	–	63	72	81	89	98	100	89	90
7	45	–	51	57	81	89	96	102	101	101	90	90
8	47	51	64	72	97	104	106	109	100	98	88	86
9	56	62	80	88	109	113	111	111	95	90	84	80
10	68	74	95	101	115	115	109	106	86	80	77	73
11	81	87	106	110	114	111	102	96	75	68	68	64
12	92	98	112	113	106	100	90	82	62	56	59	55
13	101	105	112	110	93	85	75	67	50	45	50	46
14	106	107	106	101	77	68	59	52	40	37	42	40
15	106	104	94	86	60	51	45	39	35	35	38	37
16	101	96	79	70	44	38	35	33	36	–	39	–
17	91	84	62	54	35	–	33	–	39	43	41	45
18	78	71	48	43	34	36	36	40	48	53	50	55
19	64	58	40	–	40	44	45	50	59	64	61	66
20	53	50	40	41	50	55	56	61	69	74	72	78
21	48	–	45	49	61	66	66	71	79	83	83	87
22	48	50	55	59	71	75	76	80	86	89	91	95
23	53	56	64	68	79	82	83	86	91	92	97	99
24	60	64	73	76	84	86	88	90	93	93	99	99
25	68	71	79	81	88	89	91	91	91	89	97	95
26	74	76	83	84	89	88	90	89	86	83	91	87
27	78	80	85	85	87	85	86	83	78	74	82	77
28	80	81	85	84	82	79	79	75	69	65	72	67
29	81	80	82	80	74	70	69	64	61	59	62	59
30	79	78	77	74	64	59	59	55	57	58	57	–
31	76	73	69	65			52	50			56	57